WordPerfect®
Power Pack

Ralph Blodgett

que®
CORPORATION
LEADING COMPUTER KNOWLEDGE

WordPerfect
Power Pack

Copyright © 1990 by Que® Corporation

Library of Congress Catalog No. 89-63572
ISBN 0-88022-520-3

92 91 90   8 7 6 5 4 3 2 1

Interpretation of the printing code: the rightmost double-digit number is the year of the book's printing; the rightmost single-digit number is the number of the book's printing. For example, a printing code of 90-1 shows that the first printing of the book occurred in 1990.

WordPerfect Power Pack is based on WordPerfect 5.1.

ABOUT THE AUTHOR ▼

Ralph Blodgett, M.Div, M.A., has been a magazine editor for 12 years and is the author of 15 books (including *Using WordPerfect: Macintosh Version* and *The Best Book of WordPerfect 5.1*) as well as some 300 articles published in more than 90 different magazines and newspapers—including *PC World*, *MacWorld*, *Personal Computing*, *The Washington Post*, *The Seattle Times*, *Philadelphia Enquirer*, *Pittsburgh Post-Gazette*, and Portland's *The Oregonian*. He also has been a frequent contributor to *WordPerfect Magazine*. He has received national awards for magazine feature-article writing, magazine series writing, and news writing.

The author is one of seven sysops on the WordPerfect Support Group (WPSG) forum on CompuServe who answer questions about WordPerfect from users around the world. He has worked with WordPerfect since shortly after its introduction in 1982 and has taught writing and WordPerfect seminars across the country. Currently he is employed full-time as the head of WordPerfect 5.1 tech support and training at the World Headquarters of the seven-million-member Seventh-day Adventist Church.

CONTENTS AT A GLANCE

Part VII: Desktop Publishing in the Office

TABLE OF CONTENTS ▼

II Creating General Office Correspondence

3 Writing Successful Business Letters with WordPerfect 69

V Creating Specialized Documents

12 Creating Employee and Telephone Lists ..249

13 Creating Office Forms 271

VI Creating Legal Documents

17 Creating Court Documents 397

VII   Desktop Publishing in the Office

18   Creating Camera-Ready Copy 441

19   Creating Programs, Pamphlets, and Book Pages 467

ACKNOWLEDGMENTS

Every book is a team effort, and *WordPerfect Power Pack* is no exception. Of the many people who contributed their skills, ideas, and hard work to this publication, I am particularly indebted to the following individuals:

Chuck Stewart, Product Development Manager at Que, who found my idea for a document-oriented WordPerfect book intriguing enough to "pick up the ball and run with it." Without his valuable input and encouragement from the very inception, this publication could never have been created. Thanks also to Dave Ewing, Publishing Director at Que, who appreciates innovative book ideas and who gave his approval and support for this novel approach.

Attorney Kenneth D. Chestek (of Murphy, Taylor, Trout & Chestek, Erie, Pennsylvania), who wrote Chapters 15, 16, and 17 and who provided some of the finest examples of macros ever made available to readers of a computer book.

Copy editors Ann Campbell Holcombe, Dr. Caroline Gryta, and Beth Burch. Ann Holcombe, a free-lance editor and writer, also wrote all the material related to the PRIOS model method of communication in Chapters 3, 5, 6, and 7. Caroline Gryta, who teaches business writing at Edinboro University, provided valuable assistance on the chapters dealing with business writing.

Lisa Hunt Tally, Senior Editor of the project at Que, who did much of the behind-the-scenes work to keep things organized, accurate, and moving through the editorial and production process. Thanks also to Michael McCoy, who fearlessly tech-edited the book, and designers Bill Hartman (of Hartman Publishing) and Dan Armstrong (of Que Corporation), who developed the book's final design.

My deepest thanks also go to WordPerfect Corporation's Jeff Acerson and Rebecca Mortensen, who have always been helpful to me in my book-writing projects, and likewise to Pete Peterson, Executive Vice-President of WordPerfect Corporation.

I also thank Hewlett-Packard Corporation for providing a Hewlett-Packard LaserJet IID to use for the project. I'm truly amazed at the gorgeous output one can produce by connecting WordPerfect to such a fantastic printer. Also to Bitstream Fontware (Cambridge, Massachusetts) and IQ Engineering (Sunnyvale, California) for essentially all the fonts illustrated throughout the book. And thanks also to Federal Express, who faithfully delivered these chapters back and forth halfway across the country, overnight, day after day, without the loss of a single package.

TRADEMARK ACKNOWLEDGMENTS

Introduction

In eight short years, WordPerfect has grown from a fledgling word processing program for the PC to become the undisputed "leader of the pack" in the 1990s. Every survey taken in recent years shows that WordPerfect completely dominates the business and home office environment—with usage ratings ranging from 50 to 65 percent of businesses surveyed.

Part of the reason for this unparalleled success is the amazing versatility of the program itself. It has almost every feature imaginable: a macro editor, an equation editor, a variety of graphic boxes and lines, columns, tables, math features, styles, a thesaurus, a dictionary with built-in hyphenation, auto-fonts, context-sensitive help, and the list goes on. Not surprisingly, WordPerfect was the first program to introduce these features. And all along, the program has remained easy for the beginner to learn.

Why This Book Is for You

Literally dozens of books are available on WordPerfect—so many in fact that you may find knowing which one book best fits your needs difficult to discern. Some books are for beginners, some for longtime users of WordPerfect, and some for so-called "power users" of the program.

But *WordPerfect Power Pack* is different! Never before has there been a WordPerfect publication like this book. Instead of listing all 250 or so features of the program and then discussing each feature chapter by chapter, detail by detail, through 900 and more pages, this book does something unique. It has all the information you need to create specific types of documents; the information is arranged in chapters according to the types of documents you create. In other words, this book is document-oriented, not feature-oriented—and the accompanying Applications Disk contains many sample documents, macros, and files that you can use as is or as models for customized documents.

For example, if you need to print envelopes, Chapter 8 provides proven techniques for printing envelopes on a variety of printers. The chapter even provides information for using window envelopes for your correspondence.

If you want to create interoffice memos, turn to Chapter 10. Here you find everything you need to know about creating memos (including some macros on the Applications Disk that automate the process). If you want to compose and design a company newsletter, Chapter 20 shows how to convert a plain, unattractive document into an attention-getting newsletter page in 12 easy steps. Chapter 20 also provides real-life examples of company newsletters printed on HP DeskJet, LaserJet, and PostScript printers.

If you work in a law office and want to know how to automate the work of creating legal documents such as contracts, deeds, and wills, Chapter 16 has exactly what you need. No more switching around from one book to another, trying to piece together all the necessary information to create a specific type of document.

In other words, if you create any of the documents listed below, *WordPerfect Power Pack* is a must for you:

- book pages
- brochures
- calendars (monthly, quarterly)
- credit inquiry forms
- customer invoices
- employee lists
- envelopes
- expense reports
- fax cover sheets
- fliers
- formal reports
- index cards
- labels
- letters
- memos
- minutes of meetings
- office forms
- pamphlets
- papers
- petty cash forms
- phone message forms
- phone number lists
- preprinted forms
- Rolodex cards
- two-sided documents

Because of its unique format, this book is for all WordPerfect users—those making the transition from a typewriter or another word processor, as well as those who have used the program for many years.

How To Use This Book

Whether you are new to WordPerfect or consider yourself a proficient user of the program, *WordPerfect Power Pack* helps you go beyond the manual and workbook to create the specific documents or kinds of publications you need in your office environment.

If you are a new computer user or plan to purchase your first computer or upgrade to a better model, read Chapters 1 and 2. These chapters are orientation chapters. If you are an experienced WordPerfect 5.1 user, feel free to skip these two chapters. If you are upgrading from WordPerfect 4.2 or 5.0, this book makes it easy to develop the kinds of documents you want to create without having to wade through multiple chapters. Just go to the chapter you want and start reading. Because each chapter is designed as an individual unit that contains all the information you need to create a particular type of document, you do not have to begin with any particular chapter. In fact, you may want to keep the book close to your computer and use it only when you need it. It's that kind of book.

How This Book Is Organized

This book is divided into seven parts and contains two appendixes. Part I, "Getting Started," consists of Chapters 1 and 2. Chapter 1, "Why WordPerfect Is Ideal for the Office," explains to new users of WordPerfect 5.1 how the program can speed up virtually every kind of office activity and save hundreds of hours of time creating documents. This chapter offers 12 reasons why WordPerfect 5.1 is the best word processing software choice for the business or home office. If you are a new user, the section "Using the Right Hardware" will be invaluable when you purchase your new computer, monitor, keyboard, and printer.

Chapter 2, "Reviewing WordPerfect Basics," provides a broad overview of the WordPerfect 5.1 program and features—including topics like the clean screen, hidden codes, unnamed documents, and default settings. In this chapter, you also review the many ways to move the cursor; how to use the function keys; how to manage files and printing; how to use editing commands to block, cut, copy, move, and append text; how to enhance your layout and formats; how to create columns and tables; how to create and use macros and styles; how to index a document and create a table of contents; and a variety of other things.

Part II, "Creating General Office Correspondence," spans Chapters 3 through 7. Chapter 3, "Writing Successful Business Letters with WordPerfect," provides several important letter-writing strategies for planning your documents. This chapter explains the importance of determining the purpose of your document, defining the reader or readers of your document, using the proper information to interest your readers, organizing your information for maximum impact, and using the proper style within your document.

Chapter 4, "Examining the Physical Characteristics of Your Letters," explores the importance of using proper letter-writing techniques and formats. In this chapter, you see how a letter can be used as an image maker; how to create letter balance; how to improve letter appearance; how to install and use fonts other than Courier or Pica for letter writing; how to use white space effectively; how to assemble the six basic parts of a letter into a coherent whole; and whether to use the block, modified block, semiblock, hanging indent, or simplified letter style for your correspondence. Lastly, this chapter explains how the Merge feature can save hours of letter-writing time.

Chapter 5, "Creating Letters That Inform," shows how you can use ordinary letters that inform, announce, thank, or answer questions to create goodwill toward your company or home enterprise. Sample letters discussed in this chapter (and included on the Applications Disk) are acceptance letters, acknowledgment letters, announcement letters, apology letters, appointment letters, appreciation letters, commendation letters, confirmation letters, congratulation letters, goodwill letters, instruction letters, invitation letters, order-placing letters, reservation letters, sympathy letters, and thank-you letters.

Chapter 6, "Creating Letters That Convey Bad News," provides the necessary background for writing letters that convey bad news (for example, if you have misplaced an order, delayed a payment, or refused a request). Sample bad-news letters provided in this chapter (and on the Applications Disk) include an adjustment letter, a complaint letter, a credit letter, a criticism letter, an evaluation letter, a refusal letter, and a rejection letter.

Chapter 7, "Creating Letters That Persuade," shows how you can start your persuasive letters with a central appeal, build on the appeal with persuasive evidence in the body of the letter, and conclude by suggesting a specific action you want the reader to take.

Part III, "Creating Envelopes and Labels," covers Chapters 8 and 9. Chapter 8, "Creating Business Envelopes," provides proven techniques for printing envelopes on a variety of printers: daisywheel, dot matrix, a DeskJet, or any of the Hewlett Packard printers (LaserJet, LaserJet Plus, LaserJet II, LaserJet IID, LaserJet IIP, or LaserJet III). In fact, if you use the envelope macro included on the Applications Disk, your printer can print the envelope while you write the letter itself. This chapter also shows how to create multiple envelopes with and without a merge and how to print letters for window envelopes.

Chapter 9, "Creating Labels and Rolodex Cards," takes the mystery out of two business activities that nearly every office encounters. This chapter shows you the easy way to print labels and Rolodex cards, including how to use the sheet labels found at virtually every office-supply store in the world.

Part IV, "Creating Informal and Formal Reports," consists of Chapters 10 and 11. Chapter 10, "Creating Memos and Minutes of Meetings," shows how to prepare the most frequently used form of communication within an organization: the office memo. This chapter includes descriptions of macros (included on the Applications Disk) that automate the creation of memos. In addition to memos, the chapter delves into the creation of minutes of meetings, showing the proper format for minutes.

Chapter 11, "Creating Formal Reports," provides useful information for creating formal reports for a company or educational project. The chapter details the various components of a report: the front matter, the report body, and the back matter. Examples of a letter of transmittal, an abstract, a table of contents, and other elements of a formal report are included. This chapter introduces several useful macros for creating reports and lists eight things to check when your report is written.

Part V, "Creating Specialized Documents," comprises Chapters 12 through 14. Chapter 12, "Creating Employee and Telephone Lists," provides detailed instructions that lead you gently through the steps necessary to create primary and secondary merge files—the two types of files necessary for creating employee and telephone lists. This chapter also shows how to merge information into a WordPerfect 5.1 table. The Applications Disk contains the necessary merge files for simplifying the creation of employee and telephone lists.

Chapter 13, "Creating Office Forms," includes an important-message form, petty cash form, weekly time sheet, credit inquiry form, fax transmission form, credit memo, quarterly expense summary, yearly expense summary, long-distance telephone record, one-month calendar form, and three-month calendar form. After reading this chapter and learning how to use the Tables feature to create forms, you may never again think of WordPerfect as "just another word processor."

Chapter 14, "Creating a Customer Invoice," provides step-by-step instructions for creating a common office invoice form by using the Tables feature of WordPerfect 5.1. Instructions include specific steps for removing unwanted lines, locking cells, and adding math codes. You also discover how to use the INVOICE macro to automatically fill in the table with relevant data. Using the guidelines offered in this chapter, you can create just about any form your heart desires.

Part VI, "Creating Legal Documents," covers Chapters 15 through 17. Chapter 15, "Using WordPerfect in the Law Office," details ways in which WordPerfect 5.1 can fill specific needs in a law office. Included in the chapter (and on the Applications Disk) is a legal keyboard to simplify many office activities, macros designed for common legal applications, special templates, and form documents for legal use. This chapter also shows how to organize your computer files for better file management; how to use footnote styles, paragraph numbering, and automatic cross-references; and how to create and use a special WordPerfect timesheet.

Chapter 16, "Creating Non-Court Documents," demonstrates several ways in which legal documents such as wills, deeds, contracts and other documents that use at least some standard paragraphs or language can be created and easily tailored to a specific case with WordPerfect 5.1. This chapter includes a menu-driven system for creating several documents that relate to the same case or matter, and instructions on how to use the Merge feature and macros to assist in document creation.

Chapter 17, "Creating Court Documents," shows how pleadings and court-related documents can be speedily prepared with WordPerfect 5.1. The chapter includes instructions for creating legal pleadings, captions, interrogatories, certificates of service, tables of contents, and tables of authorities. This chapter also demonstrates the two basic techniques you can use for document preparation: macros and ready-to-use forms.

Part VII, "Desktop Publishing in the Office," comprises Chapters 18 through 20. Chapter 18, "Creating Camera-Ready Copy," explains how camera-ready pages differ from the kinds of documents discussed in the previous chapters. The general guidelines presented here include the use of disk fonts and cartridge fonts, graphics, quotations, and other graphic elements that make up what is called *camera-ready copy*. The chapter also discusses how to use document preview, how to align text properly, how to use PostScript cartridges and printers, how to shade text and create shadow text, how to print white text on a black (or shaded) background, how to add graphics and text boxes, and how to add borders and rules.

Chapter 19, "Creating Programs, Pamphlets, and Book Pages," focuses specifically on fliers, pamphlets, and book-type publications. The chapter details how to print headers and two-sided documents, how to fold documents to create small brochures, how to adjust binding widths, how to print in either portrait or landscape mode, how to print fliers and program bulletins, and how to use the WordPerfect 5.1 Label feature to create "logical" pages in a flier (with correct page numbers).

Chapter 20, "Creating Newsletters and Magazine-Style Reports," shows how to convert a plain, unattractive document into an attention-getting newsletter page in 12 easy steps. In this chapter, you see how to create newsletters on everyday office equipment: a Hewlett-Packard DeskJet printer, a Hewlett-Packard LaserJet printer, a Postscript printer, and finally, a Linotronic printer.

Appendix A, "Installing the Applications Disk," explains how to install onto your hard drive or second floppy disk drive the disk that accompanies this book. Appendix B, "WordPerfect 5.1 Command Summary," lists WordPerfect 5.1 functions and details the keystrokes used to perform those functions.

Where To Find More Help

One particularly useful feature in WordPerfect 5.1 is the context-sensitive Help feature. If you want help using landscape forms, just press Help (F3) and the letter L. Listed alphabetically on the screen are entries for Landscape Fonts, Landscape Forms, and Landscape PaperSize/Type. If you are inside a menu and don't know what to do next, press Help (F3). WordPerfect provides help for the particular level of the menu at which you are located within that feature.

WordPerfect Toll-Free Telephone Support

WordPerfect Corporation provides toll-free telephone support for those times when you can't find answers through the Help feature. Call the appropriate number for help with the following features:

Feature	Telephone Number
Installation	(800) 533-9605
Features	(800) 541-5096
Graphics/Tables/Equations	(800) 321-3383
Macros/Merges/Labels/Columns	(800) 541-5129
Laser Printers	(800) 541-5170
Dot-Matrix Printers	(800) 541-5160
Other Printers	(800) 541-5097
Networks	(800) 321-3389
DrawPerfect	(800) 541-5090
WP Office	(800) 321-3253

The after-hours WordPerfect support line (call between 6 p.m. and 7 a.m. Mountain time, Monday through Friday) is (801) 226-6444.

The WordPerfect Support Group

The WordPerfect Support Group (an independent group not affiliated with WordPerfect Corporation) maintains an active user forum on CompuServe and publishes a top-notch newsletter, *The WordPerfectionist*. The newsletter contains articles by system operators and members of the WordPerfect Support Group A (WPSGA) and WordPerfect Support Group B (WPSGB) forums, as well as a wealth of "how-to" articles and information about WordPerfect. You can subscribe to *The WordPerfectionist* for $36 a year by writing to the following address:

The WordPerfectionist
Lake Technology Park
P.O. Box 130
McHenry, MD 21541
(301) 387-4500

Conventions Used in This Book

This conventions used in this book have been established to help you learn to use the program easily and quickly.

For function-key commands, the name of the command is given first, followed by the keystrokes used to invoke the command. For example: Press Format (Shift-F8) and choose **Page (2)**.

If you can access the same feature by using a mouse and the pull-down menu, that action is listed on the line below the function-key instruction as an alternative method, preceded with a special ⌦ icon. Consider the following example:

1. Press Format (Shift-F8) and choose **Page (2)**.

    ⌦ Choose **Page** from the **Layout** menu.

Where you can use either a number or a letter to activate a feature, that choice is indicated by the use of bold characters, as in the instruction "choose **Page (2)**." In this case, you can press either **2** or **P** to access the feature.

If the text mentions a file contained on the Applications Disk included at the back of the book, a ▪ icon is included in the text. Consider the following example:

 You can find both the PHONE.PF file and a sample EMPLOYEE.SF file on the Applications Disk.

Uppercase letters are used to distinguish files name, DOS (disk operating system) commands, and macro commands such as {ON CANCEL}{GO}Cancel~~.

In nearly every case, the keys on the keyboard are represented as they appear on your keyboard (for example, Enter, Tab, Shift, Backspace, Del, A, and 9). Macro variables and text that you are asked to type appear in *italics*. On-screen messages appear in a special `monospace` font.

When two or more keys are to be pressed simultaneously, they are shown connected by a hyphen. You do not type the hyphen. For example, Alt-F9 means to press the Alt key and the F9 function key simultaneously.

A series of keystrokes is shown as a numbered list. The number preceding an item in the list is for reference only. Do not type the number, just the key sequence following the number. Consider this example:

1. Press Columns/Table (Alt-F7) and Tables (**2**).

   ⌦Select **T**ables from the **L**ayout menu.

2. Press **C**reate (**1**).

3. At the `Number of Columns:` prompt, type *3* and press Enter.

4. At the `Number of Rows:` prompt, type *5* and press Enter.

This series of keystrokes creates a WordPerfect table three columns wide by five rows tall.

Maintenance Releases

WordPerfect releases "interim" or "maintenance" upgrades to a typical version of the program approximately every two months (and a totally new program approximately once every 18 to 24 months). As of this printing, WordPerfect has provided four interim releases since WordPerfect 5.1 was first released on November 7, 1989. The dates of these interim releases are 1/19/90, 3/30/90, 6/29/90, and 8/20/90. The text and macros included in this book reflect changes made to the program through the 8/20/90 release. If you have a question about which version of WordPerfect 5.1 you have, press Help (F3) and look in the upper right corner of the screen. Immediately following the text `WP 5.1` is the date of your copy of WordPerfect.

The latest interim release of the software is available from WordPerfect Corporation for approximately $15 to $25, depending on the number of disks you need. Or you can arrange to have updated versions sent automatically by calling (801) 225-5000 and asking about the WordPerfect Software Subscription Service.

A Message to the Reader

Thank you for buying my book! I take it as a compliment that you have selected this book out of a bookstore filled with hundreds of computer books.

If you have any questions about the topics covered in this book or suggestions for improving future editions, and if you are a member of CompuServe, you can send an EasyPlex message to me (my CIS number is 73767,656). As a system operator on the WPSG forums, I log on virtually every evening, usually sometime between 7 and 11 p.m. (EST). I try to post answers to my mail the same night; if that's not possible, I answer within 24 hours.

You also can send a letter to me at the following address in care of the publisher:

Ralph Blodgett
c/o Que Corporation, Suite 140
11711 N. College Ave.
Carmel, IN 46032

Best wishes with WordPerfect 5.1!

Part I

Getting Started

Why WordPerfect Is Ideal for the Office

Reviewing WordPerfect Basics

1

Why WordPerfect Is Ideal
for the Office

Six years ago, a typical business office would have included the following: a manual or electric typewriter, sheets of carbon paper, stenographic notepads, bottles of correction fluid, and an entire wall of filing cabinets.

In this setting, an office worker faced with sending a memo to 20 board members scattered around the country would have had to type the same memo 20 times (so that each recipient had an original copy); then type 20 envelopes, each with a different addresses; and, finally, file 20 different carbon copies in each of 20 folders (one for each board member).

Now, what if the person performing this time-consuming task discovered while folding the letters that the date for the meeting had been changed? Suddenly the entire operation would have to be repeated—20 new letters to type, 20 new carbon copies, 20 more folders to open, and 20 new carbons to file.

Sound familiar? Undoubtedly many office workers remember performing tasks like that at one time or another. Talk about wasted expense and time—not to mention the secretary's frazzled nerves. Of course, the perfect solution to this kind of problem is a word processor.

Note: If you are part of the new majority of offices equipped with personal computers and you are already familiar with WordPerfect 5.1, you can move immediately to Chapter 2. Chapter 1 is intended for new or potential users of WordPerfect 5.1.

What Can a Word Processor Do?

With WordPerfect 5.1 as your word processing program, you can perform numerous tasks, such as the following, with ease and efficiency:

- Correct a single error and print a perfect replacement letter moments later

- Merge a single original letter with a list of recipients to produce dozens, hundreds, or thousands of personalized individual letters

- Automatically print envelopes from a list of names and addresses

- Automatically create labels for mass mailings from a list of names and addresses

- Print as many copies of one document as needed

- "File" a copy of each of the letters in folders (called subdirectories) on a computer disk

- Automatically search through hundreds of files on disk to locate a single letter to a specific individual about a certain topic

- Select files on disk by type, account number, name, author, typist, creation or revision date, key words, or an abstract

- Create draft documents for others to review and edit, and then add those revisions without retyping the entire document

- Assemble individual articles into monthly or quarterly newsletters— complete with multiple fonts, columns, tables, justified text, and graphic images

- Alphabetize and regularly update telephone lists

- Create a variety of office forms containing vertical and horizontal lines and shaded text boxes

- Fill in preprinted forms automatically

- Print Rolodex cards for Rolodex files

- Print a variety of index cards for memo boxes

Because of these unique capabilities, the word processor is quickly becoming the standard for millions of offices around the world. And with the word processor comes a new generation of office personnel who are expected to

- Use a word processor for various office activities

- Understand the underlying concept behind the various features

- Use the proper equipment to maximize office productivity

Unfortunately, some people believe that word processors will eventually replace human operations, resulting in layoffs. Nothing could be further from the truth, of course. Computers may well be the best device ever created: they are capable of extending your hands, eyes, ears, and mind phenomenally. Nevertheless, computers *still* need human beings to tell them what to do and when to do it.

Those who take the time to learn and master new office technology, like WordPerfect 5.1, find themselves better equipped to fill the more demanding and higher-paid positions in today's business. Thus, in many offices today, learning word processing becomes a matter of survival and a means to advancement. This is especially true in business.

Why Choose WordPerfect?

One of the first questions that new users ask when they begin comparing one word processing package with another is, "What's so great about WordPerfect, and why is it so popular?" WordPerfect is the best word processing program for the office for several reasons:

1. WordPerfect dominates the business environment.

Every survey conducted over the past couple of years confirms that WordPerfect is the preferred word processor in business and home offices. Issue after issue, "Pipeline," a column in *PC Magazine* that lists the Top Ten Sellers among PC software, places WordPerfect at or very near the top of all software products sold. *Personal Computing*, after spending two months surveying the 100 U.S. companies with the greatest number of personal computers, reported in the September 1989 issue that the three dominant software programs used in business are WordPerfect (64 percent of the companies), Lotus 1-2-3 (88 per cent), and dBase III (60 percent). (The percentage total exceeds 100 percent because the respondents used more than one type of software package.)

Using the most popular program is important in an office for a couple of reasons. First, from the employee's point of view, learning a new program is never an easy accomplishment. Therefore, it is best to learn a program that is used in most offices, not only in a single company but in offices and businesses everywhere.

Second, many companies offer top pay to workers trained in WordPerfect. A quick glance at the Help Wanted section in a large city Sunday paper confirms that people trained in WordPerfect are in the greatest demand. The following ad appeared recently in the *Washington Post*:

> WORD PROCESSOR
>
> *Four positions in DC: 2 positions in legal, 80+ wpm, WordPerfect a must. 2 yrs litigation essential. Salary to low $30s; 2 positions in real estate, 80 wpm, WordPerfect a must. Salary to $24K.*

Another ad in the same paper for a job at $25K stated the following:

> *Bank needs individual for Comm'l loan department. Must have excellent phone voice, 60 wpm, and WordPerfect experience.*

Third, using the most popular word processor is also important to employers. If a company runs an unfamiliar software program, the pool of qualified new employees may be considerably reduced.

2. WordPerfect runs on many different computers.

The newest trend in business is having computer software that is compatible with various computer hardware. This compatibility not only saves training costs when employees are moved from one department to another but also makes file-sharing between noncompatible machines easier.

No other word processor offers a word processing program on so many different "platforms." Today you can run a copy of WordPerfect on Amiga, Apple IIe, Apple IIc, Apple IIGS, Atari, Data General, IBM 370 mainframe, Macintosh, OS/2, PCs, UNIX, and VAX/VMS. In addition, new versions for Windows and Presentation Manager are scheduled for release early in 1991.

Files created on any of these machines transfer cleanly to any other supported machine, even though the hardware is vastly different. A WordPerfect file created on a Macintosh computer, for example, can be saved as either a WordPerfect 4.2 or 5.0 file and opened on any of the other types of computers just listed. And vice versa. This capability saves a tremendous amount of frustration in companies that use more than one type of computer hardware or operating system.

3. WordPerfect uses a clean-screen format.

When the first PC word processing programs appeared, most displayed a screen that appeared cluttered. WordStar, for example, indicated bold, underline, subscript, superscripts, and so on with special screen codes rather than showing them, as WordPerfect does, on-screen in different colors. Bold text in WordStar was placed inside special control codes, as in

^ Bwords bolded ^ B

WordPerfect 5.1, on the other hand, does not clutter the screen in this manner; rather, all editing information appears on a keyboard overlay. This special area is about the size of a ruler (or in pull-down menus visible on-screen as you edit), leaving 23 or 24 lines for text area. Only 1 line at the bottom is used for document information (see fig. 1.1), and that line contains the document name (left), the document and page number, and the line and cursor position (right).

WordPerfect uses 16 foreground and 8 background colors to indicate font attributes and font sizes on a color monitor. You can tell at a glance exactly which font attribute or font size you are using for any given sentence, word, or individual character.

```
                    Lincoln's Address at Gettysburg

        Fourscore and seven years ago our fathers brought forth on this continent
    a new nation, conceived in liberty and dedicated to the proposition that all
    men are created equal.
        Now we are engaged in a great civil war, testing whether that nation or
    any nation so conceived and so dedicated can long endure. We are met on a
    great battle field of that war. We have come to dedicate a portion of that
    field, as a final resting place for those who here gave their lives that this
    nation might live. It is altogether fitting and proper that we should do
    this.




                                        Doc 1 Pg 1 Ln 1" Pos 1"
```

Fig. 1.1.

WordPerfect uses a "clean screen" for document pages.

The advantages to having the whole screen for editing purposes are obvious. A document that fills the whole screen looks much more like text on a page of paper in a typewriter. It is easier to read individual sentences, and it is far easier to see the context of a sentence or paragraph when you have 23 lines of text shown on the screen at one time, rather than 19 lines. The WordPerfect clean-screen format, by the way, has been copied recently by several other word processing programs.

4. WordPerfect offers excellent customer support.

When WordPerfect 3.0 came on the market in 1983, it was the first word processing program to offer free and unlimited phone support, a service virtually unheard of then. By the end of 1983, the company employed 8 support personnel. They processed an average of 15 phone calls per day. Today the company has 660 support representatives who answer more than 10,000 phone calls per day.

5. WordPerfect Support is available day and night.

WordPerfect offers eight different 800-number support lines for daytime use:

Installation	(800) 533-9605
Features	(800) 541-5096
Graphics, Tables, Equations	(800)321-3383
Macros, Merges, Labels, Tables	(800) 541-5129
Laser Printers	(800) 541-5170
Dot Matrix Printers	(800) 541-5160
Other Printers	(800) 541-5097
Networks	(800) 321-3389

WordPerfect also offers after-hours support from 6 p.m. to 7 a.m. (Mountain Standard time), Monday through Friday. The telephone number is (801) 222-9010.

In addition to having access to telephone support, WordPerfect users with a modem can access one of two WordPerfect Support Group (WPSG) forums on CompuServe and get answers day or night from 18,000 other WordPerfect users around the world. The WPSG forums (WPSGA and WPSGB), which are independently run forums not affiliated with WordPerfect Corporation, can often provide answers to the difficult questions that cannot be answered on the phone. WordPerfect 5.1 topics are covered in the WPSGA forum, which you can reach by typing *GO WPSGA* at any CompuServe prompt. CompuServe is the largest computer bulletin board in the world, having more than 500,000 registered members. The WPSG forums are 2 of 150 different user groups that can be accessed by modem in CompuServe.

6. WordPerfect supports more than 600 different printers.

WordPerfect 5.1 supports more than 600 different printers: daisywheel, dot matrix, and laser (both jet-type and PostScript). New printers are being added to the list weekly.

In addition, WordPerfect documents automatically reformat themselves when retrieved on a computer defined for a different printer. For example, if you create a document at home on a computer attached to a dot-matrix printer with only Courier font, the document prints properly with Courier font. But if you take that same document to the office and retrieve it on a computer attached to a Hewlett-Packard LaserJet IID or III, each of which has a variety of different fonts available, WordPerfect automatically selects different fonts to match the font sizes and attributes that you have selected for the document.

In other words, each time you create a new document, WordPerfect formats the document according to the printer that's currently selected. If you move documents between different computer-printer combinations, WordPerfect is intelligent enough to automatically adjust formatting and font selections so that the document can print on any of the 600 printers WordPerfect supports. WordPerfect prints with the fonts available on the printer you currently use.

Or if you create a document using Helvetica as the base font and decide to change to Times Roman or Century Schoolbook, WordPerfect automatically converts all font attributes and font sizes throughout the document to match the new base font.

Note: Various fonts are discussed and illustrated later in the book.

7. WordPerfect prints 1,600 special characters.

Many times users wish that they could use certain special characters in their documents, such as fractions, dingbats, bullets, or foreign language alphabets, but their printer does not have fonts containing these characters. WordPerfect 5.1 has solved this problem for owners of dot-matrix and LaserJet printers in a unique way. As long as you have the WP.DRS file (which stands for *device resource*) available on disk, you can print all 1,600 special characters in the 12 character sets listed in the appendix of the manual.

When you add one of these characters to your document (using the Ctrl-V command) and send that document to the printer, WordPerfect 5.1 checks to see whether you have the correct font available.

If not, then the program sends a graphic representation of that character from the DRS file to the printer, using the correct size and font attribute needed for the print job. The following are some sample characters created with the DRS file, illustrating the variety available within WordPerfect 5.1:

- ¢ © ✓ ²/₃ Π ☞ ɜ ¶ # □

These special characters can help you communicate your ideas more easily.

8. WordPerfect uses relative and absolute measurements.

Filling out preprinted forms is a common task in the office. Yet with an ordinary word processing program and a sheet printer like a Hewlett-Packard LaserJet, the task is nearly impossible. Some offices, in fact, resort to keeping an IBM Selectric typewriter on the side just for typing addresses on envelopes and filling in forms.

With WordPerfect, though, the impossible becomes possible. Using absolute measurements (that is, a measurement from the edge of the paper), you can easily position the cursor at any location on the page. Just use a ruler to measure the distance from the top and left paper edges and tell the program to print that line at that particular spot. Every time you use that form, information in that line prints exactly at the right location. In fact, you can use a keyboard merge file that prompts the user for various responses and position the replies according to the form you are using.

On the other hand, if you are working with multiple columns on the screen and you want all paragraph indentions to be one-fourth of an inch, relative tab settings (measurements from the text margin, not paper margin) keep all paragraph indents properly aligned no matter how many columns you have defined.

Another useful feature in version 5.1 is the ability to use fractions for all measurements, rather than decimals (or tenths of an inch). For example, when entering individual margin measurements, you may type the measurement as a fraction of an inch, and the program automatically converts the fraction into a decimal number for the margin setting. Thus, if you type 7/8 for the left margin and press Enter, this fraction is converted automatically into .875". The same applies to tab settings. When the Tab ruler is displayed, you type *1 5/8* and press Enter. WordPerfect inserts a tab setting at the 1.625" position.

9. WordPerfect offers tables.

Of the 60 or so new features and enhancements incorporated in WordPerfect 5.1, none is more useful in the office than Tables. If you have ever tried using tabs to create a table of numbers, a comparison chart, or an invoice, you already know how difficult this task can be in any word processing program. Adding lines and rules to such a form can be very time-consuming.

WordPerfect 5.1 Tables provides such vast opportunities for enhancing documents that one wonders how people ever got along without it all these years. Yet WordPerfect is the only word processor in the PC market that offers this new feature.

Tables are special forms with *rows* running horizontally and *columns* running vertically, as in figure 1.2. These rows and columns, separated by horizontal and vertical lines, form *cells* where information can be typed. Figure 1.2 illustrates a table of two columns and five rows, which create 10 different cells. The individual cells can hold text or numerical data or both (as in this example).

Fig. 1.2.

A WordPerfect table combining text and numerical data.

1989's Top Theme Parks	
Theme Park Name	**Attendance** (Millions)
Disney World/Epcot/MGM Studio Orlando, Florida	30.0
Disneyland Anaheim, California	14.4
Universal Studios Hollywood, California	5.1
Knotts Berry Farm Buena Park, California	5.0

Lines between the cells can be thin, thick, single, double, dotted, or dashed. And individual cells can be shaded in various percentages of gray. Text inside each cell can be positioned left, center, or right; justified both right and left; or decimal-aligned. In addition, information within a table can be sorted by individual columns.

You can even merge data into a WordPerfect table. This process is explained later in the book, but don't look for the secret in your WordPerfect manual. It isn't there.

10. WordPerfect offers interactive spreadsheet links.

Version 5.1 offers full spreadsheet importing and linking capability. With spreadsheet importing and linking you can bring information from several types of spreadsheets into a WordPerfect file; then whenever the original spreadsheet file is modified, the spreadsheet information in your WordPerfect document is automatically updated and modified. If you prepare reports that use spreadsheet data, this feature is most helpful in keeping your reports up-to-date with the latest data.

11. WordPerfect imports numerous graphic formats.

If you want to add graphic enhancements to your documents, WordPerfect cannot be surpassed. You can position a graphic box anywhere on the page and have text flow around the image automatically. Or the graphic box can be attached to the text itself so that the image "floats" up and down on the page with the copy as you edit or expand the text on the page. Moreover, WordPerfect 5.1 gives you five different categories of graphic boxes to work with:

- Figure
- Table
- Text box
- User-defined
- Equation

WordPerfect 5.1 supports 14 different graphic formats:

CGM	Computer Graphic Metafile
DHP	Dr. Halo PCI
DXF	AutoCAD
EPS	Encapsulated PostScript
GEM	GEM Draw
HPGL	Hewlett-Packard Graphics Language plotter file
IMG	GEM Paint
MSP	Microsoft Windows Paint
PCX	PC Paintbrush
PIC	Lotus 1-2-3
PNTG	MacPaint
PPIC	PC Paint Plus
TIFF	Tagged Image File
WPG	WordPerfect Graphics

12. WordPerfect offers an interactive help key.

One of WordPerfect's most competitive features is its help key. First press F3 (Help) and then any one of the 40 or so function-key combinations (F1 through F10, by itself or while pressing the Alt, Shift, or Ctrl key) at random and see what happens.

Or if you are looking for a specific feature, press Help (F3) and then any letter (A through Z). For example, the combination F3 and P offers 76 different choices under the letter *p*—items like Page Number Style, Page View, Paper Trays, Password, Preview, Print Color, Print Options, Printer Functions, and Pull Down Text. Under each of those 76 choices you can obtain information on how to use that particular feature.

To see a help screen like that in figure 1.3, follow these directions:

```
Features [S]                   WordPerfect Key   Keystrokes

Save, Clipboard                Shell             Ctrl-F1,2
Save, Fast (Unformatted)       Setup             Shft-F1,3,5
Save Text                      Save              F10
Screen                         Screen            Ctrl-F3
Screen Display                 Setup             Shft-F1,2
Screen Down                    Screen Down       +(NumPad)
Screen Rewrite                 Screen            Ctrl-F3,3
Screen Setup                   Setup             Shft-F1,2,6
Screen Split                   Screen            Ctrl-F3,1
Screen Up                      Screen Up         -(NumPad)
Scrolling Speed                Setup             Shft-F1,3,3
Search                         Search            F2
Search and Replace             Replace           Alt-F2
Search for File(s)             List              F5,Enter,9,1
Secondary File, Merge          Merge/Sort        Ctrl-F9,1
Secondary Leading              Format            Shft-F8,4,6,6
See Codes                      Reveal Codes      Alt-F3
Select Printer                 Print             Shft-F7,s
Send Printer a "GO"            Print             Shft-F7,4,4
Set Pitch (Letter/Word Spacing)  Format          Shft-F8,4,6,3
More... Press s to continue.

Selection: 0                                (Press ENTER to exit Help)
```

Fig. 1.3.

The help screen for the letter s.

1. Press Help (F3).

2. Press S.

   The help screen appears on-screen.

3. Look for the words Save Text in the left column and see what keystrokes from the right column activate that feature. In this example, pressing F10 is how you save text.

4. Press Save (F10). WordPerfect provides information on that function, as shown in figure 1.4.

5. To exit the help feature, press the space bar.

In addition, if you are in a menu or submenu when you press Help (F3), the program offers help for the particular feature you are using. This interactive help enhancement, available only in version 5.1, is most useful to new users who are not knowledgeable about the many features packed into this program.

```
 Save

       Saves the current document on disk.  The DOS filename can have up to eight
       characters plus an optional period and three-letter extension.
       (_____.___).  If a file with that name already exists on disk,
       WordPerfect will ask if you wish to replace it.

       Files may also be saved using the Long Document Names feature.  A long
       document name can contain up to 68 characters and is saved with your
       document along with the regular DOS filename (see Long Document Names on
       the Document Management/Summary screen under Setup: Environment).

       Exit may also be used to save the document that you are working on.  The
       only difference is that the Save key returns you to your document.

       WordPerfect Fast Saves documents without formatting them first, cutting
       down on save time.  You may change this option in the Setup: Environment
       menu.




 Selection: 0                                 (Press ENTER to exit Help)
```

Fig. 1.4.

*The help
screen for
Save (F10).*

As you can see, WordPerfect 5.1 offers many unique features that make it ideal for preparing a wide variety of documents in the office. The following sections discuss how to order WordPerfect 5.1 and what kind of equipment is best for using all of WordPerfect's capabilities.

Ordering WordPerfect 5.1

Although WordPerfect 5.1 lists at $495, few users pay full price for their software. Many dealers offer a significant discount, especially if you purchase the software with some computer equipment. Or you can purchase the program from one of the many mail-order companies listed in magazines like *Personal Computing*, *PC Magazine*, or *PC World*. Through mail order, you often can find WordPerfect in the range of $210 to $235, and the copy through the mail is identical to what you would receive from a dealer at twice the price.

If you already have any previous PC version of WordPerfect, you can upgrade your copy to version 5.1. Just mail the front page of your manual (the page with the copyright notice on the back), plus your registration number and a check for $87.50 (this includes $2.50 shipping), to this address:

> WordPerfect Corporation 5.1 Updates
> 1555 N. Technology Way
> Orem, Utah 84057

If you want the manual without the binder, the upgrade cost is $75. However, the larger 5.1 manual does not fit into the version 5.0 binder. For network stations that do not need the manual, the upgrade charge is $65. These prices, which are correct as this book is being written, are subject to change without notice. If you are certain of your registration number, call WordPerfect Registrations at this number: (801) 222-4555.

Using the Right Hardware

To run WordPerfect 5.1 properly, make sure that you have the right equipment. Word processing uses five basic pieces of equipment: a keyboard, a monitor, a central-processing unit (CPU), a hard disk (or C: drive), and a printer. These five items collectively are known as *hardware*. Hardware refers to the equipment on which a word processing program (the *software*) can run. These items can be purchased either as a single package or from different vendors and mixed and matched fairly easily.

In a way, buying a computer is similar to buying a car without an engine. You can put a small engine in your new car and it runs, but perhaps not too well. This is what happens if you buy low-performance software. But if you put a powerful engine into that same car, it can operate at its maximum potential.

In a sentence, WordPerfect 5.1 is the most powerful engine you can put into your computer. And with a little practice and guidance, your hardware and software working together will perform tasks once done only at a print shop filled with tens of thousands of dollars' worth of equipment.

Choosing a Computer

The two main categories of computers used in business are IBM compatibles and Macintosh computers. Because this book is about WordPerfect 5.1, only IBM-compatible PCs are discussed. (For information on how to use the Macintosh version of WordPerfect, see *Using WordPerfect: Macintosh Version* by Ralph Blodgett, published by Que Corporation.)

You can run WordPerfect 5.1 on an IBM PC or completely compatible computer with a hard disk drive. WordPerfect requires DOS 2.0 or later and a minimum of 384K of memory in which to operate.

Unless you intend to create small documents, you will find that the software performs best on a computer with 512K of RAM. A computer uses RAM to store information retrieved from a file on disk or typed from the keyboard. If you have *expanded* (not *extended*) RAM, WordPerfect uses that memory for larger files. Files too large to fit into the computer's memory will be stored partially on disk. So the more RAM you have, the less disk space will be required when working with large documents.

However, as with any powerful software program like WordPerfect, not all programs perform optimally on all computer models. Within the PC DOS environment, for example, computers come in four basic configurations:

Computer Family	Date Introduced
8088/8086	1981
80286	1984
80386	1986
80486	1989

At each level, performance increases dramatically. An AT type of machine (the 80286 family), for example, significantly outperforms the 8088/8086 family of PCs. Likewise, the 80386 computer runs circles around the AT machines. An 80386/25 MHz computer, for example, processes data at 6 mips (million instructions per second). And the newest 80486—operating at 20 mips—processes large documents, graphics, and spreadsheets in seconds. Figure 1.5 illustrates the time required to perform the same four word processing activities on nine different computer models.

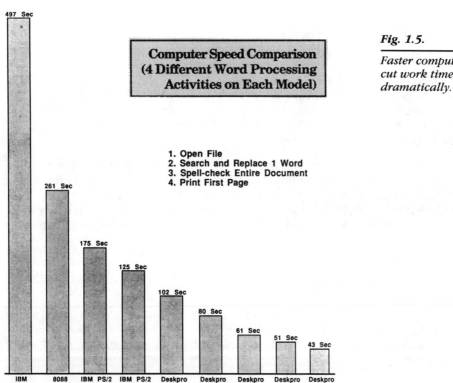

Computer Speed Comparison (4 Different Word Processing Activities on Each Model)

1. Open File
2. Search and Replace 1 Word
3. Spell-check Entire Document
4. Print First Page

497 Sec — IBM PC/XT
261 Sec — 8088 10MHz
175 Sec — IBM PS/2 Model 30
125 Sec — IBM PS/2 Model 50
102 Sec — Deskpro 286/12
80 Sec — Deskpro 386/16
61 Sec — Deskpro 386/20
51 Sec — Deskpro 386/25
43 Sec — Deskpro 386/33

Fig. 1.5.

Faster computers cut work time dramatically.

Computers using the older-style microprocessor chips can never equal the performance of the newer, more powerful models. For a word processor to work, the computer must complete a certain number of cycles of activity to carry out software instructions. And within each basic computer family, you will find subgroups of computers that run at different "clock speeds"—measured in millions of cycles per second, or *megahertz* (MHz). The higher the clock speed within each group of computers, the faster the computer can process instructions and reformat documents.

Unless you anticipate working with very large documents on a regular basis, or files containing numerous graphic images, most offices do not require the fastest and most expensive machines. At the same time, if buying new equipment, you would be wise to avoid the low-end computers (for instance, the 8088/86 models).

When purchasing a new computer, remember that computers do not wear out like a set of tires on a car. There is no elephants' graveyard of discarded machines, no secret dumping ground for useless computers. A typical PC should have a life expectancy approaching a decade or more. Therefore, considering the potential life expectancy of a computer, the quality of the unit should weigh more than the initial price when you select among different models.

Choosing a Keyboard

If you have visited one or more computer showrooms, you already know that keyboards come in two basic configurations—the older-style keyboard with 10 function keys stacked in two vertical rows along the left-hand edge of the board, and the newer style with 12 function keys stretched across the top in a single horizontal row. The older model is known as the *83-key keyboard*, and the newer is called the *101-key Enhanced Keyboard*.

If you are buying a new computer and will be running WordPerfect 5.0 or later versions, select the 12-function Enhanced Keyboard. Not only will you gain the use of two additional keys (which permit a total of 8 additional word processing commands), but you will find the WordPerfect keyboard overlay much easier to read on the 12-function keyboard. In fact, some companies no longer offer the 83-key keyboard.

Selecting a Monitor

WordPerfect 5.1 supports a variety of video systems, including Color Graphics Adapter (CGA), Enhanced Graphics Adapter (EGA), Multi-Color Graphics Array (MCGA), Video Graphics Array (VGA), Genius (full-page), IBM 8514/A, AT&T 6300, Hercules Graphic Card, Hercules Graphics Card Plus, and the Hercules InColor cards.

Because WordPerfect uses color to identify font attributes (like underline, italic, bold, redline, strikeout, and small caps) and font sizes (superscript, subscript, fine, small, large, very large, and extra large), buying a color monitor makes more sense than buying a monochrome display. A color monitor allows you to use these features and know exactly what words or characters will print in which format.

But not all color monitors are the same. Color monitors come in different types— identifiable by the number of *pixels* (or picture elements) projected on the glass horizontally and vertically. The more pixels your screen supports, the better text and graphics will appear on the screen. Monitors are grouped into five different categories, listed from worst to best:

CGA	320 × 200 pixels (4 colors)
EGA	640 × 350 pixels (16 colors)
MCGA	320 × 200 pixels (256 colors)
VGA	640 × 480 pixels (16 colors)
Super VGA	800 × 600 pixels (16 colors)

Poorer-quality CGA monitors, which have fewer pixels per screen, show distinct black horizontal stripes running through letters. Monitors with poor resolution result in user fatigue and lowered overall productivity. In fact, under poor lighting, you may have difficulty determining which character is actually being displayed on a CGA monitor. So what you save in initial purchase price may reap years of dissatisfaction.

As a result, if your office budget allows, choose a VGA monitor on which to run WordPerfect 5.1. VGA monitors are no longer merely an attractive option. They've become a necessity for many company offices and have moved into the mainstream of the business world.

Picking a Hard Disk

In business, hard disks are virtually universal now—93 percent of business users report that their computer contains a hard disk drive (*PC Magazine*, January 17, 1989). In fact, WordPerfect 5.1 simply will not run on a computer with the 360K floppy disks. It is *possible* to configure a two-disk-drive computer to use the 720K disks to run WordPerfect 5.1, but not with ease. With 3 1/2-inch disks, you must frequently swap disks in your disk drives. For this reason, you should have a machine with a hard disk drive and a minimum of 20M (megabytes).

Buying the Right Printer

Without a printer, a computer is virtually worthless. Three basic types of printers currently serve the market: daisywheel printers, dot-matrix printers, and laser printers. Although WordPerfect works with both daisywheel and dot-matrix printers, the program is most effective on laser printers.

Using a Laser Printer

A laser printer uses a laser beam to print characters on paper. An entire page is put together in the laser printer's internal memory before being printed. A laser printer can print documents at speeds of four to eight pages per minute, with eight pages per minute being the norm. Because of the excellent quality of documents that a laser printer can create, many businesses are buying laser printers.

Basically, the two types of laser printers are those compatible with PCL (printer control language) and those compatible with PostScript.

PCL Printers

The Hewlett-Packard series stands out as the leading PCL printers. The HP Series II, IIP, IID, and III printers are probably the best known. A PCL printer normally uses bit-mapped fonts, which means that each font is created by bits that form characters. If you want the font in two point sizes, then you must have two sets of fonts, one for each point size.

Relatively new to PCL printers is the scalable font. Rather than being bit-mapped, the font is outlined. Thus you can "stretch" the outline and increase the point size without losing the quality of the character. If a bit-mapped font were stretched and printed, curves would appear as jagged edges rather than smooth outlines. The HP Series III printer, among a few others, exploits scalable fonts and is the printer of choice in the PCL world, with a new level of PCL called PCL5.

Standard PCL printers are normally available with a 10-point Courier font that also prints bold, and an 8.5-point Lineprinter font. The Series III printer has the following typefaces in normal, bold, italic, and bold italic:

> CG Times
> Univers
> Courier
> Lineprinter

Many fonts are available for PCL printers. You can buy bit-mapped fonts as well as scalable fonts.

Besides printing text quickly and offering the capability to print many different "typesetter quality" fonts, PCL printers support graphics. You will be pleased with the graphics that WordPerfect can print on a PCL printer.

Many companies, including Hewlett-Packard, offer PostScript cartridges for PCL printers. So you can adapt your PCL printer to make it PostScript-compatible.

PostScript Printers

The best known PostScript printer is Apple's Laserwriter. PostScript is actually a programming language used to design a page. The language uses scalable fonts, so you can print a font in many different point sizes. One of the attractive advantages of PostScript printers is that they come with a variety of typefaces that are each available in several styles. For example, the following typefaces come in normal, bold, oblique (italic), and bold oblique styles:

Times Roman
Courier
Palatino
New Century Schoolbook
ITC Bookman
Helvetica
Helvetica Condensed
Helvetica Narrow
ITC Avant Garde Gothic
In addition, these faces are available:
Zapf Chancery Medium Italic
Symbols
ITC Zapf Dingbats

Many other fonts are also available for your PostScript printer.

PostScript printers are quite good at printing graphics. You will be pleased with the graphics that WordPerfect prints on a PostScript printer.

One additional feature that may sway you to PostScript printers is that many typesetters are PostScript devices. So you may create a document and print it on your PostScript printer for review before sending the PostScript document to the typesetter for final printing.

Which Printer Is Best?

The best printer is the one that fits your needs. Normally, daisywheel printers are out of the running because of their limited capabilities. If you do not need the best quality of print or graphics, and need to keep cost down, a dot-matrix printer may fit the bill. Also, if you must print on continuous-form paper, you must work with an impact printer, such as a dot-matrix printer. If you do decide to get a dot-matrix printer, consider a 24-pin printer for the best quality.

For high-quality, speedy printing, look seriously at laser printers. Your choice is between PCL and PostScript printers. PCL printers are much less expensive than PostScript printers, by more than $1,000. However, remember that many typefaces come built into the PostScript printer.

For the home office, you may be happy with the low-cost PCL printers. Such printers are HP's Series IIP, Epson's EPL-6000 or Okidata's OkiLaser 400.

The business office is better suited with a faster PCL printer or a PostScript printer. If you decide on a PCL printer, get one that supports PCL5, such as the Hewlett-Packard LaserJet Series III, which supports scalable fonts. PostScript printers also are scalable-font printers. You will find PostScript printers advantageous especially if you send documents out to be typeset, and the typeset house uses a PostScript device.

Summary

This chapter explained how a word processor can assist in your everyday work around the office—from simple tasks like correcting a mistake in a single letter to using merge to produce 500 letters and envelopes. You learned several reasons why WordPerfect is the perfect word processor for the office, and you learned how to order WordPerfect 5.1 and select hardware.

Chapter 2 covers the four concepts on which WordPerfect is based: the clean screen, hidden codes, the unnamed document, and default codes. The chapter also emphasizes the WordPerfect features that are particularly useful in a place of business.

2

Reviewing WordPerfect Basics

This book guides you in using WordPerfect 5.1 in an office environment to create a wide variety of documents: letters, lists, reports, papers, newsletters, forms, invoices, labels, envelopes, and various other printed business documents.

Because this book is document-related rather than feature-related, it does not detail all the various features of WordPerfect. For that kind of detail on how the program itself works, you should refer to the WordPerfect 5.1 manual and the supplemental lessons in the *WordPerfect Workbook for IBM Personal Computers*. Whether you are new to WordPerfect or have used the manual and workbook before, Que's *WordPerfect Power Pack* helps you to go beyond the manual and workbook in order to create the specific documents or publications you will need in your office environment.

Before you begin preparing business documents, however, you will want to have in mind important WordPerfect concepts and features. An assumption for the remaining chapters is that you understand clearly the concepts and features discussed in this chapter.

Understanding WordPerfect Basics

To use WordPerfect effectively, you must understand four concepts underlying the program. If you keep these four basic concepts in mind, you will be able to use the program to its fullest potential.

The Clean-Screen Concept

For users new to WordPerfect, their first surprise may be in not seeing on-screen what they are used to seeing with other word processing programs. Many word processing programs, for instance, use multiple screen lines for menu information. Of 24 screen lines, Microsoft Word 4.0 uses the bottom 4 for the "command area," plus more for lines around the text area. This leaves only 19 lines to display text on-screen. DisplayWrite 4.0 uses the top 4 lines for the status lines and menu bar.

Instead of cluttering the screen with multiple lines of menus, ruler bars, and strange codes and symbols, WordPerfect displays a "clean screen." For the function keys, WordPerfect supplies users with the software a plastic template. It shows which functions are assigned to each of the 10 or 12 function keys. In this way, all 40 WordPerfect commands are listed and visible to the user, and the screen space is free for text. If you don't have such a template, you can press F3, F3 to view WordPerfect's Help screen for the function keys.

When you start WordPerfect, all you see is a blinking cursor in the upper left corner and some letters and numbers in the lower right corner:

```
Doc 1 Pg 1 Ln 1" Pos 1"
```

This string of letters and numbers appears on the *status line* and provides four important pieces of information:

- The window you are using: `Doc 1` or `Doc 2`

- The page number: `Pg 1`

- The line number, measured in inches from the top of the paper: `Ln 1"`

- The cursor's line position, measured in inches from the paper's left edge: `Pos 1"` (which, in this instance, marks the beginning of the line)

These items appear all the time when you are using WordPerfect in editing mode.

Two other pieces of information may appear on the status line in the lower right corner:

- A column number if you are using the columns feature. WordPerfect indicates just to the left of the document number listing the number of the column where the cursor is located, as in

  ```
  Col 1 Doc 1 Pg 1 Ln 1" Pos 1"
  ```

- A table cell position if you are using the table feature. The following is an example:

  ```
  Cell A1 Doc 1 Pg 1 Ln 1" Pos 1"
  ```

Two items of information may appear on the status at the lower *left* corner of the screen:

- The document name after you have saved the document once. The path name will be included with the document name, as in

  `C:\WP51\SAMPLE.TXT`

  Note that the document name may or may not be displayed, depending on how you have configured your program.

- The typeover mode indicator. If you press the Insert key to change to typeover mode, the word `Typeover` appears in the lower left corner, masking temporarily the document name if the file has been saved.

The color used for the number following `Pos` identifies the font size or font attribute for the cursor location. For example, if you have selected pink to represent italic font, the `Pos` number will change to pink also when the cursor moves inside the italic font codes. If you press the Num Lock key, `Pos` blinks to let you know that Num Lock is activated. If instead you press Caps Lock, `Pos` changes to uppercase `POS`—warning you that any letters you type will be capital letters. If you press both Caps Lock and Num Lock, `Pos` changes to a blinking uppercase `POS`. (If you press Num Lock first and then press Caps Lock, you may have to press Num Lock again a couple of times before `POS` starts blinking.) If Block is on, `Pos` changes color or shading, again depending on what colors have been selected for fonts and screen attributes. Obviously, WordPerfect can pack a lot of information about your current document into a single line.

The clean screen has another important characteristic. When you start WordPerfect, it opens a new window where you can type information, but the window is blank and contains no codes. If you try to use the arrow keys or the mouse to move the cursor around in this window, you will discover that you cannot position the cursor where there are no text, space, tab, or other text-positioning codes.

Therefore, if you are starting with a blank screen and want to position text at the center of the first line, you must use the space bar, the Tab key, or a centering code to locate the text there. Or if you want to place your first line of text three inches from the top of the paper, you must press Enter several times, or use the Advance command (Shift-F8, **4**, **1**) to move to that location. Although this concept may take a little getting used to at first, you will soon learn to become comfortable with the idea and find it useful in some situations.

Because of WordPerfect's clean screen, you can write without visual distractions, while the program quietly deploys its technical wizardry in the background. WordPerfect is programmed to stay out of your way as much as possible so that you can concentrate your efforts on writing and editing.

The Hidden-Code Concept

Whatever you type from the keyboard becomes part of your document—mistakes and all. When you press certain keys or key combinations—such as Tab, Center, Flush Right, or Enter—WordPerfect inserts codes into your document at that point. They tell the program to do certain things to the document, either on the screen or at the printer. For Tab, Center, and Flush Right, text immediately following one of these codes appears on the screen accordingly: tabbed text is indented, centered text centered, and flush-right text placed on the right side of the screen. The Enter key moves the cursor down one line and to the left edge of the screen.

The point is that WordPerfect 5.1 does not clutter the screen with these codes as you type. It hides them, but you can view them whenever you want. For example, if you have on-screen a document containing the four preceding codes, you can view these hidden codes by using Reveal Codes (F11 or Alt-F3). In a special window in the bottom half of the screen, you will see these four codes as **[Flsh Rgt]**, **[Center]**, **[Tab]**, and **[HRt]** (see fig. 2.1). If you want to shift some text from flush right to the center, just position the cursor on the **[Flsh Rgt]** code, press the Del (Delete) key, and then use the Center command (Shift-F6).

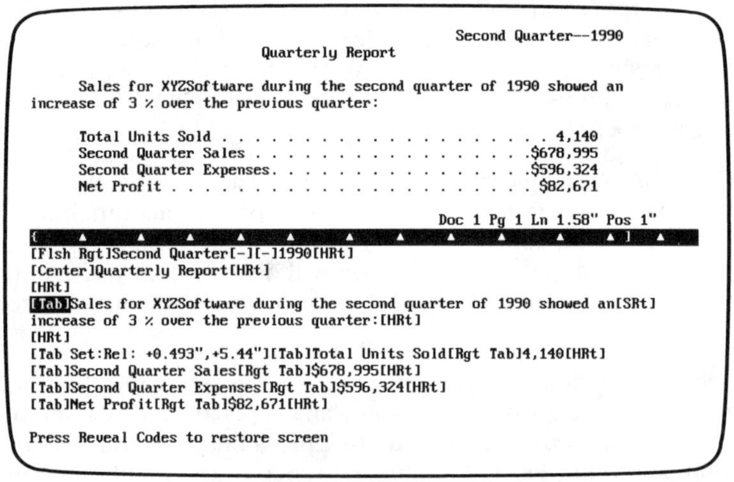

Fig. 2.1.

A WordPerfect Reveal Codes screen showing hidden codes.

```
                                             Second Quarter--1990
                           Quarterly Report
          Sales for XYZSoftware during the second quarter of 1990 showed an
     increase of 3 % over the previous quarter:

          Total Units Sold . . . . . . . . . . . . . . . . . . . 4,140
          Second Quarter Sales . . . . . . . . . . . . . . . .$678,995
          Second Quarter Expenses. . . . . . . . . . . . . . .$596,324
          Net Profit . . . . . . . . . . . . . . . . . . . . . $82,671

                                        Doc 1 Pg 1 Ln 1.58" Pos 1"
{     ▲     ▲     ▲     ▲     ▲     ▲      ▲     ▲     ▲  ] ▲
[Flsh Rgt]Second Quarter[-][-]1990[HRt]
[Center]Quarterly Report[HRt]
[HRt]
[Tab]Sales for XYZSoftware during the second quarter of 1990 showed an[SRt]
increase of 3 % over the previous quarter:[HRt]
[HRt]
[Tab Set:Rel: +0.493",+5.44"][Tab]Total Units Sold[Rgt Tab]4,140[HRt]
[Tab]Second Quarter Sales[Rgt Tab]$678,995[HRt]
[Tab]Second Quarter Expenses[Rgt Tab]$596,324[HRt]
[Tab]Net Profit[Rgt Tab]$82,671[HRt]

Press Reveal Codes to restore screen
```

Most of WordPerfect's codes are easy to interpret. For example, a code that sets the left and right margins at one and a half inches from each side of the page appears in Reveal Codes as **[L/R Mar:1.5",1.5"]**. Appendix C in the WordPerfect manual contains a complete list and description of the hidden codes.

Think of these codes as formatting instructions. Most formatting codes are *open codes*. Each open code affects all text to the right of the code or between that code and the end of the document. **[Center]** and **[Flsh Rgt]** affect all text between the code and the end of the line. A margin setting code, however, affects all text between that code and the end of the document. If you change your left and right margins on page three from 1" by 1", for example, to 1.5" by 1.5", all text following the new margin code to the end of the document will print with 1.5" margins.

Some instructions, such as boldface and italic, require two codes, a begin code and an end code. Codes to turn on attribute features (bold, italic, small font, and so on) appear as uppercase letters in Reveal Codes, and codes to turn off the feature appear as lowercase letters (for example, **[BOLD]**bold text here**[bold]**). Such codes are known as *paired codes*. Only the text between the two codes will print as the codes indicate.

While you are working in the normal editing screen (with Reveal Codes off) and are removing text with either the Backspace or Del key, you may see a message such as Delete [(Name of code)]? No (Yes) in the lower left corner of the screen. This message lets you know that you have encountered a hidden code, and the program needs to find out if you want to remove the code. To delete it, select **Y**. Press any other key to leave the code in place.

If you suspect that you have a hidden code somewhere in your document but don't know where, go to the beginning of the document (Home, Home, up arrow) and use the Search command. For example, to search for a margin setting code, press Search (F2); then specify the Margins command (Shift-F8, **1**, **7**).

Note that if you have more than one code inserted at the same spot in your document (three margin setting codes, for example), only the final code is active. The other two codes are inactive. Thus, if you insert a new tab or margin setting and it doesn't work, most likely you inserted the new code to the left of the old code. Don't keep on inserting new codes. Just use Reveal Codes, position the cursor to the right of the old code, and insert the new setting command.

Once you master the concept that virtually all formatting instructions are controlled by either open or paired codes, and that you can access these codes easily from the editing screen, you are well on your way to mastering the program and solving mysteries as to why text appears certain ways.

The Unnamed-Document Concept

With some word processing programs, the user must create a document and name it. In DisplayWrite 4, for example, the user must issue a *Create Document* command and type the path and name of the document before typing any text.

WordPerfect lets you treat a new document just as a typist treats a new page in the typewriter: you just start typing. With a typewriter, you do not place a document in a folder (thus, giving it a name) until you have finished typing it and checking it for spelling. In fact, you may never put a typed document in a folder but may throw it in the trash instead. Likewise, with WordPerfect, you can type an entire document, check the spelling, print it, and then clear the screen without once naming the document or saving it to disk.

One advantage of the WordPerfect method is that you are not locked into a specific name for any given document. You can save the same document under different names, reflecting different editing sessions or the editorial work of different people. And you can compare the different editions of the same document, using WordPerfect's Document Compare feature, which shows all additions or subtractions to the document. Or you could retrieve a document that contains a standard form, type in new information, and save the document under a new name. The WordPerfect method of document naming has many advantages.

The Default-Settings Concept

The reason why you can start typing immediately without first creating and naming a document is that WordPerfect uses preset format settings (such as paper size, initial font, justification, footnotes, margins, and tab settings) for every document you create. These settings are known as *default settings*, and they apply to all new documents created with the program. Figure 2.2 shows some default settings for a typical WordPerfect document.

Fig. 2.2.

Default settings for a standard document.

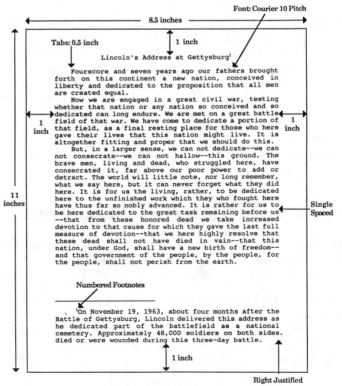

Of course, you can change the default settings for the kinds of documents you generally create. You make these changes by using the Setup command (Shift-F1) and then selecting Initial Settings (4) and Initial Codes (5).

At the Initial Codes screen, for example, you can insert a variety of default settings—margins, tabs, paper size and type, hyphenation and justification, headers, footers, and page numbers. These settings are stored in the WP{WP}.SET file and are active each time you start WordPerfect.

There are three important facts to remember about default settings. First, they are kept in a special file header (sometimes called a file preface). Since they are not viewable in either the normal editing window or the Reveal Codes window, they are invisible settings. Second, you can alter or remove them by pressing Setup (Shift-F1). Third, these settings affect all new documents, but not old documents (which already have their own default settings).

But what if you want to change the default settings of an old document to your new settings? Do you have to go in and change everything one at a time? No, and use this trick instead. Start with a clear screen and press any key—the space bar or the letter *x*, for example. Now, press Retrieve (Shift-F10), retrieve the old document into your new window (which has your new default settings), and press Backspace once to remove the space or letter *x*. The old document will take on the new default settings automatically. Save the document, using the old name or a different name if you prefer.

Moving the Cursor

Like any powerful word processing program, WordPerfect provides various ways of moving around within or between documents. Table 2.1 summarizes the most important cursor movements possible with the arrow keys.

In addition to the arrow key movements, WordPerfect lets you move the cursor by individual pages. The Page Up (or PgUp) and Page Down (or PgDn) keys, for example, move the cursor backward or forward through the document page-by-page. If you press the GoTo command (Ctrl-Home) and specify a page number, the cursor will jump to that page in the document. Or if you wan to move backward or forward five pages, press Esc, type 5, and press either Page Up or Page Down. To move the cursor to its previous location before the last major movement command was issued, press Ctrl-Home, Ctrl-Home.

Table 2.1
Cursor Movement with the Arrow Keys

Cursor Movement	Key(s)
Left one character or space	Left arrow
Right one character or space	Right arrow
Up one line	Up arrow
Down one line	Down arrow
Beginning of preceding word	Ctrl-left arrow
Beginning of next word	Ctrl-right arrow
Beginning of current or preceding paragraph[1]	Ctrl-up arrow
Beginning of next paragraph[2]	Ctrl-down arrow
Left edge of screen	Home, left arrow
Right edge of screen	Home, right arrow
Top of screen	Home, up arrow[3]
Bottom of screen	Home, down arrow[4]
Beginning of line (after any hidden codes)	Home, Home, left arrow
Far right of line	Home, Home, right arrow[5]
Top of document (after any hidden codes)	Home, Home, up arrow
Bottom of document (after any hidden codes)	Home, Home, down arrow
Beginning of line (before any hidden codes)	Home, Home, Home, left arrow
Top of document (before any hidden codes)	Home, Home, Home, up arrow
Top of current page	Ctrl-Home, up arrow[6]
Bottom of current page	Ctrl-Home, down arrow[7]

Depends on the location of the cursor. Available only on certain Enhanced Keyboards.

[2]Available only on certain Enhanced Keyboards.

[3]Repeat for Screen Up (so also Plus key on numeric keypad).

[4]Repeat for Screen Down (so also Minus key on numeric keypad).

[5]Or End key.

[6]Use PgUp for top of preceding page.

[7]Use PgDn for top of next page.

Using the Function Keys

The function keys, F1 through F10 or F12, implement different WordPerfect commands. When used alone, the 10 (or 12) function keys produce the feature or menu listed in black on the template overlay. When used in combination with the Alt (blue), Shift (green), or Ctrl (red) key, the program accesses the feature identified by that color on the overlay. Table 2.2 lists the 40 WordPerfect features accessed by the function keys.

Table 2.2
WordPerfect's Function-Key Commands

Key	Alone	Shift	Alt	Ctrl
F1	Cancel	Setup	Thesaurus	Shell
F2	Search→	←Search	Replace	Spell
F3	Help	Switch	Reveal Codes	Screen
F4	Indent	L/R Indent	Block	Move
F5	List	Date/Outline	Mark Text	Text In/Out
F6	Bold	Center	Flush Right	Tab Align
F7	Exit	Print	Columns/Table	Footnote
F8	Underline	Format	Style	Font
F9	End Field	Merge Codes	Graphics	Merge/Sort
F10	Save	Retrieve	Macro	Macro Define
F11	Reveal Codes			
F12	Block			

If you have an Enhanced IBM keyboard, F11 produces Reveal Codes, and F12 produces Block, which duplicate Alt-F3 and Alt-F4, respectively. However, you can add a total of six more commands to those two keys (with Alt, Shift, and Ctrl), using your own keyboard definitions.

Managing Files and Printing

WordPerfect's file and print management is without a doubt the most advanced in the word processing field. You can not only rename files and move them around from within the program, but also *password protect* sensitive documents so that others cannot read the contents. Likewise, you can print specific pages or ranges of pages from a document on-screen or a document on disk, or you can even print multiple copies collated or uncollated. Many of the features discussed in this section are very useful in an office setting.

Listing Files

To find out which documents you have on a disk or in a subdirectory, use the List (F5) command. Figure 2.3 illustrates how WordPerfect lists files in a subdirectory (in this case, C:\ARTICLES*.*) alphabetically in two columns.

Fig. 2.3.

A WordPerfect List Files screen showing two columns of files.

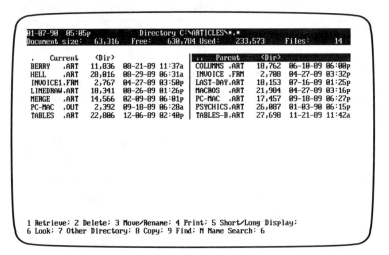

```
01-07-90  05:05p              Directory C:\ARTICLES\*.*
Document size:    63,316   Free:     630,784 Used:     233,573     Files:     14

   .     Current  <Dir>              ..      Parent    <Dir>
BERRY    .ART   11,836  08-21-89 11:37a   COLUMNS  .ART   18,762  06-18-89 06:00p
HELL     .ART   28,016  08-29-89 06:31a   INVOICE  .FRM    2,708  04-27-89 03:32p
INVOICE1.FRM     2,767  04-27-89 03:50p   LAST-DAY.ART   18,153  07-16-89 01:25p
LIMEDRAW.ART    18,341  08-26-89 01:26p   MACROS   .ART   21,904  04-27-89 03:16p
MERGE    .ART   14,566  02-09-89 06:01p   PC-MAC   .ART   17,457  09-18-89 06:27p
PC-MAC   .OUT    2,392  09-18-89 06:28a   PSYCHICS.ART   26,087  01-03-90 06:15p
TABLES   .ART   22,006  12-06-89 02:40p   TABLES-B.ART   27,698  11-21-89 11:42a




1 Retrieve; 2 Delete; 3 Move/Rename; 4 Print; 5 Short/Long Display;
6 Look; 7 Other Directory; 8 Copy; 9 Find; N Name Search: 6
```

The nine options at the bottom of the List Files screen allow you to retrieve a document (**1**), delete a document (**2**), move or rename a document (**3**), print a document (**4**), change the width of the file display (**5**), look at a file without saving it in memory (**6**), switch to another directory and make it the default directory (**7**), copy a file (**8**), or search a specific file within a directory (**9**). If many files are listed, you can search for a file by name with the Name Search command (**N**).

The Find option (**9**) enables you to search through WordPerfect document summaries for various data. With Find, you can locate files created before, after, or between certain dates; files written by one person and typed by another; or files by document name, document type, account number, keywords, or a brief abstract. The search can be limited to the document summary, the first page, or the entire document. Since conditions for the search can include one or more of the items previously mentioned, you can easily locate any particular file you might need. Files that match the search conditions are displayed on the List Files screen; the others are not displayed.

Using a Document Summary

In an office, files can often be forgotten or misplaced. The Document Summary command (Shift-F8, **3**, **5**) lets you identify files seven different ways: by the creation or last revision date (**1**), document name or type (**2**), author or typist (**3**), subject (**4**), account number or name (**5**), keywords (**6**), and abstract (**7**). Figure 2.4 shows how the document summary can contain a variety of information about a file.

```
Document Summary

        Revision Date

    1 - Creation Date   01-09-90 12:11p

    2 - Document Name   First Quarter Summary
        Document Type   Quarterly Report

    3 - Author          Lawrence Richardson
        Typist          Beverly Gibson

    4 - Subject         Sales for Ohio General Hardware

    5 - Account         #36523

    6 - Keywords        Sales, Summary, Quarterly

    7 - Abstract        Retail sales for Ohio General Hardware during the
                        first quarter of 1990 reached a total of $658,231.
                        This figure represents an increase of 9.4% in sales
                        over the same quarter one year earlier. Many factors
                        contributed to this healthy increase, among them

Press Exit when done
```

Fig. 2.4.

A sample Document Summary screen.

When you want to locate files by any of the seven Document Summary options (or combinations of these), just activate the Find command (see the preceding section).

Retrieving a File

Within the List Files screen, you highlight the document you want to retrieve and select **1**. This will load a copy of the file on disk into RAM and display the file on-screen. Of course, you do not have to use List to retrieve a document. Retrieve (Shift-F10) lets you retrieve a document without going to the List Files screen. When you press Retrieve (Shift-F10), WordPerfect prompts

```
Document to be retrieved:
```

You can either type the file path and name or press List (F5) to check the file or path name of the file you want. Note that if you have text on-screen when you press Retrieve, the document to be retrieved will be inserted at the current location of the cursor.

Saving a Document

To save the current document to disk, press Save (F10) or Exit (F7). Save makes a copy of the document on the disk but leaves the original on the screen. Exit, on the other hand, first lets you save the document, and then clears the screen. In either case, if the document already has a name, WordPerfect will offer that name and ask `Replace (filename)? No (Yes)`.

Select **Y** to replace the old version with the new version, or **N** to give the file a different name or extension. Save (F10) can also be used to save blocked sections of text to disk. Just block the section you want to place on disk, and press Save (F10). The original remains on-screen, but a copy of that section is placed on disk.

WordPerfect's Fast Save option (Shift-F1, **3**, **5**) speeds up the time it takes to store a copy of the document on disk. Fast-saved 5.1 documents, unlike version 5.0 fast-saved documents, can be printed from disk.

Save in WordPerfect 5.1 now offers a Long Display option (F5, **5**, **2**), which permits a 68-character extended file name, a portion of which can be displayed on the List Files screen.

Importing and Exporting Text

If you have documents in ASCII format to import, or want to save a WordPerfect 5.1 document to WordPerfect 5.0 or 4.2 format, Generic format, or ASCII format, you use the Text In/Out (Ctrl-F5) command. When you activate Text In/Out, a menu bar appears on-screen showing the following options:

```
1 DOS Text; 2 Password; 3 Save As; 4 Comment; 5 Spreadsheet: 0
```

If you want to save a WordPerfect 5.1 document in another format, select Save **As** (**3**). This will provide three options:

```
1 Generic; 2 WordPerfect 5.0; 3 WordPerfect 4.2: 0
```

The WordPerfect 5.0 and WordPerfect 4.2 options convert the file into either of the earlier versions. Generic format is different from DOS Text ASCII format in that all WordPerfect codes are removed, except for Tab and Indent codes. Indent codes in Generic format become Tab codes.

To import Excel, Lotus, and PlanPerfect spreadsheet documents, use the Spreadsheet Import command (Ctrl-F5, **5**, **1**).

Using Password Protection

Sensitive employee records and other personal files can be locked by the Password Add/Change command (Ctrl-F5, **2**, **1**). A *password* is a code word or phrase you supply to encrypt the entire contents of a file. Even expert DOS hackers cannot unscramble messages that have been protected with Password. This feature is widely useful in an office, especially when two or more users share the same machine. Be certain to remember your special password, or the file will remain forever locked and unreadable.

Printing

In WordPerfect 5.1 you can print individual pages or a range of pages either from a list of files (as in fig. 2.3) or from the document on-screen.

To print a document from disk, press List (F5) and then Enter, highlight the file to be printed, and select **Print** (**4**). You can also mark with an asterisk (*) several files you want printed; then select **4**. To print certain pages from a file on-screen, use Print (Shift-F7) and then select **Multiple Pages** (**5**).

To print the current document, use Print (Shift-F7). WordPerfect then provides a number of printing options, as shown in figure 2.5.

```
Print

        1 - Full Document
        2 - Page
        3 - Document on Disk
        4 - Control Printer
        5 - Multiple Pages
        6 - View Document
        7 - Initialize Printer

Options

        S - Select Printer              HP LaserJet IID (Additional)
        B - Binding Offset              0"
        N - Number of Copies            1
        U - Multiple Copies Generated by  WordPerfect
        G - Graphics Quality            Medium
        T - Text Quality                High




Selection: 0
```

Fig. 2.5.

Options available on the WordPerfect Print Screen.

If your printer has the capability, WordPerfect 5.1 lets you decide whether multiple copies of a document will be printed collated or uncollated. In an uncollated 10-page document, for example, page 8 may print x number of times before page 9 begins printing. Collated, one entire set of pages for a single document will print before another set is started. This option is found on the Print menu (Shift-F7), under Multiple Copies Generated by (**U**). If you select **P**rinter, every copy of page 1 will print before page 2 starts (uncollated). But if you select **W**ordPerfect, one entire document prints before another starts (collated).

Duplex (double-sided) printing on printers with that capability is also supported in version 5.1. To activate duplex printing, press Home, Home, up arrow (to go to the beginning of the document) and select a duplex paper size from the Format (Shift-F8) **P**age (**2**) Paper **S**ize (**7**) menu. Figure 2.6 shows a Paper Format screen for the Hewlett-Packard LaserJet Series IID printer, which permits duplex printing.

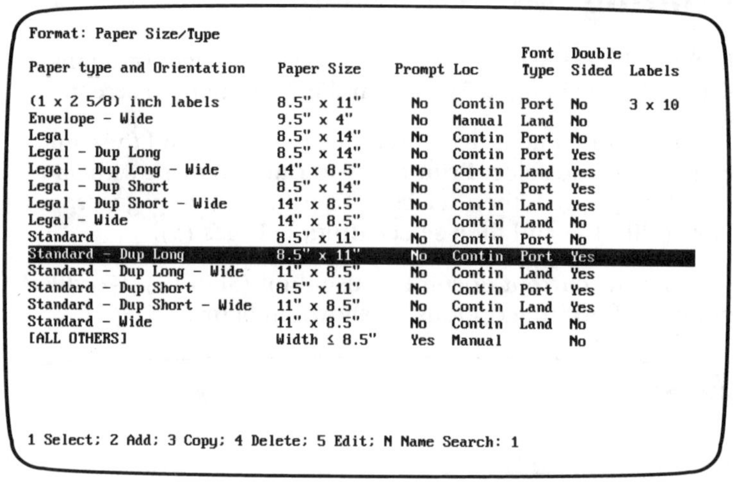

Fig. 2.6.

Paper types for a Hewlett-Packard LaserJet Series IID printer.

```
Format: Paper Size/Type

                                                         Font  Double
Paper type and Orientation    Paper Size    Prompt Loc   Type  Sided  Labels

(1 x 2 5/8) inch labels       8.5" x 11"    No   Contin  Port  No     3 x 10
Envelope - Wide               9.5" x 4"     No   Manual  Land  No
Legal                         8.5" x 14"    No   Contin  Port  No
Legal - Dup Long              8.5" x 14"    No   Contin  Port  Yes
Legal - Dup Long - Wide       14" x 8.5"    No   Contin  Land  Yes
Legal - Dup Short             8.5" x 14"    No   Contin  Port  Yes
Legal - Dup Short - Wide      14" x 8.5"    No   Contin  Land  Yes
Legal - Wide                  14" x 8.5"    No   Contin  Land  No
Standard                      8.5" x 11"    No   Contin  Port  No
Standard - Dup Long           8.5" x 11"    No   Contin  Port  Yes
Standard - Dup Long - Wide    11" x 8.5"    No   Contin  Land  Yes
Standard - Dup Short          8.5" x 11"    No   Contin  Port  Yes
Standard - Dup Short - Wide   11" x 8.5"    No   Contin  Land  Yes
Standard - Wide               11" x 8.5"    No   Contin  Land  No
[ALL OTHERS]                  Width ≤ 8.5"  Yes  Manual         No




1 Select; 2 Add; 3 Copy; 4 Delete; 5 Edit; N Name Search: 1
```

Double-sided forms are identified as either *Duplex Long* or *Duplex Short*. Duplex Long (highlighted as `Dup Long` in fig. 2.6) means that the pages are printed front and back, as if attached along the long edge of the paper—like pages in a book. Duplex Short means that the pages are printed front and back, as if the pages were attached at the top and bottom—like a stenographer's spiral-ring notebook. Either Duplex Long or Duplex Short can appear in *Wide* form, which means that the pages are printed front and back with text running in landscape mode (parallel to the 11" or 14" sides of the paper) and landscape font.

Another valuable feature offered by WordPerfect is its "intelligent printing" capability. When you create a new document, WordPerfect formats the text according to the printer you have selected, and uses the fonts available with that printer. When you change a font, WordPerfect offers only the fonts that will actually print on your machine. As a result, each document you create is printer-specific. This printer and font information is stored in a special document header (see "The Default-Settings Concept" earlier in this chapter).

Should you later retrieve that document on a computer connected to a different printer, WordPerfect will select new fonts according to the new printer and automatically adjust the document so that it will print on the new hardware combination. This unique capability allows you, for example, to create a document at the office and print it on a laser printer. In the evening at home, you can edit the document and print it again, using a dot-matrix printer.

WordPerfect 5.1 now supports more printers than any other word processor in the PC market—nearly 600 different printers.

Using Editing Commands and Windows

Word processing on a PC involves two basic stages: writing copy and editing the text after it is written. With any word processor, you can type characters into a document, but not all word processors have the same editing capabilities. With WordPerfect, users receive excellent tools for editing text.

With version 5.1, editing—blocking, moving (cutting), copying, deleting, and appending text—can be easier with a mouse. To highlight three lines of one paragraph and half of the next one, for example, just position the mouse pointer, press the left button, drag the pointer to the end of the block, and release the button. Although you can do the same thing with arrow keys and function-key commands, that method is more time-consuming. For editing typed documents, try the mouse. You may soon become addicted.

Blocking Text

In WordPerfect, Block (F12 or Alt-F4) is a powerful editing command. Once a passage of text has been highlighted, that passage can be marked, moved, copied, deleted, printed, saved, searched, formatted with a style, block-protected, converted to upper- or lowercase, spell-checked, appended to the end of another file, enhanced with a font attribute, converted to a different font size, centered, made flush right, or sorted.

Block is an easy command to use. Position the cursor at the beginning of the sentence or section to be highlighted and press Block (F12 or Alt-F4). Then move the cursor to the other end of the material to be blocked. Or turn on Block at the beginning of a sentence and type a period (.), question mark (?), or exclamation point (!) to highlight the sentence. Figure 2.7 shows how a block looks after you turn it on at the beginning of a sentence and type a period (.). To highlight an entire paragraph that ends with a **[HRt]** (hard return) code, turn on Block at the beginning of the paragraph and press Enter.

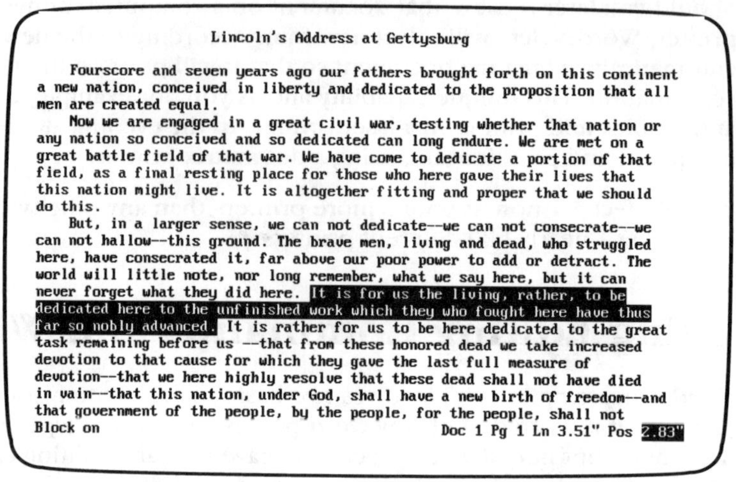

Fig. 2.7.
_____

*A blocked
sentence within
a paragraph.*

```
                     Lincoln's Address at Gettysburg
      Fourscore and seven years ago our fathers brought forth on this continent
  a new nation, conceived in liberty and dedicated to the proposition that all
  men are created equal.
      Now we are engaged in a great civil war, testing whether that nation or
  any nation so conceived and so dedicated can long endure. We are met on a
  great battle field of that war. We have come to dedicate a portion of that
  field, as a final resting place for those who here gave their lives that
  this nation might live. It is altogether fitting and proper that we should
  do this.
      But, in a larger sense, we can not dedicate--we can not consecrate--we
  can not hallow--this ground. The brave men, living and dead, who struggled
  here, have consecrated it, far above our poor power to add or detract. The
  world will little note, nor long remember, what we say here, but it can
  never forget what they did here. It is for us the living, rather, to be
  dedicated here to the unfinished work which they who fought here have thus
  far so nobly advanced. It is rather for us to be here dedicated to the great
  task remaining before us --that from these honored dead we take increased
  devotion to that cause for which they gave the last full measure of
  devotion--that we here highly resolve that these dead shall not have died
  in vain--that this nation, under God, shall have a new birth of freedom--and
  that government of the people, by the people, for the people, shall not
  Block on                                       Doc 1 Pg 1 Ln 3.51" Pos 2.83"
```

▭To block text with the mouse, place the mouse pointer at one end of the section
to be moved, click the left button, drag the pointer to the other end of the section,
and release the button.

Copying and Moving Text

The Move (Ctrl-F4) command allows you to move or copy blocked sentences,
paragraphs, columns, rectangles, or pages to a different location in a file or to
another file in Doc 2, or to append them to a file on disk. Combined with Block,
the Move command enables you to move or copy any amount of text from one
location to another, or to copy the blocked text over and over again. If you have an
Enhanced Keyboard, the shortcuts in version 5.1 for moving or copying blocked
text are Block Move (Ctrl-Del) and Block Copy (Ctrl-Ins).

Appending Text

After you have blocked text by using Block and either the arrow keys or a mouse,
you can append that document portion—short or long—to the end of any
WordPerfect file on disk. When you use Move (Ctrl-F4), select **Block (1)**; the
following menu appears at the bottom of the screen:

```
    1 Move; 2 Copy; 3 Delete; 4 Append: 0
```

When you select **Append (4)**, the prompt Append to: appears. After you type the
path and file name, WordPerfect adds the blocked text to the end of that file on
disk. If no file exists with that name, WordPerfect will create the file. Note that

highlighted text can be saved or appended also to the WordPerfect Library (Office) clipboard if you press Ctrl-F1 and select **2** or **3**.

Deleting and Undeleting Text

WordPerfect offers seven different ways to delete text:

1. Backspace (preceding character and blocked text)

2. Delete (single character and blocked text)

3. Ctrl-Backspace (preceding word)

4. Ctrl-End (to end of line)

5. Ctrl-PgDn (to end of page)

6. Home-Backspace (cursor to beginning of word)

7. Home-Del (cursor to end of word)

Remember, however, that deleted text is not gone forever. It is placed temporarily in a special delete buffer and can be undeleted (retrieved) later if you press Cancel (F1) and select **Restore** (**1**). Since the delete buffer temporarily stores up to three different deletions, you can reclaim information you deleted accidentally—as long as you do so before adding more deletions to the buffer. When you exit WordPerfect, all temporary deletions are discarded from memory.

Switching Documents

Besides providing you with editing tools, WordPerfect enables you to work with two documents at the same time: one in the Doc 1 window and another in the Doc 2 window. To jump between the two documents, just press Switch (Shift-F3).

Switch also lets you jump between a footnote and the main document body copy. If, for example, you find two documents too limiting for your editing needs, use the Switch command with a footnote in either document, and end up with four or more editable WordPerfect documents at the same time (two main documents and two footnote documents). When you have finished editing the footnote documents, you can save them to disk as a regular file, or append them to another file. This little editing trick works also with endnotes. Footnotes and endnotes are discussed later in this chapter.

Windowing Options

If you work with more than one document at a time, you may want to change the size of one of the two windows so that both documents can be seen on-screen at the same time. Figure 2.8 illustrates how you can check a table in Doc 1 while typing a letter in Doc 2, with each window taking up half of the screen.

Fig. 2.8.

Two WordPerfect windows open at the same time.

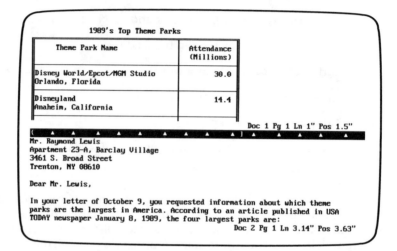

```
                    1989's Top Theme Parks

   ┌──────────────────────────────────┬─────────────────┐
   │  Theme Park Name                 │ Attendance      │
   │                                  │ (Millions)      │
   ├──────────────────────────────────┼─────────────────┤
   │ Disney World/Epcot/MGM Studio    │     30.0        │
   │ Orlando, Florida                 │                 │
   ├──────────────────────────────────┼─────────────────┤
   │ Disneyland                       │     14.4        │
   │ Anaheim, California              │                 │
   └──────────────────────────────────┴─────────────────┘
                                          Doc 1 Pg 1 Ln 1" Pos 1.5"

Mr. Raymond Lewis
Apartment 23-A, Barclay Village
3461 S. Broad Street
Trenton, NY 08610

Dear Mr. Lewis,

In your letter of October 9, you requested information about which theme
parks are the largest in America. According to an article published in USA
TODAY newspaper January 8, 1989, the four largest parks are:
                                          Doc 2 Pg 1 Ln 3.14" Pos 3.63"
```

With version 5.1, if both windows are visible at the same time and you use a mouse, you can jump between the two documents by clicking in either window. Using a mouse to copy data or move text between two windows works almost like lightning.

To make two windows equal in size, use Screen (Ctrl-F3), select **Window (1)**, type *12*, and press Enter. To return a window to its full screen size, repeat the preceding steps, but type *24* instead of 12.

Using Reveal Codes

All formatting codes are hidden in the Reveal Codes window (F11 or Alt-F3). Version 5.1 has two additional capabilities for Reveal Codes: the Reveal Codes window can be resized (Shift-F1, **2**, **6**, **6**); and the Alt-E macro on the SHORTCUT keyboard permits editing of format codes from within the Reveal Codes window. Just place the cursor in the Reveal Codes window on the code that you want to modify, and press Alt-E.

Searching for and Locating Items

When editing a document, you may need to locate a specific passage to move or copy it elsewhere. If you do not remember its page number, you could waste considerable time trying to locate the passage visually by using the cursor-movement keys. Therefore, let the computer do the searching for you. It is ideal for searching and can far outperform human effort in this activity.

Searching Forward and Backward

If you are at or near the beginning of a document, search forward by pressing F2, typing the desired word or word phrase, and pressing F2 again. Moments later WordPerfect will find the word or phrase for you—faster than any human eye could duplicate. If the cursor is past the word or phrase in the document, search backward by pressing Shift-F2, typing the word or phrase, and pressing F2 again. Or you can change a forward search into a backward search by pressing F2, up arrow, then typing the word to be seached, and pressing F2 again.

In addition to text, you can search for codes by pressing the function keys for that particular code (Center, Flush Right, Footnote, Bold, Underline, and so on). To search for a pair of codes, such as **[UND][und]**, press the function key twice; to search for just the second half of a pair, delete the first paired code—for example, **[UND]**.

Replacing Words or Phrases

If you want to change every occurrence of a certain word or phrase to another word or phrase—such as Mr. Rees to Mr. Reese or October 9 to October 19—the Replace command (Alt-F2) will do the work for you in a matter of seconds, even in a long document. With business documents, this command can save much time that otherwise would be spent locating and changing things manually. Replace also works with a number of formatting codes, such as Align, Center, Columns On/Off, Flush Right, Font Size, Graphics Box Number, Hard Page, Hard Space, Hyphen, Indent, Margin Release, Note Numbers, Outline Off, Tab Types, and Tab Align.

To search for or replace text in all headers, footers, footnotes, endnotes, and graphic and text box captions, use the Extended Search (Home, F2) or Extended Replace command (Home, Alt-F2).

Using the GoTo Command (Ctrl-Home)

If you have a 40-page report and you want to jump to a figure on page 26, just press GoTo (Ctrl-Home), type the page number, and press Enter. GoTo operates much faster than the PgUp or PgDn commands, which stop at every page in between.

GoTo is particularly useful when you are using paper copies to edit long documents on-screen. But take a tip from an expert: it always is best to edit backward from paper copy—that is, to make corrections to the last pages on-screen first and to work your way toward the beginning of the file. This way, the page sequence will remain unchanged between the paper copy and the screen version until you have completed your editing session.

Enhancing Layout and Formats

In WordPerfect the Format command (Shift-F8) offers a wide variety of options in the way text is displayed or printed. The various format options are divided conveniently into four groups: Line Format, Page Format, Document Format, and Other. Generally, Format codes are placed at the beginning of a line, Page Format codes at the beginning of a page, and Document Format codes at the beginning of a document in the document header. This section also discusses related layout features, such as Columns, Tables, Footnotes, Endnotes, Align, and Styles.

Formatting Lines

Format Line options (Shift-F8, **1**) deal with the way text is formatted horizontally on a line—that is, across the page. As shown in figure 2.9, Format Line includes such options as Line Height, Line Numbering, Line Spacing, Hyphenation, Justification, Tab Settings, Widow/Orphan Protection, and Margins Left/Right (but not Margins Top/Bottom, which is in Format Page).

Format Line in WordPerfect 5.1 includes fractional settings, four types of justification, and relative tab and indent settings.

With fractional settings, you can type fractions rather than just decimals for tab, margin, line height, and line-spacing settings. For fractional settings, for example, you may set a tab or margin at 1 5/8" by typing *1*, space, *5*, */*, *8*. This may be easier than trying to remember that 5/8" is .625".

Having available four types of line justification—left-aligned, center-aligned, right-aligned, or full justification—is very useful for certain types of documents prepared in the office environment.

```
Format: Line

     1 - Hyphenation                    No

     2 - Hyphenation Zone - Left        10%
                           Right        4%

     3 - Justification                  Left

     4 - Line Height                    Auto

     5 - Line Numbering                 No

     6 - Line Spacing                   1

     7 - Margins - Left                 1"
                  Right                 1"

     8 - Tab Set                        Rel: -1", every 0.5"

     9 - Widow/Orphan Protection        No


Selection: 0
```

Fig. 2.9.

Horizontal formatting selected from the Line Format menu.

With relative tab settings, you can now set tabs so that they are indented in relation to the edge of the text rather than the edge of the paper. This option is useful when you are working with columns, because you no longer have to set tabs for each column you create. Figure 2.10 shows a letter with the first tab setting at one quarter of an inch, and the R tab setting at the right at five and a half inches. The highlighting on the right tab indicates that it is a dot leader tab.

```
                                          October 9, 1990

    Mr. Raymond Lewis
    Apartment 23-A, Barclay Village
    3461 S. Broad Street
    Trenton, NY 08610

    Dear Mr. Lewis,

        In your letter of October 9, you requested information about which theme
    parks are the largest in America. According to an article published in USA
    TODAY newspaper January 8, 1989, the four parks with the largest attendance
    during 1989 are:

        • Disney World/Epcot/MGM Studio . . . . . . 30.0 million
        • Disneyland. . . . . . . . . . . . . . 14.4 million
        • Universal Studios . . . . . . . . . . .5.1 million
        • Knotts Berry Farm . . . . . . . . . . .5.0 million


    L..L.L. . . . . . . . . . . . . . . . . . . . . . R . . . . . . .
        ^     ┊     ^     ┊     ^     ┊     ^     ┊     ^     ┊     ^     ┊
    0"        +1"        +2"        +3"        +4"        +5"        +6"        +7"
    Delete EOL (clear tabs); Enter Number (set tab); Del (clear tab);
    Type; Left; Center; Right; Decimal; .= Dot Leader; Press Exit when done.
```

Fig. 2.10.

Relative tabs measured from the left text edge.

One useful feature with version 5.1 is that text above the Tab ruler line changes as you change tab settings in the ruler. Thus, you can more easily visualize tab and indent changes as you make them.

Moreover, you can shift tab settings (and the text aligned on those tabs) by placing the curser on the Ruler tab marker you want to move, holding down Ctrl, and pressing either the right or left arrow. The tab marker will move right or left on the Ruler, and any text aligned on that particular tab will move with the tab marker.

In figure 2.10, for instance, if you wanted to adjust the tab setting for the text following the bullets ("Disney World," "Disneyland," and so on), just position the cursor on the right L tab marker, hold down the Ctrl key, and press either the right or left arrow. The L tab (and the text aligned on that tab) shifts right or left, depending on the arrow you press.

Another feature, Line Spacing (**6**), is useful for keeping text on a single page when you have one or two lines that run to a second page. For example, if you have a letter that fills one page and runs over to a second page two or three lines, you can pull those lines back by changing the line spacing (Shift-F8, **1**, **6**) at the top of the page from 1 to .95 or .93.

Formatting Pages

Format Page options (Shift-F8, **2**), which determine how text is formatted on the page, include page centering, creating headers and footers, page numbering, selecting paper size and type, and suppressing formats. Because Format Page deals with how text appears on a page, top and bottom margin settings are located on this menu rather than the Format Line menu.

Two important enhancements to Format Page are page numbering and paper form control. Page numbering in version 5.1 now offers three styles of page numbers: Arabic, uppercase Roman, and lowercase Roman. Text may also be included with page numbers—something not possible in version 5.0 unless you put page numbers in headers and footers.

Paper size and type control, which in version 5.0 were divided between Print and Format Page, are now placed together on the Format Page menu. This makes it much easier to switch between paper types for different kinds of documents.

In version 5.1, labels selected with the Format Page Paper Size/Type command (Shift-F8, **2**, **7**) are a joy rather than a frustration. In fact, WordPerfect 5.1 even includes a special label macro to assist you in creating a variety of label forms. For example, if you need to print some 2" by 4" labels, you can use the WordPerfect *LABELS.WPM* macro to select any of 10 different Avery labels. To run this macro, you press Macro (Alt-F10), type *LABELS* at the prompt, and press Enter.

The macro displays a table of label sizes (see fig. 2.11), from which you select with a movable highlight bar the kind of label you plan to use. In figure 2.11, the D label form (2" by 4" Avery 5163) is selected.

After you have chosen a label size from the table and created the label definition, you can select that size with the Format Page Paper Size/Type command. For example, the top option in figure 2.6 is a 1" x 2 5/8" label created by this procedure.

Formatting Documents

The Format Document (Shift-F8, **3**) menu contains the features Display Pitch (**1**), Initial Codes (**2**), Initial Base Font (**3**), Redline Method (**4**), and (document) Summary (**5**).

A problem some new users have encountered in working with version 5.1 is overlapped or mispositioned text on-screen—especially within tabs or columns. You can easily correct this problem by pressing Shift-F8, **3**, **1** and changing the display pitch to a value between .085" and .095". Smaller pitch settings (.085" or less) spread text on the screen; larger pitch settings (.095" or larger) compress text on the screen.

```
        Label Page/Size Definitions

 Mnu  Label Sizes      # of labels per..
 ltr   H x W          Sheet Row Column    Examples
  A   1" x 2 5/8"       30   3    10    Avery 5160/5260
  B   1" x 4"           20   2    10    Avery 5161/5261
  C   1 1/3" x 4"       14   2     7    Avery 5162/5262
  D   2" x 4"           10   2     5    Avery 5163
  E   3 1/3" x 4"        6   2     3    Avery 5164
  F   2/3" x 3 7/16"    30   2    15    Avery 5266
  G   1/2" x 1 3/4"     80   4    20    Avery 5267
  H   2 3/4" x 2 3/4"    9   3     3    Avery 5196
  I   1 1/2" x 4"       12   2     6    Avery 5197
  J   8 1/2" x 11"       1   0     0    Avery 5165
  K   1" x 2 5/8"       30   3    10    3M 7730
  L   1 1/2" x 2 5/6"   21   3     7    3M 7721
  M   1" x 2 5/6"       33   3    11    3M 7733
  N   2 1/2" x 2 5/6"   12   3     4    3M 7712
  O   3 1/3" x 2 5/6"    9   3     3    3M 7709
  P   11" x 8 7/16"      1   0     0    3M 7701

 (↑↓), (Mnu Ltr), or (∗), then Press Enter; More=PgDn

Selection: D
```

Fig. 2.11.

WordPerfect's label selection menu.

Initial Codes (**2**) lets the user change the default formatting codes for a single document. For example, if the normal default setting (see "The Default-Settings Concept" earlier in this chapter) had justification turned on, but you wanted it off for this particular document, just press Format (Shift-F8), Document (**3**), and Initial Codes (**2**). Then add any new format codes that you want activated for the particular document (or delete unwanted codes, if any). This feature is particularly useful for primary-file documents used in merges because it prevents unwanted duplication of formatting codes.

Initial Base Font (**3**) is the typeface (Times, for example), type style (Roman, for example), and font size (10 point, for example) in which a document will be printed, unless you select a base font in the document itself. When you create a document, the initial base font for your printer (Shift-F7, **s**, **3**, **5**) is the default base font for the document. All body copy, headers, footers, endnotes, footnotes, and so on print in that font and font size, unless you specify something else.

If you want one font for all headers and footnotes in a document and a different font for all body copy, select as your Initial Base Font (Shift-F8, **3**, **3**) the font for your headers and footnotes. Then, at the top of the document, press Ctrl-F8, **4**, and select another font for your body copy. WordPerfect keeps track of the two fonts and uses the correct font for the different parts of your document.

Redline Method (**4**) refers to the method of marking text in a document, such as text to be added, so it can be easily identified. Generally, a laser printer creates redline by shading the background behind the marked words, as in this example:

This is normal; this is redlined.

Performing Other Formatting

The Format Other command (Shift-F8, **4**) displays a menu of formatting features for **Advance** (**1**), **Conditional End of Page** (**2**), **Decimal/Align** character (**3**), **Language** (**4**), **Overstrike** (**5**), **Printer Functions** (**6**), **Underline** (**7**) for spaces or tabs, and **Border** (**8**) options in recent versions of WordPerfect 5.1. This menu thus groups a variety of formatting features that do not logically fit on the Format: Line, Format: Page, or Format: Document menus. The special printer functions enable you to adjust letter and word spacing, word spacing limits with justification, leading, and the placement of the baseline.

The Leading Adjustment feature is a useful enhancement for controlling paragraph spacing. With WordPerfect 5.1, you can now define the amount of space between paragraphs. To do this, press Shift-F8, **Other** (**4**), **Printer Functions** (**6**), **Leading Adjustment** (**6**) and increase the space allowed for Secondary **[Hrt]** (hard return) codes. You do this by adding line units (.5u) or points (3p) to the Secondary **[HRt]**s. WordPerfect inserts a **[Leading Adj:]** code at that location, and all subsequent paragraphs will print according to the new setting for secondary leading.

Creating Columns and Tables (Alt-F7)

Columns (Alt-F7) in version 5.1 work essentially as they did in version 5.0, with the exception of the Column Right (Alt-right arrow) and Column Left (Alt-left arrow) commands on the Enhanced Keyboard, which let you move between columns to the right or left.

⌨ With a mouse, of course, you can jump between columns by clicking in any column where you want to work.

A number of office documents—from simple forms to monthly or quarterly newsletters—can be enhanced dramatically with columns. Part V, "Creating Specialized Documents," explores this feature in detail, as does Part VII, "Desktop Publishing in the Office".

Many business users will find the Table feature the single most useful feature in WordPerfect 5.1 because of its wide application in the business environment. The following list includes some of the most important capabilities of this feature:

- Organizing information in chart format
- Creating customer invoices
- Composing work schedules and work estimates
- Writing expense reports
- Making questionnaires, job applications, and fill-in-the-blank forms

You can make tables up to 32 columns by as many as 32,765 rows. Table 2.3 illustrates the tremendous versatility of the table feature. Shown in 16 different cells is a different font attribute (bold, italic, underline, double underline, strikeout, and redline) or font size (normal, fine, small, large, very large, extra large, superscript, and subscript.)

Using Footnotes and Endnotes

With the Footnote command (Ctrl-F7), you can make and place footnotes and endnotes. They are useful for listing sources or providing additional information on data mentioned in your body copy. Although the trend today is away from extensive use of footnotes and endnotes, they still provide a valuable function when they do not distract from the appearance of the printed document.

One practical addition to Footnotes and Endnotes in WordPerfect 5.1 is the capability to arrange data in columns within footnotes, endnotes, graphic text boxes, headers, and footers.

Even tables can be created within or added to footnotes, endnotes, text boxes, headers and footers. If, for example, you work in a medical office that requires a specific form at the top of every page in a patient's record, you can place a table in a document header. You can also include a table in a footnote or endnote. The possibilities are endless.

Table 2.3
Font Sizes and Attributes in a Table

Font Size	Font Attribute
Normal Text	**Bold Text**
Fine Text	<u>Underline Text</u>
Small Text	<u>Double Underline Text</u>
Large Text	*Italic Text*
Very Large Text	**Shadow Text**
Extra Large	SMALL CAP TEXT
Superscript^{Text}	Redline Text
Subscript$_{Text}$	~~Strikeout Text~~

Aligning Text

The F6 key—when combined with Alt, Shift, and Ctrl—provides a number of methods for aligning text. The effects of Flush Right (Alt-F6), Center (Shift-F6), and Tab Align (Ctrl-F6) are all displayed on-screen just as they appear when printed. In addition, you can use Indent (F4) and Center Indent (Shift-F4) for individual lines or paragraphs.

Using Indent (F4) and Margin Release (Shift-Tab), you can create hanging indented paragraphs. For example, if you want to create a hanging indented paragraph, first press Indent (F4) and then press Margin Release (hold down the Shift key while you press Tab). This moves the first line of the paragraph to the tab setting at the left margin and lets the rest of the paragraph indent underneath.

Using the Style Command

The Style command (Alt-F8) is a helpful feature for text and formats that you use repeatedly. Different styles can be created for different types of documents, and all the formatting for those documents can be accessed by selecting a particular set of styles.

Styles are paired, open, or outline. A *paired* style is useful for formatting a particular section of a document; an *open* style is useful for changing the format of the entire document or all text from the point of insertion on. An *outline* style is for arranging material in a hierarchical manner. With the exception of the Outline Style feature (Alt-F8, **3**, **2**, **3**), the Style command remains essentially unchanged in version 5.1.

Using the Outline Command

One useful feature for the Outline command (Shift-F5, **4**) in version 5.1 is the **Move Family** (**3**), **Copy Family** (**4**), and **Delete Family** (**5**) options. Just position the cursor in the top line of the outline section that you want to move, copy, or delete, and press Shift-F5 and select **4**. Depending on whether you select Move, Copy, or Delete, WordPerfect 5.1 adjusts your outline accordingly. Move Family, Copy Family, and Delete Family work on outlines that contain extensive sections of regular body text, provided that Outline is turned on first.

Using Fonts and Special Characters

One of WordPerfect's strong capabilities is its efficient handling of font attributes, such as font size and font appearance. Users can automatically update fonts throughout a document by (a) changing the base font at the beginning of the document or (b) retrieving the document on a computer with a different printer defined. In either case, the program will perform an elaborate and complex document conversion to match the new base font or other printer fonts. WordPerfect 5.1 also makes it possible for virtually all dot-matrix or laser printers to print all 1,542 special characters listed in Appendix P of the WordPerfect manual.

Selecting Font Size

WordPerfect's Font Size command (Ctrl-F8, **1**) lets you select seven different automatic font sizes: Superscript, Subscript, Fine, Small, Large, Very Large, and Extra Large (see table 2.3). When you use these font sizes, all text is reformatted automatically when you change the document's base font. In other words, if you create a report using all font sizes (eight including normal font size) in Times Roman and later change the document's base font to Century Schoolbook or Helvetica, all font size selections throughout the document are automatically converted to match the new base font.

The same applies if you maintain the same font but change the base font size. For example, if you change the base font from Century Schoolbook 11 point to Century Schoolbook 12 point, all other font sizes are adjusted accordingly.

Selecting Font Appearance

In addition to the seven automatic font-size selections, WordPerfect offers nine font-appearance settings: Bold, Underline, Double Underline, Italic, Outline, Shadow, Small Caps, Redline, and Strikeout (see table 2.3). These are available with the Font Appearance command (Ctrl-F8, **2**). With the exception of Bold and Underline, which can be accessed also through the F6 and F8 function keys, respectively, all font appearances are selected with the Font Appearance command.

As with automatic font sizes, the other font attributes are automatically converted to match a new base font—if you have fonts available for those attributes.

Using Special Characters

A common complaint that previous WordPerfect users had was that they could not print all 1,600 special characters that version 5.0 could create, because their printer did not have the characters available in their cartridge or downloadable fonts. In version 5.1 this limitation has been overcome: the WP.DRS (*Device ReSources*) file contains all 1,542 characters (1,700 characters with PostScript dingbats) in a graphic format. Thus, any printer that can print graphics can print any of the special characters listed in the WordPerfect manual.

To create any of the special characters listed in of the WordPerfect manual, press Ctrl-V and then type the pair of numbers that represents that particular character. For example, the cent symbol (¢) is found in Character Set 4 (Typographic Symbols), about two-thirds of the way across the first line. If you count from the left edge of Character Set 4, you will see that the cent symbol is character 19. (The numbers 1 and 2 at the top edge of the table represent 10 and 20.) Therefore, this symbol is represented by two numbers: 4 (the table number) and 19 (the position in the table). To add the cent symbol to your document, press Ctrl-V (Key = will appear in the lower left corner). Then type *4,19* and press Enter. Or use the Ctrl-V, C, / shortcut to create the same character. The Compose section of the WordPerfect manual lists more than 60 such Compose shortcuts.

To view the ¢ symbol, you may actually see it on-screen, depending on your monitor and display setup. Some characters will appear as small squares, but they can be seen as their proper character if you use the Print, View Document command (Shift-F7, 6). If you then select the 200% menu option (**2**), you can see the character plainly.

Marking Text and Linking Documents

One of the strengths of a word processor in creating multipage reports and booklets is the capability to create automatically an index, a table of contents, lists, and tables of authority—with correct page references to all items no matter how many times the document has been revised or altered. These features, plus *Master Document* and *Document Compare*, are summarized in this section.

Indexing a Document

You can index a document by identifying all entries you want to include in the index, defining where and how you want the index to appear, and then generating the index. This feature is accessed by the Mark Text command (Alt-F5, 3). Or you can create a *concordance* file, listing in that file all the words you want indexed; define the index form and location; and then generate the index. WordPerfect automatically assembles the index from the words listed in the concordance file.

For company reports and papers, *Index Generation* or *Index with Concordance* is indeed a most useful feature.

Creating a Table of Contents

If you need a Table of Contents for your company report or paper, WordPerfect's Mark Text Table of Contents command (Alt-F5, **5**, **1**) is the solution. All you do is insert a **[Def Mark:ToC]** code at the beginning of your document where you want the Table of Contents to be created (generally on a page by itself); then mark all passages you want to have included on your Contents page. When you activate the Generate feature (Alt-F5, **6**, **5**), WordPerfect automatically locates every Table of Contents entry and displays it according to the page where each line appears.

Using Cross-References

In business reports or job estimates, it is useful to be able to reference a table, footnote, or other passage of text earlier or later in the document. With the Mark Text Cross-Reference command (Alt-F5, **1**), you can include a statement like *(see footnote 3, page 14)* in a document and know that no matter how many times you edit or change the document, the cross-reference will adjust itself automatically to the correct page number. Cross-Reference can include multiple numbers, as in *(for example, see Format, pages 21, 33, 45)*.

This feature is also useful if you want to create a header that says *Page 2 of 24*. Just put a target code, like *ENDFILE*, at the end of the document, and in the header use something like *Page ^B of ?* to link all page numbers to the end. (The *?* in WordPerfect represents the ENDFILE reference code.)

Creating Lists

WordPerfect also creates lists. The List option (Alt-F5, **5**, **2**) in WordPerfect 5.1 permits 10 kinds of lists: list numbers 1 through 5 are for any list you want to create, and items 6 through 10 are for automatic WordPerfect listings. WordPerfect uses list 6 for all figures, list 7 for all tables, list 8 for text boxes, list 9 for user-defined boxes, and list 10 for equation boxes.

Creating Tables of Authority

If you create legal documents, the Table of Authority feature may prove useful in your work. A Table of Authority is used primarily for legal briefs to list where specific case-citations and statutes occur in a document. The three steps for creating a Table of Authority are the following:

1. Mark the authorities you want to include by pressing Block (Alt-F5), **4**.

2. Define the sections of the table by pressing Block (Alt-F5), **5**.

3. Generate the table by pressing Block (Alt-F5), **6**.

Using a Master Document

A *master document* is a WordPerfect document that contains multiple subdocuments—each saved as a separate file to a disk. While you may not normally need, in an office setting, to create a book-sized document made up of several smaller documents or files, someone might be assigned a project such as preparing a company handbook or house stylebook. For someone working on such a project, the Master Document feature is indispensable.

You access the Master Document feature through the Mark Text Subdoc command (Alt-F5, **2**). This allows you to identify a subdocument for your Master Document. Doing this, you can link individual chapters or sections and apply a single overall formatting style and page numbering to all chapters or sections of the book.

Comparing Documents

Another helpful WordPerfect feature in the office environment is the Mark Text, Generate, Compare command (Alt-F5, **6**, **2**), which compares different versions of the same document and marks the differences between them.

For example, you can create a document (say, version A), save it to disk, then give a copy of the document to someone else in the office to revise. When the revision is done, you can compare version B of the document with version A of the same document, and WordPerfect will mark all the additions and deletions that have occurred. Added phrases are marked with redline; deleted phrases are marked with strikeout, as in the following examples:

> This is an added phrase in a document.

> ~~This is a deleted phrase in a document.~~

Moved text is identified with comments:

    THE FOLLOWING TEXT WAS MOVED

    THE PRECEDING TEXT WAS MOVED

With a color monitor, you or other members of the staff can easily identify these changes on-screen and evaluate them to see whether the changes are acceptable.

Using Tools for Special Projects

In addition to the basic File and Print Management, Editing, Windowing, Search and Replace, Layout and Formatting, Fonts, Special Characters, Marking, Indexing, and Linking Document features, WordPerfect also offers several special *Tools* that are useful in the office environment.

Using the Speller

WordPerfect's Spell command (Ctrl-F2) is one of the most powerful in existence in the PC environment. The Speller not only checks individual words and flags double words, but in version 5.1 also checks capitalization errors, such as one uppercase letter other than the first letter in a word, or two uppercase letters in one word. For example, these two misspellings would be flagged in version 5.1: hYphenation and HYphenation. A message in the lower left corner will indicate that the case is irregular, and you are prompted to select a menu item to show how you want the irregularity handled. Figure 2.12 illustrates the variety of corrections version 5.1 may offer when it encounters just a misspelled word.

The WordPerfect 5.1 dictionary also includes hyphenation instructions that can maximize the dictionary's utility. The program almost never stops for user input, because the enlarged dictionary covers 98 percent of the words used in normal business writing. To switch hyphenation on or off, press Shift-F8, select **1**, **1**, and then select either **Y** or **N**, respectively.

Fig. 2.12.

*The WordPerfect
spell-checking
screen.*

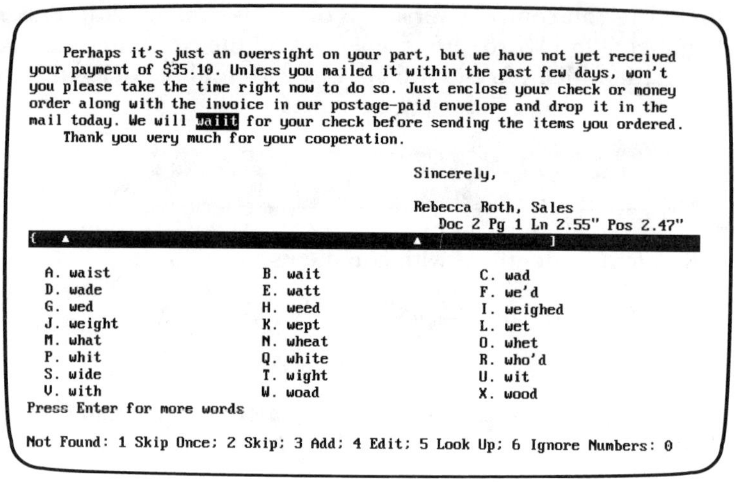

```
      Perhaps it's just an oversight on your part, but we have not yet received
   your payment of $35.10. Unless you mailed it within the past few days, won't
   you please take the time right now to do so. Just enclose your check or money
   order along with the invoice in our postage-paid envelope and drop it in the
   mail today. We will wait for your check before sending the items you ordered.
      Thank you very much for your cooperation.

                                          Sincerely,

                                          Rebecca Roth, Sales
                                             Doc 2 Pg 1 Ln 2.55" Pos 2.47"
```

```
      A. waist            B. wait            C. wad
      D. wade             E. watt            F. we'd
      G. wed              H. weed            I. weighed
      J. weight           K. wept            L. wet
      M. what             N. wheat           O. whet
      P. whit             Q. white           R. who'd
      S. wide             T. wight           U. wit
      V. with             W. woad            X. wood
   Press Enter for more words

   Not Found: 1 Skip Once; 2 Skip; 3 Add; 4 Edit; 5 Look Up; 6 Ignore Numbers: 0
```

Using the Thesaurus

The WordPerfect Thesaurus (Alt-F1) searches for and displays both synonyms and
antonyms of words in your text or words you enter from the keyboard. You can
also look up words displayed in one list, to locate just the right word that you need
to describe a product or explain an operation. Figure 2.13 shows how the
Thesaurus can display three different sets of synonyms at the same time.

The Thesaurus in version 5.1 can greatly assist you in choosing precise and
appropriate words.

Creating and Using Macros

Macros are one of the most powerful features for people who work in an office
setting. Nearly any operation you perform frequently with a word processor can be
assigned to a macro—writing, editing, drawing, merging, printing, spell-checking,
saving files, opening files, or using special formats. A macro can do a single task,
like inserting a phrase, or many tasks, like saving a copy of a letter to a file, printing
two copies of the letter, retrieving an envelope template, copying the address to
the envelope, and printing it.

Some people use WordPerfect for a year or more without ever using a macro.
However, macros are not intimidating. In fact, you already may be using something
like a macro on your office telephone if you have speed dialing. With many phones
today, you can automatically redial the last number by pressing the Redial key. Or
you can record certain frequently called numbers and have the phone dial those
numbers for you every time you press a certain key combination on your phone.

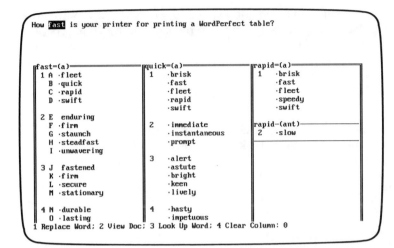

Fig. 2.13.

Word Perfect's Thesaurus offering up to three sets of synonyms.

That is how macros work in WordPerfect. You press a few keys to use a recorded macro to perform a task that might require many keystrokes if you were to perform the task manually step-by-step.

To create a macro, you turn on macro record mode, type the text or commands you want recorded in your macro, and then turn the recorder off when you are done. Specifically, creating a macro is a five-step process:

1. Press Macro Define (Ctrl-F10).

2. Type a name for the macro or press the Alt key plus a letter.

3. Give the macro a description.

4. Type text or activate commands to be included in the macro.

5. Press Macro Define (Ctrl-F10) to switch off Macro Define.

To use a recorded macro, press Alt plus the letter that is part of the macro name, or press Macro (Alt-F10), type the macro name, and press Enter. If you want to have a macro repeat several times, press Esc and type a numeral for the number of times you want the macro to repeat; then press Alt-letter, or press Alt-F10, type the macro name, and press Enter.

If you want to create a macro that repeats itself throughout a document, be sure to include one Search (F2) command in step 4; then add these steps in place of step 5.

5. Press Macro (Alt-F10).

6. Type the macro name and press Enter, or press Alt-letter.

7. Press Macro Define (Ctrl-F10) to switch off Macro Define.

Macros in version 5.1 have been enhanced and expanded, enabling you to do more with them than before. Macros can be assigned to Alt plus any of the 26 letters of the alphabet, or to Ctrl plus any of the letters; or macros can be named files on disk that you access through the Macro command. If you use Keyboards, you can create various sets of Ctrl-letter macros for different kinds of projects. In fact, the total number of macros you can create in WordPerfect is limited only by the size of your hard disk and the variety of names you can think up.

This book discusses a number of macros as they relate to various documents, and the Applications Disk included with this book offers a broad collection of macros that will speed up your work in the office environment. Many of these are ready-to-use; some you will want to modify to fit your particular needs.

Using the Date Command

Although the Date command (Shift-F5) remains relatively unchanged in version 5.1, it is still useful for documents you use repeatedly. For example, if you insert a date code in a file and save that file to disk, every time you retrieve that file and reuse it, it displays the current date rather than the date when you created it.

Merging Documents

In business, few features are more useful than Merge (sometimes called mailmerge). Merge is the process of combining information from two different files to create a new document. For example, if you merge a single-page letter with a special file that contains 50 names and addresses, WordPerfect will create 50 letters—each with a different person's name and address. Figure 2.14 illustrates how merge works.

Merge (Ctrl-F9) is particularly valuable for form letters, mailing labels, envelopes, contracts, phone lists, boilerplates, and memos, just to mention a few. In the chapters that follow, you discover the vast possibilities of using Merge in business.

Sorting Information

Sort (Ctrl-F9) lets the user select and alphabetize lines, paragraphs, rows in a table, and secondary records in WordPerfect documents or files. Sort works in ascending or descending order, and can be customized to sort data in different locations in the file (that is, sort by phone number, ZIP code, age, position, and so on).

In earlier versions of WordPerfect, many people used the Line Draw feature (Ctrl-F3, 2) to create tables and forms with text. With the addition of the Table feature (Alt-F7, 2) in version 5.1, Line Draw has been supplanted by the Table feature to create specialized forms, as you will see later on in the book.

Using Graphics and Graphics Lines

No word processor would be complete without the capability to import graphics images and highlight sections of text with graphics lines. In both WordPerfect 5.0 and 5.1, these capabilities offer tremendous potential for creating visually attractive documents that will help others understand the message you want to convey. Part VII, "Desktop Publishing in the Office," provides a number of practical examples of how graphics can be integrated with text to make more attractive products.

Figure Boxes

Figure boxes (Alt-F9) allow users to import graphics images and charts into the body of a document, with text flowing around the boxed image.

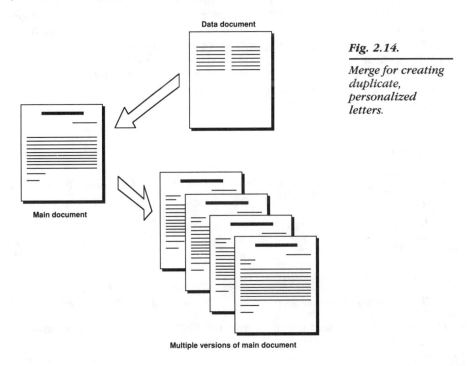

Data document

Main document

Multiple versions of main document

Fig. 2.14.

Merge for creating duplicate, personalized letters.

Graphics boxes can be many different kinds, of course, including Text boxes. Instead of containing a graphic or chart, a Text box highlights important data from the body copy so that the reader can grasp, at a glance, an important fact or piece of information that might prompt further reading.

In the magazine publishing world, these enlarged chunks of information are called *sidebars*. A Text box, unlike a Figure box, does not have lines around the box itself. The default Text box in version 5.1 is a shaded box with heavy top and bottom bars.

Graphics Lines

When you want to place horizontal or vertical lines in your document—to emphasize portions of text or to separate columns of information—use the Graphics Line command (Alt-F9, **5**). If you have a document with multiple pages of text in column format, you can place the vertical graphics lines in a header on the first page, and they will print on all pages throughout the document. Graphics lines can be placed most anywhere and also shaded and made thick or thin, depending on the emphasis you want. In fact, you can overlay a shaded graphics line over text—using the Advance command (Shift-F8, **4**, **1**)—and create some unusual effects (as you will see in later chapters).

Summary

The best way to use WordPerfect is to understand first the four underlying concepts detailed at the beginning of this chapter:

1. The clean-screen concept

2. The hidden-code concept

3. The unnamed-document concept

4. The default-settings concept

This chapter has emphasized the most useful WordPerfect features in a business environment. This discussion has followed generally the basic format of the pull-down menu bar, covering file management and printing; editing and windowing features; the Search and Replace command; layout and format features; fonts and special characters; methods of marking text and linking documents; special tools such as the Speller, the Thesaurus, and macros; and graphic elements.

Part II shows you how to create a variety of general office correspondence, with emphasis in Chapter 3 on guidelines for creating powerful letters and persuasive communications.

Part II

Creating General Office Correspondence

Writing Successful Business Letters
with WordPerfect

Examining the Physical Characteristics
of Your Letters

Creating Letters That Inform

Creating Letters That Convey Bad News

Creating Letters That Persuade

3

Writing Successful Business Letters with WordPerfect

After many long hours, your team completes the data for an important report to a district manager. If the manager likes the report, your group will be the center of growth in your company. If the report fails to attract the manager's attention, your team will be disbanded, and you may not have this opportunity again. The other team members turn to you to write the cover letter for the report because, they say, "You have all our data, and you have WordPerfect on your PC." Unlike business offices in the past, yours has no secretary to take shorthand and turn rough notes into persuasive correspondence. No, you alone will write the cover letter to help sell your team's ideas to the district manager.

You sit at your PC and pull up WordPerfect. Before you is WordPerfect's clean screen. After moving your hands to the home row of the keyboard, you must decide what to write first. So what do you do next?

With the help of WordPerfect and the toolbox of business writing guidelines provided in this chapter, you learn useful strategies and techniques for creating successful business documents. Before you begin typing, consider the following important elements, known as the PRIOS[1] model, in planning effective communication:

[1]Jeanne W. Halpern, Judith M. Kilborn, and Agnes M. Lokke, *Business Writing Strategies and Samples* (New York: Macmillan Publishing Company, 1988), pp. 42-51.

- **Purpose.** Why are you writing? What do you want your reader(s) to think or do after reading your letter?

- **Readers.** Who will read your letter? Will that reader share your letter with others?

- **Information.** What facts and data are necessary for your reader to know?

- **Organization.** How will you structure your information to make your point? Can your reader easily understand your message?

- **Style.** Will your document be relaxed or formal, friendly or objective, long or concise? Will your manager understand your technical explanations?

Used with a word processing program like WordPerfect, these business writing guidelines can help you create documents you can be proud of. This chapter gets you started by discussing the following features of letter writing:

- Writing inside addresses and salutations

- Organizing paragraphs to lead the reader to your conclusions

- Adding tracking information for your files

- Closing your letter

- Including enclosure information

After discussing how the document is written and saved in memory, this chapter shows how WordPerfect's editing functions—Move, Copy, and Search, to name just a few—can strengthen your document, making it clearer and easier to read. If you circulate your first draft to your team members, you can incorporate their WordPerfect files of additions and suggestions, producing a team-written, revised document with the best ideas from everyone.

By learning how to communicate your teams's ideas clearly and completely, you can write a convincing letter that works.

Using Good Letter-Writing Strategies

Did you ever receive an official-looking letter, on thick, rich paper with a highly embossed company logo as letterhead, but with an unimpressive misspelled word at the top of the second paragraph? First you chuckle; then you imagine how many of these letters were sent over the whole country to other chuckling readers. Whether you write weekly progress reports, dunning letters to customers who are slow in payment, letters of congratulations to contest winners, interoffice memos to keep track of responsibilities, or letters to inquire about a possible job, you create an image of yourself and the company you represent. Good planning and analysis, careful writing, precise revision, and an objective final reading can keep your company image—and your self-respect—intact.

Before you begin typing, give yourself time to plan what you want to communicate. By considering the several important issues of the PRIOS model—the purpose of your letter, the intended readers, the facts to include, the organization of the information, and the level of formality—you can develop a dynamic letter-writing strategy.

All these separate elements work together. A document's purpose statement should show that you understand your readers. Determining who your readers are helps you select the information those readers should know. And, in turn, how you organize your information depends on your purpose for writing and what your readers already know. The style of your letter, whether formal or informal, firm or friendly, detailed or concise, is determined by your purpose, your readers, and the information you convey.

Suppose that you want to write a letter to a familiar, longtime customer because an expected payment is a month overdue. Because your customer frequently orders your merchandise, your purpose statement shows three sincere concerns about your reader: (1) to discover why the customer has not paid, if a problem exists; (2) to arrange for complete payment; and (3), what is most important, to keep the customer.

If a customer regularly makes late payments, you probably won't wait for an explanation. In fact, the information you choose for a good customer and a poor customer will be the same, but your organization and style will be different. The first paragraph to a poor customer is often terse:

> Your payment is overdue.

The first sentence to a good customer shows more understanding:

> You are a valued customer with whom we have enjoyed doing business.

As you can see, all the planning elements work together. The PRIOS model thus gives you control of your message and lets you tailor your written communication to a specific audience.

Getting back to your cover letter for your team-researched project, you notice that your team has given you all the laser-printed database reports, graphs, spreadsheets, and journal entries in a binder, but you need a document that introduces these documents. Your district manager is a busy person, and you decide that a letter describing briefly but clearly what your team has been doing and containing a list of the documents in the report can save some reading time. But that big, clear screen on your desk is just as clear as it was before—what must you do first?

A good approach is to use the screen to jot down notes as you plan your document. After completing your notes, you can print them as guidelines for your document and refer to them as you type your letter.

You can even design a WordPerfect template to complete your PRIOS planning before you write a letter. For example, you can call a file simply *TEMPLATE* and type information such as that shown in figure 3.1. Whenever you must write a business document, you can simply bring up the TEMPLATE file in the Doc 2 window and fill in the blanks with your information. To keep the information on file, save this particular template under a second name, perhaps incorporating a date (*TEMP0216.90*). You can always reuse *TEMPLATE* and save the PRIOS information on disk or on paper.

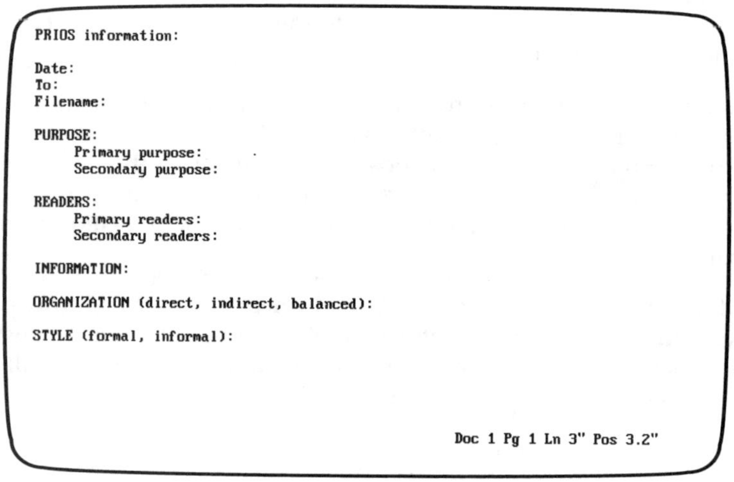

Fig. 3.1.

*A PRIOS template
to help you plan
your documents.*

```
PRIOS information:

Date:
To:
Filename:

PURPOSE:
        Primary purpose:
        Secondary purpose:

READERS:
        Primary readers:
        Secondary readers:

INFORMATION:

ORGANIZATION (direct, indirect, balanced):

STYLE (formal, informal):



                                              Doc 1 Pg 1 Ln 3" Pos 3.2"
```

Determining the Purpose of Your Document

You already know the most important reason to write the letter in this example: you want the manager to open the binder of documents and look favorably at your team's results. This is the letter's primary purpose. It indicates what you want your reader to do, how your reader should act, or what attitudes you want your reader to change.

After typing your primary purpose on-screen, ask yourself what else a cover letter can accomplish. In brainstorming sessions, your team talked about other departments in the company where management might be interested in your project. If your cover letter is informative enough, your report could easily find its way to other managers. In your mind, you can see the binder covered with colored tags and passed from mailbox to mailbox, moving higher on the wall until the binder reaches that one large mailbox at the top. But first, you must write the cover letter.

You decide that your specific primary purpose is to interest your district manager in reading your team's report and acting on the information. Your secondary purpose is to attract the attention of other managers and administrators in your business. See in figure 3.2 how this reader analysis fits your PRIOS template.

```
PRIOS information:

Date:  February 16, 1990
To:  B Platz
Filename:  COVERLET.TXT

PURPOSE:
     Primary purpose: to cause the reader to read with interest
          the accompanying documents
     Secondary purpose: to interest other managers in our new
          technology

READERS:
     Primary readers:


     Secondary readers:

INFORMATION:

ORGANIZATION (direct, indirect, balanced):

STYLE (formal, informal):

                              Doc 1 Pg 1 Ln 2.67" Pos 2"
```

Fig. 3.2.

Defining both primary and secondary purposes.

When you write a purpose, goal, or objective of a document, use such active words as "act," "compare," "follow," or "adopt." Think of other action verbs that describe not only what you plan to do but also what you want the reader to do after reading your document. Your purpose may be merely to explain data so that your reader understands.

After writing your cover letter, you can use your purpose statement as a test. Does your completed document actually do what you want? You may decide to retrieve and edit your WordPerfect document in order to strengthen its consistency of purpose.

Reaching the Reader

Your next question should be, *What do I know about my reader(s)?* You know already that your primary reader is your district manager. What do you know or have you observed about your manager? Following your statement of purpose, jot down some quick notes about your district manager. You might type the notes on your template, as in figure 3.3.

Fig. 3.3.

Notes about your primary audience.

```
PRIOS Information:

Date:  October 16, 1990
To:  B. Platz
Filename:  COVERLET.TXT

PURPOSE:
     Primary: to cause the reader to read with interest the
          accompanying documents
     Secondary: to interest other managers in our new technology

READERS:
     Primary:
          interested in saving money
          busy, with little spare time--always in hurry
          understands how machines work in system, but is not
               technically sophisticated
          dresses in three-piece suits--sees formal in informal
               situations
          wrote memo encouraging enrollment in basic writing
               courses
          impatient with details

C:\CORRECT.WP                              Doc 1 Pg 1 Ln 4.33" Pos 2.5"
```

Looking back at your purpose, however, you indicate a second audience for your letter. What do you know about other company managers? If you cannot be as specific about this secondary audience, you can generalize about them. In your template, type your description of the other managers (see fig. 3.4). After your letter is written, this short analysis can help you test how well your document works.

Fig. 3.4.

Notes about your secondary audience.

```
READERS:
     Primary:
          interested in saving money
          busy, with little spare time--always in hurry
          understands how machines work in system, but is not
               technically sophisticated
          dresses in three-piece suits--sees formal in informal
               situations
          wrote memo encouraging enrollment in basic writing
               courses
          impatient with details
     Secondary:
          relative to the following departments
               Projection
               Marketing
               Technical Maintenance
               M.I.S.
               Sales
          interested in saving money
          interested in increasing productivity
          interested in the environment if feasible
          sensitive to company criticism
          fiercely competitive

C:\CORRECT.WP                              Doc 1 Pg 1 Ln 6.67" Pos 1"
```

Write your letter with all these readers in mind. For instance, you may want to mention something about saving money and increasing productivity. You try not to be too technical in your cover letter, and you may want to add explanations of very technical descriptions in the other documents in the binder. You will not omit technical data, however, because the report may end up in technical departments that require details.

Looking back over your list of observations about your manager, you wrote "busy, with little time—always in hurry." Think about what you might do to make your document like a quick cup of coffee—swallowed with just a gulp or two.

Summarize information at the *beginning* of sections whenever you can, and use word processing features—such as bold, underlined headings and, if your printer allows, larger type or italic print—to draw the reader's eyes through a document. For readers who want more information, refer them to attached charts and reports. You may even decide to present some technical data in simple charts. Look at the example in figure 3.5.

```
     The installed apparatus can produce cost savings of 20 cents per
piece (see attached chart B). This results in savings in the following
departments, as follows:

     Department A: . . . . . . . . . $586.90 per day
     Department B: . . . . . . . . . .768.24 per day
     Department C: . . . . . . . . . .346.87 per day




                        Doc 1 Pg 1 Ln 2.17" Pos 5.87"
```

Fig. 3.5.

A simple chart to emphasize text.

Although you don't want to oversimplify technical data so that it appears that you are "talking down" to your readers, you also don't want to overwhelm your readers with uninterrupted data. Because complex data is important but difficult to read, think about your readers. If you have described your readers accurately, your data can facilitate their decision-making. If, however, you fail to target your readers, your letter and report may be pushed to one side of a desk—the side closest to the trash basket.

Figure 3.6 is an example of a technical explanation. This memo extract, which describes a test, is understood by both the person requesting the test and the person performing the test. If, however, this same memo is sent to a nontechnical department, some explanation or rewriting is necessary (see figs. 3.7 and 3.8).

Fig. 3.6.

*A technical
explanation that
may require
further
explanation.*

```
We were informed that the VDJ specification for noise was 84 db.
Also we were shown a report, dated 7/6/89 (attached), wherein VDJ
notes our line accepts 84 db. This nonconforms with our maximum
88-db level in our plant. VDJ tests indicate that 82.8 db
emanates from the rear of the machine, but might be attributable
to an absence of guards and shielding or the high ambient
background noise of 71.5 db. The machinery must be tested on-site
with all guards and shields installed.




C:\CORRECT.WP                                    Doc 1 Pg 2 Ln 4.17" Pos 1"
```

Fig. 3.7.

*A simplified
technical
explanation.*

```
We were informed that the VDJ specification for noise was 84 db.
Also we were shown a report, dated 7/6/89 (attached), wherein VDJ
notes our line accepts 84 db. This nonconforms with our maximum
88-db level in our plant. VDJ tests indicate that 82.8 db
emanates from the rear of the machine, but might be attributable
to an absence of guards and shielding or the high ambient
background noise of 71.5 db. The machinery must be tested on-site
with all guards and shields installed.

Last August, the VDJ firm apparently interpreted our proposal to
accept a noise level of 84 decibels (db). We currently operate at
a maximum of 80 db on the plant floor. The noise level at the
rear of the VDJ machine tested 82.8 db, but the loudness was
probably due to VDJ's noisy surroundings and a lack of shields or
guards around that area of the machine. Let's test a properly
shielded machine at our plant for the most accurate reading.



C:\CORRECT.WP                                    Doc 1 Pg 2 Ln 6.33" Pos 1"
```

```
Last August, the VDJ firm apparently interpreted our proposal to
accept a noise level of 84 decibels (db). We currently operate at
a maximum of 80 db on the plant floor. The noise level at the
rear of the VDJ machine tested 82.8 db, but the loudness was
probably due to VDJ's noisy surroundings and a lack of shields or
guards around that area of the machine. Let's test a properly
shielded machine at our plant for the most accurate reading.


The on-site testing took place in a noisy part of the plant
floor. The VDJ people indicated that normal shields and guards
were absent from the machine. Let's wait to make a decision about
the machine until we test it in our plant.




                          Doc 1 Pg 1 Ln 1" Pos 1"
```

Fig. 3.8.

Rewriting a technical explanation for the nontechnical reader.

Using Information To Interest Your Readers

You have decided what you want your cover letter to accomplish and for whom it is written. It's time to think about the information to include in your letter.

Written business communication contains two types of information: content information and tracking information. *Content* information is the data you want to convey. For example, your cover-letter content will probably explain who makes up your group and what you are doing. To interest your manager in reading on to the documents your team has produced, indicate your project's importance and add a descriptive list of the documents. To illustrate the competence of the team, you might add the credentials of the team members.

Tracking information, on the other hand, includes dates, copy information (*Copies to:* or *cc:*), and the paper trail within the letter (*Responding to your letter of August 5,...*). To explain tracking information, think of the following scene: You wonder what the manager knows already about your group. You move to your files and look at the early documents from the first days of the project. You notice, by looking at the copy information at the bottom of memos, that your manager was sent a copy of the memo that brought your group together. The copy statement appears as follows:

cc: Bob Platz, District Manager
  Eleanor Gomberg, Manager
  Freya Finch
  J. D. Jackson
  Fred Rolle

Note: List the names by rank in descending order, and then alphabetically within a particular rank.

Tracking information helps you determine the *communication loop*. The people listed in the copy statement form your communication loop for this document. The people in this circle will receive this information and thus be responsible for knowing what is in your letter. If you handle sensitive information—information that could be part of legal defense—accurate tracking information is crucial.

Important tracking information also appears within a business letter:

My letter of April 16 indicated my approval of the project.

By indicating to a correspondent that you have received and read a previous letter, you clarify the impetus for your current letter. If this important tracking information is missing, you may cause the correspondent to wonder whether you received the previous correspondence.

By now, your cover-letter notes may be long enough so that your screen begins scrolling. If you are new to word processing, be assured that your document is intact; WordPerfect merely allows you additional surface to type on. If you are new to WordPerfect, try saving the your growing document by pressing F10 and responding to the prompts at the bottom of the screen. You can practice naming this document and saving your guidelines.

Organizing Your Information

After writing your purpose statement, your reader analysis, and the information you plan to include, you are ready to organize your letter into recognizable parts. If you want, you can even press Shift-F3 to switch to a second document window (Doc 2) and start typing the information that will appear in your letter. Use Shift-F3 as a toggle to switch back and forth between your planning guidelines and your letter information in order to edit this data into the letter you will send.

You have three different ways of organizing information: direct, indirect, and balanced approaches. A *direct approach* places the most important information at the beginning of the letter. Use this approach for a letter that must immediately attract reader attention, such as a routine dunning letter for payment or a letter announcing an award or prize.

In the *indirect approach*, you move your readers through explanations until you announce the most important information at the end of the letter. This strategy is excellent for a persuasive letter that tries to get the reader to change an opinion or to act.

In a *balanced format*, you start politely, referring to past correspondence, leaving your most important information and explanations for the center of the document, and closing by indicating where you can be reached for further information. The balanced format makes up most of the routine or informative letters you receive.[2]

Back at your keyboard, you decide to begin your letter by relating the problem that has plagued your company for the past year—the problem that your team will solve. You briefly describe the problem and then announce that your team has an answer.

Keep in mind that most informative business letters are no longer than a page. After adding all your cover-letter information to your Doc 2 screen, you find that you have two pages of several single-spaced paragraphs. Look back at your reader analysis. How will a busy district manager react to a two-page letter? Now you can craft your information into a smaller but more effective document.

Perhaps the description of the team members' credentials would be better as an attached document. Copy the description as a block to the bottom of the page so that you can treat the credential information as a separate document. (After all, when printed, it will be a separate page.) And if your purpose is to interest the manager in reading the information in the binder, why not briefly describe the contents of the binder, referring to an attachment of a complete list of the binder's contents?

By placing the most important information at the beginning of the document and adding attachments, you can be more confident that readers will be intrigued to read further. Change this order only when you must convey bad news; then you begin with a positive *buffer* paragraph before delivering the most important information.

Furthermore, after getting your information into paragraphs, you can organize even more with some visual groupings. Format indented lists as numbered or bulleted items (see fig. 3.9). Good business writing requires that you make the document as easy to read as you can. With WordPerfect, you can draw your manager's eye to the most important information by highlighting a phrase or sentence with underlining (see fig. 3.10).

[2]Halpern, Kilborn, and Lokke, pp. 47-48.

Fig. 3.9.

Emphasizing information by using a list.

If these issues to not affect machine performance, VDJ is directed to ship the machine under the following conditions:

- Noise levels will be checked again at this plant. If the noise level exceeds 80 db, VDJ will retool the machine.

- Another run-off test of the ST 175,000 text (polygon, square, triangle) will be performed here after alignment is complete.

If you have any further comments, please call me at 3456.

Fig. 3.10.

Using underlined headings to direct the reader's attention.

The following areas of the plant must take protective measures:

Production Maintenance:

Go to the garage area, and close the double doors.

Spraying Area:

Turn off all equipment and cut breakers before leaving.

Powder Coating Controls:

Reset equipment to STASIS setting, and turn off.

If you write a memo that will be posted elsewhere in your company, you can separate information from the rest of the text by using the WordPerfect Line Draw feature (Ctrl-F3, **2**) to box in information. If you received the memo in figure 3.11 without the Army regulation in a Line Draw box, you would probably highlight this information with a colored pen.

```
NUMBER:    14-90                                28 February 1990

SUBJECT:   POLICY - Gambling


TO:        All Employees


1.   Gambling is prohibited while you are on duty or on the premises. The Standards of Conduct for
     Department of the Army Personnel state:

     ┌────────────────────────────────────────────────────────────────────┐
     │ "DA personnel will not participate in any gambling activity while on Government-owned, │
     │ contracted, or leased property or otherwise while on duty for the government." │
     └────────────────────────────────────────────────────────────────────┘

2.   Employees who gamble on duty or on Government property are subject to disciplinary or
     adverse action. Please observe the rules.


Frank Morris
Civilian Personnel Officer
```

Fig. 3.11.

Using Line Draw to highlight information on a memo to be posted.

Writing with Style

Good business writing has some accepted styles. Style pertains to the manner in which you write your letter: for example, your sentence structure, word choice, punctuation, and tone. A good style requires that you keep the following in mind:

- Make sure that your formal business letter is grammatically and mechanically correct. Your letter to one individual may be read by others.

- Write clear and concise sentences and use short paragraphs.

- Be precise and accurate. As the letter writer, you are accountable for accuracy.

- Be positive. Rewrite to avoid negative words or ideas.

- Use the active voice in your sentences. Avoid the passive voice in most business letters.

Choosing Formal or Informal Correspondence

In formal business writing, you follow the traditional letter form of an inside address and letter body, followed by a formal closing with enclosure information. Formal letters refrain from personal references, such as "Give my regards to your team members." You use full names and titles.

Although you have met the district manager, you are wise to write formally. Because team projects that affect company growth are important, the district manager may distribute your cover letter and binder of materials beyond the district management level to your company's highest administrative level. Formal writing is therefore a sound choice.

Some situations call for more personal writing. If you write letters to customers, you can soften your tone, show sincerity, and add statements of concern, as in the following:

> You have been a valued client of our company for over ten years.

> Please let me know of any concerns you may have about your account.

> Because of the interest you have shown in this company and our products, I am concerned that we have not received any payments recently.

Writing Clearly

In old Western movies, the hero said little, but what he did say was important. The average sentence in television dialogue contains nine words. Short, straightforward sentences in a business letter are easier for readers to understand. You can achieve variety and increase your letter's readability by mixing long and short sentences. In your complete letter, however, write just enough to convey your message.

After your letter is written, test each sentence for unnecessary words or phrases. For instance, suppose that your purpose statement reads, "to report recent lab work as requested." Can you simplify the following sentence?

> As per your instructions, we have constructed the focus of the study to concern the additional laboratory steps taken in the previous study performed last year.

You could shorten this to the following:

> As you requested, this report is about the extra lab work in last year's study.

You can use WordPerfect to rewrite and edit long sentences. Simply create after a long sentence a shorter version of the sentence. After you are satisfied with the shorter sentence, delete the longer sentence.

Avoiding Unnecessary, Overused, and Weak Phrases

Inexperienced business writers often use words and phrases that sound businesslike or legal, but are improper stylistically. Some of these expressions are redundancies, wordy phrases, clichés, and qualifying words and phrases.

Redundant phrases are two or more words that convey the same idea twice. When you reduce these expressions to the single word, you make your letter shorter and easier to read. The following is a list of common redundant phrases:

Redundancies:	*Replace With:*
advanced planning	planning
any and all	any (or *all*)
basic fundamentals	basics (or *fundamentals*)
cancel out	cancel
current status	status
goals and objectives	goals (or *objectives*)
in close proximity to	close to (or *near*)
merge together	merge
mutual cooperation	cooperation
regular monthly meetings	monthly meetings

For brevity, avoid wordiness. The following short list contains common wordy phrases:

Wordy Phrases:	*Replace With:*
a small number of	a few
due to the fact that	because
not in a position to	cannot
is representative of	represents
the reason is because	because (or *the reason is that*)
without further delay	immediately

Letter writers frequently use the same wording for similar situations. However, if you overuse certain phrases in letter openings, the reader will quickly glide over them to read the rest of the letter. Letter openings, especially, can weaken the entire letter if you use "pat expressions" like the following:

Overused Expressions

Reference is made to your recent meeting in which you directed . . . .
This is in response to your inquiry regarding the . . . .
This confirms our telephone conversation of April . . . .
This is to notify you that . . . .
We are in receipt of your letter dated . . . .
Per your inquiry of . . . .

When you write such expressions, you imply that your reader must be reminded of a meeting, an inquiry, a phone conversation, or a letter written on a certain day. Why insult the reader—and waste space?

Watch out for clichés—words and phrases that have lost their meaning through overuse. For example, eliminate from your letters such clichés as the following:

Clichés

back to square one
back to the drawing board
ballpark figure
bottom line
can-do
in-depth
in the bag
nail down
overkill
wrap up

Some clichés are better labeled jargon—the words of a specialized field. See the following list of examples:

Jargon

dialog (as a verb)
impact (as a verb)
interface with (as a verb)
kluge
state of the art
tapped out
wired in

Another indicator of weak writing is the use of qualifying words and phrases, such as *usually* and *generally speaking*. If you want to write a persuasive letter that shows that you have control of a situation and can be trusted to complete a job, avoid the following expressions:

Qualifying Words and Phrases

apparently
around
I feel (rather than the positive *I think*)
if you wish
it appears
it seems
give or take
maybe
more or less
perhaps
possibly
should you want
somewhere near
so to speak

Although these words or expressions are sometimes appropriate in writing, you can avoid them and thus make your point better with a few well-chosen phrases. If your letter seems long, eliminating some of these qualifying words and phrases can make your document shorter.

Adding Precision to Your Letter

A general rule for business letters is this: Avoid whatever makes your reader pause while reading. A simple difference in the way you spell out or abbreviate a term can make a reader pause and look through the text for consistency. Any inconsistency can make a reader wary of your letter's accuracy and worth.

If you have technical data in your letter, make sure that you are precise about measurements, volumes, formulas, and so on. If you discuss metric data, be certain sure that all numerical references are metric. Being precise can be as simple as being consistent. Look, for instance, at the following paragraph:

> If forty of these boxes exceed the 16 lb. limit, this office must insist that twenty-pound limits become the norm.

In this example, you must choose whether to write your numbers as words or as digits. In the past, numbers were written as words in formal writing—a carryover from an age when poor penmanship in handwritten letters might make one digit look like another. Nowadays, typed or printed digits are easy to read without confusion.

Also in this example, the pound description appears two different ways. If you abbreviate (lb.), use the abbreviation throughout a letter. If you prefer the complete word (pound), then use it consistently. Careful attention to consistency will make your letter easier to read.

Writing Positively

Communicating positive messages is excellent business practice. In all business writing, avoid a negative tone. A positive attitude suggests to readers that you are in control of a situation and are working efficiently. Rather than present a busy person with problems, offer a variety of solutions.

You can use the WordPerfect's Forward Search command (F2) to look for such negative words as *not*, *fail*, or *unable* to see whether you can make sentences more positive.

If you recall that business writing is straightforward communication, a negative tone may cause readers to pause, become upset or angry, or misinterpret your communication. The following paired sentences show how negative messages can be made positive:

Original: If you fail to make payment, this office will seek legal counsel to force payment.

Revised: Your prompt payment ensures that you continue to enjoy the cost-saving services of our organization.

Original: I can't understand why people at this end of the building can't keep the coffee pot from burning.

Revised: If the afternoon crew turns off the coffee pot after the last break, the pot should have a long and productive life.

In each set, the two sentences have the same message, but the first sentence will make the reader defensive and hostile. A negative message not only decreases the chances of a reasonable response, but also increases the possibility that your correspondent will complain to higher management or legal counsel. The second sentence emphasizes in a positive way what is possible. The reader is free to agree or disagree. If you must, use a negative message in only the most extreme circumstances, and even then ask yourself whether such a message is necessary.

Writing Letters in the Active Voice

Whenever possible, use the active voice (concerning who does what) instead of the passive voice (concerning what is acted upon). Compare these two sentences:

Passive: The Continental breakfast option should be requested of the hotel manager before 10:00 p.m.

Active: To receive a Continental breakfast, please call the main desk before 10:00 p.m.

The passive voice of the first sentence, *should be requested,* suggests anonymity. Who is speaking? Who is supposed to ask the manager? The second sentence, which indicates simply what the reader should do to have breakfast, is written in the active voice. It is more straightforward and easier to read.

Should you always avoid the passive voice? Actually, some passive sentences are unavoidable, and you may want use a few passive sentences on purpose for variety and interest. Too many passive sentences, however, produce a weak, almost "nonaccountable" document that is more difficult to read and less effective for evoking action.

The best way to find these passive verbs in your writing is to use WordPerfect's Forward Search command (F2) to look for the following variations of the verb *to be*: *am, is, are, be, was, were,* and *been*.

Writing Your Final Draft

If you have followed the letter-writing strategies so far and have typed your information in a second WordPerfect document, you are ready to produce a finished letter. If you waited until this part of the chapter to begin writing, you can retrieve the second document now and begin.

Generally, a good business letter completes communication in three or four short paragraphs. Try to keep your letter to three paragraphs:

1. Introductory paragraph
2. Main communication
3. Closing paragraph

Begin each paragraph with a topic sentence that explains what the paragraph is about.

On the letter document, type your first sentence. This introductory sentence is usually a tracking sentence, such as the following:

> As requested, a five-member group (see attached list) led by Dr. Gomberg has developed a solution to nearby groundwater contamination.

The next sentence might read as follows:

> The accompanying binder contains a history of this problem (refer to page 3).

Figure 3.12 shows the completed first paragraph.

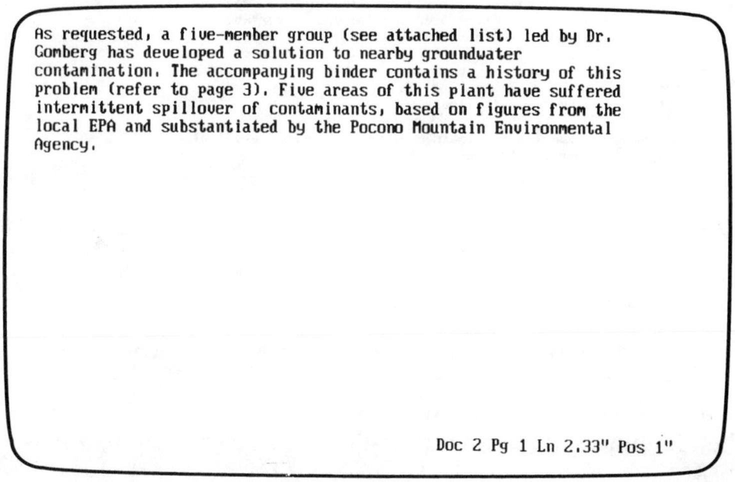

```
As requested, a five-member group (see attached list) led by Dr.
Gomberg has developed a solution to nearby groundwater
contamination. The accompanying binder contains a history of this
problem (refer to page 3). Five areas of this plant have suffered
intermittent spillover of contaminants, based on figures from the
local EPA and substantiated by the Pocono Mountain Environmental
Agency.




                         Doc 2 Pg 1 Ln 2.33" Pos 1"
```

Fig. 3.12.

First paragraph of letter draft.

In the second paragraph (see fig. 3.13), you present some of the details of your proposal solution.

Fig. 3.13.

Second paragraph of letter draft.

```
As requested, a five-member group (see attached list) led by Dr.
Gomberg has developed a solution to nearby groundwater
contamination. The accompanying binder contains a history of this
problem (refer to page 3). Five areas of this plant have suffered
intermittent spillover of contaminants, based on figures from the
local EPA and substantiated by the Pocono Mountain Environmental
Agency.

Because these contaminating spills happen in only one department
at a time, we, as a team, have been looking into a portable unit
that could be moved from department to department to treat
spillovers as the levels of waste increase. After looking at many
models of such a device, we propose using a system developed by
United Technologies of Easton, PA. This unit is the most
effective and also costs the least.




                                    Doc 2 Pg 1 Ln 3.67" Pos 1"
```

You can use your third paragraph (see fig. 3.14) to direct the reader's questions to yourself by including your phone number.

Fig. 3.14.

Directing further questions to the writer in the third paragraph.

```
As requested, a five-member group (see attached list) led by Dr.
Gomberg has developed a solution to nearby groundwater
contamination. The accompanying binder contains a history of this
problem (refer to page 3). Five areas of this plant have suffered
intermittent spillover of contaminants, based on figures from the
local EPA and substantiated by the Pocono Mountain Environmental
Agency.

Because these contaminating spills happen in only one department
at a time, we, as a team, have been looking into a portable unit
that could be moved from department to department to treat
spillovers as the levels of waste increase. After looking at many
models of such a device, we propose using a system developed by
United Technologies of Easton, PA. This unit is the most
effective and also costs the least.

If you have any questions, please call me at 555-5934 and I will
be happy to answer for the other members of the team.



                                    Doc 2 Pg 1 Ln 4.17" Pos 1"
```

If you assess your purpose and the writing situation accurately before you begin to write, you will be more efficient as you draft the letter. If time allows, or even if you are busy, wait at least an hour before attempting to reread your letter objectively, and then revise it. A helpful hint is to show your first draft to other team members for their comments.

Communicating by Inside Addresses, Salutations, and Closings

With WordPerfect, you can spend the most time working out the text of your letter, and then later add such features as the inside address, the salutation, and the closing.

Begin simply by typing the correct date. Remember to do this, because the date is often the most important information on the page.

If you use letterhead or stationery imprinted with the company logo and address, you have no need to type your own address at the top of the letter. If, however, you do not use letterhead, type this information so that your reader knows how to reach you. Current style books suggest several different ways to type the inside address, but check whether your company has its own style to follow.

After you have typed your inside address, you must decide how to type the address of the person to whom you are writing. Accuracy is most important. Be sure to spell the person's name correctly. If you are sending your letter to a person with a title (for example, District Manager), be certain that the title is accurate. A discreet phone call to the manager's company or department may help.

How do you address a person whom you know only as "T. Bateman, District Manager"? You can't tell whether this person is a man or a woman. After repeated phone calls, you discover that no one has met this person because T. Bateman is a new employee. To be perfectly safe, you write the letter to "T. Bateman, District Manager." Fine, but how do you address T. Bateman of unknown gender? Do not use the strange "Dear Sir or Madam"; this is impersonal and shows an inability to find missing information. Why not just drop the salutation altogether? This sounds like a radical idea until you see the absence of the salutation—actually, no one pays that much attention to a salutation.

Some people prefer not to use the accepted "Dear . . ." salutation and a "Sincerely yours" complimentary close. They believe that these words express a relationship that does not exist. You can solve this problem by eliminating these lines, which take up space and accomplish little. A simple "Thank you" says much more than any phrase that stresses your sincerity or truth in signing your name. Some of the nastiest letters begin with a "Dear" and end with "Very truly yours." It's time to prepare your letter writing for the 21st century.

Many of these considerations are questions of style. You should review several style books, available both in bookstores and in libraries, to determine what you are comfortable using. See also the next chapter for specific information about letter styles.

Communicating by Enclosures and Copies

After typing the closing, you are finally ready for the enclosure and copy data—part of your tracking information. Two lines below your name and title, indicate any enclosures that you are attaching to the document. Writing a cover letter for a binder of assorted materials, you may simply refer the reader to the list of documents at the beginning of the binder ("See attached list of documents"). If you have few enclosures, you can list them individually. The following example shows a letter closing with enclosure and copy information:

Thank you.

Grimms Steven
Project Director

Encl.:   Report of expenditures, December 1989-July 1990
         Long-range goals
         OSHA report

cc: B. Freed
     W. Niemoczynski
     J. East

The reader must find all three items enclosed, so make a last-minute check to ensure that these documents are included. Make certain also that the three people receiving copies of this information should be recipients of the information in the document.

Note: In interoffice memos, you often see copy information at the top of the memo. This forward listing helps office personnel distribute copies.

Editing and Revising Your Communication

As you prepare to edit and revise your document, refer to WordPerfect for help. Start with the WordPerfect Spell program. No matter how well you type, you are likely to make occasional spelling errors and typos, and you want to be sure to catch them. Your Spell program will also catch accidental word duplication, such as *the the*. Make a practice of saving your letter and promptly running the Spell program.

After you use the Spell program, your letter should resemble the one in figure 3.15. (Although your spelling may be checked, you still have to edit your letter. This rough draft is not an easy letter to read and understand.)

```
                         Plant Emissions Department
                         Hammond Engineering, Inc.
                           Stroudsburg, PA 18360

      November 5, 1990



      Mr. Robert Platz
      Hammond Engineering, Inc.
      2503 Tittabawassee Rd.
      Saginaw, MI 48604

      Dear Mr. Platz:

      As requested, a five-member group (see attached list) led by Dr.
      Gomberg has developed a solution to nearby groundwater
      contamination. The accompanying binder contains a history of this
      problem (refer to page 3). Five areas of this plant have suffered
      intermittent spillover of contaminants, based on figures from the
      local EPA and substantiated by the Pocono Mountain Environmental
      Agency.

      Because these contaminating spills happen in only one department
      at a time, we, as a team, have been looking into a portable unit
      that could be moved from department to department to treat
      spillovers as the levels of waste increase. After looking at many
      models of such a device, we propose using a system developed by
      United Technologies of Easton, PA. This unit is the most
      effective and also costs the least.

      If you have any questions, please call me at 555-5934 and I will
      be happy to answer for the other members of the team.

      Very truly yours,



      J. Denzil Jackson
      Plant Emissions Professional
```

Fig. 3.15.

A first rough draft.

Tip: You can use your WordPerfect template to check those words you commonly mistype or misspell. This time, add to the bottom of the original template a list of words you commonly misspell or misuse (see fig. 3.16). The Spell program recognizes your typos and misspellings and suggests corrections. But you must run the program for this excellent assistance.

Caution: If you mistakenly type one word for another—for example, *then* instead of *them*—and the wrong word you type is spelled correctly, the Spell program will not find the error. Therefore, proofread carefully what you have written.

In longer documents, use the Forward Search (F2) and Backward Search (Shift-F2) commands to hunt for common errors, awkward phrases, and jargon. Before a letter leaves your desk, *make sure you read it all the way through*.

Fig. 3.16.

Listing your common errors on your template.

```
STYLE (formal, informal):

     Formal
     Reader centered
     Low tech

SEARCH FOR:

     you for your                      and (comma splices)
     is (passive voice)                .  (two extra spaces)
     be (passive voice)                -- (replace)
     communication (typo)              actually (overuse)
     will (remove when possible)       impact (check use)
     exactly (overuse)                 graphics (check use)




                                   Doc 1 Pg 1 Ln 6.67" Pos 7"
```

As you read through the letter in figure 3.15, you see that the information is there, but you aren't sure of your organization. Perhaps you need to offer your actual solution in the first paragraph. To see how these ideas work on a sample file, copy your letter by selecting List Files (F5), Enter, and **8**. In the practice document, you can use Block (F11 or Alt-F4) to highlight what you want to move to another location. Next you use Move (Ctrl-F4) and select **Block (1)** and **M**ove (**1**). Then move your cursor to the new location and press Enter. Check to see whether the rewording makes the letter a better document. If your practice letter becomes a stronger letter, use it as the finished document. (It is far easier to delete an old file than to retype a new letter.)

With your guidelines beside the computer, test your letter by using the PRIOS model mentioned near the beginning of this chapter. Ask yourself the following questions:

- Is my purpose clear and consistent to the end of the letter?

- Have I written to my readers as I defined them?

- Is my information complete and clear?

- Is my letter organized so that the reader can move logically from one point to the next?

- Is my style consistent throughout the letter?

Highlight and move sentences to more effective places in the document. Delete unnecessary phrases, such as "and I will be happy to answer for the other members of the team," to pare your message to the bone. Add explanations where necessary. After you edit and revise your rough draft, compare it with the letter in figure 3.17.

Plant Emissions Department
Hammond Engineering, Inc.
1257 Main St.
Stroudsburg, PA 18360

November 5, 1990

Mr. Robert Platz
Hammond Engineering, Inc.
2503 Tittabawassee Rd.
Saginaw, MI 48604

Dear Mr. Platz:

A five-member plant emissions team led by Ms. Eleanor Gomberg has been checking the flow of contaminants into Pocono Creek, an estuary of the Delaware River. This plant has had intermittent spillover of contaminants, according to reports of the Environmental Protection Agency and local environmental groups. We propose a "watchdog" tracking of contaminant levels.

Because these contaminating spills happen in only one department at a time, the team has examined a portable unit that could be moved from department to department. After looking at many models of such a device, we propose a system developed by United Technologies of Easton, Pennsylvania. This unit is the most effective and also costs the least (see binder pages 5 and 7).

If you have any questions, please call me at 555-6934.

Sincerely,

J. Denzil Jackson
Plant Emissions Professional

Encl.:   Accompanying documentation
         Binder document list, p. 1
         Team members, p. 2

cc: Eleanor Gomberg, Manager
      Fred Rolle
      Freya Finch
      Will Nathan

Fig. 3.17.

A revised draft.

Checking your message, ask yourself whether it is positive, projects a good image for your team, and is clear business writing. The second letter looks much better.

If you compare the rough draft and the revised letter, you can see the changes. The revised letter is leaner, tighter, and more straightforward. You have produced a letter that should interest your district manager.

One last suggestion: Now that your letter is written, you have one more step. Take the letter to a co-worker and have that person read it. Ask the reader questions to make sure that all the information is clear. After that final review, you are ready to add the letter to the binder and send the package.

Summary

In this chapter you learned business-letter writing strategies, using the PRIOS model:

- Purpose
- Readers
- Information
- Organization
- Style

The chapter illustrated each of these items with examples and further ideas. You learned about listing your planning elements in a WordPerfect template you can reuse each time you plan a new document.

You learned about defining your primary purpose and your primary audience, and then looked at other purposes and readers who can affect your document.

You examined not only the information within the body of your letter, but also the tracking information that forms communication loops and "paper trails" of accountability for the information in the document.

You learned the direct, indirect, and balanced approaches to writing letters. Whether using a formal or an informal style, you saw how to add precision and consistency for accuracy in business and technical communication. You saw also how these elements work dynamically together to produce guidelines for effective communication.

After writing the letter with the correct information, you learned how to handle inside addresses, salutations, and closings. You then saw how careful revision can produce successful business communication.

4

Examining the Physical Characteristics of Your Letters

What you say in your letter—its message, the information you share, the tone and spirit of its contents—are vital elements in any letter.

But almost equally important is the overall appearance of your letter. A letter written with no regard to margins, punctuation, style, balance, or sequence of pages is substandard regardless of its content. And yet, every day thousands of letters are sent out with little or no regard to the physical characteristics of the letters themselves.

No one would think of making a business call in tennis shoes and ragged blue jeans. People dress up when they make business contacts. And for the same reason, you should "dress up" your letters so that they make the best possible impression on the readers.

This chapter discusses how to dress up your letters so that they make the best possible impression on the recipient. You will see why letter balance, letter appearance, white space, and the use of fonts and font attributes are important considerations in letter writing. Let's begin with how a letter represents the business itself.

Using a Letter as an Image Maker

Letters leaving a business office represent, in a very real sense, the organization itself. They exemplify not only the writer's ability and knowledge but also the organization's total image. In fact, the impression an individual letter creates may mean the difference between the gain or loss of a prospective client, customer, or influential friend for your company.

A corporation may spend thousands of dollars on advertising to promote its products or services and to project a positive public image. Yet this image can become seriously tarnished by careless correspondence—letters containing misspellings and inaccuracies, having illogical content, or having an out-of-date style. Carelessly prepared letters create a negative impression on their recipients.

An executive may spend as much as 50 percent of the workday on correspondence—planning what to say and how to organize the contents, determining the tone of the letters, or reading and acting on incoming correspondence. Secretaries spend as much as 80 percent of their time dealing with correspondence. With so much company time spent on one activity, it is imperative that the writer use the best style possible.

Unfortunately, style in business correspondence is not a static entity. Like language itself, letter style has changed over the years. For example, closed punctuation and indented paragraphs—once considered the standard for business letter format—have given way to Block and Simplified Letter styles. These styles are preferred today because they eliminate all tab settings and thus save typing time.

Creating Letter Balance

Have you ever received a letter that had the contents offset near the top of the page, or that had a narrow left margin and a wide right margin? This happens frequently. And these kinds of letters imply that the sender cares very little about the person receiving the letter.

Good-looking letters should be like a symmetrically framed picture with even margins working as a frame for the typed lines balanced under the letterhead. Fortunately, WordPerfect makes this symmetry easy to accomplish. You can use a standard margin setting while typing the letter, and then use the View Document command (Shift-F7, 6) to check the appearance of the letter itself. Figure 4.1 illustrates two views of the same letter: the left example shows incorrect margins; the right shows margins of 1.3" left and right, and has the Center Page feature activated.

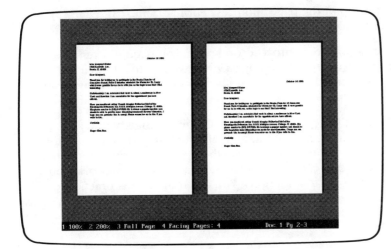

Fig. 4.1.

An incorrectly positioned letter compared with a balanced letter.

Adjusting Side Margins

One way to make letters appear more balanced is to adjust the left and right margins according to the size of the letter itself—wide margins for short letters and narrower margins for long letters. Use the following general guidelines for left and right WordPerfect margin settings:

- 1" by 1" margins for very long letters (300 words or more)

- 1.2" by 1.2" margins for medium letters (225 to 275 words)

- 1.6" by 1.6" margins for short-to-medium letters (150 to 200 words)

- 2" by 2" margins for short letters (100 words or less)

If a wider margin makes your letter run over by one or two lines onto the next page, go back to the top of your letter and change the Left/Right margin settings to a smaller number. Press Format (Shift-F8), Line (**1**), and Margins (**7**).

Tip: Remember that in WordPerfect if you have more than one margin setting code in a row, only the final code (the one on the right) is active. So if you try to change margins and nothing happens, use Reveal Codes (F11 or Alt-F3) to position properly a new margin code to the right of an existing margin code.

Adjusting Top and Bottom Margins

The text in the right-hand letter in figure 4.1 was positioned on the page vertically (that is, from top to bottom) by the Page Center command. To center a page vertically, go to the very top of the page and press Format (Shift-F8), **Page** (2), and Center Page (top to bottom) (**1**); then select **Yes** (**Y**).

If your letters sometimes run over onto a second page, you need not remove the Page Center command. It works only as long as you have less text than a full page. If your text fills the page top to bottom and spills over onto a second page, the Page Center command becomes inactive.

Tip: Some artists who sell their paintings and prints for a living say that a properly framed picture has even margins top, right, and left, but a slightly wider bottom margin. The additional 1/2 inch or inch corrects the optical illusion that the bottom margin is narrower. If you look carefully at professionally framed artwork, you will often see examples of wider bottom margins. You can transfer this practice to positioning a letter on a page. If you use the Page Center command, you can press Enter two or three times after the last line of the signature block to raise the text on the page slightly.

Improving Letter Appearance

Remember that the letters you write should represent you and your company to the best advantage. Therefore, make sure that they reflect competence and professionalism. Pay particular attention to the following items:

1. Use stationery made of high-quality paper. Nothing can do more to make a letter look bad than cheap paper and mismatched envelopes. Make certain that type from your printer prints clearly on the paper, and that the paper folds easily without cracking or rippling. Single sheets of plain white bond paper are the best, with your letterhead printed or engraved in black. The most convenient and popular size is 8 1/2 by 11 inches, although some firms now use 7 1/4-by-10 1/2-inch paper for general correspondence.

2. Keep the language clear and concise. Bad grammar, improper punctuation, and incorrect spelling will detract from your letter's message and prejudice the reader against you.

3. Check all names and addresses. No one likes to have his or her name misspelled, so be sure to use the proper form and correct spelling of names.

4. Organize the contents logically. Always keep in mind the reader's reaction to what you've written. Avoid padding and clichés.

5. Position the essential elements properly on the page. The date line, inside address, body copy, and signature block should be formatted according to an acceptable, contemporary business style (see "Using Popular Letter Styles" later in this chapter).

6. Type letters single-spaced with double-spacing between paragraphs. If characters are not clear and evenly dark, then it's time to change the ribbon or ink cartridge in your printer.

Using Different Fonts

If you are using a printer with different fonts, try creating letters with something other than Courier. A Courier font shouts *typewriter* to many readers and really is no longer the only way to create letters. Century Schoolbook 12 point, for instance, is one of the most readable and attractive fonts to use for general correspondence. But see what fonts you have available, and use a typeface that corresponds with the computer age that we now live in. Later in this chapter you will learn how to select and switch fonts so that you can print letters in a typeface that best represents your company and the products you produce.

Shortening Paragraphs

All letters—especially business letters—should be look easy to read and inviting to the eyes. Therefore, avoid long paragraphs in letters. They make reading difficult.

Paragraph breaks should come at logical points in your message. Overall, the paragraphs should present an even appearance. A letter with three short paragraphs at the top and one long paragraph at the bottom will look bottom heavy. Your letter has a far better chance at achieving its purpose if you use short, swift-moving sentences and short, swift-moving paragraphs.

Using White Space

Your letter's appearance will be enhanced by a well-planned use of white space. *White space* is a term used by journalists, magazine article writers, and book designers to refer to the blank portions of a page that assist in the overall composition. Avoid letters filled with text top to bottom and side to side. Use white space effectively so that your letters appear attractive. If a letter is brief, avoid beginning too high on the page. If the letter is long, use a second page rather than cram everything onto a single sheet.

Using Popular Letter Styles

Every well-constructed business letter contains six basic parts:

1. The heading, which includes the letterhead and the current date.

2. The inside address, which is the name and address of the person to whom the letter is written.

3. The salutation (now optional), which is the complimentary greeting.

4. The body copy, which explains the purpose of the letter.

5. The closing, which is the complimentary "good-bye."

6. The signature block, which defines who sent the letter.

Depending on the letter style used, these items may be arranged flush left, centered between the left and right margins, or flush right.

The *heading* is simply your address and the current date. Since most businesses use printed letterhead paper, the letter heading includes only the current date. Never write a letter without a heading. It's like pushing a private door open without first knocking. Letting the reader know immediately who sent the letter is both a courtesy and a custom in the business world. The date line is typed a few lines below the letterhead.

The *inside address* should include the full name and position of the person you are addressing. Remember that the envelope, which contains this information, will likely have been discarded when the letter is opened. Therefore, you want the letter itself to carry the name, position, or office of the person receiving the letter.

If you are using window envelopes (see "Using Window Envelopes" in Chapter 8), the inside address must be positioned so it appears inside the window when the letter is folded.

The *salutation* of a letter is the complimentary greeting to the person you are contacting. Long use and popular custom have made "Dear John," "Dear Martha," and "Dear Mr. Smith" the most popular form of address. If you have no way of knowing who is in charge of a particular office, it is proper to identify the person by position, as in "Dear Circulation Manager." Avoid strange-sounding salutations like "Dear Friend," "Dear Miss," or "Friend Don." Also avoid using the person's name alone, as in

Mr. Arnold Smith:

This is to inform you that the sample you ordered . . . .

The *body copy* contains your main message: the reason why you have sent the letter. Chapters 5, 6, and 7 discuss a variety of letter types that can be used as role models for your own body copy.

The *close* of the letter is the complimentary "good-bye" you include before you sign your name and slide the letter into the envelope. Of course, you can vary your closing depending on personal preference and letter type. If your closing includes more than one word, capitalize only the first word of the closing. Some popular letter closings include these:

Best regards,
Best wishes,
Cordially,
Cordially yours,
Most cordially yours,
Regards,
Sincerely,
Sincerely yours,
Very cordially yours,
Very sincerely yours,
Very truly yours,
Warmest regards,
Yours cordially,
Yours sincerely,
Yours truly,
Yours very truly,

The *signature block* defines who sent the letter. To create the signature block, press Enter five times after typing the close. The sender's name is typed on the fifth line, leaving four blank lines for the handwritten signature. The sender's title follows on the sixth line and the typist's initials on the seventh line, as in the following:

Mary Jacobs
Office Manager
MJ/rt

Under certain circumstances, the following optional elements might be added to these six basic parts:

- A reference line. A reference line containing a file or invoice number might be included in a letter replying to a specific order. Generally, a reference line is positioned either above or below the date line.

- Special mailing notations. If you send a letter by express mail or special delivery, this fact should be indicated on the envelope as well as in the letter itself. For example, if you send a letter by Federal Express, include the phrase *Federal Express* directly above the reader's address.

- An attention line. If you are sending a letter to an organization in general, but want to direct it to a specific individual within that organization, an attention line may be typed two lines below the bottom line of the address and two lines above the salutation.

- A subject line. It summarizes the subject of the letter and serves as an immediate point of reference for the reader, as well as a convenient filing tool for the secretaries at both ends of the correspondence cycle. If used, it should appear between the salutation and the body copy, separated from both by double-spacing.

- An enclosure reminder. If your letter contains additional sheets of information, a note to that effect should be typed one or two lines beneath the identification initials, if there are any, or under the last line of the signature block. Common formats for an enclosure statement include these: Enclosure, Enclosures (3), enc., encl., 3 encs., and Enc. 3.

- A carbon copy notation. Because of the wide use of computers and photocopiers, the cc: reference line at the bottom of a letter now refers to courtesy copies rather than carbon copies. Carbon paper is becoming a rare item in modern business offices. Courtesy copy notation may appear as cc, cc., Copy to, or Copies to.

- A postscript. It is aligned flush left and is typed two lines below the last notation. If the paragraphs in the body copy are indented, the postscript should likewise be indented.

Block Letter Style

In this style all principal parts are typed flush with the left margin, including paragraph openings. Double-spacing is used between the date line, the inside address, and the salutation. If you use a subject line, it should be two lines below the salutation and two lines above the first line of body copy. Paragraphs are single-spaced internally, with a double-space separating one paragraph from another. Figure 4.2 illustrates Block Letter style.

The heading for page two is blocked flush with the left margin:

Page 2
Mr. James Hoffman
November 30, 1990

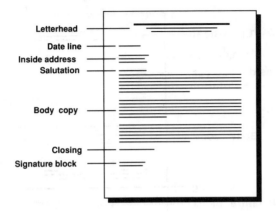

Letterhead

Date line
Inside address
Salutation

Body copy

Closing
Signature block

Fig. 4.2.

Block Letter style.

Skip two lines from the last line of the body copy to the complimentary close and leave four blank lines for the written signature. Typist's initials follow two lines below the last line of the signature block.

Modified Block Letter Style

The features of the Modified Block Letter are similar to those of the Block Letter, except for the position of the date line, the complimentary close, and the typewritten signature block. These three items should be indented, either to the center of the page or about 1/2" to the right of center. The position of the date line determines the position of the complimentary close and the signature block (see fig. 4.3).

The heading for page two in a Modified Block Letter is spread across the top of the page:

Mr. James Hoffman   - 2 -   November 30, 1990

Identification initials, such as the typist's, are placed two lines below the signature block, flush with the left margin.

Modified Semiblock Letter Style

The Modified Semiblock Letter looks similar to the Modified Block Letter, except that paragraphs are tab-indented. If a postscript is included, it is indented just like the body copy. Figure 4.4 depicts Modified Semiblock Letter style.

Fig. 4.3.

*Modified Block
Letter style.*

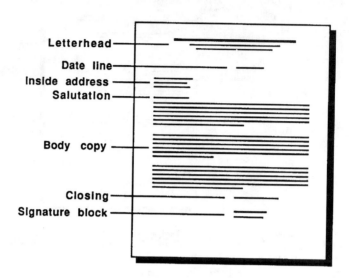

Fig. 4.4.

*Modified
Semiblock Letter
style.*

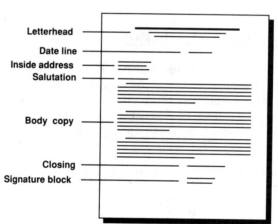

The heading for page two is the same as for the Modified Block Letter:

Mr. James Hoffman — 2 — November 30, 1990

Identification initials, as in the Modified Block Letter, appear flush with the left margins, two lines below the signature block.

Hanging-Indent Letter Style

In a Hanging-Indent Letter the date line appears flush right, with the complimentary close and typed signature block aligned under the first letter of the date line.

The Hanging-Indent Letter contains paragraphs with the top line flush with the left margin and the remaining lines indented (as in this paragraph). In WordPerfect, you create the Hanging-Indent style by pressing Indent (F4), then Shift-Tab. This format is used most often in direct-mail advertising, sales, and product promotion. Because it requires unusual indentation, the Hanging-Indent Letter style is not appropriate for general correspondence. See figure 4.5 for an example of this format.

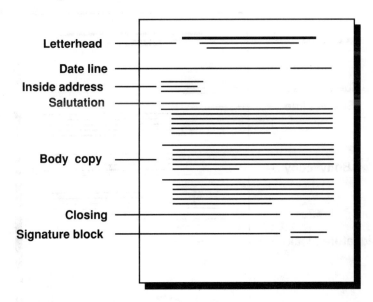

Letterhead

Date line

Inside address

Salutation

Body copy

Closing

Signature block

Fig. 4.5.

Hanging-Indent Letter style.

Continuation page headings, like those in Modified Block and Modified Semiblock Letters, must be on a single line stretched across the top of the page.

Simplified Letter Style

Simplified Letter style is a lean, clean format recommended by the Administrative Management Society. Since the format requires fewer keystrokes, it saves both time and money, boosts productivity, and enhances the look of the outgoing product.

In Simplified Letter style, the date line, inside address, body copy, and signature block are all positioned flush left, as in Block Letter style. However, the Simplified Letter contains no salutation and no complimentary close. In place of the salutation, type an all-uppercase subject line three lines beneath the final address line. At the end of the letter, type the writer's name and corporate title flush left on one line five or six lines below the last line of the body copy. The writer's name and title are separated by a single dash, as in the following:

Mary M. Smith - Senior Editor

The typist's initials are also flush left two lines beneath the writer's name. The writer's initials are not included with the typist's initials. See figure 4.6 for a representation of Simplified Letter style.

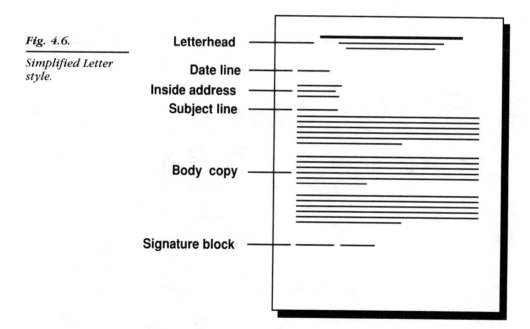

Fig. 4.6.

Simplified Letter style.

According to the Administrative Management Society, Simplified Letters require less effort, look better, are more effective, and save money.

The one drawback to Simplified Letter style is the impersonal tone it conveys. An acceptable solution is to include the reader's name at least once in the body of the letter, preferably within the first paragraph.

Half-Sheet Letter Style

Some companies use special half-sheet letterhead stationery for short notes. Half-sheet letterhead is preferred for one- or two-paragraph communications, such as short letters of appreciation or congratulation, or informal corporate invitations.

You may use any of the previous letter styles on a half-sheet letterhead. But remember to keep the letter short and to the point. Ideally, the writer's name is included in the letterhead, so that you do not need to repeat the name after the complimentary close.

Selecting Stationery Sizes

The size of stationery you use most likely will depend on the standard already established for your company. However, stationery used for office correspondence generally falls into five basic size groups: three for USA sizes and two for metric sizes:

United States Sizes:

Standard	8 1/2" by 11"
Baronial	5 1/2" by 8 1/2"
Monarch	7 1/2" by 10 1/2"

Metric Sizes:

A4	210 by 297 mm	(8.27" by 11.69")
A5	148 by 210 mm	(5.83" by 8.27")

To select (or create) a new stationery size in WordPerfect 5.1, press Format (Shift-F8), select **Page (2)**, and then choose Paper Size **(7)**. The Format: Paper Size/Type screen, as seen in figure 4.7, displays various sizes of paper. If your printer supports landscape printing and you have the fonts available, you can select between either portrait (short side at the top) or landscape (long side at the top) paper.

Using Fonts in WordPerfect 5.1

When desktop laser printers first appeared on the scene, they revolutionized the word processing market. For the first time, it became possible to combine different typefaces and fonts on a single page without sending copy to a print shop for typesetting. Hence, a new expression entered the English language: *desktop publishing*. If you have a thousand dollars or so to spend on a laser printer, your computer can now print near-typeset-quality documents for a fraction of the cost of typesetting.

Fig. 4.7.

Paper sizes available with the Hewlett-Packard LaserJet Series IID printer.

```
Format: Paper Size/Type

                                                          Font  Double
Paper type and Orientation    Paper Size    Prompt Loc    Type  Sided  Labels

Envelope - Wide               9.5" x 4"      No   Manual  Land  No
Legal                         8.5" x 14"     No   Contin  Port  No
Legal - Dup Long              8.5" x 14"     No   Contin  Port  Yes
Legal - Dup Long - Wide       14" x 8.5"     No   Contin  Land  Yes
Legal - Dup Short             8.5" x 14"     No   Contin  Port  Yes
Legal - Dup Short - Wide      14" x 8.5"     No   Contin  Land  Yes
Legal - Wide                  14" x 8.5"     No   Contin  Land  No
Standard                      8.5" x 11"     No   Contin  Port  No
Standard - Dup Long           8.5" x 11"     No   Contin  Port  Yes
Standard - Dup Long - Wide    11" x 8.5"     No   Contin  Land  Yes
Standard - Dup Short          8.5" x 11"     No   Contin  Port  Yes
Standard - Dup Short - Wide   11" x 8.5"     No   Contin  Land  Yes
Standard - Wide               11" x 8.5"     No   Contin  Land  No
[ALL OTHERS]                  Width ≤ 8.5"   Yes  Manual        No



1 Select; 2 Add; 3 Copy; 4 Delete; 5 Edit; N Name Search: 1
```

No longer is a user limited to the 10-pitch pica or 12-pitch elite of typewriter days. Typefaces like Helvetica, Times Roman, Century Schoolbook, Presentation, Broadway, Coronet, Bodoni, Cooper Black, and a hundred others are available for everyday projects.

Understanding Typefaces and Fonts

To understand the difference between typefaces and fonts, consider how different printers create text. A daisywheel or dot-matrix printer, for example, prints in a particular typeface that either is built into the printer as the internal character set or resides on a daisywheel or thimble. A *typeface* is a particular design of type, such as Courier, Times Roman, or Helvetica.

If you want to change the weight of a word—for example, to make the word appear in boldface—many of these printers will overprint each letter two or three times, sometimes even moving the print head slightly to create a bold effect. However, there are only a certain number of special effects that you can coax out of a conventional printer using a single font.

A laser printer, on the other hand, prints a special effect by switching to a different font. For a given typeface a *font* is a set of characters having a particular size, style, and weight. For example, boldface and italic for a laser printer are bold and italic fonts of a particular typeface. Superscript and subscript, likewise, are smaller fonts of the same typeface, printed offset from the baseline of regular text. In other words, a laser printer needs several different fonts for each typeface. Thus, for each font size (6 point, 8 point, 10 point, 12 point, 14 point, and so on) of a particular typeface, you can select different weights (regular, bold, extra bold, and so on) or styles (Roman or italic). See figure 4.8 for examples of different weights and styles for three different type fonts.

This is Helvetica 12 point font
This is Helvetica 12 point italic
This is Helvetica 12 point bold

Fig. 4.8.

*Different font
weights and styles.*

This is Times Roman 12 point font
This is Times Roman 12 point italic
This is Times Roman 12 point bold

This is Century Schoolbook 12 point font
This is Century Schoolbook 12 point italic
This is Century Schoolbook 12 point bold

With laser printers, typefaces and fonts are made available in three different ways: built into the printer when you buy it, added through a plug-in cartridge, or stored on disk and downloaded to the printer at the beginning of the work day. The built-in fonts are called internal fonts; the plug-in fonts are called cartridge fonts; and the disk fonts are called soft fonts. You will soon see how to put these fonts to use in the documents you create.

Selecting Your Printer

When using WordPerfect 5.1 to print documents, you must have a copy of the correct printer driver file on your hard disk. Many printer drivers are supplied with WordPerfect, and the one you need for a particular printer is copied to your program disk during installation. WordPerfect needs the printer driver for your printer to take full advantage its capabilities.

Before you can use the various fonts, you must first install your printer. To install a printer, follow these steps:

1. Press Print (Shift-F7) and choose Select Printer (**S**).

    ▭▯ Choose **Print** from the pull-down **File** menu.

2. Choose **Additional Printers** (**2**).

3. Use the up- or down-arrow key (or PgDn and PgUp) to highlight your printer.

4. Choose Select (**1**).

5. Press Exit (F7). If you see a Printer Help and Hints screen, press F7 again to exit to the Select Printer: Edit menu.

If you have previously installed your printer, do steps 1 and 2, highlight the printer you plan to use, and press **Edit (3)**. This will also take you to the Select Printer: Edit menu.

Installing Fonts

The Select Printer: Edit menu (see fig. 4.9) lets you do three activities with fonts: select individual Cartridges and Fonts (**4**), define which font will be the Initial Base Font (**5**) for all documents, and define the Path for Downloadable Fonts and Printer Command Files (**6**). Do these activities in the following order: item 6, then item 4, then item 5. If you do not have soft fonts, skip item 6.

Fig. 4.9.

Installing a font with the Select Printer: Edit menu.

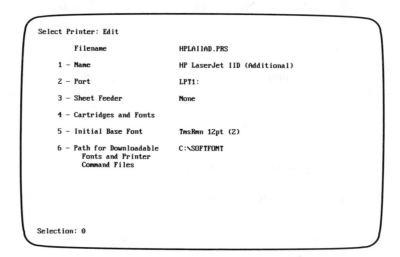

Defining the Path for Downloadable Fonts

If you have soft fonts (that is, fonts stored on disk as individual files), you must tell WordPerfect where these fonts are located on disk. At the Select Printer: Edit menu, choose Path for **Downloadable Fonts and Printer Command Files (6)**, type the full path name for the soft font subdirectory (for example, *C:\SOFTFONT*), and press Enter.

Note: You must create the soft font subdirectory and copy the font files to it before you can tell WordPerfect where they are located. If no soft font subdirectory exists, WordPerfect will not let you define a path on this menu.

Selecting Cartridges and Fonts

Next, select **Cartridges and Fonts (4)**. You will see three types of fonts like those in figure 4.10.

```
Select Printer: Cartridges and Fonts

Font Category                         Quantity        Available

Built-In
Cartridges                               2                0
Soft Fonts                            1500 K           1232 K




    NOTE: Most items listed under the Font Category (with the exception of Built-In)
    are optional and must be purchased separately from your dealer or manufacturer.

    In order to print soft fonts marked '*', you must run the Initialize Printer
    option in WP each time you turn your printer on.

    If soft fonts are not located in the same directory as your printer files, you
    must specify a Path for Downloadable Fonts in the Select Printer: Edit menu.

    1 Select; 2 Change Quantity; N Name search: 1
```

Fig. 4.10.

Three types of fonts available with most printers.

To see which internal fonts come with your printer, highlight Built-In with the up- or down-arrow key and choose **Select (1)**. In most cases, your printer will include one or more Courier fonts, and perhaps a Line Draw font or two. These should already be marked with an asterisk (*) at the left. Press Exit (F7) to return to the Select Printer: Cartridges and Font menu.

To mark the plug-in cartridge(s) installed in your printer, highlight Cartridges and press **Select (1)**. Use the up- or down-arrow key to locate which plug-in cartridge or cartridges you have installed in your printer; press **Select (1)**. See figure 4.11 for the Select Printer: Cartridges menu. Type an asterisk (*) to mark the correct cartridge. Then press Exit (F7) to return to the Select Printer: Cartridges and Font menu.

If you have soft fonts, highlight Soft Fonts on the Select Printer: Cartridges and Fonts menu (see fig. 4.10) and choose **Select (1)**. You will now see a Select Printer: Soft Fonts menu (see fig. 4.12). Use the up- or down-arrow key to highlight the soft font family installed in your soft font directory (for example, in the C:\SOFTFONT subdirectory). To select a font family, press **Select (1)**.

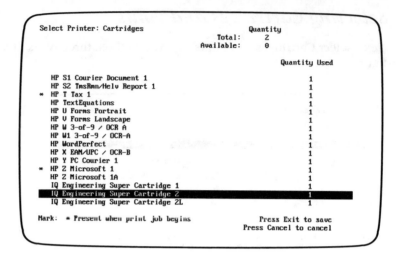

Fig. 4.11.

Cartridges available for a particular printer.

```
Select Printer: Cartridges                        Quantity
                                          Total:      2
                                      Available:      0

                                                  Quantity Used
         HP S1 Courier Document 1                      1
         HP S2 TmsRmn/Helv Report 1                    1
   *     HP T Tax 1                                    1
         HP TextEquations                              1
         HP U Forms Portrait                           1
         HP V Forms Landscape                          1
         HP W 3-of-9 / OCR A                           1
         HP W1 3-of-9 / OCR-A                          1
         HP WordPerfect                               1
         HP X EAN/UPC / OCR-B                          1
         HP Y PC Courier 1                             1
   *     HP Z Microsoft 1                              1
         HP Z Microsoft 1A                             1
         IQ Engineering Super Cartridge 1             1
         IQ Engineering Super Cartridge 2             1
         IQ Engineering Super Cartridge 2L            1

   Mark:  * Present when print job begins        Press Exit to save
                                                 Press Cancel to cancel
```

Fig. 4.12.

Selecting font families from the Select Printer: Soft Fonts menu.

```
Select Printer: Soft Fonts

Font Groups:

     HP AA TmsRmn/Helv US (P/L)
     HP AB TmsRmn/Helv R8 (P/L)
     HP AC TmsRmn/Helv US (P/L)
     HP AD TmsRmn/Helv R8 (P/L)
     HP AE TmsRmn/Helv US (P/L)
     HP AF TmsRmn/Helv R8 (P/L)
     HP AG Helv Headlines PC-8 (P/L)
   · HP DA L.Gothic/Present (P/L)
     HP DC L.Gothic/Present PC-8 (P/L)
     HP EA Prestige Elite (P/L)
     HP RA ITC Garamond US (P/L)
     HP RB ITC Garamond R8 (P/L)
   · HP SA Century Schoolbook US (P/L)
     HP SB Century Schoolbook R8 (P/L)
     HP TA Zapf Humanist 601 US (P/L)
     HP TB Zapf Humanist 601 R8 (P/L)
   · HP UA Headline Type 1 US (P/L)
     HP UB Headline Type 1 R8 (P/L)
     LTI Specialty 1-6 / Master Lib (P/L)

1 Select; N Name search: 1
```

After you have selected a font family, mark with an asterisk (*) in the Select Printer: Soft Fonts screen (see fig. 4.13) the individual fonts in the font family you plan to use all the time. Mark with a plus sign (+) the fonts you plan to use only occasionally. Fonts marked with an asterisk will be downloaded when you turn on your printer; fonts marked with a plus sign will be downloaded only when you print a document using them. Note that each font you mark with an asterisk will reduce the available printer memory (see the upper right corner under Quantity). WordPerfect will not let you exceed the total available printer memory when you are marking these fonts.

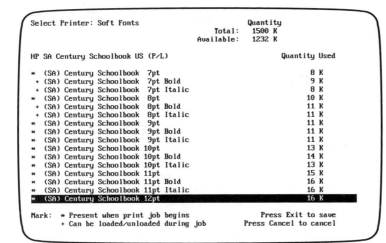

```
Select Printer: Soft Fonts                      Quantity
                                      Total:     1500 K
                                  Available:     1232 K

HP SA Century Schoolbook US (P/L)                          Quantity Used

  *  (SA) Century Schoolbook  7pt                               8 K
  +  (SA) Century Schoolbook  7pt Bold                          9 K
  +  (SA) Century Schoolbook  7pt Italic                        8 K
  *  (SA) Century Schoolbook  8pt                              10 K
  +  (SA) Century Schoolbook  8pt Bold                         11 K
  +  (SA) Century Schoolbook  8pt Italic                       11 K
  *  (SA) Century Schoolbook  9pt                              11 K
  *  (SA) Century Schoolbook  9pt Bold                         11 K
  *  (SA) Century Schoolbook  9pt Italic                       11 K
  *  (SA) Century Schoolbook  10pt                             13 K
  *  (SA) Century Schoolbook  10pt Bold                        14 K
  *  (SA) Century Schoolbook  10pt Italic                      13 K
  *  (SA) Century Schoolbook  11pt                             15 K
  *  (SA) Century Schoolbook  11pt Bold                        16 K
  *  (SA) Century Schoolbook  11pt Italic                      16 K
  *  (SA) Century Schoolbook  12pt                             16 K

Mark:  * Present when print job begins            Press Exit to save
       + Can be loaded/unloaded during job      Press Cancel to cancel
```

Fig. 4.13.

The Select Printer: Soft Fonts screen.

Press Exit (F7) to return to the Select Printer: Soft Fonts menu. If you have an additional soft font family available, repeat the selection process with that family. Press Exit (F7) to return to the Select Printer: Cartridges and Fonts menu.

When you are done marking all internal, cartridge, and soft fonts, press Exit (F7) to return to the Select Printer: Edit menu.

Selecting the Initial Base Font

The last step is to tell WordPerfect which font should serve as your *Initial Base Font*. The Initial Base Font will be the font that your printer uses for all documents unless you choose a different font for a specific document.

To select the Initial Base Font from the Select Printer: Edit menu (see fig. 4.9), do the following:

1. Choose Initial Base Font (**5**).

2. Use the up- or down-arrow key to highlight one of the fonts listed.

3. Choose Select (**1**).

4. Specific a point size if necessary.

5. Press Exit (F7) twice to return to the Print menu.

If you have any soft fonts, you must remember to initialize the printer each time you turn it on. Otherwise, WordPerfect will be unable to print text in these fonts. To initialize the printer, press Print (Shift-F7), choose Initialize the Printer (**7**), and select **Y** for yes (see option 7 in fig. 4.14).

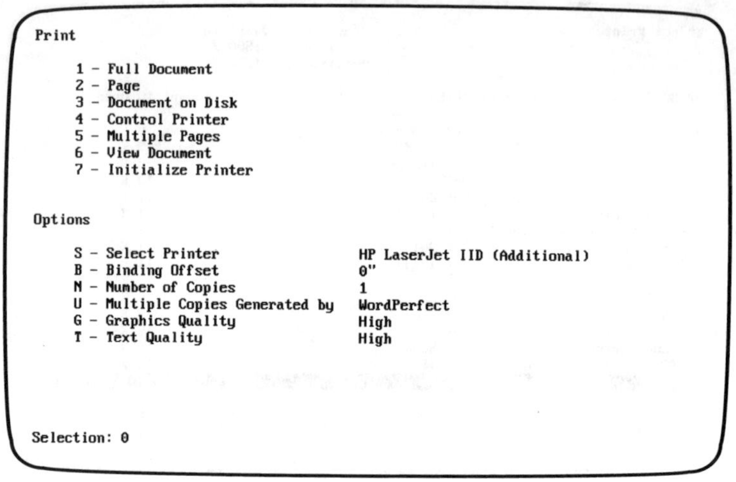

Fig. 4.14.

*Using option 7 on
the Print screen to
initialize the
printer.*

```
Print

    1 - Full Document
    2 - Page
    3 - Document on Disk
    4 - Control Printer
    5 - Multiple Pages
    6 - View Document
    7 - Initialize Printer


Options

    S - Select Printer              HP LaserJet IID (Additional)
    B - Binding Offset              0"
    N - Number of Copies            1
    U - Multiple Copies Generated by   WordPerfect
    G - Graphics Quality            High
    T - Text Quality                High




Selection: 0
```

Changing Fonts

During normal operation, WordPerfect will use the font you have identified as your
Initial Base Font for all documents. If you want to use a different font within a
document, WordPerfect 5.1 lets you change fonts three different ways: by changing
to a different font attribute (for example, bold, italic, or shadow), by using one of
the automatic font sizes (such as Fine, Small, or Large), or by changing the base
font. All three methods are accessed through the Font key (Ctrl-F8).

Changing Font Attributes

To change the appearance of a font, press Font (Ctrl-F8) and select **Appearance (2)**,
or choose Appearance from the Font pull-down menu. When you do this, you will
see nine different font attributes listed at the bottom of the screen (or in the pull-
down menu box):

1 B old 2 U ndln 3 D bl Und 4 I talic 5 O utln 6 S hadw 7 Sm C ap 8   R edln 9 S tkout

To switch to one of these font attributes, type either the number or the boldface
letter for the attribute. All text typed from that point on will print in that attribute,
provided that your printer supports the attribute. To return from one of these font
attributes to your base font, press the right-arrow key. You can also press Font
(Ctrl-F8), Normal (**3**), but the right arrow is faster. Since Bold and Underline are
the most commonly used font attributes, they are also available as single keystroke
commands: Bold (F6) and Underline (F8).

If you want to change existing text into bold, underline, italic, or another style, highlight the text with Block (F12 or Alt-F4) and then select the font attribute (for example, Ctrl-F8, **2**, **1**, for boldface).

Changing to an Automatic Font Size

WordPerfect 5.1 has a unique automatic font-sizing feature that makes it easy to switch among seven different font sizes (or eight counting the base font). These font sizes are determined by the font you have selected as your base font and are selected automatically from the fonts available for your printer (initial fonts, cartridge fonts, and soft fonts). In addition, if you use WordPerfect 5.1 to open a document containing these font sizes on a computer attached to a different printer, WordPerfect automatically selects appropriate fonts for that printer which best match the sizes you selected for your own printer. Later, when you take the document back to your own computer and printer, WordPerfect reselects the fonts you had originally.

Here are the seven automatic font sizes that are available and the percentage each differs from your base font:

Font Size	Percentage of Base Font
Superscript	60%
Subscript	60%
Fine	60%
Small	80%
Large	120%
Very Large	150%
Extra Large	200%

To change to a different font size, press Font (Ctrl-F8), **Size** (1), and select from among the seven sizes listed:

```
1 Suprscpt; 2 Subscpt; 3 Fine; 4 Small; 5 Large; 6 Vry Large; 7 Ext Large
```

Tip: If you don't like these percentages, you can change them yourself. Press Setup (Shift-F1). Select **Initial Settings** (4), **Print Options** (8), and **Size Attribute Ratio** (6). Then specify the percentage(s) you want to use.

Remember, though, that WordPerfect cannot create new fonts for you. All it can do is select the alternative fonts that come closest to the percentages listed here. For instance, if you do not have a font that is 200 percent larger than your base font, WordPerfect will select whatever font is the closest to that size from the fonts available for your printer.

Changing the Base Font

The third method of changing fonts is simply to select a specific font as your new base font. This can be for the entire document, or just for a page, paragraph, sentence, or word. If you do not plan to move your documents from one computer to another, selecting a specific font might be better than the automatic fonts, because it lets *you* decide which specific font *you* want.

To change the base font, either at the beginning of a document or anywhere within a document, press Font (Ctrl-F8) and select Base Font (4). Use the up- or down-arrow key to highlight the font you want to select; then choose Select (1). Figure 4.15 illustrates a typical Base Font menu.

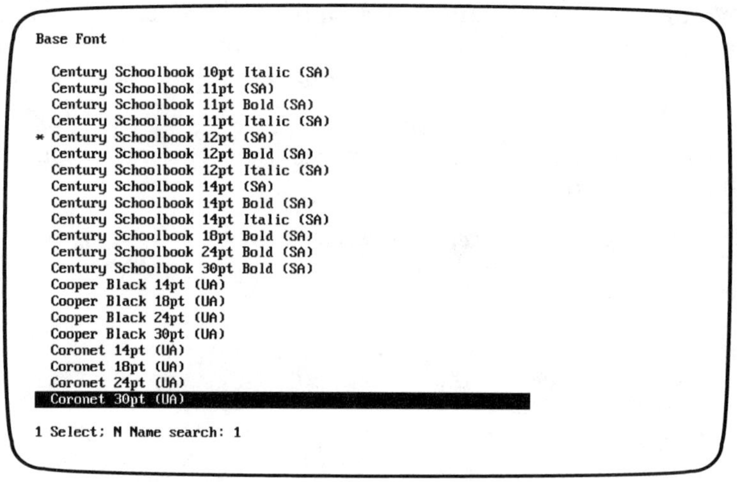

Fig. 4.15.

Selecting a different base font from the Base Font menu.

```
 Base Font

     Century Schoolbook 10pt Italic (SA)
     Century Schoolbook 11pt (SA)
     Century Schoolbook 11pt Bold (SA)
     Century Schoolbook 11pt Italic (SA)
   * Century Schoolbook 12pt (SA)
     Century Schoolbook 12pt Bold (SA)
     Century Schoolbook 12pt Italic (SA)
     Century Schoolbook 14pt (SA)
     Century Schoolbook 14pt Bold (SA)
     Century Schoolbook 14pt Italic (SA)
     Century Schoolbook 18pt Bold (SA)
     Century Schoolbook 24pt Bold (SA)
     Century Schoolbook 30pt Bold (SA)
     Cooper Black 14pt (UA)
     Cooper Black 18pt (UA)
     Cooper Black 24pt (UA)
     Cooper Black 30pt (UA)
     Coronet 14pt (UA)
     Coronet 18pt (UA)
     Coronet 24pt (UA)
     Coronet 30pt (UA)

 1 Select; N Name search: 1
```

If you use this section as your guide, you should have little problem selecting and using different font attributes and font sizes in your documents.

Creating Multiple Letters with Merge

If you ever had to type the same form letter 50 or 100 times, you already know what a boring and time-consuming task that can be. In fact, one of the first things that newcomers to word processing discover is how to use the same letter over and over again. All they do is retrieve the previous document; delete the old name, address, and date; type in a new name, address, and date; and reprint the letter.

However, what many new users do not realize is that there is an even easier method to send the same letter to 50 different people. If you set up the form letter as a WordPerfect *merge document*, you can automate the process of sending personalized copies of the letter to different individuals. The program will take your form letter and automatically insert the different names and addresses at the correct locations in every copy of the letter. In addition, you can use the same address list to print your envelopes automatically too. In fact, you can reuse the same address list repeatedly for future letters. Talk about saving time!

Understanding How Merge Works

Merge, or *mail merge* as some call it, always involves two documents: a primary file and a secondary file. The primary file can be a form letter, an envelope, a mailing label, an invoice, or even a packing slip. This file controls the merge operation. The secondary file contains a different set of names, addresses, phone numbers, and so on, for each individual who will receive a printed letter, envelope, or whatever. Figure 4.16 shows how merge combines the names and addresses from a secondary file with a primary file (the letter itself) to create multiple copies of the letter for different addresses.

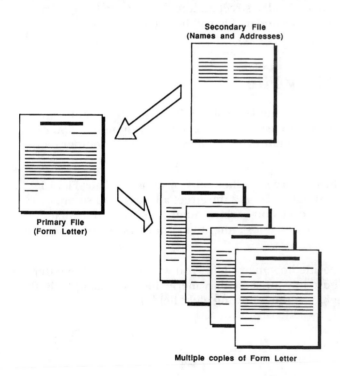

Secondary File
(Names and Addresses)

Primary File
(Form Letter)

Multiple copies of Form Letter

Fig. 4.16.

Merging a secondary file with a primary file to make multiple copies of a form letter.

You can add as many names and addresses as you want to a secondary file. And you can merge different primary files with the same secondary file. For example, a letter primary file and an envelope primary file can be merged with the same secondary address file to create 50 letters and 50 envelopes.

Both documents contain WordPerfect *merge codes*. The primary file—a form letter, for example—contains merge codes to specify where the receiver's first and last name, street address, city, state, and ZIP code are to appear, as well as where the current date should go. Another merge code is inserted to personalize the letter with the receiver's first name, as in

    Dear Jason:

The secondary file contains merge codes to identify each variable item: first and last name, street address, city, state, ZIP, and so on. WordPerfect calls these variable items *fields*. Each set of variable fields for one individual is called a *record*. Thus a secondary file may contain 100 records, with each record containing four or more fields: a last name field, a first name field, a street address field, a city field, a state field, and so on. Each record in the secondary file will be used to create a new letter, as shown in figure 4.16.

Setting Up a Secondary File

Actually, the secondary document is a simple database. It can contain many different fields, but you do not have to use all of the fields in each merge. You can select certain fields for one merge operation, and different fields for another merge later on.

In WordPerfect 4.2, different fields were identified only by number. Thus Field 1 might have been the first and last name, Field 2 the street address, and so on. Naturally this could lead to some confusion—which number represented what field? In version 5.1, you can use field names rather than numbers, making merge a much easier operation.

But first do a little planning. Decide how many fields you will need for each letter and what field names you will use in your secondary merge file. For example, in the case of a letter merge, you might use the following eight field names:

    LastName
    FirstName
    Company
    StreetAddress
    City
    State
    ZIP
    Salutation

However, since you may use this secondary file later to create a phone list, you may want to add a ninth field: PhoneNumber.

The secret to setting up a secondary file with field names is to insert a special record at the beginning of the secondary file telling WordPerfect which field names you plan to use. Begin with a clear screen and follow these steps to start a new secondary file:

1. Press Merge Codes (Shift-F9) and select **More (6)**.

   ▭ Choose the **Tools** menu and select **Merge Codes**; then select **More (6)** from the pop-out menu.

2. Use the up- or down-arrow key to move the highlight bar to {FIELD NAMES}, or start typing field names.

   ▭ Move the mouse pointer to the Merge Codes selection box. While pressing the left mouse button, drag the mouse downward to highlight the {FIELD NAMES} line.

3. With {FIELD NAMES} highlighted, press Enter or double-click that line.

4. At the Enter Field 1: prompt, type the name of the first field, or *LastName*, and press Enter.

5. At the Enter Field 2: prompt, type the name of the next field, or *FirstName*, and press Enter.

6. Repeat the process for all remaining field names—in this example, *Company*, *StreetAddress*, *City*, *State*, *ZIP*, *Salutation*, and *PhoneNumber*.

7. After typing the last field name, press Enter at the next prompt for another field name. Enter tells WordPerfect that you are finished listing field names.

After you have finished typing all the field names, WordPerfect will display the list of field names at the top of the document, as shown in figure 4.17.

Notice that each field in the FIELD NAME record is separated by a tilde (~). The tilde tells WordPerfect where one name ends and another begins. Once you have a Field Name record set up, you are ready to enter the variable data—the names, addresses, and other information—that will appear in your secondary file. Make sure your cursor is on the first line of page two, just under the double horizontal line indicating a page break.

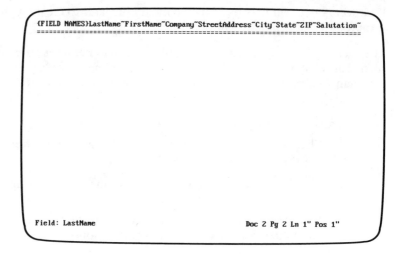

Fig. 4.17.

*Field names at the
beginning of a
secondary file.*

1. A prompt at the bottom of the screen tells you which name to type next—in this case, Field: LastName.

2. Type the last name of someone who will be included in your secondary file.

3. Don't press Enter after typing the last name. Instead, press End Field (F9). You must use F9 to mark the end of each field in a secondary file.

As soon as you press End Field (F9), the prompt at the bottom will change to the next field, Field: FirstName. Repeat steps 1 through 3 for each field in this record: Company, StreetAddress, City, State, ZIP, Salutation, and PhoneNumber.

When you have typed the last field of information (PhoneNumber), press Merge Codes (Shift-F9) and select End Record (2). An {END RECORD} code appears on a line by itself, followed by a page break. Figure 4.18 shows one complete record entered into the secondary file under the {FIELD NAMES} record at the top. Note that each record is separated by a page break (the double line).

Repeat the preceding steps for each record, making sure that you start each new record on a separate page. When you have finished creating the secondary merge file, save the file with a descriptive name like *ADDRESS.SF*. The .SF extension reminds you that the file is a secondary file, and makes that file easier to locate later when you perform a merge.

If you plan to use merge often, create a MERGE subdirectory where you can store all your primary and secondary merge files. The subdirectory, which should have a path name of C:\WP51\MERGE, can be created if you use List (F5), press Enter, and select Other Directory (7).

```
{FIELD NAMES}LastName~FirstName~Company~StreetAddress~City~State~ZIP~Salutation~
==================================================================================
Johnson{END FIELD}
Edward{END FIELD}
Ames Paper Products{END FIELD}
2639 Wabash Avenue{END FIELD}
Fort Worth{END FIELD}
Texas{END FIELD}
76109{END FIELD}
Edward{END FIELD}
{END RECORD}
==================================================================================



Field: LastName                         Doc 2 Pg 3 Ln 1" Pos 1"
```

Fig. 4.18.

Page break lines separating one record from another.

Setting Up a Primary File

After you have created a secondary merge file, you need to create a primary merge file to use with your merge. Your primary file, in this case, will be a single-page letter.

You create a primary file by typing the fixed information you want to appear in each copy of the letter you will be sending. In other words, you type the body copy of the letter itself, including the closing and signature block at the end. Where you want the variable data to appear (that is, the receiver's name, company, address, and so on), you insert a {FIELD} code and the name of each field. To include a field name, follow these steps:

1. Position the cursor where you want the variable data to appear.

2. Press Merge Codes (Shift-F9).

    ⌨ Choose **Merge** from the **Tools** menu.

3. Choose **Field (1)**.

4. At the Enter Field: prompt, type the name of the field exactly as you used it in the secondary file, and press Enter.

For example, the first field in your secondary file was named LastName, so this is how you enter the field codes. WordPerfect inserts a {FIELD} code, followed by the name of the field and a tilde (~). The tilde tells WordPerfect where each field ends.

Continue typing the primary file (your letter), inserting {Field} codes where they are needed.

Note: You can put more than one {FIELD} code in a single line if that is where you want the text to appear when the document is merged with the secondary file. Figure 4.19 illustrates how the primary file (your letter) appears on-screen with the {FIELD} codes inserted.

Fig. 4.19.

Merge codes in a primary letter file.

```
{FIELD}FirstName~ {FIELD}LastName~
{FIELD}Company~
{FIELD}StreetAddress~
{FIELD}City~, {FIELD}State~ {FIELD}ZIP~

Dear {FIELD}Salutation~:

In your particular work, you are an expert. As such, you know the value of
consulting with other experts, in order to benefit from their knowledge and
suggestions.

Suppose you had available, at any time, and at a very moderate fee, a
group of experts in the field of business, economics, finance, and
government, with whom you could consult at any time.

Suppose, too, that each of these experts continually studied and analyzed
every resource at his command, and traveled around the nation gathering
first-hand information, trends, and reactions.

Then suppose that this remarkable group sent you, every month, a clear,
concise report for your personal use and growth. You would gladly pay
$18.00 a year for their services, wouldn't you?

All this is available in COMPUTER UPDATE, the new magazine for busy
                                        Doc 2 Pg 1 Ln 1" Pos 1"
```

Performing the Merge

Once you have created a secondary file (the data file with names and addresses) and a primary file (the letter), you can merge the two files to create multiple copies of the letter—each personalized with someone's name and address. Start with an empty screen and follow these steps:

1. Press Merge/Sort (Ctrl-F9) and select **Merge** (**1**).

   ⌨ Choose **Merge** from the **Tools** pull-down menu.

2. At the `Primary File:` prompt, type the name of the primary file and press Enter. Make certain you include the correct path and full name, including extension. Instead of typing the primary file name, you can press List (F5) and locate the file that way. When you find the primary file, highlight it and press **Retrieve** (**1**).

3. At the `Secondary File:` prompt, type the name of the secondary file, including the path and extension, and press Enter. Or you can use List (F5) as in step 2.

With those two pieces of information, WordPerfect merges the primary file with the secondary file. The result of the merge will be the same number of letters as records (complete address sets) in the secondary file. Thus, with minimal effort, you can send one letter to 10, 20, 50, or 100 different people.

Summary

In this chapter, you have learned a number of important things about creating letters. You have seen that every letter is an image maker for your company, producing either a good or bad impression in the mind of the reader. This chapter has also shown the importance of creating proper letter balance by symmetrically framing the text with attractive margins.

You can improve a letter's appearance by using high-quality stationery, keeping language clear and concise, checking all names and addresses, organizing the contents logically, positioning the essential elements properly on the page, and avoiding washed-out characters. You have also learned about the various elements of a proper business letter—the heading, the inside address, the salutation, the body copy, the close, and the signature block.

With WordPerfect and the printers available today, you can use many fonts other than the old-fashioned Courier font of typewriter days. This chapter has shown you how you can install different fonts and then select cartridges and soft fonts for your letters and documents. The chapter also has shown how to use different fonts (such as Helvetica), font attributes (such as bold and italics), and font sizes (fine, small, and so on) to add interest to your documents. You have also discovered how to set up a secondary file and primary file, and how to use WordPerfect Merge to create multiple letters from those two different files.

Chapter 5 shows you how to create an informative letter with the new features of WordPerfect 5.1.

5

Creating Letters That Inform

Every day millions of business letters cross in the mail. Most are routine letters of information. The following situations fall in this category of routine letters:

- Customer Service sends an account statement to a customer.

- A staff member reports on an off-site meeting.

- A salesperson thanks a potential customer for meeting to hear a proposal.

- The Planning Committee sends an announcement of upcoming events.

- A department head reports on the status of an in-house project.

Even these routine letters, which are not problematic and not, therefore, strategically difficult for the writer to compose, are nevertheless costly to your organization. Consider, for instance, the time spent dictating, typing, and then proofreading the letter. And the more personal the letter, the more expensive it is to write.

However costly, these routine letters are the basis for business communication. A simple letter of thanks sent after a productive business meeting reflects an attitude of concern not only on the part of the writer but also on the part of the organization represented by that person. This act of politeness can help sell a product or service. Yet when funds in an organization are tight, these routine letters are usually the first to go. Far too often companies neglect to respond to inquiries or send simple letters of information because of cost restrictions. You will find that using WordPerfect on your PC for composing, printing, and revising your business correspondences can be tremendously cost-effective.

Using the PRIOS Strategy To Plan Routine Letters

You recall from Chapter 3 that a PRIOS strategy can help you plan for writing. Using this strategy, you indicate on a new document or on the PRIOS template you designed in Chapter 3 the purpose, the readers, the information, the organization, and the style of the document you must create. If you practice planning ahead for your letters, you can ensure a better document.

Suppose that you want to compose a routine letter, say a simple thank-you letter to a prospective client. Look at your PRIOS template in figure 5.1. Go to this document and fill in the information for the letter you are writing.

Fig. 5.1.

Your WordPerfect PRIOS template.

```
PRIOS information

Date:
To:
Filename:

Purpose of document:
      Primary purpose:
      Secondary purpose:
Readers:
      Primary readers:
      Secondary readers:
Information:
Organization (direct, indirect, balanced):
Style (formal, informal):

Search for:
      you for your                but also (avoid)
      is (passive voice)          and (comma splices)
      be (passive voice)          -- (replace)
      then for them (typo)        actually (overuse)
      will (remove where possible) impact (correct use)
      exactly (overuse)           graphics (correct use)

                            Doc 2 Pg 1 Ln 4.67" Pos 6.7"
```

Purpose. The purpose of most routine letters is simply to inform, to announce, to thank, or to answer. This is your primary purpose. Your secondary purpose is usually one of goodwill in doing business. As part of your purpose, decide how you want your reader to respond.

Readers. You may have a single *primary* reader or several primary readers (if you intend to send multiple copies to several readers), but if your letter is posted or passed along to other readers, you will probably have a *secondary* audience as well. In this case, you need to consider how your letter will affect them.

Information. As you look at the information to include in the letter, note on your template what information your reader needs in order to meet the purpose you set.

Be sure to include the important tracking information: the date, return address, and your phone number for a follow-up inquiry. Ask yourself whether you need to place information in lists or possibly a chart. This may be a good opportunity to use the new Table feature of WordPerfect 5.1.

Organization. Routine business letters generally follow a direct method of organization: the main idea, more information or supporting explanations, and a courteous closing. On your template, type what information you will include in each paragraph.

Style. As you consider the style of letter you write, think back to the purpose of your letter. Do you want to project a friendly attitude or a straightforward, businesslike approach? Perhaps you simply want to convey information without concern to attitude. You can adopt a neutral style, merely issuing information.

Now you are ready to write your letter, adding all the elements you listed in your PRIOS template. Look at the routine letter of information in figure 5.2.

```
Federated Commercial Products, Inc.
173 North Delaware Street
Indianapolis, IN  46204

April 10, 1990


Mr. John Digion
Network Coordinator
Bateman Management Services, Inc.
1402 New York Street
Beech Grove, IN  46107

Dear Mr. Digion:

The FCP office at 173 North Delaware will be enhancing their
telephone system by installing a new feature called Auto Phone
Dispersal (APD). This feature will be on line beginning Monday,
April 13, 1990.

When dialing FCP you may receive a recording stating that all
attendants are busy, followed by music. You call will then be
routed to the first available attendant. While we do not
anticipate delays in answering your calls, we feel this feature
will improve our telephone service. Thank you for your patience
as we continually strive to make improvements regarding our
telephone system.

Please feel free to call Toby Domenico at 555-3482 with any
comments regarding our telephone service to you.

Sincerely,



T. B. Domenico
Administration Manager

TBD/hju-4
```

Fig. 5.2.

A routine letter of information.

Sample Informative Letters

The pages that follow show examples of 16 informative letters, arranged alphabetically. Each of these letters is also on the Applications Disk. They are meant to be used as guides in composing your own messages. In some cases, you may be able to substitute your own facts and use the rest of the letter as shown here. In other cases, you may want to modify the tone or expand the content to meet your specific needs or intended reader.

Acceptance Letter

A letter accepting something should convey appreciation and, when appropriate, enthusiasm. If certain details are unclear, the acceptance must deal with these topics. Otherwise, a brief note is generally sufficient. Above all, use an appreciative tone in responding to any invitation. This letter appears on the Applications Disk in the file ACCEPT.LTR.

[Letterhead]

Dear Mr. Phillips:

I'm happy to accept your invitation to speak at the United Business Hardware annual meeting on September 20 at 3 o'clock. I've enjoyed doing business with your company and look forward to the opportunity to attend one of your meetings.

How do you feel about the topic "Computer Hardware for the 1990s"? This is just a suggestion. Since you did not indicate how long you wanted me to speak, I will limit my address to 30 minutes unless I hear otherwise from you.

I'm eager to meet you and the other members of your company. Meanwhile, if you need any information from me for your program, please give me a call.

Sincerely,

Acknowledgment Letter

When it is necessary to acknowledge the receipt of goods or work performed by someone, or to supply requested information, reply promptly and use a simple, straightforward approach. If appropriate, end with a "thank you" or an expression of interest in the company or product. This letter appears on the Applications Disk in the file ACKNOWLE.LTR.

[Letterhead]

Dear Richard:

Thanks for sending your price quote for 250 boxes of Finch Opaque Zerographic Bright White 8 1/2-by-11-inch paper. I have turned this information over to our purchasing department, and you should be receiving an order from them within a few days.

I appreciate the competitive price that you are able to offer and look forward to doing more business with your company in the months ahead.

Very sincerely,

Announcement Letter

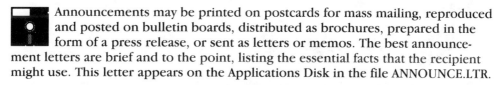 Announcements may be printed on postcards for mass mailing, reproduced and posted on bulletin boards, distributed as brochures, prepared in the form of a press release, or sent as letters or memos. The best announcement letters are brief and to the point, listing the essential facts that the recipient might use. This letter appears on the Applications Disk in the file ANNOUNCE.LTR.

[Letterhead]

Dear Mrs. Peterson:

As a valued customer at Pennsylvania Federal Credit Union, you may appreciate knowing that we have recently reduced our rates on new Home Equity loans to 9.75 percent. If you are planning on remodeling your home, have a son or daughter heading to college, or want to take that dream vacation, feel free to contact our office to see how we can help.

We are open from 8 a.m. to 5:30 p.m. Monday through Friday, and 9 a.m. to 3 p.m. on Saturdays. We would be happy to process your application for a new Home Equity loan. Our phone number is (717) 632-5674.

Very sincerely,

Apology Letter

Everyone at some time or another makes a mistake or forgets something important. A sincere letter of apology for an error, oversight, or other mistake in business is most helpful in soothing someone's ruffled feathers or hurt feelings. If possible, add a solution or suggest an alternative action if appropriate. This letter appears on the Applications Disk in the file APOLOGY.LTR.

[Letterhead]

Dear Mr. Madison:

In our recent shipment of letterhead, we incorrectly spelled your company's name. It is obvious from your order that the mistake was entirely ours and that the typo made your letterhead unusable.

Please accept my apology for the error. We have reprinted your letterhead and shipped it by overnight express so that you would have it as soon as possible. We are also extending a 25 percent discount on your order to help make up for the delay. The invoice enclosed reflects this discount from our previous quotation.

We rarely make this kind of mistake. But when we do, we do whatever possible to correct the error. I hope that you will continue using our company for your printing needs.

Very truly,

Appointment Letter

Letters concerning appointments should contain accurate details regarding the place, time, date, event, and so on. Nothing could be worse, for example, than providing incomplete details regarding a speaking engagement and causing the speaker to arrive at the wrong building or on the wrong date. This letter appears on the Applications Disk in the file APPOINT.LTR.

[Letterhead]

Dear General Archer:

Thank you for agreeing to be the guest speaker for our luncheon at the downtown Ramada Inn, Monday, November 11, in the Liberty room. Because this is Veteran's Day, we look forward to your talk about how military training prepares better workers for today's businesses.

The luncheon will start at 12:15 and run until 2 p.m. We have scheduled your remarks to begin at 1:30 p.m.

Sincerely,

Appreciation Letter

Expressing appreciation is a natural response to any thoughtful or commendable act on the part of another. Try to be warm and sincere with your appreciation, without overdoing it. State the ceremony, occasion, or activity for which thanks is being expressed. This letter appears on the Applications Disk in the file APRECIAT.LTR.

[Letterhead]

Dear Tom:

We greatly appreciate your help remodeling the downtown YMCA building. Your electrical expertise was most helpful and undoubtedly saved hundreds of dollars for the project.

Thanks ever so much, Tom. We truly are grateful for your time and effort in behalf of this community project.

Best wishes,

Commendation Letter

Everyone likes an occasional pat on the back for exemplary effort or a good deed for the company or a fellow employee. For commendation letters, concentrate on the subject's achievements and omit reference to extraneous material or topics. This letter appears on the Applications Disk in the file COMMEND.LTR.

[Letterhead]

Dear Pam:

You did a great job converting our out-of-date index card files into a WordPerfect 5.1 merge file. By making available WordPerfect's fantastic merge capability, this conversion will undoubtedly save our company hundreds of dollars in the months ahead and yet make it possible to send personalized letters to our 4,500 customers.

I have a meeting next Tuesday with Mr. Dixon, our company president, and I intend to let him know what an outstanding job you did. I will also tell him that it was your suggestion to update our customer list and convert it into a modern, computer-based list.

Congratulations, Pam, on another successful project.

Truly yours,

Confirmation Letter

If you are sending a letter to confirm a reservation or to follow up on something that must be made to order, be specific about the date and time, or item being manufactured. Specific information provides confirmation for the person who made the reservation or order, and protection for you should the customer change his or her mind. This letter appears on the Applications Disk in the file CONFIRM.LTR.

[Letterhead]

Dear Mr. Greenough:

We have reserved the Champagne Towers suite 23-A at Caesar's Poconos Resort in Paradise Streams, Pennsylvania, for the week of June 17 through June 23, 1990.

When you and your wife arrive on Sunday, please register at the front desk and receive your keys.

Very truly yours,

Congratulations Letter

Letters bearing words of congratulation relate to happy events, such as weddings, anniversaries, births, promotions, and a host of other events. Although this type of correspondence is personal, it indirectly helps in developing goodwill for the firm. An efficient secretary keeps the executive informed of happenings that should receive congratulations. This letter appears on the Applications Disk in the file CONGRAT.LTR.

[Letterhead]

Dear Mrs. Brackman:

Yesterday's edition of the Courier-Journal *announced the pleasant news of your appointment as Sales Manager at Ideal Office Supply. Congratulations!*

We greatly appreciated your contribution as assistant sales director here in our own company. The recognition you are now receiving is certainly well deserved.

Again, you have my sincere congratulations and best wishes for continued success.

Cordially,

Goodwill Letter

Friendly letters that establish goodwill and create positive impressions of a firm or person can be sent on all kinds of occasions—anniversaries, holidays, awards, achievements, outstanding service, and so on. Ideas for such events can be obtained from company records (when a first order was placed), the calendar (holidays), and newspaper accounts of community service projects. This letter appears on the Applications Disk in the file GOODWILL.LTR.

[Letterhead]

Dear Jason:

I read the story in the Minneapolis Star *titled "Local Businessmen Who Made a Difference" and saw your name listed as one of the business leaders who has contributed to the improvement of our community.*

Congratulations on your achievement. It is gratifying to find fellow businessmen who care about their community and who go out of their way to make it a better place to live.

Regards,

Instruction Letter

Instruction letters should contain clear and detailed information for readers. Never assume that the reader knows how to operate or assemble your product. Provide sufficient information for a novice to properly use the object in question. This letter appears on the Applications Disk in the file INSTRUCT.LTR.

[Letterhead]

Dear Reader:

Congratulations! The IQ Engineering Super Cartridge 2 you have purchased is an extremely versatile and valuable accessory for your laser printer. We have designed it to significantly extend the basic capabilities of your printer without your having to download soft fonts or change cartridges to obtain different fonts.

You will significantly extend the life of your font cartridge if you follow these simple guidelines:

1. *Make certain that your printer is off-line (that is, that the* On Line *light is off) and that no pages are waiting to be printed (the form feed light should be off).*

2. *Firmly insert the Super Cartridge into an empty Font Cartridge slot in the printer. Make certain that the cartridge is firmly seated. Make sure that the label side of the cartridge is face up when you insert it into the printer.*

3. *After the cartridge is firmly in place, turn the printer back on-line. Alternatively, you may turn the printer on again if you had turned it off.*

4. *Keep the cartridge away from moisture of any kind. Liquids can damage the electrical components and should be kept away from font cartridges.*

We hope that you enjoy using our product and will remember our company if we can be of further assistance.

Sincerely,

Invitation Letter

For special office events, sending an invitation by letter is more appropriate than just a general announcement. In any form of invitation, details such as the date, time, and location should be clearly stated. The tone in an invitation letter depends on to whom the letter is sent—for instance, a close personal friend (inviting someone to lunch) or a prominent personality (perhaps inviting someone to address a conference). Replies generally follow the tone and style of the initial invitation. This letter appears on the Applications Disk in the file INVITATN.LTR.

[Letterhead]

Dear Mr. Blackstone:

The Board of Directors of Gemstar, Inc., enjoyed reading your article in the July 1990 issue of The Business Times. *Your discussion of the future of word processing in the 1990s was of particular concern to the members of our corporation.*

We would like to invite you to speak about this subject at our next annual management retreat at the Oceanside Holiday Inn, Virginia Beach, Virginia, on the afternoon of October 13, 1990.

Hoping that you accept our invitation, I am enclosing a data form about our company. As you see on the form, the company provides air transportation, dinner, overnight accommodations, and an honorarium of $500 to visiting speakers.

We do hope you can join us on October 13. I would appreciate having your reply by August 30 so that we can plan air and motel accommodations.

Sincerely,

Order-Placing Letter

All correspondence ordering merchandise should provide complete information regarding the item being ordered—catalog number or page number, model number, type, shade, size, quantity, and whatever other information might be needed to process your order correctly. An incomplete or confusing order wastes time—and time is money in the business world. This letter appears on the Applications Disk in the file ORDER.LTR.

[Letterhead]

Gentlemen:

Please send the following order by standard Federal Express and charge to our account:

* *50 formatted 3 1/2-inch DS, DD 1.44M diskettes (p. 88, #88V44933)*

* *1 GTE six-outlet Computer Surge Suppresser (p. 76, #76K77669)*

* *1,000 three-part carbonless accounts payable checks (p. 47, #47K17012)*

Please include my name on the mailing label so that the order will be directed to the correct office.

Very truly yours,

Reservation Letter

The date, time, place, accommodations desired, and method of payment are crucial in making reservations and should be stated clearly—both in requests for reservations and in any change in plans that might occur. This letter appears on the Applications Disk in the file RESERVA.LTR.

[Letterhead]

Dear Reservation Desk:

My boss, Mr. Malcolm Fuller, will be flying to Chicago O'Hare International Airport on Monday, November 19, 1990, and would like a reservation at your hotel for the 19th through the evening of the 21st. He will be returning to the airport Thursday for an 11:10 a.m. flight and will require transportation to the airport.

Please confirm this reservation with me by phone at (503) 364-3386. I will provide a company Visa card number when you call to provide confirmed reservations. Thank you.

Sincerely,

Sympathy Letter

Expressions of sympathy are an unavoidable part of business as well as social life. Sympathy letters should be handled sensitively and, where appropriate, should offer additional help if needed. The death of a loved one is one of the most traumatic experiences a person can encounter. Condolence letters to a close personal friend should be written in longhand on the executive's personal stationery. This letter appears on the Applications Disk in the file SYMPATHY.LTR.

[Letterhead]

Dear Mr. Rosenberg:

Please accept my deepest sympathy on the death of your wife, Fran. Everyone at our company admired her tireless devotion to her work and her assistance with our office social activities. I know she will be greatly missed by many people here at the firm, including myself.

Please let me know if there is any way I might be of help during this difficult period.

With sincerest sympathy,

Thank-You Letter

The best thank-you letter is a brief and sincere expression of gratitude for some special act of kindness. This letter appears on the Applications Disk in the file THANKYOU.LTR.

[Letterhead]

Dear William:

I want to thank you for the time you expended during my recent trip to Atlanta. I greatly enjoyed the personal tour you gave of our new plant and the tour of the city itself. I know that this took time from your regular schedule, and I appreciate your interest in the expansion of our company in the Southeast.

Sincerely,

Summary

This chapter has illustrated a variety of information letters: the acceptance letter, acknowledgment letter, announcement letter, apology letter, appointment letter, appreciation letter, commendation letter, confirmation letter, congratulation letter, goodwill letter, instruction letter, invitation letter, order-placing letter, reservation letter, sympathy letter, and thank-you letter.

Chapter 6 deals with bad-news letters, such as credit letters, criticism letters, and refusal letters.

6

Creating Letters That Convey Bad News

Over time all businesses must be responsible for passing along bad news to a client or customer. Perhaps an order is missing, a payment is delayed, or you must simply say no to a request.

What happens if your company has sent the wrong item to a customer or if a promised delivery to a valued customer must be delayed several weeks? What sort of letter do you write when everything that can go wrong has happened? These letters are perhaps the most difficult to compose because, generally, you want to convey bad news in the most positive way, and, most important, you want to maintain the customer's confidence in your company and your product.

Other bad-news letters are those to customers who "no longer qualify for extended credit." That is a polite way of saying that you will send nothing further until you receive an overdue payment. When writing these letters, consider how what you say will affect the reader. If the customer has been a good customer and a payment or two is missing, you should cheerfully try to find out whether a problem exists. If the customer has not ordered before and shows no attempt to resolve the matter, you may write a stern message, knowing that you do not want this person as a customer.

These awkward situations may attract legal attention later, so you must choose what you say carefully. Bad-news letters call for the greatest attention to what you know about the reader. What will the reader do, and how will the reader feel about the company after reading the bad news? Except for the few readers you can do without, convey bad news in the most positive, polite, and attentive way possible.

Planning a PRIOS Strategy for Bad-News Letters

To write bad-news letters, think carefully about your PRIOS planning. As you have done before, retrieve your WordPerfect PRIOS template and start filling in the information about your purpose, your readers, your information, your organization, and your style (see fig. 6.1).

Fig. 6.1.

Filling in the PRIOS template for a bad-news letter.

```
PRIOS information

Date: April 5, 1990
To: customer (merge)
Filename: coconut.90p

Purpose of document:
     Primary purpose: To explain why advertised coconuts missing
                      from shipment
     Secondary purpose: To keep customer satisfied
Readers:
     Primary readers: customer
     Secondary readers: customer's circle
Information:
     We goofed! (Oh boy, are our faces red!)
     Explanation of correct shipment
     Explanation how we fixed problem
     What the customer can expect
     Our phone line to handle queries

Organization (direct, indirect, balanced): balanced (news in middle)
Style (formal, informal): very informal

Search for:
C:\QUE\PRIOS6.TXT                          Doc 2 Pg 1 Ln 4.33" Pos 7.7"
```

The PRIOS design in figure 6.1 is a balanced plan letter (see fig. 6.2). The writer starts off with a face-saving gesture that will probably work with most customers. The only customers who are not amused are those who strongly desired those coconuts or who have experienced other problems receiving shipments. You should know about those reactions before you write such a letter.

In this example, the company chooses a lighter-toned "oh dear" approach. Most of the news is contained in the second paragraph, where the reader learns that three coconuts were not sent. The last paragraph describes what the company will do to solve the problem, and, most important, gives the reader a direct link to the company for any complaints. Inviting the customer to communicate further is often the best apology you can make.

Other bad-news letters require more sensitivity. Before you deliver bad news, you want to say something positive and upbeat to the reader to help the person accept the bad news in the remainder of the letter. Use this beginning *buffer paragraph* with a customer you want to keep. Look at the PRIOS information in figure 6.3.

```
                                    Freedom Orchards, Inc.
                                    3568 Greenway Street
                                    Gruen, CT  08607
                                    November 1, 1990




Ms. Mathilda Plymouth
67289 Wing Rock Drive
Moreno CA  90504

Dear Ms. Plymouth:

Are our faces red!

Our regular Dessert of the Month shipment was mailed to you this
past week with the six Gruen Bay cobblers in place. We hope you
have enjoyed this special treat! But you may have wondered why you
missed the additional, advertised shipment of three coconuts.

As soon as we caught our mistake, we repackaged the coconuts, and
you should soon be opening a great holiday favorite. Be looking for
this additional shipment in the next two weeks. If you have any
further questions, please call us at (777) 555-6550.

Most sincerely,



Ted Hugh, Director
Customer Services
```

Fig. 6.2.

A bad-news letter with bad news in the middle paragraph.

```
Purpose of document:
     Primary purpose: to find out why payment has not been made
     Secondary purpose: to keep customer if possible
Readers:
     Primary readers: Mr. F. King, Acct. 746839
     Secondary readers: possible legal involvement
Information:
     note valued customer
     notice good payments
     notice of overdue payment
     several letters sent
     send account for review
     where to reach us
Organization (direct, indirect, balanced):
     indirect with buffer paragraph
     information in middle
     call-us information in last paragraph
Style (formal, informal):
     friendly and concerned
     business-like

Search for:
     you for your              but also (avoid)
C:\QUE\PRIOS6B                      Doc 2 Pg 1 Ln 5.67" Pos 3"
```

Fig. 6.3.

PRIOS information for a buffer paragraph in a bad-news letter.

Read the letter written from this PRIOS information in figure 6.4. The note about "valued customer" easily becomes the buffer paragraph. Notice that the tone of the letter is sincere and concerned. The company wants to keep this good customer if a solution to the lack of payment is found. Letting the customer compare account information offers the important communication link that builds customer trust in a business. If this matter is handled correctly, the customer may still recommend the company to friends. Satisfied customers make the best salespeople.

Fig. 6.4.

Using a buffer paragraph to soften bad news.

```
                                        Higgins Native Fruit Co.
                                        7856 South Street
                                        Gruen, CT 08609
                                        August 1, 1990

Mr. F. King
78 Windfall Road
Three Rivers, IN  46256

Dear Mr. King:

Reviewing your account, I note that you have regularly purchased
Higgins Native Raisins over the last four years. You have bought
many of our holiday items, and we have enjoyed sending you your
selections promptly in time for your gift giving.

Over the span of your account, I note that your payments have been
timely and, up until this past May, enclosed with your orders. I
note, however, that we have not received your payment due of $40.65
for our May 17, 1990, shipment of 10 pounds of preserved apricots
and 15 pounds of almonds. Several letters have been sent to you at
the above address, but we have received no answer to our inquiries.
Because you have been such a valued customer, we are sure that you
will want to clear you account of outstanding charges.

Please look over the enclosed account. If you have any questions
regarding the payment due on your account, please call me
personally at (777) 555-9056. Please let us hear from you soon so
we can send you our latest catalog of items for the upcoming
holidays.

Sincerely,


J. Arthur Campbell, Manager
Customer Services

Encl.: Acct. 746839
```

The letter in figure 6.5, however, is written to someone who is not a good customer. In this case, the same bad news is presented without a buffer paragraph. The company wants to resolve this matter and then terminate business with this customer.

If you look carefully at these letters, you can easily imagine them as paragraphs for form letters. You can see how the individual paragraphs could be kept on file and patched together to make regular form letters.

Sample Bad-News Letters

In the pages that follow, you will find examples of seven different bad-news letters, arranged alphabetically. As mentioned in the last chapter, these letters are meant as guides in composing your own messages. In some cases, you may be able to substitute your own facts and use the rest of the letter as shown here. In other cases, you may want to modify the tone or expand the content to meet your specific needs or intended reader.

```
                              Higgins Native Fruit Co.
                              7856 South Street
                              Gruen, CT 08609
                              August 1, 1990


      Mr. F. King
      78 Windfall Road
      Three Rivers, IN  46256

      Dear Mr. King:

      Reviewing your Higgins Native Fruit Co. account, I note that we
      have not received your payment due of $40.65 for our January 17,
      1990, shipment of 10 pounds of preserved apricots and 15 pounds
      of almonds. Several letters have been sent to you at the above
      address, but we have received no answer to our inquiries.

      We are sure that you will want to clear your account of
      outstanding charges. If we do not hear from you within the next
      weeks, however, it will be necessary to seek assistance
      collecting payment. If you have any questions about this matter,
      please call our Accounting office at (777) 555-9920.



      J. Arthur Campbell, Manager
      Customer Services

      Encl.: Acct. 746839
```

Fig. 6.5.

A bad-news letter to a poor customer.

Adjustment Letter

An adjustment letter responds to a complaint letter and tells the customer what your company intends to do about his or her complaint. An adjustment letter can be either a good-news letter or a bad-news letter, depending on your response.

If the complaint is a justifiable one, do your best to satisfy the customer's complaint and repair the damage that has been done. Try also to restore the customer's confidence in your company. One East Coast supermarket chain sends a $10 gift certificate along with every adjustment letter, entitling the customer to $10 worth of free merchandise the next time he or she visits the local store. Be certain that you know your company's policy regarding adjustments before you attempt to write an adjustment letter.

If you cannot replace the item purchased, however, say so as gently as possible. But be careful about what you place in print. For example, a letter containing the statement "we just received your letter of October 12 about our defective product" could be ruled in a court of law as an admission that the product is indeed defective. Also keep in mind that some adjustment letters are responses to complaints about services or charges for services rendered. This letter appears on the Applications Disk as ADJUSTMT.LTR.

[Letterhead]

Dear Mr. Fellows:

We are sorry to hear that the Minolta camera you purchased from our New York discount sales office three months ago has been damaged by water during your vacation. Our 12-month parts-and-labor warranty covers only defective parts within the camera itself, not damage due to accident after the product is received. That particular camera is not designed to be immersed in water.

The enclosed folder lists approved Minolta repair locations around the country. We suggest sending your camera to the location nearest you for an evaluation.

Sincerely,

Complaint Letter

Businesses sometimes err when providing services or goods to customers. When that happens, customers write complaint letters if they feel shortchanged by what they received from the company. The most important consideration when drafting a complaint about a product or service is the tone of your letter. Do not use a complaint letter to vent your anger. Remember that the reader of your letter probably had nothing to do with whatever went wrong, and berating that person will achieve little.

The opening paragraph of a complaint letter should clearly state the pertinent data concerning the order or transaction: date of purchase, item in question, place of purchase, cost, invoice number, and so on.

The body of the letter should explain logically and clearly why you feel the product or service was deficient. Be sure to establish any relevant facts that support the validity of your claim. Above all, avoid making accusations or threats. That will only alienate the person who receives the letter and may in fact make it more difficult to get satisfactory compensation. This letter is stored on the Applications Disk as COMPLANT.LTR.

[Letterhead]

Customer Relations Manager:

On June 7, 1990, we ordered a two-door laser printer cabinet from your company—Model W14325, listed at $169.00. It arrived by UPS on June 19th at our shipping dock and appeared to be undamaged when we opened the box.

However, after we unpacked the printer cabinet, we discovered that the two front cabinet doors stick and will not close properly. Since this defect makes the unit unsuitable for our needs, we request a replacement printer cabinet for our office.

Would you please explain the proper procedure for returning this defective printer cabinet and for obtaining a replacement as soon as possible? Thank you for your assistance.

Sincerely,

Credit Letter

Letters involving credit demand accuracy, integrity, and above all confidentiality. When you must write a letter refusing someone credit, be mindful of the reader's feelings and avoid saying things that may damage the reader's self-esteem. Try not to be negative. If possible, offer some alternative solution to the situation so that you will retain the client as a regular customer. You have already seen two examples of "dunning" letters earlier in the chapter. This letter is stored on the Applications Disk as CREDIT.LTR.

[Letterhead]

Dear Mr. Jacobson:

Over the past five years, we have valued your account with us and considered it one of our best.

Unfortunately, we have noticed in the past few months that your payments on the amounts due have run well past the normal 30-day payment period. And your June billing is now 90 days late.

It is imperative for us to keep current on our accounts receivable. Therefore, we regretfully must ask you to make future purchases on a cash-only basis until your past accounts are up-to-date.

I am enclosing a special 5 percent cash-discount card, which you may use when you make your cash purchases. Perhaps this will in some small way assist you during this period.

Sincerely,

Criticism Letter

No one likes to receive criticism, either in the social world or the business environment. Tactless criticism can wound an employee and possibly result in the loss of the worker to another organization where that person feels more needed. Therefore one must avoid a blunt or condescending tone in a criticism letter. If at all possible, begin the letter with a positive buffer paragraph that helps soften the bad news conveyed later in the letter. This letter is stored on the Applications Disk as CRITICSM.LTR.

[Letterhead]

Dear David:

I enjoyed sitting in on your WordPerfect 5.1 training class yesterday and watching the response of the trainees to the topics you presented. I am impressed with the enthusiasm you generate among the attendees toward the new version of WordPerfect. That is always good to see.

Everything moved smoothly after the class settled down. It is apparent you understand the subject well and know how to motivate the students. But it is unfortunate that the first 10 minutes of class period were spent answering individual questions raised by a few students clustered around your desk while the remainder of the class waited for the session to begin.

Next time you might ask students with individual problems to save these questions for the end of class. This way you can start right in on the lesson itself as soon as everyone arrives, and avoid taking 10 minutes of valuable lesson time.

If you gain that much training time with each lesson, you will have gained one full hour of training for every six lessons you conduct. And that time saving makes significant training time.

Please let me know if you have any further thoughts or questions on this, David. I really appreciate all you have done to make our training classes such a success.

Sincerely,

Evaluation Letter

Letters that analyze and report on the merits of something (or someone) will vary in length depending on the amount of detail necessary to evaluate properly the product in question. If the report turns out negative and you decide against using or purchasing the item, do so in a concise, straightforward style. This letter is stored on the Applications Disk as EVALUATN.LTR.

[Letterhead]

Dear Mr. Lee:

I appreciated the opportunity to evaluate and test the Microsoft Word for Windows program for possible use in our company. You are right about the program's being a major step forward from the previous version of Word, and it does have many features that make it useful in the office environment.

After considering Word for Windows, however, I feel that circumstances in our office make it difficult to change to another word processing program. These include the following:

1. *Members of our secretarial pool have been using a different word processing program (WordPerfect) for three years now and feel it would be counterproductive to change to a different software package.*

2. *Converting to Microsoft Word would require extensive retraining of all support personnel and time-consuming modifications of existing documents and files to make them compatible with a different program.*

3. *All our field offices are geared to the exclusive use of WordPerfect, and, if we changed software, future document exchange with these offices would be affected.*

4. *WordPerfect 5.1 offers more features than our present staff can use effectively, so we would experience little benefit from switching to another software package.*

As you can see, changing to a different word processing program would create problems and cause unnecessary expense in our particular situation. We have decided at this time to remain with WordPerfect rather than change to Microsoft Word.

Thank you for your time and interest.

Sincerely,

Refusal Letter

When you receive a complaint letter or an inquiry letter to which you must provide a negative reply, you need to write a refusal letter. Because it contains bad news, the refusal letter can be difficult to write. You can tactfully and courteously convey that bad news, however. As with other bad-news letters, the strategy is to delay stating the bad news directly in your opening paragraph. This letter is stored on the Applications Disk as REFUS.LTR.

[Letterhead]

Dear Mrs. Winston:

I appreciate the time you spent answering our questions about purchasing Canon laser printers for our office. I have learned much about the value of laser printers in the office environment.

Unfortunately, we just found out that our parent company, Consolidated International, signed a one-year contract with another organization that locks us into purchasing Hewlett-Packard printers during the next 12 months.

We are unable to purchase your printers at this time. Perhaps in the future, though, we can do business with your organization. Do keep in touch.

Sincerely,

Rejection Letter

A rejection letter can cause hurt feelings and alienation if it is not handled tactfully and with kindness. Never let the recipient of such a letter feel that the rejection is related to something he or she represents. This letter is stored on the Applications Disk as REJECTON.LTR.

[Letterhead]

Dear Miss Simpson:

Our president, Mrs. Susan Holden, has received your letter inviting her to speak to your membership about "Office Equipment of the 1990s" on November 3, 1990. Unfortunately, Mrs. Holden has prior commitments at that time and is unable to accept your kind invitation.

If your organization has a need for a speaker at some other time, Mrs. Holden hopes that you will remember her then.

Sincerely,

Summary

There is no easy way to convey bad news to a customer or client. When possible, try to buffer the bad news with something positive or upbeat in the first paragraph. Try to reflect sincerity and concern for the reader of the letter, even if you are unable to provide the solution that the customer seeks.

In this chapter, you examined seven different types of bad-news letters—the adjustment letter, complaint letter, credit letter, criticism letter, evaluation letter, refusal letter, and rejection letter. The solutions you see here may or may not fit the situations you face in your office experience. However, these examples suggest helpful guidelines for handling bad-news situations in your own business environment.

7

Creating Letters
That Persuade

Many of the letters you open every day seek your approval or action. Perhaps your university or religious organization requests your help or donation. The letter you open may be from some political action group or your telephone company announcing a new service you might add to your phone system. These letters are considered persuasive because they elicit action from you or seek to affect your opinions.

This chapter offers two examples of persuasive letters used in a business or organizational environment. The first is a letter asking county residents to join a state sheriffs' association; the second letter is a national magazine's subscription offer.

Persuasive letters feature an argument, or appeal, directed at your set of beliefs, your self-image, or your sense of logic. Most persuasive letters are aimed at a *population* of readers in a *mailing*. The letter writer develops a strategy to reach certain groups of readers, such as the "young" (those between 18 and 24), those in midcareer (35- to 45-year-olds), or persons nearing retirement (59- to 65-year-olds). The whole business of direct-mail marketing has made a science of *targeting* a mailing. By targeting, you use marketing research to understand your reader so that you can design a *central appeal* for the first paragraph as a "hook."

Generally, the most effective persuasive letters begin with a paragraph containing the central appeal that attracts the reader to continue reading. To support the central appeal, you then add *persuasive evidence*, or the facts or arguments that support the central appeal. If you understand your reader, you can effectively answer any questions with the persuasive evidence you add. Only after you have appealed to your reader and provided the arguments to support action can you spell out the specific action you want the reader to take. In this "taking action" section of your letter, you can list the price of your product or your phone number or address where payments can be sent.

Designing the Central Appeal

To build a central appeal for the group you want to reach, look carefully at your PRIOS analysis, particularly the purpose of your letter and your description of your readers. The central appeal is the strongest reader appeal or reader benefit, eventually your readers' most probable interest. What then would attract your readers' attention? Do your readers care more about the price of something than its attractiveness? Should you emphasize the benefits your product can deliver more than how much it costs?

Can you recall any recent "targeted" letter you chose to read through? The letter may have been a newsletter from your congressman, a description of a new housing development to be built in your neighborhood, a plea to protect a nearby bird sanctuary, or even a mailing from a group you violently oppose. Although you may have sensed that the letter was a mass mailing, it targeted the audience well enough to cause you to read it through.

As you are well aware, you are bombarded daily by requests from many different organizations. If these requests express a central appeal that you have a different opinion about, then the appeal will fail to interest you. The persuasive letter's organization, therefore, must be carefully planned around a central appeal that serves your readers' best interests.

Building the Persuasive Argument

Not all things are new; the way arguments and evidence are structured in persuasive communication is at least as old as the ancient Greeks. The "argument" in persuasive letters is not a dispute or quarrel. Argumentation is the method you use to support claims, the basis of persuasion. Three general paths of argumentation are those appealing to logic and reasoning, to rules or established policy, and to emotions.

After you decide what will affect your readers the most in your central appeal, you must decide how to support that idea. Most persuasive business letters, the kind you write directly to another person, use logic or statements of policy to be effective. Much of the sales mail that appears daily in your mail, mail targeted for a broad audience, is based on emotional appeals.

Persuasive arguments using logic and reasoning are based on evidence such as facts and clear statistics. For example, if you want to convince co-workers that a change of procedure in the workplace is desirable, emphasize relevant facts and statistics rather than using emotional appeals. WordPerfect can help you communicate statistics in orderly, graphic ways, from indented lists to highlighted and underlined information. The new Table function lets you include statistics and information in clear, side-by-side tables (see fig. 7.1).

In the following table you can see the growth of interest in the basic communications class and the need for additional rooms. This information compares spring semesters in the four years ending with the spring semester 1990.

Speech S105, 1987-1990		
Year	Hours	Classrooms Required
1987	1800	20
1988	2070	23
1989	2250	25
1990	2340	26

You can see the steady growth of these classes that compares with the overall growth in this university.

Doc 1 Pg 1 Ln 4.26" Pos 3.55"

Fig. 7.1.

A table of factual information.

If you argue on the basis of policy, you are probably writing within a large company or a government installation. The information you need is already codified in policy or written rules. You simply cite the rule that supports your argument. For instance, to stop football gambling pools the department manager in a government installation does not have to appeal to the logic or the emotions of department personnel. Merely restating the government policy about on-site gambling should make it clear that football pools will not be tolerated.

Many of the appeals seeking donations to charitable institutions or causes are based on the readers' emotions. These mailings may include pictures of children or suffering animals, or detailed forecasts of danger and doom. Because these arguments strike human sensitivities, they appeal to basic human needs, such as shelter, warmth, and food. The best of these letters combine appeals to logic as well as emotions; the worst, to emotions only.

Good persuasive letters use an *indirect approach*. Rather than beginning with the main idea, persuasive letters generally begin with a central appeal, a bond between the writer and the reader. In the central appeal, you establish what you think you as the writer and the reader agree with before indicating the specific purpose of the letter. In other words, you try to figure how your reader will react to the subject.

The central appeal in a business letter may be arguments that ensure power, growth, control, reputation, thrift, success, or career advancement. As you can see, the most important element of the central appeal is to know your audience. If you know that the manager you are writing to is a frugal person who likes growth with cost savings, you can begin your letter stressing thrifty expansion. (*"By adding two persons to this department, you can save the cost of five outside agencies."*)

Each central appeal must be augmented with persuasive evidence, the reasons your arguments should be accepted. If you seek action from the reader, you should add all important facts in as much detail as you can. If, for instance, you are requesting further consideration from a car insurance company, you might attach drawings or photos of your wrecked car to influence a claims adjuster.

Writing a sales letter, you should emphasize features of your product that directly appeal to your particular readers. If you are selling riding lawn mowers, for example, you can obviously sell larger mowers to persons with acreage than to those living in housing areas with less lawn space. If you operate a boxing gym, you should probably emphasize the vigorous nature of your exercise area's capabilities.

After you complete your arguments, state clearly what you want your readers to do. Do you want them to come to a sale? Do you want them to return an enclosed card for more information or for a call from a sales representative? Do you want them to call you for an appointment to discuss an idea in more depth? In each of these cases, make sure that you give your reader a clear-cut action to take after reading your letter.

Persuading Readers with the PRIOS Model

Suppose that you have just been elected sheriff of a rural metropolitan county. The State Sheriffs' Association has supported your candidacy, and you have been asked to encourage the people of your county to join the Sheriffs' Association and its various safety and crime-fighting programs. Your up-to-date office still has a small lockup cell and a gun cabinet, but instead of a pot-bellied stove and a small boy to run messages, you have a PC loaded with the latest software, WordPerfect 5.1. Nowadays, regional law-enforcement agencies operate as sleekly and efficiently as any business concern.

Moving to your PRIOS template, you can plan your letter's purpose, readers, information, organization, and style. Your PRIOS template looks like the one in figure 7.2. Notice that you have placed the template in your Doc 2 window so that you can move back and forth between the letter you type in Doc 1 and your letter plan in Doc 2. The ability to switch alternately between documents helps you stay with your initial plan.

```
PRIOS information:

Date:
To:
Filename:

PURPOSE:
      Primary purpose:
      Secondary purpose:

READERS:
      Primary readers:
      Secondary readers:

INFORMATION:

ORGANIZATION (direct, indirect, balanced):

STYLE (formal, informal):




C:\QUE\PER\TEMPLATE.TXT                  Doc 2 Pg 1 Ln 1" Pos 1"
```

Fig. 7.2.

Planning a persuasive letter with your PRIOS template.

After you fill in the file information at the top of the template, move to the purpose of your letter. After listing your primary purpose—to thank the voters for giving you the win—you could list a secondary purpose of encouraging county residents to join the State Sheriffs' Association. Then describe the Sheriffs' Association, its current county membership, and the new members you want to attract. Within your purpose statements, indicate what you want your readers to do (see fig. 7.3).

```
PRIOS information:

Date: May 2, 1990
To: County residents
Filename: shffasoc.let

PURPOSE:
      Primary purpose: To thank voters for voting for me. This
            letter will remind county residents who the sheriff is

      Secondary purpose: To encourage residents to join the State
            Sheriffs' Association (A letter sent to registered
            voters should reach county residents who are interested
            in public safety and improved training for sheriff
            deputies)

READERS:
      Primary readers:
      Secondary readers:

INFORMATION:

ORGANIZATION (direct, indirect, balanced):

C:\QUE\PER\TEMPLATE.TXT                  Doc 2 Pg 1 Ln 1" Pos 1"
```

Fig. 7.3.

A purpose statement for a persuasive letter.

As you describe your readers, think of the various populations in your county. Do most residents live on farms and commute to work in a nearby city, or do most residents depend on farm and small-town businesses for their income? What concerns have your readers shown in the last election? Think about the readers who will show interest in belonging to such an organization. What readers can you persuade to join who have never joined before? Describe all the readers you want to attract and their present interest in the State Sheriff's Association. See a thorough description of the audience for this letter in figure 7.4.

Fig. 7.4.

Describing the readers of a persuasive letter.

```
PURPOSE:
    Primary purpose: To thank voters for voting for me. This
        letter will remind county residents who the sheriff is

    Secondary purpose: To encourage residents to join the State
        Sheriffs' Association (A letter sent to registered
        voters should reach county residents who are interested
        in public safety and improved training for sheriff
        deputies)

READERS:
    Primary readers: Voters in past election. Rural, commuters,
        and small-town business people. Interest high in
        worsening crime rate (burglary, personal assaults,
        vandalism) and better training for deputies. See city
        problems extending to rural areas and anxious in face
        of new housing developments. Seeking solutions
    Secondary readers: Household members who were not voters.
        May generate interest in Association and make them
        familiar with new sheriff. Thank you may attract local
        reporters.

INFORMATION:
C:\QUE\PER\TEMPLATE.TXT                    Doc 2 Pg 1 Ln 5.5" Pos 2"
```

As you preplan in Doc 2, write the information to include in the letter, typing as much as you know about the subject of the letter. List how your readers can profit from joining the State Sheriffs' Association. Then, thinking carefully about the people in the district you serve, imagine what central appeals you can use to interest the citizens of your county in joining such an organization.

As you think of central appeals for county citizenry to join a statewide auxiliary organization, you might list some interests you have heard discussed in voters' meetings and the editorial pages of the local papers. You have heard rumblings about sheriff deputies' being trained to recognize illegal drug users from reckless drivers. And you know that county residents want their fair share of the state financial "pie." You decide to use both these issues to attract interest in the statewide group.

Planning your letter's organization, choose one of the patterns mentioned earlier: the direct pattern places important information first, the balanced pattern places the main point of focus at the center of the letter, and the indirect pattern focuses your main point at the end of the letter. You decide on an indirect approach, beginning with your own personal thanks, moving to the persuasive evidence of recent problems, and requesting the action to join the State Sheriffs' Association.

After planning your organization, you must decide your style of writing. Think about the image you want to convey. In this case, you want to appear professional and capable, the same qualities that attracted county voters in the first place. You can choose from the following styles:

- Friendly/informal
- Neutral
- Formal
- Imperative
- Combination of these

You decide to be friendly but professional, with a note of formality. After all, the office of sheriff is one to be respected.

Directing the Reader to Action

Building on your central appeal and the evidence and arguments to support your appeal, you must decide what you want your reader to do after reading your letter. This may be as simple as giving the address of the agency where donations may be sent or as complex as setting up a suggested course of meetings to solve a problem through negotiation. Either way, you must make clear the course of action you want the reader to take.

Drafting Your Letter

The most effective organization for persuasive letters follows the indirect plan, which features a *central appeal*, *persuasive evidence*, and the *action* you want your readers to take. You begin by affirming your resolve to be an excellent sheriff and thanking your voters. Your persuasive evidence describes changes in the county that require better deputy training and more state dollars returned to the county. Finally, you ask the readers to join the State Sheriffs' Association, a group that addresses these problems.

As you refine your central appeal with persuasive evidence, look back through your WordPerfect template and imagine what will appeal to your readers. In this case, you list the following central appeals:

- Better use of tax dollars
- Community responsibility

- Family
- Future needs
- Illegal-drug containment
- Meeting local needs first
- Peace of mind
- Safety
- Security

To use these central appeals effectively, you want to attract your readers in the first few sentences. You can appeal to most county citizens by thanking them for voting for you and assuring them of your intent to do your job well.

As you plan for your persuasive evidence, state some of the widely held concerns of county residents. Then you have to know what your readers know about the Sheriffs' Association. Try to anticipate what questions they may have about the association.

Finally, describe the Sheriffs' Association with details of how to join, describing the advantages of membership to county residents.

State clearly the action your readers must take. In this case, you want them to write a check for $30, fill out a form, and enclose both in a postage-paid envelope. Switching to the letter information you have already written in Doc 2, you can easily fill out the remainder of your letter (see fig. 7.5).

In this letter from a newly elected country sheriff to county residents, many that the new sheriff may know by name, the audience appeal is straightforward. The next section shows some different persuasive letters.

Looking at Sample Persuasive Letters

Because the words and phrasing in persuasive letters are so important, they are usually difficult to compose. Persuasive letters must be straightforward and positive and yet personal. You must include all these elements to reach your reader. Some common persuasive letters are those that seek job interviews or those that sell your own concepts or ideas. Samples of these letters are enclosed on the Applications Disk that accompanies this book.

Sheriff Mary B. Riley
Shawnee County
Techumseh, IN 46999

Dear Mr. McCullough:

On January 1, 1990, I became your new sheriff. I am thankful for the opportunity to serve you in this high and responsible office.

As you know, my job will be to uphold the laws, to preserve the peace, and to protect the lives and property of Shawnee County citizens. You know of the recent rise in drug-related incidents and the "Big City" problems that accompany Shawnee County's sky-rocketing growth.

In an effort to do my job more effectively, I am asking for your interest and aid. You can really help, and I hope you will, by joining the State Sheriffs' Association. All you have to do is send your first year's dues for $30 or more along with the form enclosed with this letter, in the enclosed postage-free envelope.

By return mail, you will receive a 1990 membership card, two star decals for your car, a $4,000 accidental death insurance benefit, and a year's subscription to our publication, *The State Sheriff.*

Your dues contribution will be used by the State Sheriffs' Association to support crime prevention and awareness programs, to promote better public safety, to provide more and improved training for sheriffs and their personnel, and to fight for more effective local law enforcement at the state level.

This is my personal invitation to you, to be a part of our efforts. Please say "yes" by sending your check today. I thank you for your support.

Sincerely,

Mary B. Riley
Sheriff, Shawnee County

P. S.   Funds raised from memberships in the Association support our local interests on a statewide basis and advance good local law enforcement through training and eduction in Indiana.

(Please make your checks out to the State Sheriffs' Association, writing "Shawnee County" in the lower left corner.

Fig. 7.5.

A persuasive letter.

Seeking a Job Interview

If any letter should express your self-confidence in a sincerely personal way, that should be the letter you write to request an interview for a position. The following letter is written to a specific person in the department you want to join. This letter appears on the Applications Disk as JOBINTV.LTR.

[Letterhead]

Dear Ms. Cramer:

I have been a production supervisor for 7 years, and I have kept track of your company's growth. I particularly like your insistence on retaining quality at the same time that you increase your output, setting new sales records.

I am seeking a new, more challenging role in production, and your company reflects the production values I appreciate.

If you are looking for a production specialist with a successful record of increased productivity and positive employee cooperation, I believe I can be an asset to your business.

My enclosed data sheet describes my supervisory accomplishments. Notice the records set in the past six years by the teams I have led.

I am certain I can produce equally strong records for you. I will call you next week to determine when we could talk.

Sincerely,

Selling an Idea

Another persuasive letter you may write is the letter to sell one of your ideas. This letter can be used to sell a service or a creative talent you are developing. In either case, you want to write a letter to spark the interest of the reader. Again, you want to be sincere and personal, but also brief. This letter appears on the Applications Disk as SELIDEA.LTR.

[Letterhead]

Dear Mr. McCaskey:

How I watch the papers for your latest toy show!

As a home woodworker and the father of three active and creative children, I own many examples of reproduction and new wooden toys. I especially like the originality of your Flying Dutchman and the Old Shoe House wooden toys.

Recently, I developed a pattern that should interest you. The flower box in my Sleeping Bee unfolds three large petals to disclose a bee, asleep in the center. The design itself is not complex, but the disclosure effect charms the children who play with the toy. Adults show great interest in this special wooden toy and ask where it may be purchased.

When you see my Sleeping Bee, I'm sure you will see how this toy could be produced to sell in specialty toy stores here in the South. Please allow me a few brief moments so you can see my handiwork.

I will call you this next week to see when I can show you the Sleeping Bee.

Most sincerely,

In figure 7.6 you are appealing to an entirely different audience. You want to capture the interest of the typical business executive who has little time to read the daily paper or watch the evening TV news. Your appeal will be based on concise but thorough coverage of current events and on a variety of news items not covered by the popular press. The action you seek is the return of the subscription card enclosed with the letter.

November 12, 190

Dear Reader:

U.S. News, of course, is a magazine you know. Business and professional people everywhere find it an ideal source of current events, financial information, and happenings around the globe. It has earned the respect (and readership) of leaders in virtually every corporation in America.

However, if you only get to see an occasional issue of *U.S. News* and have not yet subscribed, you are missing the true value of *U.S. News*—continuing update on significant events you need to know to be well informed in the 1990s. Our very next issue might just contain the information you need to help flesh out a proposal for some project or provide the spark you need for another great promotional idea.

> Here's our suggestion: accept our offer of a trial subscription, delivered either to your office or your home. Sample today's *U.S. News* for a modest 45¢ a week and see why our magazine is one of the fastest growing weekly news publications available today. Place the enclosed order card in the mail now. If *U.S. News* disappoints you, cancel your subscription and we'll gladly refund the balance of your subscription.

If you would like to keep up to date on current events and the people who shape the news, you will find that *U.S. News* is the ideal way to avoid wasting precious time scanning the daily papers.

- If you like to learn more than just the bare facts about significant stories . . .

- If you like in depth coverage by award-winning writers . . .

- If you seek more than the ordinary news story—from art to finances to religion to sports . . .

    . . . then accept our invitation to subscribe on a trial basis.

You don't even have to send money now. We will bill you after you begin receiving your copies. The order card enclosed will start your subscription.

Sincerely,

Allen J. Reynolds
Circulation Manager

Fig. 7.6.

A sample promotional letter for US News.

Summary

In this chapter, you have seen how to build the persuasive argument, how to focus on your specific audience, how to have an indirect plan with a central appeal, how to emphasize the features of your product that will appeal most to the reader of your letter, and how to state clearly what you want your reader to do. All these elements are vital to a successful persuasive letter. They contribute to the main goal—to motivate the reader to do something specific.

The next chapters illustrate some specific WordPerfect business applications you can use in your office or organization.

Part III

Creating Envelopes and Labels

Creating Business Envelopes

Creating Labels and Rolodex Cards

8

Creating Business Envelopes

Addressing envelopes for mailing is one of the most common office activities. Unfortunately, few people have tried preparing envelopes with a word processing program—because few computer programs made the activity easy. In fact, in many offices secretaries keep a regular typewriter nearby—just for the task of typing addresses on envelopes.

Now with WordPerfect 5.1, envelope printing has become a fascination rather than a frustration. Whether you are addressing a single envelope or dozens, WordPerfect can make the job easier for you.

In this chapter, you see how to create an *envelope form definition* for your printer, whether it be a daisywheel printer, a dot-matrix printer, a DeskJet printer, or any of the Hewlett Packard printers—LaserJet, LaserJet Plus, LaserJet II, LaserJet IID, LaserJet IIP, or LaserJet III. After you have created an envelope form and properly positioned the addresses, you learn how to use the envelope macro on the Applications Disk to automate the printing of envelopes.

This chapter also discusses how to position addresses for preprinted envelopes and window envelopes, how to create multiple envelopes with and without a merge, and how properly to fold business stationery for window envelopes, regular business envelopes, and small business envelopes.

Creating an Envelope Definition

Whenever you are printing on something other than a standard 8 1/2-by-11-inch piece of paper, you must tell the program what size and shape of paper you plan to use. This definition (also called a *form*) can be used a single time and deleted from the menu, or reused indefinitely.

To create an envelope form, follow these steps:

1. Press Format (Shift-F8) and select **Page** (**2**).

   ⌨Choose **Page** from the Layout menu.

2. Select Paper Size/Type (**7**).

   At this point, you see a list of definitions under Format: Paper Size/Type (see fig. 8.1). The information given for each paper type includes six items:

   - name and orientation
   - paper size in inches
   - prompt for loading (yes or no)
   - paper location
   - font type (landscape or portrait)
   - double-sided (yes or no)

Fig. 8.1.

The Paper Size/Type screen.

```
Format: Paper Size/Type

                                                  Font  Double
Paper type and Orientation   Paper Size  Prompt Loc  Type  Sided  Labels

(1 x 2 5/8) inch labels      8.5" x 11"    No   Contin Port  No     3 x 10
(2 x 4) inch labels          8.5" x 11"    No   Contin Port  No     2 x 5
Envelope - Wide              9.5" x 4"     No   Manual Land  No
Legal                        8.5" x 14"    No   Contin Port  No
Legal - Dup Long             8.5" x 14"    No   Contin Port  Yes
Legal - Dup Long - Wide      14" x 8.5"    No   Contin Land  Yes
Legal - Dup Short            8.5" x 14"    No   Contin Port  Yes
Legal - Dup Short - Wide     14" x 8.5"    No   Contin Land  Yes
Legal - Wide                 14" x 8.5"    No   Contin Land  No
Standard                     8.5" x 11"    No   Contin Port  No
Standard - Dup Long          8.5" x 11"    No   Contin Port  Yes
Standard - Dup Long - Wide   11" x 8.5"    No   Contin Land  Yes
Standard - Dup Short         8.5" x 11"    No   Contin Port  Yes
Standard - Dup Short - Wide  11" x 8.5"    No   Contin Land  Yes
Standard - Wide              11" x 8.5"    No   Contin Land  No
[ALL OTHERS]                 Width ≤ 8.5"  Yes  Manual       No

1 Select; 2 Add; 3 Copy; 4 Delete; 5 Edit; N Name Search: 1
```

The list of paper forms you have displayed depends upon the printer selected. If you have a Hewlett-Packard LaserJet II or IID, this list already includes an envelope form. In figure 8.1, a 9 1/2-by-4-inch envelope form comes already installed. If your printer includes an envelope definition, all you need to do is highlight the envelope form and choose **Select** (**1**) from the bottom menu. Skip steps 3 through 9.

If your particular printer does not include an envelope form, you can create one by following steps 3 through 9.

3. Select **Add** (**2**) from the bottom menu to create a new definition.

   The Paper Type screen (see fig. 8.2) offers eight types of paper: (**1**) **S**tandard, (**2**) **B**ond, (**3**) **L**etterhead, (**4**) **L**abels, (**5**) **E**nvelope, (**6**) **T**ransparency, (**7**) **C**ardstock, and (**8**) **A**ll others.

4. Select **Envelope** (**5**) as the paper type.

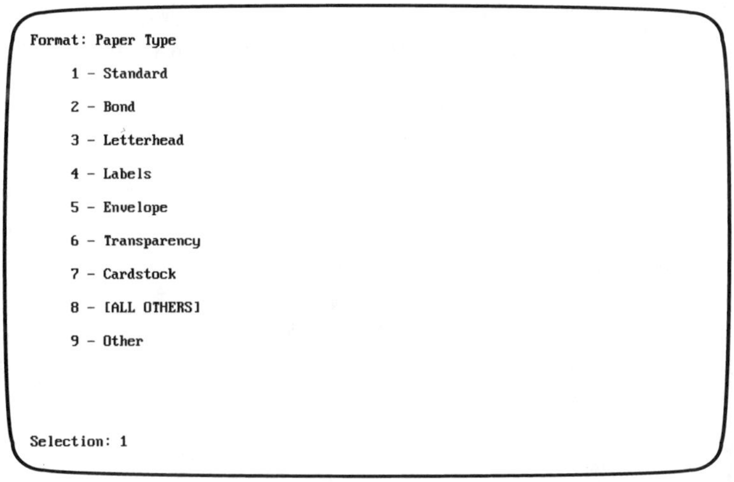

```
Format: Paper Type

    1 - Standard

    2 - Bond

    3 - Letterhead

    4 - Labels

    5 - Envelope

    6 - Transparency

    7 - Cardstock

    8 - [ALL OTHERS]

    9 - Other



Selection: 1
```

Fig. 8.2.

The Format: Paper Type screen.

5. From the Edit Paper Definition menu, select Paper Size (**1**). Figure 8.3 shows the Edit Paper Definition menu.

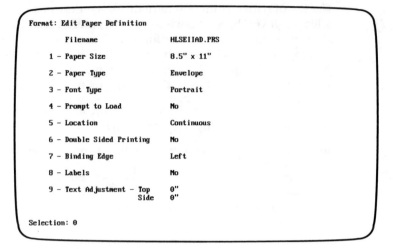

Fig. 8.3.

The Edit Paper Definition screen.

```
Format: Edit Paper Definition

        Filename                    HLSEIIAD.PRS

    1 - Paper Size                  8.5" x 11"

    2 - Paper Type                  Envelope

    3 - Font Type                   Portrait

    4 - Prompt to Load              No

    5 - Location                    Continuous

    6 - Double Sided Printing       No

    7 - Binding Edge                Left

    8 - Labels                      No

    9 - Text Adjustment - Top       0"
                          Side      0"


Selection: 0
```

6. From the Format: Paper Size screen, select **Envelope (5)** to set the size for a standard 9 1/2-by-4-inch business correspondence envelope (see fig. 8.4).

Fig. 8.4.

The Paper Size screen.

```
Format: Paper Size               Width  Height

    1 - Standard                 (8.5" x 11")

    2 - Standard Landscape       (11" x 8.5")

    3 - Legal                    (8.5" x 14")

    4 - Legal Landscape          (14" x 8.5")

    5 - Envelope                 (9.5" x 4")

    6 - Half Sheet               (5.5" x 8.5")

    7 - US Government            (8" x 11")

    8 - A4                       (210mm x 297mm)

    9 - A4 Landscape             (297mm x 210mm)

    o - Other


Selection: 0
```

At this point, you again see the Edit Paper Definition screen (see fig. 8.3). What you do next depends upon the type of printer you are using. Most dot-matrix and daisywheel printers print envelopes in the standard portrait orientation (that is, like a regular typewriter—top edge first).

The Hewlett-Packard DeskJet, an inexpensive laser printer, needs to have the envelope fed top end first (face down) into a pair of plastic guides, one on each side of the envelope. This is considered a portrait orientation, like that used on a dot-matrix printer.

However, most laser printers must have envelopes fed in short end first (usually the end that will hold the stamp). With an HP LaserJet, for example, the printer will print the address in lines down the paper (for instance, perpendicular to the leading edge), rather than across the paper (for instance, parallel to the leading edge), as is done on a typewriter. Therefore, for any HP LaserJet (Plus, II, IID, IIP, and III), you must change the font from the standard portrait (parallel) to landscape (perpendicular).

7. If your printer requires a landscape font, select **Font Type (3)**, then **Landscape (2)**. Check the following list to see which kind of font you need for your particular printer:

   - daisywheel printer .... portrait
   - dot-matrix printer .... portrait
   - HP DeskJet .... portrait
   - HP LaserJet (original) .... landscape
   - HP LaserJet Plus .... landscape
   - HP LaserJet Series II .... landscape
   - HP LaserJet IID .... landscape
   - HP LaserJet IIP .... landscape
   - HP LaserJet III .... landscape

8. If you want the computer to beep when it is time to insert the envelope, set **Prompt to Load (4)** to **Yes** rather than No. You may prefer to put your envelope in first, in which case leave the prompt set to **No**.

9. Select **Location (5)** and set it to **Manual (3)** if the printer is manually fed, or **Bin Number (2)** if you have an envelope feeder. The correct bin number for the HP LaserJet IID envelope feeder is 5. (Check your printer manual for the correct bin if you have a different printer.)

The remaining items on the Edit Paper Definition screen (items 6 through 9) should remain at their default settings. Press Enter to return to the list of paper definitions. You should see an envelope paper form defined and ready to be selected (see fig. 8.1). Highlight the envelope form and press Select (**1**).

Positioning the Address

Once you have created and selected an envelope form, you are ready to type the address. It is important to remember that on an envelope form the left and top margins are designed to include a return address in the upper left corner of the envelope.

If you use preprinted envelopes, all you need are the proper measurements for the receiver's address. Take a ruler and measure how far down from the top edge of the envelope and how far in from the left edge you want the receiver's address to begin. These measurements will be something like 2" down and 4" from the left edge.

Once you have determined these two measurements, you are ready to set the margins for your envelope form. If you want to include a return address in the upper left corner, follow Method A. If you are using preprinted envelopes and do not need a return address, follow Method B.

Method A (with a Return Address)

If you do not have preprinted stationery, you will want to type your return address in the upper left corner of the screen. Here are the steps for setting the correct margins:

1. Select **Page** (**2**) and **Margins, Top/Bottom** (**5**).

2. Type *0* for both the top and bottom margins, pressing Enter after each entry.

   Steps 1 and 2 help prevent conflicts in some printers with the Advance command, and allow for an address with more lines than normal. Again, on some printers these top and bottom margin settings may change automatically to different figures (for example, .22" and .31" on an HP LaserJet II).

3. Type the return address (your address) in the upper left corner of the page and press Enter after the last line.

4. Press Format (Shift-F8) and select **Line** (**1**).
   ⌨️Choose **Line** from the **Layout** menu.

5. Select **Margins, Left/Right (7)**.

6. Type *4.5* for the left margin and press Enter.

7. Type *0* for the right margin and press Enter twice.

   Generally, laser printers have defined minimum margins. If you type *0* for a margin and get a result like 0.3, that is the minimum allowable margin possible with your printer. You are ready to use the Advance command to place the address exactly 2" down from the top of the envelope (or any other distance you want to use).

8. Press **0**; then select **Other (4)** and **Advance (1)**.

9. Select Line (3), type *2*, and press Enter to have WordPerfect position the receiver's address 2" from the top.

10. Press Exit (F7) to return to the editing screen.

After you have selected the envelope form, keyed in the correct margin settings, and added the Advance to Line command, you should save this form to disk so you can use it again later. But first, check to see if all the settings are correct. Press Reveal Codes (Alt-F3 or F11) and see if your envelope form includes the codes shown in figure 8.5.

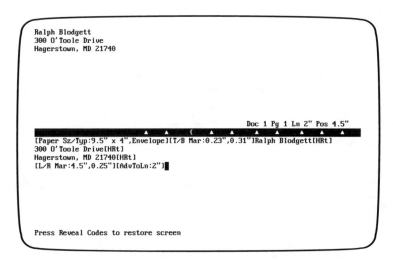

Fig. 8.5.

The proper codes for an envelope form.

If you want to save this form where you can easily retrieve it again, save it as ENVELOPE.FRM in your normal working files subdirectory, including the full path (C:\WP51\FILES\ENVELOPE.FRM or C:\WP51\TEXT\ENVELOPE.FRM, for instance). However, if you want to use this form with the envelope macro included on the Applications Disk, save it in the Macros subdirectory (C:\WP51\MACROS\ENVELOPE.FRM).

Method B (for Preprinted Envelopes)

If you are using preprinted envelopes (ones with the sender's address printed in the upper left corner of the envelope), you may use a slightly different procedure. This method is preferable to Method A because it leaves fewer codes on the form to interfere with a merge.

For Method B, you will define your margins inside the envelope form itself. To do this follow these steps:

1. Press Format (Shift-F8) and **Page** (**2**)
   ⌐⊟Choose **Page** from the Layout menu.

2. Select Paper Size/Type (**7**).

3. Highlight the envelope form and press Edit (**5**).

You see an Edit Paper Definition screen similar to figure 8.6.

Fig. 8.6.
_____

*Format: Edit
Paper Definition.*

```
Format: Edit Paper Definition

        Filename              HLSEIIAD.PRS

    1 - Paper Size            9.5" x 4"

    2 - Paper Type            Envelope - Wide

    3 - Font Type             Landscape

    4 - Prompt to Load        No

    5 - Location              Manual

    6 - Double Sided Printing No

    7 - Binding Edge          Top

    8 - Labels                No

    9 - Text Adjustment - Top 0"
                       Side   0"

Selection: 0
```

4. Select Text Adjustment (**9**).

5. Select **Down** (**2**), type *.9*, and press Enter.

6. Select Text Adjustment (**9**).

7. Select **Right** (**4**), type *3*, and press Enter twice.

Steps 4 through 7 insert the proper margin settings inside the envelope form definition itself. An alternative to method B, of course, would be to insert all the envelope format and margin codes into the document header. The steps to access the document header are as follows:

1. Press Format (Shift-F8).

2. Choose **Document** (**3**).
   ⌧Select **D**ocument **L**ayout menu.

3. Choose Initial Codes (**2**).

   You see a screen that looks like a Reveal Codes window at the bottom. Any codes you add to this screen (as in the previous steps 1 through 7) will be hidden from normal view in either the Document or Reveal Codes windows.

4. When you are finished adding codes to the Initial Codes window, press Exit (F7) twice to return to the normal document screen.

Warning: If you put *any* codes in your document header, you *cannot* use steps 1 through 4 to remove the document file name because those steps strip any initial codes.

If you want to save this form where you can easily retrieve it again, save it as ENVELOPE.FRM in your normal working files subdirectory, including the full path (C:\WP51\FILES\ENVELOPE.FRM or C:\WP51\TEXT\ENVELOPE.FRM, for instance). However, if you want to use this form with the envelope macro included on the Applications Disk, save it in the Macros subdirectory (C:\WP51\MACROS\ENVELOPE.FRM).

Methods A and B

Before you finish setting the margins, you should test the margins you have defined—either on screen as in Method A or within the form itself as in Method B. Do this by typing the following three lines on your envelope form where a normal address would appear:

Full Name
Street Address
City, State 54321

Then press Print (Shift-F7) and View Document (6). If your margins are set properly, your address should show up as in figure 8.7.

Fig. 8.7.

*A properly
positioned
address in View
Document mode.*

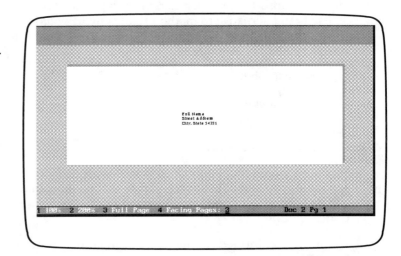

Note: Some printer definitions with version 5.1 do not properly display the set margins or advance, so if your address appears in a place different from that in figure 8.7, try printing your envelope before changing the margins from the previous settings. (See "Printing an Envelope" later in the chapter.)

If you need to change any of the margins, follow the previous directions and make the necessary adjustments. Once you have the margins defined for a typical address, delete the three dummy address lines (Full Name, Street Address, City, State 54321), taking care not to remove any final margin settings. Then save the form as ENVELOPE.FRM.

Printing an Envelope

Once you have created and selected an envelope form, and saved it to disk, you can reuse the form repeatedly if you follow these steps:

   1. Start with a clear screen and press the space bar once.

This action creates a document that contains a single space. When you retrieve a file into that single-space document, the original file name is stripped out. This ensures that you do not accidentally save an envelope address back to disk in place of ENVELOPE.FRM.

2. Press Retrieve (Shift-F10); type the full path and file name: *C:\WP51\MACROS\ENVELOPE.FRM*

3. Press Enter to start the retrieve process. The following prompt will appear at the bottom of your screen:

   ```
   Retrieve into current document? No (Yes)
   ```

4. Type *Y* for **Yes**; then press Backspace once to remove the extra space at the top of the page.

5. If you created your form with Method A, press Home, Home, down arrow to reach the location for the receiver's address. With Method B, your cursor will already be properly positioned.

6. Type the receiver's name and address. If you wish to use a different font than the default, add that code at the beginning of the address (Ctrl-F8, **4**).

7. Insert an envelope into your printer. If you have a LaserJet, insert the envelope stamp end first following the guidelines in table 8.1.

Table 8.1
Envelope Orientation in Tray

Type of Printer	*Envelope Position*
HP LaserJet (original)	Face down, right edge
HP LaserJet Plus	Face down, right edge
HP LaserJet II	Face up, centered
HP LaserJet IID	Face up, centered
HP LaserJet IIP	Face down, right edge
HP LaserJet III	Face up, centered

8. Press Print (Shift-F7) and select **Page (2)**.

   The envelope will automatically feed itself into the printer and print. If you hear a beep, this means your envelope form is set and you are ready to start printing.

9. Press Print (Shift-F7), **4**, and type *G*.

Using the Envelope Macro

The Applications Disk contains an envelope macro (named ENVELOPE.WPM) that will work with the ENVELOPE.FRM file you created, providing you saved it in your Macros subdirectory (for instance, C:\WP51\MACROS\ENVELOPE.FRM).

The macro will work from either Doc 1 or Doc 2, providing you have a clear screen in the opposite window. If the macro finds text in the opposite window, it will abort and provide the following prompt:

```
Window 2 contains a document. Exit document first and
try macro again.
```

To use ENVELOPE.WPM, type the first part of a letter, including the full address and salutation line (for instance, "Dear Allen:"). The salutation line should be separated from the address by at least one blank line. At this point you can invoke the envelope macro:

1. Press Macro (Alt-F10)

   ⌨Select **Macro** from the **Tools** menu, and choose **Execute**.

2. Type *Envelope* and press Enter. Immediately you will see the following prompt:

   ```
   Move cursor to top line of address—Press Enter.
   ```

3. Position the cursor under the first letter of the receiver's name and press Enter.

The macro copies the full address from the letter in Doc 1 (or Doc 2); switches to the opposite window; retrieves ENVELOPE.FRM, which you created earlier; pastes the address into ENVELOPE.FRM; prints the envelope; and exits that window without saving the page. Of course, all this happens faster than can be described. But the macro will save an awful lot of work on your part.

Printing Multiple Envelopes without Merge

If you want to print 5 or 10 addresses on preprinted envelopes (envelopes with the company address printed in the upper left corner), you used Method B to create ENVELOPE.FRM. You may use this envelope form for multiple envelopes. Follow these steps:

1. Retrieve ENVELOPE.FRM into a clear screen.

2. Begin typing addresses, pressing Hard Page (Ctrl-Enter) after each ZIP code.

Ctrl-Enter inserts a double-dashed line (indicating a page break) after each entry. When you have typed all the envelopes you want to send, your screen should look like figure 8.8.

```
Mr/Mrs Marvin R. Snyder
120 Huntington Avenue
Boston, MA 02116
=====================================================================
Frank J. Harrigan
135 S. 39th
Omaha, NE 68131
=====================================================================
Edna Armstrong
579 N. Pennsylvania
Indianapolis, IN 46204
=====================================================================
Spencer O'Leary
Box 10012 Riverside Sta.
Newport Beach, CA 92663
=====================================================================
Mr/Mrs Paul W. Kline
31 Lincoln Park
Newark, NJ 07102
=====================================================================
Anthony A. Ericson
1227 13th NW
Cedar Rapids, IA 52405
=====================================================================
                            Doc 1 Pg 6 Ln 1.39" Pos 2.75"
```

Fig. 8.8.

Addresses typed for six letters.

3. Print the envelopes one at a time (Shift-F7, **2**) or all at once (Shift-F7, **1**), inserting envelopes as needed for each address.

4. When done printing, press Exit (F7) to exit the document with or without saving the address.

If you mail letters to the same group of people often, such as sending an announcement to a list of board members, you will want to save the file for future use. Otherwise, exit without saving.

Printing Multiple Envelopes with Merge

If you have 20 or more envelopes to print, you can create a primary envelope merge file and merge the addresses into the envelope form. If you used Method B to create ENVELOPE.FRM, do the following:

1. From a clear screen press Retrieve (Shift-F10).

2. Type the full path and file name of your envelope form and press Enter.

3. Press Merge Codes (Shift-F9), select Field, and then type *1*.

4. Press Enter to start a new line.

5. Repeat steps 3 and 4 for each field needed for one address in your secondary file (see Chapter 4 for information on creating a secondary file).

Note: If your secondary file contains named fields, you will need to follow the instructions given in Chapter 4 for creating a primary merge file with named fields. Figure 8.9 shows a primary envelope file using named fields for the address.

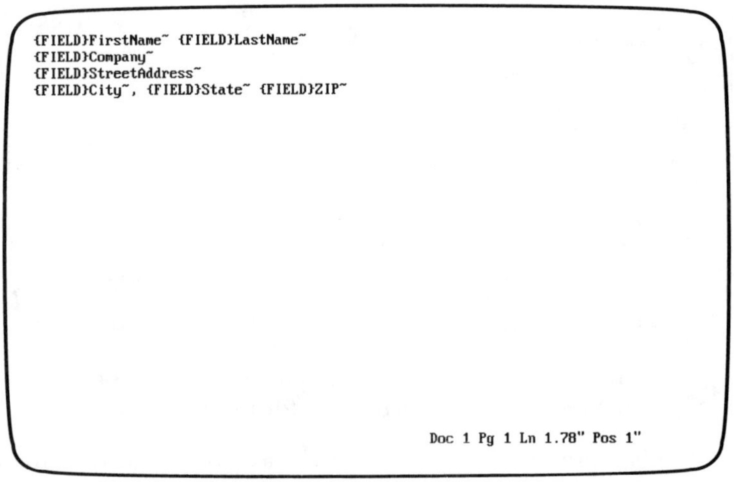

Fig. 8.9.

*A primary
envelope merge
file with named
fields.*

```
{FIELD}FirstName~ {FIELD}LastName~
{FIELD}Company~
{FIELD}StreetAddress~
{FIELD}City~, {FIELD}State~ {FIELD}ZIP~




                                          Doc 1 Pg 1 Ln 1.78" Pos 1"
```

6. Save this merge file as ENVELOPE.PF. The PF extension indicates this is a primary merge file.

Merging the Addresses

At this point you are ready to merge this primary envelope merge file with the secondary address merge file. Perform the following steps:

1. Press Merge/Sort (Ctrl-F9).
   ⌸Choose **Me**r**ge** Codes from the **T**ools menu.

2. Type *ENVELOPE.PF* as your primary file and press Enter.

3. Type *ADDRESS.SF* as your secondary file and press Enter. (See Chapter 4 for details on creating the secondary merge file.)

4. When the merge is completed, press Home twice, then up arrow to return to the top of the file.

5. Press Print (Shift-F7); then select View Document (6).

Cycle through the merged envelopes using PageUp and PageDown to check your merge before printing. Figure 8.10 shows the first address in your merged file.

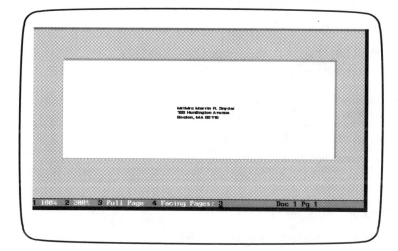

Fig. 8.10.

The first envelope of a merged envelope file.

6. If the merge worked properly, press **Full Document** (1) or **Page** (2).

If part of any address is missing, go back and check your secondary file to make sure each field has an end field code and each record has an end record code. Then perform the merge again using the corrected secondary merge file.

Cautions about Using a Merge

If you selected the correct margins and the proper Advance to Line measurement for your ENVELOPE.PF form, your envelopes should print like the sample shown in figure 8.10. If you print one letter and the address prints improperly, change the margins in your primary file and redo the merge. Nothing looks worse than having a person's name and address positioned improperly on the page.

Merging with Method B Forms

If you use merge with an envelope form created with Method B, formatting codes like margins, paper size/type, and Advance to Line get repeated in each record. This repetition will slow down the operation of the merge, as well as the printing of the file itself.

If you must include margin changes in your envelope form, these settings should be placed in the hidden document initial codes. To do this follow these steps:

1. Press Format (Shift-F8) and select Document (**3**).

   ⌨️Select **Document** from the **Layout** menu.

2. Choose Initial Codes (**2**).

3. Press Format (Shift-F8), **Page** (**2**), then Paper Size/Type (**7**).

   ⌨️Select **Page** from the **Layout** menu, then Paper Size/Type.

4. Highlight the Envelope definition, choose **Select** (**1**), and then press Exit (F7) to return to the initial codes editing screen.

5. Press Format (Shift-F8) and select Line (**1**)

   ⌨️Choose **Line** from the **Layout** menu.

6. Select **Margins, Left/Right** (**7**).

7. Type *4.5* for the left margin and press Enter.

8. Type *0* for the right margin and press Enter twice.

   Generally, laser printers have defined minimum margins. If you type *0* for the right margin and get a result like 0.3, that is the minimum allowable margin possible with your printer.

9. Select **Page** (**2**) and **Margins, Top/Bottom** (**5**).

10. Type *0* for both the top and bottom margins, pressing Enter after each entry.

With all four margins set, you are ready to use the Advance command to place the address exactly 2" down from the top of the envelope (or any other distance you wish to use). Do the following:

1. Press **0**, then select **Other** (**4**) and **Advance** (**1**).

2. Select Line (**3**), type *2*, and press Enter to have WordPerfect position the receiver's address 2" from the top.

3. Press Exit (F7) three times to return to the editing screen.

4. Save this form as ENVELOPE.PF and use it as your primary file for an envelope merge, following the directions given under "Printing Multiple Envelopes with Merge" and "Merging the Addresses" earlier in this chapter.

Using Window Envelopes

Many businesses today use window envelopes for their business correspondence and invoices. Window envelopes slash typing expenses and save time because they eliminate the need for retyping addresses on envelopes.

Some window envelopes come with dual windows, one for the sender's return address and one for the receiver's name and address. This type of envelope is the least expensive of all, because it saves printing costs. Addresses on the letter inside serve as the envelope addresses. Figure 8.11 shows the two types of window envelopes used by businesses today.

Fig. 8.11.

Window envelopes come with single or dual windows.

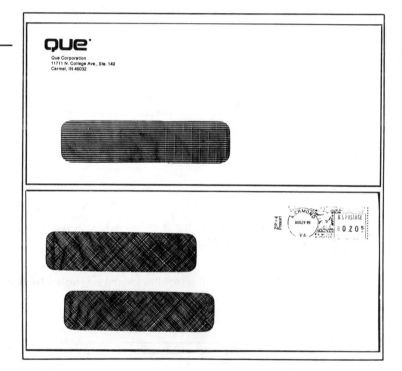

If your company uses window envelopes, you must follow five rules when creating a letter for a window envelope:

1. Make certain the paper used for the letter is no less than 1/4" narrower than the envelope being used. (If too narrow, the paper could shift inside the envelope and make the address unreadable.)

2. Measuring the height of the envelope, make certain the letter inside will be folded no less than 1/4" smaller than the envelope height. (If too

short, the paper could shift inside the envelope and make the address unreadable.)

3. Measure the distance from the left edge of the envelope to the left edge of the window (see Distance A in fig. 8.12), add 1/4", and use that figure for your left margin setting.

Fig. 8.12.

Setting the margins for a letter in a window envelope.

4. Measure the distance from the top edge of the envelope to the top edge of the window (see Distance B in fig. 8.12), add 1/4", and use that figure for the Advance to Line position for the first line of the receiver's address.

5. Fold the top third of the letter backward so the address is on the outside of the page when folded (see fig. 8.13).

Fig. 8.13.

Fold the letter so the receiver's address faces outward.

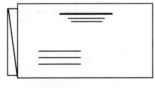
Top third of letter is folded backward

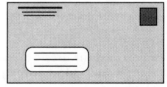
Insert so address shows in the open window

If the first page of your letter needs an address higher on the page so there is more room for body copy, use the bottom third of your letter for the height of the envelope (as in fig. 8.14) and fold the top portion short. Then you can use a folded letter to measure the proper advance needed to have the address show when inserted into the envelope.

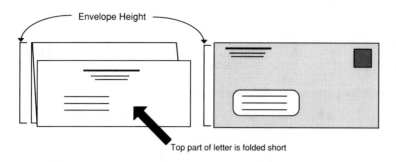

Fig. 8.14.

Folding the top of the letter short for more copy.

Using Regular Envelopes

If your company is using regular full-size envelopes, you need to fold your letters the standard way, with the bottom third folded first, then the top third folded last as shown in figure 8.15. This way, the recipient of the letter will see your letterhead and the receiver's name when he or she unfolds the top part of the folded page.

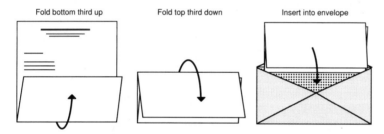

Fig. 8.15.

The proper way to fold a letter for a No. 10 business envelope.

If you must insert a sheet of regular-size paper into a short envelope, fold the letter in half first, as in figure 8.16, then into thirds. Generally, though, it is best to avoid using small envelopes with regular-size paper.

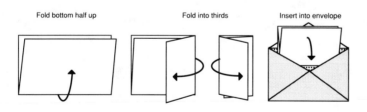

Fig. 8.16.

Folding a standard letter for a small envelope.

Summary

This chapter has explained how to perform the most common envelope addressing tasks, including these:

- How to create an envelope form definition
- How different kinds of printers use different printing methods
- How to use the envelope macro on the Applications Disk
- How to use plain business envelopes
- How to use preprinted business envelopes
- How to use window envelopes
- How to fold business stationery for different kinds of envelopes

In Chapter 9, you explore an alternative way to address envelopes—using address labels.

9

Creating Labels and
Rolodex Cards

To operate every day, many offices depend on names and addresses of customers and clients. The most up-to-date businesses still require these lists in small formats. Every business office uses labels, primarily address labels but also file folder labels, notebook labels, and labels for videotapes, computer diskettes, packages, and so on. And what office would be complete without a Rolodex index file? These phone-and-address desktop files hold special card-stock pages with two indentations along the bottom edge of each card.

Many offices still use a typewriter to prepare labels, because labels have not been easy to produce with a typical word processing program. And for years, Rolodex card addresses have been typed with a common typewriter, simply because it was too difficult to print them with a computer.

There is no such disadvantage with WordPerfect 5.1. You can now create label forms and Rolodex cards with special WordPerfect features. You can produce label forms automatically with WordPerfect's special label macro. The macro shows you a pop-up screen with a scrollable list of many standard Avery and 3M label forms. All you do is select the label size that comes closest to the labels you want to create, and WordPerfect creates the definition for you automatically.

In this chapter, you first learn how to make your own labels by creating one from scratch and then using that form to type in or merge in mailing addresses. You also see how the WordPerfect label macro works for standard label formats.

Lastly, this chapter shows you how to create a Rolodex card definition for a tractor-feed printer, how to use the text-adjustment feature to properly position text, and how to merge addresses on Rolodex cards.

Noting Types of Mailing Labels

Basically, two types of labels are used in the business environment: individual labels connected together vertically on tractor-feed paper (and used on daisywheel and dot-matrix printers) and labels that come on 8 1/2-by-11-inch sheets of paper.

Because the tractor-feed labels act much like miniature sheets of paper, they are the easiest to create. You create a label paper definition, size the paper to the actual size of the label itself, and identify the paper as continuous feed. (See fig. 9.1 for an illustration of tractor-feed paper.)

Fig. 9.1.

Tractor-feed paper is attached top to bottom in sheets.

Tractor-Feed Paper

Paper definitions for multiple labels on single sheets of paper are more complicated. For example, figure 9.2 illustrates a sheet of Avery 5260 labels, with 30 labels per sheet of 8 1/2-by-11-inch paper. These labels come either in small packages of 25 sheets per package or in larger boxes. The labels are self-adhesive and can be peeled off the paper after they are printed and affixed to the envelopes or packages as needed.

These address labels for laser printers work on a wide variety of printers—including Hewlett-Packard, Canon, Ricoh, Toshiba, Data Products, Apple, Xerox, and Corona laser printers, along with Qume, Diablo, Wang, IBM, and NBI word processing printers.

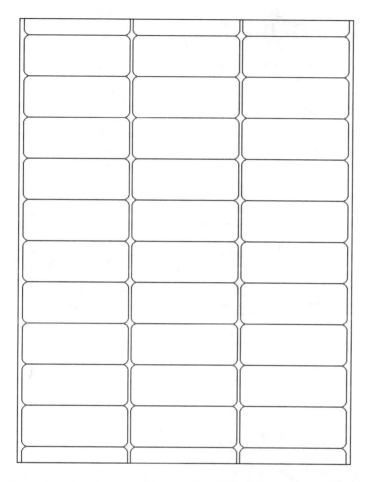

Fig. 9.2.

Avery 5260 address labels come 30 labels to a sheet.

Note that the sheet has a row of half labels at the top and another row of half labels at the bottom. Sheets that contain 33 labels (3 columns of 11 labels) and no top and bottom edges are not recommended for most laser printers, since virtually all laser printers have a small unprintable edge on all four sides that cannot be used as part of the label definition. You should avoid using label sheets that do not have a top and bottom edge.

Labels that have top and bottom spaces between them should also be avoided, as they can peel off inside the printer and create an expensive mess to repair. Use labels that touch one another from top to bottom, so that no opportunity exists for the individual labels to come off onto the printer rollers.

Creating a Label Definition

The first step in printing labels is to create a *label form definition*. You do this by defining a special paper size and type containing the number of labels per sheet, the arrangement of the labels on the paper, the dimensions of each label, and the margins for the text to be printed on the label.

You need a ruler, a sample sheet of the type of labels you want to print, and some idea where your text should appear on each label. Figure 9.3 illustrates a printed sheet of Avery 5260 labels, to give you some idea of the margins you need for each label.

Receiver's Name Street Address City, State 54321	Receiver's Name Street Address City, State 54321	Receiver's Name Street Address City, State 54321
Receiver's Name Street Address City, State 54321	Receiver's Name Street Address City, State 54321	Receiver's Name Street Address City, State 54321
Receiver's Name Street Address City, State 54321	Receiver's Name Street Address City, State 54321	Receiver's Name Street Address City, State 54321
Receiver's Name Street Address City, State 54321	Receiver's Name Street Address City, State 54321	Receiver's Name Street Address City, State 54321
Receiver's Name Street Address City, State 54321	Receiver's Name Street Address City, State 54321	Receiver's Name Street Address City, State 54321
Receiver's Name Street Address City, State 54321	Receiver's Name Street Address City, State 54321	Receiver's Name Street Address City, State 54321
Receiver's Name Street Address City, State 54321	Receiver's Name Street Address City, State 54321	Receiver's Name Street Address City, State 54321
Receiver's Name Street Address City, State 54321	Receiver's Name Street Address City, State 54321	Receiver's Name Street Address City, State 54321
Receiver's Name Street Address City, State 54321	Receiver's Name Street Address City, State 54321	Receiver's Name Street Address City, State 54321
Receiver's Name Street Address City, State 54321	Receiver's Name Street Address City, State 54321	Receiver's Name Street Address City, State 54321

Fig. 9.3.

Addresses as they should appear on the Avery 5260 sheets.

With a ruler and sheet of labels in hand, you are ready to create a label definition, following these steps:

1. Press Format (Shift-F8) and choose **Page** (**2**).

   ⌨️Choose **Page** from the **Layout** menu.

2. Select Paper Size (**7**). Next you see the Format: Paper Size/Type menu, as shown in figure 9.4.

```
Format: Paper Size/Type
                                              Font  Double
Paper type and Orientation   Paper Size   Prompt Loc   Type  Sided Labels

(2 x 4) inch labels          8.5" x 11"    No   Contin Port  No     2 x 5
Envelope - Wide              9.5" x 4"     No   Manual Land  No
Legal                        8.5" x 14"    No   Contin Port  No
Legal - Dup Long             8.5" x 14"    No   Contin Port  Yes
Legal - Dup Long - Wide      14" x 8.5"    No   Contin Land  Yes
Legal - Dup Short            8.5" x 14"    No   Contin Port  Yes
Legal - Dup Short - Wide     14" x 8.5"    No   Contin Land  Yes
Legal - Wide                 14" x 8.5"    No   Contin Land  No
Standard                     8.5" x 11"    No   Contin Port  No
Standard - Dup Long          8.5" x 11"    No   Contin Port  Yes
Standard - Dup Long - Wide   11" x 8.5"    No   Contin Land  Yes
Standard - Dup Short         8.5" x 11"    No   Contin Port  Yes
Standard - Dup Short - Wide  11" x 8.5"    No   Contin Land  Yes
Standard - Wide              11" x 8.5"    No   Contin Land  No
[ALL OTHERS]                 Width ≤ 8.5"  Yes  Manual       No


1 Select; 2 Add; 3 Copy; 4 Delete; 5 Edit; N Name Search: 1
```

Fig. 9.4.

The Format: Paper Size/Type screen.

3. Select **Add** (**2**). The Format: Paper Type screen appears (see fig. 9.5).

```
Format: Paper Type

    1 - Standard

    2 - Bond

    3 - Letterhead

    4 - Labels

    5 - Envelope

    6 - Transparency

    7 - Cardstock

    8 - [ALL OTHERS]

    9 - Other


Selection: 1
```

Fig. 9.5.

The Format: Paper Type screen.

4. Select **Labels (4)**. You next see the Format: Edit Paper Definition screen (see fig. 9.6).

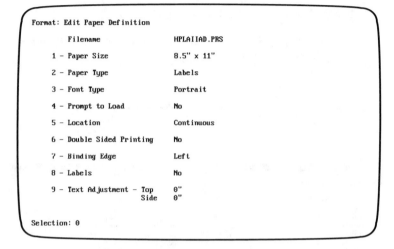

Fig. 9.6.

The Format: Edit Paper Definition screen.

```
Format: Edit Paper Definition

        Filename              HPLAIIAD.PRS

    1 - Paper Size            8.5" x 11"

    2 - Paper Type            Labels

    3 - Font Type             Portrait

    4 - Prompt to Load        No

    5 - Location              Continuous

    6 - Double Sided Printing No

    7 - Binding Edge          Left

    8 - Labels                No

    9 - Text Adjustment - Top   0"
                        Side    0"

Selection: 0
```

5. Choose **Labels (8)**. At the `No (Yes)` prompt, press Y.

After you press Y for Yes, the Format: Labels screen appears, similar to figure 9.7. The actual settings on this screen depend in part on the printer you have defined.

Fig. 9.7.

The Format: Labels screen.

```
Format: Labels

    1 - Label Size
                Width           2.63"
                Height          1"

    2 - Number of Labels
                Columns         3
                Rows            10

    3 - Top Left Corner
                Top             0.5"
                Left            0.188"

    4 - Distance Between Labels
                Column          0.125"
                Row             0"

    5 - Label Margins
                Left            0.043"
                Right           0.123"
                Top             0"
                Bottom          0"

Selection: 0
```

Measure the size of a single label on your sample sheet of labels. Determine the actual label size itself, excluding spacing between labels, if any. If the label you use is different from the sample in the Format: Labels screen, take the following steps:

1. Choose Label Size (**1**) and type the actual width (horizontal) and height (vertical) measurements, pressing Enter after each entry.

   Note: You may type tenths or hundredths of an inch, or fractions, for your label measurements. For example, 1 5/8 inches may be entered as 1.625 or 1 5/8. If you use a whole number and fractions, be sure to leave a space between the whole number and the first fraction number.

2. If the columns (side to side) and rows (up and down) of labels you plan to use are different from those shown under item 2, enter the correct figures, pressing Enter after each number.

3. Use the ruler to measure the distance from the top edge of the label sheet to where you want text to begin within the first label, and from the left edge of the label sheet to where you want text to begin within the first label. If either of these measurements is different from the Top Left Corner (**3**) option in the Labels screen, enter the correct measurements (fractions again are possible).

4. Use the ruler to measure any gaps between labels on the sheet. Type the measurements of those gaps from side to side as Distance Between Labels, Column, and from top to bottom as Distance Between Labels, Row (**4**), pressing Enter after each measurement.

5. Select Label Margins (**5**).

Look at figure 9.3 earlier in this chapter and decide where you want your mailing addresses to appear on each label. Remember, each label is treated as an individual page, so you are measuring the text margins from the left, right, top, and bottom edges of a single label. WordPerfect uses those margins for the text in every label on the sheet. Generally speaking, it is wise to leave the right and bottom margins at 0", to allow for longer names and addresses.

When you have finished entering the correct measurements for your sample label sheet, press Exit (F7). The Format: Edit Paper Definition menu reappears (see fig. 9.6), showing your newly created definition.

If you want WordPerfect to prompt you to load the paper, or if you plan to use a label sheet other than continuous-form (which is how you specify sheet paper for a laser printer), you could change other settings on the Edit Paper Definition menu. When you are ready to leave the Edit Paper Definition menu, press Exit (F7) three times to return to your document.

Using the Label Definition

Once you have correctly defined a label form, you can reuse the form continually. You do not need to re-create that same definition for the same labels. To use the new form either for a single sheet of labels or for several sheets, start with a clear screen and follow these steps:

1. Press Format (Shift-F8) and select **Page (2)**.

    ⌨ Select **Page** from the **Layout** menu.

2. Select Paper **Size (7)**. The Format: Paper Size/Type menu appears (see fig. 9.4).

3. Highlight the new label definition with the cursor keys.

4. Choose **Select (1)**.

5. Press Exit to return to the document.

Typing Labels Individually

Once you have selected the label type, you can type addresses one at a time, pressing Hard Page (Ctrl-Enter) after each complete address. However, you will be unable to print a single sheet of labels if you ask WordPerfect to print a page (Shift-F7,**2**). All you will get is a single label, even though your page contains 10, 20, or 30 addresses. To print a whole sheet of labels, you must press Print (Shift-F7) and **Full Document (1)**.

This just happens to be an idiosyncrasy of labels. Each label is considered a logical page. So if you ask WordPerfect to print a single page (Shift-F7,**2** or **P**), all you get is one label at the top of the sheet. Also, you can have WordPerfect print a group of labels by pressing Print (Shift-F7) and **Multiple Pages (5)**; typing a range of pages, such as *5-10*; and pressing Enter. Or you can print individual labels (rather than a range) by typing page numbers separated by commas, as in *5, 9, 15, 25*.

Using the WordPerfect Label Macro

If you use Avery or 3M labels, WordPerfect 5.1 comes with a special macro named LABELS.WPM, which automates the creation of 22 different Avery and 3M label forms.

To use this macro, press Macro (Alt-F10), type *LABELS*, and press Enter. If you have a version of WordPerfect shipped prior to March 30, 1990, a window like figure 9.8 pops up on your screen showing the Label Page/Size Definitions screen with 19 different label sizes. On the right are the actual Avery and 3M numbers for each label definition, and on the left the individual label sizes in inches, followed by the number of labels, columns, and rows of labels on each sheet. Pressing PgDn reveals several additional label sizes.

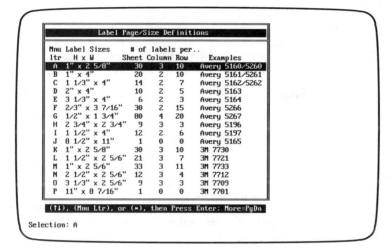

Fig. 9.8.

Avery and 3M label definitions offered by versions of WordPerfect prior to March 30, 1990.

If you have WordPerfect 5.1 dated March 30, 1990, or later, the labels macro screen appears as shown in figure 9.9.

Fig. 9.9.

The label forms available on versions of WordPerfect 5.1 dated March 30, 1990, or later.

To create one of these 22 label definitions, follow these steps:

1. Use the cursor keys to highlight the label you plan to use.

2. Press Enter to select that label definition. At the bottom of the screen, you see a prompt for three items:

   ```
   Location: 1 Continuous; 2 Bin Number; 3 Manual
   ```

3. Select one of the three options by typing the number or bolded letter. You are returned to the Format: Paper Size/Type screen (see fig. 9.4).

4. Use the cursor keys to highlight the new label definition, and press Select (**1**).

Although this label macro saves a few steps in creating up to 22 different labels, it unfortunately does not automatically include the proper margins within each label for the addresses themselves. In other words, if you use the default margins created by the LABELS.WPM macro, the addresses print in the top left corner of each label. So you will need to enter the margins within the label *page*.

Here are the steps for performing this task. Return to the Format: Paper Size/Type screen (Shift-F8,**2** or **P**, and **7** or **S**) and do the following:

1. Highlight the new Labels form and press Edit (**5**).

2. Select Labels (**8**) and press Y.

3. At the Format: Labels screen (see fig. 9.7), select Label Margins (**5**).

4. Set label margins as the following, pressing Enter after each entry:

   - Left: .4"

   - Right: 0" (printer may adjust)

   - Top: .22" (or .15" for four-line labels)

   - Bottom: 0"

5. Press Exit (F7) twice to return to the Format: Paper Size/Type screen.

6. To use this form, start with a new screen, highlight the modified labels form, and press Select (**1**).

If you press Reveal Codes (Alt-F4 or F11), you see that a paper size/type code, similar to the one shown in figure 9.10, has been added to the top of your page.

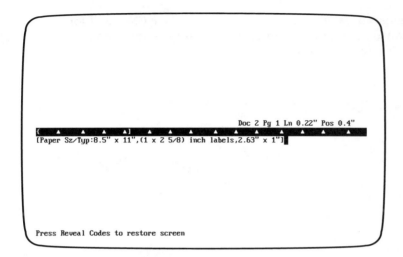

Doc 2 Pg 1 Ln 0.22" Pos 0.4"

[Paper Sz/Typ:8.5" x 11",(1 x 2 5/8) inch labels,2.63" x 1"]

Press Reveal Codes to restore screen

Fig. 9.10.

A paper size/type code as it appears in Reveal Codes.

You may use a label form at the top of a file that contains a typed address. Just make sure that a hard page break (Ctrl-Enter) separates each address from the following address. However, if you want to use any label form with a merge, you must do something different, as the following section explains.

Using a Label Form with Merge

When using a label form with a merge operation, remember to embed the label form in the hidden document preface. If you don't do this first, the label form definition shown in figure 9.10 will be repeated at the top of every label. Here are the steps for storing the label form definition in the document initial codes:

1. Press Format (Shift-F8) and select **Document** (**3**).

   ⌨Select **Page** from the **Layout** menu.

2. Select Initial Codes (**2**).

3. Press Format (Shift-F8) and **Page** (**2**).

   ⌨Select **Page** from the **Layout** menu.

4. Press Paper Size/Type (**7**).

5. Use the cursor keys to highlight the new label form.

6. Press Select (**1**).

7. Press Exit (F7) three times.

8. Add the merge codes necessary for a primary file (see Chapter 4 for more information on merge). At this point your file should look something like figure 9.11.

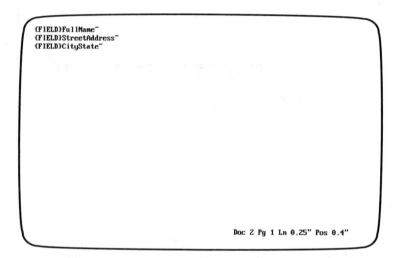

```
{FIELD}FullName~
{FIELD}StreetAddress~
{FIELD}CityState~




                                                    Doc 2 Pg 1 Ln 0.25" Pos 0.4"
```

9. Save the file to disk, supplying a .PF extension. Use a name like LABEL-30.PF (indicating 30 labels).

To perform a merge with this label form, do the following:

1. Press Merge/Sort (Ctrl-F9) and press **Merge (1)**.

   ⌨Choose **Merge** from the Tools menu.

2. At the Primary File: prompt, press List (F5), press Enter, highlight the proper .PF file, and press **Retrieve (1)** (or type the .SF file and path name and press Enter).

3. At the Secondary File: prompt, press List (F5), press Enter, highlight the proper .PF file, and press **Retrieve (1)** (or type the .SF file and path name and press Enter).

4. You'll see a * Merging * prompt at the bottom of your screen. When the merge is complete, press Home, Home, up arrow to return to the top of the file. Your screen at this point should look something like figure 9.12.

Fig. 9.12.

A sample label merge.

```
Mr/Mrs Marvin R. Snyder
120 Huntington Avenue
Boston, MA 02116
===============================================================================
Frank J. Harrigan
135 S. 39th
Omaha, NE 68131
===============================================================================
Edna Armstrong
579 N. Pennsylvania
Indianapolis, IN 46204
===============================================================================
Spencer O'Leary
Box 10012 Riverside Sta.
Newport Beach, CA 92663
===============================================================================
Mr/Mrs Paul W. Kline
31 Lincoln Park
Newark, NJ 07102
===============================================================================
Anthony A. Ericson
1227 13th NW
Cedar Rapids, IA 52405
===============================================================================
                                        Doc 2 Pg 1 Ln 0.25" Pos 0.4"
```

5. Once you have the merge document on-screen, you can print the file by pressing Print (F7) and Full Document (**1**).

Figure 9.13 shows an entire page of Avery 5260 labels (30 labels to a sheet) created with a merge operation.

Now that you know how to use WordPerfect 5.1 to make address labels, read on to find out how you can use WordPerfect with a tractor-feed dot-matrix printer to produce Rolodex cards.

Creating Rolodex Cards

Creating Rolodex cards has always been the chore you set aside until you had an hour or two free to update your file by typing each card on your typewriter. Well, that is no longer true—at least not if you have a dot-matrix or daisywheel printer sitting unused in an office closet. Now with WordPerfect 5.1 forms, printing addresses on Rolodex cards with a tractor-feed printer is simple and very efficient. In fact, you can use a merge file and merge your entire address list to Rolodex cards for immediate phone-number access.

Of course, if all you own is a LaserJet printer, then you may have to depend on the typewriter for your addresses. Apparently, few if any paper suppliers provide Rolodex-type cards on the 8 1/2-by-11-inch sheets used by LaserJets.

Mr/Mrs Marvin R. Snyder 120 Huntington Avenue Boston, MA 02116	Frank J. Harrigan 135 S. 39th Omaha, NE 68131	Edna Armstrong 579 N. Pennsylvania Indianapolis, IN 46204
Spencer O'Leary Box 10012 Riverside Sta. Newport Beach, CA 92663	Mr/Mrs Paul W. Kline 31 Lincoln Park Newark, NJ 07102	Anthony A. Ericson 1227 13th NW Cedar Rapids, IA 52405
Randal Wilson 2552 Kalakaus Avenue Honolulu, HI 96815	William Coleman 10904 W. New Haven Ave. Jacksonville, FL 32204	Deborah K. Douglas 117 W. Monroe Phoenix, AZ 85003
Donald P. Ritter 733 Sligo Ave. Silver Spring, MD 20910	Mr/Mrs Guy Pendleton 42 E. Market Akron, OH 44308	Virginia Ingram P. O. Box 729 Oak Lawn, IL 60454
Maxine Gibson 685 Peachtree NE Atlanta, GA 30309	Clarence E. Brubaker 1523 Bredell Ave. Saint Louis, MO 63117	John Yarbrough 10017 Terwilliger Blvd. Portland, OR 97219
Mr/Mrs Steven Tyler 252 N. Exchange Pkwy Dallas, TX 75235	Brent A. Richardson 5924 S. Santa Fe Drive Denver, CO 80220	Nancy K. Porter 1027 S. Capitol Blvd. Boise, ID 83706
Kenny Johnson 4219 Frederick Avenue Kansas City, MO 64106	Lyle & Karen Dixon 2420 N. Lincoln Oklahoma City, OK 73105	Charles C. Russell 2635 N. Ocean Blvd. Fort Lauderdale, FL 33308
Max E. Burkett 7156 Rutherford Rd. Baltimore, MD 21207	Patrick G. Buckley 290 E Carillo Santa Barbara, CA 93101	Mary Dwyer 336 Orange Street Albany, NY 12206
Jeffrey C. Foley 825 Sherman Street Toledo, OH 43614	Virgil W Kuck 2645 Shop Road Columbia, SC 29209	George Rogers 724 Russell Road Alexandria, VA 22305
Denise D'Anna 24213 Middlebelt Rd Farmington, MI 48024	Richard McKee 234 Hillmond Street Bethlehem, PA	Leroy Edwards Sr. 2089 Walker Road S. Pontiac, MI 49442

Fig. 9.13.

A sheet of labels created from a merge operation.

Continuous, tractor-feed Rolodex cards are available, however. One source for these continuous Rolodex-style cards is Moore Business Products, P.O. Box 5000, Vernon Hills, IL 60061, (800) 323-6230. The 5-by-3-inch size is catalog number 69K13847 and costs about $20.00 for a box of 1,000 cards. This source also has one smaller size for about the same price.

So if you have a tractor-feed printer, you will find these guidelines useful not only for Rolodex cards but also for any card stock on continuous paper with removable punched edges along the left and right sides.

Creating a Rolodex Form Definition

If you have been using a LaserJet printer, your first step in printing Rolodex cards is to select your printer and create a special Rolodex card definition. Here are the steps for doing that (the Epson LQ-2550 tractor-feed printer is the example for this chapter):

1. Press Print (Shift-F8) and choose **Select Printer** (**S**).

   ⌨ Choose **Print** from the **File** menu.

2. Use the up or down arrow to highlight the tractor-feed printer you plan to use for your cards.

3. Press **Select** (**1**) to select that particular printer (see fig. 9.14).

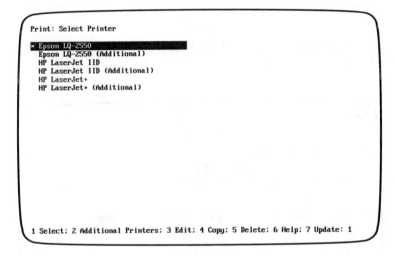

```
Print: Select Printer

■ Epson LQ-2550
  Epson LQ-2550 (Additional)
  HP LaserJet IID
  HP LaserJet IID (Additional)
  HP LaserJet+
  HP LaserJet+ (Additional)




1 Select; 2 Additional Printers; 3 Edit; 4 Copy; 5 Delete; 6 Help; 7 Update: 1
```

Fig. 9.14.

Selecting an Epson LQ-2550 tractor-feed printer.

After selecting the correct printer, you can create a Rolodex card definition. You create a new paper form definition in this manner:

1. Press Format and choose **Page** (**2**).

   ⌨ Choose **Page** from the **Layout** menu.

2. Choose Paper Size/Type (**7**).

3. Choose **Add** (**2**) and **Cardstock** (**7**). The Format: Edit Paper Definition screen appears (see fig. 9.15).

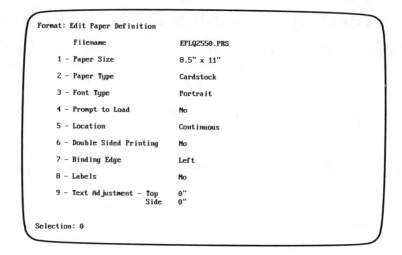

Fig. 9.15.

The Format: Edit Paper Definition screen.

```
Format: Edit Paper Definition

        Filename              EPLQ2550.PRS

   1 - Paper Size             8.5" x 11"

   2 - Paper Type             Cardstock

   3 - Font Type              Portrait

   4 - Prompt to Load         No

   5 - Location               Continuous

   6 - Double Sided Printing  No

   7 - Binding Edge           Left

   8 - Labels                 No

   9 - Text Adjustment - Top  0"
                       Side   0"


Selection: 0
```

4. Select Paper Size (**1**). At this point you should see the Format: Paper Size screen as shown in figure 9.16.

Fig. 9.16.

The Format: Paper Size screen.

```
Format: Paper Size              Width  Height

    1 - Standard                (8.5" x 11")

    2 - Standard Landscape      (11" x 8.5")

    3 - Legal                   (8.5" x 14")

    4 - Legal Landscape         (14" x 8.5")

    5 - Envelope                (9.5" x 4")

    6 - Half Sheet              (5.5" x 8.5")

    7 - US Government           (8" x 11")

    8 - A4                      (210mm x 297mm)

    9 - A4 Landscape            (297mm x 210mm)

    o - Other


Selection: 0
```

5. Choose **Other** (**o**). You should get a Width: 0" Height: prompt at the bottom of the screen, as in figure 9.17.

```
Format: Paper Size              Width  Height

    1 - Standard                (8.5" x 11")

    2 - Standard Landscape      (11" x 8.5")

    3 - Legal                   (8.5" x 14")

    4 - Legal Landscape         (14" x 8.5")

    5 - Envelope                (9.5" x 4")

    6 - Half Sheet              (5.5" x 8.5")

    7 - US Government           (8" x 11")

    8 - A4                      (210mm x 297mm)

    9 - A4 Landscape            (297mm x 210mm)

    o - Other

Width: 0"       Height:
```

Fig. 9.17.

Prompts for width and height.

6. For `Width:`, type *5* and press Enter.

7. For `Height:`, type *3* and press Enter.

8. Press Exit (F7) to return to the Format: Paper Size/Type screen.

9. Highlight the `Cardstock - Wide` form shown in figure 9.18 and press
    Select (**1**).

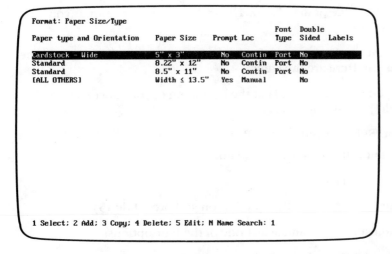

```
Format: Paper Size/Type

                                              Font  Double
Paper type and Orientation   Paper Size   Prompt Loc  Type  Sided  Labels

Cardstock - Wide             5" x 3"      No   Contin  Port  No
Standard                     8.22" x 12"  No   Contin  Port  No
Standard                     8.5" x 11"   No   Contin  Port  No
[ALL OTHERS]                 Width ≤ 13.5" Yes  Manual        No














1 Select; 2 Add; 3 Copy; 4 Delete; 5 Edit; N Name Search: 1
```

Fig. 9.18.

The newly created card-stock form.

10. Press Exit (F7) to return to the edit window.

Type a few lines on your screen; insert the first page of your tractor-feed Rolodex paper; and print one page, using this definition. Try to include a few words at the top left of your screen; at the top right of the screen, using the Flush Right command (Alt-F6); and at the bottom left of the first page (press Enter until you see a page break, and type the words on the line just above the page break).

Then measure the top left, top right, and bottom margins to see how the text fits on the card stock. If you need to make some adjustments, follow the instructions in the next section. Otherwise, skip to the section "Printing on Rolodex Cards" later in this chapter.

Tip: Remember, you do not want the standard (or default) 1-by-1-inch margins on a small 3-by-5-inch or 4-by-6-inch card. So change your margins to 1/2 inch on all four sides at the top of your document before you do any printing.

Adjusting Text Position on the Forms

Odds are you will have to make some minor text adjustments in your new card-stock form, because it is impossible for WordPerfect to provide the exact margins and paper settings for every form used in every tractor-feed printer on the market. Besides, with a wide platen in your printer, there is no way for WordPerfect to know exactly where you plan to insert your paper into your printer horizontally along the platen.

The important thing with tractor-feed printers is to place a mark somewhere on your printer so you always insert the left edge of your paper at the exact same distance in from the left edge of the platen. Then whatever paper settings you use provide consistent results.

If you find that the text needs to move left, right, up, or down on the form, use the Text Adjustment screen. Here are the steps:

1. Use Reveal Codes (Alt-F3 or F11) at the beginning of your document to delete the old paper-form setting.

2. Press Format (Shift-F8) and choose **Page** (**2**).

    ⌨Select **Page** (**2**) from the Layout menu.

3. Choose Paper Size/Type (**7**).

4. Highlight the `Cardstock - Wide` definition and press **Edit** (**5**).

5. Press Text Adjustment (**9**) and select one of the four options:

    Up (**1**), **Down** (**2**), **Left** (**3**), or **Right** (**4**)

6. With your ruler, measure how far you want the text to be moved up, down, left, or right. Type that amount for one of those four options and press Enter. For example, if you want the text moved up .75", type *.75* (or type *3/4*) and press Enter.

7. When you are finished, press Exit (F7).

8. Highlight the revised paper form and press **Select** (**1**).

9. Press Exit to return to the edit screen.

10. Print the page again and check your settings.

If one page prints correctly, type an additional page or two and print all three pages, checking the distance from the top of the text on one page to the top of the text on another page, making sure that the pages of text are printing exactly 3 inches apart (or 4 inches if you have a 4-by-6-inch form). Once you have checked all the pages and are satisfied with the results, the new card-stock form is ready for regular use. Move on to the next section.

Printing on Rolodex Cards

Once the new card-stock paper form is ready to use, you have two choices: type text for each card one at a time and print the document, or create a Rolodex primary merge file and merge the information onto your cards. The following section shows how to create and use a Rolodex primary merge file.

If you want your Rolodex cards to have last names first, then first names, at the top line of each card (like *Johnson, Blake*), you need a primary file and secondary file that contain this information on separate lines. In previous chapters, you have learned how to create a secondary file and a primary file, so it is not necessary to repeat those steps here. But the following section shows how the two files should appear so that you can properly merge onto a Rolodex file form.

A Secondary File for Rolodex Forms

If on each Rolodex card the last name should precede the first name, the secondary file must have the last names on a separate field from the first names in each record. Likewise, if your Rolodex cards include phone numbers for office and home phones, those numbers, too, must be included in both the secondary and primary files. Figure 9.19 shows how such a secondary file should look with last names in one field, first names in another, and phone numbers in their own fields.

Fig. 9.19.

A secondary file with last names in the top field.

```
{FIELD NAMES}LastN~FirstN~StreetA~CitySt~OfficeP~HomeP~~{END RECORD}
====================================================================
Armstrong{END FIELD}
Edna{END FIELD}
579 N. Pennsylvania{END FIELD}
Indianapolis, IN 46204{END FIELD}
(317) 791-4678{END FIELD}
(317) 791-2315{END FIELD}
{END RECORD}
====================================================================
Buckley{END FIELD}
Patrick G. {END FIELD}
290 E Carillo{END FIELD}
Santa Barbara, CA 93101{END FIELD}
(805) 857-1265{END FIELD}
(805) 423-8550{END FIELD}
{END RECORD}
====================================================================
Douglas{END FIELD}
Deborah K.{END FIELD}
117 W. Monroe{END FIELD}
Phoenix, AZ 85003{END FIELD}
(602) 845-1290{END FIELD}
{END FIELD}
Field: LastN                                    Doc 2 Pg 2 Ln 1" Pos 1"
```

Save the file with a .SF file extension so that you can easily identify the file later. For illustration, the file name ROLODEX.SF is assigned for a special Rolodex card secondary file.

A Primary File for Rolodex Forms

Next, you need to create the Rolodex primary file. As explained earlier in this chapter (see "Using a Label Form with Merge"), you need to put the form definition into your primary document initial codes. Do so by following these three steps:

1. Press Format (Shift-F8).

2. Select **Document** (3).

3. Choose Initial **C**odes (2).

Then select the `Cardstock - Wide` paper form as described before, and set margins for .5" on all four sides. The Initial Codes screen should look something like figure 9.20. Then exit back to your main edit window and create the rest of your primary merge file, using the merge codes shown in figure 9.21.

Note the blank line between {FIELD}CitySt~ and {FIELD}OfficeP~ as well as the tabs used for both phone numbers. The blank line and two tabs are formatting details necessary so the Rolodex cards look right when printed.

Save the primary file with a .PF extension, as in ROLODEX.PF, so that the file will be easy to identify later.

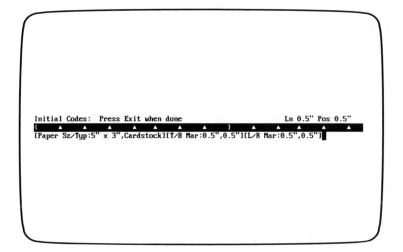

Fig. 9.20.

The Initial Codes screen for the Rolodex primary file.

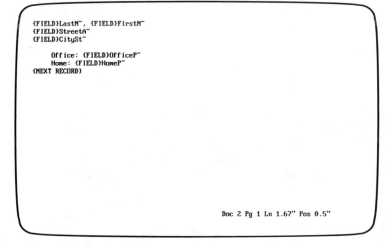

Fig. 9.21.

A primary Rolodex file with merge codes.

Merging and Printing the Cards

Once you have created the secondary and primary Rolodex files, you are ready for the merge itself. Here are the steps:

1. Press Merge/Sort (Ctrl-F9) and select **Merge** (**1**).

2. At the `Primary file:` prompt, press List (F5) and then press Enter. Now highlight ROLODEX.PF and press **Retrieve** (**1**).

3. At the `Secondary file:` prompt, press List (F5) and then press Enter. Now highlight ROLODEX.SF and press **Retrieve (1)**.

You see a `* Merging *` message in the lower left corner of your screen and then the merged file with information in the correct location on each page, as in figure 9.22.

Fig. 9.22.

One screen of a merged Rolodex file.

```
Armstrong, Edna
579 N. Pennsylvania
Indianapolis, IN 46204

      Office: (317) 791-4678
      Home: (317) 791-2315
================================================================================
Buckley, Patrick G.
290 E. Carillo
Santa Barbara, CA 93101

      Office: (805) 857-1265
      Home: (805) 423-8550
================================================================================
Douglas, Deborah K.
117 W. Monroe
Phoenix, AZ 85003

      Office: (602) 845-1290
      Home:
================================================================================
Gibxon, Maxine
685 Peachtree NE.
Atlanta, GA 30309
                                              Doc 2 Pg 1 Ln 0.5" Pos 0.5"
```

Scan down through the document, using the PgDn command, and check for any misplaced text. If you find fields missing, or misplaced, retrieve your secondary file and make the necessary repairs. It is better to fix the original secondary file itself rather than the merged file—especially if you plan to use that secondary file again. If you had to make repairs, resave the secondary file, dump your merged document, and perform the merge again.

Next send the corrected merged file to the printer, using Print (Shift-F7), **Full Document (1)**. The printed file should resemble figure 9.23.

That's all there is to it. If you have other tractor-feed card stock in different sizes, use the same steps outlined in this chapter for those forms.

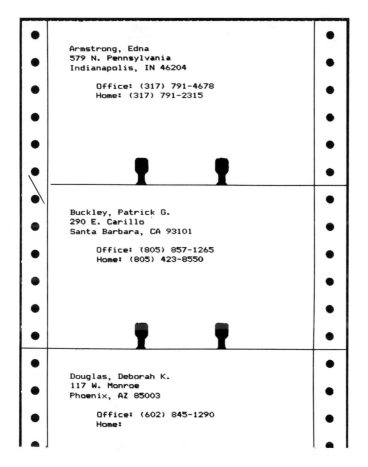

Fig. 9.23.

Several printed Rolodex cards created with WordPerfect 5.1.

Summary

This chapter has shown how easily you can create labels, using the LABELS.WPM macro provided by WordPerfect Corporation. With WordPerfect, you can print tractor-feed as well as sheet-feed labels. You can even print individual labels out of a document containing hundreds of labels or merge a list of names and addresses into a label primary file.

In this chapter, you have also discovered how easy it is to create and print Rolodex cards on a tractor-feed printer. Isn't it good news that the old printer is useful for something, even if you do have a state-of-the-art Hewlett-Packard LaserJet IID or III, or a PostScript printer with dozens of scalable fonts? This chapter has shown how to create a Rolodex paper form, how to modify the form so the text fits properly on the cards, and how to create Rolodex merge files.

Part IV

Creating Informal and Formal Reports

Creating Memos and Minutes of Meetings

Creating Formal Reports

10

Creating Memos and Minutes of Meetings

What would a company do if memos from one employee to another were suddenly banned? How would anyone follow up on assigned jobs, keep track of events and activities, inform other workers of job tasks, or record a transfer of information from one worker to another? Obviously memos are a necessary part of business operations. In fact, they are the most frequently used form of communication among members of the same organization. Likewise, minutes of meetings are important forms of communication.

In this chapter you will discover some ways to automate memo activity with the macros included on the Applications Disk. And you will learn how best to create minutes of meetings so that participants of the meeting will have an accurate record of meeting topics and motions.

Creating Office Memos

An office memo, or memo, as it is usually called, is basically an informal letter between company employees. It is intended to expedite the flow of information within an organization. Though technically memos may be short or long, single or multipaged, generally they are brief and to the point. Remember that a memo is intended as a fast, economical, and efficient way to replay important news, so stick to the point under discussion. However, if the nature, purpose, and scope of the subject demand a longer communication, exceptions are permissible.

Like all other office correspondence, memos serve a dual purpose—they transmit information from one party to another, and they provide a record of what information was transmitted. They also reduce phone calls and make it easier to convey complicated messages.

Memos can be either of two types: *interoffice memo* or *intraoffice memo*. Interoffice memos are sent between different offices or departments of a corporation; intraoffice memos are used within the same department of an organization.

Memos have numerous uses, including these:

- Announcing company policies
- Requesting information
- Exchanging information
- Instructing employees
- Delegating responsibilities
- Confirming conversations
- Reporting results

Overall, memos provide a record of decisions made and virtually all actions taken in an organization. Effective managers use memos to inform employees about company goals and to motivate them to achieve these goals.

Memo Planning

Before you create a memo, consider these questions:

- What is the primary goal of your memo?
- Who will receive your memo?
- What information do you want to send?
- What information is the most important? The least?
- Should your style be formal or informal?

The reader should see at a glance the news contained in your memo. As you organize the information to include in your memo, remember that the opening paragraph should be reserved for your most important information. Memos are intended to convey information in an easy-to-read but abbreviated format. Leave any informal, personal notes for the final paragraph ("It was great to see you again." "Enjoyed the golf—next round is at my club!").

If you are writing a memo to an employee who works under your leadership, you will want to convey enough information to enable the employee to carry out your request. A memo written to a fellow worker within your department will certainly carry a different slant from one to the president of the company or chairman of the board—whom you may never have met if you work in a large organization.

Keep in mind as you plan your memo that a written communication becomes part of a *paper trail* of evidence of your work. Managers generally keep all memos sent that concern important projects, so it is wise to consider carefully what you write in a memo. After a project is completed, good work can be documented from your reports; but, on the other hand, errors can glare from a stack of memos.

In Doc 2 you can create notes as you plan your memo, using Switch (Shift-F3) and the memo itself in Doc 1. Use the PRIOS template mentioned in Chapter 3 to keep track of your planning.

Parts of a Memo

All memos have much the same form. However, the format, or arrangement, of a memo's parts may differ from one business to another. The generally accepted elements of a memo are as follows:

1. *TO:* The intended reader of the memo
2. *FROM:* Who sent the memo
3. *DATE:* The date the memo originated
4. *SUBJECT:* The topic covered by the memo
5. *Body of the memo* The message itself

Because memos are news summaries, they never include such formal features as an inside address, salutation, complimentary close, and signature. If a memo is typed by a second person, the memo's author may initial the memo at the end of the FROM: line to indicate that he or she has read the memo before sending it, but this is not a necessary element in a memo.

Generally in the TO: and FROM: lines both the name and title of the sender and receiver should appear, as in

TO: John Jacobs, President
FROM: Jason Frank, Chairman, Board of Directors

If, however, you are sending the memo to someone within your own department or to someone outside your department with whom you have a close working relationship, you can omit the titles. And if the memo is to someone within your immediate section of a department, the use of a first name only may suffice. A courtesy title such as Mr., Mrs., or Dr. is generally omitted from all memos.

If the memo is being sent to more than one person, current usage permits the inclusion of the other names on the same TO: line, as in

TO: John Jacobs, Judy Howard, and Kevin Moss

Generally the secretary in charge of sending the memos through interoffice mail adds a check mark to the listed name of the particular person who receives that copy. In other words, if one copy of the memo is sent to Judy Howard, that copy has her name checked.

Many memos are filed by date, so make sure the date is prominently displayed. You may also add the time to this line if you are reporting progress by the hour.

The SUBJECT: line indicates briefly what topic is being covered. A good SUBJECT: line encapsulates the message that follows and makes it easy to file. The first letter of each main word may be capitalized, if you wish. Examples of typical SUBJECT lines are as follows:

SUBJECT: *July Meeting for the Planning Commission*
SUBJECT: *New Parking Policy for Workers*
SUBJECT: *Schedule for Public Relations Brochure*

Notice that the subject line is often underlined or bolded so the reader can find this information at a glance.

The *body* or message of the memo should be typed in block style (with no indentations for paragraphs), single-spaced with double spacing between paragraphs, and justified right and left. Generally the organization of facts in memos follows the direct style—where the main idea is presented first and followed by explanations or facts. An indirect memo, where the facts and explanations are presented first and the main idea or conclusion comes last, is rarely used except as a general announcement.

Brevity, courtesy, clarity, and tact are four requisites of messages in office memoranda. The final paragraph of a memo may include a request, if needed, for action or a return of information. In most cases, remind the reader how to contact the author of the memo ("If you have any questions, please call me at 555-1234.").

If the memo is short and the sender wants to use a half-page rather than a full 8 1/2-by-11-inch sheet, an alternative condensed format, as shown in figure 10.1, is permissible.

```
                    Interoffice Memo

TO: Alfred Eastman               FROM: Ralph Blodgett

SUBJECT: November 19 Meeting     DATE: November 12, 1990

Please plan to attend a special staff meeting scheduled for Monday, November
19, at 10:00 a.m., in the Conference Room. A revised agenda is attached.

Please let me know as soon as possible (extension 6217) if you will be unable
to attend. Thanks very much.




                                   Doc 2 Pg 1 Ln 3.33" Pos 3.11"
```

Fig. 10.1.

A condensed form for half-sheet memos.

How you send memos depends on whether you are mailing to only one person or a few people or, alternatively, to an overall group of people. Single, sealed envelopes are appropriate for small mailings. Place confidential memos inside sealed envelopes with the warning *CONFIDENTIAL,* followed by the recipient's name, somewhere on the front side. Large mailings can generally be routed in unsealed, string-tied interoffice mailers. These envelopes have lines for writing the recipient's name and department.

Automated Memo Macros

 Included on the Applications Disk are two macros to automate the creation of your memos—MEMOA.WPM and MEMOB.WPM. Both macros provide on-screen prompts for the recipient of the memo and the topic to be discussed.

The macros differ only in the arrangement of the TO:, FROM:, DATE:, and SUBJECT: lines. The items on the right in MEMOA.WPM are aligned on a 1" relative tab setting; the left-hand items are aligned on the left margin. MEMOB.WPM has the right-hand items aligned on a 1.2" tab setting and the left-hand items aligned by semicolon (see figs. 10.2 and 10.3).

Interoffice Memo

TO: Barrie Peterson
FROM: Frank Jones, Karen Babcock, Alfred Burbank
DATE: September 12, 1990
SUBJECT: Convention Invitation

We have been invited to make a one-hour presentation on promotional mailing at the annual convention of the International Marketing Institute. The convention will be held on December 12-15, 1990, at the Sheraton West, 2961 Wilshire Blvd., Los Angeles, CA 90010.

I don't have all the details yet, but we need to start planning the presentation as soon as possible. Please block out those days on your calendar now so as to avoid any conflicting appointments.

The invitation represents an excellent opportunity to show some of the major promotional achievements of our department during the last three years, and it could result in a number of new clients to our company. Let's do our best to make it a great presentation!

As soon as I receive more detailed information about the exact day and time for our presentation, I'll set up a meeting so the departmental leaders can discuss it.

Fig. 10.2.

The macro MEMOA.WPM memo format.

Interoffice Memo

     TO: Frank Jones, Karen Babcock, Alfred Burbank
   FROM: Barrie Peterson
   DATE: September 12, 1990
SUBJECT: Convention Invitation

We have been invited to make a one-hour presentation on promotional mailing at the annual convention of the International Marketing Institute. The convention will be held on December 12-15, 1990, at the Sheraton West, 2961 Wilshire Blvd., Los Angeles, CA 90010.

I don't have all the details yet, but we need to start planning the presentation as soon as possible. Please block out those days on your calendar now so as to avoid any conflicting appointments.

The invitation represents an excellent opportunity to show some of the major promotional achievements of our department during the last three years, and it could result in a number of new clients to our company. Let's do our best to make it a great presentation!

As soon as I receive more detailed information about the exact day and time for our presentation, I'll set up a meeting so the departmental leaders can discuss it.

Fig. 10.3.

The macro MEMOB.WPM memo format.

After you decide the format you prefer, copy the macro to your C:\WP51\MACROS subdirectory, and rename (using List [F5], Enter, 3) the macro to MEMO.WPM.

To use the macro, start with a clear screen, press Macro (Alt-F10) or press Alt-M from the Applications Disk, type *memo*, and press Enter. Answer the following two prompts and press Enter after your answer:

```
1. Type receiver's full name and press Enter:

2. Type subject of this memo:
```

The macro will then format the page, turn on full justification, add the necessary information at the top, insert a graphic line under SUBJECT:, and position the cursor for you to type the body of the memo.

Note: The supplied macros come with the standard name *John Doe* as the sender. To use either macro you must change *John Doe* to your name. But the supplied name is clearly marked inside the macro and should be fairly easy to change. Follow these steps to make this change:

1. Press Macro Define (Ctrl-F10).

    ⌨ Access the **Tools** pull-down menu, select **Macro**, and choose **Define**.

2. Type *memo*, *memoa*, or *memob* and press Enter.

3. Press **Edit (2)**.

4. Use the down arrow to reach the macro line that reads

    ```
    {Bold}FROM:{bold}{Tab}John Doe{Enter}
    ```

On the right, you will see the descriptive phrase `{;}← Change to your name~`, like the last line in figure 10.4.

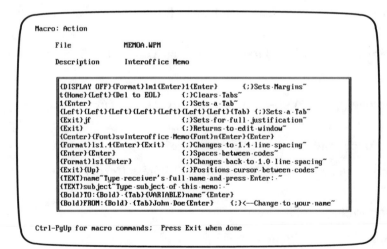

```
Macro: Action

    File            MEMOA.WPM

    Description     Interoffice Memo

    {DISPLAY OFF}{Format}lm1{Enter}1{Enter}      {;}Sets·Margins~
    t{Home}{Left}{Del to EOL}     {;}Clears·Tabs~
    1{Enter}                      {;}Sets·a·Tab~
    {Left}{Left}{Left}{Left}{Left}{Tab} {;}Sets·a·Tab~
    {Exit}jf                      {;}Sets·for·full·justification~
    {Exit}                        {;}Returns·to·edit·window~
    {Center}{Font}suInteroffice·Memo{Font}n{Enter}{Enter}
    {Format}ls1.4{Enter}{Exit}    {;}Changes·to·1.4·line·spacing~
    {Enter}{Enter}                {;}Spaces·between·codes~
    {Format}ls1{Enter}            {;}Changes·back·to·1.0·line·spacing~
    {Exit}{Up}                    {;}Positions·cursor·between·codes~
    {TEXT}name~Type·receiver's·full·name·and·press·Enter:·~
    {TEXT}subject~Type·subject·of·this·memo:·~
    {Bold}TO:{Bold}·{Tab}{VARIABLE}name~{Enter}
    {Bold}FROM:{Bold}·{Tab}John·Doe{Enter}      {;}<--Change·to·your·name~

Ctrl-PgUp for macro commands;  Press Exit when done
```

Fig. 10.4.

The edit window for MEMOA macro.

5. Use the right arrow to move to the J of John Doe.

6. Press Del eight times.

7. Type your name where John Doe was.

8. Press Exit (F7) to save the revised macro and return to the normal edit screen.

Multiple-Page Memos

If a memo continues beyond the first page, go back to the top of the first page and include a continuation header for the following pages, like this one:

John Jacobs 2   October 16, 1990

The steps for doing this are as follows:

1. Press Home, Home, up arrow to go to the top of the document.

2. Press Format (Shift-F8) and **Page (2)**
   ⌧ Choose **Page** from the **Layout** menu.

3. Press **Headers (3)**, then Header A **(1)**.

4. Press Every **Page (2)**.

5. In the header window, type the name of the first listed recipient of the memo.

6. Press Center (Shift-F6) and Ctrl-B to insert the page code ⌃**B**.

7. Press Flush Right (Alt-F6).

8. Press Date/Outline (Shift-F5), then either Date **Text (1)** or Date Code **(2)**.

9. Press Exit (F7) once to return to the Format: Page screen.

10. Choose **Suppress** (this page only) **(8)** and then Suppress Header A **(5)**; press Y for **Yes**.

11. Press Exit to return to the edit screen.

Most of your memos, however, are limited to one page and will not need the preceding addition. Next, you see how to create a set of minutes for a meeting.

Creating Minutes for a Meeting

Minutes are records of meetings and of the actions taken. They are prepared by the recording secretary of the organization, or, in the case of a workshop or committee, by any committee member who agrees to act as the secretary. Minutes must be written clearly and accurately because they are often consulted by members of the committee to confirm a previous action. Minutes should be taken in any meeting that involves voting or other important decision-making activities.

Because keeping minutes of a meeting is so important, the recording secretary should make full notes of all business decisions and actions taken during a meeting. You need not, however, record discussions that resulted in no action.

The language for minutes is fairly standard and follows traditional lines. Although notes of a company meeting need not follow the prescribed order of a formal meeting, such as a stockholder's meeting, they should generally conform to the following order:

- Name of organization holding the meeting
- Type of meeting (monthly, quarterly, board, executive, and so on)
- Date and place of meeting
- Name of presiding officer
- Names of members present for a group of 20 or fewer; if more, the total number present
- Approval of previous meeting's minutes
- Unfinished business
- Actions taken on unfinished business
- Reports of committees assigned previously
- New business, including motions made and their adoption or rejection
- Date set for next meeting
- Time of adjournment
- Name of the recording secretary at the bottom right corner
- Approval of minutes with signature of the presiding officer

Noting General Guidelines for Minutes

Minutes should always be typed as soon as possible following the meeting, while the details are fresh in your mind. Maintain an objective tone in the minutes, without adjectives expressing personal opinion (such as a "stimulating idea," a "timely suggestion," and so on).

Minutes are either double-spaced or single-spaced, depending on the practice of your particular organization. Most minutes today are prepared in a narrative style rather than the formal outline style used a few decades ago.

To produce a formal set of minutes, set justification for full (Shift-F8, 1, 3, 4) and use a proportionally spaced font like Times Roman or Century Schoolbook. Use a bolder font for the headline and major section headers within the document. If you have a larger font, use that for the headline. In other words, take advantage of the printing capability of WordPerfect itself to prepare minutes that look as if they have been printed in a print shop.

A copy of the printed-out minutes should be given to the presiding officer of the committee or meeting for confirmation of the content and accuracy of the report. Any corrections noted by the presiding officer should be added, and copies should be distributed to all committee members, including absentees, soon after the meeting. Any significant errors discovered after distribution should be corrected, and a new copy should be sent to all members of the committee with a note pointing out the change or changes in the minutes.

Minutes serve as reminders of the jobs assigned to various members and establish an impression of the activity of the group as a whole. Distributing the minutes of a meeting, moreover, allows members to think of suggestions they might offer at the next meeting concerning topics discussed earlier.

If the minutes have not been distributed, they should be read at the next meeting and approved by the group as a whole. If corrections are suggested, they should be included in the revised copy that goes into permanent records. The name of the recording secretary is added at the bottom of minutes, generally in a flush-right position. (Use Flush Right (Alt-F6) on the WordPerfect keyboard.)

Approving the Minutes

Once the minutes have been read and approved, the word *Approved* with the date of approval should be added at the bottom left margin, followed by the secretary's name as well as the president's name if the organization requires it. Some organizations include the signature of the approving officer, written adjacent to the person's typed name.

Recording Motions

The name of the person making a motion should be included in the minutes, but not that of the person who seconds the motion. Whether the motion was carried, lost, referred to a committee for evaluation, or tabled should also be recorded. If a motion fails to receive a second, it should not be included at all. Sometimes the numbers of affirmative and negative votes are stated, although this depends on the common practice of the company in question.

The secretary responsible for taking notes may want to have prepared in advance a summary sheet containing multiple entries, such as these:

Resolution 1
  Proposed by:
  Seconded by:
  Votes for:
  Votes against:

Committee Reports

Committee reports can be entered in the minutes as a summary of the report, including the committee chairperson's name, or as a copy of the entire report, or as a simple reference to the subject of the report if the report is filed separately in a different file.

Handling Special Terms

Words like *whereas*, *resolved*, and *resolved that* should be written in all capitals or in italics with the initial letter capitalized. Names like *Board of Directors*, *Corporation*, *Chairperson*, and *Comptroller* should be capitalized. If your company uses all capital letters for these words, a comma should always follow, as in

RESOLVED, that the members of this Board go on record in extending their appreciation to Sharon McWilliams for her leadership in this year's United Way campaign.

Figures 10.5 and 10.6 illustrate the minutes of two different meetings.

Fig. 10.5.

*Minutes of a
typical executive
committee.*

Meeting of the Executive Committee

May 12, 1991

Attendance

The weekly meeting of the Executive Committee was held in the office of Jason Blake, President, at 2 p.m. on May 12, 1991. Mr. Blake presided. Present were Richard Howard, Judy Peterson, Clifton Singer, Edward Simpson, and Sarah Ryan. Christopher Edwards was absent.

Items Covered

1.   Richard Howard reported on the purchase of the new transportation van approved at the last Executive Committee Meeting. The van is to be placed into service starting next Monday.

2.   Clifton Singer provided an update report on Contract 91-23. Further information is to be presented at the May 19 meeting.

3.   Kenneth Howard reported on the two estimates for new blacktop of the entrance drive way, and moved that we accept the contract from City Paving for $23,500. The motion was carried.

4.   Edward Simpson presented the proposed budget for new computers for the marketing department. The budget included four 386 UNIQ computers with color monitors, and one Macintosh CX/40 computer.

5.   Contract 91-22 was approved in the amount of $125,000.

Adjournment

The meeting was adjourned at 3:30 p.m.

_____

Sarah Ryan, Recorder

Editorial Scheduling Meeting
February 11, 1991

The weekly editorial scheduling meeting of Monday, February 11, 1991, convened at 10:00 a.m. in the conference room. Bill Johnson served as the presiding officer. Members of the staff present included Bill Johnson, Alan Myers, Arthur Ross, Betty Stacy, and David Williams. Roger Smith was unable to attend.

Minutes

The minutes of the previous meeting, held on Monday, February 4, were read and approved. There were no corrections or omissions.

Items Covered

1. Arthur Ross presented the proposed list of articles for the June issue of the magazine. With the exception of the article on the dangers of cocaine (which will not arrive back from the author in time for this issue) the list of articles were accepted. (See attached agenda for the June issue.)

2. David Williams moved that we substitute an article from our files on tobacco in place of the cocaine manuscript. The motion was carried.

3. The staff voted to reject a manuscript titled "Take Out the Fear of Being a Parent" that has been read by all members of the committee. The vote was unanimous.

4. Alan Myers said he has the ideal artist lined up to do a 4-color illustration for the article titled "Put More Life Into Your Life." The visual will be a watercolor painting of a couple having fun at the zoo.

5. Betty Stacy reminded everyone that they submit their appropriate sections to the new "Writer's Guidelines" paper by next Monday so we can move the project into copy editing and typesetting.

6. Bill Johnson outlined the current status of the budget for the first five weeks of 1991. Records indicate we are approximately $2,300 ahead of the projected expenses for this year.

7. The next meeting will be held on Monday, February 18, at 9:30 a.m.

Adjournment

The meeting was adjourned at 11:30 a.m.

Fig. 10.6.

Minutes of an Editorial Scheduling Meeting.

Summary

This chapter has discussed why memos are important in an office environment and how they can be created automatically with two WordPerfect 5.1 macros included on the Applications Disk at the back of the book. You have seen how to create minutes for a typical company or departmental meeting. Chapter 11 delves into how to create formal office reports, using WordPerfect.

11

Creating Formal Reports

Reports fill a variety of needs in the business environment. Although the goal of reports is primarily to inform, reports can also explain, justify, persuade, solicit, or launch a new product or idea.

Generally speaking, a report is an organized presentation of information gleaned from broad research or investigation, or, more simply, the details of a trip, a survey, a test, or something similar. Some reports communicate monthly or quarterly sales figures without analysis or interpretation of data. Others offer extensive analysis and specific recommendations for action. As a result, formal reports can be short or long, simple or complex, depending on the information being presented, the extent of the research, and the goals of the author.

In this chapter, you discover how to plan your report by using the PRIOS strategy, which tells you the questions you need to ask before writing a report, what points to keep in mind as you write the report, and what format to use in a formal report. You also learn how to create a table of contents with WordPerfect 5.1, how to use styles for formatting a report, and how to use quoted material and footnotes properly in a report. Finally, after you finish writing the report, you learn eight important items to check before the report is ready to present.

Using the PRIOS Strategy
To Plan Your Report

Earlier in this book, you saw how the PRIOS strategy (purpose, readers, information, organization, and style) can assist in your letter writing. Planning is even more important for a formal report, where a logical presentation is a must. Before you begin writing the report, apply the basic elements of the PRIOS strategy to your report planning:

- *Determining your purpose.* Why are you preparing this report? What do you want the reader to do as a result of reading this report? The primary purpose is what you want your reader to do or think as a result of reading your report.

- *Understanding your readers.* Consider who will be reading this report— both the immediate audience and those likely to receive a copy of it after your primary reader is finished. Is your reader friendly toward your idea, indifferent, or hostile? If you anticipate a primarily hostile or indifferent audience, you must take that into consideration when selecting and presenting data. Will the reader understand any technical information you include? What level of explanation is necessary?

  Always try to determine from the person who requests the report the approximate length, the amount of detail desired, the format (discussed later in the chapter), and the intended distribution.

  If the report will be read only by your immediate superior, an extended memo format may be sufficient. If intended for the Board of Directors or top management of the company, the report should follow a more standard and detailed report format. Likewise, a college term paper requires a simpler format than a thesis for an advanced degree. Always keep in mind that the organization of your report should be based on what your reader needs from the report, not the chronology of your research or some other pattern convenient to yourself as the writer.

  If the report must supply basic information with no recommendations, then you can use a simple format. If you are trying to persuade a variety of readers to adopt your recommendations, then you need a more formal approach, including more detailed information to support your argument.

- *Including the necessary information.* What facts are necessary for your reader to know in order to understand your report and follow its recommendations? Where will you locate this data? How will you include it in your report?

- *Using good organization.* What is the best structure to follow in order to have your information make the maximum impact? Will your reader be able to understand the points you are making?

- *Determining style.* Will your report be formal or informal, objective or friendly, warm or to the point?

Points To Keep in Mind When Planning and Writing a Report

After you have determined who your readers will be and what your general objectives will be for your report, you are ready to write. Keep the following points in mind as you plan your writing.

Place key findings up front. For maximum impact on your readers, position your key findings carefully. This point is especially important if your readers are indifferent or hostile. The indifferent reader can find the essence of your report as he begins to read, giving you the opportunity to grab his interest. If you anticipate that hostile readers will be receiving your report, build your case gradually and present your recommendations at the end of your report, rather than at the beginning.

Move from general to specific. When presenting examples and illustrations to support your case, let the emphasis shift naturally from general examples to specific examples.

Use graphic aids to strengthen your report. The expression "A picture is worth a thousand words" emphasizes the importance of adding visual elements to a report. For example, which would be more powerful in a report about the status of auto financing: the following paragraph or the graph in figure 11.1?

> Three-fourths of all car buyers use financing for their purchase. Of those who use financing, 42 percent went to the bank for their money, 38 percent got financing from an automaker, 12 percent went to a credit union, and 3 percent used other sources.

How We Finance Our Cars

Don't Know 5%
Other 3%
Credit Unions 12%

One in four of us who bought a new car in the past 12 months paid cash. This is where the rest of us got financing:

Banks 42%

Auto-makers 38%

Source: Bank Advertising News July poll of 1,000 adults

Fig. 11.1.

A graph suitable for reports.

Make the report entirely self-contained. If the reader of your report has to look up information elsewhere to understand what you have written, the report is incomplete. To be successful, a formal report must be entirely self-contained. That is, it must include all related information needed to make the presentation you want to make. You can add support material in one or more appendixes to the report.

After you have established these points and printed them out as a reference page, you are ready to consider the exact format you will be using for your report.

Formatting the Report

All reports involve, to some extent, a specific format. Formal reports are divided into three major sections—front matter, body copy, and back matter. You might think of these three sections as the opening or summary material; the discussion itself; and any attachments of appendixes, bibliographies, or glossaries. Depending on the report's length, some or all of the following parts are appropriate in a formal report.

Front Matter

As you plan your report, you can add the following items to the front of the report:

Cover: The wrapper that encloses the pages of a report

Flyleaf: A blank page inserted after the cover

Title page: The page that contains the report title, the name of the person the report was created for, the name of the preparer, the date of the report, and possibly the preparer's company name and address

Letter of transmittal: An introductory letter that identifies the report enclosed with the letter, the person to whom the report is being sent, and the reason the report was prepared

Table of contents: An outline of the main sections in the report and the page numbers where they may be found

List of illustrations: A list of titles and captions of all tables and figures in the report with the appropriate page numbers

Abstract: A brief summary or synopsis of the report

Report Body

The following sections make up the body of a standard report:

Introduction: A brief overview of the subject of the report

Background: Information needed to understand the main body of the report

Text or body: The main discussion of the report theme; the longest section of the report

Conclusion and recommendations: A summary of the report and suggestions for further action (if appropriate)

Back Matter

You can add the following information at the end of your report:

Appendix: Support material and documentation not inserted in the body of the report

Glossary: An alphabetical list of definitions of unfamiliar terms used in the report

Bibliography: Resources cited and/or used in the report

Index: An alphabetical list of names, key subjects, and terms used in the report and page numbers where they may be found

The scope and complexity of the project determine which of these items to include. Naturally, short reports of 25 pages or fewer would contain only some of these items; reports longer than 100 pages will more likely include all the listed items.

Selecting the Appropriate Format

As one might expect, the precise order within each of the three sections differs widely from one authority to another. Many companies and governmental institutions have a preferred style for formal reports and furnish guidelines that staff members must follow. If your employer has a prepared set of style guidelines, follow it. Otherwise, you might find it helpful to find file copies of previous reports and use them as guidelines. Regardless, be prepared to modify the number of report features to fit a specific situation or goal.

Creating the Front Matter

As you determine the parts of your report, think how you can achieve the overall effect you want. Use some or all of the following elements.

Cover

Most formal reports are included in some enclosure. For short reports, a simple clear plastic folder should suffice. Longer reports should be fastened together, as in a report binder with metal strips that fold down to hold the three-hole pages in a semipermanent binder.

Flyleaf

In a longer formal report, insert a blank page after the cover and before the title page. Sometimes a blank page is inserted both at the front and at the back. A flyleaf protects the rest of the document and provides a place for the reader's comments. You can omit flyleaves in a shorter report.

Title Page

The title page is the first information page of a report, containing the report title, the date of the report, the name of the preparer, and possibly the preparer's company name and address. Figure 11.2 illustrates a printed title page of a formal report, with 1/3-inch horizontal graphic lines separating the main header from the rest of the copy.

To create graphic lines like the ones shown in figure 11.2, position your cursor where you want the graphic line to appear and do the following:

1. Press Graphics (Alt-F9) and choose Line (**5**).

   ⌨ Select Line from the Graphics menu.

2. Choose Horizontal (**1**).

3. Choose Width of Line (**4**), type *33*, and press Enter.

4. Choose Gray Shading (**5**), type *70*, and press Enter.

5. Press Exit (F7) to return to the edit window.

In an academic report, include the name of the author, the instructor, the course title and number, and the date of submission.

Why Basics Food Centers Needs

a Desktop Publishing System

Prepared for:
Harry Janson
Senior Vice President

Prepared by:

Deborah Greenough
Communications Specialist
October 15, 1990

Fig. 11.2.

A sample title page for a formal report.

Letter of Transmittal

The transmittal letter, also known as a cover letter, is used to introduce the reader to the report. The letter identifies the report enclosed with the letter, the person to whom the report is being sent (often the person who assigned the report), and the reason the report was prepared.

Keep your comments brief in a transmittal letter. Open with a paragraph explaining what you are sending and why it was prepared. In an optional second paragraph, you might include a summary of the materials being sent or perhaps call attention to specific sections of particular interest to the receiver. The closing paragraph might contain acknowledgments of help received or express a willingness to provide additional information if needed. Figure 11.3 illustrates a typical transmittal letter.

Fig. 11.3.

*A sample
transmittal letter
in memo format.*

Interoffice Memo

TO: Harry Janson, Vice President
FROM: Deborah Greenough
DATE: October 15, 1990
SUBJECT: Desktop Publishing Report

I am enclosing a copy of a report titled "Why Basics Food Centers Needs a Desktop Publishing System," which you asked me to prepare for the December executive committee meeting.

The report details the amount of money Basics Food Centers can save by switching to an in-house publishing system for our monthly newsletters and other printed publications. In the appendixes at the end you will find three different hardware estimates from local computer stores which specialize in desktop systems, catalog pages of suggested computer furniture for the hardware, and a complete breakdown of our current costs for preparing a monthly newsletter.

If you need any additional information, please let me know and I'll do my best to locate it. I hope the report will make it possible for Basics Food Centers to purchase a desktop publishing system for the publications we produce.

The transmittal letter provides a permanent record of transmittal, both for the sender and for the receiver. The letter of transmittal directly follows the title page (or is attached to the title page) and can appear in any acceptable business letter or memorandum format. If the report is sent outside the company, use a standard letter format; if the report is intended only for people within the company, use a memo format.

Abstract

An abstract, which normally follows the title page in a technical report, is a brief summary or synopsis of the report, enabling the prospective reader to scan the highlights of the report at a glance. Abstracts are often published independently in periodical indexes that can be accessed by a computer. Two such monthly abstract references are *Dissertation Abstracts International* and *Work Related Abstracts*.

Keep in mind that there are two basic types of abstracts: *descriptive* abstracts and *informative* abstracts (sometimes called *summary* abstracts). A descriptive abstract lists the topics covered but does not specify the final recommendations. An informative abstract contains the thesis or recommendation and its proof, and presents the thesis or recommendation in the first paragraph. A third type of abstract, the *mixed* abstract, is a combination of the informative and descriptive abstract. This type of abstract contains part summary and part description.

Generally the abstract is from 150 to 250 words in length and should make sense by itself outside the report. Figure 11.4 illustrates a summary abstract for a desktop publishing (DTP) system proposal.

Abstract

This report describes the scope and nature of desktop publishing in business today and how it relates to publications produced by the Basics Food Centers. The report defines the seven benefits that desktop publishing offers to a company that publishes monthly newsletters and quarterly reports and explains why Basics Food Centers needs to purchase a desktop publishing system of its own.

Among the major benefits that a desktop publishing system offers are increased efficiency in the production process itself, a significant cost savings to the company, a decrease in the time needed to produce various publications, and more attractive final products. The cost savings for preparing our own company newsletters, rather than sending them out to a print shop, are sufficient that the desktop publishing system would pay for itself in less than four years.

The information for this report came from research in the current literature on desktop publishing (both books and periodicals), from interviews with three different local distributors of desktop publishing equipment, and from the actual expenses of preparing and publishing our company newsletter at an outside print shop during the past 12 months.

Fig. 11.4.

A summary abstract for a DTP proposal.

Table of Contents

A report's table of contents contains its main headings or sections and the page numbers of the first page of each section or chapter. The table always begins on a new page, often following the abstract. (The table of contents and its page number are never listed in the table of contents.)

With the abstract, the table of contents helps a reader find certain sections he may wish to examine so that he doesn't have to read the entire report itself. Figure 11.5 illustrates a typical table of contents for a report on a desktop publishing system.

Fig. 11.5.

A typical table of contents for a company report.

Table of Contents

Transmittal Memo i
List of Illustrations ii
Abstract 1
Introduction 2
Desktop Publishing Defined 3
Seven Benefits of DTP Explained 6
Why DTP System Needed 8
Other Uses of DTP System 9
Tax Write-Off Over 4-Year Period 12
DTP Equipment Needed—Detailed Analysis 13
DTP Equipment Already Owned—Savings 19
Cost Summary Breakdown of DTP System 20
Return on Investment—Detailed Analysis 21
Printing Costs 22
Conclusion and Recommendation 24
Appendixes:
Appendix A. CompuCom Systems Price Quote 26
Appendix B. Micro Services, INC. Price Quote 27
Appendix C. Everex Computer Specifications 28
Appendix D. Catalog Pictures of Computer Furniture 29
Appendix E. Breakdown of Newsletter Printing Costs 34

To create a table of contents with WordPerfect, you must mark the passages that you want included in your contents page so that WordPerfect can generate the table itself. Here are the steps for marking text:

1. Position the cursor at the left edge of the passage to be included in the table of contents.

2. Press Block (F11 or Alt-F4) and move the cursor to the right edge of the passage.

    ⌨Highlight the passage with the mouse.

3. Press Mark Text (Alt-F5) and select ToC (**1**).

    ⌨Select Table of Contents from the **M**ark menu.

4. At the prompt for ToC level, type *1* for a first-level heading or *2* for a second-level subhead; then press Enter.

5. Go through the entire report, marking each entry for the table of contents.

When you have marked all passages for your table of contents, you must define the location for the table of contents and the numbering style for each level of heading (if desired). Move the cursor to the position where you want your table of contents to appear. Generally the table of contents follows the last page of your front matter (title page, abstract, foreword, or preface, depending on what your report contains). Complete these steps:

1. Insert a hard page break by pressing Ctrl-Enter, creating a new page. The cursor is now at the top of what will become your table of contents page.

2. Press Center (Shift-F6), type a title for the table of contents, and press Enter as many times as you want to add blank lines under the title.

3. Press Mark Text (Alt-F5), select **D**efine (**5**), and then select Define Table of Contents (**1**).

    ⌨Select **D**efine from the **M**ark menu; then select Table of Contents from the pop-out menu.

4. Enter the number of heading levels you want in the table by selecting **N**umber of Levels (**1**).

5. If you selected more than one level of entries and you want the last level of entries to wrap together (rather than appear as separate lines), select **D**isplay Last Level in Wrapped Format (**2**) and press Y to wrap the last level of entries. Skip this step if you want the last level to remain on separate lines.

6. Select **P**age Numbering (**3**) and enter a numbering style for each level. The arrow keys let you move among the levels. (Figure 11.5 uses the Flush Right With Leader (**5**) page-numbering style.)

7. Press Exit (F7) to exit the Page Numbering menu.

8. Press PgDn to move to the next page following the table of contents page.

9. Press Format (Shift-F8) and select **Page** (**2**).

   ⌨Select **Page** from the **Layout** menu.

10. Select Page **Numbering** (**6**) and **New** Page Number (**2**), type *1*, and press Enter.

11. Press Exit (F7).

After you mark all the passages to be included in the table of contents and define the table of contents, you are ready to generate the table. To do so, follow these steps:

1. Press Mark Text (Alt-F5) and select **Generate** (**6**).

   ⌨Select **Generate** from the **Mark Text** menu.

2. Select **Generate Tables, Indexes, Cross-References, etc.** (**5**).

3. Press Y to continue (and replace old tables, lists, and indexes, if any).

All tables, lists, and indexes in the report are generated at the same time, and the placement of cross-references and endnotes is updated. If you change the report, you can regenerate the table of contents as many times as you like.

Because WordPerfect uses standard formatting features to format tables of contents, you can edit them as you would any other WordPerfect text. You can use both single and double spacing or even other measurements between lines. For example, if the table of contents in figure 11.5 were completely double-spaced, it would have been difficult to position all the text on a single page. So a 1.5 line-spacing code was inserted at the beginning of the line *Abstract . . . ii*, and a 1.1 line-spacing code in front of the Appendixes section at the bottom. To specify such codes, follow these steps:

1. Press Format (Shift-F8) and select **Line** (**1**).

   ⌨Choose **Line** from the **Layout** menu.

2. Select Line **Spacing** (**6**).

3. Type any number or decimal or fraction you want for line spacing, such as *1.2, 1.15, 1.75,* or *1 3/4*, and press Enter.

4. Press Exit (F7) to leave the Format:Line menu.

Wherever you have inserted a line-spacing setting, a line-spacing code like **[Ln Spacing:1.2]** will appear in Reveal Codes. From this point until the next line-spacing code, the line spacing will be 1.2 times that of the normal single-spaced line.

List of Illustrations

If a formal report includes more than five illustrations or five tables, they should be included in a list of illustrations along with the appropriate page numbers. This section should be titled *List of Illustrations* and should begin on a new page following the table of contents.

If the report contains numerous exhibits, you may want to list illustrations separately from tables. Illustrations and tables are numbered consecutively with Arabic numbers throughout the report. They can be marked and defined in the same manner as the table of contents. The generation process can then create both lists at the same time.

Creating the Report Body

You are ready to begin the body of the report, the presentation of the information in the report. The body itself can be broken down into parts: the introduction, the background statement, the central information, and the conclusion and recommendations. This section discusses these elements; explains how to use styles, quoted material, and footnotes in the report body; and offers formatting guidelines.

Introduction

An introduction supplies a brief overview of the subject of the report. In the introduction, state the subject of the report, its purpose and scope, and the way you intend to develop the topic. If a background statement is omitted (see the next section), then include in the introduction any general information the reader needs in order to understand the detailed data in the body of the report.

If a report includes individual chapters for different sections, the introduction can be either a single element on a separate page or a chapter in itself titled *Introduction*. In either case, number the introduction page as page 1 of the report. (Number the front matter with lowercase Roman numerals, such as i, ii, and iii.)

Background Statement

The optional background statement provides information needed by the reader in order to understand the main body of the report. If just a paragraph or two, this information can be included as part of the introduction.

Body of the Report

The body includes the main discussion of the report theme and is by far the longest section of the report. You can write it as a single chapter with sections, or in multiple chapters if the report is lengthy. The body includes facts needed to establish the case and details of how the topic was investigated, how the problem was solved, and how the best choice from a number of alternatives was selected by the report author or research team.

For most formal reports, there is no best way to organize the body copy. The body copy could list facts first and lead up to a conclusion, or list the conclusion first and add facts that support the conclusion, or list research in a chronological sequence. How the text is organized depends on the topic presented. Generally, though, the text is organized into sections much like chapters in a book.

If the report contains several chapters organized in sections, put a separate title page at the start of each section of the report. Center the section page horizontally and vertically, as in figure 11.6. Vertical centering in WordPerfect is activated at the top of the page; press Format (Shift-F8), **Page (2)**, and **Center Page Top to Bottom (1)**. Centering text horizontally is accomplished with Center (Shift-F6), or Format (Shift-F8), **Line (1)**, **Justification (3)**, and **Center (2)**.

Styles for the Report Body

A WordPerfect style is a special tool that you can use to format a single document or a group of documents in a certain way. Styles can include virtually any formatting code you might want to put into a document. Styles can also include text, graphic figures, and lines.

WordPerfect styles can assist in the creation of company reports and make the formatting process virtually automatic. Styles are especially useful if you print the report in a variety of different fonts or font sizes.

For example, suppose that you created a 65-page report, using 12-point Times Roman for body copy and 14-point Helvetica for all section headings. But when you submit the report, your department head says that the content of the report is acceptable but that she doesn't like Times Roman for report copy. She would rather you print the report by using Century Schoolbook for the body copy.

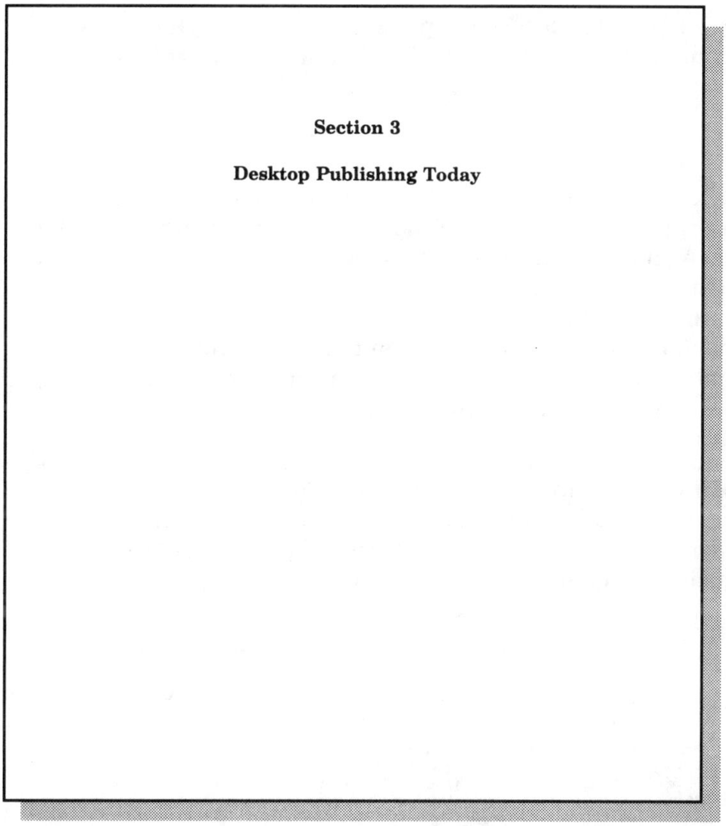

Section 3

Desktop Publishing Today

Fig. 11.6.

A sample section title page.

If you inserted the Times Roman font as a base font throughout the report, you would have to locate every wrong font code, delete it, and insert a code for the alternative font. Because you cannot use the search and replace feature to change font types or font sizes, it could be quite a chore indeed to locate every font change in that many pages.

However, if you used a paired style for all your headings, you could make that kind of change in a matter of seconds. Just modify the font definitions used in your heading style, and WordPerfect makes all the adjustments for you automatically throughout the document.

In addition to making entire-document changes an easy operation, using styles for report creation can save formatting time and keystrokes, encourage formatting consistency within the document and between similar documents, and reduce "code clutter" throughout the document.

WordPerfect offers three types of styles: open, paired, and outline. Open styles affect the document from the location of the code forward. For example, you could use open styles to change tab settings, the line spacing, or the base font, or to turn hyphenation on or off.

One excellent use for open styles in a report is the creation of a draft style and a final style. The draft style would use Courier font for the entire document, and the final style would use a proportional font like Times Roman or Century Schoolbook for the manuscript. When you create and edit the document, use the draft style to avoid "text jump," which happens when you try to display a 90-character-wide proportional font line on an 80-character-wide screen. In other words, a full page of text in a proportional font like Times Roman won't fit on a normal computer monitor, because the monitor can display only 80 characters of text (left to right) at one time. When you are through editing, switch to the final style and send the document to the printer.

Paired styles affect a particular section of text, switching on and off certain attributes. For example, you could create a paired style titled *Header* that switches up to a larger and bolder font for the section headers, and then automatically switch back to the regular font for subsequent body copy (see fig. 11.7).

Fig. 11.7.

A paired style in Reveal Codes mode.

```
In other words, for less than $5,000 a typical office worker in a couple of
hours can produce publications that 10 years ago required $200,000 worth
of printing equipment and took days to accomplish.

How Is Desktop Publishing Different?

So what sets desktop publishing apart from regular word processing? Several
things, actually. Most people think of word processing as something you do
to produce business correspondence—straight text in one font (usually
Courier) in one size running from the left margin to the right margin. For
emphasis, you underline something or type it in uppercase letters.
                                          Doc 1 Pg 1 Ln 5.05" Pos 3.99"
hours can pro-duce publications that 10 years ago required $200,000 worth[SRt]
of printing equipment and took days to accomplish.[HRt]
[HRt]
[Style On:Header]How Is Desktop Publishing Different?[HRt]
[Style Off:Header][HRt]
So what sets desktop publishing apart from regular word processing? Several[SRt]

things, actually. Most people think of word processing as something you do[SRt]
to produce business correspondence-[AdvLft:0.07"]-straight text in one font (usu
ally[SRt]

Press Reveal Codes to restore screen
```

When you use a paired style, WordPerfect inserts a **[Style On: Header]** code in front of the cursor position, and a **[Style Off: Header]** code after the cursor position. Type the text that you want placed in a larger or bolder font, and turn the style off when you are done. You will automatically be returned to the normal body style in effect before you activated the paired style. Switch paired styles on and off by pressing Styles (Alt-F8) and then either **On (1)** or **Off (2)**.

Outline styles organize and format material in a particular arrangement, or hierarchy. They offer up to eight open or paired styles assigned to a specific outline or paragraph-numbering level. Outline styles are useful, for example, for inserting customized paragraph-numbering setups.

To create a style, complete the following steps:

1. Press Style (Alt-F8).

   ⌨Chose **Styles** from the **Layout** menu.

2. Press Create (**3**). The Styles: Edit menu appears (see fig. 11.8). Two items on the menu contain default values.

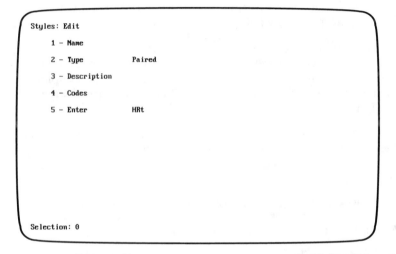

Fig. 11.8.

The Styles: Edit menu.

3. Select **Name** (**1**), type a name for your styles, and press Enter. For example, you could name the style *DRAFT.* Make sure that the name is something you can remember and easily identify months later. Because the name is not a file name, you can enter up to 12 characters for the style name.

4. Select **Type** (**2**). Three choices appear:

   ```
   Type: 1 Paired; 2 Open; 3 Outline: 0
   ```

5. Select the style type you want to use—for example, **Open** (**2**).

6. Select **Description** (**3**); type a short description (up to 54 characters) to help identify this style later. For example, type *Uses Courier font for draft editing mode* and press Enter.

7. Select Codes (**4**). For an open style, you next see a screen that looks like a Reveal Codes window. As you insert codes in your style, the codes appear in the lower half of the screen. If you add text to your style, the text appears in both halves of the screen. For a paired style, you see a box that reads `Place Style On Codes above, and Style Off Codes below.`

8. Insert any formatting codes (as for tab settings, margin settings, line spacing, font type) that you want to appear in your style. If you want to insert a Courier font code, for example, press Font (Ctrl-F8) and **B**ase Font (**4**) and then select Courier 10 cpi. If you're using a PostScript printer, you will be asked to specify a point size after selecting the font. (For a paired style, you need not turn off the codes. WordPerfect will turn off all codes automatically when you turn the style off.)

9. For an open style, press Exit (F7) three times to return to the document. For a paired style, press Exit (F7) once, select Enter (**5**), and select the effect that pressing Enter has with a paired style. For example, select **O**ff (**2**) if you want the paired style to switch back to normal when you press the Enter key.

Note that, when you create a set of styles, the styles become a part of the document you are editing. When you save the document, that set of styles is saved with the document and not in your style subdirectory. If you anticipate using this style or set of styles again, do the following:

1. From the Styles list screen, select **S**ave (**6**).

2. At the `Filename:` prompt, type a file name and press Enter.

3. If a style file already exists by that name, WordPerfect asks whether you want to replace the old style file with the newer style file. If you press N, WordPerfect prompts for another file name.

4. Press Exit (F7) to return to the document.

As you become proficient in working with WordPerfect 5.1, you may find many useful things styles can be used for in creating and formatting documents.

Quoted Material and Footnotes

Quoted material four lines or longer should be indented on both the right and left sides, through the use of the →Indent← key (Shift-F4), as in the following example:

Let's dispel the myth that design solutions appear like magic in a burst of creative energy or like a light bulb illuminating over the head of a cartoon character. Successful graphic design usually emerges from trial-and-error experimentation. Complicated solutions are the result of a willingness to try various design alternatives until the solution looks right. *Looking Good in Print*, by Roger C. Parker (Ventana Press, Chapel Hill, NC, 1988), page 7.

Footnotes created with the Footnote key (Ctrl-F7) are numbered automatically according to their position in the document. If you move a paragraph containing a footnote to a new location with WordPerfect, the footnote automatically moves with the paragraph and is renumbered automatically. The following is a typical footnote created with WordPerfect:

[2]Tom Lichty, *Design Principles for Desktop Publishers* (Scott, Foresman and Company: Glenview, Illinois, 1989), p.56.

General Guidelines for the Report Body

Headings within a chapter or section have the main words capitalized and come in three styles:

A *centered* head is placed on a line by itself, with two lines above and one line underneath. The head can be in either a larger or bolder font.

A *side* head is flush left on a line by itself and bolded, with one or two blank lines above and one blank line underneath.

A *run-in* head forms the first sentence of a paragraph and is generally bolded, underlined, or italicized, depending on its position in the structure. Following are samples of these three types of headings:

This is a Centered Head

This is a Side Head

A ***run-in head*** makes up the first few words or first sentence of a paragraph and is flush with the left margin.

If you want to arrange the body of your report in an outline format rather than with heads and subheads, use a combined Roman numeral/alphabet system for the general outline of the body copy, as used by students when writing term papers. Following is a sample outline style:

    I. Main Heading
        A. Subheading
            1. Sub-subheading
            2. Sub-subheading
        B. Subheading
            1. Sub-subheading
            2. Sub-subheading
   II. Main Heading

WordPerfect's outline feature—Shift-F5, **Define** (6)—offers a variety of choices for your outline, as shown in figure 11.9.

Fig. 11.9.

Menu for defining an outline.

```
Paragraph Number Definition

    1 - Starting Paragraph Number              1
        (in legal style)
                                      Levels
                            1    2    3    4    5    6    7    8
    2 - Paragraph           1.   a.   i.   (1)  (a)  (i)  1)   a)
    3 - Outline             I.   A.   1.   a.   (1)  (a)  i)   a)
    4 - Legal (1.1.1)       1    .1   .1   .1   .1   .1   .1   .1
    5 - Bullets             •    o    -    ■    *    +    .    x
    6 - User-defined

    Current Definition      I.   A.   1.   a.   (1)  (a)  i)   a)
    Attach Previous Level        No   No   No   No   No   No   No

    7 - Enter Inserts Paragraph Number         Yes

    8 - Automatically Adjust to Current Level  Yes

    9 - Outline Style Name


Selection: 0
```

In version 5.1, you can copy or move entire sections of your outline along with related text—a feature not incorporated in earlier versions of the program.

Provide ample margins around a report. If the report is to be bound or fastened on the left side, make the left margin 1.5 inches or perhaps 1.75 inches wide, with 1-inch margins on the remaining sides.

Conclusion and Recommendations

The conclusion summarizes the report, pulling together the results of the study into one location. Here you, the reader, are told what you have learned and its implications. The conclusion can include suggestions for further action (if appropriate), or the recommendations—if numerous—can be put into their own section following the conclusion. In a report containing several chapters, the conclusion is a chapter by itself.

Creating the Back Matter

Several different items can make up the back matter of your report. In general, back matter can comprise appendixes, a glossary of terms, a bibliography, and an index. You can use any of these in a formal report to supplement the information in the body of your report.

Appendix

An appendix includes support material and documentation not inserted in the body of the report. Generally, information that is too detailed to go in the body is added to the report as an appendix. Material for an appendix includes survey results, questionnaires, text of interviews conducted, pertinent correspondence, charts, and other supplementary data. A report can contain one or more appendixes, with each appendix containing similar types of material.

If appendixes are labeled, they are generally referred to alphabetically—Appendix A, Appendix B, and so on. However, never title a single appendix in a report as Appendix A. If you have an Appendix A, you logically must include an Appendix B in the report.

Glossary

A glossary is an alphabetical list of definitions of unfamiliar terms used in the report. Include a glossary only if your report contains many words and expressions that might be unfamiliar to your intended audience. Arrange the glossary entries alphabetically, each on a new line, with the definitions following the dictionary entry style. The glossary must begin on a new page. It can be a separate section or included as one of the appendixes. The glossary included at the back of this book provides an example of a typical glossary for a publication.

Bibliography

A bibliography is a list in alphabetical order of all sources that were consulted in preparing the report, but excluded from the body copy itself. If the report references all sources used, then the bibliography is excluded.

Like most other elements in either the front matter or the back matter, the bibliography starts on a page by itself and, if short, can be centered on the page through the WordPerfect page-center feature discussed earlier in this chapter.

A bibliography is formatted through the use of hanging indents. In WordPerfect, you create a hanging indent by pressing the Indent key and then Shift-Tab. Here are two examples of hanging-indent bibliography entries:

Mary A. DeVries, *Complete Secretary's Handbook*. Prentice Hall: Englewood Cliffs, NJ, 1988.

L. E. Frailey, *Handbook of Business Letters*. Prentice Hall: Englewood Cliffs, New Jersey, 1989.

Index

An index is an alphabetical list of names, key subjects, and terms used in the report, as well as page numbers where these items can be found. Although most normal office reports do not contain an index, large reports containing hundreds of pages might. An index makes it possible for a reader to quickly locate primary references to a specific topic in the report itself and is useful for reports of unusual length. The index to this book serves as an example of a publication index. Indexes are useful especially for large reference works and manuals.

WordPerfect makes indexing large reports fairly easy. There are two basic ways to index a report: create a concordance file that contains all the terms to be indexed, or manually mark all entries you want indexed throughout the document.

The concordance method is easier, of course. Start with a clear screen, type a word or phrase you want indexed, and press Enter. Repeat this procedure for every word or phrase that you want indexed. Don't worry about arranging the words alphabetically; WordPerfect will do that for you automatically when it creates the index.

To use the concordance method of developing an index, follow these steps:

1. Save the file to disk.

2. Open the file you want indexed.

3. Move to the end of the document (if that is where you want your index created) and create a new page by pressing Ctrl-Enter.

4. Press Center (Ctrl-F6), type *Index* at the top of the page, and press Enter several times to move to where you want the index to begin.

5. Press Mark Text (Alt-F5) and select **Define** (**5**).

   ⌨Select **Define** from the **Mark** menu.

6. Choose Define Index (**3**); the Mark Text: Define screen appears (see fig. 11.10).

   ⌨Select **Index** from the pop-out menu.

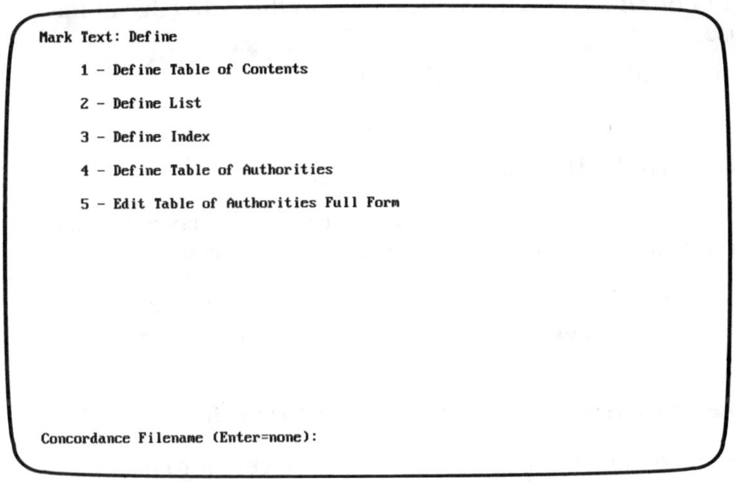

```
Mark Text: Define

     1 - Define Table of Contents

     2 - Define List

     3 - Define Index

     4 - Define Table of Authorities

     5 - Edit Table of Authorities Full Form




Concordance Filename (Enter=none):
```

Fig. 11.10.

The Mark Text: Define screen.

7. At the `Concordance Filename (Enter=none):` prompt, type the name of the file containing your concordance-index words (including the full path).

8. Select the type of page numbering—for example, Flush Right Page Numbers with **Leader** (**5**).

You are then returned to the edit window of the file that you plan to index. But if you press Reveal Codes (F11 or Alt-F3), you will see that the program has inserted a **[Def Mark: Index,5;*filename*]** code where your cursor was located in step 4. Generate the index with these three steps:

1. Press Mark Text (Alt-F5) and **Generate** (**6**).

   ⌨Choose **Generate** from the **Mark** menu.

2. Select **Generate Tables, Indexes, Cross-References, etc.** (**5**).

3. Press Y at the `Existing tables, list, and indexes will be replaced. Continue? Yes (No)` prompt.

During the generation process, every page containing the words and phrases in your Concordance file will be noted and included in the index.

The second method for creating an index is to mark each reference individually for inclusion in the index and then generate the index. To mark words or passages for inclusion in an index, follow these steps:

1. Position the cursor at the left edge of the word to be included in the index.

2. Press Block (F11 or Alt-F4) and move the cursor to the right edge of the word or phrase.

   ⌨Highlight the word or phrase with the mouse.

3. Press Mark Text (Alt-F5) and select Index (3).

   ⌨Select Index from the Mark menu.

4. Press Enter at the `Index heading:` prompt to use the displayed text as an index heading, or enter your own heading for the passage.

5. Press Enter to use the displayed text (if any) for the subheading, or enter your own text for a subheading. Or press Cancel (F1) to skip the subheading.

6. Go through the entire report, marking each entry for the index.

When you are finished marking text for the index, move the cursor to the end of the document. Then create an index definition on a new page, following these steps:

1. At the very end of the document, press Ctrl-Enter to create a new page.

2. Press Center (Shift-F6) and type *Index* at the top of the new page. Press Enter several times to move to the location where you want the index created.

3. Press Mark Text (Alt-F5) and select Define (5).

   ⌨Choose Define from the Mark menu.

4. Select Index (3).

5. Press Enter at the `Concordance Filename (Enter=none):` prompt.

6. Select the type of page numbering—for example, Flush Right Page Numbers with Leader (5).

You are returned to the edit window of the file that you plan to index. Generate the index with these three steps:

1. Press Mark Text (Alt-F5) and Generate (6).

   ⌨Choose Generate from the Mark menu.

2. Select Generate Tables, Indexes, Cross-References, etc. (5).

3. Press Y at the `Existing tables, list, and indexes will be replaced. Continue? Yes (No)` prompt.

Using Macros To Create a Report

The Applications Disk contains a number of macros that can help in the writing and formatting of a formal report. In particular, try the Alt-B macro (accesses the Base Font menu), the Alt-C macro (centers text right and left in a line), the Alt-F macro (a pop-up window for inserting fractions into your text), the Alt-H macro (turns on hyphenation), the Alt-I macro (italic font), the Alt-J macro (switches on justification), the HEADER macro (inserts the name of the document and page number on every page of your report except the page where the macro is activated), the NOTE macro (a pop-up window for taking notes for a report), and the FOOTNOTE macro (prompts for book reference information and inserts the data into a footnote).

Eight Things To Check When Your Report Is Written

1. Has someone else read the report word for word to see that it makes sense and uses proper language?

2. Are the pages properly numbered?

3. Are the margins, paragraph spacing, and other organizational matters attractive and consistent throughout the report?

4. Are proper names correctly spelled?

5. Have all quoted statistics been checked on the printed copy with the original source?

6. Are all mathematical tables and computations accurate?

7. Are all the pages firmly attached in the binding?

8. Is the overall appearance of the report attractive and professional-looking?

Summary

Formal reports fill an important place in the office setting. They summarize research, investigation, a trip, a survey, a test, or the like and often make specific recommendations for action. Formal reports contain three basic sections of information: the front matter, the body, and the back matter. In addition, each part is traditionally composed of different sections, described in this chapter.

Formal reports are the way workers in a corporation share information with workers in other departments or their own superiors, and obtain funding for new projects or for new products. Employees who know how to organize and write professional reports will find themselves in high demand in progressive companies, and these people may even be placed in charge of new projects because of the quality of their report that launched the project.

Part V

Creating Specialized Documents

Creating Employee and Telephone Lists

Creating Office Forms

Creating a Customer Invoice

12

Creating Employee and Telephone Lists

Every business except the very smallest keeps a list of employees and their departments, as well as a list of employee phone numbers or phone extensions. A small company might simply combine the information onto one list. But a large company with hundreds or thousands of workers often must create multipage documents or small handbooks to maintain this employee information.

Every business also has a turnover of employees—some moving to different departments (and different phone extensions), some leaving to take jobs elsewhere, and new workers arriving to fill job vacancies and new positions. Keeping an up-to-date list of employees, the departments where they work, and their correct phone extensions can be quite a chore. And the larger the company, the more often the lists have to be updated and reprinted.

Before computers, these lists had to be revised and retyped every time personnel changes made the former lists invalid. With a computer, though, maintaining the lists is much simpler. The employee list and phone list are maintained as separate files, with a single line per employee in each file. When it comes time to update the files, lines are removed and new lines added to both files one name at a time.

But even with computers, there is no practical way to update a phone list and automatically update the department list at the same time. For example, if you had only a phone list and wanted to make a department/employee list, you would have to retype the employee list to arrange the employees by the departments where they work.

However, if you already had the list of employees in a WordPerfect merge file, you could extract the data you needed in the order you needed it and create the exact kind of employee list or phone list you wanted. In this chapter you will see how to use a merge file to maintain both a department/employee list and an employee/phone list from the same file. You will also explore how to merge employee and phone data into a WordPerfect table.

Creating a Secondary Merge File

As you learned in Chapter 4, the secret to setting up a secondary file with field names is to insert at the beginning of that file a special record telling WordPerfect which field names you plan to use. Because the information in this chapter is different from what was used in previous chapters for correspondence, envelopes, and labels, this file begins from scratch. Start with a clear screen and follow these steps to start a new secondary file:

1. Press Merge Codes (Shift-F9) and select More (6).

   Choose the Tools menu and select Merge Codes.

2. Use the up- or down-arrow keys to move the highlight bar to {FIELD NAMES}, or start typing field names.

   Move the mouse pointer to the Merge Codes selection box; while pressing the left mouse button, drag the mouse downward to highlight the {FIELD NAMES} line.

3. With {FIELD NAMES} highlighted, press Enter.

   Double-click the {FIELD NAMES} line.

4. At the Enter Field 1: prompt, type the name of the first field, or *Employee*, and press Enter.

5. At the Enter Field 2: prompt, type the name of the next field, or *Department*, and press Enter.

6. At the Enter Field 3: prompt, type the name of the next field, or *PhoneNumber*, and press Enter.

7. After typing the last field name, press Enter at the next prompt for another field name. Pressing Enter tells WordPerfect that you are finished listing field names.

After you have finished typing all the field names, WordPerfect displays the list of field names at the top of the document (see fig. 12.1).

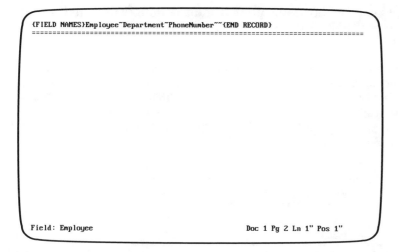

```
{FIELD NAMES}Employee~Department~PhoneNumber~~{END RECORD}
===============================================================================




















Field: Employee                          Doc 1 Pg 2 Ln 1" Pos 1"
```

Fig. 12.1.

The field names for the secondary merge file.

Each field in the FIELD NAME record is separated by a tilde (~). The tilde tells WordPerfect where one field ends and another begins.

If you think that you may need the employee home addresses in this file, add them now rather than later. These addresses and ZIP codes could be useful for future mailings to the employee homes. If you want to do these addresses, add the street address as one field and the city, state, and ZIP as another field. Because you can sort by items within a field, you do not need to break the categories into those smaller than street address and city/state/ZIP. Also, if you want to use this list later to build a larger database file for other projects, you may want to list the employees' first and last names as separate fields (such as FirstName~ LastName~). But this step is not necessary for either a phone list or an employee list. For current purposes, the fields are kept to a minimum to make these steps easier to follow.

Once you have a Field Name record set up, you are ready to enter the variable data—the names, departments, phone numbers or extensions, and other information that will appear in your secondary file. Make sure that your cursor is on the first line of page two—just under the double horizontal line indicating a page break. Then complete these steps:

1. A prompt at the bottom of the screen tells you which name to type—in this case, `Field: Employee`. Type the last name of an employee who will be included in your secondary file.

2. Type a comma and then the first name.

3. Don't press Enter after typing the first name. Instead, press End Field (F9). You must use F9 to mark the end of each field in a secondary file.

As soon as you press End Field (F9), the prompt at the bottom changes to the next field, Field: Department. Repeat steps 1 through 4 for both Department and PhoneNumber.

When you have typed the last field of information (PhoneNumber), press Merge Codes (Shift-F9) and select End Record (2). An {END RECORD} code appears on a line by itself, followed by a page break. For each record (that is, for each employee in the company), repeat the steps just given, making sure that you start each new record on a separate page. Figure 12.2 shows how the first five records look in a typical employee secondary merge file.

Fig. 12.2.

A sample employee secondary merge file.

```
{FIELD NAMES}Employee~Department~PhoneNumber~~{END RECORD}
==================================================================
Eastman, Alfred{END FIELD}
Marketing{END FIELD}
2435{END FIELD}
{END RECORD}
==================================================================
Howard, Kenneth{END FIELD}
Treasury{END FIELD}
2673{END FIELD}
{END RECORD}
==================================================================
Peters, Christine{END FIELD}
Public Relations{END FIELD}
2853{END FIELD}
{END RECORD}
==================================================================
Cohen, Morton{END FIELD}
Treasury{END FIELD}
2344{END FIELD}
{END RECORD}
==================================================================
Jacobson, Thomas{END FIELD}
Treasury{END FIELD}
                                        Doc 1 Pg 1 Ln 1" Pos 1"
```

When you have finished creating the secondary merge file, save the file under a descriptive name like EMPLOYEE.SF. The .SF extension reminds you that the file is a secondary file and helps you locate the file later on when you are ready to merge.

Setting Up a Primary File

After creating a secondary merge file, you need to create a primary merge file to use with your merge. If all you want is an alphabetized list of employees, with their phone numbers on the right, your primary file can be very simple. Just place the {FIELD}Employee~ merge code at the top left margin. Then press Flush Right twice (to create dot leaders) and insert the {FIELD} PhoneNumber~ at the right margin, along with the {PAGE OFF} code, as shown in the following line:

    {FIELD}Employee~............{FIELD}PhoneNumber~
    {PAGE OFF}

Now you are ready to add the merge field codes to your document:

1. Position the cursor at the left margin of the first line.

2. Press Merge Codes (Shift-F9).

   ⌨Choose Me**r**ge Codes from the **T**ools menu.

3. Choose **Field (1)**.

4. At the `Enter Field:` prompt, type the name of the field exactly as you used it in the secondary file and press Enter.

   For example, if the first field in your secondary file was named *Employee*, that is how you type the first field code name. WordPerfect inserts a {FIELD} code, followed by the name of the field and a tilde (~), into the document. The tilde tells WordPerfect where the field ends.

5. Press Flush Right (Alt-F6) twice to extend dot leaders to the right margin.

6. Press Merge Codes (Shift-F9).

   ⌨Choose **M**erge from the **T**ools menu.

7. Choose **Field (1)**.

8. At the `Enter Field` prompt, type *PhoneNumber* and press Enter.

9. Press Merge Codes (Shift-F9) and then **P**age Off (**4**).

Using flush right with dot leaders works well for phone numbers, because phone numbers generally have the same number of characters: 765-4321 or Ex. 1234. However, flush right does not look proper with most other types of data, as when short names are mixed in with long names. For example:

```
....................................John Smith
...............................Frank Jacobson
```

This format extends Frank's name farther to the left than John's. For variable-length data placed on the right with dot leaders, you need to use a tab setting with dot leaders, as in the following:

```
..............................John Smith
...............................Frank Jacobson
```

Using Tab Codes with a Merge

In a normal document, adding a dot-leader tab setting is no problem. Just position your cursor at the left margin where you want the dot-leader tabs to begin and press Format (Shift-F8), Line (**1**), and Tab Set (**8**).

But you should not include tab and margin settings in a merge document that will contain information from multiple records on a single page. If you do, you will end up with a merged phone list like the one shown in figure 12.3—with a new margin and tab set code for every employee name. If you have 300 names, you would end up with 300 margin and tab codes in the final document.

Fig. 12.3.

A sample of an improperly merged file.

```
Eastman, Alfred . . . . . . . . . . . . . .2435
Howard, Kenneth . . . . . . . . . . . . . .2673
Peters, Christine . . . . . . . . . . . . .2853
Cohen, Morton . . . . . . . . . . . . . . .2344
Jacobson, Thomas. . . . . . . . . . . . . .2746
Moss, Kevin . . . . . . . . . . . . . . . .2975
Ryan, Clifton . . . . . . . . . . . . . . .2789
Stephens, Neil. . . . . . . . . . . . . . .2145
Riley, Betty. . . . . . . . . . . . . . . .2658
McDowell, David . . . . . . . . . . . . . .2687
Hilliard, Anthony . . . . . . . . . . . . .2556
                                   Doc 1 Pg 1 Ln 1" Pos 1.1"
[                                   ▲                       ]
[L/R Mar:1.1",1.1"][Tab Set:Rel: -1",-0.5",+4.13"]Eastman, Alfred[Tab]2435[HRt]
[L/R Mar:1.1",1.1"][Tab Set:Rel: -1",-0.5",+4.13"]Howard, Kenneth[Tab]2673[HRt]
[L/R Mar:1.1",1.1"][Tab Set:Rel: -1",-0.5",+4.13"]Peters, Christine[Tab]2853[HRt
]
[L/R Mar:1.1",1.1"][Tab Set:Rel: -1",-0.5",+4.13"]Cohen, Morton[Tab]2344[HRt]
[L/R Mar:1.1",1.1"][Tab Set:Rel: -1",-0.5",+4.13"]Jacobson, Thomas[Tab]2746[HRt]

[L/R Mar:1.1",1.1"][Tab Set:Rel: -1",-0.5",+4.13"]Moss, Kevin[Tab]2975[HRt]
[L/R Mar:1.1",1.1"][Tab Set:Rel: -1",-0.5",+4.13"]Ryan, Clifton[Tab]2789[HRt]
[L/R Mar:1.1",1.1"][Tab Set:Rel: -1",-0.5",+4.13"]Stephens, Neil[Tab]2145[HRt]

Press Reveal Codes to restore screen
```

You need to put tab settings in the document where they will be unaffected by the merge. You do so by adding them to the document preface. Here are the steps for hiding codes in a document from a merge operation:

1. Press Format (Shift-F1) and select Document (**3**).

   ⌨Choose **Document** from the Layout menu.

2. Press Initial Codes (**2**).

   Your screen will split into two windows like the screen shown in figure 12.4. If any codes there are unwanted, press Backspace to remove them.

3. Press Format (Shift-F8) and Line (**1**).

   ⌨Choose **Line** from the Layout menu.

4. Press Tab Set (**8**).

5. Press Home, left arrow; then press Delete to End of Line (Ctrl-End) to remove all current tab settings.

6. Type *4.5*; then press Enter to set a tab at the 4 1/2-inch mark.

7. Type a period (.) to make that tab a dot-leader tab.

8. Press Exit (F7) two times. You should see a tab setting like the one in figure 12.4.

9. Press Exit (F7) two more times to return to the edit window.

Actually, you may want to include a margin setting between steps 7 and 8. Doing so ensures that your phone list maintains the same margins each time you create it, rather than any current default margins you might have set. Figure 12.4 includes a margin code, but the code is an optional entry and is not necessary for the merge operation.

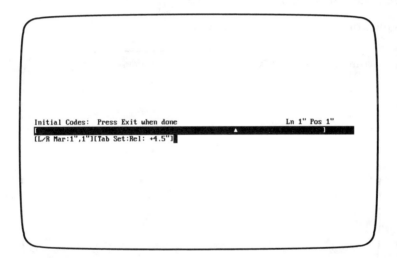

Fig. 12.4.

Margin and tab setting codes in the hidden document preface.

Adding the Merge Codes

Now you are ready to add the merge field codes to your document. Complete the following steps:

1. Position the cursor at the left margin of the first line.

2. Press Merge Codes (Shift-F9).

   ▭Choose Merge from the Tools menu.

3. Choose Field (**1**).

4. At the Enter Field: prompt, type the name of the field exactly as you used it in the secondary file and press Enter.

For example, if the first field in your secondary file is named *Employee*, that is how you type the first field code name. WordPerfect inserts a {FIELD} code, followed by the name of the field and a tilde (~), into the document. The tilde tells WordPerfect where the field ends.

5. Press Tab to move to the 4.5" tab location.

6. Press Merge Codes (Shift-F9).

    Choose **Merge** from the **Tools** menu.

7. Choose **Field (1)**.

8. At the Enter Field: prompt, type *PhoneNumber* and press Enter.

9. Press Merge Codes (Shift-F9) and then **Page Off (4)**.

Figure 12.5 shows the primary file for a simple phone list.

Fig. 12.5.

Merge codes needed in a telephone primary file.

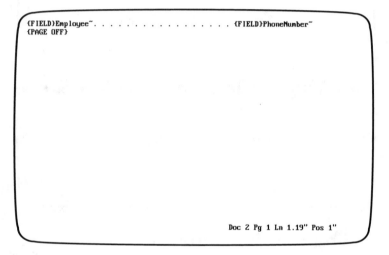

When the primary file is completed, press Exit (F7) and give the file a name like PHONE.PF. The .PF extension helps you locate the file when the time comes for a merge. You will find both the PHONE.PF file and a sample EMPLOYEE.SF file on the Applications Disk.

Sorting the Secondary File

Before you perform the merge operation, you need to make sure that the secondary file (the list of employees and phone extensions) is arranged alphabetically. Here are the steps for sorting a merge file:

1. Retrieve the EMPLOYEE.SF file to the screen.

2. Press Merge Sort (Ctrl-F9) and choose **Sort (2)**.

   ▭⧉Select **Sort** from the **Tools** menu.

3. At the `Input file to sort: (Screen)` prompt, press Enter.

4. At the `Output file for sort: (Screen)` prompt, press Enter.

   At this point you should see a sort window at the bottom with `Sort by Line` at the top of this second window, as in figure 12.6. Because this is a merge file, you need to change the sort from a line sort to a secondary merge sort.

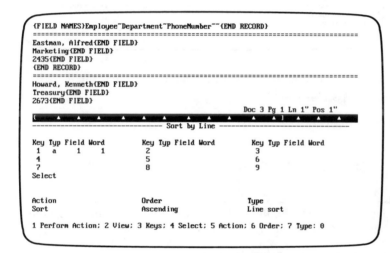

Fig. 12.6.

A sort window at the bottom with the secondary merge file above.

5. Press **Type (7)** to change the type of merge from Sort by Line to Sort Secondary Merge File.

6. Press **Merge (1)**.

7. Press **Keys (3)**; the cursor jumps to the first key.

8. Press the right arrow five times and type *2* to change `Word 1` to `Word 2` for `Key 2`.

9. Press **Exit (F7)** once and then **Perform (1)** to start the sort operation.

Figure 12.7 shows the sorted secondary merge file after an alphabetical sort.

Fig. 12.7.

The EMPLOYEE.SF file after a merge file sort.

```
{FIELD NAMES}Employee~Department~PhoneNumber~~{END RECORD}
================================================================================
Alexander, John{END FIELD}
Treasury{END FIELD}
2890{END FIELD}
{END RECORD}
================================================================================
Babcock, Karen{END FIELD}
Marketing{END FIELD}
2577{END FIELD}
{END RECORD}
================================================================================
Brown, Ruth{END FIELD}
Treasury{END FIELD}
2546{END FIELD}
{END RECORD}
================================================================================
Burbank, Alfred{END FIELD}
Marketing{END FIELD}
2855{END FIELD}
{END RECORD}
================================================================================
Cohen, Morton{END FIELD}
Treasury{END FIELD}
                                                    Doc 2 Pg 1 Ln 1" Pos 1"
```

10. Press Exit (F7), resave the file under the same name, and clear the screen without exiting WordPerfect.

Now you are ready to create the phone list.

Performing the Merge

Once you have created a secondary file (the data file with employee names and phone numbers) and a primary file (the file with merge fields), you can merge the two files to create a phone list. Start with an empty screen and follow these steps:

1. Press Merge/Sort (Ctrl-F9) and select **Merge (1)**.

   ⌨Choose **S**ort from the **T**ools pull-down menu.

2. At the Primary File: prompt, press List Files (F5) and Enter, select the correct primary file, and press **R**etrieve (**1**). (Or type the name of the primary file and press Enter. Make certain that you include the correct path and full file name, including the extension.)

3. At the Secondary File: prompt, press List Files (F5) and Enter, select the correct secondary file, and press **R**etrieve (**1**). (Or type the name of the secondary file, including the path and extension, and press Enter.)

With those two pieces of information, WordPerfect will merge the primary file with the secondary file and create a phone list. Figure 12.8 shows a properly merged telephone list on-screen.

```
Alexander, John . . . . . . . . . . . . . . . . 2890
Babcock, Karen. . . . . . . . . . . . . . . . . 2577
Brown, Ruth . . . . . . . . . . . . . . . . . . 2546
Burbank, Alfred . . . . . . . . . . . . . . . . 2855
Cohen, Morton . . . . . . . . . . . . . . . . . 2344
Edwards, Bessie . . . . . . . . . . . . . . . . 2561
Eastman, Alfred . . . . . . . . . . . . . . . . 2435
Gonzales, Edward. . . . . . . . . . . . . . . . 2674
Graybill, Judith. . . . . . . . . . . . . . . . 2765
Handy, Christopher. . . . . . . . . . . . . . . 2544
Hilliard, Anthony . . . . . . . . . . . . . . . 2556
Howard, Judy. . . . . . . . . . . . . . . . . . 2799
Howard, Kenneth . . . . . . . . . . . . . . . . 2673
Hunter, Joan. . . . . . . . . . . . . . . . . . 2911
Isaacs, Sarah . . . . . . . . . . . . . . . . . 2354
Jacobson, Thomas. . . . . . . . . . . . . . . . 2746
Lacy, Nancy . . . . . . . . . . . . . . . . . . 2637
McDowell, David . . . . . . . . . . . . . . . . 2687
Moore, Peter. . . . . . . . . . . . . . . . . . 2722
Moss, Kevin . . . . . . . . . . . . . . . . . . 2975
Norman, Ralph . . . . . . . . . . . . . . . . . 2779
Peters, Christine . . . . . . . . . . . . . . . 2853
Peterson, Barrie. . . . . . . . . . . . . . . . 2888
Riley, Betty. . . . . . . . . . . . . . . . . . 2658
                              Doc 2 Pg 1 Ln 1" Pos 1"
```

Fig. 12.8.

A merged telephone extension list alphabetically arranged.

After the merge you can press Home, Home, up arrow to go to the top of the screen; press Enter two or three times; and add a header such as *Company Phone List*. Figure 12.9 shows a printed page with a header in a different font and a bolded caption for Employee and Extension.

Company Phone List

Employee	Extension
Alexander, John	2890
Babcock, Karen	2577
Brown, Ruth	2546
Burbank, Alfred	2855
Cohen, Morton	2344
Edwards, Bessie	2561
Eastman, Alfred	2435
Gonzales, Edward	2674
Graybill, Judith	2765
Handy, Christopher	2544
Hilliard, Anthony	2556
Howard, Judy	2799
Howard, Kenneth	2673
Hunter, Joan	2911
Isaacs, Sarah	2354
Jacobson, Thomas	2746
Lacy, Nancy	2637
McDowell, David	2687
Moore, Peter	2722
Moss, Kevin	2975
Norman, Ralph	2779
Peters, Christine	2853
Peterson, Barrie	2888
Riley, Betty	2658
Ryan, Clifton	2789
Singer, Charles	2588
Stephens, Neil	2145

Fig. 12.9.

A typical phone list created with a merge.

The merge operation that produced figure 12.8 is fairly uncomplicated. Now try going one step further and create a company department/employee list from the same secondary merge file.

Creating a Department/Employee List with a Merge

For this next document, all employees should be arranged under their departments. That is, you arrange the department names alphabetically as well as the names of the employees within each department.

 Using the special merge file included on the Applications Disk, you can perform this difficult chore easily. But first you need to re-sort the secondary merge file.

Sorting the Secondary File by Department

Here are the steps for re-sorting the secondary merge file by department and then by employee within department:

1. Retrieve the EMPLOYEE.SF file to the screen.

2. Press Merge Sort (Ctrl-F9) and choose Sort (2).

    ▭Select Sort from the Tools menu.

3. At the Input file to sort: (Screen) prompt, press Enter.

4. At the Output file for sort: (Screen) prompt, press Enter.

    If the sort screen reads Sort by Line, you need to change the sort from a line sort to a secondary merge sort. If the sort window indicates a Sort Secondary Merge File, skip steps 5 and 6.

5. If necessary, press Type (7) to change the type of merge from Sort by Line to Sort Secondary Merge File.

6. Press Merge (1).

7. Press Keys (3); the cursor jumps to the first key.

8. Press the right arrow once and change Field 1 to Field 2.

9. Press Enter six times until you reach the end of Key 2. You want Key 2 to read a, 1, 1, 1.

10. Press Enter four more times and change Word 1 to Word 2 in Key 3.

Steps 8 through 10 tell WordPerfect to sort first by field 2 (the Department field), to sort next by the first word in field 1 (the Employee field), and then to sort any duplicates by the first name in field 1 (the Employee field).

11. Press Exit (F7) and then **P**erform Action (**1**).

You will briefly see the prompt n Records transferred.

12. Save the file again, using the same name as before.

Using the Department/Employee Primary File

 Because creating the primary file for the next step requires the use of some advanced merge commands, the primary file has already been created for you and included on the Applications Disk. During the merge operation, the primary file first selects a department title and then adds the first name in that department under the department name.

Then the primary file checks to see whether any more employees work in that department. If the file finds any, it adds their names under the department name without repeating the department title. This process continues throughout the file until the entire list is created. Figure 12.10 shows what this DEPARTMT.PF file looks like. If you want to create the DEPARTMT.PF file yourself, first be sure that you understand the advanced merge commands in WordPerfect 5.1.

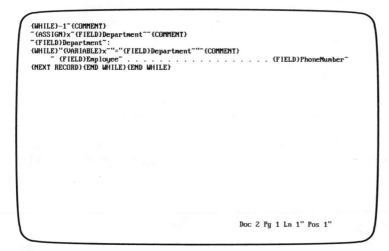

Fig. 12.10.

A primary merge file created with advanced merge language.

 To use this file, copy it to the same directory where your EMPLOYEE.SF file is located. Then do the following:

1. Press Merge/Sort (Ctrl-F9) and select **Merge (1)**.

   ▢◧Choose **Merge** from the **Tools** pull-down menu.

2. At the `Primary File:` prompt, press List Files (F5) and then Enter, choose the `DEPARTMT.PF` file, and press **Retrieve (1)**. (Or type *DEPARTMT.PF* and press Enter. Make certain that you include the correct path for the subdirectory and the full file name, including the extension.)

3. At the `Secondary File:` prompt, press List Files (F5) and then Enter, choose the `EMPLOYEE.SF` file, and press **Retrieve (1)**. (Or type *EMPLOYEE.SF* and press Enter. Make certain to include the correct path and full file name, including the extension.)

In a minute the screen will show a merged file that lists all the department names, with workers listed alphabetically underneath the department where they work, as shown in figure 12.11.

Fig. 12.11.

An employee list organized by company departments.

```
Administration:
        Handy, Christopher . . . . . . . . . . . . . . . 2544
        Moore, Peter . . . . . . . . . . . . . . . . . . 2722
        Norman, Ralph. . . . . . . . . . . . . . . . . . 2779
        Peterson, Barrie . . . . . . . . . . . . . . . . 2888
Advertising:
        Lacy, Nancy. . . . . . . . . . . . . . . . . . . 2637
        Ryan, Clifton. . . . . . . . . . . . . . . . . . 2789
Cafeteria:
        Edwards, Bessie. . . . . . . . . . . . . . . . . 2561
        Howard, Judy . . . . . . . . . . . . . . . . . . 2799
        Riley, Betty . . . . . . . . . . . . . . . . . . 2658
Computer:
        McDowell, David. . . . . . . . . . . . . . . . . 2687
Library:
        Isaacs, Sarah. . . . . . . . . . . . . . . . . . 2354
Mail Room:
        Hunter, Joan . . . . . . . . . . . . . . . . . . 2911
Maintenance:
        Gonzales, Edward . . . . . . . . . . . . . . . . 2674
        Hilliard, Anthony. . . . . . . . . . . . . . . . 2556
        Singer, Charles. . . . . . . . . . . . . . . . . 2588
Marketing:
        Babcock, Karen . . . . . . . . . . . . . . . . . 2577
                                        Doc 2 Pg 1 Ln 1" Pos 1"
```

Figure 12.12 is a printout of the merged file, to which a header was added. Note that the document is off-center to the left so that it can be printed on regular sheets of paper and trimmed to make the list easier to use.

Merging Data to a Table

Now you are ready to explore more fully the capabilities of WordPerfect 5.1. Try doing a merge to a WordPerfect table, so that you have employee names on the left side of the table, the department where each employee works in the middle column, and each employee's phone extension in the right column.

Company Employee List

Administration:
      Handy, Christopher 2544
      Moore, Peter 2722
      Norman, Ralph 2779
      Peterson, Barrie 2888
Advertising:
      Lacy, Nancy 2637
      Ryan, Clifton 2789
Cafeteria:
      Edwards, Bessie 2561
      Howard, Judy 2799
      Riley, Betty 2658
Computer:
      McDowell, David 2687
Library:
      Isaacs, Sarah 2354
Mail Room:
      Hunter, Joan 2911
Maintenance:
      Gonzales, Edward 2674
      Hilliard, Anthony 2556
      Singer, Charles 2588
Marketing:
      Babcock, Karen 2577
      Burbank, Alfred 2855
      Eastman, Alfred 2435
      Moss, Kevin 2975
Public Relations:
      Graybill, Judith 2765
      Peters, Christine 2853
Transportation:
      Stephens, Neil 2145
Treasury:
      Alexander, John 2890
      Brown, Ruth 2546
      Cohen, Morton 2344
      Howard, Kenneth 2673
      Jacobson, Thomas 2746

Fig. 12.12.

A printout of the employee list.

Sorting the Secondary File

Because the secondary file needs to be in alphabetical order again, repeat the first merge given in this chapter:

1. Retrieve the EMPLOYEE.SF file to the screen.

2. Press Merge Sort (Ctrl-F9) and choose **Sort (2)**.

   ▭ Select **Sort** from the **Tools** menu.

3. At the `Input file to sort: (Screen)` prompt, press Enter.

4. At the `Output file for sort: (Screen)` prompt, press Enter.

   If the sort window reads `Sort Secondary Merge File`, skip steps 5 and 6.

5. Press Type (7) to change the type of merge from Sort by Line to Sort Secondary Merge File.

6. Press **Merge (1)**.

7. Press **Keys (3)**; the cursor jumps to the first key.

8. Press the right arrow once and change Field 2 in Key 1 back to Field 1.

9. Press the right arrow six times and type *2* to change Word 1 to Word 2 for Key 2.

10. Press Del once to clear all entries in Key 3 (from the previous merge operation).

11. Press Exit (F7) once and then **Perform (1)** to start the sort operation.

Your screen should look like figure 12.7 now. One nice feature about Sort: you can perform the operation repeatedly in different combinations to get the kind of secondary file needed for the particular merge operation. Save the EMPLOYEE.SF file back to disk under the same name.

Creating the Primary Table Merge File

The table you are about to create has three columns—one for employees, one for departments, and one for phone extensions. Included are the steps for adding a header to this table so that it looks better when merged. Start with a clear screen and follow these steps to create a primary table merge file:

1. Press Columns/Table (Alt-F7) and choose **Tables (2)**.

   ⌨Choose **Tables** from the Layout menu.

2. Choose **Create (1)**.

3. For Number of Columns: type *3* and press Enter.

4. For Number of Rows: type *4* and press Enter.

5. Press F12 or Alt-F4 to turn on Block in cell A1.

6. Press End to highlight the entire upper row.

7. Press **Join (7)** and then press Y in response to the question Join Cells?

8. Press the down arrow once; then press Block (Alt-F4 or F12) and the End key.

9. Press **Lines (3)**, select **Top (3)**, and choose **None (1)**.

10. Press **Lines (3)**, select **Left (1)**, and choose **None (1)**.

11. Press the left arrow once to move to the center column.

12. Press Lines (**3**), select Left (**1**), and choose None (**1**).

Now you are ready to add titles to the table. First you can add a header, then a title for each of the three columns of information.

1. Press the up arrow, Format (**2**), and then Cell (**1**).

2. Press Justify (**3**) and Center (**2**).

3. Press Exit (F7) to return to the edit screen.

4. In cell A1 type *Company Employee List*.

5. Press Tab to go to cell A2 and type *Employee*.

6. Press Tab to go to cell B2 and type *Department*.

7. Press Tab to go to cell C2 and type *Extension*.

During the merge operation, the bottom row is duplicated as many times as there are records in the secondary file. Therefore, you need to change the rule on the bottom row from double-line to single-line. Here are the steps for making this change:

1. Press Tab to move to cell A4.

2. Press Columns/Table (Alt-F7) to modify the table.

3. Press Block (F12 or Alt-F4) and the End key to highlight the bottom row.

4. Press Lines (**3**), Bottom (**4**), and Single (**2**).

5. Press Exit (F7) to return to the edit screen.

At this point your table should look like figure 12.13.

Adding Merge Codes to the Primary Table Merge File

The last step in creating a primary merge file is to add the merge codes to the table. Complete these steps to perform this operation:

1. Press Shift-Tab five times to move back to cell A3.

2. Press Merge Codes (Shift-F9) and choose More (**6**).

   ⌨Choose Merge Codes from the Tools menu; then choose More.

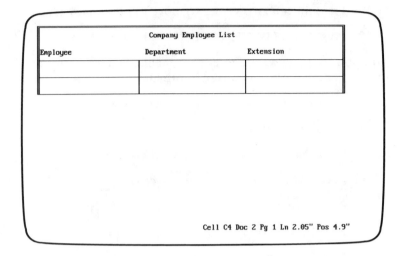

Fig. 12.13.

*A primary merge
table with
headers for each
column.*

3. Use the down arrow to reach {LABEL}label~ in the codes window.

4. Press Enter, type *loop*, and press Enter again.

5. Press Merge Codes (Shift-F9) and choose Field (**1**).

    ⌨Choose **Merge** Codes from the **Tools** menu; then choose **Field**.

6. Type *Employee*, press Enter, and then press Tab once to move to the center column.

7. Press Merge Codes (Shift-F9) and choose Field (**1**).

    ⌨Choose **Merge** Codes from the **Tools** menu; then choose **Field**.

8. Type *Department*, press Enter, and then press Tab once to move to the right column.

9. Press Merge Codes (Shift-F9) and choose Field (**1**).

    ⌨Choose **Merge** Codes from the **Tools** menu; then choose **Field**.

10. Type *PhoneNumber* and press Enter.

11. Press Merge Codes (Shift-F9) and choose Next Record (**5**).

    ⌨Choose **Merge** Codes from the **Tools** menu; then choose **Next** Record.

12. Press Tab to move to cell A4 on the bottom row.

13. Press Merge Codes (Shift-F9) and choose More (**6**).

    ⌨Choose **Merge** Codes from the **Tools** menu; then choose **More**.

14. Use the up arrow to reach the `{GO}label~` entry in the merge codes window; then press Enter.

15. Type *loop* and press Enter.

At this point you may need to adjust your monitor to display properly the information in the table. The steps for adjusting the display pitch for the screen are these:

1. Press Format (Shift-F8) and Document (3).

   ⌨Choose **Document** from the Layout menu.

2. Choose **Display Pitch (1)** and press N.

3. Type *.065* for Width and press Enter.

4. Press Exit (F7) to return to the edit window.

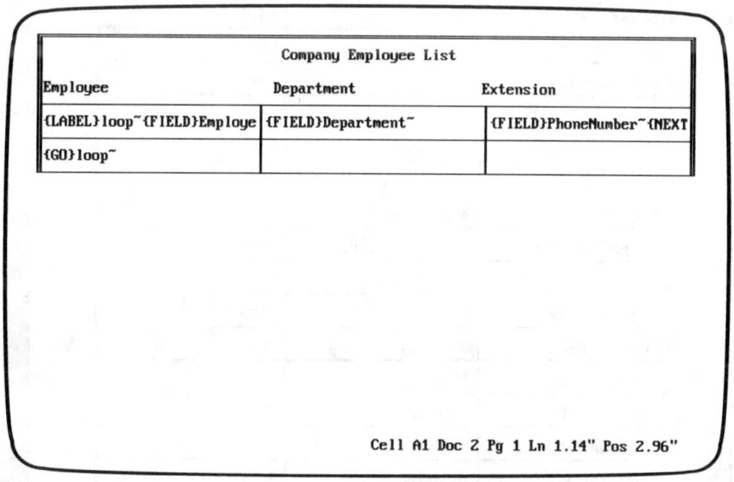

Company Employee List		
Employee	Department	Extension
{LABEL}loop~{FIELD}Employe	{FIELD}Department~	{FIELD}PhoneNumber~{NEXT
{GO}loop~		

Cell A1 Doc 2 Pg 1 Ln 1.14" Pos 2.96"

Fig. 12.14.

The completed primary table merge file.

Now your primary table merge file should look like figure 12.14.

5. Press Exit (F7) and save this file in the same subdirectory as your other merge files, naming the file TABLEMRG.PF.

Merging the Data into the Primary Table File

You are now ready to merge information from the EMPLOYEE.SF file into the newly created primary table file. Here are the steps to follow:

1. Press Merge/Sort (Ctrl-F9) and select **Merge (1)**.

   ▢▤Choose **Merge** from the **Tools** pull-down menu.

2. At the `Primary File:` prompt, press List Files (F5) and Enter, highlight the `TABLEMRG.PF` file, and press **Retrieve (1)**. (Or type *TABLEMRG.PF* and press Enter. Make certain that you include the correct path for the subdirectory and the full file name, including the extension.)

Fig. 12.15.

A printed table that lists employee information.

Company Employee List		
Employee	**Department**	**Extension**
Alexander, John	Treasury	2890
Babcock, Karen	Marketing	2577
Brown, Ruth	Treasury	2546
Burbank, Alfred	Marketing	2855
Cohen, Morton	Treasury	2344
Eastman, Alfred	Marketing	2435
Edwards, Bessie	Cafeteria	2561
Handy, Christopher	Administration	2544
Gonzales, Edward	Maintenance	2674
Graybill, Judith	Public Relations	2765
Hilliard, Anthony	Maintenance	2556
Howard, Judy	Cafeteria	2799
Howard, Kenneth	Treasury	2673
Hunter, Joan	Mail Room	2911
Isaacs, Sarah	Library	2354
Jacobson, Thomas	Treasury	2746
Lacy, Nancy	Advertising	2637
McDowell, David	Computer	2687
Moore, Peter	Administration	2722
Moss, Kevin	Marketing	2975
Norman, Ralph	Administration	2779
Peters, Christine	Public Relations	2853
Peterson, Barrie	Administration	2888
Riley, Betty	Cafeteria	2658
Ryan, Clifton	Advertising	2789
Singer, Charles	Maintenance	2588
Stephens, Neil	Transportation	2145

3. At the Secondary File: prompt, press List Files (F5) and Enter, highlight the EMPLOYEE.SF file, and press **Retrieve (1)**. (Or type *EMPLOYEE.SF* and press Enter. Make certain to include the correct path and full file name, including the extension.)

In a minute the screen will show a merged file that lists all the workers alphabetically in the first column, the department where they work in the middle column, and their phone extension in the right column. The printed list should look like figure 12.15.

Using the steps just given, you should be able to construct a table for your own employee list or a similar list of information from a secondary merge file.

Summary

As you can see, the WordPerfect merge feature can save a lot of work in a typical office environment. In this chapter you discovered how to create a primary file for a simple employee/phone number list and how to use a department/employee primary file to create a different kind of company list. You also learned how to create a WordPerfect 5.1 table with columns of employee names, their departments, and their phone extensions by merging these data with a primary table file. Now that you know these steps, you should be able to create a variety of lists for use in a typical company environment.

13

Creating Office Forms

Most businesses, offices, and organizations use printed forms of one kind or another. Businesses need job-estimate forms, customer invoices, credit-inquiry forms, credit-memo sheets, and long-distance telephone sheets. Salespeople rely on sales-order forms and expense reports—weekly, quarterly, and yearly. Secretaries need fax cover sheets, phone-message forms and petty-cash forms. Office workers need daily and weekly time sheets and calendars for appointments. High school and college teachers require class-attendance forms and questionnaire forms. Clubs need application and membership forms, score cards, and so on.

Of course, you could purchase a separate software program to create office forms, but some are expensive and all take time to learn. Fortunately, WordPerfect 5.1 offers you a way to create the kinds of forms you need without an additional program.

If you use a variety of forms in your office, the money in learning to use WordPerfect 5.1's form-creation feature more than pays for itself in a few months' time. You can use WordPerfect 5.1 to create and print the master forms, which can be duplicated on any photocopier whenever needed. In fact, the forms you could create in WordPerfect 5.1 are limitless.

This chapter offers an array of office forms—all of which you can copy from the Applications Disk and then modify within WordPerfect. All the forms in this chapter make use of the WordPerfect Tables feature.

In this chapter, you find the following forms:

- Important Message Form
- Petty Cash Form
- Weekly Time Sheet
- Credit Inquiry Form
- FAX Transmission Form
- Credit Memo
- Quarterly Expense Summary
- Yearly Expense Summary
- Long-Distance Telephone Record
- Calendar Form (3-month)
- Calendar Form (1-month)

Chapter 14, on the other hand, provides a detailed hands-on example of how to create a single office form from beginning to end with all the necessary steps listed so you can create and modify your own forms. In Chapter 14, you also learn how to set spacing between text and the table lines, how to set cell justification, how to switch fonts in a table, how to lock table cells, how to remove unwanted lines, how to adjust the size of the columns, how to add column headers, and how to add math codes to a table. If you are interested in creating your own forms, study Chapters 13 and 14 as a unit.

Understanding Table Basics

Tables are special forms made from a grid of empty boxes. The grid contains rows of boxes running horizontally and columns of boxes running vertically, as in figure 13.1. These rows and columns of horizontal and vertical lines, form cells where information can be typed. Cells are identified by their column letter, then their row number. Figure 13.1 shows four columns and four rows, creating 16 cells. The first cell, highlighted in figure 13.1, is named Cell A1 on the status line near the bottom of the page (just to the left of Doc 2 Pg 1).

Cell lines can be thin, thick, single, double, dotted, or dashed, as you soon discover. And individual cells can be shaded in various percentages of gray.

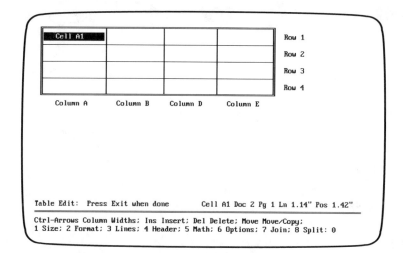

Fig. 13.1.

Tables are made up of rows and columns of cells.

Creating Your First Table

The default settings for a WordPerfect table look like figure 13.1—with double lines around the outside and single lines inside the form. You create a WordPerfect table be following these steps:

1. Press Columns/Table (Alt-F7) and **Tables** (**2**).

   ⌨Select **Tables** from the Layout menu.

2. Press **Create** (**1**).

3. At the Number of Columns: prompt, type *3* and press Enter.

4. At the Number of Rows: prompt, type *5* and press Enter.

At this point, you see a screen like figure 13.2, with the first cell highlighted and a menu of 8 items along the bottom.

Tip: If you have created a table and exited the Table Editor, you can return to the editor by placing your cursor somewhere inside the table and pressing Alt-F7. Otherwise, you will have to type extra keystrokes to enter the screen.

Within a table cell, you can use any font, font attribute, or font size used elsewhere on the page. Figure 13.3, for example, illustrates a printed table with 16 different font attributes: bold, italic, underline, double underline, small cap, superscript, subscript, redline, strikeout, fine, small, normal, large, very large, and extra large.

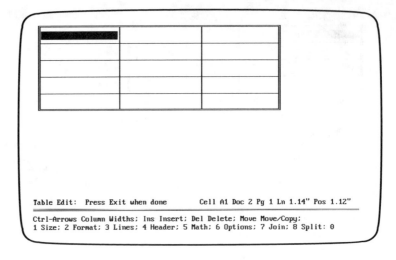

```
Table Edit:   Press Exit when done        Cell A1 Doc 2 Pg 1 Ln 1.14" Pos 1.12"

Ctrl-Arrows Column Widths; Ins Insert; Del Delete; Move Move/Copy;
1 Size; 2 Format; 3 Lines; 4 Header; 5 Math; 6 Options; 7 Join; 8 Split: 0
```

Fig. 13.3.

*Sixteen different
font attributes in a
single table.*

Attributes Within a Table

Regular Text	**Bold Text**	*Italic Text*
Fine Text	Small Text	**Large Text**
Very Large	**Extra Large**	text^{Superscript}
text$_{\text{subscript}}$	Redline	~~Strikeout~~
<u>Underline Text</u>	<u>Double Underline</u>	SMALL CAP

Tables can be as small as a single cell, or as large as 32 columns wide by 32,765 rows high (or a table with more than a million cells). An individual cell can be as small as a single character in a tiny font, or as large as an entire 8 1/2-inch-by-11-inch page.

Changing Line Thickness and Line Shading

Within a table, you can use a variety of line types for the sides of the cells and even shade the cells with gray.

Adjusting Line Styles

Tables are made of six different types of lines, illustrated later in this section. To change any line in your table to one of these six options, do the following:

1. Place your cursor inside the table.

2. Press Columns/Table (Alt-F7).

    ⬚Select **Tables** from the Layout menu.

3. Select **Line (3)** from the menu at the bottom of the screen.

4. Select one of the first six line options you want to change (see fig. 13.4). The seventh option makes all lines the same:

   Left (1)
   Right (2
   Top (3)
   Bottom (4)
   Inside (5)
   Outside (6)
   All (7)
   Shade (8)

   (The eighth option, **Shade**, is discussed in the next section.)

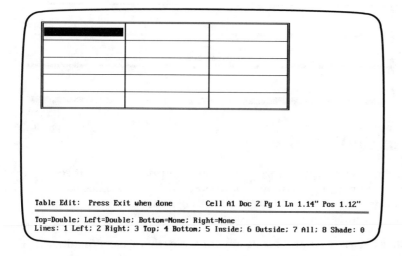

Fig. 13.4.

The line edit menu offers eight choices.

```
Table Edit:  Press Exit when done        Cell A1 Doc 2 Pg 1 Ln 1.14" Pos 1.12"

Top=Double; Left=Double; Bottom=None; Right=None
Lines: 1 Left; 2 Right; 3 Top; 4 Bottom; 5 Inside; 6 Outside; 7 All; 8 Shade: 0
```

After you select any of the first seven choices, a line-style menu appears, like the one shown at the bottom of figure 13.5. From a laser printer, the six line styles look like the ones in figure 13.6.

Fig. 13.5.

The line-choices menu.

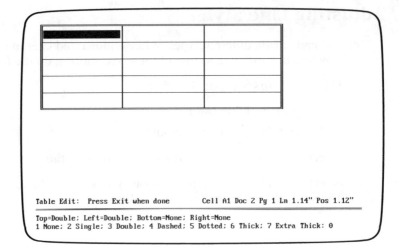

Table Edit: Press Exit when done   Cell A1 Doc 2 Pg 1 Ln 1.14" Pos 1.12"

Top=Double; Left=Double; Bottom=None; Right=None
1 None; 2 Single; 3 Double; 4 Dashed; 5 Dotted; 6 Thick; 7 Extra Thick: 0

Types of Table Lines

Fig. 13.6.

A printed sample of the six types of table lines.

	Dotted Line	
	Dashed Line	
	Single Line	
	Double Line	
	Thick Line	
	Extra Thick Line	

Adjusting the Cell Shading

If you have ever purchased preprinted forms at an office supply store, or if you have order forms from a print shop, you may have noted that many office forms contain shaded sections for emphasis and to make filling in forms easier. In this chapter, you will find several examples of shaded cells within office forms.

If you want to shade a cell or a group of cells in your table, then select Shade (option **8** in fig. 13.4).

If you use a laser printer like the Hewlett-Packard LJ, LJ Plus, or LJ series II, IID, IIP, or III, you can print only eight different levels of shading: 5, 10, 15, 30, 50, 70, 90, or 100 percent. All other percentages default to one of these 8 settings when the document is printed, because that is all an HP LJ can utilize.

If you plan to put text inside your table, stick to the lighter shades of gray so the text can be easily read. Figure 13.7 illustrates all eight shades of gray produced on a Hewlett-Packard LaserJet IID.

Types of Table Shading

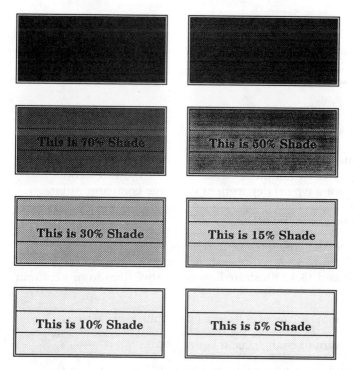

Fig. 13.7.

The eight possible shades of gray available with an HP printer.

Set the level of shade for your table with the Table Options selection (see this menu in fig. 13.2). The Table Options screen, as shown in figure 13.8, lets you set gray shading by percentage points—anything from 1 percent to 100 percent. However, remember only the eight shades shown in figure 13.7 can be printed on a Hewlett-Packard printer.

Fig. 13.8.

*Table shading is
set from the Table
Options screen.*

```
Table Options

    1 - Spacing Between Text and Lines
            Left                    0.083"
            Right                   0.083"
            Top                     0.1"
            Bottom                  0"

    2 - Display Negative Results       1
            1 = with minus signs
            2 = with parentheses

    3 - Position of Table           Left

    4 - Gray Shading (% of black)   10%




Selection: 0
```

Removing Lines from a Table

In addition to adjusting line thickness and line shading, you can also remove lines from a table so that it looks like two or more tables. Figure 13.9, for example, illustrates the office layout for a typical department in a large company. Although figure 13.9 looks like three tables placed together on one page, it was actually created from two tables, one above the other.

But in the top table in figure 13.9, the lines were removed from Column C (as shown in figs. 13.10, 13.11, and 13.12) to suggest two tables side by side on the page. Figures 13.10, 13.11, and 13.12 illustrate how to remove lines from a column or row of cells in a table.

To remove lines from a column or row of cells in a table, follow these steps:

1. Block the cells you want to change, as in figure 13.10.

   You can block multiple cells by turning on Block (F12 or Alt-F3) in the cell on one end or corner, and pressing any of the four arrow keys (up, down, left, or right) to stretch the block to the other end or corner. You can also use End, Home, Down Arrow, Home, Home, Down Arrow, etc., to block many cells quickly.

2. Choose Lines (**3**), Inside (**5**), and None (**1**).

3. Next, position the highlight bar in the bottom cell of the column (see fig. 13.11), and select Lines (**3**), Bottom (**4**), and None (**1**).

4. Position the highlight bar in the top cell of the column. (Your center column should now look like figure 13.12.) Select Lines (**3**), Top (**3**), and None (**1**).

OFFICE LAYOUT

Eric Armer (Ex 6976)	Harold Baasch (Ex 6964)
Alan Adams (Ex 6975)	Tanda Moyer (Ex 6965)
(Training) (Ex 6974)	James Jordan (Ex 6967)
Gloria Mansfield (Ex 6973)	Richard O'Ffill, Jr. (Ex 6968)
Ralph Blodgett (Ex 6972)	Kevin von Gersdorff (Ex 6969)
David Engelkemier (Ex 6971)	Art Fuller (Ex 6970)

Ron Pherigo (Ex 6952)	Jake Randall (Ex 6962)
Don Freesland (Ex 6953)	Bettie Dahlberg (Ex 6950)
Stacey Kuhlman (Ex 6954)	Louise Smith (Ex 6961)
Fely Ann Rugless (Ex 6957)	Wendy Gates (Ex 6960)
Buddy Ward (Ex 6956)	Bill Onuska (Ex 6959)
Mussie Gebregziabihar (Ex 6955)	Larry Stokenbury (Ex 6958)

Fig. 13.9.

Making two tables look like three tables.

Joseph Marcellino (Ex 6987)	(Work Room) (Ex 6986)	Richard Christian (Ex 6983)	Ron Macomber (Ex 6981)	Richard Peters (Ex 6979)
Jerry Penner (Ex 6988)	Tom Taylor (Ex 6985)	David Eide-Altman (Ex 6984)	Bob Sowards (Ex 6982)	Carl Friday (Ex 6988)

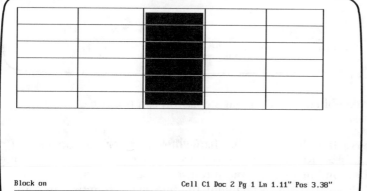

Fig. 13.10.

Blocking the center column of cells.

```
Block on                        Cell C1 Doc 2 Pg 1 Ln 1.11" Pos 3.38"
Ctrl-Arrows Column Widths; Ins Insert; Del Delete; Move Move/Copy;
1 Size; 2 Format; 3 Lines; 4 Header; 5 Math; 6 Options; 7 Join; 8 Split; 0
```

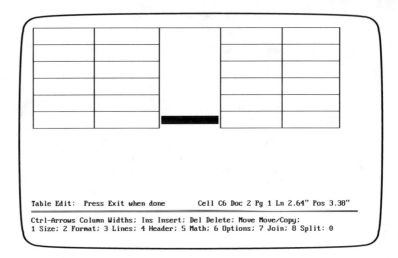

Fig. 13.11.

Inside lines and bottom line changed to none.

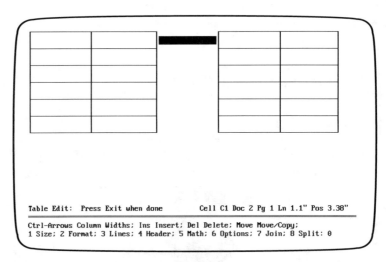

Fig. 13.12.

Removing the top line from column C.

Using these steps, or combinations of similar steps, you can remove or modify any line in any table you have created.

Note: If you encounter a line that cannot be changed, remember that top and left lines in WordPerfect Tables are the easiest to remove or change. So if you are trying to modify a right or bottom line of a cell and it refuses to be changed, jump to the cell to the right or underneath, and try changing the line again. In most cases, this method should work if the line you want to change is to the left or above the cell.

Examples of Tables WordPerfect Can Create

Now that you have seen how easy it is to change the types of lines used to form a table, how to remove lines from a form, and how to change the shading of the table itself, let's look at a number of table examples WordPerfect 5.1 can create.

You will find all the following forms on the Applications Disk that accompanies this book. (Installation places these forms in a \QTABLES subdirectory.)

Important Message Form

The Important Message form, illustrated in figure 13.13, began as a table 8 columns wide and 13 rows tall. To create a form like the Important Message form, create a table 8 columns wide by 13 rows tall. Block cells A1 through H1 and join them (option **7**, **Y**). Block and join the following groups of cells:

A2-D2   A3-H3
E2-F2   A4-F4
G2-H2   A5-F5

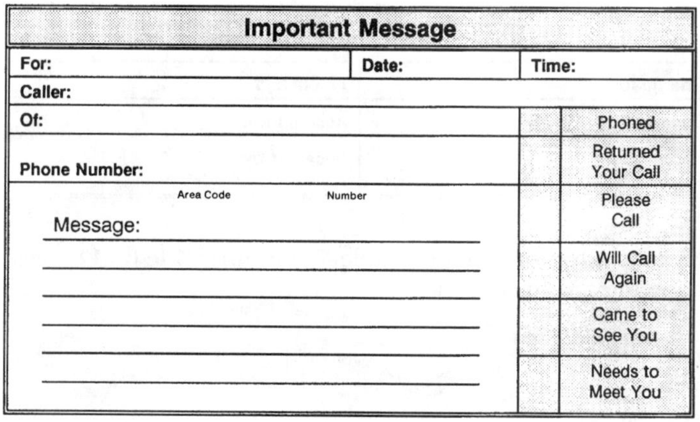

Important Message		
For:	Date:	Time:
Caller:		
Of:		Phoned
Phone Number:		Returned Your Call
Area Code Number		Please Call
Message:		Will Call Again
		Came to See You
		Needs to Meet You

Fig. 13.13.

A sample phone message form.

Block cells A6 through F6 and remove the bottom and inside lines (Lines [3], Bottom [4], None [1]) then (Lines [3], Inside [5], and None [1]). To create the "floating" lines following *Message:* refer to the section "Creating a Table Note Box." Then, where you want text centered, press Format (2), Cell (1), Justify (3), and Center (2). Row 1 at the top and columns G and H on the right are shaded with a 10 percent gray screen.

Petty Cash Form

The Petty Cash form, shown in figure 13.14, began as a table 3 columns wide and 11 rows tall. Row 2, which contains the large letters *Petty Cash*, is shaded with a 10 percent gray screen.

Fig. 13.14.

A Petty Cash table form.

Receipt No:		Date:	
	Petty Cash		
Expended for:			
Charge to:		Amount: $	
Department:		Account No:	
Approved by:		Received by:	

To create a form like the Petty Cash form, create a table 4 columns wide by 11 rows tall. Block and join the following groups of cells:

C1-D1	A10-B10
A2-D2	C10-D10
A9-B9	A11-B11
C9-D9	C11-D11

The "floating lines" under *Expended for:* are explained and illustrated in the section "Creating a Table Note Box." Only one cell, A2, contains centered text, which you achieve by pressing Format (2), Cell (1), Justify (3), and Center (2).

This heading centered in Row 2 appears in 24-point Century Schoolbook, bold font. All other text in the Petty Cash form is 12-point Helvetica bold. For an explanation of how to create the "floating" lines in the center of the box, look ahead to the section "Creating a Table Note Box."

Weekly Time Sheet Form

The Weekly Time Sheet form shown in figure 13.15 shows how to can use two different tables to create a single form. The large table that composes the major portion of the form contains 11 columns and 10 rows. Column A on the left and rows 1 and 2 of this table are shaded with a 10 percent gray screen.

Weekly Time Sheet

Name of Employee_____ For Week Ending_____, 199__
Department_____ Exemptions_____

Day of Week	Morning		Afternoon		Overtime		For Office Use Only	
	IN	OUT	IN	OUT	IN	OUT	Regular Hours	Overtime Hours
Sunday								
Monday								
Tuesday								
Wednesday								
Thursday								
Friday								
Saturday								
Totals								

No employee is permitted to work overtime without authorization! This time sheet must be filled out and signed by the employee.

Authorization:	Employee:

Fig. 13.15

A Weekly Time Sheet form.

To create the top table for the Weekly Time Sheet form, create a table 11 by 10 columns. Block cells A1 and B1 and join (**7, Y**). Block and join the following cells:

B1-C1 H1-K1
D1-E1 H2-I2
F1-G1 J2-K2

Except for the days of the week and the "Totals" at the bottom, all other cells have justification turned to center. To center-justify a cell or adjacent group of cells, start from the table edit mode and do the following:

1. Place the cursor in the cell to be modified (or press F12 or Alt-F4 to block a group of cells).

2. Choose Format (**2**).

3. Choose Cell (1).

4. Choose Justify (3).

5. Choose Full (4).

To change from simple lines to double lines inside the table, block a row or column of cells next to the line you want to change and do the following:

1. Choose Lines (3).

2. Choose which line (Left, Right, Top, or Bottom) to change.

3. Choose Double (3) or any other line type you want.

The small bottom table for signatures contains 2 columns and 1 row. This table is shaded with a 10 percent gray screen.

Cooper Black, 18-point, is used for *Weekly Time Sheet* at the top of the table. The rest of the form uses Helvetica, 12-point, except for the days of the week, which are Helvetica, 12-point, bold. The *No Employee...* line between the top and bottom forms is Helvetica, 8-point.

Credit Inquiry Form

 Increasing in complexity is the Credit Inquiry form, which contains five different tables in a single form:

1. A table for information about the sender

2. A table for who is being investigated

3. A shaded table on the left with check boxes for different kinds of information

4. A table on the right for financial information

5. A table at the bottom for the signature of the sender

Figure 13.16 illustrates a printed copy of the Credit Inquiry form.

The two unique features of this table are the check boxes in the third table and the side-by-side positions of the third and fourth tables. Check boxes are created in this manner:

1. Position the cursor where you want the check box.

2. Press Compose (Ctrl-V).

3. At the Key = prompt, type *4,38* (with no spaces between the numbers).

4. Press Enter.

Credit Inquiry

FROM:
COMPANY:
ADDRESS:
CITY/STATE/ZIP:

REGARDING:
ADDRESS:
CITY/STATE/ZIP:

The customer above has applied for a line of credit with our company. **Please provide us with** the following confidential information regarding the above individual or individuals.

Check Kind of Payments:	Largest Amount Owed:	$	
□ Prompt & Satisfactory	Total Amount Now Owed:	$	
□ Up to ____ Days Slow			
□ Pays on Account	Amount Past Due:	$	
□ Asks for More Time	Recent Trends: □ Promptness	□ Slowness	
□ Slow But Collectable			
□ Slow & Unsatisfactory	Credit Refused: □ Yes	□ No	
□ Notes Paid at Maturity	If Credit Refused, State Why:		
□ Accepts CODs Promptly			
□ Account Secured			
□ Collected by Attorney			
□ In Hands of Attorney			

□ If you have had no experience within the past 12 months, please check this box and return form.	We will be happy to reciprocate in providing information we have regarding credits. Yours truly,

A stamped, self-addressed envelope is enclosed for your reply. Thank you.

Fig. 13.16.

The Credit Inquiry form contains five different tables.

To position table boxes side by side, you have two options. You can create two side by side figure boxes using the Graphics feature (Alt-F9) and import a table into each figure box. Or you can place the two boxes one above the other on the screen and issue an Advance to Line command in front of both boxes, which tells WordPerfect to print the boxes side by side on the paper when the table is sent to the printer (see fig. 13.17). Generally speaking, it is easier to use the Advance to Line command, because you can see the contents of both boxes on the screen in the text mode. With figures, you cannot see the text inside the figure box, except in print preview.

To print two tables together on the same line, add an Advance to Line command at the upper left corner of each of the tables. Do this by first locating the **[TblDef:]** code at the beginning of each table, highlighted in figure 13.18. Then, to the immediate left of this table code, you insert an Advance to Line command, using these steps:

Fig. 13.17.

How two side-by-side tables look on the screen.

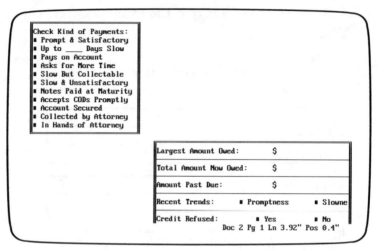

Fig. 13.18.

Place the Advance to Line command in front of the [Tbl Def] code.

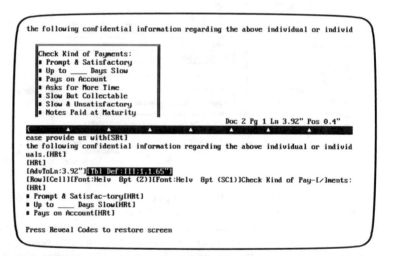

1. Press Format (Shift-F8) and select Other (**4**).

   ⌨Choose **Other** from the Layout menu.

2. Select **Advance** (**1**).

3. Choose **Line** (**3**).

4. At the Adv to Line: prompt, type the position measured in inches from the top of the page where you want each of the tables to appear.

5. Press Enter to add the Advance code.

Changing Line Thickness and Line Shading

If you want to create forms using different kinds of lines than the six shown in figure 13.6, you can do this in WordPerfect 5.1 by inserting a special format code in front of the table or tables you want to change. Here are the steps to insert the table line format code:

1. Press Format (Shift-F8) and choose **Other (4)**.

2. Select **B**order Options **(8)**.

When you choose Border Options, a Border Options screen like figure 13.19 appears. The best line to change for tables is **Thick (5)**. Note the default settings for a thick like are a line width of 0.063 inch and a shading of 100 percent. However, in many cases a line that thick doesn't look right in a typical table (see fig. 13.6).

```
Format: Border Options

    1 - Single -      Width           0.013"
                      Shading         100%

    2 - Double -      Width           0.013"
                      Shading         100%
                      Spacing Between 0.013"

    3 - Dashed -      Width           0.013"
                      Shading         100%
                      Dash Spacing    0.013"
                      Dash Length     0.053"

    4 - Dotted -      Width           0.013"
                      Shading         100%
                      Dot Spacing     0.013"

    5 - Thick -       Width           0.063"
                      Shading         100%

    6 - Extra Thick - Width           0.125"
                      Shading         100%

Selection: 0
```

Fig. 13.19.

The Format: Border Options screen.

By changing the width of the thick line, you can create a thick line that better fits the form you are creating. Figure 13.20 is a printed sample of seven different thickness settings—from .025 inch to .055 inch. Note that all the examples in figure 13.20 are thinner lines than the default line thickness of .063 inch.

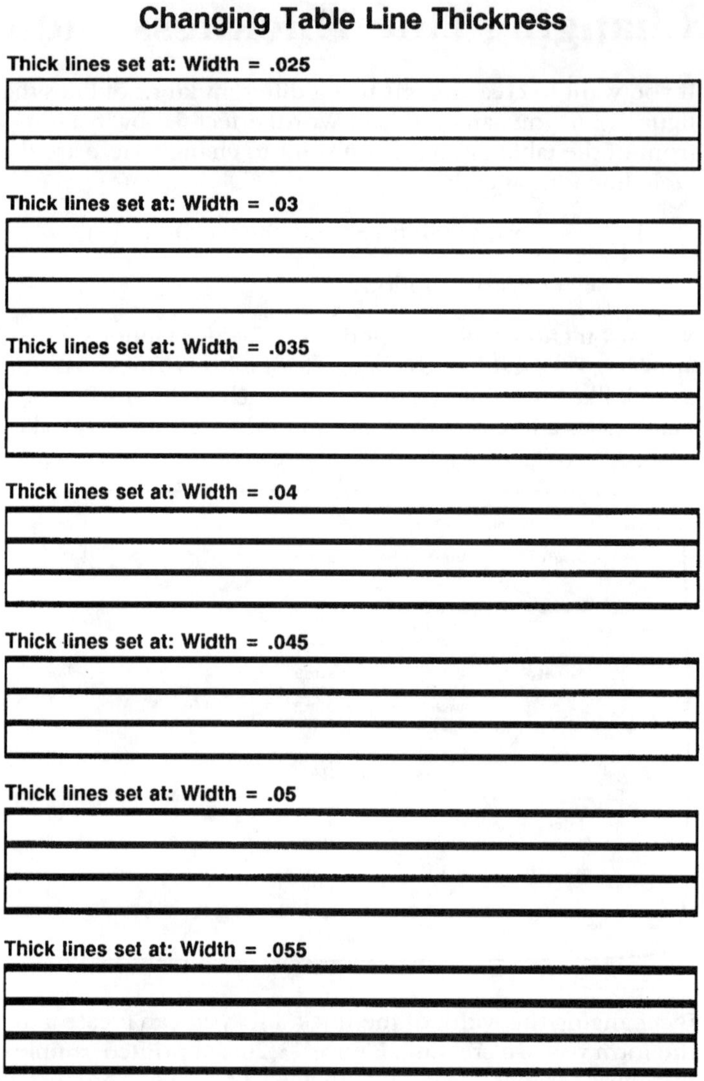

Changing Table Line Thickness

Fig. 13.20.

Printed samples of different table line thicknesses.

Thick lines set at: Width = .025

Thick lines set at: Width = .03

Thick lines set at: Width = .035

Thick lines set at: Width = .04

Thick lines set at: Width = .045

Thick lines set at: Width = .05

Thick lines set at: Width = .055

If in addition to line thickness, you want to change line shading from the default shading of 100 percent, you can do that from the same menu. Figure 13.21, for example, is a printed sample of line shading from 100 percent down to 10 percent.

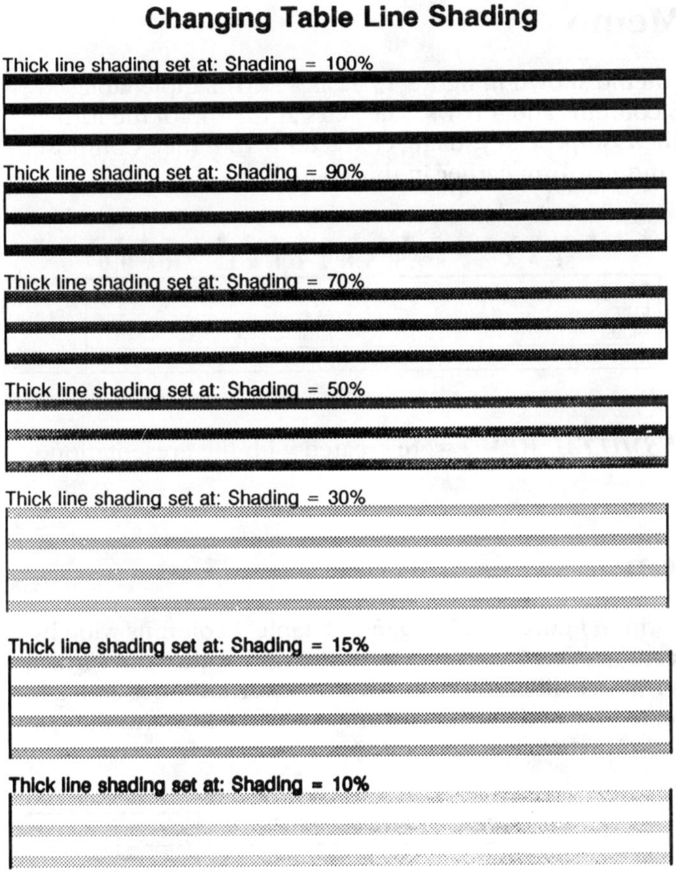

Changing Table Line Shading

Thick line shading set at: Shading = 100%

Thick line shading set at: Shading = 90%

Thick line shading set at: Shading = 70%

Thick line shading set at: Shading = 50%

Thick line shading set at: Shading = 30%

Thick line shading set at: Shading = 15%

Thick line shading set at: Shading = 10%

Fig. 13.21.

Table line shading from 100 percent to 10 percent.

Samples of Tables with Thick Lines

Now that you know how to change line thickness from the default .063-inch line to something more attractive, lets look at a few examples of forms created with thick lines set at .03 inch.

Fax Transmittal Memo

The fax transmittal memo shown in figure 13.22 is a fairly simple table, which began with 3 columns and 4 rows. The stars at the top of the form were created with the Compose key, using character 6,184. (See Compose mentioned with the Credit Inquiry form earlier in this chapter.)

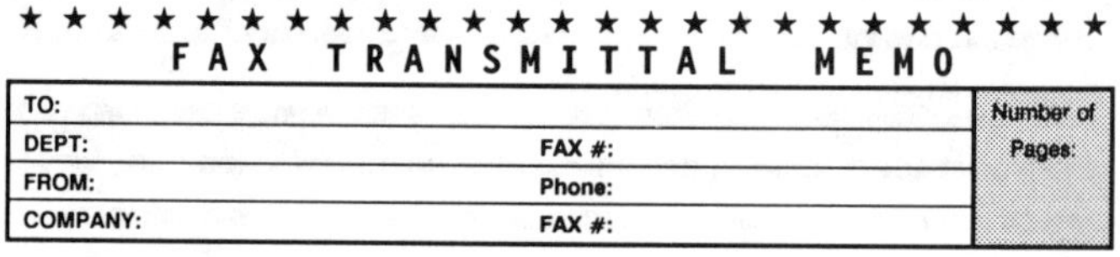
★ ★

FAX TRANSMITTAL MEMO

TO:		Number of Pages:
DEPT:	FAX #:	
FROM:	Phone:	
COMPANY:	FAX #:	

Fig. 13.22.

A fax transmittal form created from a WordPerfect table.

The large letters ***FAX TRANSMITTAL MEMO*** were created with the Presentation, 8.1-cpi font.

Credit Memo Form

The Credit Memo form in figure 13.23 began as a table 7 columns wide by 16 rows tall. This form needed 7 columns to start with because the vertical lines in the bottom row are different from any of the vertical lines above it. Separate cells had to be created for each of the bottom-row's two lines (to the left of ***Credit Approved by:*** and ***Condition & Remarks***).

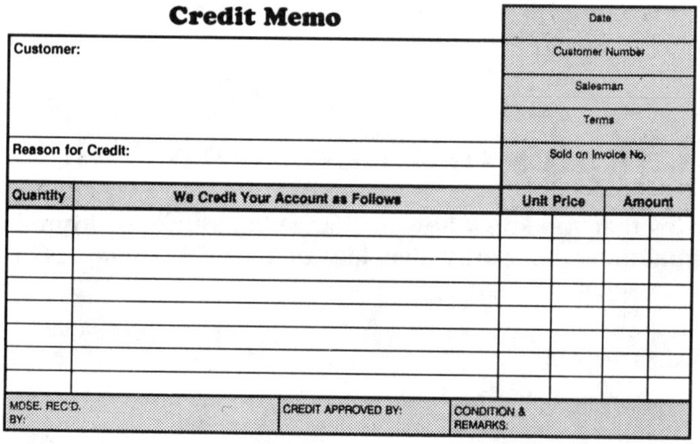
Credit Memo

Customer:		Date	
		Customer Number	
		Salesman	
		Terms	
Reason for Credit:		Sold on Invoice No.	
Quantity	We Credit Your Account as Follows	Unit Price	Amount
MDSE. REC'D. BY:	CREDIT APPROVED BY:	CONDITION & REMARKS:	

Fig. 13.23.

A Credit Memo using thick and single lines.

To create a form like the Credit Memo, start with a table 7 columns wide by 16 rows tall. Block cells A1-D1 and choose Join (**7**), Yes (**Y**). Then remove the top and left lines (Lines [**3**], Left [**1**], None [**1**]; and then Lines [**3**], Top [**3**], and None [**1**]). Block cells A2-D2, then press the down arrow two times to include row 4, and join.

In lines 1-6, join cells E-H. Block cells E5 and E6 and join vertically. For lines 5 and 6, join cells A-D. For lines 7-15, join cells B-D. For line 16, join cells A16 and B16; then join cells D16 through H16.

To change from single lines to thick lines, move your cursor outside the table to the left or on a line immediately above. (Use Reveal Codes to make certain the cursor is left of or above the [**TblDef:**] code.) Then follow the directions given earlier in this chapter for changing line thickness. Figures 13.23-25 and 13.27 all use the thickness of .03".

Then return inside the table and switch to the table edit mode (Alt-F7). Block and highlight a row or column of cells alongside the line you wish to change and do the following:

1. Choose Lines (**3**).

2. Choose which line (**Left**, **Right**, **Top**, or **Bottom**).

3. Choose Thick (**6**).

You will see the line thickness change from a single line to a shaded bar.

Cooper Black 18-point font was used for the ***Credit Memo*** heading on this form. The five boxes at the upper right uses Helvetica, 8-point; the ***Quantity...Amount*** (line 5) uses Helvetica, 10-point, bold, and the bottom section (row 16) uses Helvetica, 8-point.

Quarterly and Yearly Expense Summaries

The Quarterly Expense Summary and Yearly Expense Summary forms in figures 13.24 and 13.25 are fairly similar forms. However the most unique feature in both of these forms is the *Notes:* box at the bottom. Although normally all horizontal lines inside a table stretch from one vertical line on the left to another vertical line on the right, you can mimic the appearance of fill-in-the-blank lines by using a little trick to remove unwanted lines. The next section explains how to create such a box.

Quarterly Expense Summary

Fig. 13.24.

*A Quarterly
Expense Summary
form.*

For Month_____ Through_____   Year 199___

Preparer's Name	Branch/Region/Zone			Territory No.			Product Line	
	Air Fare	Auto	Hotel	Meals	Phone	Entertainment	Miscel.	Totals
First Week								
Second Week								
Third Week								
Fourth Week								
Fifth Week								
1st Month's Total								
First Week								
Second Week								
Third Week								
Fourth Week								
Fifth Week								
2nd Month's Total								
First Week								
Second Week								
Third Week								
Fourth Week								
Fifth Week								
3rd Month's Total								
Total for Quarter								

Notes:
_____
_____
_____

To create the Quarterly or Yearly Expense Summary, do the following. Create a table 9 columns wide by 21 rows high. In the Quarterly Expense Summary, join cells B1-D1, D1-G1, and H1-I1. To create the Yearly Expense Summary, start with a table 9 columns wide by 19 columns high. Then block and join cells B1-D1, E1-G1, and H1-I1. Cells containing *Month's Total* or *Quarter's Total* use right justification. To change to right justified cells, choose **F**ormat (**2**), **C**ell (**1**), **J**ustify (**3**), and **R**ight (**3**).

Yearly Expense Summary

For Year 199___   Preparer's Name_____

Fig. 13.25.

A Yearly Expense Summary form.

Department Name	Branch/Region/Zone			Territory No.			Product Line	
	Air Fare	Auto	Hotel	Meals	Phone	Entertainment	Miscel.	Totals
January								
February								
March								
1st Quarter's Total								
April								
May								
June								
2nd Quarter's Total								
July								
August								
September								
3rd Quarter's Total								
October								
November								
December								
4th Quarter's Total								
Yearly Total								

Notes:
_____
_____
_____

Creating a Table Note Box

After you understand the principle behind the Table Note Boxes shown in figures 13.24 and 13.25, you will find this box easy to create. Figure 13.26 illustrates the five steps necessary to create a box with what appear to be *floating lines* or horizontal lines unconnected to either side of the box.

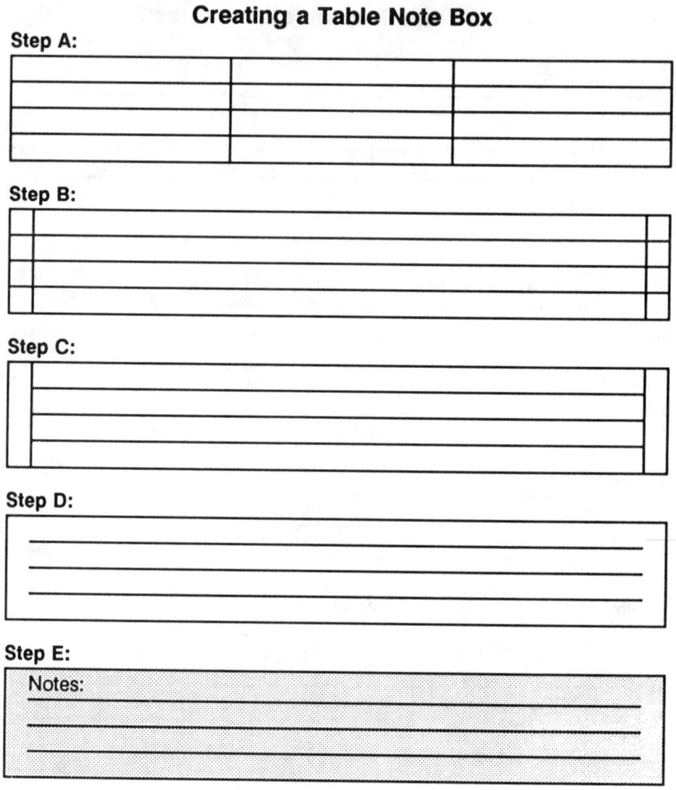

Creating a Table Note Box

Fig. 13.26.

How to create a box with "floating" lines.

Step A:

Step B:

Step C:

Step D:

Step E:

Notes:

The steps for creating this box follow:

1. Start with a box three columns wide by as many rows tall as you need. Go to the Table Options menu (see fig. 13.8) and change the Spacing Between Text and Lines (**1**) to 0.0 for each entry. This makes the spacing between the lines as little as possible. Change **P**osition of Table (**3**) from **L**eft to **F**ull. Now you are ready to modify the table itself.

2. Use the cell adjustment commands (Ctrl-Left arrow for smaller; Ctrl-right arrow for larger) to make the center column very wide and the left and right columns skinny.

3. Highlight the cells in column A and remove the inside and right lines.

4. Highlight the cells in column A and remove the right lines. Highlight the cells in column C and remove the inside and left lines.

5. Add text to cell B1 and, if desired, shading to the entire table. Your table should look like the bottom table in figures 13.24 and 13.25.

Now add the table to any form you might wish to create.

Long-Distance Telephone Form

 The Long Distance Telephone Record in figure 13.27 is an example of a table of many rows from the top to the bottom of a page. Shading appears in columns E, F, G, and H.

LONG DISTANCE TELEPHONE RECORD				REPORTING PERIOD From_____ To_____			
Date	Caller	Person or Firm Called	Number Called	Person to Person	Collect Call	Personal Call	Billed Elsewhere

Fig. 13.27.

The Long Distance Telephone Record form.

Monthly and Quarterly Calendars

Figures 13.28 and 13.29 illustrate how you can create different kinds of calendars with WordPerfect tables. Figure 13.28 contains a three-month calendar on one page, with white text in a black box for the heading *1990 Calendar*.

Fig. 13.28.

A three-month calendar on one sheet of paper.

1990 Calendar

October

Sunday	Monday	Tuesday	Wednesday	Thursday	Friday	Saturday
	1	2	3	4	5	6
7	8	9	10	11	12	13
14	15	16	17	18	19	20
21	22	23	24	25	26	27
28	29	30	31			

November

Sunday	Monday	Tuesday	Wednesday	Thursday	Friday	Saturday
				1	2	3
4	5	6	7	8	9	10
11	12	13	14	15	16	17
18	19	20	21	22	23	24
25	26	27	28	29	30	

December

Sunday	Monday	Tuesday	Wednesday	Thursday	Friday	Saturday
						1
2	3	4	5	6	7	8
9	10	11	12	13	14	15
16	17	18	19	20	21	22
23	24	25	26	27	28	31

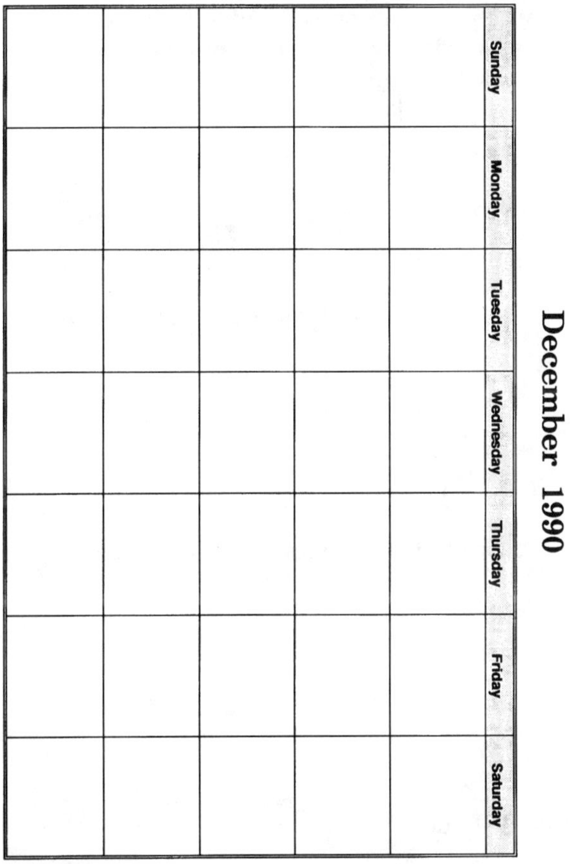

Fig. 13.29.

A one-month calendar printed in landscape mode.

The one-month and three-month calendars are included on the Applications Disk as CALENDAR.TBL (one-month) and CALENDAR.3M (three-month). (Installation puts these files in the \QTABLES subdirectory.)

Adding Dates to the Calendar with a Macro

On the Applications Disk are two macros that automatically insert numbers 1-31 in these calendar forms. (Installation puts these macros in the \QMACROS subdirectory.) If you want to add dates to the one-month calendar, do the following:

1. Retrieve the CALENDAR.TBL form to your screen.

2. Press Macro (Alt-F10).

3. Type *CALENDAR* and press Enter.

4. The macro prompts for the month and year you want added, and for which day of the week (Sunday–Saturday) that you want numbers 1-31 to begin. (For example, if you want 1 to begin on a Tuesday, type *Tuesday* at the prompt for day of the week.)

If you want to add dates to the three-month calendar, do the following:

1. Retrieve the CALENDAR.3M form to your screen.

2. Change the name of each month to the months you want to use.

3. Position your cursor in the first table where you want numbers 1-31 to begin.

4. Press Macro (Alt-F10).

5. Type *CALENDAR2* and press Enter.

6. The macro will add the dates to the first month.

7. Repeat Steps 2 through 4 for the two remaining months on the page.

Creating Landscape Forms

Figures 13.29 (in the earlier section "Monthly and Quarterly Calendars") and 13.30 illustrate how to use a landscape table to create a form printed sideways on the page.

To create a landscape table like figure 13.30, do the following.

1. Press Format (Shift-F8) and select **Page** (**2**)
   ⌨Choose **Page** from the **Layout** menu.

2. Choose Paper Size/Type (**7**).

3. Use the up or down arrow to highlight the Standard-Wide paper size on the Format: Paper Size/Type screen.

4. Press **Select** (**1**) to choose the landscape form.

5. Press Exit (F7) to return to the edit window.

6. Press Columns/Table (Alt-F7) to begin creating a landscape table.

7. Choose **Table** (**2**).

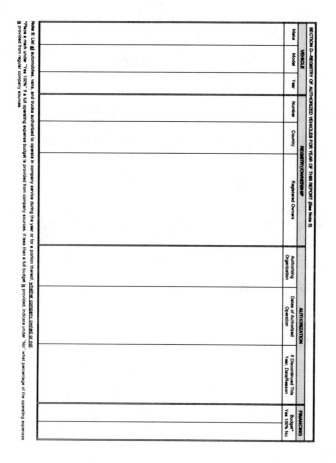

Fig. 13.30.

*A landscape
Registry of Vehicles
form.*

8. Choose **Create** (**1**).

9. Type 7 and press Enter to specify the number of columns.

10. Type 6 and press Enter to specify the number of rows.

11. Move the cursor to cell A1 and turn on Block.

12. Press the End key to highlight every cell in row 1.

13. Choose **Format** (**2**).

14. Choose **Cell** (**1**).

15. Choose **Justify** (**3**).

16. Choose **Center** (**2**).

17. Press Exit (F7) to return to the text mode.

18. Type the days *Sunday* through *Saturday* in cells **A1** through **G1**.

19. You can make rows 2 through 6 (the days of the week) taller by pressing Enter three or four times in one day of each row (for example, pressing Enter three times in a cell in Sunday will make the entire row taller by three lines).

To create a landscape table like figure 13.30, the Vehicle Registry form, follow Steps 1 through 8 above, except use 11 for number of columns and 4 for number of rows. Then add these steps:

1. Type *11* and press Enter to specify the number of Columns.

2. Type *4* and press Enter to specify the number of Rows.

3. Block all the cells in row 1 and join into one cell (**7**, **Y**).

4. Block and join cells A2-C2, D2-F2, G2-I2, and J2-K2.

5. Move the cursor to cell A1 and turn on Block.

6. Press Home, Home, down arrow to highlight the entire form.

7. Choose **Format** (**2**).

8. Choose **Cell** (**1**).

9. Choose **Justify** (**3**).

10. Choose **Center** (**2**).

11. Type the information shown in figure 13.30.

Changing Dash Spacing and Dash Line Length

What if you want to use a table with dashed lines? Can you adjust the length of the dashes or their distance apart? You can if you use the Border Options screen (see fig. 13.19) and change the defaults for **Dashed** (**3**) from a dash spacing of .013 inch and dash length of .053 inch. Figure 13.31 illustrates what you can create using different settings for these two dash options.

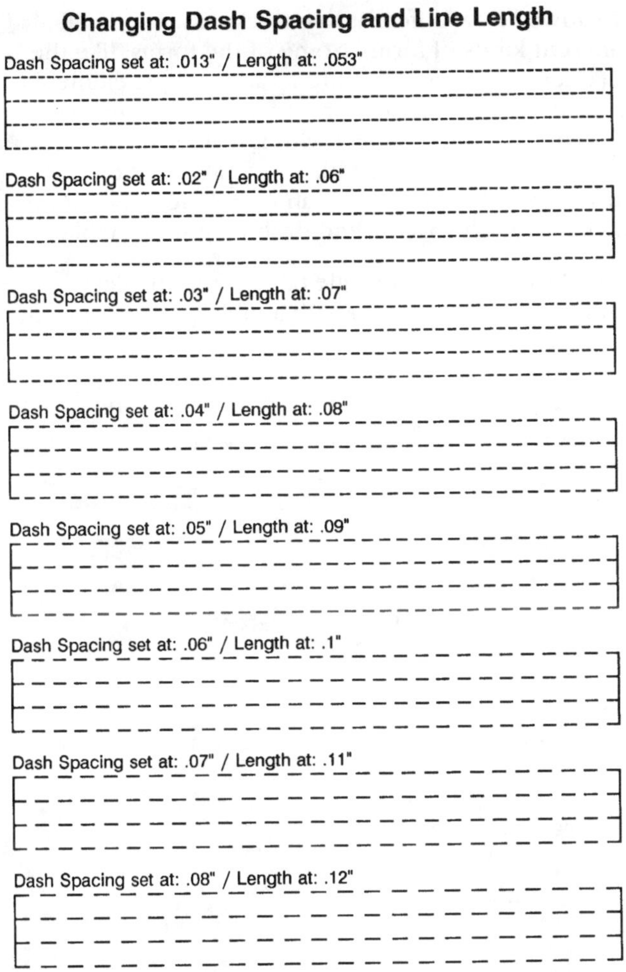

Changing Dash Spacing and Line Length

Dash Spacing set at: .013" / Length at: .053"

Dash Spacing set at: .02" / Length at: .06"

Dash Spacing set at: .03" / Length at: .07"

Dash Spacing set at: .04" / Length at: .08"

Dash Spacing set at: .05" / Length at: .09"

Dash Spacing set at: .06" / Length at: .1"

Dash Spacing set at: .07" / Length at: .11"

Dash Spacing set at: .08" / Length at: .12"

Fig. 13.31.

How different settings affect dashed lines.

Summary

In this chapter, you have learned the basics of a WordPerfect table, how to create a table, and how to select and modify the table line thickness and table line shading. You have also discovered how to change and remove lines from a table, and how to make one table look like two tables. The table examples included in this chapter illustrate the variety of forms that can be created using one or more WordPerfect tables on a single page of paper. With the Credit Inquiry form you saw how to create side-by-side tables within a single form using the Advance to Line command.

Additional forms in this chapter showed how different line thicknesses and cell shading could produce many different kinds of forms. Some of the forms, like the fax transmittal form, used WordPerfect's Compose feature to add unique elements like stars to the form. This chapter also revealed the secret of how to create a table with "floating lines"—lines that do not seem to connect with any lines within the form. Also, the calendar examples showed how to combine several tables on one page to create a multiform document and how to create tables in landscape mode. Lastly, you saw how easy it is to change dash spacing and dash length in a table.

Chapter 14 shows you step-by-step how to create a single table—and invoice form—from beginning to end and how to use a macro with a table to fill in specific information.

14

Creating a Customer Invoice

Businesses keep track of individual sales or transactions with an invoice form that serves as the buyer's proof-of-purchase form. An invoice describes the item sold or service rendered and notes the total cost, including the basic cost plus any tax, price discounts, or special payment arrangements. The invoice generally lists the address and phone number of the business and can also show the name and address of the customer or client. The invoice can show the number of the individual sale as well as the number of any purchase order used for payment.

Earlier word processing programs lacked the power to create the many formats required for a complex invoice or a statement of account. To produce customized forms on the PC, businesses had to invest in special invoice-creation programs or have their invoices custom-printed at a local print shop.

With the tables feature, WordPerfect 5.1 now has the capability to both print a customized invoice form and fill in the form as it prints. This chapter shows you how to create a typical customer-invoice form and how to use the INVOICE macro included on disk to fill in the top portion of the form. (Although this chapter includes complete instructions for creating and modifying an invoice, the form itself is available completely prepared on the Applications Disk, under the title INVOICE.TBL.)

The INVOICE macro retrieves the INVOICE.TBL invoice from the C:\WP51\MACROS subdirectory, prompts the user for pertinent information, and fills in the form automatically. All you have to do is enter the purchased items and their prices in the lower section of the form (see fig. 14.1).

<table>
<tr><td colspan="4">Company Name
123 Main Street
Anytown, ST 54321</td><td colspan="2">Invoice Number
@
Invoice Date</td></tr>
</table>

Fig. 14.1.

The complete invoice form.

Company Name 123 Main Street Anytown, ST 54321	Invoice Number @
	Invoice Date
Sold To:	Customer Number
	Purchase Order Number

Code	Description	Quantity	Price	Total
%%				0.00
			Total Due	0.00

Creating the Invoice Header

The first part of an invoice is the *invoice header*. All invoices have a section at the top of the page that lists the following:

- The company's name and address
- The purchaser's name and address
- The date of the transaction
- The invoice number
- Any customer number
- Any purchase-order number

These items are fairly standard in the business world and should be included in your invoice, unless your company has a different accepted format.

Creating the First Table

In the INVOICE.TBL form, the header is a separate WordPerfect table with different entries in each of the table's cells. You can "lock" certain cell information to make it inaccessible by the user. The invoice can then be used with or without the INVOICE macro.

Start creating the invoice header by following these steps:

1. Press Columns/Table (Alt-F7) and Tables (**2**).

    ⌨Select **Tables** from the **Layout** menu.

2. Press **Create** (**1**).

3. For the prompt Number of Columns:, type *2* and press Enter.

4. For the prompt Number of Rows:, type *8* and press Enter.

5. In cell A1, press Block (Alt-F4 or F12); then press the down arrow two times.

6. Press Join (**7**) and **Yes** (**Y**); then press the down arrow two times.

7. In cell A5, press Block (Alt-F4 or F12); then press the down arrow three times.

8. Press Join (**7**) and **Yes** (**Y**).

9. Press **Options** (**6**).

At this point you should see the Table Options screen shown in figure 14.2.

Fig. 14.2.

Table Options menu.

```
Table Options

        1 - Spacing Between Text and Lines
                    Left                    0.083"
                    Right                   0.083"
                    Top                     0.1"
                    Bottom                  0"

        2 - Display Negative Results        1
                    1 = with minus signs
                    2 = with parentheses

        3 - Position of Table               Left

        4 - Gray Shading (% of black)       10%




        Selection: 0
```

Setting the Proper Spacing

To position information properly in the invoice header, you must adjust the spacing between the text and the table lines. The following steps adjust text spacing inside the table (all settings in this menu affect all cells in the table):

1. Choose Spacing Between Text and Lines (**1**).

2. Press Enter two times to reach the Top setting.

3. Change the default 0.1" to .09" by typing *.09*.

4. Press Enter once and then Exit (F7) twice to return to cell A5.

Setting the Cell Justification Options

1. Press the up arrow two times to reach cell A1.

2. Press Format (**2**) and Cell (**1**).

3. Press Justify (**3**). At this point your table should look like figure 14.3, with cell A1 highlighted.

4. Press Center (**2**) and then the right arrow to reach cell B1.

5. Press Format (**2**) and Column (**2**).

6. Press Justify (**3**) and Center (**2**).

Fig. 14.3.

The Cell Justification menu at the bottom of the screen.

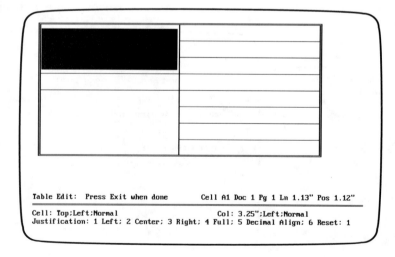

```
Table Edit:  Press Exit when done        Cell A1 Doc 1 Pg 1 Ln 1.13" Pos 1.12"

Cell: Top:Left:Normal                     Col: 3.25":Left:Normal
Justification: 1 Left; 2 Center; 3 Right; 4 Full; 5 Decimal Align; 6 Reset: 1
```

7. Press the left arrow once to reach cell A1.

8. Press Exit (F7) to leave table edit mode.

Typing Information into the Table Header

The next step is to type permanent information in the table header. This information appears in every copy of the table that is printed—your company name; the various cell prompt lines, such as `Invoice Number`; and so on. Complete the following steps to add text to the table header:

1. In cell A1, press Font (Ctrl-F8) and choose Base Font (4).

   ⊡ Select Base Font from the Font menu.

2. Select Helvetica 14-point bold or a similar large font.

3. Type your company's name on the first line.

4. Press Font (Ctrl-F8) and choose Base Font (4).

   ⊡ Select Base Font from the Font menu.

5. At the end of your company name, select Helvetica 12-point bold or a smaller font.

   This second font will be used for the rest of the permanent information in the invoice.

6. Press Enter twice and type the street address.

7. Press Enter and type the city, state, and ZIP code.

8. Press Tab once to enter cell B1.

9. In cell B1, type *Invoice Number* and press Tab twice.

10. In cell B3, type *Invoice Date* and press Tab once.

11. In cell A4, type *Sold to:* and press Tab three times.

12. In cell B5, type *Customer Number* and press Tab twice.

13. In cell B7, type *Purchase Order Number*.

14. Press Home, up arrow, and then down arrow to reach cell B1.

Locking the Permanent Information

After typing permanent information into the invoice header, you can lock those cells to keep the user from changing the text accidentally. The following are the steps for locking certain cells:

1. Press Columns/Table (Alt-F7).

    ▭Select Tables from the Layout menu.

2. Choose Format (**2**) and Cell (**1**). The Cell Type menu should appear, as in figure 14.4.

3. Press Lock (**5**) and On (**1**).

4. Press Tab twice to reach cell B3; repeat steps 2 and 3.

5. Press Tab once to reach cell A4; repeat steps 2 and 3.

6. Press Tab three times to reach cell B5; repeat steps 2 and 3.

7. Press Tab twice to reach cell B7; repeat steps 2 and 3.

Fig. 14.4.

The Cell Type menu includes a lock option.

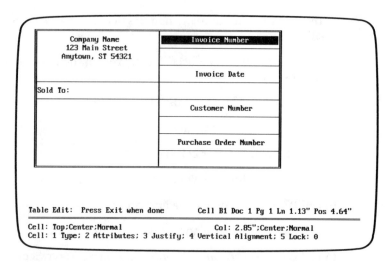

Removing Unwanted Lines

After you lock any cells that contain permanent information, you must remove unwanted lines from the table. Complete these steps to remove lines you no longer need:

1. Press the up arrow six times to reach cell B1. (Or press GoTo [Ctrl-Home], type *b1*, and press Enter.)

2. Press Block (Alt-F4 or F12) and the down arrow once.

3. Press **Lines (3)**, **Inside (5)**, and **None (1)**.

4. Press the down arrow once and repeat steps 2 and 3.

5. Press the left arrow once and repeat steps 2 and 3.

6. Press the right arrow once and repeat steps 2 and 3.

7. Press the down arrow once and repeat steps 2 and 3.

8. Press the down arrow once and repeat steps 2 and 3.

9. Press Home, left arrow to reach cell A5.

10. Press Ctrl-right arrow 12 times to expand the left half of the table.

11. Press Exit (F7) to leave table edit mode.

12. Press Shift-Tab twice to return to cell B2.

13. In cell B2 type an "at" code (@), which will indicate to the INVOICE macro the starting point for inserting information.

    Your table header should look like figure 14.5 now, with the unwanted lines removed and an @ under Invoice Number.

14. Press Home, Home, down arrow to position the cursor underneath the table header; then press Enter to insert a blank line under the table.

Creating the Body of the Invoice

Now that the header is properly formed, it's time to add the main part of the invoice—the section to be filled in with specific information about the item or service being purchased. (Now is a good time to save a copy of the work you have done so far, in case something goes wrong.) Making certain that the cursor lies beneath the previously created table, complete these steps to create the bottom half of the invoice:

1. Press Columns/Table (Alt-F7) and **Tables (2)**.

    ⌨Select **Tables** from the Layout menu.

2. Press **Create (1)**.

3. At the prompt Number of Columns:, type *5* and press Enter.

Fig. 14.5.

*The finished
header with
unwanted lines
removed.*

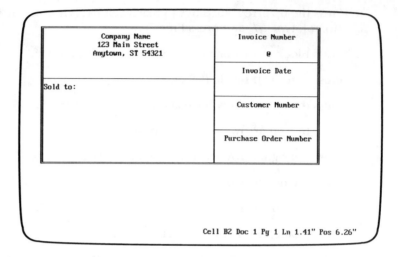

```
            Company Name              Invoice Number
            123 Main Street
            Anytown, ST 54321                0

                                         Invoice Date
Sold to:

                                       Customer Number


                                    Purchase Order Number




                            Cell B2 Doc 1 Pg 1 Ln 1.41" Pos 6.26"
```

4. At the prompt `Number of Rows:`, type *20* and press Enter. Figure 14.6 shows this second table.

5. In cell A1, press Block (Alt-F4 or F12), End.

6. Select **Lines (3)**, **Bottom (4)**, and **Double (3)**.

7. In cell E1, press Block (Alt-F4 or F12); then press the left arrow twice.

Fig. 14.6.

*A second table for
the bottom half of
the invoice form.*

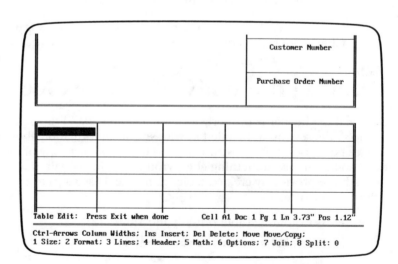

```
                                       Customer Number


                                    Purchase Order Number




Table Edit:  Press Exit when done        Cell A1 Doc 1 Pg 1 Ln 3.73" Pos 1.12"
Ctrl-Arrows Column Widths; Ins Insert; Del Delete; Move Move/Copy;
1 Size; 2 Format; 3 Lines; 4 Header; 5 Math; 6 Options; 7 Join; 8 Split: 0
```

8. Press Format (**2**), Column (**2**), Justify (**3**), and Decimal Align (**5**).

9. Press the left arrow once to reach cell B1.

10. Press Format (**2**), Column (**2**), Justify (**3**), and Center (**2**).

11. Press the left arrow once to reach cell A1.

12. Press Block (Alt-F4 or F12) and then End to highlight the first row.

13. Press Format (**2**), Cell (**1**), Justify (**3**), and Center (**2**).

Adjusting the Size of the Columns

Next, make room for a product-description column by adjusting the size of the columns in the lower table. To do this, you must shrink columns A, C, D, and E, and expand column B. Follow these steps to adjust the various columns:

1. In cell A1, press Ctrl-left arrow four times.

2. In cell C1, press Ctrl-left arrow four times.

3. In cell D1, press Ctrl-left arrow four times.

4. In cell E1, press Ctrl-left arrow four times.

5. Press the left arrow three times to reach cell B1.

6. In cell B1, press Ctrl-right arrow 16 times. (When finished, you want the right edge of the lower table to match the right edge of the upper table.)

7. Press Exit (F7) to leave table edit mode.

Adding Headers to the Lower Table

The lower section now needs column headers. The following steps add column headers to the table:

1. Press the left arrow to reach cell A1.

2. In cell A1, type *Code*.

3. In cell B1, type *Description*.

4. In cell C1, type *Quantity*.

5. In cell D1, type *Price*.

6. In cell E1, type *Total*.

7. Press Columns/Table (Alt-F7).

☐ Select Tables from the Layout menu.

Figure 14.7 illustrates how your bottom table should look with headers added to each column.

Fig. 14.7.

The bottom table with columns defined.

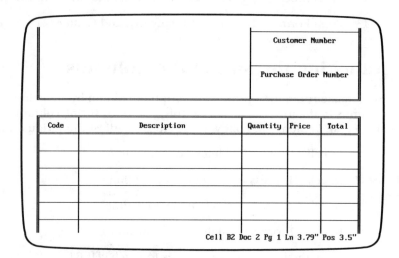

Cell B2 Doc 2 Pg 1 Ln 3.79" Pos 3.5"

Locking the Header Cells

To lock the cells containing column headers so that they cannot be changed by a user, do the following:

1. In cell E1, press Block (Alt-F4 or F12) and then Home, left arrow to highlight the entire row.

2. Press Format (2), Cells (1), Lock (5), and On (1).

In table edit mode, cells that have been locked display a cell number in square brackets, such as Cell [A1]. Figure 14.8, for example, shows that cell A1 is locked. When table edit mode is not in effect, the cursor cannot enter any locked cell.

˙ng the Total Line

˙he table, you need to fix a section for the total cost or charges
ᴊle. You can do this by removing some lines from line 20.
˙t mode, with one cell highlighted, do the following:

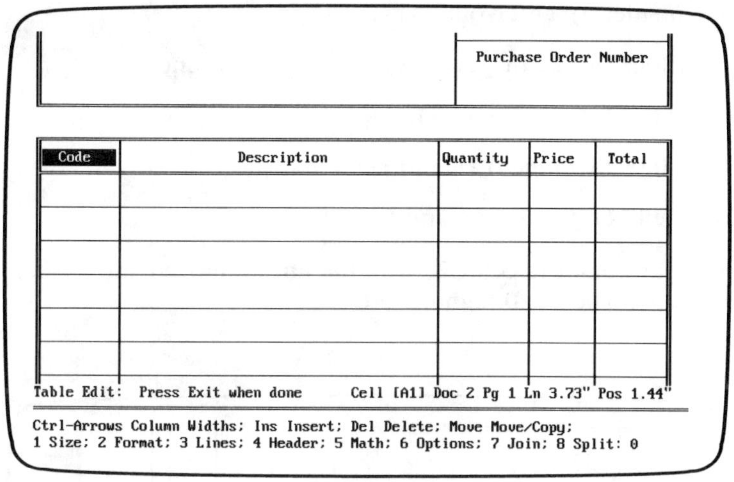

Fig. 14.8.

A locked cell displays a cell number in square brackets.

1. Press Home, Home, down arrow to reach cell E20.

2. Press the up arrow once to move to cell E19.

3. Press Block (Alt-F4 or F12) and then Home, left arrow to highlight row 19.

4. Press **Lines (3)**, **Bottom (4)**, and **Double (3)**.

5. Press the down arrow once to move to cell A20.

6. Press Block (Alt-F4 or F12) and the right arrow once.

7. Press **Join (7)** and **Yes (Y)**.

8. Press the right arrow once to reach cell C20.

9. Press Block (Alt-F4 or F12) and the right arrow once.

10. Press **Join (7)** and **Yes (Y)**.

Removing Lines from the Table

To remove lines from row 20, follow these steps:

1. In cell C20, press Block (Alt-F4 or F12) and the left arrow once.

2. Press Lines (**3**), Outside (**6**), and None (**1**).

3. In cell A20, press Block (Alt-F4 or F12) and the right arrow once.

4. Press Lines (**3**), Inside (**5**), and None (**1**).

5. In cell C20, press Lines (**3**), Right (**2**), and Double (**3**).

6. Press Format (**2**), Cell (**1**), Justify (**3**), and Left (**1**).

   Figure 14.9 shows the cursor in cell C20 with the lines removed and table edit mode on, with cell C20 highlighted.

Fig. 14.9.

Row 20 with lines removed from the left side.

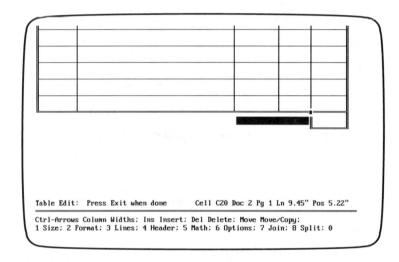

```
Table Edit:  Press Exit when done        Cell C20 Doc 2 Pg 1 Ln 9.45" Pos 5.22"

Ctrl-Arrows Column Widths; Ins Insert; Del Delete; Move Move/Copy;
1 Size; 2 Format; 3 Lines; 4 Header; 5 Math; 6 Options; 7 Join; 8 Split: 0
```

7. Press Exit (F7) and type *Total Due* in cell C20.

Figure 14.10 shows the bottom portion of the table in normal text-screen mode, with a `Total Due` entry to the left of the bottom right cell. Don't worry about the double-line intersection display between rows 19 and 20. The display appears this way because the intersection includes a single line at the top. The table will print properly, however.

Adding the Math Codes to the Invoice

The last step is to add math formula codes to the table so that all entries can be multiplied by quantity and unit price and added vertically for a total with a macro:

1. Press Columns/Table (Alt-F7).

   Select **Tables** from the **Layout** menu.

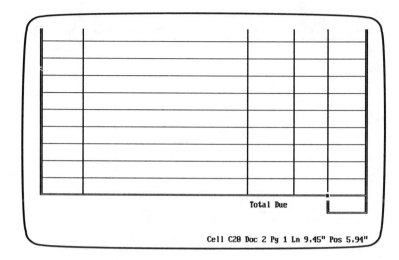

Fig. 14.10.

The bottom of the invoice table with text added.

2. Press Home, Home, up arrow to reach cell A1 of this table.

3. Press the down arrow once and then End to reach cell E2.

4. Press **Math (5)** and select **Formula (2)** from the Math menu at the bottom of the page (see fig. 14.11).

5. At the Enter Formula: prompt, type *C2*D2* and press Enter.

   This code tells WordPerfect to multiply whatever appears in cell C2 by whatever appears in cell D2 and to place the result in cell E2.

   0.00 appears in cell E2, and the code =C2*D2 is displayed in the lower left corner of the screen, as in figure 14.12.

6. Press Home, Home, down arrow to reach cell E20.

7. Press **Math (5)** and 4 .0.00 appears in cell E20, and the code =+ appears in the lower left corner.

8. Press Home, Home, up arrow and then Exit (F7).

9. Press the down arrow once and type %% in cell A2.

   The INVOICE macro needs these characters in this cell as a search string for completing the macro. The completed invoice table should look like figure 14.13.

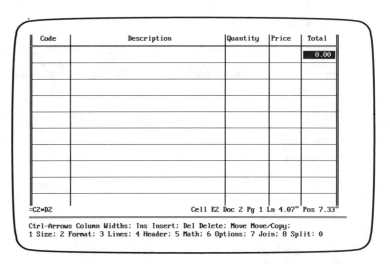

Fig. 14.11.

The table math menu at the bottom of the screen.

Code	Description	Quantity	Price	Total

Table Edit: Press Exit when done Align Cell E2 Doc 2 Pg 1 Ln 4.07" Pos 7.11"

Math: 1 Calculate; 2 Formula; 3 Copy Formula; 4 +; 5 =; 6 *: 0

Fig. 14.12.

The math code for a cell is displayed in the lower left corner.

Code	Description	Quantity	Price	Total
				0.00

=C2*D2   Cell E2 Doc 2 Pg 1 Ln 4.07" Pos 7.33"

Ctrl-Arrows Column Widths; Ins Insert; Del Delete; Move Move/Copy;
1 Size; 2 Format; 3 Lines; 4 Header; 5 Math; 6 Options; 7 Join; 8 Split: 0

10. Save the invoice as INVOICE.TBL in the C:\WP51\MACROS subdirectory (or copy the INVOICE.TBL from the disk into that subdirectory).

Using the Invoice Macro

To use the INVOICE.WPM macro, copy the macro INVOICE.TBL and the Alt-T macro to the C:\WP51\MACROS subdirectory. Then follow these steps:

1. Start with a clear screen.

Code	Description	Quantity	Price	Total

Company Name
123 Main Street
Anytown, ST 54321

Sold To:

Invoice Number

@

Invoice Date

Customer Number

Purchase Order Number

Code	Description	Quantity	Price	Total
%%				0.00
		Total Due		0.00

Fig. 14.13.

The completed invoice form.

Note: If you do not have a clear screen, the macro shows the prompt in figure 14.14 when run.

2. Press Macro (Alt-F10).

3. Type *INVOICE* at the `Macro:` prompt.

4. The macro then retrieves the INVOICE.TBL file and searches for @ in cell B2 (under the Invoice Number header).

   Should the INVOICE.TBL file be missing, the macro shows a prompt like that shown in figure 14.15.

5. The macro next offers a series of prompts to assist filling in the invoice.

6. When done, the macro searches for the %% code and leaves the cursor in row 2 of the lower invoice table, ready for you to type the product code, product description, quantity, and price.

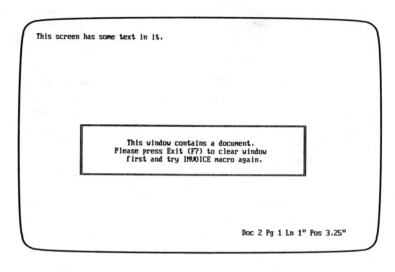

Fig. 14.14.

*Prompt provided
by the INVOICE
macro.*

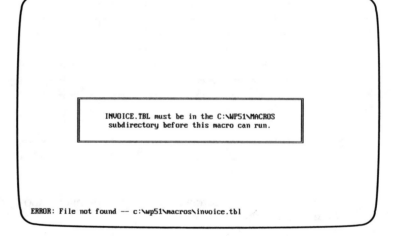

Fig. 14.15.

*The prompt if the
INVOICE.TBL is
missing from
C:\WP51\MACROS.*

7. After you type the price, run the Alt-T macro to multiply the price by the
   quantity, enter the proper sum in the Total column, calculate the Total
   Due at the bottom of the form, and advance the cursor to the next line.

For each line, press Alt-T after you have typed the Price (and before you enter the
Total column), and each line will calculate. That's all there is to it. If you haven't
already done so, be sure to save the invoice under a different name when you are
done.

Examining the Text of the Invoice Macro

For those readers who want to edit the macro, here is the complete text of the INVOICE.WPM used in this chapter:

Macro: Action

    File   INVOICE.WPM

    Description   Fills in the INVOICE.TBL

```
{DISPLAY OFF}
{ON ERROR}{GO}notfound~~
{IF}{SYSTEM}document~=256~  {;}Checks·window·for·a·document~
   {GO}do-invoice~
{ELSE}
   {BELL}{BELL}{DISPLAY ON}     {;}If·not·clear,·display·message~
{PROMPT}
{^P}δδ
{^P}δ9
{^P}δſ ·············This·window·contains·a·document.···········
{^P}δπ ·······Please·press·Exit·(F7)·to·clear·window··········
{^P}δ* ···········first·and·try·INVOICE·macro·again.···········
{^P}δ►
{^P}δ◄
~
{WAIT}40~
{DISPLAY OFF}{DISPLAY ON}      {;}Clears·and·restores·screen~
{END IF}
{QUIT}

{LABEL}do-invoice~
{ON CANCEL}{CALL}confirm~~
·{Retrieve}c:\wp51\macros\invoice.tbl
{Enter}{Backspace}             {;}Retrieves·INVOICE.TBL~
{Search}@{Search}{Backspace}   {;}Enters·Invoice·Cell~
{DISPLAY ON}                    {;}Displays·the·invoice·table~
{TEXT}Number~Type·invoice·number·and·press·Enter:·~
{VARIABLE}Number~              {;}inserts·the·Invoice·Number~
```

```
{DISPLAY OFF}{Tab}{Date/Outline}
t{DISPLAY ON}                    {;}inserts the current date~
{Tab}{TEXT}Name~Type customer's name and press Enter: ~{Enter}
{Home}{Tab}{VARIABLE}Name~{Enter}    {;}inserts the customer's name~
{TEXT}Company~Type company name and press Enter: ~
{Home}{Tab}{VARIABLE}Company~{Enter}    {;}inserts the company name~
{TEXT}Address~Type customer's street address and press Enter: ~
{Home}{Tab}{VARIABLE}Address~{Enter}    {;}inserts the address~
{TEXT}CityState~Type city, state, ZIP and press Enter: ~
{Home}{Tab}{VARIABLE}CityState~         {;}inserts the city and state~
{TEXT}CustNum~Type the customer's number and press Enter: ~
{Tab}{VARIABLE}CustNum~         {;}inserts the customer number~
{TEXT}PurOrder~Type the purchase order number and press Enter: ~
{Tab}{VARIABLE}PurOrder~        {;}inserts the purchase order number~
{DISPLAY OFF}                   {;}hides the following activity~
{Search}%%{Search}             {;}moves to the second table~
{Backspace}{Backspace}         {;}deletes the %% codes~

{DISPLAY ON}                    {;}restores the screen~
{RETURN}


{LABEL}confirm~    {;}Checks to see if user wants to cancel macro~
{CHAR}cancel~Do you wish to cancel this invoice and clear
 the screen?  No (Yes)~
{IF}"{VARIABLE}cancel~"="Y"|"{VARIABLE}cancel~"="y"~   {;}If Yes~
   {DISPLAY OFF}
   {Exit}nn        {;}User wants to cancel, so clear screen~
   {QUIT}          {;}Return control to WordPerfect~
   {DISPLAY ON}
   {END IF}
{RETURN}           {;}Continues macro~


{LABEL}notfound~    {;}User told that INVOICE.TBL not found~
   {BELL}
{PROMPT}
{^P}δδ
{^P}δ9   ...................................................
{^P}δſ   ...... INVOICE.TBL must be in the C:\WP51\MACROS .....
{^P}δſ   ....... subdirectory before this macro can run. ......
{^P}δ*   ...................................................
{^P}δ►
~{WAIT}40~        {;}Leave message displayed 40 seconds~
{Cancel}
```

Ctrl-PgUp for macro commands; Press Exit when done

As you learned in Chapter 13, you can modify tables fairly easily. For example, figure 14.16 shows a printed table that has thick lines rather than double lines.

To change the double lines to thick lines, do the following:

1. Inside cell A1 of the top table, press Columns/Table (Alt-F7).

2. Press Block (Alt-F4 or F12).

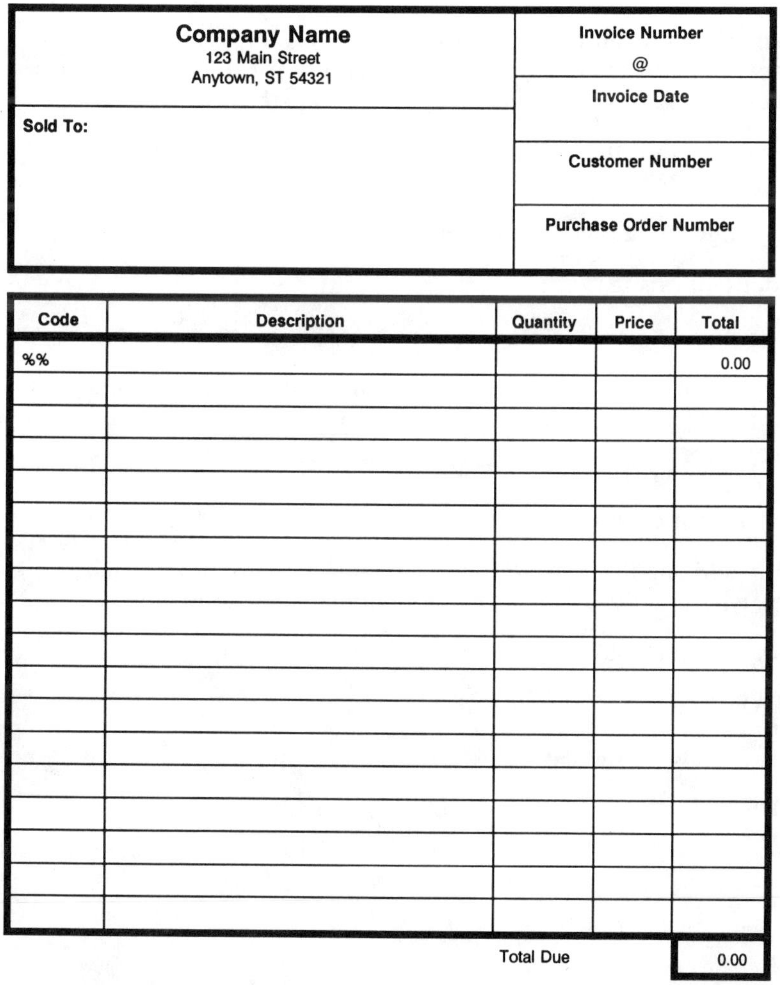

Fig. 14.16.

An invoice with thick border lines.

3. Press Home, Home down arrow to highlight the top table.

4. Press **Lines** (**3**) and **Outside** (**6**).

5. Press **Thick** (**6**).

6. Press Exit (F7).

Repeat the process in the lower table, changing every double line to a thick line. Print the table.

Unfortunately, WordPerfect's default setting for thick lines produces lines that, usually, look too thick. But you can easily change the settings for thick lines. Here's how to make the thick lines less prominent:

1. Go to the top of the INVOICE.TBL page by pressing Home, Home, up arrow.

2. Press Format (Shift-F8) and choose **Other** (**4**).

3. Choose **B**order Options (**8**).

4. Select **Thick** (**5**).

5. The default line width for thick lines is 0.063"; about half that thickness looks best. Type *.03* and press Enter.

6. Press Exit (F7) twice to return to edit mode.

Now when you print the same table, the line looks much better (see fig. 14.17).

In addition, you could add shading to certain cells in your table to indicate cells where no text will be typed. For example, in the top table, do the following:

1. Press Columns/Table (Alt-F7).

2. Move to cell A1.

3. Choose **Lines** (**3**) and **Shade** (**8**).

4. Press **On** (**1**).

5. Press Exit F7.

Company Name 123 Main Street Anytown, ST 54321	Invoice Number @
	Invoice Date
Sold To:	Customer Number
	Purchase Order Number

Fig. 14.17.

Invoice table with modified thick lines.

Code	Description	Quantity	Price	Total
%%				0.00
		Total Due		0.00

Repeat the process in cells A1 through E1 in the lower table. When you print the invoice this time, it should look like figure 14.18.

Of course, you may also change the text used in the invoice and add or remove as many lines as you want. But at least these examples give you an idea of the possibilities available with the WordPerfect table feature.

Fig. 14.18.

Invoice table with shaded cells.

Company Name 123 Main Street Anytown, ST 54321	Invoice Number @
	Invoice Date
Sold To:	Customer Number
	Purchase Order Number

Code	Description	Quantity	Price	Total
%%				0.00
		Total Due		0.00

Summary

This chapter has covered a lot of ground. Although the invoice table itself is included on the Applications Disk, the steps for creating the table should make it possible to create any other kind of invoice or statement form by using a WordPerfect 5.1 table.

In this chapter, you have seen how to create a table, how to adjust column spacing within a table, how to define the justification of a cell (center, left, and decimal), how to add information to a table header, how to lock information in cells so that it cannot be changed by the user, how to remove unwanted lines from inside and outside a table, how to add math inside a table, and how to use a macro to automate table entry.

In Chapters 15 through 17, you will learn how to create a variety of legal forms by using WordPerfect features and the macros included on the Applications Disk.

Part VI

Creating Legal Documents

Using WordPerfect in the Law Office

Creating Non-Court Documents

Creating Court Documents

15

Using WordPerfect in the Law Office

In law offices around the country, and indeed around the globe, WordPerfect is the word processing market leader. Many of its features, such as the tables of authorities and redlining, seem to be designed specifically for legal applications. But many other WordPerfect features have equally significant use in the law office.

This chapter discusses some of the ways WordPerfect can fill the specific needs of a law office. You will see how WordPerfect 5.1 can save both time and money in everyday legal practice. The chapter focuses on the following:

- A legal keyboard to simplify many office activities
- Macros designed for common legal applications
- Special templates
- Form documents in legal use

You also learn how to perform these tasks:

- Organize your computer files for better file management
- Use footnote styles, paragraph numbering, and automatic cross-references
- Create and use the special WordPerfect time sheet (included on the Applications Disk)
- Use the legal keyboard to effortlessly insert special symbol characters into your legal documents

Looking ahead, Chapter 16 demonstrates several ways in which legal documents, such as wills, deeds, contracts and other documents that use at least some standard paragraphs or language, can be created and easily tailored to a specific case; Chapter 17 shows how pleadings and court-related documents can be speedily prepared.

Although the information in these three chapters is useful primarily to attorneys and secretaries working in a law office, the principles of keyboards, document assembly, symbols, and forms outlined in these chapters can be used in most any office to speed up a variety of office activity.

Using This Book in Your Law Office

The macros, form documents, and other techniques discussed in Chapters 15 through 17 are designed for use by both legal secretaries and lawyers. It will take you some time to create all the documents and forms, install and modify the macros, and learn the techniques required to become proficient in producing the documents you need in your practice. Learning this material is best shared by secretary and lawyer alike.

When you are through, however, you will have a system that produces better-looking, more thorough, and more accurate documents far easier and in less time than you ever thought possible. The process of organizing your form documents will probably cause you to adopt standard procedures for certain types of cases. And once the forms are in place, putting those procedures into routine practice is a simple matter.

Don't expect the start-up process to be fast. When you look hard at all the forms you use now and think of ways to automate their preparation, you will be amazed at how much can be done.

Don't expect to reduce the size of your secretarial staff. Although the office staff members can generate documents much faster (and produce better-looking documents at that), they will probably generate more documents than before and spend more time helping you manage your caseload, using the systems you develop together.

Don't expect your rush projects to be completed earlier. They can be completed much faster, but you will soon become so accustomed to the speed that you will delay starting such projects.

The suggestions contained in this and the next two chapters are useful in two ways. If you are new to WordPerfect 5.1 and are setting up your system from a clean disk, you can adopt these macros and methods and use them as they have been written. If you are an experienced WordPerfect user and have an established system of forms, macros, and file management, you can use these materials for new ideas on how to further automate your work, and modify them to suit your needs. Some of the ideas and techniques discussed in this section may have no application at all to your practice; pick and choose from them as you need.

Acquiring the Basic Tools

The techniques described in this section of the book make use of several types of files and documents. Some are provided on the Applications Disk; others you must create yourself. Remember that you must first install the Applications Disk before you can use these files (see Appendix A). They are generally as follows:

- *A special legal keyboard*

  This keyboard definition produces special characters useful to a law practice and provides a method to start several of the more important macros discussed in this section. The legal keyboard definition is on the Applications Disk under the filename LEGAL.WPK. Make sure you have a copy in your main macro directory.

- *A set of macros*

  Macros range from simple recordings of keystrokes to complex, miniature computer programs. Many macros are discussed in the pages to come, and are included on the disk. After installation, they should all be copied to your main macro directory. Macros files all have the extension .WPM.

- *Menu templates*

  A menu template is a list of form documents that creates a menu of options. The menu templates described in these chapters are all WordPerfect documents you create to help you prepare documents quickly. These templates list various form documents you have created and where they are stored on the disk. Several sample templates appear on the disk.

- *Form documents*

  These, too, are your own WordPerfect documents, set up to work with the various macros and templates and speed up the process of creating finished documents. Rather than specific names or other information, these forms contain merge codes that correspond to specific "fields," or types of information to be inserted in each final document. For instance, the names of the parties to a lawsuit may be represented in a form complaint by specific merge codes. Several sample form documents are also included on the disk.

- *Variables lists*

  These WordPerfect documents simply list the types of information that go into the fields you establish for your form documents. You need these lists to help you insert the correct information in the blanks in the form documents, a task to be automated with a macro that uses the WordPerfect Merge feature. Several sample variables lists are included on the disk.

The Applications Disk accompanying this book includes three files, each with the primary file name of README. These files (one for each of the three chapters in this section of the book) are WordPerfect documents containing instructions on how to install the forms and files for each chapter, and how to edit the several macros which may require editing. Print out each of these files and follow the instructions to be sure your system is set up correctly.

All of the macros and form documents supplied on the Applications Disk are in WordPerfect 5.1 format. Many of them will not work properly with WordPerfect 5.0 because many take advantage of new 5.1 features.

Organizing Your Files

Take some time when you first organize your computer files to create a directory structure that helps you find your files. There are several reasons for doing this.

First, grouping similar types of documents in directories makes your file management easier. You can find documents more readily to update or to delete obsolete files established for old cases.

But more importantly, many of the techniques described in the next two chapters rely heavily on merge forms, templates, and other documents that work together. You will have a much easier time creating a set of interrogatories if you remember that, for example, the interrogatory forms for product liability cases (a file called PRODUCTS stored in the forms directory) works with the variable template for that type of case (a file also called PRODUCTS, but stored in the template directory). Likewise, in preparing a deed and mortgage for a closing, you may want to store the deed description under a file name in the deeds directory, and a variable list for other information for the same closing under the same file name in your variables directory, making it easy to ensure that the right information is merged into your final documents. Remember that you can use identical file names only if you store those files in different directories.

Many macros on the Applications Disk require WordPerfect to look for certain types of files in specific subdirectories of your system. However, your system may be configured differently (for example, you may designate your hard disk as D: or F: rather than C:), or you may have an existing directory structure that you are accustomed to.

Keep in mind that each of the Applications Disk legal macros that requires information about your computer's directory structure must read a macro called INSTALL.WPM. *To make the macros work, you must first edit INSTALL.WPM to provide accurate drive and directory information.* Make sure that you edit this macro very carefully, or most of the other macros on the Applications Disk for these chapters will not operate.

To edit INSTALL.WPM, first read the detailed instructions found in the file README.15 on the Applications Disk. Also, INSTALL.WPM itself contains comments marking the locations for editing to occur. These appear in the macro editing screens as {;} codes, followed by an editing note and a tilde (~), ending the comment.

A sample directory structure for a system is shown in figure 15.1. This structure would allow you to run all the macros described in these three chapters. Some of the directories shown would not be necessary if you do not use the corresponding macros.

SUGGESTED DIRECTORY STRUCTURE

```
\ROOT
    └─WP51                              WordPerfect program files
        ├─COUNSEL                       Lists of counsel to serve in various cases
        ├─DEEDS                         Deed descriptions
        ├─FORMS                         Form documents
        ├─MACROS                        All macros
        ├─MENUS                         Menus of user-prepared forms
        ├─TIMESHEE                      Time records
        ├─VARLISTS                      Lists of variable information to insert in forms
        ├─VARTEMP                       Templates of variables for specific cases
        ├─[VARIOUS DATA DIRECTORIES]    Finished documents
```

Fig. 15.1.

A sample directory structure.

The directories shown in figure 15.1 are of four basic types:

1. *Main macros directory*

   This directory contains the keyboard definition and your macro programs. In figure 15.1, this appears as directory C:\WP51\MACROS.

2. *Forms directories*

   These contain general-purpose form documents and the templates that work with those forms. In figure 15.1, the directories C:\WP51\FORMS, C:\WP51\MENUS, and C:\WP51\VARTEMP are forms directories.

3. *Variables directories*

Variables directories contain specific information geared to particular cases in your office. This information will be inserted into your general-purpose documents. In figure 15.1, the directories C:\WP51\COUNSEL, C:\WP51\DEEDS, and C:\WP51\VARLISTS are variables directories.

4. *Data directories*

The data directories contain your finished documents. You can name these directories according to any scheme that makes sense to you. You may have directories for types of documents, areas of practice, large cases, important clients, or any other method. The directory C:\WP51\TIMESHEE in figure 15.1 is an example of a data directory.

The operation of the macros, creation of form documents, and the uses of variable lists and templates are all described in detail in the next two chapters.

Using the LEGAL Keyboard

The keyboard definition function of WordPerfect is one of the most useful tools the program provides. It enables you to redefine any key on the keyboard or key combination to behave in any way you want it to. You can assign new characters to any key on the keyboard, or you can assign any macro you want to any key or combination of keys that you want.

If you want to use the LEGAL keyboard provided on the Applications Disk at the back of this book, be sure to copy the file LEGAL.WPK from the \QLEGAL subdirectory (created during the installation of the Applications Disk) into your main macro directory (for instance, C:\WP51\MACROS). Then choose Setup (Shift-F1), select **Keyboard (5)**, and use the arrow keys to move the highlight bar to LEGAL. Choose **Select (1)** or press Enter to select that keyboard. Your Setup screen should now show the LEGAL keyboard as currently selected under the option **Keyboard Layout (5)**.

If you want to edit the LEGAL.WPK keyboard definition to suit your own needs and tastes, follow these steps:

1. Press Setup (Shift-F1) and choose **K**eyboard Layout (**5**).

   ⌨ Choose Se**t**up from the **F**ile menu, then **K**eyboard Layout.

2. Using the arrow keys, highlight LEGAL.

3. Choose Edit (**7**).

The Keyboard: Edit screen appears listing the new assignments for various keys on the LEGAL keyboard. The screen shows the altered keys or key combinations, the new actions for those keys, and a description of each new action. The screen for the LEGAL keyboard available on the Applications Disk appears in figure 15.2.

```
Keyboard: Edit

  Name: LEGAL

  Key           Action            Description

  Ctrl-F7       {KEY MACRO 1}     Footnote formatting
  Alt--         {KEY MACRO 2}     Em-dash
  Ctrl-C        {KEY MACRO 3}     Long form captions
  Ctrl-D        [°:6,36]          Degree symbol
  Ctrl-K        {KEY MACRO 4}     Time and date pop-up
  Ctrl-M        {KEY MACRO 5}     Merge assist
  Ctrl-N        {KEY MACRO 6}     Automatic paragraph numbers
  Ctrl-O        [■:4,23]          Copyright symbol
  Ctrl-P        [¶:4,5]           Paragraph symbol
  Ctrl-R        [■:4,22]          Registered trademark symbol
  Ctrl-S        [§:4,6]           Section symbol
  Ctrl-T        [■:4,41]          Trademark symbol
  Ctrl-X        {KEY MACRO 7}     Short form captions
  Ctrl-Z        {KEY MACRO 8}     Document assembly "trigger"
  "             {KEY MACRO 9}     Close quotes ''
  `             {KEY MACRO 10}    Open quotes ``

  1 Action; 2 Dscrptn; 3 Original; 4 Create; 5 Move; Macro: 6 Save; 7 Retrieve: 1
```

Fig. 15.2.

The Keyboard: Edit screen for the LEGAL keyboard.

4. Use the menu at the bottom of the Keyboard: Edit screen to edit, delete, or move existing key definitions, or to create new key definitions as you need to.

The LEGAL keyboard has two basic types of key definitions. One set of definitions assigns new characters (referred to by their WordPerfect character set number on the Keyboard: Edit screen) to given keys or key combinations. The second set assigns entire macros to different key combinations, shown as {KEY MACRO} numbers. Both are discussed next.

Creating Special Characters in WordPerfect

WordPerfect provides an extensive set of special characters that can be included in any WordPerfect document. You can insert a special character by pressing Compose (Ctrl-2) and specifying the character set, a comma, and the number of the character in that set. The Appendix to your WordPerfect manual contains a list of the 12 special-character sets.

For example, if you wanted to create the section marker §, you can see that it is found in character set 4, and is listed as character number 6 in that set. To enter it on-screen, do the following:

1. Place your cursor where you want the character to be inserted; then press Compose (Ctrl-2). Press the numeral 2 in the top row of your keyboard, not the function key F2.

   Nothing appears to happen on your screen.

2. Type *4*. Then type *6: 4,6*. Still nothing shows up on your screen.

3. Press Enter; the character symbol will appear on-screen. In Reveal Codes it will look like a section marker until you place the cursor directly on the character; it will then look like this:

   ` / :4,6 `

Starting Macros from Hot Keys

Many of the characters provided in the special character sets are quite useful to lawyers, but looking them up constantly in the manual (since you can never remember the exact character set and number) and entering an arcane string of keystrokes to retrieve the single character gets old fast.

The LEGAL keyboard takes care of the problem by assigning those characters to special *hot keys* that insert these characters with a simple Alt-letter or Ctrl-letter combination. If you have been using WordPerfect for a while, you probably have written several hot-key macros using Alt-letter combinations. But you can also create hot keys with the Ctrl key. By using the Keyboard Layout feature, you can assign any macro you want to any key combination.

Note: Whether or not the characters appear on your screen depends upon the type of screen and screen driver installed on your computer. However, if your printer can print graphics and you have installed the WP.DRS file, you can print all the characters on the legal keyboard, whether or not those characters are part of any font installed in your printer.

Using the LEGAL Keyboard Macros

The LEGAL keyboard on the Applications Disk comes with 13 new key assignments. As you can see in figure 15.2, 7 of those 13 keys create the following special characters useful to a law practice.

Key Combination	Character Created
Ctrl-D	The degree mark (∘)
Ctrl-O	The copyright symbol (©)
Ctrl-P	The paragraph symbol (¶)
Ctrl-R	The registered trademark symbol (®)
Ctrl-S	The section marker (§)
Ctrl-T	The trademark symbol (™)
Alt-hyphen	The em-dash (—)

Some of those characters may appear as a *slug*, or a little black box (■), on your screen. However, if your printer can print graphics, you can print the characters using WordPerfect 5.1.

Note that these keyboard assignments are different from hot-key macros that you may have already assigned to Alt-key combinations and stored in your macros directory. Except for Alt-hyphen, all the keyboard assignments use Ctrl-letter, rather than Alt-letter combinations, so as not to conflict with any Alt-key macros you may already use. You use Alt-hyphen because WordPerfect already uses Ctrl-hyphen to create a soft hyphen.

The other six special key assignments start complex macros, as follows:

- Ctrl-C (for **C**aption) invokes the macro LONGCAP, discussed in detail in Chapter 17. LONGCAP helps you create legal pleadings with long-form "captions," or case names.

- Ctrl-K invokes **K**LOCK. This macro momentarily displays the current date and time (the system date entered as you booted your computer) on-screen, then vanishes. It is useful when you want to check what date will appear if you use a date code or when you simply want to check the current time.

- Ctrl-M invokes **M**ERGE, a macro to help you use the WordPerfect Merge function to create custom-made documents from forms. Further discussion of this key assignment appears in more detail in both Chapters 16 and 17.

- Ctrl-N invokes PARANO, a macro designed to assist with the insertion of automatic paragraph number codes in documents. When you press Ctrl-N, a pop-up window lists the levels of automatic paragraph numbers in the outline paragraph-numbering format (definition **3** on the Paragraph Number Definition screen). By pressing the number of the numbering level you want to insert, you insert the code with a space behind it. If you want the third level, you can press either **3** or Enter. If you change your mind and don't want any code, press Cancel (F1). You must select number 1 through 8, Enter, or F1; the macro will reject any other key.

If you want to use any other paragraph-numbering definition, you can edit the pop-up window in the macro to display the definition you prefer. Instructions on how to do this are included in the file README.15 on the Applications Disk. Be sure, however, that your system is set for the numbering pattern you prefer before you use the Ctrl-N key or PARANO macro. You can do this either by setting your initial codes for all documents—using the Setup function (Shift-F1, **5**)—or by changing the definition for each specific document, using the Paragraph Number Define key (Shift-F5, **6**). For more information, see "Using Automatic Paragraph Numbering" later in this chapter.

- Ctrl-X invokes the macro SHORTCAP, an alternative to the LONGCAP macro described earlier. SHORTCAP assists you in preparing "short form" captions for legal pleadings. Its operation is described in detail in Chapter 17.

- Ctrl-Z invokes the macro TRIGGER. It is used in a "point-and-shoot" document assembly technique described in Chapters 16 and 17. Essentially, TRIGGER is the device that "shoots at" (or zaps) the block of text in which the cursor is located, retrieving that block into the document you are creating.

To deselect the LEGAL keyboard, press Ctrl-6 from any screen within WordPerfect.

If you want to assign some of your own macros to Ctrl keys, you can do so as follows:

1. Press Shift-F1 (Setup); then press **Keyboard Layout (5)**.

   ⌨ Choose Se**t**up from the **F**ile menu; then select **K**eyboard Layout.

2. Highlight LEGAL and press Edit (7).

3. Press **C**reate (**4**).

4. Enter the key or key combination to which you want to assign the macro. At the Description: prompt, enter a brief description of what the macro does and press Enter.

5. A window similar to WordPerfect's internal macro editor appears.

6. The cursor appears within the editing window. The current "action" or key assignment is displayed. For example, if you have not previously

redefined the key combination Ctrl-N, the screen shows { ^N} as the
current definition of that key. Delete the current contents of the editing
window, using the Del or Backspace key.

7. Now assign the new function to that key.

    For example, suppose you want to assign the macro PARANO.WPM on
    the Applications Disk to Ctrl-N on a keyboard you're already using. To
    do this, you would enter the following in the editing window:

    {Macro}parano{Enter}

    Note: Insert the {Macro} command by pressing Alt-F10; the {Enter}
    command, by pressing Ctrl-V, Enter. Do not try to enter the codes by
    typing those words in brackets.

8. When you are finished, press Exit (F7) three times to return to the main
    editing screen.

The Ctrl-V key in step 7 tells the keyboard or macro editor how to interpret
keystrokes that could be ambiguous. Several keys on the keyboard affect cursor
movement in the macro editing window, or have some special uses in in the macro
editor. For example, when you press an arrow key, Tab, or Enter, you may want to
move the cursor within the macro or keyboard editing window, or you may want
the macro to insert a tab or hard return, or move the cursor with the arrow. If you
press any of those keys (or any of the other "dual-purpose" keys) without first
pressing Ctrl-V, the keys act on the cursor or the macro editor but not the
operation of the macro.

Where, as in the previous example, you want to insert a code into the macro rather
than simply to move the cursor within the macro editing window, you must press
Ctrl-V first. Ctrl-V tells the macro editor that the next keystroke is intended as a
command to be issued by the macro. The appropriate code will then appear in the
macro editing screen and will be executed by the macro as the macro executes.

In the example given in step 7, when you return to the main editing screen and
press Ctrl-N, that key behaves as if you had pressed Alt-F10, typed *parano*, and then
pressed Enter to execute the PARANO macro.

The editing screen showing the PARANO macro assigned to the Ctrl-N key appears
in figure 15.3. You enter the {DISPLAY OFF} code from the Macro Commands
window, described later. The code speeds up execution of the macro and prevents
the word *parano* from flashing at the bottom of your screen when you press Ctrl-N.

Fig. 15.3.

The PARANO macro Keyboard Assignment screen.

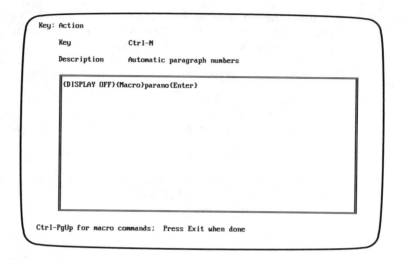

```
Key: Action

     Key              Ctrl-N

     Description      Automatic paragraph numbers


  {DISPLAY OFF}{Macro}parano{Enter}











Ctrl-PgUp for macro commands;  Press Exit when done
```

Another way to assign macro functions to a Ctrl-key is to actually enter the macro commands from the keyboard edit screen. The Ctrl-PgUp key combination brings up the Macro Commands pop-up into the key editing screen, from which you can select any of the standard macro commands to write a macro as you normally would.

This technique, however, was not employed in creating the LEGAL keyboard for this book. You may have several keyboard definitions that you switch between, and you might want to have the same macros assigned to keys in several keyboard definitions. By leaving the macros in the main macro directory and having the keyboard definitions simply call the existing macros, you can have several keyboards using the same macros without your having to retype them.

You can import any macro into your existing keyboard assignments if you choose. Follow these steps:

1. Press Setup (Shift-F1) and select **Keyboard Layout** (**5**).

   ⌨ Choose Setup from the File menu and select **Keyboard Layout**.

2. Highlight the keyboard into which you want to import the macro; then press **Edit** (**7**).

3. Select **Retrieve** (**7**).

4. The status line prompts you for a Key: where you want to assign the macro. Type in the key or key combination you want to define.

5. The status line then prompts you for the name of the macro you want to assign to that key. Type in the macro name. If it is not located in the main macro directory, type in its full path as well. Press Enter when you are done.

If you do not wish to use some of the macros assigned to the LEGAL keyboard, it is a simple matter to cancel those reassignments. Do the following:

1. Press Setup (Shift-F1) and select **Keyboard Layout (5)**.

   ⌨ Choose **Setup** from the **F**ile menu and select **Keyboard Layout**.

2. Select the LEGAL keyboard with the highlight bar.

3. Press **E**dit (**7**) and move the highlight bar to the key you wish to delete.

4. Press Original (**3**) to delete the key definition (answer Y to the `Delete?` prompt).

Using Special Keys for Quotation Marks

The LEGAL keyboard also redefines two other keys, the one for the open single quotation mark (') located to the left of the numeral 1 on most keyboards, and the one for the straight double quotation mark ("). The LEGAL keyboard defines the ' key to produce two open single quotation marks, ", whereas the " key is redefined to produce two close single quotation marks, ".

If you use a proportionally spaced font, the two single open quotation marks print so close together that they appear as a single open quotation mark (although they look a little funny on your nonproportionally spaced computer screen); likewise the two close single quotation marks produce a single close quotation mark. If you do not use a proportionally spaced font on your printer, or do not want to distinguish between open and close quotation marks, simply delete those two key definitions from the LEGAL keyboard.

Formatting Footnotes with Ctrl-F7

Lawyers love footnotes. Not all lawyers, however, love how WordPerfect formats them. Although the Footnote Options feature gives you a small measure of control over how your footnotes look, that feature is not particularly flexible (in sharp contrast to almost everything else WordPerfect does). For example, if you want the footnote text to appear in smaller type than the rest of the document, you cannot enter the codes you need to do that in the Footnote Options screen. Although you could do this manually as you create each footnote, this is burdensome to do and very time-consuming if you decide later to change the size again.

You can, however, combine the Style feature with a macro to do the job for you. To make its operation even simpler, you can assign the macro to the Ctrl-F7 key to make its operation absolutely invisible to the user. This technique works just as if WordPerfect had programmed more functionality into the Footnote (Ctrl-F7) key to begin with.

The Applications Disk contains a macro called FOOTNOTE. It mimics the screens that appear when you press Footnote (Ctrl-F7). The macro essentially "intercepts" the standard operation of the original Ctrl-F7 key and inserts a footnote style code (which you define) each time you create a new footnote. In all other ways FOOTNOTE behaves exactly like the WordPerfect Footnote key.

The codes entered by the Footnote style are inserted in the footnote immediately after the **[NoteNum]** code produced by the Footnote feature itself. If you want to change the location or style of the footnote number itself, follow these five steps:

1. To change the appearance or location of the footnote number in a specific document, retrieve that document to your screen (or, if you want to change the appearance of the document already on your screen, move the cursor to the top of the document, using Home, Home, Home, up arrow, in order to make it easier to locate the **[Ftn Opt]** code).

2. Press Footnote (Ctrl-F7) and select **Footnote** (**1**).

   ⌨ Choose **Footnote** from the **Layout** menu.

3. Select **4** or choose **Options** to bring the Footnote Options screen up.

4. To edit the appearance of the note number in the footnote, select Style for Number in Note (**4**) and delete or add spaces and font codes to control the appearance of the footnote number. The Footnote Options feature does not accept tab or indent codes, although it accepts characters and spaces. Press Enter when done.

5. Press Exit (F7) when finished.

Tip: If you want the appearance of footnote numbers to be the same in all new documents you create, you can accomplish this by placing these Footnote Option codes in the prefix of all new documents through the Setup feature (Shift-F1, **4**, **5**).

After you have edited the appearance of the footnote number to your liking, you need to create a Footnote style in your styles library. The Footnote style will then insert whatever formatting codes you select into the text of all of your footnotes.

To create a Footnote style, follow these steps:

1. First determine the name of your styles library, if one exists. Press Setup (Shift-F1) and then Location of Files (**6**).

   ⌨ Choose **Setup** from the **File** menu and select **Location of Files**.

2. Check the listing, if any, after **Style Library Filename** (**5**). If one exists, note its name.

3. If no styles library exists, create one by pressing **Style (5)**. Provide the path to the directory where you want to store your styles library; then type in the name you wish to assign to your styles library at the `Library Filename:` **prompt.**

4. Press **Exit (F7)** to return to a blank document (exit from any document that may be on-screen).

5. Create a paired style called Footnote for the formatting codes you wish to insert in your footnotes. Press **Style (Alt-F8)** and type **Create (3)**.

   The Styles: Edit screen will appear. The Styles: Edit screen for the Footnote format included on the Applications Disk is shown in figure 15.4.

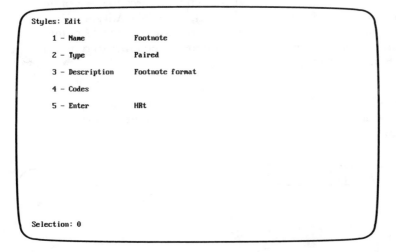

Fig. 15.4.

The Styles: Edit screen for formatting footnotes.

6. Press **Description (3)**, and enter a description for your footnote style.

7. Now enter the formatting codes for your footnotes. Press **Codes (4)**; a screen very similar to the Reveal Codes screen will appear.

8. Enter the formatting codes for your footnotes.

   The formatting codes you enter are entirely up to your personal preference. For example, you may want all footnotes to appear in 9-point type, or a different typeface; enter a font selection code to accomplish this. You may want to change the line or word spacing; you can enter these codes. All of the standard WordPerfect formatting codes are available to you.

Tip for Advanced Users: Suppose, for example, that you wish to indent the entire footnote one quarter of an inch on the left side only, leaving the footnote number at the left margin. Although you could use an [→Indent] code to do this, that would become a problem if your footnote contains more than one paragraph. The [HRt] at the end of each paragraph would cancel the indentation. Another way to do this is to change the left margin to 1.25", but a slight problem develops if you do this immediately after the footnote number. WordPerfect will not allow you to change the left margin in the middle of a line. If you try to do so, it will insert a [HRt] immediately before the margin change so that the margin change takes effect at the beginning of the next line. This would leave the footnote number one line higher than the body of the footnote text.

To resolve that problem, use an [AdvUp:x] code to force the text of the footnote up one line. Press Format (Shift-F8), Other (4), Advance (1), and Up (1). Enter the line height of the font you are using (a 12-point Courier font, for example, is .157"). Press Enter three times to return to the Styles: Edit [Codes] screen.

Figure 15.5 shows the codes entered in Styles: Edit [Codes] for the Footnote style just described. The [AdvUp:0.167"] code that appears after the [Comment] code in figure 15.5 eliminates a line of space between any footnotes that appear on the same page.

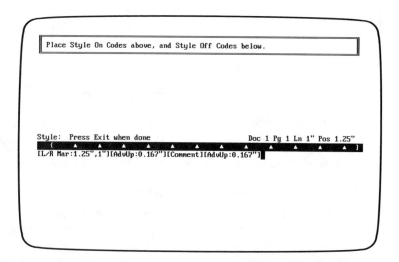

Fig. 15.5.

Inserting codes to eliminate an empty line in a footnote.

Place Style On Codes above, and Style Off Codes below.

Style: Press Exit when done   Doc 1 Pg 1 Ln 1" Pos 1.25"
[L/R Mar:1.25",1"][AdvUp:0.167"][Comment][AdvUp:0.167"]

9. Once you have finished entering your formatting codes, press Exit (F7) twice to return to the Styles screen.

10. You must now save your Footnote style to your styles library. Press Save (**6**). The status line will prompt for a `Filename:`. Enter the path and file name of the styles library you have chosen in step 2. Answer Y to any Replace? prompt that appears.

11. Press Exit (F7) until you return to your blank screen.

This Footnote style appears in the file STYLES.LIB included on the Applications Disk. Instructions on how to install the Footnote style from that file into your own standard styles library appear in the file README.15 on the Applications Disk.

The FOOTNOTE macro automatically inserts the Footnote style from the document you are working on. The style is saved with each document in which it is used. If you decide to change your footnote style in any specific document, you can edit it easily as follows:

1. With the document on-screen, press Style (Alt-F8).

    Choose Styles from the Layout menu.

2. Using the highlight bar, select the Footnote style.

3. Press Edit (**4**) and select Codes (**4**).

4. Insert your new codes.

5. Now press Exit (F7) three times to return to the main editing screen.

When you save your document, the new footnote style for that document is saved with it. All footnotes in that document will follow the new footnote format. This does not affect the standard Footnote style you saved in your styles library, nor does it affect footnotes using that style in other documents.

If you want to change the standard style in your styles library, begin from a blank screen; then follow steps 1 through 4. When you have completed editing your formatting codes, press Exit (F7) only twice, leaving you at the Styles screen. Select Save (**6**) and type in the name of your styles library to save the edited Footnote style for use with future documents.

If you want your existing documents to use this newly edited format, you must retrieve the edited styles into any document using those styles. To do this, follow these steps:

1. With the document to be updated on-screen, press Style (Alt-F8).

   ▣ Choose **Styles** from the Layout menu.

2. Select the Footnote style with the highlight bar.

3. Press **Retrieve (7)**, and type in the name of your styles library containing the edited Footnote style. If the document on-screen uses any style in the library, the status line asks, `Style(s) already exist. Replace? No (Yes)`.

4. Press Y to retrieve the edited styles into your document. All the footnotes using the Footnote style will be modified accordingly.

5. Press Exit (F7) to return to your document. The new Footnote style will be saved with your document.

Note: Because the Footnote style is defined as a *paired* style (that is, with both **[Style On]** and **[Style Off]** codes), be careful to insert your footnote text between those two codes. Any text inserted after the **[Style Off]** code will not be affected by formatting codes in the style. The Footnote macro leaves you between the two codes so that when you type your text initially it should appear between the codes. But if you return to the footnote for editing later, be careful to use the Reveal Codes screen to place your cursor in front of the **[Style Off]** code before editing.

The LEGAL keyboard provided on the Applications Disk assigns the FOOTNOTE macro to the Ctrl-F7 key. Using this key assignment, Ctrl-F7 works in exactly the same way as it would without the FOOTNOTE macro, except when you select Footnote **(1)**, then Create **(1)**. In that case, when you are at the Footnote edit screen, the FOOTNOTE macro turns on the Footnote style you have defined. If you do not wish to assign this macro to that key, simply delete that key assignment from your keyboard. You can still invoke the FOOTNOTE macro directly if you wish to use it, or you can turn off the Footnote style manually as you see fit.

Using Automatic Paragraph Numbering

One of the most useful features of WordPerfect is its automatic paragraph-numbering codes. This feature is particularly useful in a law office where many documents go through various drafts and revisions. If you want to insert or delete paragraphs of a contract, for example, as you do so the subsequent paragraphs can renumber themselves. Used in conjunction with automatic cross-references (discussed later on), this saves a great deal of time in making revisions and ensures that numbering sequences are correct.

To best use the automatic paragraph-numbering feature, select the paragraph-numbering definition that most suits your preferences. WordPerfect gives you four standard definitions, but allows you to define your own numbering scheme using any combination of Roman or Arabic numerals and capital or lowercase letters.

To select a paragraph-numbering definition, follow these steps:

1. Press Shift-F5 (Date/Outline); then select **Define** (6).

   ▢ Choose **Define** from the **Tools** menu.

2. If you wish to use any of the standard numbering sequences (listed on the Paragraph Number Definition screen on lines 2 through 5), press the number for the line containing the definition you like. The Current Definition line in the middle of your screen should then reflect your selection.

3. If you do not like any of the standard definitions, press User-Defined (6) and enter the numbering sequence you prefer, starting from Level 1 and working down in priority.

4. Press Exit (F7) twice to return to your document. In Reveal Codes, note that a **[Par Num Def]** code appears at your cursor location. All paragraph-numbering codes which follow that code will then follow the sequence you specified.

Hint: The standard Outline definition is fine for most purposes, but there may be times when you would like to modify it only slightly. For example, in the example of the simple will discussed later in Chapter 16, you may wish to use a Level 1 paragraph definition mark (**[Par Num:1]**) to mark the number of the various Articles in the will form. However, the Outline definition supplies a period after the capitalized Roman numeral in Level 1 of that definition:

   I.

If you do not want a period after the numeral, follow steps 3 and 4. In Level 1, simply type a capital *I* (Roman numeral I) without a period, and leave the rest of the numerals at the other levels exactly as they appear in the Outline definition.

Tip: If you want your computer to default to a particular numbering sequence for all future documents, insert a **[Par Num Def]** code in your Initial Settings (Shift-F1, **4, 5**).

Note: You can insert paragraph codes automatically using the PARANO macro included on the Applications Disk. This macro is assigned to the Ctrl-N key on the LEGAL keyboard. For more information on using PARANO, see the previous discussion of the LEGAL keyboard.

Using the Automatic Cross-Reference Feature

In many types of legal documents, lawyers must refer to other paragraphs, sections, pages, or footnotes within the document. As the document is revised, page and footnote numbers may change. If you created your document with automatic paragraph numbers, those numbers change as well. This would ordinarily make cross-referencing a nightmare, but WordPerfect has a cross-referencing feature that keeps track of these changes for you.

Suppose you are drafting a will. Article II creates a testamentary trust and appoints a trustee; Article III appoints an executor. You want both officers to have broad powers of administration, which you describe in Article IV. In Article II, you provide that the executor shall have all powers conferred under Article IV, while in Article III you provide that the executor shall have all powers provided in Article IV except several enumerated powers set forth in that Article.

If you have used **[Par Num:x]** codes for all the Article numbers and paragraphs and subparagraphs in the will, the Auto Ref feature of WordPerfect makes it easy to create cross-references that will change as the document is revised. The reference to administrative powers in Article II would look like this on your screen (and on paper):

> *The Trustee shall have all of those powers specified in Article IV.*

This sentence contains a *reference* in WordPerfect parlance, because it *refers* to Article IV. Article IV itself is the *target* to which the reference relates. Since the number of the target article may change if you add an Article to the will in revision, you will want this reference to change with it. To insert the proper cross-reference codes to accomplish this, follow these steps:

1. Delete the manual reference in your document (in this example, delete the Roman numeral IV). Be sure to leave the cursor exactly where you want the reference to appear.

2. Press Alt-F5 (Mark Text); then select Cross **Ref** (**1**).

   ⌨ Choose Cross **Reference** from the **Mark** menu.

3. If you are using the function keys, the Mark Text: Automatic Reference screen then appears. If you are using the pull-down menu, another window appears listing your options.

4. Type Mark **Both** Reference and Target (**3**).

   ⌨ Choose **Both** from the pull-down menu.

5. Because you want to tie this reference to the automatic numbering code for the Article dealing with administrative powers, select Paragraph/ Outline Number (**2**).

   Note: You can tie references to page numbers, paragraph codes, footnote or endnote numbers, or graphics box numbers. You cannot tie the reference to a paragraph you have numbered manually; it will cross-reference only to paragraphs beginning with **[Par Num:x]** codes.

6. Your document reappears on the screen. The status line reads `Auto Ref: Move to Paragraph; Press Enter.` Move the cursor to a position immediately following the **[Par Num:x]** code that marks the Article referred to. Press Enter.

7. The status line prompts you for a `Target Name:`. Give the target-reference pair a unique but descriptive name, such as *powers*. The reference code will be inserted at the reference point, and a target code will be inserted at the location of the item referred to.

At the reference point, your screen should still look as it did before. But in Reveal Codes, you will see *not* the Roman numeral IV, but this:

```
The Trustee shall have all of those powers specified in Article
[Ref(POWERS):Par IV]
```

If you refer to the same item at several places in your document, you can insert just a reference code at the appropriate place. In Article III of the example, when you want to refer to the same Article on administrative powers, you need mark only the reference, because that target has already been marked.

To insert only the reference code, do the following:

1. At the point in Article III where you would refer to the administrative powers described in Article IV, delete the original reference to Article IV as discussed earlier.

2. Press Mark Text (Alt-F5) and select Cross **Ref** (**1**).

   Choose Cross **Reference** from the **Mark** menu.

3. If you are using the function keys, the Mark Text: Automatic Reference screen then appears. If you are using the pull-down menu, another window appears listing your options.

4. Choose option Mark **Reference** (**1**).

   Choose **Reference** from the pull-down menu.

5. Press Paragraph/Outline Number (2) and enter the target name *POWERS* (or whatever target name you have chosen). Press Enter.

Notice that once you press Enter, WordPerfect returns to the main editing screen. A question mark appears at your cursor location. The correct paragraph number will be inserted there when you generate your tables and references.

WordPerfect does not automatically change all cross-references as your document is revised; you must do so before printing, by *generating* the document. To do this, follow these steps:

1. Press Mark Text (Alt-F5) and select Generate (6).

   ⌨ Choose **Generate** from the **Mark** menu.

2. From the Mark Text: Generate screen, select **Generate** (5) and then Y to update all cross-references.

If you forget to generate your cross-references before printing your document, WordPerfect will remind you before allowing you to print. If you have made changes to the document since the last time it was generated, when you try to print the document you will get the prompt

```
Document may need to be generated. Print? No (Yes)
```

If you have made changes in the document that may affect your references, press N at that reminder and execute the steps to generate the document; otherwise press Y to continue printing the document.

Keeping Track of Document Revisions

No matter what sort of practice you have, from time to time you need to create documents that go through several different drafts. As you print successive revisions of the document, you run the risk that earlier versions that have not been discarded might be mistaken for the more recent versions. You may also want a way to keep track of the various revisions and their authors.

The Applications Disk includes a macro called REV that creates this revision history for you quickly. If a document is going to go through several revisions, run the macro immediately prior to each printing of the document. The macro creates a "cover sheet" containing the revision history, but automatically resets the page numbering for subsequent pages so that, when you have finished the document, the pagination of the body of the document will be correct. At that time, you can simply put your cover sheet in a file or discard it and use the final document without reprinting it.

Each time you use REV, it moves to the top of the document and searches for the string **[UND][BOLD][und][bold]Revision number: 1**. If the macro does not find that string, it knows that the document is in its first draft, and it prompts you for a title to put on the cover sheet (so you can quickly identify what the document is) and, if the document has not been previously saved, a file name. It asks for the author, then creates the cover sheet, showing the document title, file name, author, and revision number: 1; it then adds a hard page code, resets the page number for the body of the document, and moves to the exit options.

Note: If you look in Reveal Codes at the cover sheet, you will see that the legend *Revision number: 1* is preceded by the nonsense codes **[UND][BOLD][und] [bold]**. These codes do nothing to the appearance of the document; they simply ensure that the macro is not misled into thinking that the document has been revised before if you happen to use the exact words *Revision number: 1* in the body of your document. Do *not* delete those codes from the cover sheet, or the next time you run the macro it will presume that the document has not been revised before and will start numbering again from number one.

After the first revision, every time that the macro finds the

    [UND][BOLD][und][bold]Revision number 1:

legend, it will simply ask for the name of the author, increment the revision number by one, and move to the exit options.

When REV is done running, it gives you three options. You can choose **S**ave (**1**), **E**xit (**2**), or **R**eturn to document without saving (**3**). If you choose option 1, **S**ave, on the first revision the macro will save the document to the file name you gave it in responding to the earlier prompt and return you to the document.

Using WordPerfect To Keep Track of Time

Most law offices have computerized timekeeping and billing systems already in place. The macro, math, and other capabilities of WordPerfect make it theoretically possible to write an entire time and billing "program" using only WordPerfect. Doing so, however, would be akin to using a spreadsheet program for word processing; just because it is theoretically possible does not make it the best tool for the job.

WordPerfect, however, can be used to assist the lawyer (or secretary) with the daily chore of keeping track of work performed during the day. Any timekeeping system begins on the lawyer's desk, where he records the work he performs during the day. Most lawyers use preprinted forms on which they make handwritten entries (if they can find the sheet); these forms are later given to the billing staff to be typed into the "numbers" computer. Other lawyers dictate their time entries on tape, giving the tapes to their secretaries or directly to the billing staff for input into the computer. (The practice of providing erasable tapes directly to the billing staff is not a good one. Tape involves a high risk of accidental erasure, and there is no hard copy of the lawyer's time entries to fall back on.)

If the lawyer has a computer at his desk, the screen can become the "preprinted" form for time entries, with the following advantages:

- The computer screen is harder to lose on a cluttered desk than a piece of paper.

- Most timekeeping systems break down on the input side; that is, lawyers tend to put off making entries on their sheets until long after the work is performed, then forget much of what they did. This is largely due to the fact that finding the time sheet and making the entry often interrupts some other activity. The macro described in this chapter allows a lawyer to make a time sheet entry at any time, from within any document on his screen, without forcing him to exit from that document.

- With a proper set of macros for standard timekeeping entries, the lawyer can make more consistent time entries; in fact, language for time entries can be standardized among all lawyers in the office in this way. Even a poor typist using a well-developed macro library can make time entries as fast as or faster than by hand.

- Lawyers rarely have the opportunity to work on one project without interruption during a busy day. They may undertake three or four tasks on the same file, but perform them at different parts of the day because of phone calls, meetings, and other interruptions. The "electronic time sheet" is much more forgiving than papyrus; the entry for that file for that day can be edited or rearranged on-screen before it goes to the billing staff, where editing becomes far more difficult.

- The simple timekeeping system demonstrated in this chapter is an easy way for a "computerphobe" to try out WordPerfect and become proficient in using it.

The timekeeping system suggested here is designed to help expedite the recording of the hours you work. The end product is a series of daily time sheets for each attorney, which can then be turned over to the billing staff to use with your existing billing software.

This system relies primarily on a time sheet form that you prepare in WordPerfect and store in your forms directory. A macro on the Applications Disk, TIME, will retrieve the form and insert the correct date for the sheet being prepared; allow you to make time sheet entries at any time without exiting from your current work; and automatically calculate the number of hours reported on any daily time sheet. Additional sample macros for standard time sheet entries are also included on the disk and are described next.

Creating Your Time Sheet Form

The time sheet form you create can appear any way you like it. (Or you can use or modify the one provided on the Applications Disk.) It is a WordPerfect document to be stored in your forms directory and retrieved every time you make a new time sheet. The time sheet provided on the Applications Disk is shown, in Reveal Codes format, in figure 15.6.

Fig. 15.6.

The time sheet form seen from Reveal Codes.

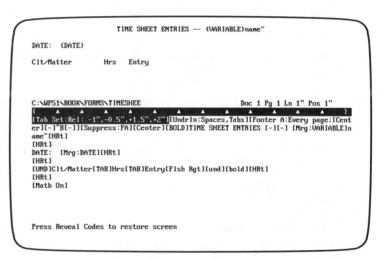

```
                        TIME SHEET ENTRIES -- {VARIABLE}name~

        DATE:  {DATE}

        Clt/Matter       Hrs   Entry




C:\WP51\BOOK\FORMS\TIMESHEE                            Doc 1 Pg 1 Ln 1" Pos 1"
[      ▲    ▲    ▲    ▲    ▲   ▲    ▲    ▲    ▲    ▲    ▲    ▲      ]
[Tab Set:Rel: -1",-0.5",+1.5",+2"][Undrln:Spaces,Tabs][Footer A:Every page:[Cent
er][-]^B[-]][Suppress:FA][Center][BOLD]TIME SHEET ENTRIES [-][-] [Mrg:VARIABLE]n
ame~[HRt]
[HRt]
DATE:  [Mrg:DATE][HRt]
[HRt]
[UND]Clt/Matter[TAB]Hrs[TAB]Entry[Flsh Rgt][und][bold][HRt]
[HRt]
[Math On]



Press Reveal Codes to restore screen
```

For the form to work correctly with the TIME macro described in this section, the form you use should observe a few rules. You can see these guidelines in the codes shown in figure 15.6.

Wherever you want to include the date to be used in the time sheet, include a {DATE} merge code. In this way, you (or the TIME macro) can retrieve your form by using the Merge function, and the current date (from your computer's clock) will be automatically inserted at that location. You should not use a **[Date:x]** code (Shift-F5, **2**) to do this, because that code will change the date of your time sheet every time you retrieve it to your screen. Because you will probably want to save time sheets from day to day, it could become confusing if they all redated themselves as you retrieved them. To insert the {DATE} merge code, position your cursor where you want the code to appear, and follow these steps:

1. Press Merge Codes (Shift-F9).

   ⌨ Choose **Me**rge Codes from the **T**ools menu.

   If you are using the function keys, the status line will give you a selection of merge codes, not including {DATE}. If you are using the pull-down menus, another window appears, listing some of the merge codes.

2. Press **M**ore (**6**).

   ⌨ Choose **M**ore from the pull-down menu.

3. Move the highlight bar down to the {DATE} code, using the down-arrow key. Or use the Name Search feature; simply press D, and the highlight bar will move to the {DATE} code. Press Enter; the code will appear in your document at your cursor location.

The tab settings for your time sheet are important, too. The TIME macro is designed so that the client, file name, or other identifying matter is typed at the left margin; the hours worked will be inserted at the next tab stop, and the description of the work performed is typed, in indented format, after the hours. Your sheet therefore requires only two tab stops. The first should be far enough to the right of the margin to accommodate your file naming or identification system, and the second should be just enough farther right to leave a small space between the hours worked and the description.

Include a page-numbering footer so that, if the time sheet exceeds one page, the pages can be kept in order. Follow these steps:

1. Press Format (Shift-F8) and then select **P**age (**2**).

   ⌨ Choose **P**age from the **L**ayout menu.

2. Press **F**ooters (**4**).

3. Press Footer **A** (**1**).

4. Select Every **P**age (**2**) to print the footer on every page.

5. Type in the footer you wish to place at the bottom of each page, but include a Ctrl-B character (which will appear as ^B on your screen). That instructs WordPerfect to print the page number at the Ctrl-B code. You might specify a simple page-numbering footer by pressing Center (Shift-F6) and then -^*B*- (hyphen, Ctrl-B, hyphen).

6. Press Exit (F7) twice to return to the main editing screen.

You can suppress this footer on the first page if you want it to print only if the time sheet exceeds one page; press Format (Shift-F8), P, U, F, Y, and then Enter until you return to the main editing screen.

Use WordPerfect's Math function to provide a total of the hours worked on the day covered by the time sheet. When you create your form, set your first tab stop at the location where you will enter the hours to be recorded. After you complete your document, place a **[Math On]** code immediately before the expected location of the first time entry. To do so, simply perform this step:

Press Math/Columns (Alt-F7) and then press **Math On** (**1**).

▢ Choose **Math** from the **Layout** menu, select **On**, and press Enter.

To set up your system to take advantage of the TIME macro and the form you have just created, follow these steps:

1. Prepare your own time sheet as described earlier (or use the TIMESHEE form provided on the Applications Disk) and store it in your forms directory. Be sure you modify the INSTALL macro to provide the correct path to your particular forms directory. The macro TIME will look in that directory for the file name TIMESHEE when it creates a new time sheet, so the form you select must use that file name and be placed in your standard forms directory.

2. Create a special directory to store your finished time sheets in (such as C:\WP51\TIMESHEE); then modify the INSTALL macro to provide the correct directory name. The TIME macro will repeatedly refer to time sheets (one for each day), and needs to know in what directory they can be found. It is simplest to isolate them in a directory of their own for easy retrieval.

3. Decide on a file-naming convention for time sheets. The simplest thing to do is to use the date of the time sheet as the file name. Thus, the time sheet for November 19, 1990, might use the file name 11-19-90. The complete path to the document might therefore be C:\WP51\TIMESHEE\11-19-90.

4. If time sheets for more than one timekeeper are to be stored in the same directory, consider using the extension (the last three characters after the period in the file name) for the initials of the timekeeper involved. Thus, the November 19, 1990, time sheet for attorney David C. Dean would be found at C:\WP51\TIMESHEE\11-19-90.DCD.

5. Be sure the TIME macro is copied to your main macros directory. If you find the macro useful, you may consider assigning it to a hot key for ease of use. For help on how to do this, see the earlier section "Using the Legal Keyboard."

Now you are ready to use the TIME macro to create time sheets and record your time. The macro behaves differently depending on whether or not it is started from a "clean" screen.

If you invoke TIME from a blank screen, the following status line menu appears:

```
1 Create timesheet; 2 M ake entry; 3 Calculate hours: 0
```

Each of these options is discussed next. If you invoke TIME with a document already on-screen, you will not scc this menu. TIME assumes that you wish to choose **Make a time entry (2)**, and goes directly to that function.

Option 1 - Create timesheet

Use this option when you simply want to create a new time sheet form for you to look at and work with manually. The option lets you create a time sheet for the current date (as determined by the system clock) simply by pressing Enter. Or you can type in any other date if you wish to create a time sheet for another date. The macro will use your TIMESHEE form to create a time sheet with the date you provided in the correct place, and will quit with the time sheet on your screen.

Option 2 - Make entry

Use this option, either from the menu or automatically, to make entries to any time sheet. If you wish to make an entry to a time sheet that has not been created yet, TIME will detect that and create that time sheet for you, if you choose.

The macro first asks you what time sheet you wish to make an entry to. At the prompt, type the file name (the date of the time sheet, if you use the file-naming convention suggested earlier) for the time sheet you wish to place the entry in. TIME checks to see whether that time sheet already exists; if it does not exist, it will ask if you want to create that time sheet. If you answer Y, the sheet will be created as if you had selected Option 1; then TIME will continue on to allow you to make your time entry.

After confirming that the sheet you want exists, or after creating it, TIME will ask you for the identity of the client and matter to which the entry relates. It will then ask you for the number of hours you worked on that matter. **Important:** Be sure to include a decimal point after the hours worked, even for a round number (for example, 8.0). TIME uses WordPerfect's Math feature to tabulate the hours on each sheet for you, and uses the decimal point to align the hours correctly.

TIME then temporarily "breaks" your screen to allow you to enter a description of the work you have done. The client/matter and hours you entered will be displayed for you, and the cursor will be placed after an **[->Indent]** code to allow you to type your entry. There is no limit to the length of the entry you can make, but be sure to use two **[->Indent]** codes to realign the text if you choose to make your entry in two or more paragraphs.

Note: When the macro stops for entry of the work performed, it is actually "paused." If you press Cancel (F1), the macro stops, but leaves the time entry in the middle of whatever document was on-screen at the time. You can restore your document to its original condition by deleting everything between, and including, the two **[HPg]** codes that separate the time sheet entry from your document.

Note also that while the macro is paused you can run any of the "standard language" macros described later. However, they will not be displayed on the screen unless you include a {DISPLAY ON} code at the end of those macros.

When you have completed your time sheet entry, press Exit (F7). TIME will append the entry to the time sheet you designated in response to the first prompt, then restore your screen to its original condition.

Option 3 - Calculate

The third option provides a convenient way to total up the hours reported on each time sheet.

From a "clean" screen, invoke TIME and choose Calculate (3). The macro asks for the file name of the time sheet you want to calculate. It then retrieves that file, inserts the word TOTAL at the bottom of the sheet, and adds up the total hours reported.

If you save the time sheet with the TOTAL, you can still add entries to that sheet. If you do so and later use the WordPerfect Retrieve (Shift-F10) feature or retrieve the file from the List Files screen, the later entries will show up underneath the TOTAL line. However, if you use TIME's Calculate option to retrieve the file, the TOTAL line moves to the bottom of the screen and recalculates for you.

A sample of a completed time sheet using the form from figure 15.6 is shown as figure 15.7.

		TIME SHEET ENTRIES — David C. Dean
DATE: November 19, 1990		
Clt/Matter	**Hrs**	**Entry**
15462.301	1.25	Receipt and review of Amended Complaint in Civil Action against our client. Telephone conference with client re same; discussion of possible avenues of defense and possible attempt to seek early dismissal of action. Telephone conference with Plaintiff's counsel re theories of case and time for response to Complaint.
RE246.25	2.25	Review of title search, noting possible problem with easement. Preparation of preliminary title certificate; forward to title insurance company. Telephone conference with attorney for seller discussing results of title search, including easement problem.
Smith/will	1.0	Conference with clients re preparation of will, possible tax consequences of various proposed bequests.
PB-23	2.0	Attendance at district magistrate hearing on behalf of pro bono client.
Admin	1.25	Firm administration/nonbillable time.
TOTAL	7.75	

Fig. 15.7.

A sample time sheet.

Expediting Time Entries

Most lawyers have favorite phrases or standard time sheet entries for certain types of work. These can be easily automated through the use of simple macros. Several suggestions are shown in figure 15.8. With a little creativity you can come up with a much longer list of entries tailored to your own practice.

Fig. 15.8.

Using macros to automate common time sheet descriptions.

Sample Macros for Standard Time Sheet Entries

Macro	Entry
rr	Receipt and review of
ra	Review and analysis of
rf	Receipt and review of fax transmission from
tc	Telephone conference with
ip	Initial preparation of
cc	Conference with client regarding
dep	Preparation for and attendance at deposition of
ac	Attendance at closing

To write a simple standard language macro, follow these steps:

1. Press Macro Define (Ctrl-F10).

   ⌨ Choose **Macro** from the **Tools** menu and select **Define**.

2. The status line prompts you to `Define macro:`. Enter the name of the macro at the prompt. Try to choose a short, easy-to-remember name— the fewer the letters the better. Press Enter.

3. The status line then prompts you to enter a `Description:`. Enter a brief description (up to 39 characters) of what the macro is for.

4. WordPerfect now returns you to your document, with the message `Macro Def` blinking in the status line. Type in the standard language as you want it to appear in your pleadings; WordPerfect records each keystroke.

5. When you have finished your standard language, press Macro Define (Ctrl-F10).

   ⌨ Choose **Macro** from the **Tools** menu and select **Define**.

This turns off the "tape recorder" and saves your macro to the name you gave it in step 2.

Note: If you intend to use these macros with the TIME macro described earlier, you need to include one further step in order to allow the language to be displayed during creation of a time sheet entry. That is, you must include a {DISPLAY ON} code at the end of the standard language. Press Macro Define (Ctrl-F10), type in the name of your macro, and press E to indicate you wish to edit the macro. Then move the cursor to the end of the language you entered, press Ctrl-PgUp to bring up the Macro Commands window, move the cursor to the {DISPLAY ON} code, and press Enter. Then press Exit (F7) to exit from the macro editor and save your modified macro. The macro *rr* on the Applications Disk is a sample of how such a standard language macro should be created.

Hint: Remember that the point of macros is to save keystrokes. If, for example, you had a macro named "conf" which simply typed the word *conference*, by the time you press Macro Define (Alt-F10), type in the macro name, press Enter, and wait for the computer to retrieve and run the macro, you really haven't saved any time at all. Your macro names should therefore be short (two or three characters are ideal) and easy to remember. Consider adding a space after the last word in the macro so that, when it finishes running, the macro will be in the correct position to start the next word.

To use the macro you have just created to insert the language you typed, place the cursor at the exact location in your document where you want the language to appear, and then do this:

1. Press Macro (Alt-F10).

   ▭ Choose **Macro** from the **Tools** menu and select Execute.

2. At the Macro: prompt, type in the name of the macro and press Enter. The language you typed will be inserted into your document.

Summary

In this chapter, you have discovered how computers have invaded the law office and how the right word processing tools can improve law-office activities and save both time and money. Some of the tools discussed included a legal keyboard, macros, templates, and form documents. You have also learned how to organize your word processing files for better file management, and how to create special characters and quotation marks for legal documents. Other topics included special footnote styles, paragraph numbering, automatic cross-references, and how to use special WordPerfect time sheets.

In Chapter 16, you discover three ways to build legal documents—the cut-and-paste method, the merge method, and the menu-driven system of form creation. Chapter 16, as you will see, is most valuable for people who work in law offices.

16

Creating Non-Court Documents

Many legal documents, including leases, deeds, mortgages, and contracts, are prepared on preprinted, fill-in-the-blank forms, used by lawyers and professionals who work with lawyers. This chapter provides specific examples of these documents, created with merge forms, macros, and other WordPerfect tools. You first see a will that illustrates assembling documents by "cutting and pasting."

Next, you look at the special problems that arise from preparing a special group of documents: deeds, mortgages, and related papers. These problems are described and resolved with a macro designed just for such papers.

The chapter concludes with a menu-driven system for creating a large number of documents that all relate to the same case or matter. The example given is that of a system of form letters, pleadings, and other papers relating to a collections practice, but the system works with any group of documents you may wish to create.

Although the methods described in this chapter are geared toward law offices, they can be easily adapted, with only slight modification, to any other office setting.

In this chapter, you learn how to do the following:

- Prepare form documents from which you can select portions to "assemble" into a custom document for a particular case

- Assemble a custom-made document from one or more forms you have created

- Use a special macro to help you speedily and accurately prepare secondary merge files to insert correct names, addresses, pronouns, and other specific information into your form documents

- Build a library of form documents and a menu to allow you to select and prepare standard documents quickly

An Overview of Methods for Creating Documents from Forms

The most straightforward way to create custom-made documents for specific cases is to take an almost complete document with blanks for case-specific information, and then fill in the blanks with necessary information. A more complicated method (now becoming fairly common through word processing) is to assemble standard paragraphs (or other blocks of text) from a form document, and then insert specific client information. This method is called "cut and paste."

This chapter illustrates both the fill-in and cut-and-paste methods; you may want to use both methods for the same document. You can easily prepare paragraph by paragraph such cut-and-paste forms as wills, contracts, settlement agreements, or similar documents. Then you simply fill in the blanks. This chapter shows you how to set up such forms and how to use a "point-and-shoot" macro to speed assembly, and finally provides a macro to help you fill in the blanks. This chapter illustrates a will preparation, but the same technique and same macros work for virtually any type of document you routinely prepare.

The examples in this chapter use WordPerfect's Merge function to insert specific information into general forms. The basic tools for doing this are the following:

- *A list of variable fields to go with each form you create*. You may create multipurpose lists of variables (such as names, addresses, phone numbers, and so on) that work with related forms in your library, or you may decide on separate lists for each form.

- *A library of form documents.* Two types of form documents appear in this chapter. The first forms are a collection of standard paragraphs, clauses, or other segments to be assembled into more specific documents, the "cut-and-paste" forms. The second form is the "fill in" type with specific-case information to enter in the blanks. This chapter uses a simple will as the example of a cut-and-paste form and a deed as an example of a fill-in form. The macros described later in this chapter use these files as primary merge files.

- *A secondary merge file*, containing the specific variable information to insert into your form documents that create the will, contract, deed, or other form specific to your case.

The chapter begins by showing how to create these tools and use them manually to create top-quality legal documents. You then see macros to help you prepare and use these documents. (If you are unfamiliar with the Merge function of WordPerfect 5.1, you may want to review the function in the reference section of the WordPerfect manual.) In this chapter, a *primary file* is a document that contains standardized information (such as a form letter), and a *secondary file* is a document that contains variable information (such as names and addresses).

Assembling Documents by Cutting and Pasting

One familiar way to create form documents is to *cut* standard language paragraphs, clauses, or other blocks of information from a form document and *paste* those elements together to create a new document specific to your case. WordPerfect has several features to help you do this. With properly prepared form documents, you can use a macro or macros to cut and paste automatically. For documents prepared with merge codes for incorporating specific information into the document, you can use the Merge function to insert that information correctly. You can also use macros to help you with this second process.

This section uses a simple will as an example to demonstrate the *cut-and-paste* method. The method easily adapts to any other document that you can create by incorporating blocks of standard text from a form document. Examples of other types of documents where this technique would work well are contracts, corporate bylaws, and divorce-settlement agreements. The TRIGGER macro in this section works equally well on such types of documents.

The cut-and-paste method of document assembly involves the following five steps:

1. Creating a list of variable information

2. Creating the cut-and-paste form

3. Assembling the primary document

4. Creating a secondary merge file

5. Merging the variable data into the final document

After you have worked through these five steps, you can use the method for any other similar forms.

Step 1: Creating Variable Lists

To automate the creation of cut-and-paste forms, study the forms you now use to determine what variable information you must include. Notice in your existing forms the many places the same information is called for on each form. (Does one area on a form always require a client's phone number after the client's name?) By using {FIELD} merge codes in your form, you can ensure that the correct information appears in the right spaces during the merge.

Note: In WordPerfect 5.0, {FIELD} codes were the ^Fn^ merge codes.

Hint: Type your variable list as a WordPerfect document and save it on disk. You can modify that list into a variable template to use with the MERGE macro described later.

Each type of information to be included in your form is called a *field*. A field can contain anything from a single letter (such as an *s* to insert for plural words) to several paragraphs or more. Any information that changes from case to case can be a field for merging.

After you list the different fields required by each type of document you wish to prepare, decide whether each form should have its own special list or whether you want to create a *master* variable list to use with a group of related form documents. (See the section on preparing deeds and mortgages.) In making this decision, consider your own practice and the way in which the forms are to be used.

- *Individual variable lists.* Generally, using different variable lists for each form results in shorter secondary merge files because there are fewer fields in each list. A master list of variables may contain fields that do not relate to every form. To prepare the secondary merge file to use with a particular form, you must include a blank field at every place on the variable list that calls for information not needed in that particular form. If you do not include the proper number of blank fields in the proper place, the information will not be inserted in your document at the right location. The more blank fields needed in a secondary merge file, the more difficult it is to quickly and accurately prepare these files.

- *A master variable list.* If you routinely create closely related documents from different forms, consider using a master variable list that works with all related forms. You can thus create a single secondary merge file (containing the specific information to be inserted into your form documents) that can produce correct documents from all of the related forms. This saves you the trouble of creating separate secondary merge files for each document you create. In many cases, preparing a master variable list can be a major time-saver. The collections system described later is a good example of using a single variable list with a wide variety of documents to save a great deal of time.

The list of variables to be used with the sample will included in this chapter appears in figure 16.1. This information is used later on to create a secondary merge file that automatically inserts the variable data into your finished document.

Variable List for Simple Will

1. Name of testator
2. Testator's town of residence
3. Testator's county of residence
4. Names of testator's children
5. Name of executor/trix
6. Testator/trix
7. He/she/it (gender of executor/trix)
8. His/her (possessive gender for testator/trix)

Fig. 16.1.

Variables used in a sample will.

Step 2: Creating Cut-and-Paste Form Documents

After preparing your list of variables, or fields, to be included in your form document, you are ready to prepare the form document itself. Use as a model the document or documents from which you made your list of variables. The first page of the sample will to be created appears in figure 16.2. This document was probably created manually, but you now want to modify it to use as a cut-and-paste form.

First, retrieve your form to the screen and insert unique {FIELD} codes corresponding to the variables on the list you created earlier. This enables WordPerfect to determine what information to place in each place in your form document.

WordPerfect gives you two ways to identify the variables. In WordPerfect 5.0, you were limited to numbered fields. WordPerfect 5.1 still works with the 5.0 numbered codes, but now you can name your fields if you prefer. Therefore, if the name of the person making the will were the first field on your list of variables, the code for that field in 5.0 might have been ^F1^. In 5.1, you can use numbers, such as {*FIELD*}*1*~, or you can use a name, such as {*FIELD*}*testator*~ (or some other descriptive name).

In deciding whether to use named or numbered fields, consider these points:

- When you create your secondary merge file, numbers are somewhat faster to enter and involve less risk of a typographical error. However, numbers make the primary merge file (your form document) harder to read because the designation {FIELD}1~ has no meaning by itself, whereas the designation {FIELD}testator~ has inherent meaning.

- Named fields have the advantage of making the primary merge document more easily understandable without reference to outside lists.

Fig. 16.2.

*First page of the
sample will.*

LAST WILL AND TESTAMENT

David C. Lorn

I, David C. Lorn, having my residence and domicile in the City of Erie, County of Erie and State of Pennsylvania, being of sound mind and memory, do hereby make, publish and declare this my Last Will and Testament, and I hereby revoke and declare to be null and void all Wills, Codicils, and Testamentary Dispositions formerly made by me.

ARTICLE I

I direct my Executor to pay out of the principal of my residuary estate all federal estate, state inheritance, estate and succession taxes imposed upon or with respect to my estate or any property in which I may have an interest and any expenses of administration of my estate. I direct that all my just debts and funeral expenses be paid as soon after my death as practical.

ARTICLE II

I give, devise and bequeath all the rest, residue and remainder of my property, wheresoever situated, whether real, personal or mixed, in equal shares so that one of such shares shall be paid over to each of my children who survive me, and one of such shares shall be paid to the issue of each child of mine who predeceases me, leaving issue surviving me, per stirpes and not per capita. My children at the time of this will are: Linda, James, Richard, Pamela and Jeffrey.

ARTICLE III

I nominate, constitute and appoint Virginia K. Lorn to be the Executor of this my Will and I direct that she shall serve in such capacity without filing a bond in the Orphans' Court of Erie County or such similar court of competent jurisdiction of the jurisdiction in which I may be domiciled at the time of my death.

ARTICLE IV

I hereby give and grant unto my said Executor full power and authority to sell and convey any and all real estate of which I may die siezed, to such person or persons for such price or prices and on such terms and conditions as she may deem best and give a good and sufficient deed or deeds of conveyance therefor.

However, named fields are more difficult to enter, both in the primary and secondary files, and involve greater risk of typographical errors. Any error in the field name causes the merge to overlook information to be inserted in the field where the error occurred.

You use the Merge Codes key to enter the {FIELD} codes. To insert a field code, follow these steps:

1. Call your form document to the screen, and delete the first bit of information to be replaced with new information for your specific document. In the example in figure 16.2, that is the name of the testator, or person making the will. Move the cursor to that spot and delete the name of the testator.

2. At the exact place where you want new information to be inserted in your document, press Merge Codes (Shift-F9).

   ⌨ Choose Merge Codes from the Tools menu.

3. If you use the function keys, the status line displays the various types of merge codes available. If you use the pull-down menu, a box containing the codes appears.

4. Press **Field (1)**. The status line then prompts you for a field name or number.

5. At the Enter Field: prompt, type the name or number corresponding to that variable on your list and press Enter. The correct {FIELD} code then appears in your document at the place where that information is to be inserted. In the example here, the name "testator" is assigned to the first field on the list shown in figure 16.1. You would type *testator* and press Enter.

   You should now see the following on your screen in place of the Testator's name:

   {FIELD}testator~

   Note: You can edit the field name or number later on from the main editing screen, but be sure you do not delete the tilde (~) character following the field.

6. Repeat the process at all places where variable information must be inserted, always taking care to put the correct field name or number from your list of variables.

   Next, you must separate the form into smaller segments that can be individually retrieved as needed for your specific document. Think carefully about the way you need to retrieve blocks of information when you create specific documents. What should be your basic building block? Should you separate each paragraph so you can retrieve information paragraph by paragraph? Should you separate information by sentences or clauses? Are there larger sections, such as a group of paragraphs, that always need to go together?

The idea is to visually separate the different building blocks of your document so that when you look at the form on your screen, you can easily move to a section and retrieve that language for your special document. In the will example, the basic building block is the Article, or the paragraphs that relate to a single subject.

Next, you must decide how you want to separate the blocks. If your basic blocks are always going to be paragraphs, then the sequence of two hard returns is enough to separate the blocks. However, you can work with the forms easier if you separate the paragraphs with some sort of line to show the joining. The will example shown in figure 16.3 separates the segments with a hard page (**[HPg]**) code (press Ctrl-Enter). Note the hard-page code preceding the introductory paragraph; this code is necessary for the TRIGGER "point and shoot" macro described later.

Fig. 16.3.

First page of will with codes.

==

LAST WILL AND TESTAMENT

{FIELD}testator~

I, {FIELD}testator~, having my residence and domicile in the {FIELD}testown~, County of {FIELD}testcounty~ and State of Pennsylvania, being of sound mind and memory, do hereby make, publish and declare this my Last Will and Testament, and I hereby revoke and declare to be null and void all Wills, Codicils, and Testamentary Dispositions formerly made by me.

==

ARTICLE I

I direct my Executor to pay out of the principal of my residuary estate all federal estate, state inheritance, estate and succession taxes imposed upon or with respect to my estate or any property in which I may have an interest and any expenses of administration of my estate. I direct that all my just debts and funeral expenses be paid as soon after my death as practical.

==

ARTICLE II

I give, devise and bequeath all the rest, residue and remainder of my property, wheresoever situated, whether real, personal or mixed, in equal shares so that one of such shares shall be paid over to each of my children who survive me, and one of such shares shall be paid to the issue of each child of mine who predeceases me, leaving issue surviving me, per stirpes and not per capita. My children at the time of this will are: {FIELD}children~.

==

ARTICLE III

I nominate, constitute and appoint {FIELD}executrix~ to be the Executor of this my Will and I direct that {FIELD}genderex~ shall serve in such capacity without filing a bond in the Orphans' Court of Erie County or such similar court of competent jurisdiction of the jurisdiction in which I may be domiciled at the time of my death.

The following tips on setting up your form documents can make them easier to use:

- If your finished document includes paragraph numbers, consider using Automatic Paragraph Numbering codes (**[ParNum:x]**) to produce those numbers. Then, when you assemble documents in a different order from the original form or if you insert or delete paragraphs, the paragraphs still number themselves correctly. See Chapter 15 for more information on using these codes. An automatic paragraph-numbering macro is included as the hot key Ctrl-N on the LEGAL keyboard described in Chapter 15.

- You can make it easier for the person assembling documents to identify the correct paragraph or block to include by making use of WordPerfect's Comment feature.

To add comments to your document, follow these steps:

1. Press Text In/Out (Ctrl-F5); then select **Comment** (**4**).

   ⌨ Choose **Comment** from the **E**dit menu and select **Create** (**1**).

2. Type a brief title or description of the block of information, such as the following:

   Introductory paragraph

3. Press Exit (F7) when you are through.

   The comment stays on your screen, but does not print with the document. You can leave the comments in the final assembled document or delete them if you choose.

   An example of the will form with comments included is shown in figure 16.4.

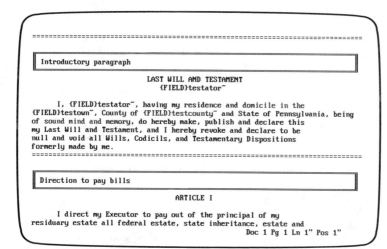

Fig. 16.4.

The will with comments added.

When you have completed your form document, store it in your forms directory. For easy reference, store in a single directory all form documents that you create. The macro that follows looks for such documents in whatever directory you specify as your forms directory when you modify the INSTALL macro (see the file README.16 on the Applications Disk for more information on how to modify that macro).

Step 3: Assembling the Final Document

The Applications Disk includes a handy macro, TRIGGER, to help assemble paragraphs or other blocks of information from cut-and-paste forms into new documents. TRIGGER is assigned to the hot key Ctrl-Z on the LEGAL keyboard. If you choose not to use the LEGAL keyboard, you can still use this macro by invoking it by its full name. Better yet, rename it to an Alt-letter combination as a hot key that does not conflict with any of your existing hot-key macros.

The TRIGGER macro works with forms where the blocks of information are separated by hard-page codes. The macro operates quite simply. It switches between Doc 2 (your cut-and-paste form) and Doc 1 (where your final document is being created). Your form can be in either Doc 1 or Doc 2.

To use TRIGGER, follow these steps:

1. Create the title or introductory information for your new document (unless your cut-and-paste form supplies that); then place your cursor at the location where you want the blocks of text to appear.

2. Switch to Doc 2 (Shift-F3) and retrieve your cut-and-paste form.

3. Place the cursor anywhere within the block information you wish to paste into your new document, except on the last character of that block.

4. Invoke TRIGGER by pressing Ctrl-Z or any other hot key to which you have assigned the macro. TRIGGER copies that block of information over to your final document at the point where you left the cursor, then returns to the cut-and-paste form and moves to the next block of information. (All of this is done in the background; you do not actually see the macro work until it is through and the cursor has moved to the next block on your form.)

You can repeatedly invoke TRIGGER to retrieve every block that you need in your new document. You can skip form paragraphs you don't need by pressing PgDn or GoTo (Ctrl-Home). When you have inserted all of the paragraphs that you want from your form, press Exit (F7) to exit from the form in Doc 2 without saving it. You can then retrieve another form in Doc 2 and add more blocks if you want.

When you are through assembling blocks from your cut-and-paste form, switch back to your final document in Doc 1. All of the hard-page codes from the form document now appear in your final document in Doc 1. Although the codes can be easily deleted, you may want to leave them for a few moments while you edit the final document. If, for example, you want to rearrange the order in which the information appears, the hard-page codes help. Follow these steps to rearrange the order:

1. Place the cursor within the paragraph or block of information that you wish to move.

2. Press Move (Ctrl-F4) and select **Page** (**3**) to indicate that you wish to move a "page."

   ⌨ From the **E**dit menu, press Select, then **Page**. That block of information is then highlighted.

3. Press **Move (1)** to indicate that you wish to move that "page," and it disappears from your screen. The status line prompts

   `Move cursor; press Enter to retrieve.`

4. Move the cursor to the location where you want the block to appear and press Enter.

If the block of information you want to move is more than a page long, you cannot use this shortcut, but you can accomplish the same thing with the Block function. Move the cursor to the beginning of the block you want to move and do this:

1. Press Block (Alt-F4).

   ⌨ Choose **Block** from the **Edit** menu.

2. Press Search (F2) followed by Ctrl-Enter, to indicate that you want to search for a **[HPg]** code.

3. Press Search (F2) a second time. WordPerfect then moves to the next **[HPg]** code that should be the end of the block you want to move.

4. Press Move (Ctrl-F4), and select **Block (1)** and then **Move (1)**.

   ⌨ Choose **Move** from the **Edit** menu.

   The block of text disappears from your screen.

5. Move the cursor to the exact place where you want to insert the block of information, and press Enter. The block then reappears at that location.

After all of the information is in the order you want it to appear, you can easily delete the hard-page codes through a simple search and replace. Do the following:

1. Move the cursor to the top of the document by using Home, Home, up arrow.

2. Press Replace (Alt-F2).

   ⌨ Choose **Replace** from the **Search** menu.

3. Press **N** at the `w/Confirm? No (Yes)` prompt.

4. Press Ctrl-Enter. The **[HPg]** code appears after the `Srch:` prompt.

5. Press Search (F2) to indicate that Replace should search for hard-page codes. The status line then prompts `Replace with:`.

6. Press Search (F2) again to indicate that the **[HPg]** codes should be replaced with nothing. WordPerfect then strips your document of all **[HPg]** codes.

You can strip any comments you inserted in the same way.

Hint: The macro MERGE described later can perform this function for you automatically if you prefer. If you intend to use MERGE to finish your document, you can skip this step.

After you add any nonstandard language, signature lines, or other information to the document, store the file in the directory where you keep such documents. This file becomes your primary merge file when you fill in the blanks left by your form document. (The macro MERGE described next refers to this document as a *custom form*.)

Step 4: Creating Secondary Merge Files

Now that you have completed the basic document, you must replace the {FIELD} codes with specific information for your new document. To do this, use the Merge feature. Basically, the primary merge file you just created will be merged with a secondary merge file containing all of the data to be inserted in the primary file. To explain this, you first see how to make a secondary merge file manually, and then you see a macro that makes this job easier.

To create a secondary merge file manually, be sure you keep a printed copy of your variable list handy. If you chose to use named fields, you must begin your secondary merge file with a {FIELD NAMES} statement. This statement identifies the names of the fields in the forms, but prepare the statement very carefully.

To create a secondary merge file manually, follow these steps:

1. Begin from a clean document. Press Merge Codes (Shift-F9), then **More (6)**.

    ⌨ Choose **Merge** Codes from the **Tools** menu, then **More**.

2. The Merge Commands window then appears. Move the cursor to the {FIELD NAMES} by using the arrow key or by pressing F, down arrow. Press Enter.

3. The status line prompts you for Field Number 1:. Type the name for the first variable on your list and press Enter.

4. The status line asks for the next field number. Keep entering the fields from your list. When you have entered the last field from your list, press Exit (F7).

5. The {FIELD NAMES} statement then appears at the top of your screen, all on one line, with tildes (~) separating the fields you entered. The

last field is followed by a second tilde, an {END RECORD} code, and a **[HPg]** code. Do not delete the second tilde or either code.

You can clean up the appearance of this statement by separating each field into separate lines. Do this simply by moving the cursor to the first letter of each field and pressing Enter.

After making your {FIELD NAMES} statement, or if you choose to use numbered fields, continue by entering the information to be inserted in each field. You must be extremely careful here to place it in the same sequence as the named or numbered fields you have established. Refer to your form.

To enter information in the fields, follow these steps:

1. Immediately below the **[HPg]** (or from a blank screen, if you are using numbered fields), type the information to insert in the first field on your list.

2. Press End Field (F9). An {END FIELD} merge code appears, and the cursor drops to the next line. The status line shows Field: (name or number), indicating you are ready to insert information for the next field on your list.

3. Insert the proper information for the next field, and press End Field (F9) again. Note that the status line now shows Field: (another name or number).

4. Continue on through all the fields, inserting correct information in the fields in your variable list.

5. If you get to a field where no information is to be inserted, simply press End Field (F9) to create a blank field. This is extremely important. If you fail to add a blank field, all of the information in fields subsequent to the one that should be blank is inserted in the wrong places in your finished document.

    Note: It does not matter how long each field is. Insert the information as you wish it to appear in the final document, although this is not critical. You can go into the merged final document and edit it as you would any other WordPerfect document later if you wish. You can then add tabs, indents, hard returns, or other formatting codes, such as boldface or italic codes. All are merged in the final document.

    When you are through inserting information in your secondary merge file (say that you get to the end of your variable list), end the document with an {END RECORD} code:

6. Press Merge Codes (Shift-F9); then press End Record (**2**).

    ▭ Choose **Merge** from the **T**ools menu and select **End Record**.

    The {END RECORD} code appears.

Save your secondary file in a separate directory under some file name that is associated with the file you are working on (such as a client name or file number). The MERGE macro discussed later looks for such files in the directory you designate for variable lists when you modify the INSTALL macro.

The secondary merge file to be used with the sample will appears in figure 16.5.

Fig. 16.5.

The will's secondary merge file.

```
{FIELD NAMES}
testator~
testown~
testcounty~
children~
executirx~
testatrix~
genderex~
gendertest~
~{END RECORD}
======================================================
David C. Lorn{END FIELD}
City of Erie{END FIELD}
Erie{END FIELD}
Linda, James, Richard, Pamela and Jeffrey{END FIELD}
Virginia K. Lorn{END FIELD}
testator{END FIELD}
she{END FIELD}
his{END FIELD}
{END RECORD}
```

Step 5: Creating the Final Document

The last step in manually creating your final document is to merge the primary and secondary merge files into a single document. From a blank screen, follow these steps:

1. Press Merge/Sort (Ctrl-F9); then type **Merge** (**1**).

    ▭ Choose **Merge** from the **T**ools menu.

2. The status line prompts you for the primary file. Enter the path and file name for the primary merge file (your final document) you created. If you can't remember the file name, press List (F5) and retrieve the file from the list of files.

3. The status line then asks for the name of the secondary file you just created. Type in the path and file name for that file as well. Again, in WordPerfect 5.1, you can enter the file name for the secondary merge file by using List (F5).

4. After you press Enter, your final document with all of the blanks properly filled in appears on your screen. You can then edit it, print it, or save it as you want.

Using a Macro To Assist the Process

The Applications Disk includes a macro entitled MERGE (assigned to the hot key Ctrl-M on the LEGAL keyboard) that speeds up this process considerably. It uses the documents you created in the section "Step 3: Assembling the Final Document" as the primary merge file. The macro creates the secondary merge file by prompting you for the information required by your form, then asks you for the name of your primary merge file. Finally, the macro automatically merges the two files and, if you choose, deletes any hard-page codes or comments that you did not delete manually.

In order for the MERGE macro to know what information to ask for, you must create a template file. This is simply a list of the variables (or fields) you created when you first wrote your form documents (see fig. 16.1). You must set up this template, however, in a special way.

To create a variable template to use with MERGE, follow these steps:

1. If you decided to use named fields, create a {FIELD NAMES} statement for your form first. MERGE copies this statement into all secondary files that it creates. Follow the five steps discussed earlier in the chapter to create this statement.

2. Retrieve the variable list you created earlier (see "Step 1: Creating Variable Lists"). Be sure that each item on the list appears on a line by itself and is no more than one line long. Also be sure that no blank lines appear in the document. Each field you place on this template will become a prompt when you use the MERGE macro.

3. The first field should be on the very first line after the **[HPg]** code that follows the {FIELD NAMES} statement. If you use numbered fields, the first field should be on the very first line of the document. Delete any title or introductory matter you may have placed in your list.

4. The very last line of the document *must* be simply, in all capital letters, the word *END*. Do not include any spaces or any characters other than the three *capital* letters of that word on that line. The MERGE macro uses this line to determine when to stop building the secondary merge file.

A sample variable template for use with the will form appears in figure 16.6. The template is derived from information listed in figure 16.1.

```
{FIELD NAMES}
testator~
testown~
testcounty~
children~
executirx~
testatrix~
genderex~
gendertest~
~{END RECORD}
==================================================
1. Name of testator
2. Testator's town of residence
3. Testator's county of residence
4. Names of testator's children
5. Name of executor/trix
6. Testator/trix
7. He/she/it (gender of executor/trix)
8. His/her (possessive gender for testator/trix)
END
```

Store your variable template in a directory reserved for similar templates. To make it easy, give the template the same file name as the form to which it relates (this is why a special directory is required for templates). For example, you could name your simple will form XWILL and store it in the directory C:\WP51\FORMS. Its corresponding variable template would also be named XWILL, to be stored in the directory C:\WP51\TEMPLATE. MERGE looks for variable templates in the directory you specify for such documents when you modify the INSTALL macro. For instructions on how to do this, see the file README.16 on the disk.

MERGE uses both Doc 1 and Doc 2 during its operation. To guard against accidentally retrieving templates or writing merge information into a document that may be on-screen in Doc 2, MERGE checks both screens to see whether anything is there. If it finds anything at all, MERGE quits immediately and asks you to save your work before completing your merge.

To create your secondary merge file with the MERGE macro, follow these steps:

1. Create and save your basic document (the primary merge file) with the TRIGGER macro.

2. From a blank screen, invoke MERGE by pressing Macro (Alt-F10).

    ⌨ Choose **Macros** from the **Tools** menu and select **Execute**.

3. Type *Merge* and press Enter. (If you are using the LEGAL keyboard, invoke MERGE simply by pressing Ctrl-M.)

4. The Document Assembly Main Menu appears, as shown in figure 16.7. Select the option **Create list of information to insert in form (1)**.

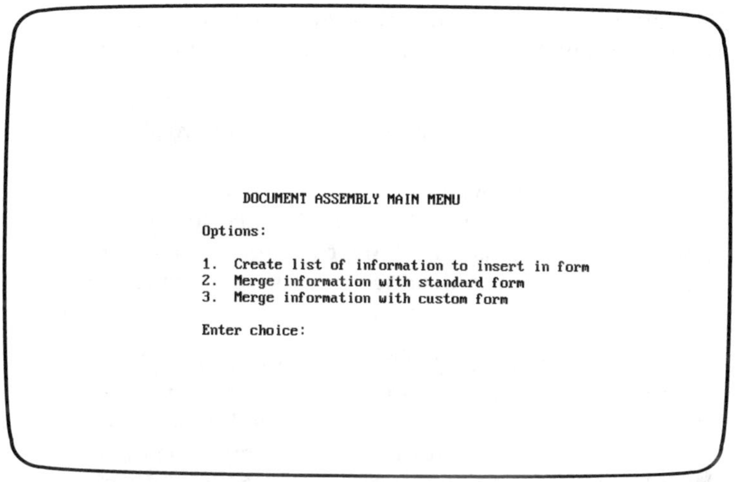

```
        DOCUMENT ASSEMBLY MAIN MENU

    Options:

    1.  Create list of information to insert in form
    2.  Merge information with standard form
    3.  Merge information with custom form

    Enter choice:
```

Fig. 16.7.

The Document Assembly Main Menu.

5. MERGE then asks you for the name of the variable template you want to use. If you named the file for the form it works with, enter the name of the form you are preparing; MERGE supplies the path.

6. MERGE then retrieves the template you created. Each line of the template becomes a prompt, signaling you to type in the information needed for each field.

7. Enter the requested information.

   Note: You are limited to 129 characters with MERGE.

8. When MERGE encounters the END line in your template, it asks for a file name for the secondary merge file just created. Assign a name that you can identify with the document you are preparing (such as a file number). If a file already exists with that name, MERGE prompts you for another name. MERGE then saves the secondary merge file to the name you provide.

9. MERGE then returns to the Document Assembly Main Menu.

To create your final document, select the option Merge with custom form (3). MERGE then prompts you for the names of the primary and secondary merge files and merges them. It then asks if you want to delete all hard-page codes and comments. After you press Y or N, MERGE offers your finished document.

Creating Deeds and Mortgages

As noted before, the cut-and-paste form works well for documents that incorporate standard blocks of information in different sequences. Some types of documents, however, do not lend themselves well to this technique. Deeds and mortgages are good examples.

Ever since the printing press came into widespread use, lawyers have almost exclusively used preprinted forms for deeds, mortgages, and other such papers. More often than not, the blank spaces provided with such forms are either too large or too small for the information to be inserted. But with WordPerfect and a laser printer, reliance on preprinted deed forms is no longer necessary. You can easily create your own forms with merge codes to produce custom-made papers suitable for recording.

Like the cut-and-paste method, the *standard form* method described here relies on the Merge function. You must begin by creating variable lists for each of the documents you want to make a form for, evaluating the possibility of making a master list of variables to use with numerous forms. As an example, a single variable list could supply information to be incorporated in a general warranty deed, several types of special warranty deeds, an estate or fiduciary deed, a corporate deed, a quitclaim deed, various types of mortgages, and other certificates routinely used in a real estate practice.

An example of this technique is shown in figures 16.8 and 16.9. Figure 16.8 is a list of the variables to be inserted in a general warranty deed and a related mortgage to be prepared for the same closing. Note that not all of the variables are used in the general warranty deed shown in figure 16.9 (for example, the name of the lender, field *lender*, does not appear in the deed), nor do all of the fields appear in the mortgage (for example, the name of the seller or grantor of the property). If, however, you create a secondary merge file containing all of the variables listed in figure 16.8, you could merge that file with both your deed form and your mortgage form, and each would print correctly.

Creating Form Documents

After creating your list or lists of variables to use with each document, you are ready to create your primary document forms. By using correct field codes at each location where variable information is to be inserted, you can accelerate the creation of your final documents.

You probably already have form documents in WordPerfect. The easiest way to create a form document is to take a sample of the type of document you want to create and edit the changes into your standard form. Simply work through the document, deleting the specific information, replacing it with a corresponding {FIELD} code. (See the earlier discussion of form preparation.)

Variable List for Deeds/Mortgages

1. Day of deed (Date only)
2. Month, year of deed
3. Name of Seller(s)
4. "y" or "ies" (seller: party or parties)
5. Name of Buyer(s)
6. "y" or "ies" (buyer/borrower: party or parties)
7. Name of lender
8. Amount of consideration for deed
9. Amount of mortgage
10. Gender of seller(s) (him/her/them)
11. Municipality where property is located
12. Name of first seller
13. Name of second seller
14. Name of first buyer/borrower
15. Name of second buyer/borrower

Fig. 16.8.

List of variables for a deed and mortgage.

WARRANTY DEED

THIS INDENTURE, made this {FIELD}day~ day of {FIELDS}mo-yr~, by and between

{FIELD}seller~, part{FIELD}sellnum~ of the first part [the Grantor(s)]

AND

{FIELD}buyer~, part{FIELD}buynum~ of the second part [the Grantee(s)]

WITNESSETH, That the said part{FIELD}sellnum~ of the first part, for and in consideration of the sum of:

{FIELD}price~

lawful money of the United States, to {FIELD}sellgen~ in hand paid by the said part{FIELD}6~ of the second part, at and before the ensealing and delivery of these presents, the receipt and payment whereof is hereby acknowledged, has/have granted, bargained, sold, released and confirmed, and by these presents do/does grant, bargain, sell, release and confirm unto the said part{FIELD}buynum~ of the second part, and to his, her, their, its, heirs/successors and assigns,

All that certain piece or parcel of land situate in the {FIELD}where~, bounded and described as follows, to-wit:

{NEST MACRO}getdescr~
{DOCUMENT}{VARIABLE}deeds~\{VARIABLE}descrip~~

Grantor(s) has/have not disposed of solid waste or hazardous waste on the above-described property and has/have no knowledge whether or not any solid waste or hazardous waste was deposited on the above-described property prior to acquisition of title thereto by the Grantor(s).

TOGETHER with all and singular the rights, liberties, privileges, hereditaments, improvements, and appurtenances, whatsoever thereto belonging, and the reversions and remainders, rents, issues and profits thereof; and also, all the estate and interest whatsoever of the said part of the first part, in law or equity, of, in, to or out of the same;

TO HAVE AND TO HOLD the same, together with the premises hereby granted, or intended

Fig. 16.9.

A general warranty deed form.

Note: The variables do not have to appear in sequential order in the form document to print correctly. You must, however, use the correct field name or number corresponding to the formation needed at that place in your form.

The new merge codes in WordPerfect 5.1 are useful for retrieving the correct legal description of the property being sold into your deed form. If you include a *{DOCUMENT}filename~* merge code in your form, WordPerfect retrieves the named file into the deed form during the merge. By setting up each legal description as a separate WordPerfect document, you can use a {DOCUMENT} code to automatically retrieve the full legal description into any form document.

For this feature to work, however, you must provide the correct file name of your legal description during the merge. You can do this with another of the new features of Merge in WordPerfect 5.1, its capability to *nest* macros and use variables in much the same way that macros do.

 The Applications Disk includes a macro called GETDESCR that asks you for the name of the deed-description file. If you enter a file name that does not exist, the macro prompts for another name. Once you enter a valid file name, that file is pulled into your deed by the {DOCUMENT} merge command.

GETDESCR assumes that you have stored all deed descriptions as WordPerfect documents in a special directory. GETDESCR reads the INSTALL macro to learn where to find deed descriptions—you can edit INSTALL to provide the correct directory for those files. For more information, see the file README.16 on the Applications Disk.

At the location in the deed where you want the property's legal description to be inserted, insert a {NEST MACRO} command. First place any formatting codes you want to insert for the legal description. For example, you may want the description to be indented an extra inch on both sides. Because many legal descriptions are more than one paragraph long, you cannot use an **[>Indent<]** code to do this: the **[HRt]** at the end of the first paragraph would terminate the indentation. You must therefore change the margins for the legal description to two inches (or whatever you choose) to accomplish this.

Next, place the {NEST MACRO} code in the document at the location where you want the legal description to be inserted. Do the following:

1. Press Merge Codes (Shift-F9).

   ⌨ Choose Me**r**ge Codes from the **T**ools menu.

2. From the list of options, type **M**ore (**6**) or press Merge Codes (Shift-F9) again.

   ⌨ Choose **M**ore.

   The Merge Commands window appears.

3. Move the cursor to the {NEST MACRO} code with the down-arrow key. Or use the Name Search feature: simply press N to move the cursor automatically to that code (because the code is the first merge code beginning with the letter N.)

4. Press Enter.

5. The status line prompts you to `Enter Macro Name:`. Type *getdescr* and press Enter. The {NEST MACRO} command appears in your document, together with the name of the GETDESCR macro.

Press Enter to move down a line, then insert the {DOCUMENT} code to retrieve the file name entered at the {TEXT} prompt. To do this, follow these steps:

1. Press Merge Codes (Shift-F9).

   ⌨ Choose Me**r**ge Codes from the **T**ools menu.

2. From the list of options, press **M**ore (**6**).

   ⌨ Choose **M**ore from the pull-down menu.

   The Merge Commands window appears.

3. Move the cursor to the {DOCUMENT} code with the down-arrow key. Or use the Name Search feature: simply type *do* to move the cursor automatically to that code (because it is the only merge code beginning with the letters DO).

4. Press Enter.

5. The status line prompts you to `Enter Filename:`. Because the actual file name depends on what you enter in response to the GETDESCR macro during merge, you cannot enter a specific file name here. You must, however, enter a path to show where your legal descriptions are stored. The INSTALL macro uses the variable {VARIABLE}deeds~ to refer to the your directory for legal descriptions. Because you cannot enter the {VARIABLE} code at this point, simply press Enter for now.

The {DOCUMENT} code appears on your screen, followed by a tilde (which marks the end of the {DOCUMENT} command). You must now insert the proper {VARIABLE} codes inside of the {DOCUMENT} code to tell WordPerfect where to find the specific file you want during merge.

Note: If you plan to use this deed without the DEED macro described next, you have to either type the correct path to your deed descriptions instead of the {VARIABLE}deeds~, or add the merge command {NEST MACRO}install~ immediately before the {NEST MACRO}getdescr~ command. The macro INSTALL inserts the correct path in the variable {VARIABLE}deeds~. The DEED macro nests the INSTALL macro and sets the contents of {VARIABLE}deeds~ for you.

1. Move the cursor to the left of the tilde (~) that follows the {DOCUMENT} code by pressing left arrow.

2. Press Merge Codes (Shift-F9).

   ⌨ Choose Merge Codes from the Tools menu.

3. From the list of options that appears, press More (6) or press Merge Codes (Shift-F9) again.

   ⌨ Choose More from the pull-down menu.

   The Merge Commands window appears.

4. Move the cursor to the {VARIABLE} code with the down-arrow key. Or use the Name Search feature: simply press V to move the cursor automatically to that code (because it is the only merge code that begins with the letter V.)

5. Press Enter.

6. The status line prompts you to Enter Variable:. Type the word *deeds* to designate the variable where the path to your deed description directory is stored.

7. Press Enter. The designation {VARIABLE}deeds~ appears, followed by a second tilde (marking the end of the {DOCUMENT} command).

8. Type a backslash between the two tildes.

9. Enter another {VARIABLE} code by repeating steps 2 through 6. At the Enter Variable: prompt, type *descrip*. This is the variable that GETDESCR uses to store the name of the file you provide. Press Enter.

In this example, the complete string of codes should now appear on your screen like this (as shown in figure 16.9):

```
{NEST MACRO}getdescr~
{DOCUMENT}{VARIABLE}deeds~\{VARIABLE}descrip~~
```

The two tildes at the end are necessary. One marks the end of the {VARIABLE} command, and the second marks the end of the {DOCUMENT} command (which includes {VARIABLE}).

Now, when you retrieve your merge form with these merge codes inserted, WordPerfect runs the macro GETDESCR. The macro asks you for the file name of the legal description. The file name you enter should be the name only because the {DOCUMENT} command supplies the path to your deeds directory. The {DOCUMENT} command then retrieves the file name in that variable from the deeds directory and inserts it automatically into your deed form.

Dressing Up Your Forms

If you have a laser printer, consider using its font capabilities or WordPerfect's graphics features to dress up the appearance of your form documents. Consider the deed form shown in figure 16.9, which uses a 24-point Times Roman font for the W and D characters, and 18-point type for the rest of the title *Warranty Deed*. These are the default fonts for the extra large and very large size attributes in the printer file that printed this form.

You can see the size-change codes in Reveal Codes. The codes used to create the deed form (shown in fig. 16.9) appear in figure 16.10.

To add size attributes to your forms, follow these steps:

1. Press Block (Alt-F4).

   ⌨ Choose **Block** from the **Edit** menu.

2. Using the arrow keys, move the cursor to highlight the letter or letters whose size you want to change.

3. Press Font (Ctrl-F8).

   ⌨ Choose **Font** from the pull-down menu.

4. If you use the function keys, the status line asks whether you want to change the size or some other appearance attribute of the letters you have marked with the Block (for example, whether to underline or italicize). Select **Size (1)**. If you use pull-down menus, skip to step 5.

5. Select the size attribute you want from the status line or the pop-up menu that appears.

You may also include graphics or lines (with Line Draw) to improve the appearance of your final documents.

Creating Secondary Merge Files

After creating your variable lists and form documents, you are ready to use your new forms. To do this, you must create the secondary merge file for each new document you want to create with your forms.

It is extremely important that the information you insert in the secondary merge file match the field type you established when you created your variable list, even if you must insert blank fields in your secondary merge file. In the example given in figure 16.8, you may want to create a deed for a cash transaction (with no mortgage). You would have to leave fields 7 and 9 blank to properly merge your deed form with the secondary merge file; otherwise the merge inserts information in fields 8 through 15 in the wrong places.

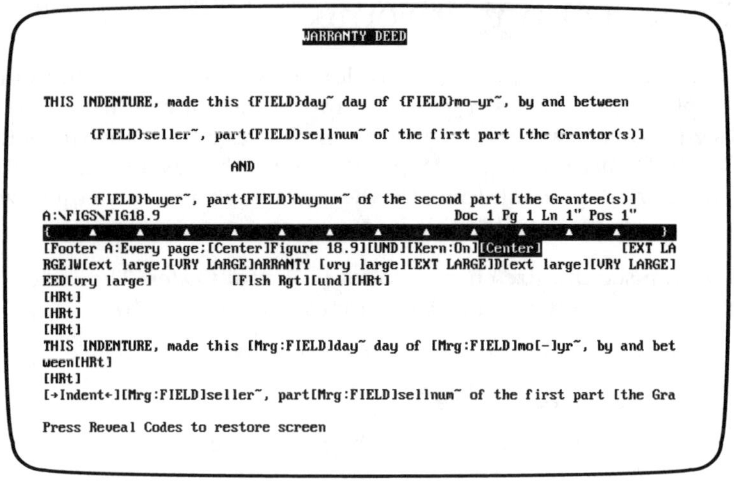

Fig. 16.10.

The codes used to create the warranty deed.

```
                              WARRANTY DEED

  THIS INDENTURE, made this {FIELD}day~ day of {FIELD}mo-yr~, by and between

        {FIELD}seller~, part{FIELD}sellnum~ of the first part [the Grantor(s)]

                              AND

        {FIELD}buyer~, part{FIELD}buynum~ of the second part [the Grantee(s)]
  A:\FIGS\FIG18.9                                   Doc 1 Pg 1 Ln 1" Pos 1"
  {      ▲     ▲     ▲     ▲     ▲     ▲     ▲     ▲     ▲     ▲     ▲     }
  [Footer A:Every page;[Center]Figure 18.9][UND][Kern:On][Center]          [EXT LA
  RGE]W[ext large][VRY LARGE]ARRANTY [vry large][EXT LARGE]D[ext large][VRY LARGE]
  EED[vry large]          [Flsh Rgt][und][HRt]
  [HRt]
  [HRt]
  [HRt]
  THIS INDENTURE, made this [Mrg:FIELD]day~ day of [Mrg:FIELD]mo[-]yr~, by and bet
  ween[HRt]
  [HRt]
  [→Indent←][Mrg:FIELD]seller~, part[Mrg:FIELD]sellnum~ of the first part [the Gra

  Press Reveal Codes to restore screen
```

For a discussion of how to create a secondary merge file manually, see "Step 4: Creating Secondary Merge Files." A secondary merge file for the deed form shown in figure 16.9 is shown in figure 16.11.

Creating Legal Description Files

Because legal descriptions are generally lengthy and require careful proofreading, take great care entering such descriptions in your deeds, mortgages, and other documents. The deed form you have just created allows you to create a separate WordPerfect document consisting of just the legal description of the property involved in the sale. The deed form then retrieves that description into your deed or mortgage just as typed. In this way, you can type and proofread the description once and then use it for any document that requires the full legal description (including mortgages, mechanics lien waivers, and any of the various certificates that might be required at a closing).

For help locating and identifying legal description files, create a special directory for legal descriptions, making sure you provide the correct information when you modify the INSTALL macro. Before you prepare your first deed, type the legal description for that deed on a blank screen and save it as a standard WordPerfect document to your legal descriptions directory under an easily recognizable and recallable file name (the name of the seller or the office file number might be good file names).

```
{FIELD NAMES}
day~
mo-yr~
seller~
sellnum~
buyer~
buynum~
lender~
price~
loan~
sellgen~
where~
1sellname~
2sellname~
1buyname~
2buyname~
~{END RECORD}
=====================================================
18th{END FIELD}
August, 1989{END FIELD}
WARREN B. WORTHINGTON and MARIA G. WORTHINGTON, his wife{END FIELD}
ies{END FIELD}
DAVID C. LORN and VIRGINIA K. LORN, his wife, as tenants by the entireties{END
FIELD}
ies{END FIELD}
{END FIELD}
Ninety-five thousand nine hundred dollars ($95,900){END FIELD}
{END FIELD}
them{END FIELD}
City of Erie{END FIELD}
Warren B. Worthington{END FIELD}
Maria G. Worthington{END FIELD}
{END FIELD}
{END FIELD}
{END RECORD}
```

Fig. 16.11.

A secondary merge file for the warranty deed.

Creating the Final Document

Now that you have created the form document, the specific secondary merge file to combine with it, and the legal description file, creating the final document using WordPerfect's Merge function is a simple matter. Refer to the steps shown previously in the will example to see how to merge the deed form with the secondary merge file. The merge form itself prompts you for the name of the legal description file, as discussed earlier.

The first page of the deed created by merging figure 16.9 with figure 16.11 is shown in figure 16.12.

Easier Data Input with the DEED Macro

Creating the secondary merge file for each document can be a time-consuming job. The potential for mistakes is great, particularly where the same variable list is used for several documents. It is easy to forget adding a blank field where information is

WARRANTY DEED

Fig. 16.12.

*The first page of
the general
warranty deed
after the merge.*

THIS INDENTURE, made this 18th day of August, 1990, by and between

> **WARREN B. WORTHINGTON** and **MARIA G. WORTHINGTON**, his wife,
> parties of the first part [the Grantor(s)]

> AND

> **DAVID C. LORN** and **VIRGINIA K. LORN**, his wife, as tenants by the
> entireties, parties of the second part [the Grantee(s)]

WITNESSETH, That the said parties of the first part, for and in consideration of the sum of:

Ninety-five thousand nine hundred dollars ($95,900)

lawful money of the United States, to them in hand paid by the said parties of the second part,
at and before the ensealing and delivery of these presents, the receipt and payment whereof is
hereby acknowledged, has/have granted, bargained, sold, released and confirmed, and by these
presents do/does grant, bargain, sell, release and confirm unto the said parties of the second part,
and to his, her, their, its, heirs/successors and assigns,

All that certain piece or parcel of land situate in the City of Erie, bounded and described as
follows, to-wit:

> Lot number 27 in the Golf Park Subdivision recorded in Erie County Map Book
> A42, page 201.

> Being the same premises acquired by the said parties of the first part by deed
> recorded April 19, 1974 in Erie County Deed Book 4098, page 142.

Grantor(s) has/have not disposed of solid waste or hazardous waste on the above-described
property and has/have no knowledge whether or not any solid waste or hazardous waste was
deposited on the above-described property prior to acquisition of title thereto by the Grantor(s).

TOGETHER with all and singular the rights, liberties, privileges, hereditaments, improvements,
and appurtenances, whatsoever thereto belonging, and the reversions and remainders, rents,
issues and profits thereof; and also, all the estate and interest whatsoever of the said part of

not needed, causing the merge to put information in the wrong places in your final
document.

With macros, you can expedite the process of creating the secondary merge
file and indeed the merge process itself. The Applications Disk includes a
macro called DEED that automates the entire process for you. The macro
works equally well with mortgage forms or any form you create.

DEED is actually a derivative of the MERGE macro, and it operates similarly. DEED,
however, is specifically designed to produce deeds, mortgages, or other forms that
use lengthy legal descriptions, avoiding (for certain fields) the 129-character
limitation inherent in the MERGE macro.

The DEED macro looks for certain types of files in specific directories. You can
modify DEED to conform to your directory structure, or you can modify your
directory structure to that setup in DEED. For instructions on how to do this, see

the file README.16 on the Applications Disk. If you modify DEED, however, you should probably set up separate directories for the types of documents called by the macro, as described next.

DEED needs four types of files to create a final product; it is suggested that each type be stored in separate directories because related files may have the same file name. The types of files needed are these:

- A variable template (created by modifying your variable list)
- A deed or mortgage merge form (created earlier)
- A legal description (created in WordPerfect) for each specific file
- A secondary merge file (written by the DEED macro)

Remember to edit the INSTALL macro to provide the correct path to the directories where you store each of these types of documents. For help with editing INSTALL, see the file README.16 on the disk.

Creating Secondary Merge Files with DEED

The most useful thing DEED does for you is to walk through the creation of your secondary merge file with a series of on-screen prompts. It also allows you to type your legal description only once, store it in a directory reserved for legal descriptions, and refer to that same description from any form that you establish that requires a legal description. This ensures accuracy in preparation of papers because you can retrieve the same description into every document you create for a particular closing.

Creating a Variable Template

To help create a secondary merge file, DEED needs to know what information needs to be inserted in which fields. You can use your variable list to prepare a template that DEED can refer to. DEED prompts you for the correct information to insert, in the correct order, to create a secondary merge file that works correctly with the related primary merge form.

You can easily modify the variable list in figure 16.8 to work as a variable template for the DEED macro. To create the template, follow the steps outlined in creating the MERGE macro. Each line of the template appears as a prompt on your status line as DEED works through the template. Your responses to those prompts is then written by DEED into a secondary merge file that can then fill in the blanks on your standard deed or mortgage form.

There are exceptions, however. Because DEED makes use of the WordPerfect variables, the responses you give to the prompts must be 129 characters or fewer and cannot contain formatting codes (such as **[BOLD]** or **[UND]**). Although this is not a problem for most types of information to be included in a secondary merge file, in three areas this limitation is a significant problem. That is, the names of the buyers and sellers and the legal description itself can exceed 129 characters, and you may want to include formatting codes. The DEED macro therefore treats those fields slightly differently.

For DEED to recognize these three fields and operate correctly, your variable template must be set up in a specific way. Follow these steps:

1. If you used named fields (instead of numbered fields) to create your deed forms, remember to include a {FIELD NAMES} statement at the beginning of your variable template. (See the earlier discussion of setting up a template for the MERGE macro.)

2. The DEED macro pauses for you to enter the sellers' names when it encounters a line in your template containing the exact string SELLER— nothing more, nothing less. From your original variable list, delete the line where you called for the name of the sellers and replace it with the single word *SELLER* in all capital letters. It does not matter where in the template this word appears, so long as it is in the place corresponding to the field number on your variable list.

3. Likewise, the macro pauses for the buyers' names when it finds the string BUYER. Replace the buyers' names variable with *BUYER* in capital letters. (Even if you are creating a template for use with a mortgage form, use the word "BUYER" instead of "borrower" or "mortgagor.")

4. To expedite inserting a legal description into your final document, DEED assumes you have typed it and stored it as a separate document. DEED also assumes that the {NEST MACRO} and {DOCUMENT} codes have been inserted into your deed form.

5. The template must end with the word *END* on the last line, by itself. Failure to include this word causes the macro to become an unending loop, from which you can exit only by pressing Cancel (F1). Again, *it is extremely important to have only the three letters END on the last line*; if you include so much as a space before or after the word END, the macro does not recognize it as the signal to stop and becomes a loop.

A sample of a deed template appears in figure 16.13. It shows how figure 16.8, the original variable list, has been modified as a template for the deed form shown in figure 16.9.

```
{FIELD NAMES}
day~
mo-yr~
seller~
sellnum~
buyer~
buynum~
lender~
price~
loan~
sellgen~
where~
1sellname~
2sellname~
1buyname~
2buyname~
~{END RECORD}
==================================================
1. Day of deed (Date only)
2. Month, year of deed
SELLER
4. "y" or "ies" (seller: party or parties)
BUYER
6. "y" or "ies" (buyer/borrower: party or parties)
7. Name of lender
8. Amount of consideration for deed
9. Amount of mortgage
10. Gender of seller(s) (him/her/them)
11. Municipality where property is located
12. Name of first seller
13. Name of second seller (<Enter> if none)
14. Name of first buyer/borrower
15. Name of second buyer/borrower (<Enter> if none)
END
```

Fig. 16.13.

A deed template sample.

Create a template for each form you use, or group of related forms, and store them in your template directory.

Creating Deed and Mortgage Forms

In the previous section, you saw the creation of form documents with {FIELD} codes for blanks to be filled in. Those forms work with DEED as long as you use the same variable list to create your variable template.

Creating the Final Document

You are now ready to create the final document. DEED speeds this process tremendously. Perform the following steps:

1. Start with Doc 1 and Doc 2 empty. If you invoke DEED with text in either document, the macro detects that and quits, allowing you to save your work before continuing.

2. Invoke the DEED macro by pressing Macro (Alt-F10), typing *DEED*, and pressing Enter.

    Choose **Macro** from the **Tools** menu, select **Execute**, type *DEED*, and press Enter.

   Tip: If you have an active real estate practice and will be using this macro frequently, you may want to assign this macro to a key in your LEGAL keyboard, or to an Alt-letter hot-key macro, to make it easier to invoke.

3. The DEED menu appears, as shown in figure 16.14. If you have not already created a secondary merge file (the list of information to insert in your deed form), choose **Create list of information to insert in form (1)**.

Fig. 16.14.

The DEED menu.

```
                    DEEDS ASSEMBLY MAIN MENU

          Options:

          1.  Create list of information to insert in form
          2.  Merge information with form

          Enter choice:
```

4. The macro then asks you for the type of document you want to prepare. Type the name of the variable template you want to use. The macro supplies the path.

5. DEED then retrieves your template in Doc 2 and begins working through it, prompting you to enter the information set forth on the template.

6. When the DEED macro encounters the "name of sellers" field, it pauses and shows you the secondary merge file as it exists so far. A prompt in the status line asks that you enter the name of the seller for the closing. You can enter as much text as you want, formatted in any way you want. Press End Field (F9) when done.

7. The macro pauses in a similar fashion at the "name of buyers" field.

8. Once the macro gets to the end of the template (designated by the END line), it exits from the template and asks you for a name for the secondary merge file it has just created for you. For ease of reference, you can give it the same name as the legal description because the list is stored in a different directory.

   Note: If you create two or more documents for the same closing, but the documents use different variable templates, consider giving each secondary merge file an extension. The extension is the three digits after the period that designate the template from which the list was created.

9. After you name the file, DEED stores it in the directory that you designate for variable lists by modifying INSTALL.

10. DEED then asks you what form (primary merge file) you want to use, and merges that file with your new secondary merge file to create a finished document.

11. At the legal description field, the macro asks for a file name, retrieves the previously stored legal description, and places the description in the secondary merge file. DEED uses the {NEST MACRO} and {DOCUMENT} codes you placed in the form document.

If the variable template you used to create the secondary merge file works with more than one primary form, you can easily create these documents next. Simply invoke DEED, choose option **2** from the menu, and then enter the name of the form and the secondary file to be merged. The finished document is created immediately. You can edit or print the document and then store it in any directory you want.

Hint: To avoid confusion with your forms files or your legal description files, store the finished deed in a directory reserved for finished documents of that type, or with other files for that client, or however you arrange your document files. Avoid storing the finished documents in your form, templates, deeds, or variable directories.

Preparing Forms with a Menu-Driven System

If you have a large group of documents for which a single variable list can be used, you can further automate the document preparation by using a system of forms driven by the MENU macro provided on the Applications Disk accompanying this book.

The example used is a typical collections practice. Lawyers who do collections work typically have a highly developed system of form letters, notices, complaints, pleadings, and other documents that must be generated from time to time as the case progresses through the office. The MENU system allows you to create a standard list of variables for all of the standard documents that may be prepared during the handling of a claim. The system then allows you to prepare any document simply by selecting the appropriate document from a menu and entering the file number for the claim. The variable list and the menu of forms are all custom-designed by you.

Although the example provided is for a collections practice, the methods and the MENU macro work with any group of documents that you may want to create.

The essential files for this system are these:

- *The menu*, listing all form documents that use the variable template. The suggested directory for these files is C:\WP51\MENUS; you can designate your own directory by modifying INSTALL. The menu documents lists all of the various forms you create that use the variable lists, and tells the MENU macro where to find them.

- *The template of variables* (or fields) to be included in all case files. The recommended directory for these files is C:\WP51\VARTEMP. These templates can create lists of information for each case to be merged into your form documents.

- *The form documents* you want to use for your system; the suggested directory for these documents is C:\WP51\FORMS.

- *The secondary merge files*, or "case files," containing the specific information to be stored in various fields for a particular case. These files will be repeatedly merged with the various forms to produce the documents you need during the handling of the particular case. The recommended directory for these files is C:\WP51\VARLISTS.

The final documents generated by the MENU macro can be printed without being saved, or can be saved to any directory you want to create.

Creating the Variable Template

You create the variable template for this system exactly the same way as the MERGE macro. Because this macro must work with a large group of related documents, consider the needs of all of the related documents, and make a variable list that covers all possibilities. Excerpts from a sample variable template for the collections practice are shown in figure 16.15.

```
{FIELD NAMES}
filenum~
debtorname~
debtoradd1~
debtoradd2~
debtorcity~
creditorname~

. . .

atty~
~{END RECORD}
==================================================
1. Our file number
2. Name of debtor(s)
3. Debtor address (line 1) (if necessary)
4. Street address for debtor(s)
5. City, state and zip code for debtor(s)
6. Name of creditor(s)

. . .

24. Attorney handling file
END
```

Fig. 16.15.

A sample variable template.

The variable template is not technically required because you could create the variable lists for all of your cases manually. However, it is highly recommended that a template be created in the format discussed earlier, because the MENU macro can refer to that template and help accurately create the variable lists for each of your cases.

 The complete variable template excerpted in figure 16.15 is included on the disk as a file named COLLECT.TMP.

Creating Your Form Documents

You create the form documents in the same way as those you created for the MERGE macro. Again, insert the proper {FIELD} code in your form documents so that correct information is inserted.

A sample collections letter to be used in the MENU system is shown in figure 16.16. It is also provided on the disk in DEBTOR1.

Fig. 16.16.

*A sample
collections letter.*

{DATE}

{FIELD}debtorname~
{FIELD}debtoradd1~
{FIELD}debtoradd2?~
{FIELD}debtorcity~

Re: {FIELD}creditorname~
       {FIELD}amount~

Dear Sirs:

Please be advised that this office has been retained by {FIELD}amount~ to represent it in legal proceedings to collect the debt shown above that you owe.

You can avoid the additional expenses associated with these legal proceedings only by making immediate arrangements through this office to pay the debt in full. Please contact us immediately to make such arrangements. If we do not hear from you within seven days of the date of this letter, we will be forced to bring suit on behalf of our client without further notice to you.

Very Truly Yours,

{FIELD}atty~

Note the question mark that follows {FIELD}debtoradd2~ in figure 16.16. That field reserves an extra line for an address that might be blank in some records if the address to be inserted does not require the second line. If the variable list for the case you are working on does not use that field, the question mark in that field on the form document causes that field to be skipped during a merge. This prevents an unwanted blank line from showing up in the middle of the address on the letter. If something does exist in that field in another variable list, it prints correctly for that case.

You can store the form documents in any directory you choose so long as you give the proper path to them when you make your menu listing. Creating this list is discussed next.

Creating Your Menu Listing

The key to the operation of the MENU macro is creating the menu itself. The menu is a WordPerfect document and can be any length at all, but you must observe a few essential rules in creating the menu.

When first invoked, MENU asks you which menu document you want to work from, and then displays it on screen. MENU then prompts you for the number of the document you want to prepare (if your menu is larger than a single screen, press M to see more selections). The macro then searches for the first occurrence of the number you have selected. (The number must follow a greater than [>] character.) The macro then moves to the end of the line where that number is found, copies the word at the end of the line (which is the path and file name for the form document you want to prepare), then merges that document with the variable list for the case you are working on to produce your final document.

To work properly, your menu must therefore observe these rules:

1. All form documents included on the menu must be numbered, and each number must follow a greater than (>) sign. (The > sign guards against a search finding the wrong string because you use numbers in your document descriptions or file names.)

   Note: Do not use **[Par Num]** codes for these numbers because MENU needs to search for the Arabic number, not a **[Par Num]** code.

2. Each document must appear on a single line, and only one document can appear on any single line.

3. The proper path and file name for the form document must appear at the end of each line. This information need not be flush right, although you may place it there to dress up the appearance of your menu screen.

4. One of the numbered selections should be an exit from the system. Instead of a file name, that line must end with the word EXIT. It does not matter what number or where in the document this selection occurs. Once MENU produces one document, it returns to the menu screen so you can prepare the next document. You need an "escape route" to end the macro.

   Note: If you fail to include this escape route, use the Cancel (F1) key to stop the macro and leave you with the menu on-screen. You can then exit from the menu document manually.

5. One selection (the first being the most likely) should be an option to create the variable list (case file) for a new case. This can help you prepare your variable lists correctly. That selection must end with the word OPEN.

A sample menu for the sample collections system appears in figure 16.17. This menu is included on the disk under the file name COLLECT.MEN. You can create as many menu documents for as many forms systems as you desire, but you should store any menus that you create in a separate directory reserved for such documents. Remember to note the proper path for that directory in the INSTALL macro.

COLLECTION SYSTEM – MAIN MENU

Fig. 16.17.

A sample menu for a collections system.

>1.	Set up variables for new file	OPEN
>2.	Acknowledgement to forwarder	c:\wp51\forms\forward1
>3.	First demand letter to debtor	c:\wp51\forms\debtor1
>4.	Second demand letter to debtor	c:\wp51\forms\debtor2
>5.	Suit requirements letter to forwarder	c:\wp51\forms\forward2
>6.	Complaint -- goods sold and delivered	c:\wp51\forms\complain.gsd
>7.	Complaint -- landlord and tenant	c:\wp51\forms\complain.lt
>8.	Complaint -- insurance premiums	c:\wp51\forms\complain.ins
>9.	Complaint -- services rendered	c:\wp51\forms\complain.svc
>10.	Affidavit for client	c:\wp51\forms\affidavi.col
>11.	Forwarding letter for complaint	c:\wp51\forms\forward3
>12.	Instructions to sheriff	c:\wp51\forms\instruct
>13.	Notice of Intention to Take Default	c:\wp51\forms\notice.def
>14.	Praecipe for Default Judgment	c:\wp51\forms\default
>15.	Exit system	EXIT

Creating Your Secondary Merge Files with MENU

As in the MERGE macro, you can create secondary merge files manually for all files that use your form set. An easier way to do this is to insert the OPEN option in your menu listing, as discussed earlier. MENU can then retrieve the variable template for the menu you designate, display each template line sequentially to allow you to insert the correct information for each case, and ask you for a file number. MENU then assigns that file number to the variable list and saves the list in the directory you have designated for such documents by modifying INSTALL. The macro refers to this file repeatedly as it generates the various documents listed in your menu.

If a variable list already exists under that file number, the macro warns you of the problem and asks for a new file name. You may want to assign a three-digit extension (after the period in the file name) to designate the menu from which the variable list was prepared.

After MENU finishes writing and storing the variable list, it returns to the main document selection menu and awaits further instructions.

Creating Documents from the MENU

After your menu, variable template, and forms are created and stored in their proper directories, MENU makes creating your final documents a simple task. Starting with a blank screen, do the following:

1. Invoke MENU by pressing Macro (Alt-F10), typing *MENU*, and pressing Enter.

   ▭ Choose **Macro** from the Tools pull-down menu, select Execute, type *MENU*, and press Enter.

2. MENU then asks you which menu you want to use. Type the name of the menu you want and press Enter.

3. MENU then retrieves and displays the documents menu you specified and asks you to enter your selection. If the menu is more than one screen long, press M to display the next screenful of selections.

4. If you have not already created a variable list for the file you are working on, type the number for the OPEN option (typically selection number **1**) and respond to the prompts.

5. If a variable list already exists for the file you are working on, type the number of the document you want to prepare (do not type the greater than [>] character).

6. The macro asks for the file number and then merges the selected document with the proper variable list, producing a finished document in Doc 2.

7. The macro then displays the finished document and pauses, allowing you to edit. When you are through editing, or if there are no changes, press Exit (F7). The macro then gives you three choices:

   a. *Print document without saving.* You may want to simply send your finished documents (especially short form letters) directly to the printer without wasting disk space saving documents that can easily be re-created. If you select this option, the document is sent to the printer and erased from Doc 2 without being saved to disk. The macro then returns to the main document selection menu to allow you to prepare your next document.

   b. *Save document and print document.* This option first saves the document to a directory and file name that you specify (any legal directory works). If you inadvertently give it the name of a file that already exists, it simply asks for a different name. The document is then sent to the printer, and the macro returns to the document selection menu.

   c. *Save document without printing.* This works like the second option but does not send the document to your printer.

Creating Multiple MENU Systems

Because MENU works with any template and menu form you create, you may decide to create several independent systems for the various types of cases you handle. For example, you may have one macro to run your collections forms; a second macro to generate the various letters, certificates, and applications needed for administering an estate; and still another to help prepare corporate bylaws, minutes, and other documents for your business clients. The possibilities are limited only by your own creativity.

Summary

In this chapter, you learned how to create and use form documents, and how WordPerfect can be used as a fairly sophisticated document-assembly tool. These techniques will be expanded in Chapter 18, where the word processing needs of a litigation practice are addressed.

Chapter 17 shows how you can use WordPerfect in a law practice to automate the creation of such court documents as pleadings, interrogatories, captions, certificates of service, tables of contents, and tables of authorities.

The two methods of document creation discussed and illustrated in Chapter 17 are a macro-driven system and a form-driven system.

Although it may take some time to set up a system like that outlined in Chapters 16 and 17, after it has been created, the system can remove much of the drudgery of legal document creation that most offices experience. And this frees up office staff for other, more productive, activities.

17

Creating Court Documents

In the last chapter, you learned several techniques for creating legal documents. This chapter discusses some specific documents used in a litigation-oriented practice, or documents for court. You will learn how to automate the creation of the following documents for court:

- Legal pleadings
- Captions
- Interrogatories
- Certificates of service
- Tables of contents
- Tables of authorities

These documents illustrate various techniques; the same techniques can be used to prepare virtually any kind of court document.

This chapter demonstrates two basic techniques for document preparation, both used in Applications Disk macros. The macro SHORTCAP is *macro-driven*, meaning that macros do most of the work, including writing text for the document. The macro LONGCAP is *form-driven*: you create form documents in WordPerfect and merge them with lists of variable information.

More difficult to develop, a macro-driven system relies heavily on programming in macro code. Moreover, its output is rigid; the macro writes a caption only one specific way. The primary advantage of the macro-driven system is ease of use. After a complex macro is written to a macro-driven system and debugged, even a beginning user can prepare the most complex documents in a very short time.

Easier to set up initially, the form-driven system relies on standard WordPerfect documents and merge codes entered directly from the program. A form-driven system produces far more flexible output because you can set up many different forms to create specific types of captions. The main disadvantage is that a form-driven system requires that you know how WordPerfect operates its merge function and is therefore somewhat more difficult to use.

The two techniques are not, however, necessarily independent of each other. You can write macros to help the user create variable lists and activate the merge function. Both SHORTCAP and LONGCAP use merge documents at various points in their operation.

Creating Legal Pleadings

Virtually all court documents begin with a caption that identifies the court where the suit is pending, the names of the plaintiffs and defendants, and docket information. Because the basic case caption doesn't change from pleading (a paper filed in a lawsuit) to pleading, most legal secretaries devise a manual system to retrieve captions from prior pleadings to save retyping. WordPerfect can automate both the initial creation of the caption and the retrieval of an existing caption. This chapter shows two alternative ways to create captions and a system of macros and forms to automate the creation of the body of the pleading as well.

This chapter describes two basic macro systems that automate caption creation. The first system is SHORTCAP, which asks a series of questions about the parties and inserts the responses in a caption. You can modify the macro to use for the courts in which you typically practice. To customize, you must modify the macro INSTALL. For detailed instructions on how to do this, see the file README.15 after you install the Applications Disk.

The second macro, LONGCAP, uses a set of merge-document forms that you create in WordPerfect. Although a macro helps LONGCAP operate, the heart of this system is the forms you create. This system is particularly useful if the courts you practice are very specific about the appearance of pleadings or if you practice in various courts with differing caption formats.

Both SHORTCAP and LONGCAP work with another macro, PLEAMENU, that helps create a pleading's title and introductory paragraph or paragraphs. Other macros, described later in the chapter, can help you prepare the body of your litigation documents.

These macros create pleadings in the following way:

- They create a new caption or retrieve an existing caption (a function performed by SHORTCAP and LONGCAP macros).

- They write and/or retrieve the title and introductory paragraph or paragraphs into a pleading (a function performed by the PLEAMENU macro and form documents you create).

- They create the body of the pleading (assisted by macros you may write, with samples discussed in this chapter).

- They create signature lines (through macros you create for each attorney in your office).

The system begins with either SHORTCAP or LONGCAP. SHORTCAP creates pleadings with the *short form* caption shown in figure 17.1. This form, which usually occupies half a page or less, is popular with many courts. LONGCAP creates a *cover sheet*, or full-page caption, with more detailed information, used in some jurisdictions. A sample cover-sheet caption appears in figure 17.2. You can use LONGCAP with any form you design, as described later.

IN THE COURT OF COMMON PLEAS
OF ALLEGHENY COUNTY, PENNSYLVANIA

JOSEPH T. CARVER, an individual; and MARY
C. CARVER, his wife,

    Plaintiffs

    vs   No. 2861 of 1989

NATIONAL MUTUAL INDEMNITY COMPA-
NY, a Delaware corporation;

    Defendant

Fig. 17.1.

A "short-form" caption.

Fig. 17.2.

A "cover-sheet" caption.

```
                    IN THE COURT OF COMMON PLEAS
                   OF ALLEGHENY COUNTY, PENNSYLVANIA


JOSEPH T. CARVER, an individual;  and  :    CIVIL DIVISION
MARY C. CARVER, his wife,                :
                                         :
              Plaintiffs                 :    No.  2861 of 1989
                                         :
               vs                        :
                                         :    FILED ON BEHALF OF:
NATIONAL   MUTUAL   INDEMNITY  :
COMPANY, a Delaware corporation;         :    Defendant,  National  Mutual  Indemnity
                                         :    Company
              Defendant                  :
                                         :
                                         :
                                         :
                                         :    TYPE OF PLEADING:
                                         :
                                         :
                                         :    ANSWER  OF  NATIONAL  MUTUAL
                                         :    INDEMNITY   COMPANY   TO
                                         :    COMPLAINT  OF  JOSEPH  T.  AND
                                         :    MARY C. CARVER
                                         :
                                         :
                                         :    COUNSEL  OF  RECORD  FOR  THIS
                                         :    PARTY:
                                         :
                                         :    David C. Dean, Esq.
                                         :    I.D. No. 96271
                                         :    DEAN, LORN AND OVERSTREET, P.C.
                                         :    356 Main Street
                                         :    Erie, Pennsylvania 16501
                                         :    (814) 555-0000
                                         :
                                         :
```

Creating a Caption with SHORTCAP

SHORTCAP is assigned the hot key Ctrl-X on the LEGAL keyboard definition on the Applications Disk. The macro lets you write a new caption or retrieve an existing caption from a special file called CAPTIONS in your forms directory. SHORTCAP then starts a macro that allows you to write a new title for the type of pleading you request.

Note: For the macro to retrieve an existing caption or save the new caption, Doc 2 *must* be empty. SHORTCAP is designed to prevent accidental retrieval of form documents into documents already on-screen in Doc 2. Thus if you start SHORTCAP while Doc 2 contains something, the macro notifies you that Doc 2 is not empty and quits, leaving you in Doc 2 so that you can safely exit that document.

Customizing SHORTCAP to Your Tastes and Needs

Unlike LONGCAP, SHORTCAP sets up tabs, margins, widow/orphan protection, and similar codes at the beginning of all documents. It does so by including a **[Style On]** code at the beginning of all pleadings. Thus, for SHORTCAP to work correctly, you must create a style called "Pleading" and store it in your styles library.

The topic of styles and a styles library is discussed in relation to formatting footnotes in Chapter 15. However, the pleading style differs slightly from the footnote style described in that chapter because pleading is an *open* (rather than *paired*) style.

To create a pleading style, follow these steps:

1. First determine the name of your styles library, if one exists, by pressing Setup (Shift-F1) and then Location of Files (**6**).

    ⌨Choose Set**up** from the Files menu; select **L**ocation of Files.

2. Check the listing, if any, after Style Library Filename (**5**). If a styles library exists, note its name.

3. If no styles library exists, create one by pressing Style (**5**). At the Files: prompt, provide the path to the directory where you want to store your styles library. Then, at the Library Filename prompt, type the name you want to assign to your styles library.

4. Press Exit (F7) to return to a blank document (exit from any document that may be on-screen).

5. Create an open style called "Pleading" for the formatting codes you want to enter in your pleadings. Do this by pressing Style (Alt-F8) and then choosing Create (**3**).

    ⌨Choose **S**tyles from the **L**ayout menu; then choose **C**reate (**3**).

    The Styles: Edit screen appears.

6. Press **N**ame (**1**) and type *Pleading*.

7. Press **T**ype (**2**), followed by **O**pen (**2**), to indicate that this is an *open* type of style (that is, once turned on it remains on for the entire document).

8. Press **D**escription (**3**) and enter a description for your pleading style.

9. Press Codes (4).

    A screen similar to the Reveal Codes screen appears. Enter the
    formatting codes for your pleadings. The formatting codes you type are
    largely your personal preference. (Note, however, that when
    SHORTCAP writes a caption, it inserts tabs at various places. You must
    experiment with the tab settings of your pleading style to make the
    caption look the way you want.) All the standard WordPerfect
    formatting codes are available to you. You may want to set a 1 1/2-inch
    top margin, set Widow/Orphan Protect on, modify the hyphenation
    zone, or include any other code that you would normally include in
    your document.

10. After entering your formatting codes, press Exit (F7) twice to return to
    the Styles screen.

11. You must now save your pleading style to your styles library. Press **Save**
    (**6**); the status line prompts `Filename:`. Type the name of the styles
    library you chose in step 2. Press Y in response to any `Replace?` prompt
    that appears.

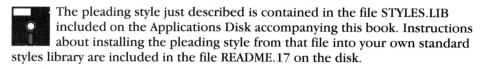
The pleading style just described is contained in the file STYLES.LIB
included on the Applications Disk accompanying this book. Instructions
about installing the pleading style from that file into your own standard
styles library are included in the file README.17 on the disk.

Note that after SHORTCAP inserts a pleading style in a document, that style is saved
with the document. You can modify the pleading styles in each document without
affecting the standard style saved in your styles library. And the standard style itself
can be modified without affecting existing documents using that style. (For help
with these, refer to the discussion of the footnote style in Chapter 15.)

SHORTCAP also expects the CAPTIONS form file to be stored in your forms
directory. You can specify the path to that directory on your system by modifying
the macro INSTALL, as described in the file README.15.

You must also modify the names of the courts where you regularly practice,
because SHORTCAP supplies these from a pop-up menu. You can accomplish this,
too, by editing the INSTALL macro.

Using SHORTCAP

To create a new short form caption by using SHORTCAP, follow these steps:

1. If you have not used SHORTCAP or LONGCAP before and have not
    created a CAPTIONS form file, create a "skeleton" CAPTIONS file first.
    From a blank screen, simply type a **[HPg]** code (Ctrl-Enter) and save it
    to a file called CAPTIONS in your forms directory (for example,
    C:\WP51\FORMS\CAPTIONS).

2. With the LEGAL keyboard selected, press Ctrl-X. If you choose not to use the keyboard, invoking the macro SHORTCAP starts the system. To start the macro, press Alt-F10, type *SHORTCAP*, and then press Enter.

   ⌨Choose **Ma**cro from the **To**ols menu, select **Ex**ecute, type *SHORTCAP*, and press Enter.

   Note: SHORTCAP could be renamed to an Alt key if you choose.

3. The first screen is a menu, shown in figure 17.3. It allows you to choose between creating a new caption from scratch or retrieving an existing caption from your CAPTIONS file. Select **Cr**eate new caption (**1**).

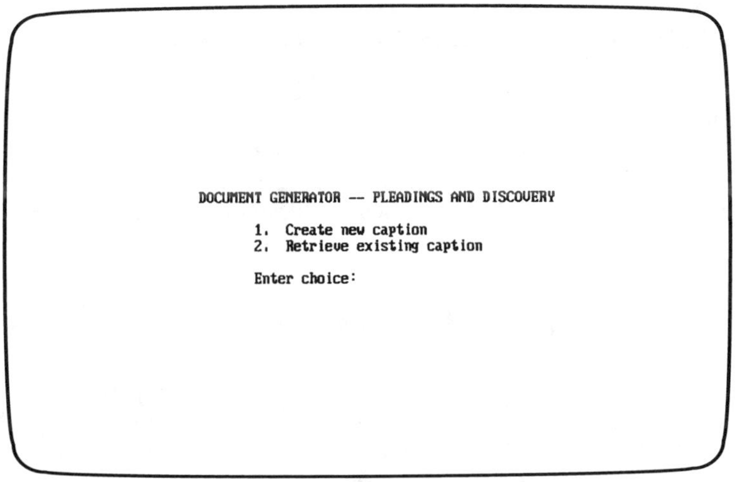

Fig. 17.3.

The first menu in the SHORTCAP macro.

```
DOCUMENT GENERATOR -- PLEADINGS AND DISCOVERY

     1.  Create new caption
     2.  Retrieve existing caption

     Enter choice:
```

4. SHORTCAP then walks you through the creation of a caption for a new case. The macro starts by asking that you choose the court for which you are preparing the pleading. You can choose two trial courts (federal and state) and four appellate court selections. Select the number or letter corresponding to the court for which the pleading is being prepared.

5. SHORTCAP then asks a series of questions about the identity and status of the parties, with loops built in for any number of parties. For example, if you have multiple plaintiffs, you can press Y in response to the question Are there any other Plaintiffs? until you have exhausted your list; the number of parties you can list is limitless.

6. If you are creating a caption for an appellate court pleading, SHORTCAP asks which parties are the appellants and which are the appellees so

that it can accurately reflect that information in the caption. The macro also detects whether more than one party of a given type is present (for instance, whether there is more than one plaintiff), and automatically supplies any plural *s*.

7. After you have entered all plaintiffs, defendants, and any third-party defendants, the macro pauses and shows the caption it has written. You can then use the cursor keys to correct or change whatever you like.

8. After reviewing the caption, press Exit (F7). The macro resumes by asking whether you want to save this caption to your standard CAPTIONS form file. If you press Y, the macro retrieves that file in Doc 2, writes the new caption to the end of that file, and resaves the file automatically. (Note that before you can use this option, you must have created the CAPTIONS file, if only the skeleton **[HPg]** code, discussed in step 1.)

9. After storing the new caption (or not), SHORTCAP starts the macro PLEAMENU that calls up a menu that helps create the title and introductory paragraphs of different pleadings you use in your practice. A complete discussion of how PLEAMENU works appears later in this chapter.

Using Existing Captions with SHORTCAP

If your pleading is for a case where a standard caption already exists in your CAPTIONS file, select **Retrieve existing caption (2)** from the menu. The macro retrieves the standard CAPTIONS form file into Doc 2, asks you for a name to look for in that file, searches for the name you type, and retrieves the appropriate caption.

When responding to the prompt Enter case/name to search, choose a unique name, docket number, or other string of text out of the caption. SHORTCAP searches the CAPTIONS form file for the first occurrence of that name, number, or string; shows it to you; and pauses. The status line prompts the following:

```
Move to caption; <Enter> to accept or search
```

You then have several options. If the caption that appears on the screen is the correct one, simply press Enter and then press Y at the next prompt. If the caption is not correct, move the cursor with the cursor keys, PgUp, or PgDn. When you locate the correct caption, press Enter and then press Y.

If the name appears in several captions in the CAPTIONS form file, keep searching for the correct caption simply by pressing Enter. The status line then prompts the following:

```
Is this the correct caption? (Y to accept, N to search for next
occurrence)
```

If you press N, the macro proceeds to the next occurrence of the name you entered and stops again. If the macro does not find the name you typed, you have the following three options:

1. Enter a new name and search again.

2. Create a new caption.

3. Quit.

Note that the CAPTIONS form file on each machine in your office is different (unless you run on a network and share the CAPTIONS form file). Note also that the CAPTIONS form file gets larger and larger over time. The captions appear in chronological order, not alphabetical, so use Search (F2) for the easiest way to find the caption you want. As the file grows, SHORTCAP must work harder to search the file, slowing down the process. Periodically, then, you should call up the file and remove inactive captions (cases settled or disposed of). You can recall the CAPTIONS file like any other WordPerfect document and edit it (for example, if a caption changes because of the addition of parties).

The CAPTIONS file can contain not only captions written by SHORTCAP and LONGCAP but also captions created manually from your existing cases. (See the discussion of the CAPTIONS file later in this chapter.)

After retrieving the caption, SHORTCAP starts the macro PLEAMENU and awaits your instructions.

Creating a Caption with LONGCAP

LONGCAP works a little differently from SHORTCAP. Whereas SHORTCAP uses a highly complex and lengthy macro to write the caption, LONGCAP takes a standard WordPerfect document and merges it with information entered from the keyboard. LONGCAP's basic technique is the *keyboard merge*, using the {PROMPT}message~{KEYBOARD} codes. (Instructions on creating documents with these codes appear in steps 1 through 10, which follow.)

Before you can use LONGCAP, you must create a merge form for your captions. You create the merge form in WordPerfect and store it like any other document file. In actual practice, you can create a library of such forms for different courts, different types of pleadings, different attorneys, or any variation you choose.

Figure 17.4 shows a sample merge form for a "cover sheet" caption. The Applications Disk contains a modified version of this form as LONGFORM.CAP. You can create any number of similar files to work with LONGCAP (as practice, start by working with a caption from an existing case).

Fig. 17.4.

A sample merge form for a cover-sheet caption.

IN THE COURT OF COMMON PLEAS
OF {PROMPT}Name of County~{KEYBOARD} COUNTY, PENNSYLVANIA

{PROMPT}Names and capacities of all Plaintiffs~{KEYBOARD}	:	{PROMPT}Which division?~{KEYBOARD} DIVISION
	:	
Plaintiff{PROMPT}*Add*	:	
"s" if more than one Plaintiff~{KEYBOARD}	:	No. {PROMPT}Enter Docket Number~{KEYBOARD}
	:	
vs	:	
	:	
{PROMPT}Names and capacities of all Defendants~{KEYBOARD}	:	FILED ON BEHALF OF:
	:	{PROMPT}Name of our client~{KEYBOARD}
D e f e n -	:	
dant{PROMPT}*Add "s" if more than one Defendant*~{KEYBOARD}	:	
	:	
{PROMPT}Type "vs" if any additional defendants (F9 if none)~{KEYBOARD}	:	TYPE OF PLEADING:
	:	
{PROMPT}Names and capacities of all Additional Defendants (F9 if none)~{KEYBOARD}	:	{PROMPT}Title of Pleading~{KEYBOARD}
	:	
{PROMPT}Type	:	COUNSEL OF RECORD FOR THIS PARTY:
"Additional Defendant(s)" if any (F9 if none~{KEYBOARD}	:	
	:	{PROMPT}Name of Attorney~{KEYBOARD}
	:	I.D. No. {PROMPT}I.D. Number~{KEYBOARD}
	:	DEAN, LORN AND OVERSTREET, P.C.
	:	356 Main Street
	:	Erie, Pennsylvania 16501
	:	(814) 555-0000

To work with LONGCAP, follow these steps:

1. Retrieve a copy of an existing pleading and discard everything but the caption. Include the pleading's tab settings, footers, hyphenation codes, or any other code you would routinely use, because LONGCAP does not supply such codes.

2. At every place in the caption where information can change, replace the case-specific information with merge codes. For example, if you used figure 17.2 as your starting form and you wanted to prepare a form for

any Pennsylvania county, you would first delete the county name *ALLEGHENY* in the second line.

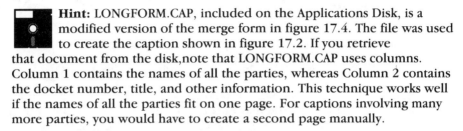 **Hint:** LONGFORM.CAP, included on the Applications Disk, is a modified version of the merge form in figure 17.4. The file was used to create the caption shown in figure 17.2. If you retrieve that document from the disk, note that LONGFORM.CAP uses columns. Column 1 contains the names of all the parties, whereas Column 2 contains the docket number, title, and other information. This technique works well if the names of all the parties fit on one page. For captions involving many more parties, you would have to create a second page manually.

3. Insert a {PROMPT} merge code to tell the user what information needs to be inserted at that location. Do this by pressing Merge Codes (Shift-F9).

   Choose Me**r**ge Codes from the **T**ools menu.

4. From the status line or pull-down menu that appears, type **More (6)** or press Merge Codes (Shift-F9) a second time. The Merge Commands window appears in the upper right corner of your screen.

5. Move the cursor to the {PROMPT} code by pressing the down-arrow key. Or use the Name Search feature by typing the first few letters of the word *PROMPT*; the cursor moves to that command. Press Enter when the cursor is positioned on the {PROMPT} command.

6. Type the message that you want to display on the status line to prompt the user to enter the variable information. In this example, type *Name of County*; then press Enter. WordPerfect inserts the {PROMPT} code and your message, followed by a tilde (~) to mark the end of the message. You can edit the message from the main editing screen, but be careful not to delete the tilde.

7. Next, place a {KEYBOARD} code after the tilde to temporarily stop the merge so that you can enter the information called for in the message. Do this by pressing Merge Codes (Shift-F9).

   Choose Me**r**ge Codes from the **T**ools menu.

8. From the status line or pull-down menu that appears, type **More (6)** or press Merge Codes (Shift-F9) a second time. The Merge Commands window appears in the upper right corner of your screen.

9. Move the cursor to the {KEYBOARD} code by using the down-arrow key. Or use the Name Search feature by pressing K to move the cursor to that command. Press Enter.

10. Continue through your form, repeating steps 3 through 9 to enter messages everywhere you want to prompt the user to insert information in the caption.

After the {KEYBOARD} merge codes are entered in this example, the line for the name of the plaintiff in your on-screen pleading might look like this:

{PROMPT}Name of Plaintiff(s); Press F9 when done~{KEYBOARD}

An aesthetic problem can arise if the input called for by the {PROMPT} code extends more than one line. You may encounter a longer line when you the form to create an actual caption. As soon as the entry "wraps" to the next line and the screen is rewritten, the message in your {PROMPT} command disappears and is replaced by the message *Merging* in the status line. This message may distract the user, especially when the instruction Press F9 when done disappears prematurely.

WordPerfect 5.1 contains a new Merge command that can solve this problem. The {STATUS PROMPT} command lets you place whatever message you want on the status line. The message remains until another {STATUS PROMPT} command replaces it or turns it off. The following command string makes the message Name of Plaintiff(s); Press F9 when done stay on the screen until the user has entered the names of all plaintiffs and pressed F9:

{STATUS PROMPT}Name of Plaintiff(s); Press F9 when done~{KEYBOARD}{STATUS PROMPT}~

You enter the {STATUS PROMPT} command exactly as the {PROMPT} message was entered, except that you move the cursor to the {STATUS PROMPT} command in the Merge Commands window.

In the example, the first {STATUS PROMPT} displays, as a message in the status line, everything before the next tilde. {KEYBOARD} pauses the merge so that the user can type information in response to the prompt. The merge remains paused, and the message remains on-screen until the user presses End Field (F9). After the user presses End Field (F9), the {STATUS PROMPT}~ command is executed, canceling the prior {STATUS PROMPT} message.

Note that if your message extends more than halfway across the screen, it is overwritten by the standard Doc x Pg x Ln x Pos x information line provided by WordPerfect. If you want to use prompts longer than 30 or 40 characters, you can force them to wrap a line (creating the effect of a two-line prompt) by inserting a hard return in the middle of the prompt, at the location where you want the message to break and wrap. The sample merge form LONGFORM.CAP provided on the disk uses this technique in several places.

After you have created your merge form, save it in your forms directory under some descriptive file name. For example, you may have a form for federal court filings saved under the name C:\WP51\FORMS\USDIST, an Allegheny County form filed under C:\WP51\FORMS\ALLEG, a form for Erie County under C:\WP51\FORMS\ERIE, and a generic form (where the name of the county is left blank with a merge code) under C:\WP51\FORMS\COUNTY.

To see how these merge forms work, try creating a caption by doing a merge manually. (LONGCAP automates this function later). To do this, take the following steps:

1. Press Merge (Ctrl-F9) and select **Merge** (**1**).

   ⌨Choose **Merge** from the **Tools** menu.

2. The status line prompts you for the name of the primary merge file, the merge form you just created. Type the name (with path if necessary) of your form. If you enter an incorrect name, or if WordPerfect can't find the file in the path indicated, the merge tells you and stops.

3. The status line then prompts you for the name of the Secondary merge file. Because these forms will merge information typed from the keyboard rather than from a pre-existing secondary file, simply press Enter.

4. The form you created appears on your screen, with the first message from the first {PROMPT} or {STATUS PROMPT} code displayed in the status line. Simply respond with the information requested; then press End Field (F9).

5. The merge then moves to the next code, displays the next message, and again awaits your input. If no information needs to be inserted at a prompt, press End Field (F9) to move to the next location. Thus, in the example given in figure 17.4, if the case has no additional defendants, just press End Field (F9) for all messages relating to additional defendants.

After the merge has run through the entire form and found no more message codes, the merge stops. Your caption should be complete.

Using LONGCAP

After creating a merge form or two and moving them to the forms directory on your system, you are ready to use LONGCAP to expedite the process. Like SHORTCAP, LONGCAP lets you either create a caption with your merge forms or retrieve the caption with the CAPTIONS form file. Any new captions you create with LONGCAP can, at your option, be stored in your CAPTIONS file from within LONGCAP. (Remember to edit the INSTALL macro so that LONGCAP can find your CAPTIONS file.)

LONGCAP has been assigned to Ctrl-C on the LEGAL keyboard. To create a new caption with LONGCAP, follow these steps:

1. With the LEGAL keyboard active, invoke LONGCAP by pressing Ctrl-C or Macro (Alt-F10), typing *LONGCAP*, and pressing Enter.

   ⌨Choose **M**acro from the **T**ools menu, select **E**xecute, type *LONGCAP*, and press Enter. Again, you may want to reassign this macro to an Alt-key combination you choose.

2. LONGCAP's first screen is a menu identical to the first screen of SHORTCAP (see fig. 17.3). Press **C**reate new caption (**1**).

3. LONGCAP then prompts you for the file name of the form you want to use. Type the file name only (the macro supplies the path automatically).

4. Fill in the blanks on your form, using the End Field (F9) key as you did in the SHORTCAP macro.

5. After the blanks are filled, LONGCAP pauses to allow you to review and edit the caption. You can correct typos or make any changes you want to the caption at this point. Press Exit (F7) when done.

6. LONGCAP then gives you the option of saving the new caption to your CAPTIONS file. Press Y if you want the caption to be saved; otherwise, press N.

7. LONGCAP then starts the PLEAMENU macro that helps you prepare the body of your pleading. PLEAMENU is discussed later in this chapter.

Using an Existing Caption with LONGCAP

LONGCAP retrieves existing captions from your CAPTIONS form file just as SHORTCAP does. See the earlier discussion of how SHORTCAP retrieves captions.

Note that you are not limited to using only SHORTCAP or LONGCAP; you can use either as needed. Captions created with either macro can be stored together in the CAPTIONS form file and later retrieved with either macro.

Creating a CAPTIONS Form File

SHORTCAP and LONGCAP work with captions created manually as well as those the macros generate on their own. You probably already have a captions file, or at least some standard location on your hard disk for pleadings. You can take existing captions and create your own CAPTIONS form file to make immediate use of SHORTCAP or LONGCAP without having to rewrite all your captions.

The key to setting up the CAPTIONS form file is to be sure that each caption is separated from every other one by a hard page (**[HPg]**) code. SHORTCAP and LONGCAP retrieve existing captions from the CAPTIONS form file by searching for such codes. The macros retrieve a caption of any length from the CAPTIONS form file, even those that exceed one page, so long as it is followed by the **[HPg]** code (or is the last caption in the file).

To create a CAPTIONS form file from your existing pleadings, follow these steps:

1. Start with both Doc 1 and Doc 2 empty.

2. In Doc 1, press Ctrl-Enter to insert a **[HPg]** code.

3. Press Switch (Shift-F3) to switch to Doc 2.

    ▭Choose **Switch Document** from the **Edit** menu.

4. Retrieve your first document with a caption you want to save by pressing List (F5) or Retrieve (Shift-F10).

    ▭Choose **Retrieve** from the **File** menu and type the path and file name for the document you want to retrieve.

5. Press Block (Alt-F4) and use the cursor keys to mark the caption only. (Exclude any title or nonstandard information that may be in your source document.) Remember to capture any formatting codes that may be at the top of the document that you want to retain with the caption. Press Home, Home, Home, up arrow to move the cursor in front of any such codes (or look at the codes in Reveal Codes) to be sure.

6. Copy the marked caption to the buffer: press Move (Ctrl-F4) and then press **Block (1)** and **Copy (2)**.

    ▭Choose **Copy** from the **Edit** menu.

7. Press Switch (Shift-F3) to switch back to Doc 1.

    ▭Choose **Switch Document** from the **Edit** menu.

8. Retrieve the block by pressing Enter. The block should appear after the **[HPg]** code you placed there in step 2.

9. Move to the bottom of the caption you have just retrieved by pressing Home, Home, down arrow.

10. Press Ctrl-Enter to add another **[HPg]**.

11. Switch back to Doc 2, exit that document (without saving), and retrieve your next caption.

12. Repeat steps 4 through 11 for all captions you want to place in your CAPTIONS form file. You do not need a **[HPg]** code after the last caption in the file.

For a sample of how the CAPTIONS form file should look, retrieve the sample CAPTIONS form file included on the disk.

Creating Title and Introductory Paragraphs for Pleadings

After writing a new caption or retrieving an existing one, both SHORTCAP and LONGCAP invoke another macro, called PLEAMENU. This macro displays a menu you create that shows the types of pleadings you use frequently in your practice. The macro then merges standard titles, opening paragraphs, or other matters that you specify and places them into your pleading immediately below the caption you have just written or retrieved.

To use PLEAMENU, you must create several forms. You need a group of form documents stored in your forms directory, containing formatting codes, titles, and standard opening language for each specific type of a pleading that you want to prepare. You also need a template, or menu, listing the various forms for opening paragraphs and their location on the disk.

PLEAMENU is a simplified version of the MENU macro discussed in Chapter 16. PLEAMENU's operation is discussed here. (For a more complete discussion of the related MENU macro, see Chapter 16.)

Creating Standard Titles and Opening Paragraphs for Pleadings

First consider the types of pleadings you might need to create routinely in your practice. The following is a sample list:

- Complaint
- Answer
- Motion to dismiss
- Other motion
- Brief
- Interrogatories
- Requests for production of documents
- Affidavit
- Verification
- Certificate of service

Create your own list in WordPerfect and save it, because your list will become the basis for the PLEAMENU template later on. You can make the list as long and specific as you want, or as simple and general as the list shown here. You can easily add to or delete from the list at any time later on.

For each of the types of pleadings you list, you need to create a separate form file of the formatting codes, the title (complete or with blanks to be filled in), the opening paragraph or paragraphs, and any other standard information that goes with a pleading of that type. You are not limited by space; the forms can be as long or as short as you want.

To make the best use of PLEAMENU, however, you should follow these guidelines in creating your forms:

- To decide what to put into your standard opening forms, imagine a typical pleading with the caption removed. Remember that PLEAMENU picks up where SHORTCAP or LONGCAP quits, right after the caption has been placed in your document. Your form should begin with the very next thing that appears after the caption. In most cases, this is the title of the pleading (although the title may be incorporated in your long form caption, as described in the LONGCAP discussion).

  For example, if one of the options on your list of pleadings is a general-purpose opening for a motion, write a standard opening or retrieve it from an existing pleading. A sample opening paragraph for a motion for summary judgment is shown in figure 17.5.

NOW COMES {status of our client(s)}, {name of our client}, by and through {gender of our client(s)} attorneys, DEAN, LORN AND OVERSTREET, P.C., and moves this Honorable Court for {type of motion being filed} against {status of opposing party}, {name of opposing party}, setting forth as follows:

Fig. 17.5.

A sample opening paragraph for a motion.

- Because PLEAMENU uses WordPerfect's Merge capabilities to insert the standard form into your document, you can use the macro code {PROMPT}message~{KEYBOARD} or {STATUS PROMPT} for prompts to help the user insert information in the correct places in a new pleading. (To learn how to insert these codes at the correct location, see the previous discussion of creating long form captions.)

Figure 17.6 shows how the standard paragraph for the motion for summary judgment shown in figure 17.5 can be modified to include merge codes at the proper places.

Fig. 17.6.

*A sample opening
paragraph for a
motion as a merge
file.*

NOW COMES {STATUS PROMPT}Status of our client(s); press F9 when
done~{KEYBOARD}, {STATUS PROMPT}Name of our client; press F9 when
done~{KEYBOARD}, by and through {STATUS PROMPT}Gender of our client(s); press F9
when done~{KEYBOARD} attorneys, DEAN, LORN AND OVERSTREET, P.C., and moves
this Honorable Court for {STATUS PROMPT}Type of motion being filed; press F9 when
done~{KEYBOARD} against {STATUS PROMPT}Status of opposing party; press F9 when
done~{KEYBOARD}, {STATUS PROMPT}Name of opposing party; press F9 when
done~{KEYBOARD}{STATUS PROMPT}~, setting forth as follows:

Notice that figure 17.6 makes use of the {STATUS PROMPT} codes in the
place of the {PROMPT} codes. This keeps the special message on-screen
no matter how much information is inserted at each {KEYBOARD}
pause. Each time the merge encounters a new {STATUS PROMPT}
message, the status line changes to display the new message. After the
last {KEYBOARD} pause, insert a final {STATUS PROMPT}~, with no
message, to return the status line to its original state. If you fail to
include such a code, the last {STATUS PROMPT} message from your
merge form remains on the status line, even after you exit the document.

- Store the forms in the forms directory specified when you modified the
  INSTALL macro. Give each form a good descriptive file name. For
  example, you may want to store the motions form shown in figure 17.6
  in a file called C:\WP51\FORMS\MOTION.INT.

Tip for advanced users: You can also take advantage of WordPerfect 5.1's
capability to nest macros within merge documents to expedite the creation
of a title and introductory paragraph. The Applications Disk contains a
simple primary merge file called P-INTRO and a macro of the same name. The
P-INTRO document shown in figure 17.7 does nothing more than position the
cursor at the correct location below the caption and then start the P-INTRO macro.
The macro uses a paired style called Title (also included in the STYLES.LIB file) to
write the title; the macro then writes the introductory paragraph by asking a series
of questions about the parties and the nature of the pleading being prepared.

The information gathered by P-INTRO is stored in your computer's memory until
you turn off your machine (or until the contents of the variables are replaced by
another macro). The macro WHERE4, described later, can use this information to
automatically prepare a "wherefore" clause with the correct identity of the parties.

You may want to make multiple copies of P-INTRO, stored under different file
names relating to the different types of pleadings you typically prepare, and edit
the questions and the text to suit your needs.

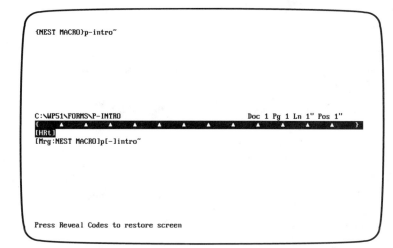

```
{NEST MACRO}p-intro~




C:\WP51\FORMS\P-INTRO                    Doc 1 Pg 1 Ln 1" Pos 1"
{   ▲    ▲    ▲    ▲    ▲    ▲    ▲    ▲    ▲    ▲    ▲   }
[HRt]
[Mrg:NEST MACRO]p[-]intro~




Press Reveal Codes to restore screen
```

Fig. 17.7.

The P-INTRO file.

Creating Your Menu of Pleadings

Like the MENU macro described in Chapter 16, PLEAMENU uses a menu you create in WordPerfect to locate and retrieve the forms you just made. To make your menu, follow these steps:

1. Retrieve the list of forms you just made.

2. Number all form documents on the menu, preceding each number with a greater-than (>) sign. (The > guards against a faulty search, because numbers may appear in your document descriptions or file names.)

   Note: Do not use **[Par Num]** codes for these numbers, because PLEAMENU must search for the Arabic number, not a **[Par Num]** code.

3. Put each document on a single line; only one document can appear on any line. However, the documents need not begin on the first line. You can provide descriptive information (a menu title, for example) at the top of the document if you want.

4. At the end of each line, include the proper path and file name for the form document. This information need not be flush right, although you may want to consider placing it at that location to "dress up" the appearance of your menu screen.

5. Make one numbered selection an exit from the system. Instead of a file name, that line should end with the word EXIT. It does not matter what number is given this selection or where in the document this selection occurs. Having an exit selection is advisable so that you have a quick

way to exit from PLEAMENU and return to the bare caption you have written or retrieved.

Note: If you fail to include this escape route, the (F1) Cancel key stops the macro and leaves you with the menu on-screen. You can then exit from the menu document manually.

6. Save your menu to your menu directory under the file name PLEAMENU.

A menu created from the sample list of pleading types shown earlier appears in figure 17.8.

DEAN, LORN AND OVERSTREET DOCUMENT PREPARATION
Main Menu

Fig. 17.8.

A sample menu of documents.

Type of pleading to prepare:

>1.	Complaint	c:\wp51\forms\complain
>2.	Answer	c:\wp51\forms\answer
>3.	Motion to Dismiss	c:\wp51\motdisms.int
>4.	Other Motion	c:\wp50\forms\motion.int
>5.	Brief	c:\wp50\forms\brief.int
>6.	Interrogatories	c:\wp50\forms\interrog.int
>7.	Requests for Production of Documents	c:\wp50\forms\request.int
>8.	Affidavit	c:\wp50\forms\affidavi
>9.	Verification	c:\wp50\forms\verifi
>10.	Certificate of Service	c:\wp50\forms\certifi
>11.	Exit from system	EXIT

Using PLEAMENU

Recall that PLEAMENU automatically starts when SHORTCAP or LONGCAP finishes writing or retrieving the caption for your case. The PLEAMENU template you just created is retrieved and placed in Doc 2 (assuming that your caption was written or retrieved in Doc 1; it does not matter whether the caption is Doc 1 or Doc 2). To use PLEAMENU, follow these steps:

1. PLEAMENU prompts you to enter the number of the pleading you want to prepare. Type the number and press Enter. Do not type the greater-than (>) character.

2. PLEAMENU then reads the location and file name of your form document (at the end of the numbered line you selected) and recalls it into Doc 1 (where your caption is) with the Merge function.

3. If you have used {PROMPT}message~{KEYBOARD} codes in your form documents, PLEAMENU pauses at each code, displays the document, and prompts you with the message you placed inside the codes. Type the information requested and press End Field (F9) when done.

4. If you used {NEST MACRO} codes in your form documents (see the discussion of P-INTRO), those macros are executed.

5. When you reach the final prompt or message code, PLEAMENU ends, and your document, with the caption, title, and introductory paragraph, appears on your screen.

You can now create the "meat" of the document you are preparing.

Creating Standard Language Macros

After the introductory paragraph is in place, prepare the remainder of your document as you normally would. You may find it useful, especially when drafting complaints, motions, or other initial pleadings, to use automatic paragraph number codes at the beginning of each paragraph. This is especially true if you expect to revise the document before filing it, because WordPerfect can then handle paragraph renumbering for you automatically. For a fuller discussion of automatic paragraph numbering, see Chapter 15.

You can also use any macro of your own choosing to help create the text of the pleading. You can write simple macros to insert standard phrases such as *Admitted*, *Denied upon lack of knowledge*, or *Defendant <insert name of defendant> was negligent in the following respects:*. Some suggested macros and the averments that they produce appear in figure 17.9. You can easily write simple macros similar to these to write the standard types of averments repetitively used in your practice and in your jurisdiction.

Averment Macros

Macro	Averment	
Ad	"Admitted."	*Fig. 17.9.*
Ad-den	"Admitted in part and denied in part; in further answer, "	*Sample averment macros.*
Contrib	"The <prompts for status of negligent party>, <prompts for name of negligent party>, was contributorily negligent in the following respects:"	
Neg	"The <prompts for status of negligent party>, <prompts for name of negligent party>, was negligent in the following respects:"	
Noknow	"After reasonable investigation, this Defendant is without information sufficient to form a belief as to the truth or falsity of the matters alleged in this paragraph; the allegations are therefore denied, strict proof demanded at trial."	
Nolaw	"This averment is denied as containing conclusions of law."	
Notme	"This allegation is addressed to another Defendant, and requires no response from this Defendant. To the extent any answer is required from this Defendant, after reasonable investigation this Defendant is without information sufficient to form a belief as to the truth or falsity of the matters alleged, and the matters are therefore denied, strict proof demanded at trial."	

To write a simple standard language macro, follow these steps:

1. Press Macro Define (Ctrl-F10).

   ⌨Choose **Macro** from the **Tools** menu; select **Define**.

2. The status line prompts `Define macro:`. Enter the name of the macro at the prompt. Try to choose a short, easy-to-remember name; the fewer letters, the better. Press Enter.

3. The prompt `Description:` appears. Enter a brief description (up to 39 characters) of what the macro is to do.

4. WordPerfect now returns you to your document, with the message `Macro Def` blinking in the status line. Type the standard language you want to appear in your pleadings. WordPerfect "records" each keystroke.

5. When you have finished your standard language, press Macro Define (Ctrl-F10) again.

   ⌨Choose **Macro** from the **Tools** menu; select **Define**.

This last step turns off the "tape recorder" and saves your macro to the name you gave it in step 2.

Hint: Remember that the point of macros is to save keystrokes. If, for example, you had a macro named PLF that simply typed the word *plaintiff*, by the time you press Alt-F10, type the macro name, press Enter, and wait for the computer to retrieve and run the macro, you really haven't saved any time at all. Your macro names should therefore be short (two or three characters are ideal) and easy to remember. Consider adding a space after the last word in the macro so that when it finishes running, the macro is in the correct position to start the next word.

To use the macro you just created to insert the language you typed, place the cursor at the exact location in your document where you want the language to appear; then do this:

1. Press Macro (Alt-F10).

   ⌨Choose **Macro** from the **Tools** menu; select **Execute**.

2. At the `Macro:` prompt, type the name of the macro and press Enter. The language you typed is inserted into your document.

To complete your pleading, use the WHERE4 macro provided on disk. WHERE4 produces a typical clause asking for judgment in favor of your client and against your opponent, inserting appropriate information in the correct places. WHERE4 then chains to your signature block macros (which will be discussed in a minute). An option to quit without adding a signature block is also provided (for those wherefore clauses tucked at the end of each separate count where you do not need a signature block).

If you created the title and introductory paragraph with P-INTRO or its derivative, the information necessary to complete the wherefore clause may already reside in your computer's memory. WHERE4 displays the current contents of the system variables. If the variables are correct, you need only press Y or Enter to create the wherefore clause. If the information is not correct, you can enter whatever new or corrected information you need.

A Special Problem: Creating Interrogatories

The preparation of interrogatories, or written questions to be posed to your opponent in a lawsuit, is a good example of a repetitive task that can be made quite simple with both macros and merge documents. This section describes setting up form interrogatories, using templates for inserting variable case-specific information through a merge document, and generating the document to be filed or served.

The macro INTERROG can help you with this job. After you have created the caption, title, and introductory paragraph for your interrogatories by using SHORTCAP, LONGCAP, or PLEAMENU, you can run INTERROG to produce the final document. Once invoked, INTERROG gives you the following three options:

1. Assemble form questions from any standard set of interrogatories to create a custom set of questions for a particular case.

2. Merge a standard set of interrogatories with a variable list to create instantly a standard set of interrogatories for the case you are working on.

3. Exit if you change your mind.

You can produce the final set of interrogatories by using the MERGE macro described in Chapter 15. MERGE's role in interrogatory preparation is discussed later in the chapter.

The secret to efficiency in preparing interrogatories in this fashion is to create a good forms library, stored systematically on your computer for easy access. See Chapter 16 for a suggested directory structure to help you.

Before INTERROG and MERGE can work properly, you must set up a set of form interrogatories using {FIELD} merge codes. (For a discussion of these codes, see Chapter 16.) The Applications Disk contains two skeleton sets, entitled PRODUCTS and INJURY (for products-liability cases and personal-injury cases, respectively). These forms are provided for illustrative purposes only and should be reviewed carefully and supplemented by the attorney directing the preparation of the interrogatories.

For each set of interrogatories to create, you need two form documents. The first document is for the questions themselves, with the appropriate merge codes placed at the proper locations. The second is a *template*, or an index of what each variable for that set is. For easiest reference, both documents should have the same file name but be stored in different directories. For example, your standard set of interrogatories for a products-liability case might bear the file name C:\WP51\FORMS\PRODUCTS, whereas its corresponding template or list of variables would be named C:\WP51\VARTEMP\PRODUCTS. This device makes it easier for the computer operator to remember which variable list goes with which set of questions.

To create a template to help you make variable lists for your specific cases, follow these steps:

1. First, consider the types of information that you want to include in the various questions you will be entering in your form interrogatories.

   Hint: If you plan to frequently assemble interrogatories from two or more sets of standard interrogatories, you may want to consider creating only one list of variables for each set of standard interrogatories. For example, most products-liability cases also involve personal injuries, so you may have a set of interrogatories specifically designed for products liability and a second set for personal injuries. If you use one variable list for both sets, when you assemble your special set you must run the MERGE macro only once. But if the two sets use different variable lists, you must run MERGE immediately after selecting the questions from each standard set you use.

2. Decide whether you want to use named or numbered {FIELD} codes. See the discussion of this topic in Chapter 16. If you decide to use numbered fields, skip to step 8.

3. If you use named fields, your variable list must begin with a {FIELD NAME} statement. From a clean document, press Merge Codes (Shift-F9); then press **More** (6).

   ▭🖱Choose **Merge** Codes from the **Tools** menu; then choose **More.**

4. The Merge Commands window appears. Move the cursor to the {FIELD NAME} by using the arrow keys or by pressing F, down arrow, and then Enter.

5. The prompt `Field Number 1:` appears. Type the name for the first variable on your list and press Enter.

6. The status line asks for the next field number. Keep entering the fields from your list. When you have entered the last field from your list, press Exit (F7).

7. The {FIELD NAME} statement then appears at the top of your screen, all on one line, with tildes (~) separating the fields you entered. The last field is followed by a second tilde, an {END RECORD} code, and a **[HPg]** code. Do not delete the second tilde or either code.

8. On the very first line after the **[HPg]** code (or at the first line of the document if you are using numbered fields), type the prompt for each variable (field). Be sure to put only one field on each line, and do not leave any blank lines between fields.

9. It is a good idea (although not essential) to use the field name or number in each prompt (this helps you set up your form questions). There is no limit to the number of variables you can have on your list.

10. It is also important to place the word *END* in capital letters on a separate line at the very end of the list. When you use the template to create your final interrogatories, you invoke the macro MERGE to create a list of the information to be inserted in the final document. If you do not include END at the end of your template, MERGE becomes stuck in an endless loop.

11. Store the template you have created in the directory you designate for templates. Be sure that the macro INSTALL has been modified correctly to provide the path to that directory.

See figure 17.10 for a sample template file intended to work with both the PRODUCTS and INJURY sets of interrogatories.

Fig. 17.10.

A sample template to work with PRODUCTS and INJURY.

```
{FIELD NAMES}
client~
clientstat~
clientgender~
serve~
servestat~
injured~
injuredgender~
injuredspouse~
spousegender~
product~
date~
location~
~{END RECORD}
==================================================
1. Name of our client:
2. Position in lawsuit of our client (e.g., Plaintiff, Defendant):
3. Gender of our client (his, her, its, their):
4. Name of party being served:
5. Position in lawsuit of party being served:
6. Gender of party being served (his, her, its, their):
7. Name of injured person:
8. Gender of injured person:
9. Name of spouse of injured person:
10. Gender of spouse of injured person:
11. Product causing injury:
12. Date of injury:
13. Location of injury:
END
```

Now prepare your standard interrogatory sets. To do this, follow these steps:

1. Start with a good set of interrogatories you have already used in a case.

2. At each location where you must insert variable information, place a {FIELD} merge code. To use the example in figure 17.11, at every place in your form interrogatories where you want the name of your client to appear, place a {FIELD}client~ code; wherever you want to refer to the name of the injured person, place a {FIELD}injured~ code. To insert these codes, first press Macro Codes (Shift-F9).

    ▢▤Choose **Merge** Codes from the **Tools** menu.

3. Then press F, type the number for the specific field, and press Enter.

4. If you want to use these form sets to assemble interrogatories for specific cases, choosing only some questions from the form, separate each question from the prior question with a hard page (**[HPg]**) code (Ctrl-Enter). This step enables you to use the "point-and-shoot" macro described in the next section to quickly select those specific questions that you would include in your custom-made set. For more discussion of the point-and-shoot method of document assembly, see Chapter 16.

5. You should also begin each question with an automatic paragraph-numbering (**[Par Num:x]**) code, especially if you intend to use your form for assembling. In this way, you can insert additional questions using similar codes, and all paragraphs automatically renumber

themselves. For more information on using automatic paragraph-numbering codes, see Chapter 15.

6. In the directory you have designated for forms, store each set of form interrogatories you create. A sample page of a form interrogatory appears in figure 17.11.

<u>INTRODUCTION AND DEFINITIONS</u>

A. The term "document" is used in its customary broad sense, covering items which are printed or recorded, filmed, or reproduced by any other mechanical or electrical process, or are written or produced by hand, and whether or not claimed to be privileged against discovery. It includes, but is not limited to, contracts and memoranda of agreements or understandings; purchase orders, receipts, order acknowledgements and invoices, assignments, subrogation receipts, correspondence, notes, memoranda, charts, plans, sketches and drawings, photographs, motion pictures, audio and video tapes and disks, models and mock-ups, reports and/or summaries of investigations, opinions and reports of experts and consultants, books of account, statements, bills, checks and vouchers, computer disks and/or data, and drafts of originals and marginal comments appearing on any document covered by this definition.

B. The terms "{FIELD}serve~", "you" or "your" shall be deemed to include {FIELD}servestat~ and {FIELD}servegender~ attorney(s), agent(s), employee(s), etc.

C. The terms "incident" or "accident" shall be synonymous and shall refer to the occurrence which caused the injuries to {FIELD}injured~ which forms the basis of this lawsuit.

==
1. Identify all persons known to you or believed by you to have knowledge or information relevant to this lawsuit, and give a brief description of the relevant knowledge or information of each person.

<u>ANSWER:</u>

==
2. State the date, time and exact location at which the incident occurred.

<u>ANSWER:</u>

==
3. As to {FIELD}injured~ please state: (a) his date of birth; (b) his social security number; (c) his employee I.D. Number, if any; and (d) Worker's Compensation case number, if any.

<u>ANSWER:</u>

==
4. Please state the marital status and spouse's name for {FIELD}injured~ as of the (a) incident date and (b) the present.

<u>ANSWER:</u>

Fig. 17.11.

A sample of a form interrogatory.

Preparing Interrogatories with INTERROG

First, create or retrieve your caption by using SHORTCAP or LONGCAP as described before. Add any title and introductory paragraph from the PLEAMENU macro. Move the cursor to the end of the introductory paragraph and invoke INTERROG by pressing Alt-F10, typing *I-intro*, and pressing Enter.

INTERROG displays a menu of options. The menu appears in figure 17.12. The three options listed on the menu are discussed next, in the order that they appear on the menu.

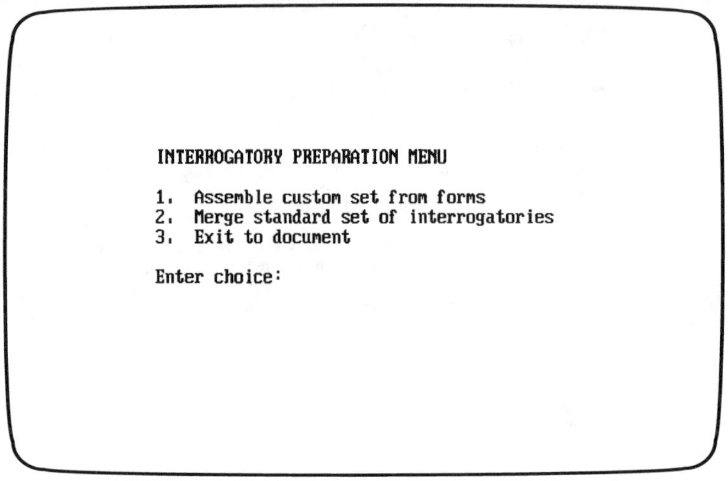

Fig. 17.12.

The INTERROG menu of options.

```
          INTERROGATORY PREPARATION MENU

          1.  Assemble custom set from forms
          2.  Merge standard set of interrogatories
          3.  Exit to document

          Enter choice:
```

Preparing Interrogatories from a Form Set

You may prefer to be selective in the questions you include in your interrogatories, or you may want to combine questions from several different forms. To combine questions, select option 1, or *a*, from the Interrogatory Preparation Menu and assemble a set of questions specifically tailored to your case.

When you select the first option, INTERROG asks you which set of interrogatories to load into Doc 2. The macro quits with those interrogatories on-screen. (If you switch back to Doc 1, you can see the caption and title you have created.) Into your document in Doc 1, you can assemble standard interrogatory questions from your standard questions in Doc 2 by using a point-and-shoot macro called TRIGGER (assigned to the Ctrl-Z on the LEGAL keyboard). Do so by placing the cursor anywhere within the question you want to incorporate and pressing Ctrl-Z. The macro automatically copies that question to Doc 1 and moves the cursor down to the next question. For more information on TRIGGER, see Chapter 16.

Hint: The macro should automatically retrieve the proper interrogatory form file into Doc 2 and leave you there to assemble your interrogatories from the standard questions in that file. If the macro does not, it has not located the file where it expected to find it. You can then enter another file name or press Cancel (F1) to quit.

Complete the assembly of your interrogatories in the following way:

1. Move the cursor down to the INTRODUCTION AND DEFINITIONS page (if any) in your form set and press the Ctrl-Z trigger. Doing so selects the definitions section and places it in your interrogatories.

2. Then move the cursor in succession to the numbered paragraphs desired, executing the Ctrl-Z trigger on each question. The cursor may be anywhere in the interrogatory except on the very last character of the paragraph.

3. After all the desired paragraphs are copied, exit from your form set in Doc 2 (without saving it) and return to your custom interrogatories in Doc 1. You can now add any special or unique questions, remembering to number each paragraph with an automatic paragraph-numbering code. By doing this, if you choose to rearrange the order of the questions, you can ensure that they renumber automatically.

4. After you add all the questions, retrieve the signature block for the attorney who will execute the interrogatories by executing the appropriate signature block macro or by copying from a previous pleading. Signature blocks are discussed later in this chapter.

5. Save your custom interrogatories to any directory that you want.

6. Complete the interrogatories by using the MERGE macro, which replaces all the variables in the form questions with appropriate information specific to the case. Do this by pressing Macro (Alt-F10), typing *MERGE*, and pressing Enter or (if you are using the LEGAL keyboard) Ctrl-M.

   ⌨Choose Macro from the **T**ools menu, select Execute, and then type *MERGE* and press Enter.

   The MERGE menu then appears (see fig. 16.7 in Chapter 16).

7. If you have not previously created a variable list for the case you are working on, select **C**reate list of information (**1**).

8. MERGE then asks you for the name of the variables template you created for the interrogatory form you want to use. The macro then works through that list, creating a variable list for your case with the answers you provide. If you want nothing entered in a particular field, simply press Enter at the prompt for that variable field.

9. When the macro reaches the END marker on your template, the macro asks for a file name for your variable list. Give it a name you easily recognize, such as the office file number for that case. The macro then saves the variable list to the directory C:\WP51\VARLIST or any other directory you specify in INSTALL. If the macro finds another file in that directory with the same name, the macro asks you for a new file name. The file stored in that directory is in the format of a secondary merge file. A sample of such a file is shown in figure 17.13.

```
{FIELD NAMES}
client~
clientstat~
clientgender~
serve~
servestat~
injured~
injuredgender~
injuredspouse~
spousegender~
product~
date~
location~
~{END RECORD}
==================================================
National Mutual Indemnity Company{END FIELD}
Defendant{END FIELD}
its{END FIELD}
Joseph T. Carver and Mary C. Carver, his wife{END FIELD}
Plaintiffs{END FIELD}
their{END FIELD}
Joseph T. Carver{END FIELD}
him{END FIELD}
Mary C. Carver{END FIELD}
her{END FIELD}
Stockman Model 146 drill press{END FIELD}
January 12, 1990{END FIELD}
Allegheny Sheet Metal Products, Inc.{END FIELD}
{END RECORD}
```

Fig. 17.13.

A secondary merge file created by MERGE.

10. After storing the variable list, MERGE returns to the menu. Select Merge with custom form (**3**); then type the path and file name of the custom interrogatories you created for that file.

11. MERGE then merges that form with the variable list it has just created and asks whether you want to remove any **[HPg]** or **[Comment]** codes left in your form. After you respond to that prompt, MERGE quits, leaving you with complete interrogatories.

Note: If you press N when MERGE asks whether to delete **[HPg]** codes, the macro leaves those codes between all questions, so that each question appears on a separate page when printed. If you do not like this, you can delete any or all hard-page codes and replace them with sufficient hard returns to leave space for the answers. You can do this easily by using the WordPerfect Replace feature. Simply press Replace (Shift-F2), press N, press Ctrl-Enter (to indicate that WordPerfect should search for **[HPg]** codes) and Search (F2), and then press Enter as many times as you want to create additional space for the answers. When you now press Search (F2) one last time, the **[HPg]** codes are replaced with the number of **[HRt]**s that you entered.

Merging with a Standard Set of Interrogatories

If you have prepared a complete set of interrogatories to be used intact (for instance, without assembling or adding case-specific questions), after you create your caption, title, and introductory paragraph, select **2** or **M** from the Interrogatory Preparation Menu. INTERROG then asks for the name of the standard interrogatory set you want to use, and appends that set to the caption and introductory matter you created. The macro then asks you for the name of a file in which to store the interrogatories.

After INTERROG stores your interrogatories, it automatically starts the MERGE macro. From there, you can create the variable list (a secondary merge file) if needed to retrieve the interrogatories you just created. You can then merge them with your variable list, leaving you with a finished set of interrogatories.

The final option on the Interrogatory Preparation Menu is to simply exit from the INTERROG macro, leaving you with the caption and title only. If you choose this option, simply choose **3** or **E** from the menu.

Preparing Certificates of Service

In many jurisdictions, courts require all pleadings to be accompanied by a certificate, signed by the attorney, stating the identity of all persons on whom the pleading has been served or delivered. If you prepare your form certificate of service to take advantage of some of the new features of WordPerfect 5.1, you can automate the creation of these documents. To do so, follow these steps:

1. Include a "Certificate of Service" form in your PLEAMENU template as discussed earlier.

2. Create your certificate form as your jurisdiction or practice requires.

3. At each point where you must specify variable information (for example, the manner in which service was made), use the merge code {PROMPT}message~{KEYBOARD} or {STATUS PROMPT}.

4. You can insert a {DATE} code at the location where you want to insert the date on which service is being made. To do this, press Merge Codes (Shift-F9).

   ⌨Choose Merge Codes from the Tools menu.

5. From the status line or pop-up menu that appears, press More, press T, and then press Enter.

6. At the location where you want to insert the names and addresses of the attorneys being served, use a {TEXT}var~message~ code to prompt the user to enter the file name for the list of counsel to be retrieved into the form. Do this by pressing Merge Codes (Shift-F9).

   ⌨Choose Merge Codes from the Tools menu.

7. From the status line or pop-up menu that appears, press More, press T, and then press Enter.

8. Type a variable name (*counsel*, for example) and press Enter.

9. Type a message to prompt the user to enter the file number for the counsel list and press Enter again.

10. Now use a {DOCUMENT} code to retrieve the counsel list into your certificate of service by pressing Merge Codes (Shift-F9).

    ⌨Choose Merge Codes from the Tools menu.

11. From the status line or pop-up menu that appears, press More (or, if you are using the function keys, press Shift-F9 again), type *DO*, and then press Enter.

12. Do not provide a file name at the prompt. Instead, simply press Enter a second time. You will provide a file name with the {VARIABLE} merge command next.

13. Press the left-arrow key once to move the cursor inside the tilde that appears immediately after the {DOCUMENT} code.

14. Type the path where you plan to store counsel lists (the suggested directory is C:\WP51\COUNSEL). Leave a backslash after the directory name; the {VARIABLE} command supplies the file name.

15. Now enter a {VARIABLE} merge code (to enter into the {DOCUMENT} command the file name called for by the {TEXT} code) by pressing Merge Codes (Shift-F9).

    ⌨Choose Merge Codes from the Tools menu.

16. From the status line or pop-up menu that appears, press More, press V, and then press Enter.

17. Type the name of the variable you chose in step 8 and press Enter. The {VARIABLE} command should appear, followed by the name of your variable and two tildes.

At the end of the form, you can nest a macro to insert a signature block. Use a {TEXT} command to assign to a variable the initials of the lawyer who will sign the pleading; then use a {NEXT MACRO} command to execute the macro assigned to those initials. Follow these steps:

1. Press Merge Codes (Shift-F9).

   ⌨Choose Me**r**ge Codes from the **T**ools menu.

2. From the status line or pop-up menu that appears, press **More** (or, if you are using the function keys, Shift-F9 a second time), press T, and press Enter.

3. Type a different variable name (*sign*, for example) and press Enter.

4. Type a message to prompt the user to enter the initials of the attorney who will sign the certificate, and press Enter again.

5. Now use a {NEST MACRO} code to invoke the macro assigned to those initials by pressing Merge Codes (Shift-F9).

   ⌨Choose Me**r**ge Codes from the **T**ools menu.

6. From the status line or pop-up macro that appears, press **More** (or, if you are using the function keys, Shift-F9 again). Move the cursor to the {NEST MACRO} command and press Enter.

7. Do not provide a file name at the prompt. Instead, simply press Enter a second time. You will provide a file name with the {VARIABLE} merge command, discussed next.

8. Press the left-arrow key once to move the cursor inside the tilde that appears immediately after the {NEST MACRO} code.

9. Now enter a {VARIABLE} merge code (to enter into {NEST MACRO} the initials called for by the {TEXT} code) by pressing Merge Codes (Shift-F9).

   ⌨Choose Me**r**ge Codes from the **T**ools menu.

10. From the status line or pop-up menu that appears, press **More** (or, if you use the function keys, Shift-F9 again), press V, and then press Enter.

11. Type the name of the variable you chose in step 3 and press Enter. The {VARIABLE} command should appear, followed by the name of your variable and two tildes.

Store your form in your forms directory. Be sure that you provide the correct path and file name in your PLEAMENU template.

A sample merge form, prepared as described, appears in figure 17.14. This merge form is included as the file CERTIF on the Applications Disk that accompanies this book.

Fig. 17.14.

A sample certificate of service.

CERTIFICATE OF SERVICE

The undersigned certifies that a true and correct copy of the foregoing {STATUS PROMPT}Name of pleading; press F9 when done~{KEYBOARD}{STATUS PROMPT}~ was served on {DATE}, by first class mail, postage pre-paid, on the following counsel:

{TEXT}filename~Enter filename for counsel list: ~

{DOCUMENT}c:\wp51\counsel\{VARIABLE}filename~~

{TEXT}sign~Who will sign? Type initials: ~
{NEST MACRO}{VARIABLE}sign~~

Next, you must make your lists of counsel to be served in each of your litigation cases. These lists can be easily modified with any change in the list of counsel for a particular case. Each case should have its own list of counsel to be routinely served with pleadings or other matters. To create these lists, do the following:

1. Create a directory on your disk to store files consisting only of lists of counsel to be served in your cases. Be sure that the certificate form you just created contains the correct directory information in the {DOCUMENT} code.

2. For each litigation file in your office, create a list of the names and addresses of all parties or counsel who should be served with pleadings, in the exact format you want them to appear in the certificate of service. Thus if you want the names centered, in two or more columns, or in any other format, put these codes into this document.

3. Store each list in the counsel directory under a recognizable file name (the file number might be a good name).

Now when you select the certificate option from the PLEAMENU screen, your certificate generates automatically and requires you to follow this procedure:

1. The form asks you for the file name of your counsel list. Don't type the path; the form you created supplies that. Just type the file name you gave the list and press Enter.

2. Insert any information asked for by the messages you entered when you created your form. Press End Field (F9) after each entry.

3. The form then asks you for the name of the attorney who will sign the pleading. Enter the initials; the appropriate signature block macro will then run. (Signature block macros are discussed next.)

For help with creating merge documents, see the discussion of creating a long form caption earlier in this chapter.

Finishing Your Pleading

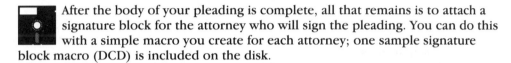 After the body of your pleading is complete, all that remains is to attach a signature block for the attorney who will sign the pleading. You can do this with a simple macro you create for each attorney; one sample signature block macro (DCD) is included on the disk.

Like WHERE4, this macro checks the computer's memory to see whether the name of the client has been stored in a specific variable. If it has, the macro asks whether this is the name to use for this signature block. If you answer no, or if the macro cannot find the information it needs, the macro prompts you for the name of your client and then inserts that information on the last line of the signature block, immediately after the words *Attorney for*.

Name each signature block macro with the initials of the attorney to whom it relates. Doing so helps you remember the name of the macro but also helps your signature-block macros to work with several of the macros described previously that automatically chain to your signature blocks. For example, if you use WHERE4 and press Y in response to the prompt Add signature block: Y/N?, the next prompt asks you for the initials of the attorney who will sign the pleading. The macro then invokes the macro with those initials.

The easiest way to create signature block macros similar to the form DCD.WPM provided on the disk is to make multiple copies of DCD.WPM, saved under file names corresponding to the initials of the attorneys in your firm. Then edit the macros to insert the correct names and addresses of the attorneys to whom the macros are assigned.

Creating Tables of Contents and Tables of Authorities

WordPerfect includes a wonderful utility for creating both tables of contents and tables of authorities for briefs. However, the program expects you to search through your document manually and decide (a) what headings go in a table of contents and (b) what text is a citation to be included in your table of authorities.

You can automate both these functions if a little care is taken in typing the original brief. The disk includes a group of macros that search for and mark table of contents headings and table of authorities citations, both long and short forms. Their operation is discussed next.

Using the TOC Macro

The TOC macro creates the table of contents. It works by searching for automatic paragraph-numbering codes (**[Par Num:x]**) because it assumes that each item you want to list in your table of contents begins with such a code.

Thus when you type a brief for which you intend to create a table of contents, you must begin each heading that you want to incorporate in the table with a paragraph-numbering code. These can be easily entered with the PARANO paragraph-numbering macro, assigned to Ctrl-N on the LEGAL keyboard.

TOC first asks whether you want to delete any existing **[Mark:ToC]** codes that may have been placed in your document manually (or placed in a prior document that you are revising). It then asks whether you want to begin the table of contents on page *i*; if you answer yes, TOC sets the page number for *i* and resets the page number for the first page after the table to 1.

TOC then creates a table of contents page at a location selected by you and begins searching for all automatic-numbering codes. After finding a numbering code, the macro pauses to allow you to block the text you want to enter in the table of contents. After you press Enter, the macro asks for the level of the item being marked and then moves on to the next entry until it finds no more numbering codes.

Using the TOA Macro

TOA is the primary macro for creating tables of authorities. If you have not already defined a table of authorities, this macro does so and then calls the remaining three macros in sequence to mark all references to constitutions, cases, statutes, and rules.

TOA begins by asking whether you want to strip existing long- and short-form citation markings from the document. This stripping guards against duplicate entries in the final table that can result if you run TOA more than once on the same document or if you copy text from one brief to another and inadvertently include such codes. If you do not want to lose such codes already in your document, simply answer no at the prompt.

TOA then asks where you want to place the table of authorities. If it detects that a table of contents has been created through the TOC macro, it asks whether you want to place the table of authorities immediately after the table of contents. If you answer yes, the table of authorities is placed automatically. Otherwise, you can move the cursor to the exact location where you want the table to be created.

If you have not already set the page numbering for a table of contents to *i*, TOA asks whether you want to reset the page numbers. If page numbering has already been set by TOC, TOA skips this step.

The table of authorities created by TOA has up to four levels, corresponding to the four types of citations it looks for and marks. If other types of citations are to be incorporated, the table can be amended to add further levels after TOA has run. Of course, citations in those levels must be searched for and marked manually. If TOA does not find one or more of the four types of citations, that level will not be defined in the table of authorities.

After you have run TOA once to create the table of authorities page, any of the nested macros for marking citations can be run separately if needed. More information on how they work follows.

Using the CONST Macro

The CONST macro helps you locate and mark references in your brief to constitutional citations. The operation of CONST (whether called by TOA or invoked directly by you) is as follows:

1. CONST begins by searching the document for all occurrences of the string `Const`. The macro skips over `const`, so words like `constitutional` are not found; however, the macro may mistake `Constitutional` for a citation to a constitution.

   Tip for advanced users: If you want to edit CONST to have it search for a different string, the place to edit the search string is marked within the macro by the comments `{;}Edit search string here~`.

2. When the macro finds the string `Const`, it pauses, backs up one word, and inserts an arrow (**—>**). The macro then asks you whether the string following the arrow is a constitutional citation.

3. If the string is, press Y. The macro then defines level 1 of the table of authorities as "Constitutional Provisions" and instructs you to block the full citation.

4. Press Block (Alt-F4) and use the cursor keys to highlight the entire constitutional reference. Now press Enter. The citation you have marked becomes the table of authorities full form, level 1.

5. The macro then pauses, with Reveal Codes on, to allow you to edit the full form (for example, to correct italicization, correct spelling errors, delete specific page references, or change the appearance in any way necessary for the primary table).

6. The macro then asks you to create a short form. Enter a unique string that identifies the provision cited.

7. After that is done, the macro asks whether you want to mark all references with the short form citation. Answer yes or no as you need.

8. After you mark the short form references to that provision, or if you choose not to mark them, CONST proceeds to search for the next occurrence of the string Const, and continues as before.

9. If CONST "hits" on something that is not a citation to a constitutional provision, simply press N. The macro will continue on to the next occurrence.

After you are through marking constitutional references, the TOA macro switches to CASES and works on case citations.

Using the CASES Macro

CASES helps you locate and mark citations in your brief to cases. This macro takes the most time to operate because it has the most work to do. Its operation is as follows:

1. CASES begins by searching the document for all occurrences of the **[ITALC]** code, the first code in most citations. Unfortunately, it also occurs naturally in headings, emphasized words, and so on, so there will be a fair number of errant "hits" during the operation of this macro. Simply pressing N moves the arrow to the next italicized word or phrase.

 Note: If you underline your case citations instead of italicizing them, you must modify CASES to search for an **[UND]** code. The point to edit is marked within the macro by a comment, shown in figure 17.15. For more information on editing this macro, see the file README.17.

Fig. 17.15.

The editing comment within the CASES macro.

```
Macro: Action

    File           CASES.WPM

    Description    Create table of authorities

{LABEL}start~
    {DISPLAY OFF}
    {ASSIGN}loop1~0~
    {WHILE}{VARIABLE}loop1~=0~
        {ASSIGN}loop2~0~
        {DISPLAY OFF}
        {ON NOT FOUND}{CALL}notfound~~
        {Home}{Search}{Font}ai{Search}          {;}edit·search·criterion~
        {WHILE}{VARIABLE}loop2~=0~
            {Left}-->
            {DISPLAY ON}
            {ASSIGN}ok~0~
            {WHILE}{VARIABLE}ok~=0~
                {ASSIGN}ok~-1~
                {CHAR}cite~Is·this·a·citation?·(Y/N)··
```

Ctrl-PgUp for macro commands; Press Exit when done

2. If —> is in front of a case citation, press Y. The first time (and only the first time) that you press Y at this prompt, CASES will define level 2 of the table of authorities as Cases.

3. Next, you must highlight the citation with Block. Press Block (Alt-F4) and use the cursor keys to highlight the citation you want to mark. Press Enter when you have highlighted the whole citation. This becomes the table of authorities full-form reference for level 2.

    A minor problem may arise if the case citation is preceded immediately by additional italicized words. For example, the citation may be preceded by a call such as *see e.g.* or *cf.* In that case, you may get something that looks like this on your screen:

    >see, e.g., Stoneking vs Bradford Area School District, 874 F.2d 1234 (3rd Cir. 1988).

    If you move the cursor to the first word of the case citation (in this example, *Stoneking*), your full form does not include the **[ITALC]** code for turning on italics. In this situation, you can do one of two things. You can block the whole reference beginning at the arrow (including the **[ITALC]** code and the call *see, e.g.*) and then edit the full form to omit the call on the next screen. Or you can move the cursor to the first word of the case and edit the full form on the next screen to italicize the case name.

4. After the full form of the citation has been entered and marked, the macro asks you for the short form and pauses to allow you to enter it as you normally would.

5. The macro then asks you whether you want to mark all references. If you press Y, the macro asks you for a case name to search for. You should enter here the shorthand name that the author of the brief has used in the body of the brief. The macro then searches out that shorthand name and enters a short form citation at every occurrence.

6. The macro then returns to the arrow, erases it, and starts over again, looking for the next citation. Repeat steps 1 through 5 as often as necessary.

When CASES finds no more **[ITALC]** codes, TOA starts STATS.

Using the STATS Macro

STATS marks all statutory citations. It does so by searching for a § character, then backing up two words and inserting the arrow (—>). (As with CONST, you can edit the search string if you choose). The macro asks whether it has found a statutory citation. If the macro has, press Y and mark the citation manually by using Block, just as you did with the CONST macro. The macro also flags later references in the same way as the previous two macros.

STATS defines statutory references as level 3; the heading in the table of authorities (if any such references are found) is "Statutes."

When STATS can find no more statutes, TOA starts RULES.

Using the RULES Macro

RULES searches for occurrences of R, which should appear in citations to rules. The macro then stops and asks whether it has found a rule citation and asks you to mark it if the macro has. You can edit the search criterion if you want to search for a more specific string.

RULES defines the references to rules as level 4. The heading in the table of authorities (if any such references are found) is "Rules."

Generating Your Tables

After the macros complete their work, you can generate your table of contents and table of authorities and edit them as needed. To generate the tables, follow these steps:

1. Press Mark Text (Alt-F5) and select **Generate (6)**.

2. Press **Generate (5)**.

3. WordPerfect warns you that existing tables will be replaced. Press Y to continue generating.

WordPerfect then runs through the document several times, correcting cross-references and noting page numbers for the various items you marked in using TOA. WordPerfect ends by writing a table of contents and a table of authorities at the locations you designated.

Summary

As you can see, WordPerfect 5.1 is an extremely powerful word processor that can automate numerous activities in a law office or practice. With WordPerfect macros and the merge capability, nearly any repetitive legal activity—from time sheets to pleadings to captions to interrogatories—can be accomplished quickly and easily. That is why WordPerfect has consistently been the word processor of choice for the legal environment.

In the next section, you explore another kind of forms that can be created with WordPerfect: newsletters, office publications, news releases, brochures, programs, and pamphlets. Although WordPerfect is very productive in the legal setting, it is equally productive in almost any office environment—especially where camera-ready copy is needed for publication purposes.

Part VII

Desktop Publishing
in the Office

Creating Camera-Ready Copy

Creating Programs, Pamphlets,
and Book Pages

Creating Newsletters and
Magazine-Style Reports

18

Creating Camera-Ready Copy

Virtually every office at one time or another produces news releases, programs, schedules, reports, newsletters, brochures, manuals, and other materials to be given away, sold, or sent to people outside the office. Generally this information is copied or printed in sufficient quantity—perhaps 50, 500, or 10,000 copies—to meet the intended audience.

A few years ago, preparing material for reproduction was a labor-intensive and costly activity. Typewritten copy was sent to a typesetter who entered the information into a typesetting terminal, fonts were specified by a graphic designer, and galleys of single-column pages were printed on proof copy paper. The designer then would cut apart these columns, paste them on large sheets of "dummy pages," and add ruled boxes where illustrations and photographs would be positioned. If everything fit properly and received the customer's approval, the designer or paste-up person would then prepare a second set of pages just like the "dummy," but this time use proof galleys pasted on clear acetate sheets and ready-to-reproduce illustrations or red amberlith overlays where the publisher would later strip in photographs.

With the advent of computers, word processing programs like WordPerfect 5.1, and laser printers, all these various steps are now being done on-screen rather than on paper. This process of combining a variety of fonts, graphic images, tables of information, charts, quotes set in shaded boxes, and vertical and horizontal bars and lines on a computer rather than on paper is called desktop publishing. With desktop publishing (or DTP, for short), the final appearance of the printed page is in your hands, not the hands of graphic artists and designers. And for most applications in the typical office, you won't need to use PageMaker or Ventura to get quality desktop publishing-type documents.

Desktop publishing involves combining a variety of publishing elements onto pages that are ready to be photographed by the printer and duplicated. These ready-to-photograph pages are called camera-ready copy.

This chapter indicates some of the ways in which camera-ready pages differ from the kinds of documents discussed in the previous chapters. The general guidelines presented here include the use of fonts, graphics, quotations, and other graphic elements that make up what is called camera-ready copy. Chapters 19 and 20 will provide specific examples of how these elements can be combined to make attractive publications for your office.

Using Document Preview

Over the years, WordPerfect has become famous for its clean-screen approach to text editing. The monitor screen is not cluttered with menu bars at the top and bottom as with some programs, or scroll bars along the side as with desktop publishing programs. On a regular monitor, the user sees 24 lines of text—a full screen minus a single line at the bottom for necessary document and cursor-position information.

Although this clean-screen design has good points, the one drawback is the user's inability to see fonts, font sizes, and page elements like headers, footnotes, and the contents of figure boxes on-screen while editing the document. WordPerfect 5.1, of course, offers an alternative. Font sizes and attributes can be assigned to any of 16 different foreground colors and 8 different background colors. But if you have a monochrome monitor, even this option provides little useful information. After all, how many different shades of gray can one easily distinguish?

Another alternative is to install the Hercules In-Color Card, or Hercules Plus-Card for monochrome monitors. These cards allow on-screen representations of font sizes, basic font types, and font attributes like bold and italic. Many users find these cards useful when working with WordPerfect documents. But even with a Hercules Card addition, you still will not see other important document elements like the various special characters created with Compose, headers, footers, footnotes, endnotes and graphic lines, as well as figures and scanned photographs. WordPerfect does not show these screen elements in edit mode.

Fortunately, this negative aspect can be easily corrected with the View Document feature. You can access this mode by pressing Print (Shift-F7) and then selecting **View Document (6)**. Figure 18.1 shows one page in view mode at its actual (100%) size.

Fig. 18.1.

Fonts and graphics in the View Document screen.

However, even better than the normal steps for document preview would be a mnemonic Alt-letter macro that would pop up view mode with a simple keystroke. Here are the steps for creating a View Document macro, which will let you see the fonts, rules, graphics, columns, footnotes, and so on with a single key command:

1. Press Macro Define (Ctrl-F10) to start macro definition.

2. To name the macro, hold down the Alt key and press V (for View Document).

3. For a description, type *Look at Doc in View mode* and press Enter.

4. Press Print (Shift-F7) and then select View Document (6).

5. Press Macro Define (Ctrl-F10) to end macro definition.

In many cases, you may want to view a full page of a document, but you do not need to select the level of view as part of the macro. WordPerfect will automatically default to the most recently used level of view: (**1**) 100%, or actual size; (**2**) 200%, or twice the size; (**3**) Full Page; or (**4**) Facing Pages. To return to the document after you use this macro, press Exit (F7). You may find 100% the most convenient size to use, as it provides a half-page view. To view the bottom half, press the gray plus (+) key; to view the top half, press the gray minus (–) key.

On an 80386 machine, this macro generally works very fast—certainly faster than if you were using the Print menu. Even on an 8088 or 80286 machine, the macro is faster than keyboard commands and menus. The Alt-V macro included on the Applications Disk has been modified to speed up view mode slightly and make its operation smoother.

Aligning Text Properly

Although no single rule governs all printed material, most publications have fully justified text—that is, lines of text aligned vertically at both the right and left margins. The following examples illustrate each kind of text:

> Documents created on a typewriter, or made to look as if they came from a typewriter, have left-justified text and ragged right margins for each of the lines. Typed documents are rarely hyphenated because that requires extra effort on a typewriter.

> Text in books and magazines generally is justified at both the left and right margins. Except for short lines that don't reach the right margin, justified text has no ragged ends. It often contains hyphens, however, to minimize between words the wide gaps caused by justification.

Unless you want your publications to appear "newsy," personal, and informal, fully justified text looks best. You just turn on justification at the beginning of the document by using Format (Shift-F8) and selecting Line (1), Justification (3), and Full (4).

Note that the Full Justification ([Just:Full]) code must be put at the beginning of a line. If the code is added elsewhere on the line, WordPerfect inserts a Deletable Soft Return ([DSRt]) code and moves the Full Justification code to the beginning of the next line.

Using Different Fonts

Chapter 4 discussed the difference between typefaces and fonts. It also delved into how to select a printer, install fonts, change font attributes, use different cartridges and soft fonts, select an Initial Base Font, change base fonts, and work with WordPerfect's automatic font sizes.

However, because this section deals with desktop publishing, which uses a variety of fonts and font attributes, the fascinating world of fonts should be explored in more detail.

If all you plan to create with WordPerfect 5.1 are memos, letters, reports, forms, and similar office-type documents, you likely will not need anything fancier than a standard laser printer, a single font cartridge, and perhaps one set of soft fonts on disk for more demanding jobs.

Alternative Font Options

If, however, you are serious about desktop publishing, you will need to consider some font alternatives. A laser printer with a single font cartridge is far too limited for true desktop publishing. You have access to only 16 or 18 different font sizes in two typefaces. For example, here are the typefaces and font sizes available on each of three popular HP font cartridges:

Fonts on the HP WP Cartridge:

CG Times 6 point
CG Times 8 point
CG Times 8 point Bold
CG Times 8 point Italic
CG Times 10 point
CG Times 10 point Bold
CG Times 10 point Italic
CG Times 12 point
CG Times 12 point Bold
CG Times 12 point Italic
CG Times 14 point
CG Times 14 point Bold
CG Times 14 point Italic
CG Times 18 point Bold
CG Times 24 point Bold
Univers 14 point
Univers 18 point
Univers 24 point

Fonts on the HP Z1 Cartridge:

Helv 8 point
Helv 10 point
Helv 10 point Bold
Helv 10 point Italic
Helv 12 point
Helv 12 point Bold
Helv 12 point Italic
Helv 14 point Bold
TmsRmn 8 point
TmsRmn 10 point
TmsRmn 10 point Bold
TmsRmn 10 point Italic
TmsRmn 12 point
TmsRmn 12 point Bold
TmsRmn 12 point Italic
TmsRmn 14 point Bold

Fonts on the Z1A Cartridge:

Helv 8 point
Helv 10 point
Helv 10 point Bold
Helv 10 point Italic
Helv 12 point
Helv 12 point Bold
Helv 12 point Italic
Helv 14 point Bold
TmsRmn 8 point
TmsRmn 10 point
TmsRmn 10 point Bold
TmsRmn 10 point Italic
TmsRmn 12 point
TmsRmn 12 point Bold
TmsRmn 12 point Italic
TmsRmn 14 point Bold

If you are doing desktop publishing, you will certainly need some headline sizes larger than 14 point, typefaces other than Times Roman and Helvetica, and odd font sizes like 7 point, 9 point and 11 point. Figure 18.2, for example, shows how three different font sizes larger than 14 point Times Roman look in Print View Document mode so that you can see the difference size makes:

Fig. 18.2.

Four different font sizes seen in View Document mode.

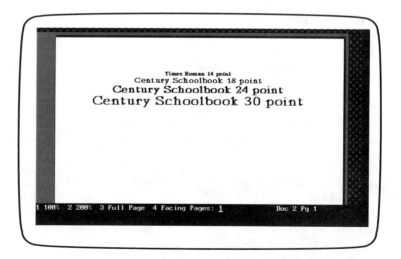

Special Font Cartridges

Two useful font alternatives for desktop publishing are the Super Cartridge 1 and Super Cartridge 2, developed by IQ Engineering, P.O. Box 60955, Sunnyvale, CA 94086. Super Cartridge 1 contains 55 different fonts, and Super Cartridge 2 contains 70 different fonts—in sizes ranging from 6 point to 30 point. These cartridges include the equivalent number of fonts as found on 10 or 12 regular font cartridges. Figure 18.3 shows printed samples of some of the different fonts available on the Super Cartridge 2.

Super Cartridge 1 contains many of the same fonts as Super Cartridge 2, but offers two sizes of Presentation instead of Ribbon.

Soft Fonts

A second alternative is soft fonts—fonts kept on a hard disk and downloaded to the printer at the beginning of the day or as needed for individual print jobs.

Soft fonts are easy to use in addition to a regular cartridge. Since they include no mechanical parts, they never break down. The main disadvantages of soft fonts are the disk space they consume, the time it takes to download them, and the extra memory needed by the printer if different fonts are combined in a single document.

Depending on your printer, you can print text that is up to 144 points in height (approximately 2 inches tall) with PCL printers, or 975 points tall (approximately 11 inches) with PostScript printers. Bitstream Fontware, for example, lets you generate any size font you want (in 1/10-point increments, if desired) between the sizes in the following list:

- HP DeskJet and DeskJet Plus: between 2 and 30 points
- HP LaserJet Plus: between 2 and 36 points
- HP LaserJet Series II: between 2 and 144 points
- Canon LBP-8II and III: between 2 and 144 points
- PostScript printers: between 2 and 975 points

Choosing the right typefaces for specific printing jobs can be difficult. Fortunately, Bitstream has put together six Fundamental packages of soft fonts for specific applications: newsletters, books and manuals, fliers, reports and proposals, presentations, and spreadsheets. Each package contains 12 typefaces specifically selected for the type of publication you want to print.

Figures 18.4 through 18.9 show the types of fonts from four of the the soft font Fundamentals packages provided by Bitstream (Bitstream, Inc., 215 First Street, Cambridge, MA 02142; [800] 522-FONT). The fonts in every package can be generated in any point size your printer can use.

Times Roman 6 pt
Times Roman 6 pt bold
Times Roman 6 pt italic

Times Roman 8 pt
Times Roman 8 pt bold
Times Roman 8 pt italic

Times Roman 10 pt
Times Roman 10 pt bold
Times Roman 10 pt italic

Times Roman 11 pt
Times Roman 11 pt bold
Times Roman 11 pt italic

Times Roman 12 pt
Times Roman 12 pt bold
Times Roman 12 pt italic

Times Roman 14 pt
Times Roman 14 pt bold
Times Roman 14 pt italic

Times Roman 18 pt
Times Roman 18 pt bold

Times Roman 24 pt bold

Times Roman 30 pt bold

Ribbon 14 point

Ribbon 18 point

Ribbon 24 point

Ribbon 30 point

Fig. 18.3.

Kinds of fonts available on Super Cartridge 2.

Helvetica 6 pt
Helvetica 6 pt bold
Helvetica 6 pt italic

Helvetica 8 pt
Helvetica 8 pt bold
Helvetica 8 pt italic

Helvetica 10 pt
Helvetica 10 pt bold
Helvetica 10 pt italic

Helvetica 11 pt
Helvetica 11 pt bold
Helvetica 11 pt italic

Helvetica 12 pt
Helvetica 12 pt bold
Helvetica 12 pt italic

Helvetica 14 pt
Helvetica 14 pt bold
Helvetica 14 pt italic

Helvetica 18 pt
Helvetica 18 pt bold

Helvetica 24 pt bold

Helvetica 30 pt bold

Letter Gothic 30 cpi
Letter Gothic 16.67 cpi
Letter Gothic 12 cpi
Letter Gothic 12 cpi bold

Fig. 18.3.

Continued

Line Printer 27.27

Prestige Elite 16.67 cpi

Line Draw 12 cpi

Prestige Elite 12 cpi
Prestige Elite 12 cpi bold
Prestige Elite 12 cpi italic

Broadway 14 pt

Broadway 18 pt

Broadway 24 pt

Broadway 30 pt

Cooper 14 pt Black

Cooper 18 pt Black

Cooper 24 pt Black

Cooper 30 pt Black

Fig. 18.3.

Continued

Some of the collections include special fonts for headlines. For example, the Fliers Collection includes two sets of headline fonts: Headlines 2 (Blippo, Brush Script, and Windsor) and Headlines 4 (Clarendon, Coronet, and ITC Zapf Chance) (see fig. 18.4).

The Newsletters Collection includes Headlines 1 (Cooper Black, Broadway, Cloister, and University Roman), as illustrated in figure 18.5.

The Presentations Collection, as shown in figure 18.6, includes Headlines 5 (Park Avenue, Handel Gothic, Futura Black, and Dom Casual).

The Reports and Proposals Collection features three different typefaces, each in regular (roman), italic, bold, and bold italic: Activa, Zapf Humanist, and Amerigo (see fig. 18.7).

As you can see, soft fonts provide a wide variety of types and sizes of fonts for virtually any printing need you might have. And Bitstream provides 52 different typeface packages (most containing four different font styles: regular, bold, italic, and bold italic) for PC users. Bitstream fonts are highly recommended for attractive desktop-published documents.

Futura Light
Futura Condensed
Blippo Black
Brush Script Italic
Hobo
Windsor
Clarendon
Coronet Bold
ITC Zapf Chance Italic

Fig. 18.4.

Samples of fonts available in the Fliers Collection.

Fig. 18.5.

Samples of fonts available in the Newsletters Collection.

Charter Black
Swiss Black
Cooper Black
Broadway
Cloister
University Roman

PostScript Cartridges and Printers

If you intend to use many different fonts and you want them in the broadest range of sizes, the best alternative is either buying a PostScript printer or purchasing a PostScript cartridge for your standard laser printer. With a PacificPage PostScript Emulation Cartridge, for example, you can print 35 different fonts in any size you want. Figure 18.8 illustrates 14 of the 35 different fonts available on the PacificPage cartridge.

Each of these 35 fonts can be printed in full and partial sizes all the way from 2 points to 999 points. Figure 18.9 shows one Postscript font in different sizes in landscape mode, and figure 18.10 shows fonts up to 900 points. (Note: Both figures have been reduced somewhat.)

Fig. 18.6.

*Samples of fonts
available in the
Presentations
Collection.*

Slate Medium

Slate Bold

Slate Extra Bold

Swiss Condensed

Swiss Condensed Italic

Swiss Condensed Black

Park Avenue

Handel Gothic

Futura Black

Dom Casual

Another advantage of PostScript is the capability to print the same fonts in either portrait or landscape format. Figure 18.11 shows a certificate awarded for WordPerfect 5.1 proficiency. The certificate is printed in landscape Century Schoolbook font on an HP LaserJet Series II printer with the Pacific Page PostScript cartridge. The stock-style background paper came blank from a print shop and generally is available in a variety of colors.

Fig. 18.7.

*Samples of fonts
available in the
Reports and
Proposals
Collection.*

Activa Roman
Activa Italic
Activa Bold
Zapf Humanist Bold
Zapf Humanist Bold Italic
Bitstream Amerigo
Bitstream Amerigo Italic

Using Shading and Shadow Type

In addition to a large variety of fonts and font sizes, PostScript printers and cartridges let the user print type in a variety of shades, or screens of gray. Figure 18.12 shows some of the screen effects possible with WordPerfect and the PacificPage PostScript cartridge.

Sample PostScript Fonts

Fig. 18.8.

Fourteen different fonts available in PostScript.

Helvetica (24 Pt)

Helvetica Bold (24 Pt)

Helvetica Narrow (24 Pt)

Avant Garde Gothic (24 Pt)

Bookman Demi (24 Pt)

Bookman Light (24 Pt)

Zapf Chancery (24 Pt)

Century Schoolbook (24 Pt)

C. Schoolbook Bold (24 Pt)

Palatino (24 Pt)

Palatino Bold (24 Pt)

Times Roman (24 Pt)

Times Roman Bold (24 Pt)

Symbol Font (24 Pt)

Fig. 18.9.

One font in different sizes.

Schoolbook (9 Pt)
Schoolbook (11 Pt)
Schoolbook (11.5)
Schoolbook (12 Pt)
Schoolbook (14 Pt)
Schoolbook (18 Pt)
Schoolbook (24 Pt)
Schoolbook (30 Pt)
Schoolbook (36 Pt)
Schoolbook (42 Pt)
Schoolbook (60 Pt)

Fig. 18.10.

PostScript fonts to 900-point.

Fig. 18.11.

An example of a PostScript font in landscape mode.

WordPerfect 5.1 Certificate

This is to certify that on January 31, 1991, **Annette Thomas** successfully completed all the requirements of an **Intermediate Level Training Seminar** in WordPerfect 5.1. The six-week seminar included training on new WordPerfect features like Pull-down Menus, Working with Fonts, Creating Tables, Creating and Using Macros, Creating and Using Styles, Using the Merge Feature, Creating and Using Keyboards, Using Graphics and Figure Boxes, Adding Graphic Lines, and Introduction to Desktop Publishing (DTP).

This **WordPerfect 5.1 Certificate** has been presented to **Annette Thomas** in recognition of this accomplishment by the Seminar instructor, Ralph Blodgett, author of *The Best Book of WordPerfect 5.1* (by Hayden Books) and *WordPerfect 5.1 Power Pack* (by Que Corporation).

Ralph Blodgett, Instructor
January 31, 1991

Fig. 18.12.

Screened text printed with the PacificPage PostScript cartridge.

Helvetica Bold 0% White
Helvetica Bold 10 % White
Helvetica Bold 20 % White
Helvetica Bold 30 % White
Helvetica Bold 40 % White
Helvetica Bold 50 % White
Helvetica Bold 60 % White
Helvetica Bold 70 % White
Helvetica Bold 80 % White
Helvetica Bold 90 % White
Helvetica Bold 95 % White

Shaded text with a PostScript printer or cartridge is created through the Print Color feature of WordPerfect. To shade text, do these steps:

1. Position the cursor in front of the text you want to screen.

2. Press Font (Ctrl-F8).

3. Choose Print Color (**5**). The Print Color screen shown in figure 18.13 will appear.

```
Print Color

                            Primary Color Mixture
                            Red      Green     Blue

          1 - Black         0%       0%        0%
          2 - White         100%     100%      100%
          3 - Red           67%      0%        0%
          4 - Green         0%       67%       0%
          5 - Blue          0%       0%        67%
          6 - Yellow        67%      67%       0%
          7 - Magenta       67%      0%        67%
          8 - Cyan          0%       67%       67%
          9 - Orange        67%      25%       0%
          A - Gray          50%      50%       50%
          N - Brown         67%      33%       0%
          O - Other

          Current Color     0%       0%        0%



Selection: 0
```

Fig. 18.13.

The WordPerfect Print Color screen.

4. Select Gray (**A**) if you want the text to be printed as 50 percent of normal, or Other (**O**) if you want a percentage of gray other than 50 percent, as illustrated in figure 18.13.

5. Press Enter to return to the edit screen.

Note in figure 18.13 that black text (**1**) has a primary color mixture of 0% red, 0% green, and 0% blue. White text (**2**) has a mixture of 100% red, 100% green, and 100% blue; and gray text (**A**), 50% red, 50% green, and 50% blue. As you can see in figure 18.13, the greater the amount of white text, the lighter the printed text will appear.

Going one step further, you can create a shadowed effect with PostScript fonts by overprinting black text on the same text in a gray screen. Figure 18.14 shows the results of such a text overprint.

Fig. 18.14.

Black text overlaid on 50%-shaded text.

To create the shadow effect shown in figure 18.14, change to the Gray option (50% red, 50% green, and 50% blue) in the Print Color screen the text shading for the word or phrase you wish to shadow. Make note of the line and cursor position for the first letter of the word being shaded. For example, the S of "Shade" begins on a line 2 1/2 inches from the top of the page and at a position 2 inches from the left page edge. Now follow these steps to create a shadow type:

1. On the next line underneath that line, type the word or phrase again; then move the cursor to the beginning of the word or phrase

2. Press Format (Shift-F8) and select **Other** (**4**) and **Advance** (**1**).

3. Choose **Line** (**3**) and at the `Adv. to line` prompt specify a line .05" higher than the gray text; in this example, type *2.45* (WordPerfect will supply the inch mark) and press Enter.

4. Select **Advance** (**1**) again and now choose **Position** (**6**) to specify a line location .05" farther left than the gray text, or to position 1.95" in this example.

5. Press Exit (F7) to return to the edit screen.

6. Using the previous steps for changing color, change the font back to **Black** (**1**).

What these commands do is tell WordPerfect to lay black text on top of gray text, but slightly offset the black so that the gray appears to be a shadow of the black. If you press Reveal Codes (F11 or Alt-F3), you will see the codes you created for the shadowed text (see fig. 18.15).

Using Inverse Type

With PostScript printers and with the new fonts available on the Hewlett-Packard LaserJet III printer, you can now can print white text on a black background, as in figure 18.16.

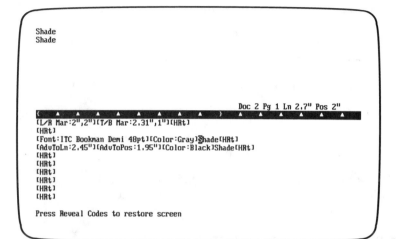

Fig. 18.15.

Codes for shadowed text.

```
Shade
Shade




                                    Doc 2 Pg 1 Ln 2.7" Pos 2"
{   ▲   ▲    ▲    ▲    ▲    ▲    }   ▲    ▲    ▲    ▲    ▲    ▲
[L/R Mar:2",2"][T/B Mar:2.31",1"][HRt]
[HRt]
[Font:ITC Bookman Demi 48pt][Color:Gray]Shade[HRt]
[AdvToLn:2.45"][AdvToPos:1.95"][Color:Black]Shade[HRt]
[HRt]
[HRt]
[HRt]
[HRt]
[HRt]
[HRt]

Press Reveal Codes to restore screen
```

This is white text on a black background.

Fig. 18.16.

White text on a black background.

To do inverse printing, follow these steps.

1. First use the Graphics command (Alt-F9) and select **Figure (1)** and **Options (4)** to create a figure option box.

2. Change the settings in the figure option box to **Gray Shading (9)**, setting it for 100%.

3. Press Exit (F7) to return to the edit window.

4. Create a figure box the size you want for the black background. To make a sample figure box, follow steps 5 through 9.

5. Press Graphics (Alt-F9) and Select **Figure (1)**.

6. Choose **Create (1)**.

7. Choose Size **(7)** and **1** (Set **Width/Auto Height**).

8. Type the width you want the box to appear and press Enter.

9. Choose **Edit** (**9**) to enter the Figure Box Edit screen.

10. Press Font (Ctrl-F8) and choose Print **Color** (**5**).

11. Select **White** (**2**) and press Exit (F7).

12. Type the text you want inside the box.

13. Select Print **Color** (**5**) again and change the text color back to Black (**1**).

14. Press Exit (F7) to return to the edit screen. Either preview or print the page to see how the color looks in the box.

If you want to be even more creative, use different shades for the box itself, or a shade of text color other than pure white, or a combination of each.

Adding Graphics and Text Boxes

Another way to enhance your documents' appeal to readers is to integrate graphics, charts, and text boxes with your text. Boxes can add impact to important quotations, illustrations, charts, and photographs. In Chapters 19 and 20, you will see how graphics and text boxes can increase the dramatic appeal of your publications. But adding a quotation in a shaded box is quite easy to accomplish. Here are the steps:

1. Press Graphics (Alt-F9) and select Text **Box** (**3**).

2. Choose **Create** (**1**).

3. Select the Anchor **Type** (**4**)—**Page** (**2**) if you want text to float around the box, or **Paragraph** (**1**) if you want the box to stay with a particular paragraph.

4. If you choose a **Page** box, set the vertical position (**5**) where you want the box to appear (top, center, bottom, or set position).

5. If you choose a **Page** box, set the horizontal position, generally either **Margins** (**1**) or Set Position (**3**), measured from the left edge of the page.

6. Set the Size (**7**) of the box.

7. Press **Edit** (**9**) to insert text into the box itself.

The advantage of using text boxes is that WordPerfect has already defined a text box as having rules top and bottom, and a shaded background, as in figure 18.17.

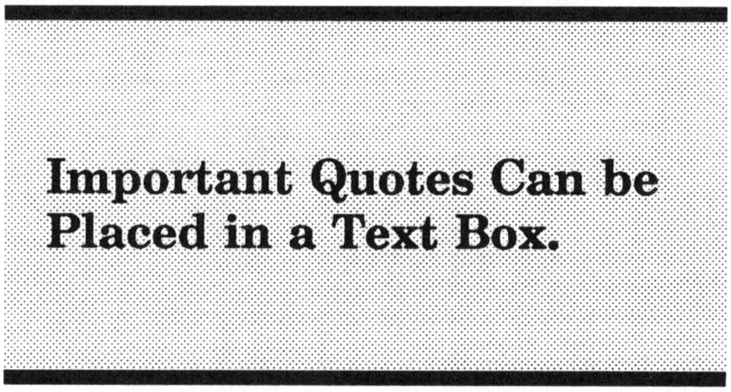

Important Quotes Can be Placed in a Text Box.

Fig. 18.17.

A typical shaded text box created in WordPerfect 5.1.

Figure 18.17, for example, is a text box 3 inches wide by 1 1/2 inches tall, containing 14-point Century Schoolbook bold font. Two **[HRt]**s were used to position the text vertically inside the box.

Adding Borders and Rules

In addition to fonts, font sizes, font shades, and other special effects, graphic rules and borders can add a lot to a document, as you will see in Chapters 19 and 20.

For example, the FULL_BOX.STY file on the Applications Disk includes 10 different ready-to-use document border styles that can be printed on every page of your document. Figure 18.18 shows the styles available in the FULL_BOX.STY file.

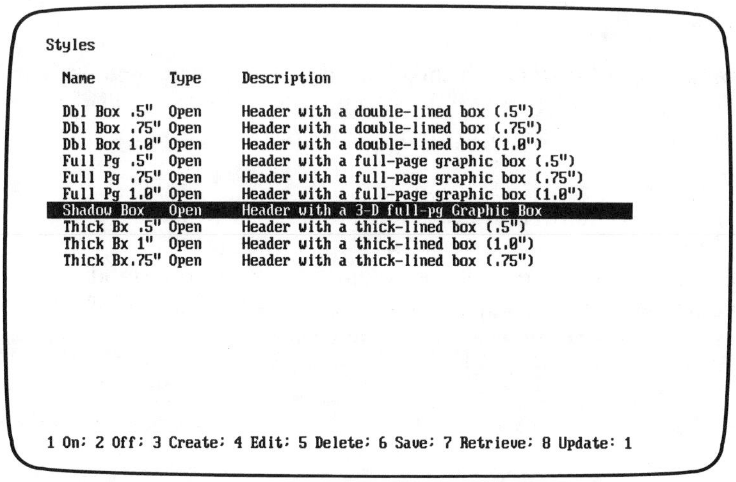

```
Styles

Name            Type    Description

Dbl Box .5"     Open    Header with a double-lined box (.5")
Dbl Box .75"    Open    Header with a double-lined box (.75")
Dbl Box 1.0"    Open    Header with a double-lined box (1.0")
Full Pg .5"     Open    Header with a full-page graphic box (.5")
Full Pg .75"    Open    Header with a full-page graphic box (.75")
Full Pg 1.0"    Open    Header with a full-page graphic box (1.0")
Shadow Box      Open    Header with a 3-D full-pg Graphic Box
Thick Bx .5"    Open    Header with a thick-lined box (.5")
Thick Bx 1"     Open    Header with a thick-lined box (1.0")
Thick Bx.75"    Open    Header with a thick-lined box (.75")




 1 On; 2 Off; 3 Create; 4 Edit; 5 Delete; 6 Save; 7 Retrieve; 8 Update: 1
```

Fig. 18.18.

Ten full-page box styles in the FULL_BOX.STY file.

Figure 18.19 illustrates 4 of the 10 full-page box styles available in the FULL_BOX.STY file.

Fig. 18.19.

*Four box styles
from the
FULL_BOX.STY file.*

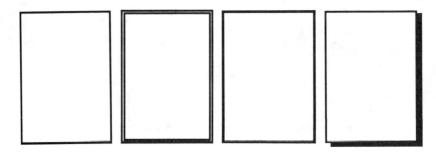

To use any of these styles, simply copy the FULL_BOX.STY file to the subdirectory C:\WP51\STYLES. Then go to the very beginning of your document, in front of all codes, and follow these steps:

1. Press Style (Alt-F8).

2. Choose **Retrieve** (**7**).

3. At the Filename: prompt, type

    C:\WP51\STYLES\FULL_BOX.STY

    or press List Files (F5) and Enter to view the style files inside the style subdirectory. (Note: You must have already copied FULL_BOX.STY from the QSTYLES subdirectory to the C:\WP51\STYLES subdirectory.)

4. Press Enter. The screen shown in figure 18.19 will appear.

5. Highlight with the up- or down-arrow key the style you want, and press **On** (**1**).

A special style code containing a header with the desired graphic image will appear. Since the graphic box is in a header, it will automatically print on all pages of your document. This is how to use a style to improve the looks of your desktop published documents.

Two additional styles contained on the Applications Disk will make it easy to use graphic lines in your documents: GRAPH-LN.STY and PG-NUMBER.STY. The Graphic Lines style offers nine types of horizontal lines—from dotted and dashed lines to shaded and black lines in a variety of sizes. Figure 18.20 illustrates the nine graphic lines available with GRAPH-LN.STY.

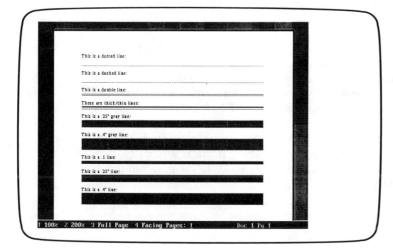

Fig. 18.20.

GRAPH-LN.STY offers nine types of graphic lines.

PG-NUMBERS.STY provides four types of page-numbering methods: bottom page numbers with right and left gray lines, bottom page numbers with right and left black lines, bottom page numbers with a top and bottom horizontal line, and bottom page numbers with a thick and a thin top horizontal line. Figure 18.21 shows four types of page numbers available with PG-NUMBER.STY. All three styles (FULL_BOX.STY, GRAPH-LN.STY, and PG-NUMBER.STY) are included on the Applications Disk inside the back cover of this book.

Style: Page number with R/L shaded bars:

1

1

1

1

Fig. 18.21.

PG-NUMBER.STY provides four types of page numbers.

Summary

In this chapter, you have seen how WordPerfect can use different typefaces, font sizes, font shadings, and font colors to produce the unusual effects found in documents published with desktop publishing programs like PageMaker or Ventura. This chapter has also discussed the different kinds of font cartridges you can purchase, including the Super Cartridges 1 and 2. You have also discovered a variety of fonts available with soft fonts, such as the Bitstream Sontware collections. A major section of the chapter dealt with the unique advantages of PostScript, including shaded text and inverse type. Adding borders and rules is another way to add appeal to pages, features that we will explore in more detail in Chapters 19 and 20.

19

Creating Programs, Pamphlets, and Book Pages

In previous chapters you learned how to prepare a wide variety of documents, such as letters, envelopes, labels, formal reports, telephone lists, office forms, invoices, and legal documents. Now you are ready for a group of documents called publications. In this chapter you explore how to create camera-ready pages for book-style publications: pamphlets, bulletins, manuals, and books. You also learn a few tricks that printers use to create books. The topics covered in this chapter include the following:

- Printing headers

- Adjusting binding widths

- Printing two-sided documents

- Determining portrait- or landscape-mode printing

- Printing fliers and program bulletins

- Using the label feature to create "logical" pages on fliers

When you finish this chapter, you will be able to prepare many different types of fliers, pamphlets, or book-style publications. In the following chapter, you learn about creating magazine-style publications—newsletters and similar documents.

Establishing a Background for Printing

Because this chapter deals with book-style publications, both large and small, take a moment to learn the background of modern printing. You can use this information to create a wide variety of documents with WordPerfect 5.1.

Before the invention of personal computers and desktop printers, printing could be done only at printing establishments that had the necessary hardware for setting type and printing large sheets of paper—17 inches by 22 inches or larger. A sheet of paper was prepared so that when it was folded in half three times and trimmed, the result was a *signature* containing 8 pages (16 sides) of paper (see fig. 19.1) or, if folded four times, a signature containing 16 pages (32 sides) of paper.

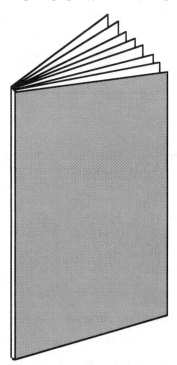

Fig. 19.1.

A sheet of paper folded three times yields an 8-page signature.

If text were printed on both sides of these 8 or 16 pages prior to folding and trimming, you would end up with the standard 16- or 32-page signature used at the larger printing houses.

A printer preparing a small book would print several sets of these 16- or 32-page signatures. In the bindery, a worker would then clamp one copy of each signature together in a set, trim and roughen the folded edges, and apply glue (see fig. 19.2).

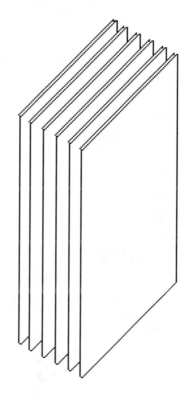

Fig. 19.2.

Six signatures arranged together for a book.

After the pages were glued, the worker then added the cover, which had already been printed with the book title and author's name. This type of binding, shown in figure 19.3, is \called *perfect binding*.

Another type of binding, *case binding*, is more expensive but has proved more durable because it uses stitched signatures rather than glued ones. Figure 19.4 illustrates case binding.

Of course, technology hasn't created a $2,000 printer that handles 17-by-22-inch sheets of paper. But with a LaserJet or similar printer and with programs like WordPerfect 5.1, you can prepare all the text for this type of book and take it elsewhere to be printed. Such pages, prepared on your computer and printed with the correct page numbers and headers, are called *camera-ready pages*. At the print shop, the printer would take your finished pages and photograph them with a special camera, which creates negatives. The negatives are used to make the printer's plates for your book or pamphlet. By using camera-ready pages, you can slash your printing bill by 60 percent or more.

Fig. 19.3.

A perfect-bound book uses glue as the binding medium.

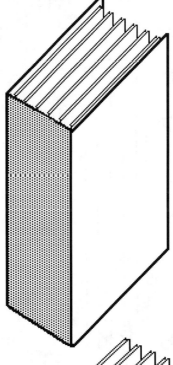

Fig. 19.4.

Case binding uses stitched signatures.

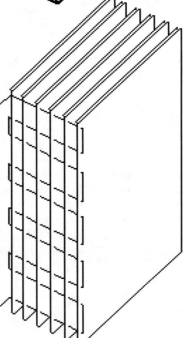

An even better option, if you have only a few publications to print (a *small print run*), is to substitute your own binding. Suppose that you are conducting an in-service training seminar at your company and want to give a syllabus to each of your 25 students. Instead of having 25 or 50 copies printed and bound (an expensive option for a small print run), print the pages yourself and put them in three-ring binders. You can print on both sides of the paper and use the same page numbering and page headers, but omit the printing, folding, and binding expense of a print shop. The pages might look like those in figure 19.5.

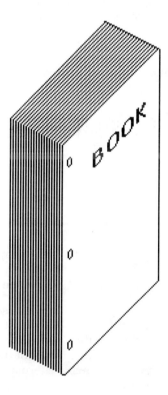

Fig. 19.5.

Inexpensive books created for three-ring binders.

If you print your own material, you want to use the least amount of paper possible, printing on both sides of the paper. This practice creates new signature-printing problems. In an ordinary book or manual printed on both sides of the pages, you print the name of the document and page number on all the left pages; the chapter name and page number go on all the right pages. Also, all left pages are even-numbered, and all right pages are odd-numbered. To observe this type of printing, look at the open 16-page signature in figure 19.6.

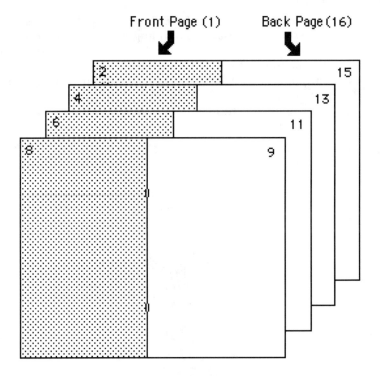

Fig. 19.6.

Numbering scheme for an open 16-page signature.

You can set WordPerfect to create headers for this type of layout automatically—no matter how many changes you make to the copy. If on a regular printer you try to duplicate the book-page layout shown in figure 19.6, you end up with a page sequence like the one in figure 19.7.

Headers not only provide page numbers for your documents but also can be used to include the document name and the date the document was created. Some headers include a horizontal graphic line at the bottom of the header (or, for a footer, at the top). Shortly, you'll see how to make alternative headers for book-style publications.

If you are preparing camera-ready copy for a printer, you may want the name of the book or manual (and page number) on every even-numbered page and the name of the section or chapter (and page number) on every odd-numbered page. For even pages, the page number needs to be on the far left of the header; for odd pages, the page number should be on the far right, as shown here:

2—Title of Book   (even pages)

                                           (odd pages)   Chapter Name—3

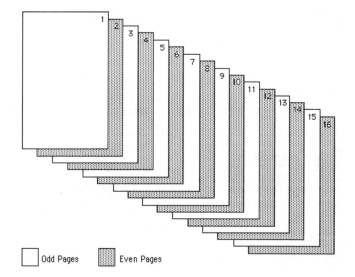

Fig. 19.7.

Odd-even page layout for a 16-page signature.

If you plan to print these pages yourself for a three-ring syllabus binder—with copy on both sides of the paper—the paging problem becomes more complicated. Later in this chapter, you learn a neat shortcut for adjusting headings for pages to be copied on both sides. (The shortcut is so fantastic that you will wonder why businesses and schools haven't been using it for years.)

Alternating Page Headers

For some projects, you need to print two different types of page headings—one for every even-numbered page and another for every odd-numbered page. And the pages between the two need to be interactive so that each page reflects what number precedes it and what number follows it.

WordPerfect 5.1 lets you identify two different headers (and two footers, if you want). Figure 19.8 shows how these will be identified in the program.

Notice that in figure 19.8 the even-numbered page has Header A flush left, but the odd-numbered page has Header B flush right. This placement of headers is another formatting detail that WordPerfect automatically performs if you tell it to do so.

Note: These methods for creating and printing alternating headers apply to any multipage document printed on both sides—reports, papers, manuals, even a syllabus for a class. These methods also apply for publications that are punched and bound with a plastic spiral.

Fig. 19.8.

WordPerfect lets you have different headers on your pages.

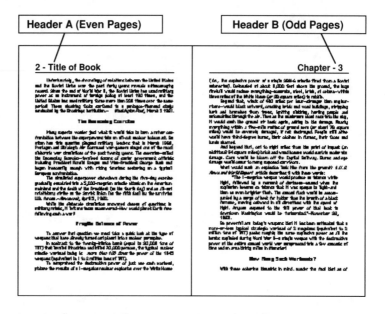

With this background, you are ready to create alternating page headers automatically. If you have a document on-screen that doesn't have headers or page numbers, you need to move to the document's beginning (using Home, Home, Home, up arrow) before inserting the commands. Here are the steps for creating Header A (page number and book title flush left):

1. Press Format (Shift-F8) and choose **Page** (**2**).

   ⌨Choose **Page** from the **Layout** menu.

2. Choose **Headers** (**3**).

3. Choose Header **A** (**1**).

4. Choose Even Pages (**4**) as illustrated in figure 19.9.

   Next, you see a header window where you type the text for your header. The following prompt appears at the bottom of the new window:

   ```
   Header A: Press Exit when done
   ```

5. At the top left edge of the window, hold down Ctrl and press B to insert a ^B code—an automatic page-numbering code.

6. Type *--title* (using the name of your publication). Or, as an alternative, use Compose (Ctrl-V) and substitute character 4,34 in place of the double hyphens (--), followed by the title of your publication.

7. Press Exit (F7) to return to the Format: Page screen.

```
Format: Page

      1 - Center Page (top to bottom)    No

      2 - Force Odd/Even Page

      3 - Headers

      4 - Footers

      5 - Margins - Top                  1"
                    Bottom               1"

      6 - Page Numbering

      7 - Paper Size                     8.5" x 11"
                    Type                 Standard

      8 - Suppress (this page only)




 1 Discontinue; 2 Every Page; 3 Odd Pages; 4 Even Pages; 5 Edit: 0
```

Fig. 19.9.

Screen for selecting odd or even pages.

Note: The page number precedes the title in Header A but follows the title in Header B.

Follow these steps to create Header B (chapter title and page number flush right):

1. Choose **Headers** (**3**).

2. Choose Header **B** (**2**).

3. Choose **Odd Pages** (**3**).

   The following prompt appears at the bottom of the new header window:

   Header B: Press Exit when done

4. At the top left edge of the window, press Flush Right (Alt-F6).

5. Type *chapter title--* (using the chapter name). Or use Compose (Ctrl-V) and substitute character 4,34 in place of the double hyphens (--).

6. Hold down Ctrl and press B to insert a ^B code page-numbering code at the right end of the line.

7. Press Exit (F7) twice to return to the edit screen.

If you press Reveal Codes (Alt-F3 or F11), you should see codes for **[Header A:Even pages]** and **[Header B:Odd pages]** at the beginning of the document. (These codes look like the first codes in the lower half of fig. 19.10.) When you print a document containing these codes, all even-numbered pages have a header with the page number and book title, and all odd-numbered pages have a header with the chapter (or section) title and a page number.

Fig. 19.10.

WordPerfect codes for Header A and Header B.

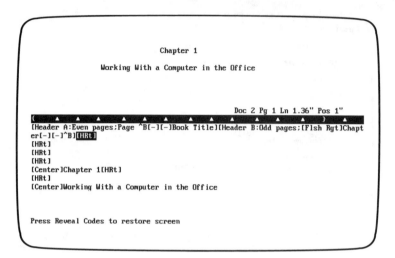

Printing Offset Pages

If you want to print pages for a three-ring notebook, you need to use WordPerfect's Binding feature to provide room for the hole punches. (The same is true if your book pages will be stitched together, as shown in fig. 19.4, or bound with a plastic spiral.) Setting a binding width shifts all odd-numbered pages to the right on the paper and all even-numbered pages to the left on the page. For example, in figure 19.11, room has to be left on all pages for three-ring notebook holes. So the even pages (left side) must have text shifted slightly to the left, and the odd pages (right side) must have text shifted slightly to the right.

Fig. 19.11.

Extra space is needed for three-ring notebook pages.

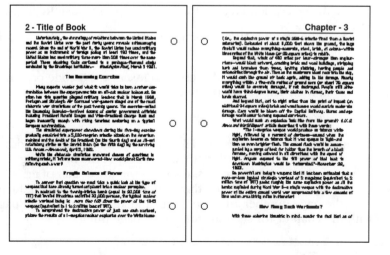

How much space you set for binding depends on how much room you need for binding space or hole punches. In figure 19.12, for example, the inside shaded area represents the binding-width setting. If, for example, you set text margins at the top of your document for 1-inch left and 1-inch right margins, and you print the document after specifying a .25-inch binding, WordPerfect subtracts .25 inch from all outside margins and adds .25 inch to all inside margins.

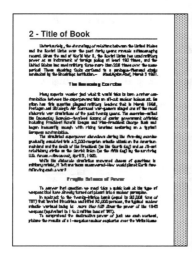 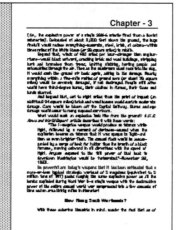

Fig. 19.12.

Text area is shifted left and right to allow for binding.

In this case, your outside text margins will be .75 inch (1 inch minus .25 inch), and your inside text margins will be 1.25 inch (1 inch plus .25 inch). This arrangement should be nearly ideal for notebook-type paper containing three-ring holes.

To set a binding width for printing a document, complete these steps:

1. Press Print (Shift-F7) and select **B**inding Offset (**B**).

    Choose **Print** from the **File** menu and select **B**inding Offset.

2. Type a binding-width decimal value or type a fraction (for instance, *1/4*).

3. Press Enter.

4. Press **Full Document** (**1**) or **Page** (**2**).

Keep in mind that the binding-width setting is like the number-of-copies setting— the setting stays with the document only until you change the setting or exit the document. WordPerfect does not insert a binding-width code in your document. If you want to use this feature with the same document a week later, you need to enter the settings again.

Also, in WordPerfect 5.1 maintenance releases dated 6/19/90 or later, renumbered pages are printed with the binding width set according to their *new* page number, rather than to which page they follow. For example, if you renumber page 11 as page 12, the binding edge will print as an even-numbered page (even though page 12 actually follows page 10 and was previously an odd page).

Printing Odd and Even Pages

The 3/30/90 and later updates of WordPerfect 5.1 include the capability to print either odd or even pages. This option makes printing on both sides of the paper easy. For example, you can print all odd pages first, reinsert the pages in your paper tray, and print all the even pages. You must adjust the pages in the tray for the second printing so that page 1 is the top sheet stacked face down (for most printers) and that the last page is the bottom sheet.

If you do not have the 3/30/90 (or later) edition of WordPerfect, or if you want to print the front and back of many pages at the same time, consider using the following trick to accomplish your goal.

Suppose that you are a seminar teacher for a class of 20 students or employees and that you want to print a 10-page summary of class notes to distribute to each student at the end of this week's classes. To save paper, you decide to print on both sides of the pages.

If your printer paper tray holds only about 100 pages at a time, that plan should work just fine for this project. To illustrate:

```
20 students . . . . . . . . . . . . . . . . . . . . . . . 20
Times 10 pages per lesson . . . . . . . . . . . x 10
Subtotal . . . . . . . . . . . . . . . . . . . . . . . . 200
Divided by 2 (because you are using
both sides of the paper). . . . . . . . . . . . . . 2
Equals . . . . . . . . . . . . . . . . . . . . . . . . . .100
```

Fill the paper tray and complete the following steps. Be sure that you have included some kind of headers (or footers) with page numbers as explained earlier in this chapter.

1. Press Print (Shift-F7) and select Multiple Copies Generated by (**U**).

   Choose **Printer (2)** to print pages uncollated.

2. Choose **Printer (2)** to print pages uncollated.

3. Choose **N**, type *10*, press Enter, and choose **Full Document (1)**.

4. Restack the printed pages (the first side) as shown in figure 19.13.

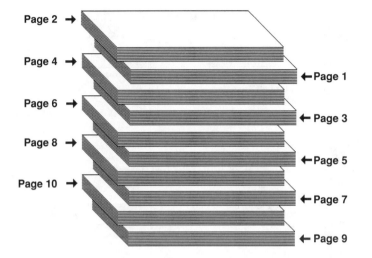

Page 2 →
Page 4 →
Page 6 →
Page 8 →
Page 10 →

← Page 1
← Page 3
← Page 5
← Page 7
← Page 9

Fig. 19.13.

Secret for printing on both sides of the paper.

5. Put the paper back in (top edge of page first), but with the printed side facing down in the tray.

6. Print 10 more copies of the document.

That's all there is to it! You will now have 20 sets of your document—exactly enough for each employee or student in your seminar. This tip really does work! However, be sure to use the right quality of paper so that the ink from one side does not seep through or show on the reverse side.

Multipage Documents on Single Sheets of Paper

So far in this chapter, you have seen how to print multipage documents on both sides of many different sheets of paper (that is, one sheet per page). But what if you want to create a small flier or bulletin for the office that uses only a single sheet of paper folded in half or into thirds? No problem: WordPerfect can handle that with a breeze. And it can even provide the proper page numbers for each page on your folded sheet!

First think about how most pages are printed in the office today. The paper goes into the printer short-end first, and text is printed on the sheets in *portrait mode*. The word *portrait* indicates that the text on the printed sheet is oriented like ordinary portrait paintings: with a shorter width than length. The sides are long, and the top and bottom relatively short. Figure 19.14 shows the standard (or default) settings for a WordPerfect document printed in portrait mode.

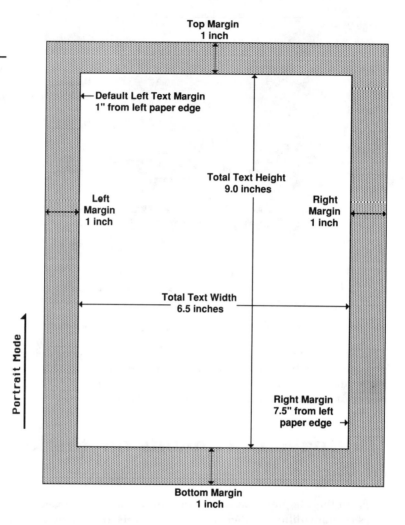

Fig. 19.14.

Default margins and text area for portrait printing.

But if you want to prepare a flier for a handout or bulletin for a special program, you should print in *landscape mode*, or lengthwise on the paper, as illustrated in figure 19.15. The term *landscape*, of course, refers to a landscape painting, which generally is wider than it is tall (to fit in the width of landscape a painter would want to capture).

To select landscape page format, do the following:

1. Press Format (Shift-F8) and choose **Page** (**2**).

   ⌨Choose **Page** from the Layout menu.

2. Choose **Paper Size** (**7**).

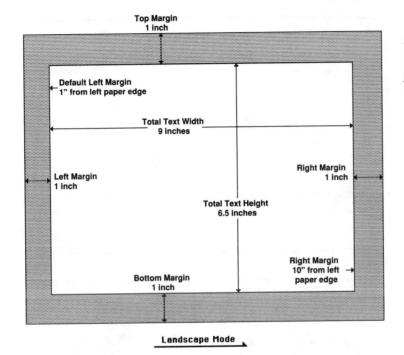

Fig. 19.15.

Text area for sheets printed in landscape mode.

The Format: Paper Size/Type menu appears, as shown in figure 19.16.

3. Using the arrow keys, highlight either of these choices:

    Standard - Wide   11" x 8.5"

    Legal - Wide   14" x 8.5"

4. Press Select (**1**).

5. Press Exit (F7) to return to the edit window.

Printing Pages Two-Up

Using this type of paper form, if you select .75 inch (or even .5 inch) for top, bottom, right, and left margins, and if you create a columns definition containing two columns per page, you should be able to fit two pages of text on the page, as shown in figure 19.17. Note the fold line indicated in the middle of the page.

Of course, what makes these "pages" of text are the individual columns of a page that contain two columns of text. Thus the left column becomes the left page and the right column becomes the right page. If you print on both sides of such a sheet of paper and fold it in half, you create a simple program bulletin, as in figure 19.18.

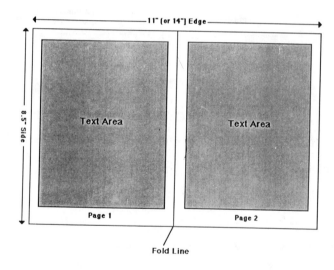

Fig. 19.16.

Selecting landscape paper from the Format: Paper Size/Type menu.

```
Format: Paper Size/Type

                                                                Font  Double
Paper type and Orientation    Paper Size   Prompt Loc     Type  Sided Labels

2-up (Narrow Binding) - Wide  11" x 8.5"   No     Contin  Land  No    2 x 1
2-up Landscape - Wide         11" x 8.5"   No     Contin  Land  No    2 x 1
2-up West - Wide              11" x 8.5"   No     Contin  Land  No    2 x 1
Envelope - Wide               9.5" x 4"    No     Manual  Land  No
Labels                        8.5" x 11"   No     Contin  Port  No
Legal                         8.5" x 14"   No     Contin  Port  No
Legal - Dup Long              8.5" x 14"   No     Contin  Port  Yes
Legal - Dup Long - Wide       14" x 8.5"   No     Contin  Land  Yes
Legal - Dup Short             8.5" x 14"   No     Contin  Port  Yes
Legal - Dup Short - Wide      14" x 8.5"   No     Contin  Land  Yes
Legal - Wide                  14" x 8.5"   No     Contin  Land  No
Standard                      8.5" x 11"   No     Contin  Port  No
Standard - Dup Long           8.5" x 11"   No     Contin  Port  Yes
Standard - Dup Long - Wide    11" x 8.5"   No     Contin  Land  Yes
Standard - Dup Short          8.5" x 11"   No     Contin  Port  Yes
Standard - Dup Short - Wide   11" x 8.5"   No     Contin  Land  Yes
Standard - Wide               11" x 8.5"   No     Contin  Land  No
Video Labels                  6.31" x 11.25" No   Contin  Port  No    2 x 5
[ALL OTHERS]                  Width ≤ 8.5" Yes    Manual        No

1 Select; 2 Add; 3 Copy; 4 Delete; 5 Edit; N Name Search: 1
```

Fig. 19.17.

Two "pages" of text on one sheet of paper.

Note: Look at the page numbers in figure 19.18. If you print on both sides of a landscape sheet of paper and fold the paper in half, the left outside page becomes the cover (like a church bulletin), the two inside pages become pages 1 and 2, and the right outside page becomes either page 3 or the back cover.

Printing Pages Three-Up

If you wanted a dual-fold bulletin or flier, you could select three columns in landscape mode and create a sheet that can be folded twice, into thirds, as in figure 19.19.

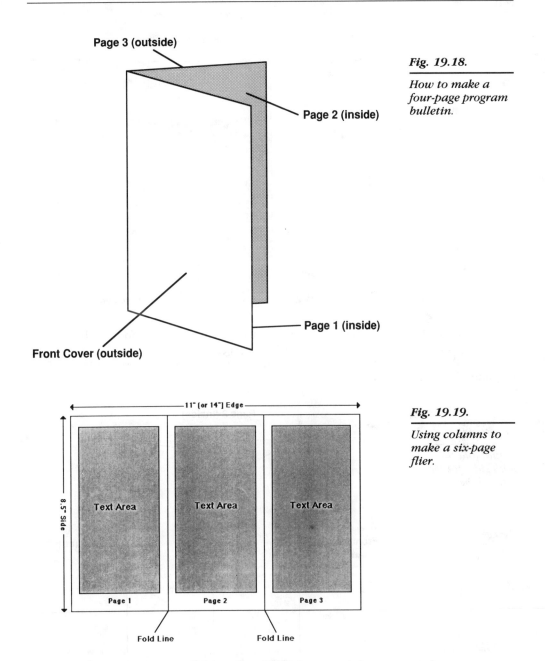

Page 3 (outside)

Page 2 (inside)

Page 1 (inside)

Front Cover (outside)

Fig. 19.18.

How to make a four-page program bulletin.

Fig. 19.19.

Using columns to make a six-page flier.

11" (or 14") Edge

8.5" Side

Text Area

Text Area

Text Area

Page 1   Page 2   Page 3

Fold Line   Fold Line

To visualize the page layout in a dual-fold flier, look at figure 19.20. Again the front cover is on the outside at the left, pages 1, 2, and 3 are inside the flier, and pages 4 and 5 are on the reverse side.

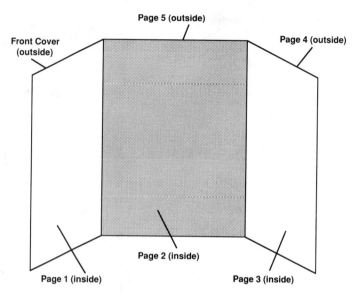

Fig. 19.20.

The page make-up of a six-page flier.

One advantage to making a six-page flier—especially if you print on 8 1/2-by-14-inch legal-size paper—is the various ways a six-page flier can be folded. For example, if the left and right sides both fold toward the center, then you have a flier or pamphlet that looks like figure 19.21.

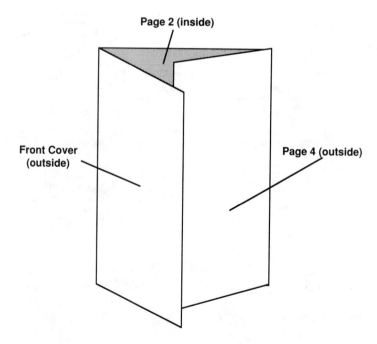

Fig. 19.21.

A dual-fold flier with sides folded toward the center.

Alternatively, you could fold the right-hand page backward rather than forward and create a much different flier without changing the arrangement of text whatsoever, as in figure 19.22.

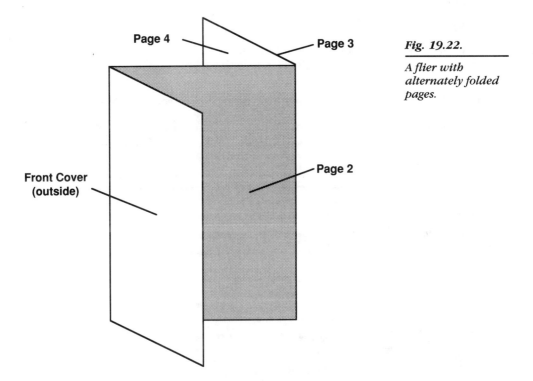

Page 4 — Page 3

Front Cover (outside) — Page 2

Fig. 19.22.

A flier with alternately folded pages.

Dealing with Page Numbers

Figures 19.17 through 19.22 all have one common problem that has been a problem of every version of WordPerfect since 1983—when you create bulletins and fliers by using newspaper columns on landscape-style paper, there is no good way to add the correct page number to each page. The reason is that each "page" is nothing more than a column of text, and WordPerfect will not paginate columns of text.

But in version 5.1, you can use another feature to get around that problem. You can create a label definition that puts two or three labels on each page, rather than two or three columns of text on each page. And labels created in WordPerfect are considered logical pages. That is, each label can be numbered anywhere on the label—top, bottom, right lower corner, left lower corner, and so on.

So rather than using columns for your fliers and bulletins, use the label format. And use page numbers for each page, just as they appear in figures 19.17 through 19.22. Start with a clear screen and follow these steps to create a landscape label definition:

1. Press Format (Shift-F8) and choose **Page** (2).

    ⌨Choose **Page** from the Layout menu.

2. Select Paper Size (7).

3. Choose Add (2) from the Paper Size/Type Screen (see fig. 19.16).

4. Press Other (9) from the Format: Paper Type menu. At the `Other form type:` prompt, type *2-up Landscape* and press Enter. The Format: Edit Paper Definition menu appears, as in figure 19.23.

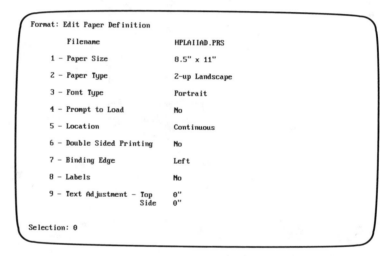

Fig. 19.23.

The Format: Edit Paper Definition.

```
Format: Edit Paper Definition

         Filename               HPLAIIAD.PRS

    1 - Paper Size              8.5" x 11"

    2 - Paper Type              2-up Landscape

    3 - Font Type               Portrait

    4 - Prompt to Load          No

    5 - Location                Continuous

    6 - Double Sided Printing   No

    7 - Binding Edge            Left

    8 - Labels                  No

    9 - Text Adjustment - Top   0"
                        Side    0"

Selection: 0
```

5. Choose Paper Size (1). You will now see the Format: Paper Size menu, as shown in figure 19.24.

6. Choose Standard Landscape (2). The Format: Edit Paper Definition menu reappears.

7. Choose Font Type (3). Select Landscape (2) from this menu:

    Orientation: 1 Portrait; **2** Landscape: **0**

8. Choose Labels (8) and press Y for **Yes**.

9. Next appears the Format: Labels menu, as in figure 19.25. The settings you see here depend on the printer selected.

```
Format: Paper Size              Width  Height

     1 - Standard               (8.5" x 11")

     2 - Standard Landscape     (11" x 8.5")

     3 - Legal                  (8.5" x 14")

     4 - Legal Landscape        (14" x 8.5")

     5 - Envelope               (9.5" x 4")

     6 - Half Sheet             (5.5" x 8.5")

     7 - US Government          (8" x 11")

     8 - A4                     (210mm x 297mm)

     9 - A4 Landscape           (297mm x 210mm)

     o - Other


Selection: 0
```

Fig. 19.24.

*The Format:
Paper Size menu.*

```
Format: Labels

     1 - Label Size
                    Width       11"
                    Height      8.5"

     2 - Number of Labels
                    Columns     1
                    Rows        1

     3 - Top Left Corner
                    Top         0"
                    Left        0"

     4 - Distance Between Labels
                    Column      0"
                    Row         0"

     5 - Label Margins
                    Left        0.25"
                    Right       0.22"
                    Top         0.31"
                    Bottom      0.23"

Selection: 0
```

Fig. 19.25.

*The Format:
Labels menu.*

10. Select Label Size (**1**). Type *5.5* (for `Width`) and press Enter; type *8.5* (for `Height`) and press Enter.

11. Select **Number of Labels** (**2**). Type *2* (for `Columns`) and press Enter; type *1* (for `Rows`) and press Enter.

12. Make certain that Top Left Corner (**3**) and Distance Between Labels (**4**) are set for 0" for all settings.

13. Select **Label Margins** (**5**). Type *.6* and press Enter for all four settings. (Or use slightly wider or narrower margins, as desired.)

14. Press Exit (F7). The Format: Edit Paper Definition menu reappears.

Figure 19.26 shows the settings for the Format: Labels window (as explained in steps 10 through 13). These provide even margins of .6 inch on all four sides of each logical page of the paper (that is, for the left and right halves of the sheet of paper).

Fig. 19.26.

Settings for the Format: Labels screen.

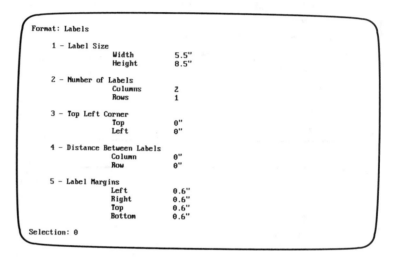

```
Format: Labels

    1 - Label Size
                    Width          5.5"
                    Height         8.5"

    2 - Number of Labels
                    Columns        2
                    Rows           1

    3 - Top Left Corner
                    Top            0"
                    Left           0"

    4 - Distance Between Labels
                    Column         0"
                    Row            0"

    5 - Label Margins
                    Left           0.6"
                    Right          0.6"
                    Top            0.6"
                    Bottom         0.6"

Selection: 0
```

Unfortunately, one disadvantage of the settings in figure 19.26 is that if you are creating a church bulletin type of publication, the left margin for page 2 and the right margin for page 3 are each .6 inch, which is proper. But the two center margins for page 2 and 3 (.6 inch each) add up to a combined center space of 1.2 inches for the physical sheet of paper. And to many users, this large center gap between the two sections of text (the left side and right side of the sheet) looks incorrect.

If you want a narrower gap between the two sections of text on each sheet of paper, figure 19.27 shows corrected settings, which yield outside left and right margins of .6 inch, but inside left and right margins of .4 (or a combined center margin gap of .8 inch). If you prefer a more balanced appearance of your text on the sheet, use the settings in figure 19.27. If you want a wider center area between your two sides, use the settings in figure 19.26.

If the paper you plan to use in your printer is not continuous, or if you want a prompt for paper loading, change the appropriate menu selections for those two items.

```
Format: Labels

    1 - Label Size
                  Width          5.1"
                  Height         8.5"

    2 - Number of Labels
                  Columns        2
                  Rows           1

    3 - Top Left Corner
                  Top            0"
                  Left           0"

    4 - Distance Between Labels
                  Column         0.2"
                  Row            0"

    5 - Label Margins
                  Left           0.6"
                  Right          0"
                  Top            0.6"
                  Bottom         0.6"

Selection: 0
```

Fig. 19.27.

*Adjusted settings
for the Format:
Labels screen.*

To use the 2-up page definition, follow these steps:

1. Position the cursor at the beginning of your document or at the top of the page where you want to start using the logical pages. Or, if you prefer, specify this code in the Document Initial Codes screen: Shift-F8, **3**, **2**.

2. Press Format (Shift-F8) and select **Page** (**2**).

3. Select Paper Size (**7**). The Format: Paper Size/Type menu appears (see fig. 19.28).

4. **Highlight the** 2-up Landscape **paper form and press Select** (**1**) to return to the editing screen (see fig. 19.28).

5. If you want to add page numbers, press Format (Shift-F8) and select **Page** (**2**).

6. Select Page **Numbering** (**6**).

7. Select from the various settings in the Format: Page Number Position screen (see fig. 19.29).

8. Press Exit (F7) to return to the regular edit screen. You are now ready to print numbers on your logical pages (the left and right sides of each sheet of paper).

Fig. 19.28.

Selecting the 2-up landscape form.

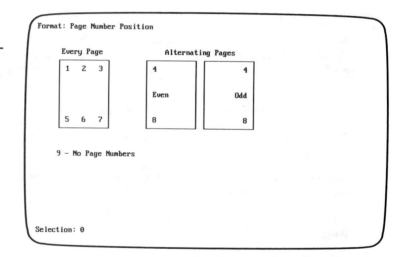

```
Format: Paper Size/Type

                                                                    Font   Double
Paper type and Orientation          Paper Size    Prompt Loc        Type   Sided  Labels

(1 x 2 5/8) inch labels             8.5" x 11"    No     Contin     Port   No     3 x 10
(2 x 4) inch labels                 8.5" x 11"    No     Contin     Port   No     2 x 5
2-up (Narrow Binding) - Wide        11" x 8.5"    No     Contin     Land   No     2 x 1
2-up Landscape - Wide               11" x 8.5"    No     Contin     Land   No     2 x 1
Envelope - Wide                     9.5" x 4"     No     Manual     Land   No
Labels                              8.5" x 11"    No     Contin     Port   No
Legal                               8.5" x 14"    No     Contin     Port   No
Legal - Dup Long                    8.5" x 14"    No     Contin     Port   Yes
Legal - Dup Long - Wide             14" x 8.5"    No     Contin     Land   Yes
Legal - Dup Short                   8.5" x 14"    No     Contin     Port   Yes
Legal - Dup Short - Wide            14" x 8.5"    No     Contin     Land   Yes
Legal - Wide                        14" x 8.5"    No     Contin     Land   No
Standard                            8.5" x 11"    No     Contin     Port   No
Standard - Dup Long                 8.5" x 11"    No     Contin     Port   Yes
Standard - Dup Long - Wide          11" x 8.5"    No     Contin     Land   Yes
Standard - Dup Short                8.5" x 11"    No     Contin     Port   Yes
Standard - Dup Short - Wide         11" x 8.5"    No     Contin     Land   Yes
Standard - Wide                     11" x 8.5"    No     Contin     Land   No
[ALL OTHERS]                        Width ≤ 8.5"  Yes    Manual            No

1 Select; 2 Add; 3 Copy; 4 Delete; 5 Edit; N Name Search: 1
```

Fig. 19.29.

Possible page number positions.

```
Format: Page Number Position


     Every Page                   Alternating Pages

    ┌──────────────┐       ┌──────────────┐  ┌──────────────┐
    │ 1   2    3   │       │ 4            │  │            4 │
    │              │       │              │  │              │
    │              │       │ Even         │  │ Odd          │
    │              │       │              │  │              │
    │ 5   6    7   │       │ 8            │  │            8 │
    └──────────────┘       └──────────────┘  └──────────────┘


     9 - No Page Numbers






Selection: 0
```

Summary

This chapter has focused specifically on how to create camera-ready pages for book-style publications—pamphlets, bulletins, manuals, and books. You have discovered how printed pages are folded to create book signatures and how signatures are combined to create books—both perfect-bound books (bound with glue) and case-bound books (bound with stitching). You have also learned how to create inexpensive books by printing the pages on prepunched paper and inserting them into three-ring binders.

Because books are generally printed with copy on both sides of the paper, you have learned how to create alternating page headers for right and left pages. Also, this chapter has explained how to print text offset on the paper so that there is room for binding or for prepunched paper. If you have WordPerfect version 3/30/90 or later, you learned how to print odd pages first and then even pages. For those whose copy predates the 3/30/90 version, this chapter also offered an alternative method of printing both sides of the paper.

The final section in this chapter illustrated how single sheets of paper in landscape mode can be folded to create 4- and 6-page bulletins and fliers. It also provided details on how to use the "logical pages" of WordPerfect 5.1 labels to create multipage documents on single sheets of paper, with page numbers on each folded "page" of the sheet.

20

Creating Newsletters and Magazine-Style Reports

What would an organization be without a newsletter? Businesses and groups of all kinds produce newsletters—companies, departments within companies, headquarters of large organizations, churches, schools, academies, clubs, societies, associations, leagues, fraternities, lodges, industries, granges, and syndicates. Newsletters promote unity, convey information, and announce upcoming events. An estimated 200,000 newsletters are produced regularly every year in the United States alone, and the total grows annually.

In this chapter, you learn how to convert a plain document into an attractive newsletter in 12 easy steps. Then you examine a few existing WordPerfect 5.1 newsletters to see what you can do daily with WordPerfect 5.1, using a laser printer such as a Hewlett-Packard DeskJet, a Hewlett-Packard LaserJet, or a PostScript printer with a Linotronic printer. Finally, you see six different ways to make the front page of a newspaper article attractive.

Creating a Newsletter in 12 Easy Steps

Suppose that you have a WordPerfect 4.2 document and that it is ready to be converted into WordPerfect 5.1 for your company's newsletter. You have access to a laser printer—a Hewlett-Packard LaserJet, a LaserJet-compatible printer, or a PostScript printer.

A draft printout of your WordPerfect 4.2 document has Courier pica type (10 characters per inch, or cpi), with underlining for emphasis and italic (see fig. 20.1). For the moment, let's avoid a newsletter logo or title and concentrate on article beginnings and format.

Fig. 20.1.

Original copy with Courier pica (10 cpi) type.

What Is Desktop Publishing?

Today we live in an era of mass-produced information. In fact, we're so productive that the volume of information we produce doubles every four and a half years. In 1923 Willard Kiplinger published the nation's first newsletter: The Kiplinger Washington Letter. Now approximately 200,000 newsletters are published regularly--a total that grows by 30 percent every year.

No wonder desktop publishing is so popular. With a personal computer (PC), a word processing program like WordPerfect 5.1, and a laser printer, almost anyone can produce reports, proposals, presentation overheads, letterheads, memos, office forms, programs, promotional literature, brochures, manuals, catalogs, and newsletters at a fraction of the cost of having a print shop set copy, do page layout, and strip in illustrations and page numbers.

In other words, for less than $5,000 a typical office worker in a couple of hours can produce publications that 10 years ago required $200,000 worth of printing equipment and took days to accomplish.

How Is Desktop Publishing Different?

So what sets desktop publishing apart from regular word processing? Several things, actually. Most people think of word processing as something you do to produce business correspondence--straight text in one font (usually Courier) in one size running from the left margin to the right margin. For emphasis, you underline something or type it in uppercase letters.

Desktop publishing, on the other hand, tastefully mixes together a variety of fonts and font sizes (including italic and bold) together within multiple columns on the page. The pages themselves contain large-font headlines, graphic images, charts, tables of information, quotations set in shaded boxes, as well as vertical and horizontal bars and lines (called "rules").

Graphic images can be locked to a particular spot on the page with text flowing around them, like water around a rock in a stream, or they can be attached to a specific paragraph and "float" up and down the page with the text as it is edited.

And text is almost always printed "full-justified," meaning that it is aligned vertically along the right margin as well as along the left margin.

One other nice feature--with desktop publishing, you have full control over the production schedule. No longer are you a slave to an outside printer who may take days or weeks to do what you can do in an afternoon. As a result, you can use the most up-to-date information for your project.

Step 1: Adding Proportional Spacing

The first step in improving the appearance of this document is to select a font for proportional spacing. Compared to monospaced fonts, which provide the same amount of space for each character on a line no matter how narrow or wide the character is, proportionally spaced fonts allot each letter only the space it needs on the line. As a result, proportionally spaced text is easier to read and more attractive.

To select a font for proportional spacing, you must first decide what typeface to use. Undoubtedly, the most popular typeface for proportional spacing is Times **Roman**, which is included with many printers. Times Roman, however, was created in the 19th century to fit a lot of copy into a small space to save printing costs. Because Times Roman crams information into each line, the text is more difficult to read than text set in other proportional fonts. For body copy, a better choice is a typeface such as Century Schoolbook or Palatino.

You must also select the type's size, a choice that depends on your objectives. If you have a lot of information that you want to fit in limited space, you should select a relatively small size, such as 10 point. If you want to make your newsletter easy to read and pleasing to the eye, however, 11- or 12-point type is better for this project. If you are using Bitstream fonts, you can create fonts in virtually any size you like, including fractions down to 1/10th of a point.

To select a typeface and type size for proportional spacing in your document, follow these steps:

1. Press Home, Home, Home, up arrow to go to the very top of your document.

2. Press Font (Ctrl-F8) and choose Base Font (4).

    ⌨Choose the Font pull-down menu and select Base Font.

    You soon see a list of fonts available for your printer. Highlight for your body text the font you want to use, such as Century Schoolbook, and press Select (**1**) or Enter.

3. If you have a PostScript or LaserJet III printer, WordPerfect asks you for the size. At the Point size: prompt, type the size you want and press Enter.

4. Press Exit (F7) to return to your document.

If you want to use a different font for all your footnotes, endnotes, and figure captions, select that font (such as italic) as your Document Initial Base Font. The following are the steps for selecting a Document Initial Base Font:

1. Press Format (Shift-F8) and choose Document (3).

    ⌨Choose the Layout pull-down menu and select Document.

2. Choose Initial Base Font (3).

3. Highlight the font you want to use for footnotes, endnotes, and figure captions.

4. Press Select or Enter.

5. Press Exit (F7) to return to your document.

For example, if you select Helvetica italic 11-point as your Initial Base Font (in your document preface), and at the beginning of the body copy you select Century Schoolbook 12-point Roman, the main body copy prints in Century Schoolbook 12-point Roman. Any footnotes and figure captions print as Helvetica italic 11 point. Using two different fonts in this way is a simple method for setting footnotes and headers in a font different from the body copy's.

If you want to include headers, footers, and page numbers in the same Initial Base Font (Helvetica 11-point italic), make sure that those codes are the first codes at the top of your document—before the Century Schoolbook font code. Otherwise, if Century Schoolbook (in this example) is the very first code at the beginning of your document, headers, footers, and page numbers will print in Century Schoolbook.

Step 2: Increasing the Size of Headlines

To make a headline larger, you have two options: (1) you can use WordPerfect's automatic fonts, discussed in Chapters 2 and 4; or (2) you can select a base font specifically for the headline. Note that if you use the second method, you will need to select another base font for the text that follows the headline.

To use an automatic font to increase the size of a headline, complete the following steps:

1. Move the cursor to the first character of the headline.

2. Turn on Block (F12 or Alt-F4) and press the End key to highlight the line.

   If the headline occupies more than one line, move the cursor until the entire headline is highlighted.

3. Press Font (Ctrl-F8) and select Size (1).

   In addition to Superscript and Subscript, you see a selection of five sizes: Fine, Small, Large, Very Large, and Extra Large. Each size is relative to the current size of your base font. When you first start WordPerfect, Fine is set to be 60% of the size of your base font. Small is set to 80%, Large to 120%, Very Large to 150%, and Extra Large to 200%. Thus, if your base font is 12 point, Fine is about 7 point; Small, 10 point; Large, 14 point; Very Large, 18 point; and Extra Large, 24 point. If these point sizes are not available on your system, WordPerfect uses the closest size it can find.

4. Select Vry Large (6). You don't have to press Enter, for WordPerfect returns you to the document screen.

The advantage to using these automatic font sizes is that if you change your mind about your body text and want to use a different size or typeface, WordPerfect automatically adjusts the size of your headlines when you change your base font.

To increase the size of a headline by changing the base font, follow these steps:

1. Move the cursor to the first character of the headline.

2. If your headline is underlined and you want to remove the underlining, use Reveal Codes (F11 or Alt-F3), move the cursor to the [UND] code, and delete it. The **[und]** code will be deleted as well. Press F11 or Alt-F3 to turn off Reveal Codes.

3. Press Font (Ctrl-F8) and select Base Font (**4**).

    ▢⊟Choose Base Font from the **F**ont menu.

    You soon see a list of fonts available for your printer.

4. Highlight the font you want to use for your headline, such as Century Schoolbook 18-point Bold, and press **S**elect (**1**) or Enter.

5. If you have a PostScript or LaserJet III printer, WordPerfect asks you for the size. At the `Point size:` prompt, type the size you want and press Enter.

The advantage to using this method is that if your printer has the capability of scaling font sizes, you can specify the size of a headline with precision. Remember that if you use this second method, you need to change the base font for the text that follows the headline.

Step 3: Replacing Underlining with Italic

In the illustration for this chapter, your WordPerfect 4.2 document contains underlining. In most cases, underlining in a document is how users emphasize information when they cannot use an italic font. With WordPerfect 5.1 and a printer that prints italic font, you can now print italics directly. You first, however, must change the underlining to italic. Unfortunately, WordPerfect's Replace feature cannot make this change for you. You must do so manually or with a macro.

To change underlining to italic manually, complete the following steps:

1. Press Search (F2).

2. Press Underline (F8).

3. Press Search (F2) again.

4. Press Backspace; at the `Delete [UND]? No (Yes)` prompt, press Y.

5. Now press Block (F12 or Alt-F4).

6. Use the right-arrow key (or Ctrl-right arrow) to move the cursor to the end of the block to be changed into italic.

7. Press Font (Ctrl-F8) and select **Appearance (2)** and **Italc (4)**.

8. Repeat steps 1 through 7 until all underlining in your document is replaced with italic.

If your document is long, the preceding procedure can be time-consuming. You can save time by using a macro that makes all the changes for you automatically. Installation placed a macro named UND_ITAL.WPM, which searches through any document and converts any underlining to italic, in the QMACROS subdirectory. Copy this macro to your main macros subdirectory. To run the macro, press Macro (Alt-F10), type *UND_ITAL*, and press Enter. The macro will then make the conversions automatically.

Step 4: Replacing Inch Marks with Double Quotation Marks

The fourth step is to replace any inch mark (") that has been used for a double quotation mark—a practice left over from typing classes. When you use a proportional font, you should use true double quotation marks, which are a set of double opening quotation marks (") and double closing quotation marks ("). Again, you can replace any inch marks manually or with a macro.

To replace inch marks manually, complete these steps:

1. Press Home, Home, up arrow to move the cursor to the beginning of the document.

2. Press Search (F2).

3. Press Shift-' to type an inch mark (").

4. Press Search (F2) again.

5. Replace the opening quotation inch mark with opening double quotation marks ("). The left curved single quote mark is generally on the same key as the tilde (~) character and just above the Tab key; press the left single quote twice to produce the opening double quote marks.

6. Then move the cursor to the closing quotation inch mark and replace it with closing double quotation marks (").

The right curved single quote mark is generally on the same key as the inch mark; press the right single quote twice to create the closing double quotes.

7. Repeat steps 2 through 6 until you have replaced all of the inch marks throughout the document.

This procedure, too, can be time-consuming, but a macro can make the process easier and faster. On the Applications Disk is a macro called QUOTES.WPM. It searches for an inch mark and then asks whether you want to change it to an opening or a closing double quotation mark. The macro also lets you skip the replacement of the character if you want.

To replace inch marks by using the QUOTES.WPM macro, first copy it to your main macros subdirectory. (Installation puts the macro in the QMACROS subdirectory.) To run the macro, press Macro (Alt-F10), type *quotes*, and press Enter. As the cursor pauses on each inch mark, select **O**pen or **C**lose if you want to convert the opening or closing quotation inch mark, respectively. Or select **S**kip if you want to skip a conversion. After correcting the quote marks, press Home, Home, up arrow again and then search for and replace all double spaces between sentences with a single space. In general, double spacing between sentences—a habit left over from high school typing class—should not occur in a document printed with proportional fonts. After you have fixed the quotation marks and double spacing, your document should look like figure 20.2.

Step 5: Adding Newspaper Columns, Full Justification, and Hyphenation

Most typeset documents arrange text in columns. The principal advantage of this arrangement is that text is easier to read because the human eye tends to lose its place on long lines of text. An additional advantage is that more text can be placed on the page.

To arrange your text in columns, you must first define the margins. Because the best place for margin codes is at the top of your document, press Home, Home, up arrow to reach the top of your document. Then complete these steps:

1. Press Format (Shift-F8) and select **L**ine (**1**) and **M**argins (**7**). Type .75 for the left margin and press Enter; then type .75 for the right margin and press Enter.

2. Press Exit (F7) to return to the Document window.

*The newsletter page
after step 4 has
been performed.*

2

What Is Desktop Publishing?

Today we live in an era of mass-produced information. In fact, we're so productive that the volume of information we produce doubles every four and a half years. In 1923 Willard Kiplinger published the nation's first newsletter: *The Kiplinger Washington Letter*. Now approximately 200,000 newsletters are published regularly—a total that grows by 30 percent every year.

No wonder desktop publishing is so popular. With a personal computer (PC), a word processing program like WordPerfect 5.1, and a laser printer, almost anyone can produce reports, proposals, presentation overheads, letterheads, memos, office forms, programs, promotional literature, brochures, manuals, catalogs, and newsletters at a fraction of the cost of having a print shop set copy, do page layout, and strip in illustrations and page numbers.

In other words, for less than $5,000 a typical office worker in a couple of hours can produce publications that 10 years ago required $200,000 worth of printing equipment and took days to accomplish.

How Is Desktop Publishing Different?

So what sets desktop publishing apart from regular word processing? Several things, actually. Most people think of word processing as something you do to produce business correspondence—straight text in one font (usually Courier) in one size running from the left margin to the right margin. For emphasis, you underline something or type it in uppercase letters.

Desktop publishing, on the other hand, tastefully mixes together a variety of fonts and font sizes (including italic and bold) within multiple columns on the page. The pages themselves contain large-font headlines, graphic images, charts, tables of information, quotations in shaded boxes, as well as vertical and horizontal bars and lines (called "rules").

Graphic images can be locked to a particular spot on the page with text flowing around them, like water around a rock in a stream, or they can be attached to a specific paragraph and "float" up and down the page with the text as it is edited.

And text is almost always printed "full-justified," meaning that it is aligned vertically along the right margin as well as along the left margin.

One other nice feature—with desktop publishing, you have full control over the production schedule. No longer are you a slave to an outside printer who may take days or weeks to do what you can do in an afternoon. As a result, you can use the most up-to-date information for your project.

Next, add full justification and hyphenation to your document. When working with columns, printers often use full justification to avoid large gaps at the ends of lines. Full justification takes all the space left at the end of the line and divides it among the words on the line to make the text fill the entire line.

However, full justification creates another problem: uneven gaps among words on the line. This problem can be partially solved by hyphenating words. One of WordPerfect 5.1's new features is dictionary hyphenation. WordPerfect now automatically checks its dictionary to find the appropriate place for the hyphen. If a word is not in the dictionary, WordPerfect asks you to place the hyphen.

To apply full justification and turn on hyphenation, do the following:

1. Press Format (Shift-F8) and select Line (**1**), Justification (**3**), and Full (**4**).

2. Select Hyphenation (**1**) and Yes.

3. Now press Exit (F7) to return to your document.

The final task is to define and turn on the columns. Complete these steps:

1. Place your cursor at the beginning of the first paragraph of your body text.

2. Press Columns/Table (Alt-F7) and select Columns (**1**).

3. Select Define (**3**).

   You can see that Type and Number of Columns are already set to give you two newspaper columns. However, you need to reduce the distance between the columns by performing the next step.

4. Select Distance Between Columns (**3**), type *.3*, and press Enter.

   Note that the margins automatically change to reflect the new distance between the columns.

5. Press Exit (F7) to return once again to the document.

6. From the Columns: menu at the bottom of the screen, select On (**1**).

Now press Home, Home, down arrow; the screen displays your document in two columns. The document should now look like figure 21.3.

Step 6: Placing Text in a Box

Seeing column after column of nothing but body text can quickly discourage a reader. To help break the monotony, as well as to emphasize a particular idea, you can place text in a shaded box and use the box to break up text in columns.

For the text for the box, you can either select an important phrase or sentence from the article itself, or later (in step 7, which follows) create a phrase or sentence for the box. In your document, locate an important quotation for the box and copy the selection by performing the following steps:

1. Position the cursor at the beginning of the phrase or sentence to be used for the box.

2. Turn on Block (F12 or Alt-F4) and highlight the selection.

3. Copy the selection by pressing Save (F10) and then pressing Enter without typing a block name. This step copies the blocked selection to the cut/copy memory area.

Fig. 20.3.

The document reformatted in two columns.

3

What Is Desktop Publishing?

Today we live in an era of mass-produced information. In fact, we're so productive that the volume of information we produce doubles every four and a half years. In 1923 Willard Kiplinger published the nation's first newsletter: *The Kiplinger Washington Letter*. Now approximately 200,000 newsletters are published regularly a total that grows by 30 percent every year.

No wonder desktop publishing is so popular. With a personal computer (PC), a word processing program like WordPerfect 5.1, and a laser printer, almost anyone can produce reports, proposals, presentation overheads, letterheads, memos, office forms, programs, promotional literature, brochures, manuals, catalogs, and newsletters at a fraction of the cost of having a print shop set copy, do page layout, and strip in illustrations and page numbers.

In other words, for less than $5,000 a typical office worker in a couple of hours can produce publications that 10 years ago required $200,000 worth of printing equipment and took days to accomplish.

How Is Desktop Publishing Different?

So what sets desktop publishing apart from regular word processing? Several things, actually. Most people think of word processing as something you do to produce business correspondence straight text in one font (usually Courier) in one size running from the left margin to the right margin. For emphasis, you underline something or type it in uppercase letters.

Desktop publishing, on the other hand, tastefully mixes together a variety of fonts and font sizes (including italic and bold)

within multiple columns on the page. The pages themselves contain large-font headlines, graphic images, charts, tables of information, quotations in shaded boxes, as well as vertical and horizontal bars and lines (called "rules").

Graphic images can be locked to a particular spot on the page with text flowing around them, like water around a rock in a stream, or they can be attached to a specific paragraph and "float" up and down the page with the text as it is edited.

And text is almost always printed "full-justified," meaning that it is aligned vertically along the right margin as well as along the left margin.

One other nice feature with desktop publishing, you have full control over the production schedule. No longer are you a slave to an outside printer who may take days or weeks to do what you can do in an afternoon. As a result, you can use the most up-to-date information for your project.

Now move your cursor between two paragraphs of text in either column. You use GoTo (Ctrl-Home) with the right- or left-arrow key to move the cursor between columns. Find a position about one-third of the way from the top or bottom of the page, because such a location allows you to place breaks in both columns without having the breaks line up across the page.

Next change the options for your text box so that it will print from margin to margin. Do the following steps:

1. Press Graphics (Alt-F9) and select Text **B**ox (**3**) and **O**ptions (**4**).

2. Select **O**utside Border Space (**2**) and change Left and Right to *0*" to let the box fill the entire width of the column.

   At this point the Options: Text Box screen should look like figure 20.4.

```
Options: Text Box

     1 - Border Style
              Left                             None
              Right                            None
              Top                              Thick
              Bottom                           Thick
     2 - Outside Border Space
              Left                             0"
              Right                            0"
              Top                              0.167"
              Bottom                           0.167"
     3 - Inside Border Space
              Left                             0.167"
              Right                            0.167"
              Top                              0.167"
              Bottom                           0.167"
     4 - First Level Numbering Method          Numbers
     5 - Second Level Numbering Method          Off
     6 - Caption Number Style                  [BOLD]1[bold]
     7 - Position of Caption                   Below box, Outside borders
     8 - Minimum Offset from Paragraph         0"
     9 - Gray Shading (% of black)             10%

Selection: 0
```

Fig. 20.4.

The Options: Text Box screen.

3. Press Exit (F7) three times to return to the document. Now create the box itself by performing steps 4 and 5.

4. Press Graphics (Alt-F9) and select Text **B**ox (**3**) and **C**reate (**1**).

5. Select **H**orizontal Position (**6**) and **F**ull (**4**).

   You should see on-screen a Definition: Text Box menu like the one in figure 20.5.

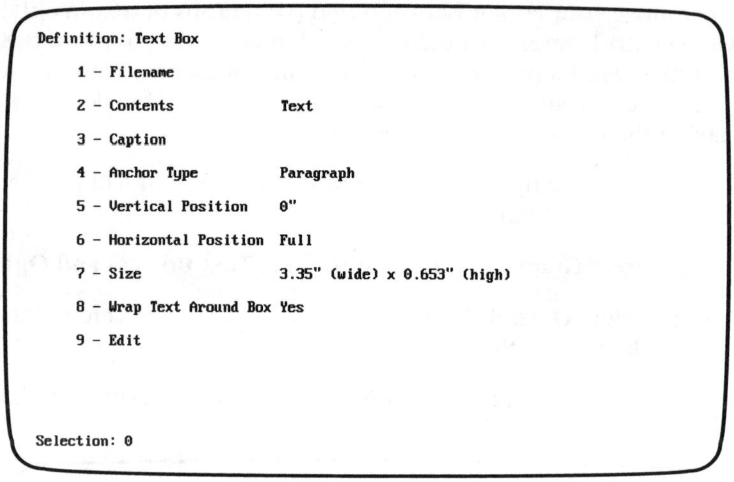

Fig. 20.5.

*The Definition:
Text Box screen.*

```
Definition: Text Box

    1 - Filename

    2 - Contents              Text

    3 - Caption

    4 - Anchor Type           Paragraph

    5 - Vertical Position     0"

    6 - Horizontal Position   Full

    7 - Size                  3.35" (wide) x 0.653" (high)

    8 - Wrap Text Around Box  Yes

    9 - Edit



Selection: 0
```

6. Select Edit (9).

   You are ready to retrieve the selection you copied or to create a phrase or sentence specifically for the box. Before you do either, however, you may first want to turn on Bold (F6) or select a larger type size to make the boxed text stand out. After making any such adjustment, perform one of the two actions noted in step 7.

7. If you have a copied a selection, press Retrieve (Shift-F10) and press Enter without typing a file name.

   or

   If you have waited until now to create text for the box, type the text now on the Edit screen.

8. Press Exit twice to return to the document.

9. If you want to view the text in a box, press Print (Shift-F7) and select View Document (6).

Step 7: Adjusting Paragraph Indentations

One step that helps transform a normal file into a desktop-published document involves formatting paragraphs so that they flow together and are easy to read. Notice that the paragraph beginnings in figures 20.1, 2, and 3 are flush left with the margins and that the paragraphs themselves are double-spaced. For readability, the blank spaces between paragraphs should be removed, and the first line of each paragraph indented (so that the reader knows where the paragraph starts). Here are the steps for formatting paragraphs into text paragraphs:

1. Move to the first line of body text, press Format (Shift-F8), and choose Line (**1**).

   ⌨Choose the **L**ayout pull-down menu and select **L**ine.

2. Choose **T**ab set (**8**); press Home, left arrow, and Ctrl-End to erase all current tab settings for the document.

3. Type *1/4* and press Enter to insert a tab at .25 inch. (Or if you prefer deeper paragraph indents, type *1/3* rather than *1/4*.)

4. Press Exit (F7) twice to return to the editing screen.

5. Press Tab to indent the first paragraph.

6. Choose Search (F2) and press Enter twice to insert **[HRt][HRt]** as the search string for the next paragraph break.

7. Press Search (F2) to locate the next paragraph break.

8. Press Backspace to remove the second **[HRt]** code.

   When you press Backspace, the second paragraph jumps up one line and appears to immediately follow the previous paragraph. For readability, the first line needs to be indented.

9. Press Tab to indent the second paragraph.

Press Search (F2) twice in a row to locate the each of the remaining paragraphs, repeating steps 8 and 9 at the beginning of each paragraph.

Step 8: Editing Side Headings

Another way to break up the text columns is to add side headings. Note that a long side heading like "How Is Desktop Publishing Different?" should be broken into two or three lines of two, three, or four words each. In this chapter's example, the side heading is broken after the word *Desktop*. Your printed page should now look like figure 20.6.

Fig. 20.6.

A newsletter page with a text box and side heading.

What Is Desktop Publishing?

4

Today we live in an era of mass-produced information. In fact, we're so productive that the volume of information we produce doubles every four and a half years. In 1923 Willard Kiplinger published the nation's first newsletter: *The Kiplinger Washington Letter*. Now approximately 200,000 newsletters are published regularly—a total that grows by 30 percent every year.

No wonder desktop publishing is so popular. With a personal computer (PC), a word processing program like WordPerfect 5.1, and a laser printer, almost anyone can produce reports, proposals, presentation overheads, letterheads, memos, office forms, programs, promotional literature, brochures, manuals, catalogs, and newsletters at a fraction of the cost of having a print shop set copy, do page layout, and strip in illustrations and page numbers.

> **Approximately 200,000 news-letters are published on a regular basis every year.**

In other words, for less than $5,000 a typical office worker in a couple of hours can produce publications that 10 years ago required $200,000 worth of printing equipment and took days to accomplish.

How Is Desktop Publishing Different?

So what sets desktop publishing apart from regular word processing? Several things, actually. Most people think of word processing as something you do to produce business correspondence—straight text in one font (usually Courier) in one size run-ning from the left margin to the right margin. For emphasis, you underline something or type it in uppercase letters.

Desktop publishing, on the other hand, tastefully mixes together a variety of fonts and font sizes (including italic and bold) within multiple columns on the page. The pages themselves contain large-font headlines, graphic images, charts, tables of information, quotations in shaded boxes, as well as vertical and horizontal bars and lines (called "rules").

Graphic images can be locked to a particular spot on the page with text flowing around them, like water around a rock in a stream, or they can be attached to a specific paragraph and "float" up and down the page with the text as it is edited.

And text is almost always printed "full-justified," meaning that it is aligned vertically along the right margin as well as along the left margin.

One other nice feature—with desktop publishing, you have full control over the production schedule. No longer are you a slave to an outside printer who may take days or weeks to do what you can do in an afternoon. As a result, you can use the most up-to-date information for your project.

Step 9: Adding Graphics

Yet another way to break up text is to add graphics. This example uses one of the graphics that comes with WordPerfect. As with the text box, the first step is to change the graphics options so that the graphic extends across the column. To do this, position the cursor where you want the graphic to appear and then perform the following steps:

1. Press Graphics (Alt-F9) and select **F**igure (**1**) and **O**ptions (**4**).

2. Select **O**utside Border Space (**2**) and change Left and Right to *0"* to let the figure box fill the entire width of the column.

The Options: Figure screen should look like figure 20.4.

3. Press Exit (F7) three times to return to the document. Now you are ready to create the graphic itself.

4. Press Graphics (Alt-F9); select Text **Figure (1)** and **Create (1)**.

5. Select **Horizontal Position (6)** and **Full (4)**.

6. Choose **Filename (1)** and press List (F5).

7. Make sure that the subdirectory which contains your graphics files is listed; then press Enter.

8. Highlight the graphic you want. This example uses PRINTR-3.WPG.

9. Press **Retrieve (1)**.

10. Now choose **Caption (3)** and type whatever caption you want for your figure. You can use any text attributes for the caption. In figure 20.8 the caption is in italic, which is a common style for a caption.

   At this point your Definition: Figure screen should look like figure 20.7.

```
Definition: Figure

      1 - Filename          PRINTR-3.WPG

      2 - Contents          Graphic

      3 - Caption           Figure 1. An HP LaserJet Series IID...

      4 - Anchor Type       Paragraph

      5 - Vertical Position    0"

      6 - Horizontal Position  Full

      7 - Size              3.35" wide x 2.43" (high)

      8 - Wrap Text Around Box Yes

      9 - Edit


Selection: 0
```

Fig. 20.7.

Settings for a graphic figure.

11. Press Exit (F7) to return to the editing screen.

   When printed, your page should look like the one shown in figure 20.8.

12. If you want to view the graphic image on-screen, press Print (Shift-F7) and select **View Document (6)**.

Fig. 20.8.

A newsletter page with a graphic image.

5

What Is Desktop Publishing?

Today we live in an era of mass-produced information. In fact, we're so productive that the volume of information we produce doubles every four and a half years. In 1923 Willard Kiplinger published the nation's first newsletter: *The Kiplinger Washington Letter.* Now approximately 200,000 newsletters are published regularly—a total that grows by 30 percent every year.

No wonder desktop publishing is so popular. With a personal computer (PC), a word processing program like WordPerfect 5.1, and a laser printer, almost anyone can produce reports, proposals, presentation overheads, letterheads, memos, office forms, programs, promotional literature, brochures, manuals, catalogs, and newsletters at a fraction of the cost of having a print shop set copy, do page layout, and strip in illustrations and page numbers.

> **Approximately 200,000 newsletters are published on a regular basis every year.**

In other words, for less than $5,000 a typical office worker in a couple of hours can produce publications that 10 years ago required $200,000 worth of printing equipment and took days to accomplish.

How Is Desktop Publishing Different?

So what sets desktop publishing apart from regular word processing? Several things, actually. Most people think of word processing as something you do to produce business correspondence—straight text in one font (usually Courier) in one size run-

ning from the left margin to the right margin. For emphasis, you underline something or type it in uppercase letters.

Figure 1. An HP LaserJet Series IID Printer.

Desktop publishing, on the other hand, tastefully mixes together a variety of fonts and font sizes (including italic and bold) within multiple columns on the page. The pages themselves contain large-font headlines, graphic images, charts, tables of information, quotations in shaded boxes, as well as vertical and horizontal bars and lines (called "rules").

Graphic images can be locked to a particular spot on the page with text flowing around them, like water around a rock in a stream, or they can be attached to a specific paragraph and "float" up and down the page with the text as it is edited.

And text is almost always printed "full-justified," meaning that it is aligned vertically along the right margin as well as along the left margin.

One other nice feature—with desktop publishing, you have full control over the production schedule. No longer are you a slave to an outside printer who may take days or weeks to do what you can do in an

Step 10: Adding Larger and Shaded Fonts

You learned in Chapter 18 that you can use larger fonts for emphasis—particularly if you have soft fonts or a PostScript printer. In step 10, you alter the top line even more by increasing the font size considerably and adding a screen for shading.

In Chapter 18, you learned also how to screen (or shade) words. Briefly, the steps are these:

1. Position the cursor in front of the words you want to screen.

2. Press Font (Ctrl-F8).

3. Choose Print Color (5).

4. Select Gray (**a**) if you want the words to be printed as 50 percent of normal, or Other (**O**) if you want a percentage of gray other than 50 percent.

5. Press Exit (F7) to return to the Edit screen.

6. Position the cursor after the words to be changed to gray, repeat steps 2 and 3, select Black (**1**), and press Exit (F7) to change the print color back to black.

The top line in figure 20.9 is Century Schoolbook 60-point bold that is shaded, or screened, 50 percent. The second line is in the same typeface but is 42-point bold without shading. If this were a newsletter front page, you could use similar sizes inside a box or table form to create a newsletter logo.

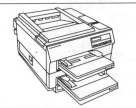

What Is Desktop Publishing?

6

Today we live in an era of mass-produced information. In fact, we're so productive that the volume of information we produce doubles every four and a half years. In 1923 Willard Kiplinger published the nation's first newsletter: *The Kiplinger Washington Letter*. Now approximately 200,000 newsletters are published regularly——a total that grows by 30 percent every year.

No wonder desktop publishing is so popular. With a personal computer (PC), a word processing program like WordPerfect 5.1, and a laser printer, almost anyone can produce reports, proposals, presentation overheads, letterheads, memos, office forms, programs, promotional literature, brochures, manuals, catalogs, and newsletters at a fraction of the cost of having a print shop set copy, do page layout, and strip in illustrations and page numbers.

Approximately 200,000 newsletters are published on a regular basis every year.

In other words, for less than $5,000 a typical office worker in a couple of hours can produce publications that 10 years ago required $200,000 worth of printing equipment and took days to accomplish.

How Is Desktop Publishing Different?

So what sets desktop publishing apart from regular word processing? Several things, actually. Most people think of word processing as something you do to produce business correspondence——straight text in one font (usually Courier) in one size running from the left margin to the right margin. For emphasis, you underline something or type it in uppercase letters.

Figure 1. An HP LaserJet Series IID Printer.

Desktop publishing, on the other hand, tastefully mixes together a variety of fonts and font sizes (including italic and bold) within multiple columns on the page. The pages themselves contain large-font headlines, graphic images, charts, tables of information, quotations in shaded boxes, as well as vertical and horizontal bars and lines (called "rules").

Graphic images can be locked to a particular spot on the page with text flowing around them, like water around a rock in a stream, or they can be attached to a specific paragraph and "float" up and down the page with the text as it is edited.

And text is almost always printed "full-justified," meaning that it is aligned vertically along the right margin as well as along the left margin.

Fig. 20.9.

Larger and shaded fonts.

Step 11: Adding Graphic Lines to a Page

To make your columns more evident when they are printed, you can add vertical and horizontal graphic lines to different pages in the text. Figure 20.10 illustrates one page with three vertical graphic lines added—one on each side of the text and one between the two columns.

Fig. 20.10.

Vertical graphic lines on a page.

What Is Desktop Publishing?

7

Today we live in an era of mass-produced information. In fact, we're so productive that the volume of information we produce doubles every four and a half years. In 1923 Willard Kiplinger published the nation's first newsletter: *The Kiplinger Washington Letter*. Now approximately 200,000 newsletters are published regularly—a total that grows by 30 percent every year.

No wonder desktop publishing is so popular. With a personal computer (PC), a word processing program like WordPerfect 5.1, and a laser printer, almost anyone can produce reports, proposals, presentation overheads, letterheads, memos, office forms, programs, promotional literature, brochures, manuals, catalogs, and newsletters at a fraction of the cost of having a print shop set copy, do page layout, and strip in illustrations and page numbers.

> Approximately 200,000 newsletters are published on a regular basis every year.

In other words, for less than $5,000 a typical office worker in a couple of hours can produce publications that 10 years ago required $200,000 worth of printing equipment and took days to accomplish.

How Is Desktop Publishing Different?

So what sets desktop publishing apart from regular word processing? Several things, actually. Most people think of word processing as something you do to produce business correspondence—straight text in one font (usually Courier) in one size running from the left margin to the right margin. For emphasis, you underline something or type it in uppercase letters.

Figure 1. An HP LaserJet Series IID Printer.

Desktop publishing, on the other hand, tastefully mixes together a variety of fonts and font sizes (including italic and bold) within multiple columns on the page. The pages themselves contain large-font headlines, graphic images, charts, tables of information, quotations in shaded boxes, as well as vertical and horizontal bars and lines (called "rules").

Graphic images can be locked to a particular spot on the page with text flowing around them, like water around a rock in a stream, or they can be attached to a specific paragraph and "float" up and down the page with the text as it is edited.

And text is almost always printed "full-justified," meaning that it is aligned vertically along the right margin as well as along the left margin.

The following are the steps for adding vertical graphic lines to a page. Start with a printed copy of the page without graphic lines and have a ruler handy.

1. Press Graphics (Alt-F9) and select Line (**5**).

   ⌨Choose **Line** from the **Graphics** menu.

2. Select Create Line, **Vertical** (**2**).

3. Choose **Horizontal Position** (**1**).

4. Choose **Set Position** (**4**)

5. Type the measurement in inches from the left edge of the paper where you want the line printed.

6. Press Enter.

7. Press **Vertical Position** (**2**).

8. Choose **Set Position** (**5**).

9. Type the beginning point for the line in inches, measured from the top edge of the paper.

10. Press Enter.

11. Select **Length of Line** (**3**).

12. Type the length of the line in inches and press Enter.

Figure 20.11 shows how the Graphics: Vertical Line screen looks for the left line in figure 20.10.

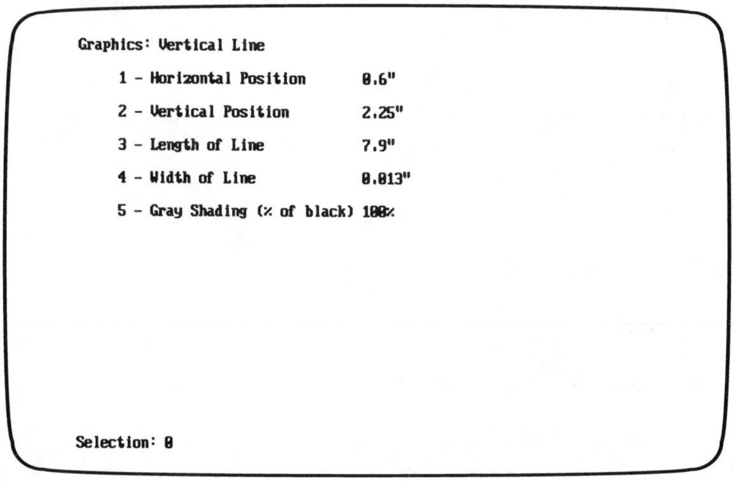

```
Graphics: Vertical Line

     1 - Horizontal Position      0.6"

     2 - Vertical Position        2.25"

     3 - Length of Line           7.9"

     4 - Width of Line            0.013"

     5 - Gray Shading (% of black) 100%




Selection: 0
```

Fig. 20.11.

The Graphics: Vertical Line screen.

Using steps 1 through 12, you can add more vertical lines to a page. If you want them to appear at the same locations on each page of your newsletter, put the three vertical graphic lines in a header on page 1. When the document is printed, the three lines will appear in their proper locations on every page.

Step 12: Adding a Full-Page Graphic Box

Chapter 18 showed several examples of the FULL-BOX.STY file included on the Applications Disk. If you copy the FULL-BOX.STY file from the QSTYLES subdirectory to your style files subdirectory, such as C:\WP51\STYLES, you can use that style for this document. Here are the steps:

1. Press Home, Home, Home, up arrow to move the cursor to the very top of the document.

2. Press Style (Alt-F8).

3. Press **Retrieve** (7) to select a style file.

4. Press List Files (F5) and make sure that the path, such as C:\WP51\STYLES*.*, is correct for your style files.

5. Press Enter to look inside the STYLES subdirectory.

6. Highlight the FULL-BOX.STY and press **Retrieve** (1).

The FULL_BOX.STY file on the Applications Disk includes 10 different ready-to-use document border styles that will print on every page of your document. Figure 20.12 shows how the 1/2-inch box style looks when added to the same page as in figure 20.9.

You now know how to improve the appearance of newsletter pages so that they look much better than a page typed with a simple Courier font. To see how much the appearance is improved, compare figure 20.10 or 20.12 with figure 20.1. The difference is considerable.

Sample Newsletters Created in WordPerfect 5.1

Now look at some specific examples of newsletters created with WordPerfect 5.1 on different printers.

8

What Is Desktop Publishing?

Today we live in an era of mass-produced information. In fact, we're so productive that the volume of information we produce doubles every four and a half years. In 1923 Willard Kiplinger published the nation's first newsletter: *The Kiplinger Washington Letter.* Now approximately 200,000 newsletters are published regularly——a total that grows by 30 percent every year.

No wonder desktop publishing is so popular. With a personal computer (PC), a word processing program like WordPerfect 5.1, and a laser printer, almost anyone can produce reports, proposals, presentation overheads, letterheads, memos, office forms, programs, promotional literature, brochures, manuals, catalogs, and newsletters at a fraction of the cost of having a print shop set copy, do page layout, and strip in illustrations and page numbers.

> Approximately 200,000 newsletters are published on a regular basis every year.

In other words, for less than $5,000 a typical office worker in a couple of hours can produce publications that 10 years ago required $200,000 worth of printing equipment and took days to accomplish.

How Is Desktop Publishing Different?

So what sets desktop publishing apart from regular word processing? Several things, actually. Most people think of word processing as something you do to produce business correspondence——straight text in one font (usually Courier) in one size running from the left margin to the right margin. For emphasis, you underline something or type it in uppercase letters.

Figure 1. An HP LaserJet Series IID Printer.

Desktop publishing, on the other hand, tastefully mixes together a variety of fonts and font sizes (including italic and bold) within multiple columns on the page. The pages themselves contain large-font headlines, graphic images, charts, tables of information, quotations in shaded boxes, as well as vertical and horizontal bars and lines (called "rules").

Graphic images can be locked to a particular spot on the page with text flowing around them, like water around a rock in a stream, or they can be attached to a specific paragraph and "float" up and down the page with the text as it is edited.

And text is almost always printed "full-justified," meaning that it is aligned vertically along the right margin as well as along the left margin.

One other nice feature——with desktop publishing, you have full control over the

Fig. 20.12.

A full-page graphic box around a text page.

A Newsletter Printed on a Hewlett-Packard DeskJet Printer

Figures 20.13 and 20.14 illustrate how a newsletter can be prepared successfully even on an HP DeskJet printer. The newsletter *The Sundae Times* is a monthly publication of High's Ice Cream Corporation.

Fig. 20.13.

The front page of The Sundae Times, *printed on an HP DeskJet printer.*

The newsletter editor, Oscar W. Smith, Jr., describes the publication's origin and production this way:

> *The Sundae Times* began life as a fun internal communication to get a few things across to our employees. It developed into a marketing tool with a circulation of about 1,000. All 26 monthly issues since January 1988 have been done with WordPerfect in various incarnations.

> I use a hand scanner and PC Paint+ for the few non-WordPerfect Graphics. I print it with my HP DeskJet using the Times Roman cartridge, and take the camera-ready pages to the printer.

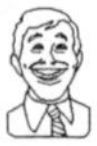

is a real breakthrough in research. As always we caution you not to leap to the supermarket without consulting your doctor and to remember that a well balanced diet, including ice cream and moderate exercise (such as walking), are about the only guarantees of extended health.

THE YEAR OF THE HORSE in China started just a few days ago. Many of you have, no doubt, wondered what the other Chinese years are named. Well, *The Sundae Times* is happy to satisfy your curiosity and contribute to your education. The other Chinese years are sheep (or goat), monkey, hen (or rooster), dog, pig, rat, ox (or bull), tiger, rabbit (or hare or cat), dragon, and, last but not least, snake.

OUR DENTIST TELLS US that Mayo Clinic Research shows that keeping your own teeth in healthy, functioning condition can add years to your life. It seems that people who consistently wear dentures have trouble chewing. Because of this discomfort, they make subconscious changes in their diet which have a

long term negative effect on overall health.

WE ALL WONDER where the time goes. We're heard to say, on many occasions, "I just don't have time!" We grew up with predictions of a four day work week. When we first heard about computers, we were told they were going to take over all the mundane jobs and save us time. When PCs first became widely available (which was only nine years ago, dear hearts), everyone predicted that they would make information faster and more readily available. According to a recent article in "Compuserve Magazine," the average American work week has increased from 41 to 49 hours. The average amount of time not working has gone down by 32%. According to a 1989 survey, over 85% of the work force works more than 45 hours per week and 65% of us work at least one weekend a month (**High's** best employees, who work *every* weekend, would sign a contract for one weekend). How has all this happened? According to the survey, *paperwork* has increased *600%* in the same 20 year period! Yeah, the computers are great, but we obviously never got a chance to use them the way they were intended. If

we didn't have them, we'd be doing nothing but paperwork all day.

IN THE SAME VEIN, we've always felt that one of the greatest figures in American business was James Ling who merged several companies in different businesses during the late 1968-72 period and formed the first mega corporation with multiple business aims–Ling, Tempco, Vaught. We don't think he was great because LTV was the fist conglomerate (which it was) nor because it was successful (which it wasn't). We think Jimmy Ling was great because he accomplished it all *before* the first four-function electronic calculator was invented.

75% OF HIGH'S CUSTOMERS make some comment about calories or their diet as they buy our great products. They've obviously figured out what Bryce Thompson, one of the great mavens of the ice cream and frozen dessert industry, said in this month's Sundae School Newsletter, "It's not how many calories, it's how many units of joy per scoop!" Thanks Bryce.

The Sundae Times
High's Ice Cream Corp.
1063 West Thirty Eighth Street
Norfolk, VA 23508

BULK RATE
U.S. POSTAGE
PAID
NORFOLK, VA
Permit No. 411

Fig. 20.14.

The back page of The Sundae Times, *printed on an HP DeskJet printer.*

Note that you can produce attractive newsletter pages by using one of the lowest-priced laser printers on the market. At today's prices, you can purchase an HP DeskJet for the price of a good-quality dot-matrix printer.

A Newsletter Printed on a Hewlett-Packard LaserJet

Figures 20.15 through 20.18 are sample pages of the newsletter *Letter to the Editors*, which is printed photo-offset from a laser-printed mechanical. Headlines are in Helvetica Bold and Helvetica Narrow Bold. The body text is in Times Roman 10 point. One ad is in Palatino.

Newsletters Printed with PostScript Fonts on a Linotronic Printer

Figures 20.19 through 20.24 illustrate how a newsletter can look when printed with PostScript fonts. *The WordPerfectionist* is the official newsletter of the WordPerfect Support Group and costs $36 per year. Address correspondence to *The WordPerfectionist*, Lake Technology Park, P.O. Box 130, McHenry, MD 21541.

Steven M. Schafer, editor of *The WordPerfectionist*, provided the following information about his publication:

> The front-page logo [letterhead] for the newsletter began in WordPerfect 5.1 as italic Times Roman 185-point font. The newsletter title was then scanned, taken to the Arts and Letters graphic program, auto-traced, and modified. Then the rectangular box around the logo was added in Arts and Letters. All nonitalic text used in the logo and main section headings (as at the top of page 2) is Times Roman.
>
> *The WordPerfectionist* body copy is Bitstream, Charter 9.5-point, with Bitstream News Gothic for headers, footers, and smaller article headings. The small font text used inside the figures boxes on pages 2 and 3 is Helvetica 8-point. Fonts for the various section headings and article headings throughout the publication are activated by use of WordPerfect styles.

The WPCorp Report is published quarterly and is sent out free of charge to registered users of WordPerfect products. Figures 20.25 through 20.29 show five pages from the January 1990 issue. Paul Scousin, the new editor of *The WPCorp Report*, says this about the publication:

> *The WPCorp Report* is published to inform registered WordPerfect users of company and product changes—new releases, updates, pricing, and anything else of interest to WordPerfect users. The headline at the top of page 1 was created in Adobe Illustrator, using a Macintosh computer. Text body copy for the publication is Palatino 10-point font; headlines were created using Optima 16-point font. The lines beneath each headline are WordPerfect horizontal graphic lines.

LETTER TO THE EDITORS

Motion Picture & Video Tape Editors   *Local 771*   *Vol. 2, No. 1, Spring 1990*

Local 771
Motion Picture & Videotape Editors
*International Alliance of Theatrical
Stage Employees and Moving Picture
Machine Operators of The United
States and Canada*

INSIDE

IATSE/NABET Merger
In The Works
Page 2

President's Report
Page 2

New ABC Contract Approved
Page 3

US & Canadian Editors
Deplore Excessive Hours
Page 3

Business Agent's Report:
Is A National Contract In Our
Future?
Page 5

Videotape Caucus Report:
Reaching Out to
Non-Union Editors
Page 7

AFL-CIO Legislative Agenda
Page 8

FILM SEARCH STRIKERS CONTINUE THEIR FIGHT

The picket lines went up at 111 Fifth Avenue on February 27, 1990, at the headquarters of Film Search, a stock footage house, wholly-owned subsidiary of *The Image Bank*, a stock still archive with offices worldwide.

In meetings prior to the walkout, *Film Search* employees expressed no doubts about their desire to be represented by **Local 771** and sought the most expedient means of gaining our representation. After signing authorization cards designating **Local 771** as their union, they marched into their general manager's office to demand union recognition.

An hour later, elected shop steward **Don Fedynak**, a **Local 771** member since 1970, was summoned to the president's office and discharged for union activity. Upon hearing of Don's unlawful termination, the Film Search workers walked out in protest, and the Steenbecks, video editing equipment and other tools of the trade fell silent.

More Than a Picket Line

The striking Film Search workers haven't been content to simply wait for the National Labor Relations Board to act on their unfair labor practice charges. Rather, they've transformed themselves into full-time organizers, activists, press agents and fundraisers. A full campaign is under way to maximize pressure on the company. Letters are coming in informing them that Local 771's picket line and its call for a boycott will be honored. Union members and other industry professionals have canceled orders and cited the strike as their reason for doing so. Articles

Alcides Wilson, Doris Salek, Lisa Damon, Mark Bottino and Don Fedynak picketing in front of 111 Fifth Avenue. Photo by fellow striker Lisa Orberg.

covering the strike have appeared in *Backstage*, *Photo District News*, *Flatiron* and the AFL–CIO's *Labor News*.

You Can Help

As the strike enters its second month, it's all the more important to have the active support of your fellow Union brothers and sisters. Picketing is being conducted 9:00 AM to 5:00 PM, Monday through Friday. The Executive Board has allocated from our Help Fund $20 per day for any member who walks a minimum of four hours a day. Letters protesting the company's actions should be addressed to: **Mr. Stanley Kanney, Chairman of the Board, *The Image Bank*, 111 Fifth Avenue, New York, NY 10003.** Please send a copy to the union. Be acutely aware of the source of any stock footage you may use. If it is *Film Search* stock, cancel the order and let the company and the union know about it. For more information, please contact **Tim Lally** at the union office.   *Tim Lally*

The Effects House Corporation/The Optical House will be conducting seminars on VistaVision and optical effects during May and June at their new facilities at 111 Eighth Avenue. Anyone interested in attending should contact Patty Barry at The Effects House, 924-9150.

Fig. 20.15.

The front page of Letter to the Editors, printed on a LaserJet.

Fig. 20.16.

A page from Letter to the Editors.

TODD-AO
STUDIOS EAST

254 W. 54th St.
New York, NY 10019
(212) 265-6225

S.M. HASSANEIN
President

ERIC ALBERTSON
Vice President

Academy Awards
1955 OKLAHOMA
1957 SPECIAL
      ACHIEVEMENT:
      TODD-AO SYSTEM
1958 SOUTH PACIFIC
1960 THE ALAMO
1961 WEST SIDE STORY
1965 THE SOUND OF MUSIC
1972 CABARET
1973 THE EXORCIST
1982 E.T.
1985 OUT OF AFRICA

Emmy Awards
1970 MISSION IMPOSSIBLE
1980 THE ORDEAL OF
      DR. MUDD
1982 HILL STREET BLUES
1983 HILL STREET BLUES
1984 HILL STREET BLUES
1984 A STREETCAR NAMED
      DESIRE
1984 REAL PEOPLE
1985 CONTRACT FOR LIFE:
      THE S.A.D.D. STORY
1985 CAGNEY AND LACEY
1985 SPACE: PART 5
1985 CHEERS

Sound Editing
1979 FRIENDLY FIRE
1983 SCARLET AND THE
      BLACK
1985 CHEERS
1987 MAX HEADROOM
1987 UNNATURAL CAUSES

TODD-AO STUDIOS is proud to announce the relocation of *Richard Portman* to our New York facility, where he will join sound mixer *Rick Dior* and our new ADR and Foley mixer, *Paul Zydel.*

Our New York facility offers:

• 40 editing rooms

• 3 transfer rooms

• 40—seat luxury screening room

• The largest dubbing stage/mixing studio in the east

Our facility also has the newest film & tape ADR/Foley stage in New York. In addition, our new Dubbing Stage/Mixing Studio includes an SSL 500M console with a Series G Total Recall Computer. We are proud of our high standards of quality and competitive pricing. To tour and book our facility services, please call (212) 265-6225.

Hollywood
P.O. Box 38931
Hollywood, CA 90038

Fig. 20.17.

A page from Letter to the Editors.

Business Agent's Report

Is a National Feature Contract In Our Future?

Over the last eight months, *President* **Troll** and Business Agent **Bill Hanauer**, with guidance from the National Feature Contract Committee, and, through them, the Caucuses, have met with Local 776 Executive Director **Ron Kutak** and Local 780 Business Agent **Andy Younger** to develop a compromise position to present to the IATSE leadership and, in time, as contract proposals, to the AMPTP. Much work remains to be done.

The last West Coast Basic Agreement (WCBA) brought sweeping changes for members of 776 (e.g., the elimination of two tiers of the roster system). The next WCBA, currently being negotiated, will also have great impact. Its signing will leave the majors with little incentive to negotiate on a national level. To bargain from a strong position, we must begin to negotiate a national feature contract before the west coast negotiations are completed. We must do this even if it means reopening our own contract *before* it expires in December.

If we want a national feature film (and episodic) contract we must agree—for the purposes of negotiating and holding that contract **only** to co-bargain with the other two Locals and IATSE President **DiTolla**, who holds the bargaining right of Local 776.

WHAT IS CO–BARGAINING?

Co–bargaining means forming a bargaining committee with equal representation for all three locals, with the president of IATSE as its chief negotiator. If only one local ratifies, there is no contract. If two ratify, the third is not bound by the contract. However, if all three locals ratify the same agreement, we have a national contract.

Possible advantages of a co-bargained national feature contract could be:
- Greater bargaining strength.
- National working conditions.
- More signatories.
- A larger jurisdiction.
- Stronger, richer welfare and pension funds through equitable regionally pro–rated distribution of residuals.
- An end to the roster for editorial personnel.
- Stronger inducement to use local crews.
- Greater co–operation in organizing non–union and runaway productions.

Possible disadvantages could include:
- In our local, nothing bars a member from moving from apprentice to editor, or from picture to sound. If we join with 776 and 780, specific eligibility requirements might be introduced.
- Some working conditions guaranteed in our contract which are thought to be

better than those for 776 and 780, might have to be re–negotiated.
- Since no collective bargaining agreement exists in a vacuum, any conditions agreed to in this contract will surely be on the table for all other contracts.

These issues must be discussed fully. At a roll–call meeting in March, called expressly for that purpose, we attempted to do so. Unfortunately, the evening's agenda was too full to devote sufficient time, so we decided to reconvene the caucuses. They will meet at the union office at 7:00pm on the following dates:

Thursday, April 19   Assistant Editors Caucus
Wednesday, April 25   Sound Editors Caucus
Thursday, April 26   ERAs Caucus
Monday, April 30   Picture Editors Caucus

Any member is welcome at any of the meetings. We must act quickly so that Business Agent Hanauer can meet again with Mr. Younger and Mr. Kutak as soon as possible and continue our joint work. Please plan to attend.

New York Women in Film Accepting Applications

NYWIF is a nonprofit organization for professionals in film and television. As a network for the exchange of information and resources, *NYWIF* presents over 40 workshops and seminars a year on every aspect of film and television production, in addition to exclusive screening and special events. Our programs have featured such industry leaders as Barry Levinson, Meryl Streep, Jonathan Demme, Glenn Close, Martin Scorsese, Susan Seidelman, John Sayles, Jay Presson Allen, Mike Nichols, Charlayne Hunter–Gault, Lee Grant and Joan Micklin Silver.

Membership is open to those with a minimum of five years experience, above entry level, and applicants must be sponsored by two *NYWIF* members. *Deadline for applications: August 1.*

For membership applications call *NYWIF Hotline* at (212) 675–0898 and leave a message.

- *New York Women in Film* • 274 Madison Avenue • Suite 1603 • New York NY 10016 • (212) 679–0870

Fig. 20.18.

A page from Letter to the Editors.

Welfare Plan Cost Reduction Announced by Trustees

Through seemingly unceasing negotiations, the Welfare Trustees have gotten a small reduction in the price of the indemnity plans for the second quarter of 1990. We will continue to try to lower the cost while upgrading the plan, when possible.

ACTIVE PARTICIPANTS		1st Quarter	2nd Quarter
PLAN A	Individual	$700.11	$692.52
	Family	1,515.27	1,496.28
	Family—Income equal to or less than $12,500	1,164.77	1,125.78
PLAN B	Individual	214.89	207.30
	Family	430.41	411.42
PLAN C	Individual	351.80	343.41
	Family	728.07	709.68

RETIREES	1st Quarter	2nd Quarter
PLAN A Individual under 65	659.19	651.60
Family under 65	1,474.35	1,455.36
Individual over 65	466.23	458.64
Family over 65	940.47	921.48
Retiree under 65/	1,004.85	991.23
Retiree over 65/ Spouse under 65	1,151.04	1,137.42

Videotape Caucus Report

The small—but dedicated—Videotape Caucus met on Thursday, March 15, to discuss a proposed Open House, now tentatively scheduled for early fall. The objective of the Open House, or Town Meeting, is to reach out to our own members and any non–union editors who want to know how Local 771 can address their needs in a changing employment environment. Since most freelance editors working with video or other electronic/digital equipment find it nearly impossible to get a contract or letter of adherence (and therefore no benefits), we're looking for a forum in which our colleagues can speak freely about their perceptions— good and bad—of unions, in hopes of learning how to turn this non–union trend around. We need to dispel the myths of how unions interfere in the work place, and consider what changes need to be made in our contract to make it more appealing to editors and employers.

This committee has taken on a seemingly impossible task, and each member has at one time or another felt it to be a futile fight. Yet we know that if we don't try to make changes—if the membership doesn't express its needs and if it is not heard—the freelance editor will be shut out of a union that has, until now, assured us decent wages and working conditions.

A questionnaire for the membership is being developed. It will help the committee identify problems, frustrations, hopes for the future, etc. If you have any suggestions about what should be included, contact Richard Milner.

It's going to take more that our 15 member committee to organize the "event", locate non-union editors to invite them to talk with us, suggest contract changes, and formulate the questionnaire. Our next meeting is scheduled for Monday, April 23 at 6:30. If you would like to participate, check with the office to confirm the date before coming over.

And, we repeat the plea for names (and addresses) of non-union editors. At the appropriate time, we'd like to send out fliers to as many people as possible announcing the Open House. Send your list to the Union office (Attention: Videotape Caucus). *Sharon Kaufman*

THE

WordPerfectionist

Newsletter of the WordPerfect Support Group   Volume IV. Number 1

Richard P. Wilkes 76701.23
Publisher

Alessandra B. Wilkes 76701.22
Managing Editor

Steven M. Schafer 76702.506
Editor

Bonnie R. Thomas 74020.10
Customer Service Manager

Dee Lewis   Jeanne Kissner   Dana Adams
Julie Kitzmiller   Ellie Mitchum
WPSG Customer Service

Joan Friedman 76701.145
Compuserve Forum Manager

Guerri Stevens 76702.1070   Bruce Parrello 76702.511
Bruce Rodgers 70416.115   Ralph Blodgett 73767.656
Marilyn Horn Claff 74020.103
CompuServe Forum Assistants

Purpose: To provide concise and timely information and
guidance to business and computer professionals dedicated to
the effective use of WordPerfect-brand software tools.

The WordPerfectionist (ISSN 0747-6094) is published twelve times
per year for the WordPerfect Support Group by Support Group, Inc.
Please address all correspondence and address changes to The
WordPerfectionist, Lake Technology Park, P.O. Box 130, McHenry,
Maryland 21541. Phone (301) 387-4500, FAX (301) 387-7322. Or,
use your modem to contact our forum on the CompuServe Information
Service (GO WPSG) 74020.10.

Subscriptions are $36 for twelve issues, $48US to Canada & Mexico,
$68US overseas. Orders only toll free (800) USA-GROUP. Group rates
are available. 100% Money Back Guarantee.

The views of this independent group do not necessarily reflect the
official positions of WordPerfect Corporation of Orem, Utah, its officers,
or its employees.

WordPerfect is a trademark of WordPerfect Corporation. "The
WordPerfectionist" is used under exclusive license from WPCorp.

The newsletter is written from start to finish using WordPerfect 5.1.
Page proofs are printed on an HP LaserJet Series II with the QMS
JetScript PostScript board. Camera-ready copy is printed directly by
WP on the WPSG's Linotronic L100P typesetter at 1270 dpi.
Duplication is by Community Press, Provo, Utah.

Entire contents Copyright © 1990 by Support Group, Inc.
Reproduction without written consent is forbidden.

In This Issue

Fig. 20.19.

*The front page
of* The
WordPerfectionist,
*printed with
PostScript fonts.*

Fig. 20.21.

A page from The WordPerfectionist.

---

using a program like QEMM's LOADHI. This program works only on 386 machines, although a companion program QRAM is supposed to work on LIM 4.0 equipped 286 machines. We use LOADHI on all our 386 machines here and end up with over 500K free after loading the network and Shell.

Virtual File Access

After WP runs out of RAM, it starts swapping parts of the document, graphics, etc., out to the virtual files. These file are placed in the default directory unless you redirect them using the /D-pathname start-up option.

Avoid RAM Disks

A lot of people think that the way to speed up WP is to use a RAM disk. That is seldom a good choice. A RAM disk in expanded memory takes away memory from WP. So, all you're doing is adding the overhead of the RAM disk when WP could have simply used the expanded memory instead.

If you have extended memory, converting that memory to EMS is ideal. Otherwise a disk cache is a better use of this memory. Remember that if you use a RAM disk for virtual files, you may run into a disk full error when loading or printing large files. The only time we use RAM disks are on floppy-only laptops with lots of RAM.

Disk Cache

I've mentioned disk caches a couple of times without really explaining what they are. Disk caches like the superb Super PCKwik takes a portion of RAM (conventional, extended, or expanded) and keeps the most recently read and written sectors of your disk in it. Every time a program wants to read the disk, the cache looks to see if the information is already in RAM.

By taking the information from RAM rather than disk, the cache can be 100 times faster than re-reading the same information from the hard drive. In our testing we've found that even a small disk cache can avoid two-thirds of all disk requests. In the chart (created using DrawPerfect) you'll note that a small 64K cache made a huge difference.

We highly recommend you purchase a disk cache program if you have the memory to spare.

Buffers: Poor Man's Cache

If you don't have the memory for a disk cache, be *sure* to have your CONFIG.SYS file modified to include the line BUFFERS=32 or higher. Running with fewer than 32 is a waste, and more than 40 will probably not improve performance much and could slow things down on a slow computer.

Disk Fragmentation

Your hard disk is separated by DOS into sections 2K in size (some DOS versions use 4K or 8K). So, a 100K file will need 50 of these sections. However, DOS can store the file spread over 50 different places on the hard drive, requiring a lot of disk drive head movement to read the file. Such a file would be called "fragmented." You can speed up your disk access by defragmenting your hard drive using a utility like PC Tools. The process is painless—unless it blows up. *Always back up your hard drive before defragmenting!* It is worth doing, but please be careful.

Interpreting the Results

The chart below shows two time trials. The slowest time was given a value of 100. If another test shows a value of 50, it took half as long as the longest time. Tests were done with and without disk cache and EMS. Clearly, the more memory the better.

If memory is not sufficient to hold the entire document and virtual files on disk, add a disk cache. Even a small one will help. Remember that a disk cache will make all your applications run faster, as well as saving wear and tear on the hard drive. The cache helps with virtual files as well as the WP.FIL overlay file and the WP.DRS driver resource (both are accessed constantly by WP 5.1).

Keeping the whole document in memory is ideal. You won't use virtual files on disk, so the cache won't come into play there. You'll get the best 5.1 performance if you have expanded memory for 5.1 to use. The chart shows that EMS alone makes WP 5.1 three to ten times faster than the minimal configuration.

Loading WP with the /R option is a mixed bag. Loading /R uses up over 700K of EMS that could be used for virtual memory. Since WordPerfect really slows down if virtual files are needed, I'd skip the /R unless I had gobs of EMS or a very slow network. A slow hard drive can be "solved" with a disk cache smaller than 700K!

Armed with this information, you can decide the performance level you need and what it will cost to get it. Clearly, some machines could operate two to ten times as fast as they are now. It just takes knowledge, time, and money. A few dollars on a disk cache might save you from trading in a perfectly adequate computer. ❖

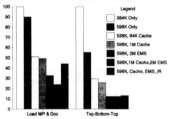

WP 5.1 Time Trials

Legend:
- 384K Only
- 596K Only
- 538K, 64K Cache
- 596K, 1M Cache
- 596K, 2M EMS
- 596K, 1M Cache, 2M EMS
- 596K, Cache, EMS, /R

Load WP & Doc   Top-Bottom-Top

Alessandra B. Wilkes

WPSG Forums

The WPSG opened the first WordPerfect forum on the CompuServe Information Service almost three years ago. Since then, over two hundred thousand messages have been written. The libraries contain over 1300 files—over 50 megabytes. In order to help control this enormous amount of traffic, we have split the original forum into WPSGA and WPSGB.

CompuServe is limited to 18 separate sections in a forum. You can have only 999 messages in a forum before old messages are replaced by new ones. In order to keep the "scroll" rate (the speed at which old messages disappear) reasonably slow, a new forum was needed. We didn't want to force people to connect with CompuServe every day for fear of missing ongoing conversations.

A second advantage to the new forum is that it allows us to arrange topics more precisely. Now it is easier to find a subject of interest by going to the correct section. For example, if you want to ask a question about a 5.1 macro, you can leave a message in section 4 of WPSGA. If you need more information on WP Training you can read the messages in section 5.

WPSGA has sections for members who are interested in the IBM PC WordPerfect versions. The main emphasis of the forum is WordPerfect 5.1. Sections 14 and 15 are for discussions on WP 5.0 and 4.2. For each section there is a corresponding library of files, utilities, and macros.

The new WPSGB forum is for all other WordPerfect products on all other platforms. Not only can you participate in discussions on PlanPerfect, DataPerfect, Library/Office, and the new DrawPerfect, but you can also share information with other Unix, Macintosh, and VAX users.

Some History

Why did we open a forum? We were looking for a meeting place where our diverse membership could get together on a daily basis to exchange ideas, problems, and solutions. Our widespread international membership makes local meetings impractical. We needed an easy, electronic means for keeping in touch.

We chose CompuServe for several reasons. As the largest of the electronic information services, it offers easy access from most parts of the U.S. and overseas. Since CompuServe is a multiuser system, members can call in virtually 24 hours a day without dealing with busy signals.

On CompuServe, messages are read in "thread" order rather than sequentially by number as our old BBS system did. A thread keeps the original message and all its responses together.

TAPCIS

The deciding factor in our decision to open a forum on CompuServe was the communications package TAPCIS—a program designed exclusively for saving time and money on CompuServe.

TAPCIS features include: a split-screen text editor with WordPerfect-like editing and word wrap; an address book of names and user IDs; and automatic downloading of messages and files.

CompuServe charges $12.50 an hour for the time you are online (connected to the service). This is comparable to the cost of calling long distance to a BBS. TAPCIS helps you conserve cost by painlessly gathering information and staying offline as much as possible. TAPCIS costs $59 for members of the WPSG ($79 for non-members). Like all WPSG products, TAPCIS has a 90-day money back guarantee.

The WPSGA and WPSGB forums can provide you with technical assistance, problem updates, and a friendly user group atmosphere. If you'd like a free IntroPak to get you connected with CompuServe, give us a call at 800-USA-GROUP. Come and visit!   ❖

Sec	The WordPerfect A Forum	The WordPerfect B Forum
1	WordPerfect 5.1 Gen	Library/Office
2	Printers/Fonts	PlanPerfect
3	Graphics/Tables/DTP	DrawPerfect
4	Macros/Merges	DataPerfect
5	Training	WP Executive/Other
6	Conversion	Macintosh WP
7	Village Inn	Village Inn
8	Networks	Unix
9	Hardware/DOS	VAX/DG/Mainframe
10	WordPerfectionist	WPCorp News/Info
11	WPCorp News/Info	Amiga/Atari/Apple 2
12	Forum/CompuServe	Forum/CompuServe
13	Problem Reports	Problem Reports
14	WordPerfect 5.0	3rd Party Programs
15	WordPerfect 4.2	

Section Topics of The WPSG Forums

Fig. 20.22.

A page from The WordPerfectionist.

Fig. 20.23.

A page from The WordPerfectionist.

Figure 2: The PagePak "Newspaper" design.

6) Choose [C-Borders & Page Treatments], [A-Newspaper Front Page]. The macro retrieves the "Newspaper" template.

7) Type or retrieve text where the comments specify. You can use any font supported by your printer. Additional graphics can be added to the design if you like.

8) Preview the page ([Print/F7], [6-View Document]) and print.

Practical Uses

MGI has designed three styles of letterhead pages. Each design also has matching envelopes, business cards, and diskette labels. Just a few keystrokes and you've assembled a collection of matching business forms.

Several pages are included that can be used to accentuate graphs, advertisements, or handouts. A cover and inside pages for a "directory" are also provided (see figure 3).

Other designs include shipping labels, brochures (cover and inside), maps for the United States, England, Canada, and the world, calendars, invitations, and an assortment of subject borders.

Problems

MGI has done a terrific job in designing and implementing PagePak. In using the product I encountered only two small problems.

MGI should figure out a way to have the pathname where PagePak is installed permanently recorded into the macro; having to enter the path each time is absurd.

No provision is given to keep text from running off the crop marked areas. This deficiency is demonstrated at the bottom of the left hand page in Figure 3. The user has no idea whether the text is going to fit in the space provided. The page must be previewed to see if the text runs into a graphic or outside of the crop marks. However, the page can be quickly previewed and corrected if necessary.

Conclusion

Since PagePak uses only WP macros and styles, it does not require any memory above and beyond what WP itself requires. This is the type of

application the WPSG has been hoping to see—a complete package that builds upon WordPerfect's own capabilities to make appealing documents easier to produce. We are starting to see similar products in the works for specific fields like law, medicine, and accounting, as well as general business.

Such applications represent the true power of WordPerfect version 5.0 and 5.1. The more we can automate the tedious and difficult chores of formatting, the more enjoyable working with a word processor becomes.   ❖

Graphic Credits

The WPSG used Arts & Letters and DrawPerfect to assemble most of the graphics accompanying articles.

Various clip-art products were used to provide images. The people in the graphic on page 15 were taken from *Cliptures* by Dream Maker software. MGI's PagePak graphics were used to in the review of PagePak (pp. 11-12).

HiJaak was used to capture and convert all screen images.

The WordPerfectionist used Bitstream Charter and News Gothic PostScript fonts for headlines and body text. Adobe Times Roman was used for all main article headlines.

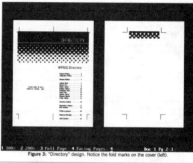

Figure 3: "Directory" design. Notice the fold marks on the cover (left).

WordPerfect Support Group Order Form Phone (800) USA-GROUP

Name _____

Company _____

Address _____

City _____

State _____ Zip _____

Country _____

Phone ( ) _____

Member/Acct # (or "New") _____

Newsletter Subscriptions

Sign me up for a subscription to *The WordPerfectionist*, the newsletter of the WordPerfect Support Group, for the term I have checked below. I understand that I may cancel my subscription at any time and receive a full refund.

❏ New Subscription ❏ Renewal (include member# above)

12 Issues U.S.: ❏ 3rd Class $36 ❏ 1st Class $48
24 Issues U.S.: ❏ 3rd Class $69 ❏ 1st Class $93
12 Issues Canada: ❏ 1st Class $48 U.S. Funds
12 Issues Airmail: ❏ $68 U.S. Funds

Payment Method

❏ Check
❏ Purchase order
❏ MasterCard ❏ Visa ❏ American Express ❏ Discover

Card # _____ Exp. _____

Signature _____
       Please make checks payable to "WordPerfect Support
       Group" and mail to address below.

Credit Card Orders: 1 (800) USA-GROUP (872-4768)
                     1 (301) 387-4500
                     1 (301) 387-7322 (Fax)

The WordPerfectionist   ❖   Volume IV, Number 1

Products

TAPCIS, The Complete Communications Program for Accessing CompuServe, for IBM PC's and compatibles, requires modem. Includes a free IntroPak with CompuServe User ID, sign-on password, and $15 usage credit.
❏ WPSG Members $59 ❏ Non-members $79

Disk Subscription including WP printer drivers, macros and utilities (2-5.25" or 1-3.5" disk per set)
❏ 6 months $60 ❏ 12 months $110 ❏ One disk set $15
❏ Send more information incl a description of the last 6 sets

Pacific Page PostScript cartridge for LaserJet II
❏ $495 IIP ❏ $465

Pacific 2-meg LaserJet II expansion board
❏ $495 IIP ❏ $425

GoScript Plus ❏ $295

Hewlett-Packard WordPerfect cartridge
LaserJet II ❏ $167 DeskJet Plus ❏ $130

Hewlett-Packard ProCollection cartridge ❏ $249

HOTLINE w/special WP directory ❏ $69

HiJaak ❏ $119

Fresh Technologies
LAN Assist ❏ $269 MAP Assist ❏ $319

MGI PicturePak Clip art Graphics 565 images ❏ $245
MGI PagePak ❏ $108

Soft Fonts (Adobe and Bitstream). Specify volume, title and format. ❏ 25% off retail ❏ two or more 30% off

Theory and Practice of DataPerfect by Parrello ❏ $21.95

WP 5.1: The Complete Reference by Karen Acerson ❏ $24.95

WordPerfect from 5.0 to 5.1 by Karen Acerson ❏ $16.50

Mastering WordPerfect 5.1 by Alan Simpson ❏ $24.95

WPSG products are offered with a 90 day unconditional money back guarantee.

All prices include UPS shipping within the U.S. and airmail to Canada. Overseas products will be shipped surface mail unless additional airmail postage is included.

2nd day delivery for all orders over $100, TAPCIS, and HOTLINE.

Maryland residents add 5% sales tax.

THE
WordPerfectionist
Newsletter of the WordPerfect Support Group

Lake Technology Park
P.O. Box 130
McHenry, MD 21541

Address Correction Requested
Forwarding Postage Guaranteed

BULK RATE
U.S. POSTAGE
PAID
SALT LAKE CITY, UT
Permit No. 3280

Fig. 20.24.

The back page of The WordPerfectionist.

Fig. 20.25.

*The headline
WordPerfect 5.1 is
the Optima 16-
point font.*

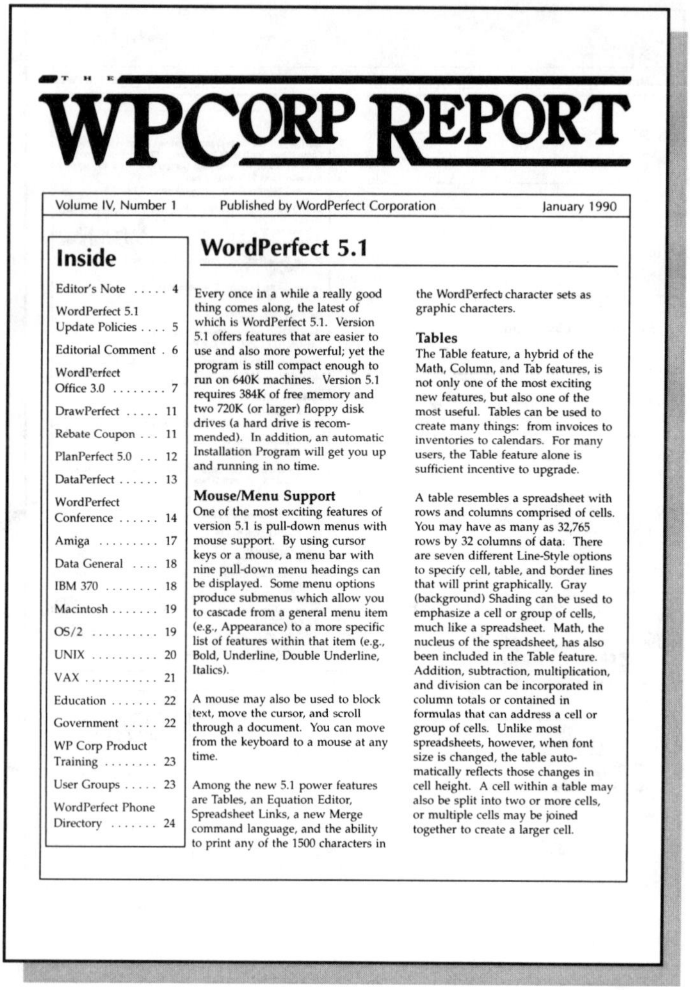

THE WPCORP REPORT

Volume IV, Number 1   Published by WordPerfect Corporation   January 1990

Inside

WordPerfect 5.1

Every once in a while a really good thing comes along, the latest of which is WordPerfect 5.1. Version 5.1 offers features that are easier to use and also more powerful; yet the program is still compact enough to run on 640K machines. Version 5.1 requires 384K of free memory and two 720K (or larger) floppy disk drives (a hard drive is recommended). In addition, an automatic Installation Program will get you up and running in no time.

Mouse/Menu Support

One of the most exciting features of version 5.1 is pull-down menus with mouse support. By using cursor keys or a mouse, a menu bar with nine pull-down menu headings can be displayed. Some menu options produce submenus which allow you to cascade from a general menu item (e.g., Appearance) to a more specific list of features within that item (e.g., Bold, Underline, Double Underline, Italics).

A mouse may also be used to block text, move the cursor, and scroll through a document. You can move from the keyboard to a mouse at any time.

Among the new 5.1 power features are Tables, an Equation Editor, Spreadsheet Links, a new Merge command language, and the ability to print any of the 1500 characters in

the WordPerfect character sets as graphic characters.

Tables

The Table feature, a hybrid of the Math, Column, and Tab features, is not only one of the most exciting new features, but also one of the most useful. Tables can be used to create many things: from invoices to inventories to calendars. For many users, the Table feature alone is sufficient incentive to upgrade.

A table resembles a spreadsheet with rows and columns comprised of cells. You may have as many as 32,765 rows by 32 columns of data. There are seven different Line-Style options to specify cell, table, and border lines that will print graphically. Gray (background) Shading can be used to emphasize a cell or group of cells, much like a spreadsheet. Math, the nucleus of the spreadsheet, has also been included in the Table feature. Addition, subtraction, multiplication, and division can be incorporated in column totals or contained in formulas that can address a cell or group of cells. Unlike most spreadsheets, however, when font size is changed, the table automatically reflects those changes in cell height. A cell within a table may also be split into two or more cells, or multiple cells may be joined together to create a larger cell.

WordPerfect 5.1 *(continued)*

WPCorp Report is published quarterly by WordPerfect Corporation, Orem, UT (801) 225-5000, and is distributed to all registered owners of WordPerfect Corporation software.

Editor:

Jacque White

Associate Editors:

Beth McGill
Rebecca Mortensen
Kathryn Pond-Sargent

Contributing Editors:

Julie Harrison
Sandy Modersitzki
Liz Tanner

Contributing Writers:

Dave Clare
W.E. "Pete" Peterson
Rich Running

Designer:

Randy B. Nelson

Typographer:

Alan L. Murray

©WordPerfect Corporation 1989

WordPerfect, DataPerfect, DrawPerfect, PlanPerfect, and WPCorp are registered trademarks of WordPerfect Corporation.

All other brands and product names are trademarks or registered trademarks of their respective companies.

WPCorp Report is created using WordPerfect 5.1 and DrawPerfect.

If you've ever tried to add a new column in the middle of a group of tabs, you will welcome the Table feature. Adding another column to a table simply involves a few keystrokes, or a few clicks of the mouse. You can move data in a table by blocking and copying—just like moving within the document itself.

Equations

The WordPerfect Equation Editor offers more than 60 functions and commands, and more than 300 symbols. You can enter an equation and immediately preview its printed appearance. The equation editing screen includes an editing window, a preview area, and a pallet which contains math, Greek, and many other types of symbols.

The size of an equation may be determined by the base font, and it can be graphically displayed using scaleable font sizes (up to 1067 point). Spacing is determined by a set of mathematical rules so that only fine tuning is needed to adjust the letter spacing within an equation.

If you have a printer capable of printing graphics, WordPerfect 5.1 will also print every character available in the equation pallet (as well as any of the 1500 characters in the WordPerfect character sets). Even if the character or symbol font isn't built into your printer or included in your soft fonts or font cartridges, WordPerfect 5.1 will print

the character as a bit-mapped graphic image. (If printed graphically, more than 250 fonts may be printed per page.)

UKALALI TOURS
-Travel Packages-

	A	B	C	D	E
Oahu	✓		✓	✓	
Maui	✓		✓		✓
Hawaii		✓		✓	✓
Kauai	✓	✓			✓
Hotel		✓			✓
Condo	✓	✓		✓	
Luau		✓	✓	✓	✓
Car		✓	✓	✓	✓

Spreadsheet Import

WordPerfect 5.1 will import spreadsheet information directly from PlanPerfect, Lotus 1-2-3 (WKS and WK1 formats), and Microsoft Excel. (WordPerfect Corporation is currently developing support for Lotus WK3 files.) Not only will version 5.1 import the information into tabs or tables, but by linking the spreadsheet, you can update your imported information at any time. Links can retrieve an entire spreadsheet or a range of cells. Named spreadsheet ranges may be listed and selected from within WordPerfect.

Mailing Labels

Mailing Labels can be easily created in WordPerfect 5.1 by simply specifying the dimensions of your labels and the number of labels on each page. WordPerfect 5.1 also includes a macro that will create mailing label forms for you. Once invoked, this macro will list (by size and manufacturer) 19 of the most popular label form sizes. After marking the label forms you wish to create, WordPerfect does the rest.

Merge

Now you can name the fields in your WordPerfect Merge files, making them more descriptive and easier to understand. The new WordPerfect

2

Fig. 20.26.

The WordPerfect Tables feature was used to create the table between columns 2 and 3.

Fig. 20.27.

The figures show a PlanPerfect Spreadsheet (top box) and a WordPerfect table imported from a spreadsheet (bottom box).

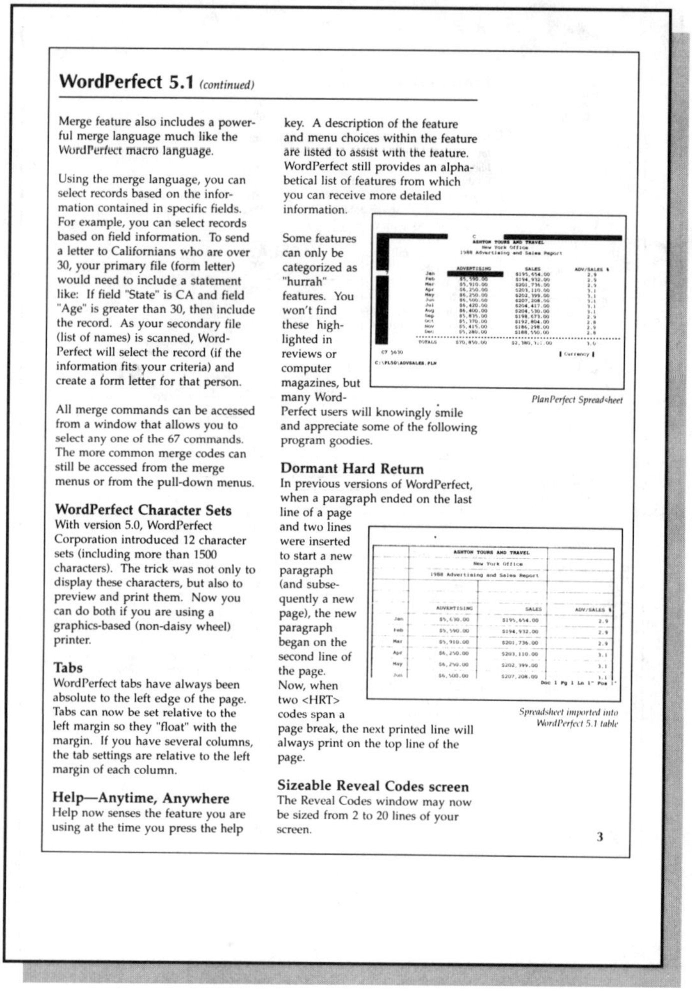

WordPerfect 5.1 *(continued)*

Merge feature also includes a powerful merge language much like the WordPerfect macro language.

Using the merge language, you can select records based on the information contained in specific fields. For example, you can select records based on field information. To send a letter to Californians who are over 30, your primary file (form letter) would need to include a statement like: If field "State" is CA and field "Age" is greater than 30, then include the record. As your secondary file (list of names) is scanned, WordPerfect will select the record (if the information fits your criteria) and create a form letter for that person.

All merge commands can be accessed from a window that allows you to select any one of the 67 commands. The more common merge codes can still be accessed from the merge menus or from the pull-down menus.

WordPerfect Character Sets
With version 5.0, WordPerfect Corporation introduced 12 character sets (including more than 1500 characters). The trick was not only to display these characters, but also to preview and print them. Now you can do both if you are using a graphics-based (non-daisy wheel) printer.

Tabs
WordPerfect tabs have always been absolute to the left edge of the page. Tabs can now be set relative to the left margin so they "float" with the margin. If you have several columns, the tab settings are relative to the left margin of each column.

Help—Anytime, Anywhere
Help now senses the feature you are using at the time you press the help key. A description of the feature and menu choices within the feature are listed to assist with the feature. WordPerfect still provides an alphabetical list of features from which you can receive more detailed information.

Some features can only be categorized as "hurrah" features. You won't find these highlighted in reviews or computer magazines, but many WordPerfect users will knowingly smile and appreciate some of the following program goodies.

PlanPerfect Spreadsheet

Dormant Hard Return
In previous versions of WordPerfect, when a paragraph ended on the last line of a page and two lines were inserted to start a new paragraph (and subsequently a new page), the new paragraph began on the second line of the page. Now, when two <HRT> codes span a page break, the next printed line will always print on the top line of the page.

Spreadsheet imported into WordPerfect 5.1 table

Sizeable Reveal Codes screen
The Reveal Codes window may now be sized from 2 to 20 lines of your screen.

3

Editorial Comment

What Does the WordPerfect/Lotus Agreement Mean to Our Customers?

W.E. "Pete" Peterson
Executive Vice President

At a press conference during Fall COMDEX, WordPerfect Corporation and Lotus Development Corporation announced an agreement of cooperation. After almost a year of discussions, we agreed to work together so that the interfaces for our OS/2 PM products, WordPerfect and Lotus 1-2-3/G, will be similar, and so that data can be easily exchanged between the two products.

Some of you, especially those who have purchased PlanPerfect, may wonder why we entered into the agreement. The answer is simple. While we have worked on WordPerfect and WordPerfect Office for PM, we have not started working on a PM version of PlanPerfect. We do not expect to have a PM version of PlanPerfect ready before late 1991. Because many of our PM customers will want to purchase a spreadsheet program before that date, we feel it necessary to integrate well with 1-2-3/G. We are impressed with the Lotus PM product and their interface design. We also feel that 1-2-3/G will be a good choice for our PM WordPerfect customers until we introduce our own spreadsheet. We also know that many of our DOS customers use 1-2-3/G, and that many of those customers who move to OS/2 PM will welcome a tighter integration of our product with 1-2-3/G.

Does this mean we are ending our PlanPerfect DOS development? Not at all. We expect to have a minor release of PlanPerfect ready in the first half of next year, which will use the 5.1 printer drivers and support a mouse. We are also working on a major update of the product. If this new product is well-received, we intend to create a PM version.

Does this kind of strategy mean we are schizophrenic—cooperating with Lotus and continuing development on PlanPerfect at the same time? Perhaps a little. It has taken a long time to realize how important it is for us to integrate well with other products, and we want to work more closely with other, well-accepted software products. With WordPerfect 5.1, for example, you can retrieve a Lotus 1-2-3 or an Excel 2.1 worksheet directly into a document without any conversion steps.

We also feel it is important to offer other business software applications. Obviously, we need to make careful decisions with our resources so that we can continue to improve WordPerfect (and there will be more versions of WordPerfect for DOS). We think we can do a good job with WordPerfect, and at the same time produce other fine software tools. For example, DrawPerfect, DataPerfect, and PlanPerfect each have a place in the marketplace, especially for WordPerfect customers. WordPerfect Office, which is already a best-selling product for local area networks, will shortly become a very attractive mail/calendaring/scheduling program for wide area networks.

We are now the third-largest personal computer software company and sell a lot of software for mini-computers and mainframes. As time goes on we will work more closely with other software companies and continue to develop our own products.

6

Fig. 20.28.

Shaded figure boxes are used to indicate where photos will appear in final copy.

Fig. 20.29.

DrawPerfect is used to add graphical illustrations to the publication.

Presenting DrawPerfect

Who needs DrawPerfect? Anyone interested in creating business presentations, adding visuals to any WordPerfect document, or producing charts and graphs. DrawPerfect is a new graphics package designed to enhance any presentation or document. The program is scheduled for a first quarter 1990 release. Bundled with each package of DrawPerfect will be a copy of the WordPerfect Office 3.0 Shell program that will let you "hot-key" between DrawPerfect and WordPerfect 5.1, allowing you to share graphics between the two programs with a single keystroke.

Transparencies
With DrawPerfect, you can turn graphics and text that you create into an overhead transparency. Just put transparency film into the paper bin of your printer, and print. Or, you can print on paper and then make transparencies by using a copy machine or professional service.

Slides
You can send the images created in DrawPerfect to several different slide service bureaus who can turn your illustrations into high-quality slides within 24 hours. To turn Draw-Perfect files into slides, select Export from the File pull-down menu, select CGM or SCODL as your export format, and Spread then enter the filename.

Presentations
DrawPerfect includes many ways to present the visuals you've created. You can begin a presentation sequence by specifying the filenames you want included. After specifying the amount of time each file will be displayed, you can choose how each image leaves the screen. You can have images fade from the screen,

overlay images, or erase from one side to the other. DrawPerfect will demonstrate your presentation, and you can make changes until you have exactly what you want.

You can select a shaded background that fades from one color at the top of the screen to another color at the bottom, move forward as well as backward through a presentation, and create self-running presentations which can be shown on the screen, or printed on overhead transparencies or as slides.

Charts and Graphs
With a complete set of graph and chart types including pie, bar, line, scatter, hi-lo, stacked bar, area, and mixed, you can create illustrations in no time, and they can be incorpo-rated into any WordPerfect document. You can also add legends or grid lines, and overlap bars and label axes. It's easy to insert your own data or retrieve information from PlanPerfect, Lotus, or Excel spreadsheets. You can also turn these into transparencies.

Figure Library
DrawPerfect also includes a figure library containing more than 500 ready-to-use objects, banners, backgrounds, arrows, maps, flags, symbols, computers, animals, busi-ness graphics, and other clip-art images that print in color or in black and white. All images are com-pletely compatible with WordPerfect versions 5.0 and 5.1. Additional figure libraries are being created and will be sold separately.

Drawing
You have flexibility and control in creating and modifying images with the drawing tools in DrawPerfect. Creating lines, boxes, circles, arcs,

10

Examples of Different Headline Styles on Newsletter Pages

Of course, article headlines do not need to be positioned at the top of the page and centered. You can use different article headline styles in your newsletters in order to break up the monotony caused by having everything exactly the same on every page. What follows in figures 20.30 through 20.35 are examples of different ways to lay out headlines on newsletter pages.

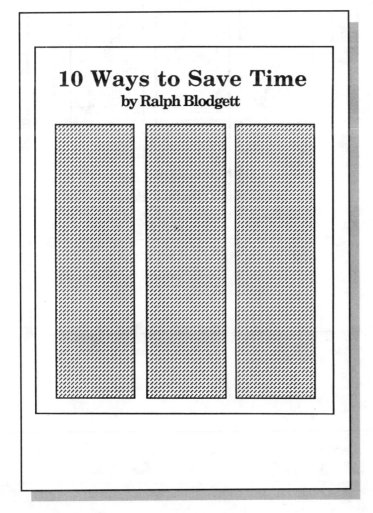

Fig. 20.30.

Headline at top, centered.

Fig. 20.31.

Headline at top, flush right.

Fig. 20.32.

Headline at top, flush left.

Fig. 20.33.

"Vertical" headline surrounded by text.

Ten
Ways
to
Save
Time

by
Ralph
Blodgett

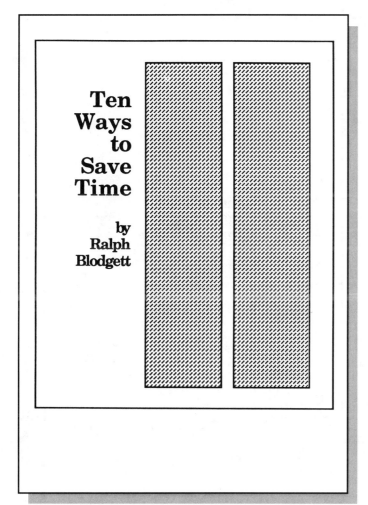

Fig. 20.34.

"Vertical," flush-right headline to the left of copy.

Fig. 20.35.

Headline at top, surrounded by text on three sides.

**Ten Ways
to
Save Time**

by Ralph Blodgett

Summary

In this final chapter you learned how to convert a plain WordPerfect 4.2 document that uses Courier font into an attractive newsletter page in 12 easy steps. These steps included adding a proportional font; changing the headline size; replacing underlining with italic font and inch marks with double quotation marks; adding newspaper columns, full justification, and hyphenation; placing a quotation into a text box; editing section headings; adding paragraph indentions, graphics, and shaded fonts; adding graphic lines between columns; and adding a full-page graphic box.

Next the chapter showed newsletters printed on a Hewlett-Packard DeskJet printer (*The Sundae Times*), a Hewlett-Packard LaserJet printer (*Letter to the Editors*), and a Linotronic printer (*The WordPerfectionist* and *The WPCorp Report*). Last, you saw six examples of headline placement for a newsletter page ("10 Ways to Save Time").

After reading the guidelines provided in this chapter, you should have some new ideas on how to modify and enhance your text and turn it into an attractive, informative newsletter for your company or home business.

A

Installing the Applications Disk

WordPerfect Power Pack comes with one 5 1/4-inch, 360K IBM PC format disk. The disk contains macros, styles, templates, forms, letters, merge files, and supporting documents described in this book.

The following files are contained on the Applications Disk:

WPPOWPAK.EXE   Self-extracting ZIP file containing this book's files in compressed format

INSTALL.BAT   Batch file to install files

GETKEY.EXE   Utility program used by the installation batch file

You must install the Applications Disk before you can use the files on the disk. You can install the Applications Disk to a hard disk or a high-capacity floppy disk on a dual-floppy-disk system (hard disk installation is recommended). The files on the Applications Disk are stored in compressed format. When you run the INSTALL batch file, the files are "extracted" and copied to your hard disk or to a high-capacity floppy disk, depending on which you choose. You can elect to install all the files or selected sets of files by subdirectory. The following subdirectories are created when you install the Applications Disk:

\QLEGAL   Contains macros, form documents, and other files for legal applications

\QLETTERS   Contains 26 sample business letters

\QMACROS	Contains 56 macros and supporting files
\QMERGE	Contains primary and secondary merge files
\QSTYLES	Contains styles for boxes in headers, various types of horizontal lines, and page numbering
\QTABLES	Contains a number of useful form templates created with the Table feature

The README files in the \QLEGAL and \QMACROS subdirectories provide additional suggestions on how to use the macros in these subdirectories.

After installation, put the Applications Disk in a safe place. If you accidentally delete material in a file or delete a file entirely, you can restore the file by selectively reinstalling files from the Applications Disk. If at any time you need to reinstall files, follow the installation directions in this appendix.

Hard Disk Installation

To install the files on your hard disk, under your WordPerfect directory, follow these steps:

1. Place the Applications Disk in drive A or B.

2. Log onto the drive by typing *a:* or *b:* and pressing Enter.

3. Type *install d:\path* and press Enter, where *d:* is the drive you want the files to be installed on and *\path* denotes the directory you would like them installed under. For example, to install all the files under your WordPerfect directory on drive C, type *install c:\wp51* and press Enter. The menu shown in figure A.1 is displayed.

   To the right of the menu, the drive/path (d:\path) combination you have selected is displayed for your convenience. If this information is not correct, use option 8 (Exit to DOS) and restart the installation.

4. If you want to install individual subdirectories (options 1 through 6), choose the number of the subdirectory you want to install. If you want to install all subdirectories, select option 7. To install all subdirectories, you will need approximately 600K of disk space available.

Errors made during installation are trapped and reported to you with suggested corrective action.

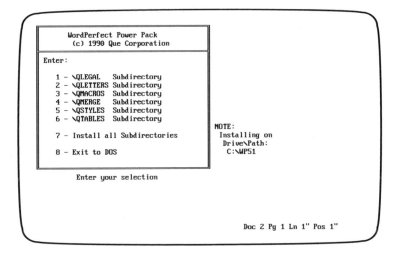

Fig. A.1.

The installation menu.

Dual-Floppy-Disk Installation

If you are installing on a dual-floppy-disk system, first prepare a blank, high-capacity disk before the installation process. (Note: The Applications Disk files require at least 600K of floppy disk space.) Follow these steps:

1. Place the Applications Disk in drive A and the blank, formatted target disk in drive B.

2. Log onto the drive by typing *a:* and pressing Enter.

3. Type *install b:* and press Enter, where *b:* is the drive you want the files to be installed on. The main installation menu is displayed (see fig. A.1).

   To the right of the menu, the drive information you have selected is displayed for your convenience. If this information is not correct, use option 8 (Exit to DOS) and restart the installation.

4. If you want to install individual subdirectories (options 1 through 6), choose the number of the subdirectory you want to install. If you want to install all subdirectories, select option 7. To install all subdirectories, you will need approximately 600K of disk space available.

Errors made during installation are trapped and reported to you with suggested corrective action.

B

WordPerfect 5.1
Command Summary

Feature	Command	Keystrokes
Absolute tab settings	Format	Shift-F8,1,8,T,1
Acceleration factor (mouse)	Setup	Shift-F1,1,5
Add password	Text In/Out	Ctrl-F5,2
Additional printers	Print	Shift-F7,S,2
Advance (to position, line, and so on)	Format	Shift-F8,4,1
Advanced macro commands (macro editor)	Macro Commands	Ctrl-PgUp
Advanced merge codes	Merge Codes	Shift-F9,6
Align/decimal character	Format	Shift-F8,4,3
Align text on tabs	Tab Align	Ctrl-F6
Alphabetize text	Merge/Sort	Ctrl-F9,2
Alt/Ctrl key mapping	Setup	Shift-F1,5
Appearance of printed text	Font	Ctrl-F8
Append text to a file (Block on)	Move	Ctrl-F4,1-3,4
Append to clipboard (Block on)	Shell	Ctrl-F1,3
ASCII text file	Text In/Out	Ctrl-F5,1
Assign keys	Setup	Shift-F1,5

Assign variable	Macro Commands	Ctrl-PgUp
Attributes, printed	Font	Ctrl-F8
Attributes, screen	Setup	Shift-F1,2,1
Authorities, table of (define)	Mark Text	Alt-F5,5,4
Authorities, table of (edit full form)	Mark Text	Alt-F5,5,5
Authorities, table of (mark)	Mark Text	Alt-F5,4
Automatically format and rewrite	Setup	Shift-F1,2,6,1
Backspace (erase)	Backspace	Backspace
Backup directory location	Setup	Shift-F1,6
Backup files, automatic timed	Setup	Shift-F1,3,1,1
Backup files, location of	Setup	Shift-F1,6,1
Backup options	Setup	Shift-F1,3,1
Backward search	<-Search	Shift-F2
Base font	Font	Ctrl-F8,4
Base font (Document)	Format	Shift-F8,3,3
Base font (Printer)	Print	Shift-F7,S,3,5
Baseline placement for typesetters	Format	Shift-F8,4,6,5
Beep options	Setup	Shift-F1,3,2
Binding offset	Print	Shift-F7,B
Binding offset (default)	Setup	Shift-F1,4,8,1
Black and white, view document in	Setup	Shift-F1,2,5,1
Block	Block	Alt-F4 or F12
Block, assign variable (with Block on)	Macro Commands	Ctrl-PgUp
Block, append (Block on)	Move	Ctrl-F4,1,4
Block, center (Block on)	Center	Shift-F6
Block, comment (Block on)	Text In/Out	Ctrl-F5
Block Copy (Block on)	Move	Ctrl-F4,1,2
Block Copy (Block on)	Block Copy	Ctrl-Ins
Block, delete (Block on)	Del or Backspace	Del or Backspace
Block, move (Block on)	Move	Ctrl-F4,1,1
Block Move (Block on)	Block Move	Ctrl-Del
Block, print (Block on)	Print	Shift-F7
Block Protect (Block on)	Format	Shift-F8

Bold	Bold	F6
Bold (print attribute)	Font	Ctrl-F8,2,1
Border Options (table and graphic box)	Format	Shift-F8,4,8
Bottom margin	Format	Shift-F8,2,5
Box (fig., table, text, user, equation)	Graphics	Alt-F9,1-4 or 6
Cancel	Cancel	F1
Cancel hyphenation code	Home	Home,/
Cancel print job(s)	Print	Shift-F7,4,1
Capitalize Block (Block on)	Switch	Shift-F3,1
Cartridges and fonts	Print	Shift-F7,S,3,4
Case conversion (Block on)	Switch	Shift-F3
Center	Center	Shift-F6
Center with dot leaders	Center	Shift-F6,Shift-F6
Center block (Block on)	Center	Shift-F6
Center justification	Format	Shift-F8,1,3,2
Center page (top to bottom)	Format	Shift-F8,2,1
Center tab setting	Format	Shift-F8,1,8,C
Centimeters, units of measure	Setup	Shift-F1,3,8
Change comment to text	Text In/Out	Ctrl-F5,4,3
Change default directory	List	F5,=,*name*,Enter
Change font (part of document)	Font	Ctrl-F8
Change font (entire document)	Columns/Table	Alt-F7,1,1 or 2
Change supplementary dictionary	Spell	Ctrl-F2,4
Change text to comment (Block on)	Text In/Out	Shift-F5
Character sets	Compose	Ctrl-V or Ctrl-2
Character spacing	Format	Shift-F8,4,6,3
Clear screen (without saving)	Exit	F7,N,N
Clear screen (and save)	Exit	F7,Y,N
Clipboard (with shell program)	Shell	Ctrl-F1,2-4
Codes, default	Setup	Shift-F1,4,5
Codes, merge	Merge Codes	Shift-F9
Codes, reveal	Reveal Codes	Alt-F3 or F11
Color print	Font	Ctrl-F8,5

Colors (display)	Setup	Shift-F1,2,1
Columns	Columns/Table	Alt-F7,1
Columns, define	Columns/Table	Alt-F7,1,3
Columns, movement among	GoTo	Ctrl-Home,arrow
Columns, movement among (Enhanced Keyboard)	Item Right/Left	Alt-right arrow, Alt-left arrow
Columns, on/off	Columns/Table	Alt-F7,1,1 or 2
Columns, side-by-side display	Setup	Shift-F1,2,6,7
Commands, programming (macro editor)	Macro Commands	Ctrl-PgUp
Comment in document	Text In/Out	Ctrl-F5,4
Comment to text	Text In/Out	Ctrl-F5,4,3
Comments display	Setup	Shift-F1,2,6,2
Compare screen and disk documents	Mark Text	Alt-F5,6,2
Compose	Compose	Ctrl-V or Ctrl-2
Concordance	Mark Text	Alt-F5,5,3
Condense master document	Mark Text	Alt-F5,6,4
Conditional end of page	Format	Shift-F8,4,2
Control characters	Merge Codes	Shift-F9
Control printer	Print	Shift-F7,4
Convert documents (5.1 to 5.0 or 4.2)	Text In/Out	Ctrl-F5,3,2 or 3
Convert old merge codes	Merge/Sort	Ctrl-F9,3
Copy block (Block on)	Move	Ctrl-F4,1,2
Copy block (Block on)	Block Copy	Ctrl-Ins
Copy file(s)	List	F5,Enter,8
Copy keyboard definition	Setup	Shift-F1,5,5
Copy text (Block on or off)	Move	Ctrl-F4,1-3,2
Count words	Spell	Ctrl-F2,6
Create spreadsheet link	Text In/Out	Ctrl-F5,5,2
Cross-reference	Mark Text	Alt-F5,1
Cross-references, generate	Mark Text	Alt-F5,6,5
Ctrl/Alt key mapping	Setup	Shift-F1,5
Cursor movement	Home and arrow keys	Arrow keys
Cursor movement by page	PgUp or PgDn	PgUp or PgDn

Cursor movement by screen	Screen Up or Down	+ or – (numeric keypad)
Cursor movement to a page	GoTo or Repeat	GoTo or Esc
Cursor speed	Setup	Shift-F1,3,3
Cut text (Block Off)	Move	Ctrl-F4,1-3,1
Date format	Date/Outline	Shift-F5,3
Date format (default)	Setup	Shift-F1,4,2
Date of file creation	Format	Shift-F8,3,5,1
Date/time	Date/Outline	Shift-F5
Decimal/align character	Format	Shift-F8,4,3
Decimal tab setting	Format	Shift-F8,1,8,D
Default codes	Setup	Shift-F1,4,5
Default directory	List	F5
Default settings	Setup	Shift-F1
Define macros	Macro Define	Ctrl-F10
Define paragraph/outline numbering	Date/Outline	Shift-F5,6
Define printer	Print	Shift-F7,S
Define text (highlight)	Block	Alt-F4
Define ToC, lists, ToA, index	Mark Text	Alt-F5,5
Delete	Delete	Del or Backspace
Delete block (Block on)	Block Delete	Del or Backspace
Delete file	List	F5,Enter,2
Delete text (Block Off)	Move	Ctrl-F4,1-3,3
Delete to end of page	Delete to End of Page	Ctrl-PgDn
Delete to end of line	Delete to End of Line	Ctrl-End
Delete word	Delete	Ctrl-Backspace
Diacriticals/digraphs	Compose	Ctrl-V or Ctrl-2
Dictionary	Spell	Ctrl-F2
Directories	List	F5,Enter
Display	Setup	Shift-F1,2
Display attributes	Setup	Shift-F1,2,1
Display disk space	List	F5,Enter
Display document comments	Setup	Shift-F1,2,6,2
Display file names, short/long	List	F5,Enter,5

Display pitch	Format	Shift-F8,3,1
Display setup	Setup	Shift-F1,2
Document backup	Setup	Shift-F1,3,1
Document comment	Text In/Out	Ctrl-F5,4
Document compare	Mark Text	Alt-F5,6,2
Document format	Format	Shift-F8,3
Document management/summary	Setup	Shift-F1,3,4
Document preview	Print	Shift-F7,6
Document, retrieve	Retrieve	Shift-F10
Document summary, create/edit	Format	Shift-F8,3
Document summary, create on save/exit	Setup	Shift-F1,3,4,1
Documents directory	Setup	Shift-F1,6,7
DOS command	Shell	Ctrl-F1,5
DOS text file	Text In/Out	Ctrl-F5,1
Dot leader tab	Format	Shift-F8,1,8
Double underline	Font	Ctrl-F8,2,3
Download fonts to printer	Print	Shift-F7,7
Downloadable fonts	Print	Shift-F7,S,3,4
Downloadable fonts path	Print	Shift-F7,S,3,6
Draw lines	Screen	Ctrl-F3,2
Dual document editing	Switch	Shift-F3
Edit find conditions	List	F5,Enter,9,5
Edit screen options	Setup	Shift-F1,2,6
Edit spreadsheet link	Text In/Out	Ctrl-F5,5,3
Encrypt a document	Text In/Out	Ctrl-F5,2
End of field	End Field	F9
End of line, delete to	Delete to End of Line	Ctrl-End
End of line, move to	End	End
End of page, delete to	Delete to End of Page	Ctrl-PgDn
End of record	Merge Codes	Shift-F9,2
Endnote	Footnote	Ctrl-F7,2
Endnote placement	Footnote	Ctrl-F7,3
Endnotes, generate	Mark Text	Alt-F5,6,5

Enhanced Keyboard definition	Setup	Shift-F1,5
Enter, inserting paragraph number with	Date/Outline	Shift-F5,6,7
Environment	Setup	Shift-F1,3
Equation editor	Graphics	Alt-F9,6,1,9
Equation options	Setup	Shift-F1,4,3
Execute macro	Macro	Alt-F10
Exit WordPerfect	Exit	F7,N or Y,Y
Expand master document	Mark Text	Alt-F5,6,3
Extended characters	Compose	Ctrl-V or Ctrl-2
Extended replace	Replace	Home, Alt-F2
Extended search	Search	Home,F2
Extra-large print	Font	Ctrl-F8,1,7
Fast save (unformatted)	Setup	Shift-F1,3,5
Fast text display	Setup	Shift-F1,2,1,2
Field, end of code	Merge Codes	Shift-F9,1
Figure box	Graphics	Alt-F9,1
File, DOS text	Text In/Out	Ctrl-F5,1
File location	Setup	Shift-F1,6
File management	List	F5,Enter
File, mark	List	F5,Enter,*
File search	List	F5,Enter,9
File name on status line	Setup	Shift-F1,2,6,3
Files, backup	Setup	Shift-F1,3,1
Find	List	F5,Enter,9
Find file name	List	F5,Enter,9,1
Fine print	Font	Ctrl-F8,1,3
Flush right	Flush Right	Alt-F6
Flush-right text with dot leaders	Flush Right	Alt-F6,Alt-F6
Font appearance	Font	Ctrl-F8,2
Font attributes	Font	Ctrl-F8,(1,2, or 5)
Font, base	Font	Ctrl-F8,4
Font color	Font	Ctrl-F8,5
Font, initial (document)	Format	Shift-F8,3,3

Font, initial (printer)	Print	Shift-F7,S,3,5
Font size	Font	Ctrl-F8,1
Fonts directory	Print	Shift-F7,S,3,6
Fonts, download to printer	Print	Shift-F7,7
Fonts, downloadable	Print	Shift-F7,S,3,4
Footers	Format	Shift-F8,2,4
Footnote	Footnote	Ctrl-F7,1
Force odd/even page	Format	Shift-F8,2,2
Forced insert (macro define)	Ins	Home,Home,Ins
Forced typeover (macro define)	Typeover	Home,Ins
Foreign characters	Compose	Ctrl-V or Ctrl-2
Foreign languages (international)	Format	Shift-F8,4,4
Format line/page/document/other	Format	Shift-F8
Format screen	Screen	Ctrl-F3,3
Format screen, automatically	Setup	Setup,2,6,1
Forms (paper size)	Format	Shift-F8,2,7
Forward search	->Search	F2
Full justification	Format	Shift-F8,1,3,4
Generate tables, indexes, etc.	Mark Text	Alt-F5,6,5
Generic word processor format	Text In/Out	Ctrl-F5,3,1
Global search and replace	Replace	Home, Alt-F2
Go to	GoTo	Ctrl-Home
Go to DOS/Shell	Shell	Ctrl-F1,1
Graphics	Graphics	Alt-F9
Graphics box options	Graphics	Alt-F9,1-4 or 6,4
Graphics files directory	Setup	Shift-F1,6,6
Graphics quality	Print	Shift-F7,G
Graphics quality (default)	Setup	Shift-F1,4,8,3
Graphics screen type	Setup	Shift-F1,2,2
H-zone	Format	Shift-F8,1,2
Hanging indent	Indent	F4,Shift-Tab
Hard hyphen	Hard Hyphen	Home,-
Hard page break	Hard Page	Ctrl-Enter

Hard return display character	Setup	Shift-F1,2,6,4
Hard space	Space bar	Home,space bar
Hard tab	Tab	Home,Tab
Headers	Format	Shift-F8,2,3
Help	Help	F3
Help, printer	Print	Shift-F7,S,6
Hidden codes	Reveal Codes	Alt-F3
Hide document comments	Setup	Shift-F1,2,6,2
Hyphen character	Hyphen	-
Hyphen, hard	Hard Hyphen	Home,-
Hyphen, soft	Soft Hyphen	Ctrl,-
Hyphenation	Format	Shift-F8,1,1
Hyphenation dictionaries	Setup	Shift-F1,3,6
Hyphenation files, location of	Setup	Shift-F1,6,3
Hyphenation prompt	Setup	Shift-F1,3,7
Hyphenation rules	Setup	Shift-F1,3,6
Hyphenation zone	Format	Shift-F8,1,2
Import spreadsheet	Text In/Out	Ctrl-F5,5,1
Inches (units of measure)	Setup	Shift-F1,3,8
Indent left and right	->Indent<-	Shift-F4
Indent left only	->Indent	F4
Index, define	Mark Text	Alt-F5,5,3
Index, generate	Mark Text	Alt-F5,6,5
Index, mark text for (Block on)	Mark Text	Alt-F5,3
Initial base font, printer	Print	Shift-F7,S,3,5
Initial base font, document	Format	Shift-F8,3,3
Initial codes, default	Setup	Shift-F1,4,5
Initial codes, document	Format	Shift-F8,3,2
Initial settings, default	Setup	Shift-F1,4
Initialize printer	Print	Shift-F7,7
Input, merge	Merge Codes	Shift-F9,3
Insert special character	Compose	Ctrl-V or Ctrl-2
Insert, forced (macro define)	Forced Insert	Home,Home,Ins

Insert page number	Format	Shift-F8,2,6,3
Insert /Typeover mode	Ins	Ins
Insert subdocument	Mark Text	Alt-F5,2
International characters	Compose	Ctrl-V or Ctrl-2
Interrupt print job	Print	Shift-F7,4,5
Invisible soft return	Enter	Home,Enter
Italics print	Font	Ctrl-F8,2,4
Item down	Item Down	Alt-down arrow
Item left	Item Left	Alt-left arrow
Item right	Item Right	Alt-right arrow
Item up	Item Up	Alt-up arrow
Justification	Format	Shift-F8,1,3
Justification limits	Format	Shift-F8,4,6,4
Keep lines together	Format	Shift-F8,4,2
Kerning	Format	Shift-F8,4,6,1
Keyboard definitions/layout	Setup	Shift-F1,5
Keyboard/macro files, location of	Setup	Shift-F1,6,2
Keyboard map	Setup	Shift-F1,5,8
Labels	Format	Shift-F8,2,7,5,8
Landscape fonts	Print	Shift-F7,S,3,4
Landscape forms	Format	Shift-F8,2,7
Landscape paper size/type	Format	Shift-F8,2,7
Languages	Format	Shift-F8,4,4
Large print	Font	Ctrl-F8,1,5
Leaders (centered text)	Center	Shift-F6,Shift-F6
Leaders (flush-right text)	Flush Right	Alt-F6,Alt-F6
Leading	Format	Shift-F8,4,6,6
Left and right margins, specify	Format	Shift-F8,1,7
Left justification	Format	Shift-F8,1,3,1
Left margin release	<-Margin Release	Shift-Tab
Left tab setting	Format	Shift-F8,1,8,L
Letter/word spacing	Format	Shift-F8,4,6,3
Line (border) appearance	Format	Shift-F8,4,8

Line draw	Screen	Ctrl-F3,2
Line format	Format	Shift-F8,1
Line, graphics	Graphics	Alt-F9,5
Line height	Format	Shift-F8,1,4
Line numbering	Format	Shift-F8,1,5
Line spacing	Format	Shift-F8,1,6
Link options	Text In/Out	Ctrl-F5,5,4
Link, update	Text In/Out	Ctrl-F5,5,4,3
Links, spreadsheet	Text In/Out	Ctrl-F5,5,2-4
List files	List	F5,Enter
List printer files	Print	Shift-F7,S,2,4
Lists, mark text for (Block on)	Mark Text	Alt-F5,2
Lists, define	Mark Text	Alt-F5,5,2
Lists, generate	Mark Text	Alt-F5,6,5
Locked document	Text In/Out	Ctrl-F5,2
Long document name	Setup	Shift-F1,3,4,3
Long form, table of auth (Block on)	Mark Text	Alt-F5,4
Long/Short file name display	List	F5,Enter,5
Look at a file	List	F5,Enter,6
Lower-/uppercase (Block on)	Switch	Shift-F3
Macro editor	Macro Define	Ctrl-F10
Macro commands (in macro editor)	Macro Commands	Ctrl-PgUp
Macros, define	Macro Define	Ctrl-F10
Macros, execute	Macro	Alt-F10
Macros, keyboard definition	Setup	Shift-F1,5
Mail merge	Merge/Sort	Ctrl-F9,1
Main dictionary location	Setup	Shift-F1,6,3
Map, keyboard	Setup	Shift-F1,5,8
Map special characters	Setup	Shift-F1,5
Margin release	<-Margin Release	Shift-Tab
Margins, left and right (specifying)	Format	Shift-F8,1,7
Margins, top and bottom (specifying)	Format	Shift-F8,2,5
Mark text for index (Block on)	Mark Text	Alt-F5,3

Mark text for list (Block on)	Mark Text	Alt-F5,2
Mark text for ToA (Block on)	Mark Text	Alt-F5,4
Mark text for ToC (Block on)	Mark Text	Alt-F5,1
Master document	Mark Text	Alt-F5,2
Math	Columns/Table	Alt-F7,3
Menu bar	Menu Bar	Alt-=
Menu options	Setup	Shift-F1,2,4
Merge	Merge/Sort	Ctrl-F9,1
Merge codes	Merge Codes	Shift-F9
Merge codes (convert old codes)	Merge/Sort	Ctrl-F9,3
Merge codes display	Setup	Shift-F1,2,6,5
Merge options	Setup	Shift-F1,4,1
More merge codes	Merge Codes	Shift-F9,6
Mouse	Setup	Shift-F1,1
Mouse, type	Setup	Shift-F1,1,1
Move block (Block on)	Move	Ctrl-F4,1,1
Move block (Block on)	Block Move	Ctrl-Del
Move down one paragraph	Paragraph Down	Ctrl-down arrow
Move down one item (columns and tables)	Item Down	Alt-down arrow
Move left one item (columns and tables	Item Left	Alt-left arrow
Move one word right	Word Right	Ctrl-right arrow
Move one word left	Word Left	Ctrl-left arrow
Move/rename file	List	F5,Enter,3
Move right one item (columns and tables)	Item Right	Alt-right arrow
Move text (Block Off)	Move	Ctrl-F4,1-3,1
Move up one item (columns and tables)	Item Up	Alt-up arrow
Move up one paragraph	Paragraph Up	Ctrl-up arrow
Multiple copies generated by	Print	Shift-F7,U
Multiple copies generated by (default)	Setup	Shift-F1,4,8,2
$n=$ (default)	Setup	Shift-F1,4,6
$n=$ (set temporarily)	Repeat Value	Esc,#,Enter
New page	Hard Page	Ctrl-Enter
New page number	Format	Shift-F8,2,6,1

New supplementary dictionary	Spell	Ctrl-F2,4
Newspaper columns	Columns/Table	Alt-F7,1,3,1
Next document	List	F5,Enter,6,1
Normal font	Font	Ctrl-F8,3
Number lines	Format	Shift-F8,1,5
Number of copies (default)	Setup	Shift-F1,4,8,2
Number of copies	Print	Shift-F7,*n*
Number pages	Format	Shift-F8,2,6,4
Page break, hard	Hard Page	Ctrl-Enter
Page down	PgDn	PgDn
Page format	Format	Shift-F8,2
Page format, suppress	Format	Shift-F8,2,8
Page length	Format	Shift-F8,2,7
Page number, go to	GoTo	Ctrl-Home,#,Enter
Page number in text	^B (Ctrl-B)	Ctrl-B
Page number in text (using style)	Format	Shift-F8,2,6,3
Page number, new	Format	Shift-F8,2,6,1
Page number style	Format	Shift-F8,2,6,2
Page numbering	Format	Shift-F8,2,6,4
Page offsets	Format	Shift-F8,2,7,5,9
Page up	Page Up	PgUp
Page view	Print	Shift-F7,6
Paper location	Format	Shift-F8,2,7
Paper size/type	Format	Shift-F8,2,7
Paper trays	Print	Shift-F7,S,3,3
Paragraph down	Down	Ctrl-down arrow
Paragraph numbering, automatic	Date/Outline	Shift-F5,5
Paragraph up	Paragraph Up	Ctrl-Up
Parallel columns	Columns/Tables	Alt-F7,1,3,1
Password	Text In/Out	Ctrl-F5,2
Path for downloadable fonts	Print	Shift-F7,S,3,6
Path for printer command files	Print	Shift-F7,S,3,6

Percent of optimal spacing	Format	Shift-F8,4,6,3
Pitch, display	Format	Shift-F8,3,1
Port, mouse	Setup	Shift-F1,1,2
Port, printer	Print	Shift-F7,S,3,2
Portrait fonts	Format	Shift-F8,2,7
Portrait forms	Format	Shift-F8,2,7
Portrait paper size\type	Format	Shift-F8,2,7
Preview	Print	Shift-F7,6
Previous document	List	F5,Enter,6,2
Primary file, merge	Merge/Sort	Ctrl-F9,1
Primary leading	Format	Shift-F8,4,6,6
Print	Print	Shift-F7
Print (cancel, rush, display, go, stop)	Print	Shift-F7,4,1-5
Print block (Block on)	Print	Shift-F7,Y
Print color	Font	Ctrl-F8,5
Print document on disk	Print	Shift-F7,3
Print from disk	Print	Shift-F7,3
Print from disk	List	F5,Enter,4
Print full document	Print	Shift-F7,1
Print list files	List	F5,Enter,Shift-F7
Print multiple pages	Print	Shift-F7,5
Print options (default)	Setup	Shift-F1,4,8
Print options (document)	Print	Shift-F7
Print page	Print	Shift-F7,2
Print preview	Print	Shift-F7,6
Print quality, graphics	Print	Shift-F7,G
Print quality, graphics (default)	Setup	Shift-F1,4,8,3
Print quality, text (default)	Setup	Shift-F1,4,8,4
Print quality, text	Print	Shift-F7,T
Printed attributes	Font	Ctrl-F8
Printer command	Format	Shift-F8,4,6,2
Printer command files path	Print	Shift-F7,S,3,6

Printer control	Print	Shift-F7,4
Printer edit	Print	Shift-F7,S,3
Printer files location	Setup	Shift-F1,6,4
Printer fonts (location)	Print	Shift-F7,S,3,6
Printer functions	Format	Shift-F8,4,6
Printer, initialize	Print	Shift-F7,7
Printer name	Print	Shift-F7,S,3,1
Printer port	Print	Shift-F7,S,3,2
Printer, select	Print	Shift-F7,S
Program macro commands (macro editor)	Macro Commands	Ctrl-PgUp
Prompt for hyphenation	Setup	Shift-F1,3,7
Prompt for document summary	Setup	Shift-F1,3,4,1
Protect a document	Text In/Out	Ctrl-F5,2
Protect block (Block on)	Format	Shift-F8
.PRS files, edit	Print	Shift-F7,S,3
.PRS files, view	Print	Shift-F7,S,2,4
Quality of text or graphics	Print	Shift-F7,T or G
Quality of text and graphics (default)	Setup	Setup,4,8,3 or 4
Quit WordPerfect	Exit	F7,Y or N,Y
Reassign keys	Setup	Shift-F1,5
Recover deleted text	Cancel	F1,1
Rectangle, move/copy (Block on)	Move	Ctrl-F4,3
Redline method	Format	Shift-F8,3,4
Redline method (default)	Setup	Shift-F1,4,8,5
Redline print	Font	Ctrl-F8,2,8
Redline, remove	Mark Text	Alt-F5,6,1
Reformat screen	Screen	Ctrl-F3,3
Relative tab settings	Format	Shift-F8,1,8,T,2
Remove password	Text In/Out	Ctrl-F5,2,2
Remove redline and strikeout	Mark Text	Alt-F5,6,1
Rename/move file	List	F5,Enter,3
Repeat value (default)	Setup	Shift-F1,4,6

Repetition number (*n*)	Repeat Value	Esc
Replace	Replace	Alt-F2
Replace, extended	Replace	Home,Alt-F2,
Report printer status	Print	Shift-F7,4
Restore deleted text	Cancel	F1,1
Retrieve a file	List	F5,Enter,1
Retrieve a file	Retrieve	Shift-F10
Retrieve clipboard	Shell	Ctrl-F1,4
Retrieve tabular column	Move	Ctrl-F4,4,2
Retrieve document	List	F5,Enter,1
Retrieve document	Retrieve	Shift-F10
Retrieve DOS text file	Text In/Out	Ctrl-F5,1,2 or 3
Retrieve Text (Move key)	Move	Ctrl-F4,4,1-3
Reveal codes	Reveal Codes	Alt-F3
Reveal Codes window size (Reveal on)	Screen	Ctrl-F3,1
Reveal Codes window size (default)	Setup	Shift-F1,2,6,6
Reverse search	<-Search	Shift-F2
Rewrite screen	Screen	Ctrl-F3,3
Right justification	Format	Shift-F8,1,3,3
Right margin	Format	Shift-F8,1,7
Right tab setting	Format	Shift-F8,1,8,R
Ruler	Screen	Ctrl-F3,1,23,Enter
Save, clipboard	Shell	Ctrl-F1,2
Save, fast (unformatted)	Setup	Shift-F1,3,5
Save text	Save	F10
Screen	Screen	Ctrl-F3
Screen display options	Setup	Shift-F1,2
Screen down	Screen Down	+ (numeric keypad)
Screen rewrite	Screen	Ctrl-F3,3
Screen setup	Setup	Shift-F1,2
Screen split	Screen	Ctrl-F3,1
Screen up	Screen Up	- (numeric keypad)
Scrolling speed	Setup	Shift-F1,3,3

Search	Search	F2
Search and replace	Replace	Alt-F2
Search for file(s)	List	F5,Enter,9,1
Secondary file, merge	Merge/Sort	Ctrl-F9,1
Secondary leading	Format	Shift-F8,4,6,6
Select printer	Print	Shift-F7,S
Send printer a "go"	Print	Shift-F7,4,4
Set tabs	Format	Shift-F8,1,8
Settings, initial (default)	Setup	Shift-F1,4
Setup	Setup	Shift-F1
Shadow print	Font	Ctrl-F8,2,6
Sheet feeder	Print	Shift-F7,S,3,3
Sheet feeder help	Print	Shift-F7,S,6,Shift-F3
Shell, go to	Shell	Ctrl-F1,1
Short form, table of authorities	Mark Text	Alt-F5,4
Short/long file name display	List	F5,Enter,5
Side-by-side columns display	Setup	Shift-F1,2,6,7
Size attribute ratios	Setup	Shift-F1,4,8,6
Size of print (attributes)	Font	Ctrl-F8,1
Small capitalized print	Font	Ctrl-F8,2,7
Small print	Font	Ctrl-F8,1,4
Soft hyphen	Soft Hyphen	Ctrl,-
Sort	Merge/Sort	Ctrl-F9,2
Space, hard	Space bar	Home,space bar
Spacing justification limits	Format	Shift-F8,4,6,4
Spacing lines	Format	Shift-F8,1,6
Spell	Spell	Ctrl-F2
Speller files location	Setup	Shift-F1,6,3
Split screen	Screen	Ctrl-F3,1
Spreadsheet, import	Text In/Out	Ctrl-F5,5,1
Spreadsheet, link	Text In/Out	Ctrl-F5,5,2-4
Status line file-name display	Setup	Shift-F1,2,6,3

Stop printer	Print	Shift-F7,4,5
Strikeout	Font	Ctrl-F8,2,9
Style	Style	Alt-F8
Style files directory	Setup	Shift-F1,6,5
Style library file location	Setup	Shift-F1,6,5
Style library file name	Setup	Shift-F1,6,5
Style, outline	Date/Outline	Shift-F5,6,9
Subdocument	Mark Text	Alt-F5,2
Subject search text	Setup	Shift-F1,3,4,2
Subscript print	Font	Ctrl-F8,1,2
Summary, document	Format	Shift-F8,3,5
Summary prompt	Setup	Shift-F1,3,4,1
Superscript print	Font	Ctrl-F8,1,1
Supplementary dictionary, location	Setup	Shift-F1,6,3
Suppress numbering, headers, and so on	Format	Shift-F8,2,8
Swappable fonts and cartridges	Print	Shift-F7,S,3,4
Switch documents	Switch	Shift-F3
Tab	Tab	Tab
Tab align	Tab Align	Ctrl-F6
Tab, hard	Tab	Home,Tab
Tab ruler	Screen	Ctrl-F3,1,23,Enter
Tab set	Format	Shift-F8,1,8
Tab type	Format	Shift-F8,1,8,T
Table	Columns/Table	Alt-F7,2
Table box	Graphics	Alt-F9,2
Table of authorities (default)	Setup	Shift-F1,4,7
Table of authorities, mark (Block on)	Mark Text	Alt-F5,4
Table of authorities, define	Mark Text	Alt-F5,5,4
Table of authorities, generate	Mark Text	Alt-F5,6,5
Table of contents, mark (Block on)	Mark Text	Alt-F5,1
Table of contents, define	Mark Text	Alt-F5,5,1
Table of contents, generate	Mark Text	Alt-F5,6,5

Target	Mark Text	Alt-F5,1,2
Text box	Graphics	Alt-F9,3
Text columns	Columns/Table	Alt-F7,1
Text in/out	Text In/Out	Ctrl-F5
Text quality	Print	Shift-F7,T
Text quality (default)	Setup	Shift-F1,4,8,4
Text screen type	Setup	Shift-F1,2,3
Text to comment (Block on)	Text In/Out	Ctrl-F5
Thesaurus	Thesaurus	Alt-F1
Thesaurus, file location	Setup	Shift-F1,6,3
Thousands' separator	Format	Shift-F8,4,3
Time/date	Date/Outline	Shift-F5
Timed document backup	Setup	Shift-F1,3,1,1
Top and bottom margin	Format	Shift-F8,2,5
Typeover, forced (Macro Define)	Insert	Home,Ins
Typeover mode	Insert	Ins
Undelete	Cancel	F1,1
Underline spaces and tabs	Format	Shift-F8,4,7
Underline text	Underline	F8
Underline text	Font	Ctrl-F8,2,2
Units of measure	Setup	Shift-F1,3,8
Unlock a document	Text In/Out	Ctrl-F5,2
Update spreadsheet link	Text In/Out	Ctrl-F5,5,4,3
Update printer driver	Print	Shift-F7,S,7
Update references	Mark Text	Alt-F5,6,5
Upper-/lowercase (Block on)	Switch	Shift-F3
User-defined box	Graphics	Alt-F9,4
Variable	Macro Commands	Ctrl-PgUp
Very large print	Font	Ctrl-F8,1,6
View codes	Reveal Codes	Alt-F3
View document	Print	Shift-F7,6
View-document options	Setup	Shift-F1,2,5
Widow/orphan protection	Format	Shift-F8,1,9

Window	Screen	Ctrl-F3,1
Word count	Spell	Ctrl-F2,6
Word left, cursor movement	Word Left	Ctrl-left arrow
Word/letter spacing	Format	Shift-F8,4,6,3
Word look up	Spell	Ctrl-F2,5
Word right, cursor movement	Word Right	Ctrl-right arrow
Word spacing justification limits	Format	Shift-F8,4,6,4
Word spell	Spell	Ctrl-F2,1
WP 4.2 format, save as	Text In/Out	Ctrl-F5,3,3
WP 5.0 format, save as	Text In/Out	Ctrl-F5,3,2

Glossary of Word Processing Terms

As word processors like WordPerfect invade the office, a whole new vocabulary has emerged—a vocabulary that often sounds dazzling or intimidating to the new user. The following glossary provides brief definitions of the key terms and concepts you may encounter when working with a word processor on a computer. Throughout the definitions below, *DTP* refers to desktop publishing—using a computer and printer to produce text like the text produced at a print shop. Words in italic are defined elsewhere in the glossary.

Access. To call up information or data stored in a file on a computer's hard or floppy disk.

Access time. The amount of time required to locate and retrieve data from a particular hard disk. The smaller the access time, the better the hard disk. A disk with an access time of 17 ms, for example, is far superior to a disk with an access time of 32 ms.

Align. In DTP terminology, to align text right or left means to select the proper justification. Left-aligned text is flush left with a ragged right margin; right-aligned text is flush right with a ragged left margin; fully justified text is aligned on both the left and right margins.

Art. In DTP terminology, all nontext material.

ASCII (pronounced "*as*-key"). An acronym for the American Standard Code for Information Interchange. ASCII refers to a method of translating computer information into a series of eight-digit codes. The method is often used to exchange data from one program to another.

AT clone. A computer that has an Intel 80286 microprocessor and is both hardware- and software-compatible with the IBM PC AT.

Automatic file sort. The rearrangement by a word processor of a collection of information into alphabetic or numeric order on the basis of the characters that appear in certain positions. For example, WordPerfect can sort a secondary file of names and addresses by last name, by state, by ZIP code, or by almost any other type of information in the file.

Backup file. A copy on disk of the current file in use.

Banner. Any large headline or title.

Baseline. The lowest point a character reaches on a line (excluding characters with descenders, such as *g*, *p*, and *q*).

Baud rate. The speed at which data is transmitted over a phone line or cable.

BIOS. An abbreviation for basic input-output system, a series of programs in ROM that controls the low-level operation of the computer.

Bit. The smallest, most basic unit of information used in a personal computing system. A bit always has the binary value of 0 or 1. The term comes from the phrase *binary digit*.

Bleed. To print a photo so that it extends to the edge of the page. To create a full bleed, print the photo on a larger-sized page and trim off the excess paper so that the photo extends to the cut edge.

Body copy. The main part of the text of a publication, as distinguished from *headers, footers,* footnotes, *captions*, and so on.

Body size or **body height.** The total height used for a particular typeface, measured in points (a measurement equal to approximately 1/72 inch). A typeface's height is measured from the top of the tallest character to the bottom of the lowest descender character.

Boldface. A heavy-faced type that is darker, with thicker and more pronounced strokes, than normal text. On a dot-matrix printer, boldface (or bold) is created by the double-striking of the letters; on a LaserJet, a thicker font is used for bold.

Box. A section of text set off with rules—either top and bottom, top alone, or on all four sides. Sometimes text in a box is shaded in gray.

Brochure. A small, folded pamphlet.

Budget. The total editorial expense (including art and text) for a publication or single issue.

Bullet. A small black circle (•) used to mark entries in a list.

Byte. A group of *bits* that forms a single unit of information. A byte consisting of eight bits, for example, makes up a single letter or character on the screen.

c&lc. An abbreviation for text set in both capital letters and lowercase letters, as in a headline.

Camera-ready. Describing material that is fully ready for plate-making, with no additional adjustments on the pages being necessary. The term refers to the first step in the plate-making process, in which the pages are photographed and turned into the negatives used in making the printing plates. In DTP, the term also refers to pages printed from a DTP system that are ready for reproduction.

Caps. An abbreviation for capital letters, the familiar uppercase form of alphabet letters.

Caps/small caps. An instruction to cast, in a heading, the first letter of each word in capital letters and to cast the remaining letters in small caps, which are smaller than the normal capital letters. The following shows the use of caps/small caps:

THIS PHRASE CONTAINS CAPS AND SMALL CAPS

Caption. A line or lines of text accompanying and identifying a figure, photo, or other illustration.

CD-ROM drive. A drive that uses a laser beam to scan tracks of microscopic pits in a rotating compact disk.

Cell. The intersection of a column and row in a spreadsheet or table.

Central processing unit (CPU). The portion of a personal computer that manipulates data according to a set of software instructions.

Color Graphics Adapter (CGA). One of the two original display adapters introduced with the original IBM PC in 1981. The CGA monitor provides a resolution of 320 by 200 *pixels* with four colors.

Click. To press and release a mouse button quickly.

Close up (pronounced "cloze-*up*"). A proofreading instruction to reduce the amount of space between words, either in general throughout the document or between two words (or characters) individually.

Column. A vertically running section of a page, generally so called if more than one column is in a section.

Column inch. In newspaper and magazine production, the vertical inch of printed text one column wide. Most publishers charge advertisers either by column inch or by portions of a page (for example, half-page, one-third page, or one-quarter page).

Column rule. A thin vertical line placed between columns of text.

Composition. The setting of type and the arranging of the type on a page.

Constants. Layout elements that remain the same from one issue to another of the same publication.

Context-sensitive help. An on-line help feature that gives information about the operation the user is currently performing. For example, in WordPerfect 5.1, pressing Help (F3) while creating a footnote calls up a screen of information about the footnote feature.

Conventional memory. The RAM that MS-DOS uses directly. The maximum usable conventional memory is one megabyte, of which only 640K is available for running a single application.

Copy fitting. Estimating the size of the material to be included in a publication and making allowances for the text by properly selecting the typeface and leading.

CPU. See **Central processing unit**.

Cursor. A blinking horizontal line or square on the computer monitor that marks the place where characters appear on-screen when you type.

Cut and paste. An operation that once required manually cutting sections of text and pasting them into a new location. You can accomplish this task on-screen by using your word processor's "move" feature.

Daisywheel. A printing element made of plastic or metal and used inside certain impact printers to produce text. Each character is affixed to the end of a spoke on the wheel.

Dash. Any of a variety of horizontal-line characters. These include the hyphen (-), the em dash (—), and the en dash (–). (See *em dash* and *en dash*.)

Database. A collection of individual records stored in an organized format on a computer disk. A database program can sort, select, merge, and otherwise manipulate the records to produce mailing lists and other related printouts.

Delete. In computer terminology, to erase or eliminate characters or entire sections of text.

Desktop publishing. The use of a personal computer to produce high-quality printed output that is *camera-ready* for the printer. Often referred to as DTP.

Diagnostics. Software programs that test the operational status of hardware components.

Directory. An index of the location of files on a disk.

Disk. A revolving plate on which information and programs are stored.

Disk drive. An internal or external machine that stores and retrieves information on magnetic disks.

Display. The monitor screen that displays characters you type from your keyboard.

Documentation. A user manual or set of instructions that comes with a piece of hardware or software and that tells how to use the material.

DOS. An abbreviation for disk operating system, a collection of programs designed to operate the computer and move data to and from a disk.

Dot-matrix printer. A printer that uses closely spaced dots to create characters on a sheet of paper. Dot-matrix printers come in two basic types: 9-pin and 24-pin. The 24-pin printers produce better printed quality.

Dot pitch. Refers to the space, measured in millimeters (mm), between *pixels* on the screen. Standard VGA dot-pitch measurements include 0.28mm, 0.31mm, and 0.41mm. A lower dot-pitch number indicates that the dots are closer together and thus form a tighter, crisper image.

Drag. To press a mouse button and move the mouse in order to highlight text on-screen.

Em dash. A special horizontal line used to indicate an abrupt change of sentence structure. Generally, an em dash is the same width as a capital M in that particular font.

EMS. An abbreviation of Expanded Memory Specification. The term refers to a system by which extended memory is converted into expanded memory.

En dash. A horizontal line longer than a hyphen and shorter than an *em dash*. An en dash is used to separate numbers that show a range, as in "pages 12–20." An en dash is half the width of an em dash.

Enhanced Graphics Adapter (EGA). The Enhanced Graphics Adapter, which first appeared in 1984, offers 16 out of 64 colors at 640-by-350-pixel resolution.

Expanded memory. Memory above the base 640K memory that DOS directly addresses. WordPerfect can use expanded memory to hold larger documents in *RAM*.

Fax. The short form for *facsimile*, the copy of a printed page transmitted between two locations through the use of a phone line.

Field. A single unit of data in a record. (See **Record**.)

Floppy disk. A transportable disk—generally 5 1/4 or 3 1/2 inches in size and sealed in a square plastic jacket—used to record and store information. You must use floppy disks with a disk drive to store or retrieve data.

Font. A typeface of a particular design and size.

Footer. One or more lines of information printed along the bottom margin of every page of a document, such as a page number.

Format. As applied to publications, the overall size, layout, typestyle, and sequence of materials used in those publications.

Function keys. The keys to the left or along the top of the keyboard, marked F1 through F10 or F12. In WordPerfect, function keys are preset to provide 40 or 42 WordPerfect commands.

G. See **Gigabyte**.

Gigabyte. One billion bytes.

Gutter. The area between two printed pages that face each other. Although it is possible to continue a heading across the gutter, the practice in not recommended unless your publisher has precise control over registration and binding.

Hacker. A very technical person in the computer field. The term generally refers to someone who gains unauthorized access to other computers and data banks.

Hardware. Hardware refers to the physical components of a computer system—the keyboard, monitor, central processing unit, printer, and modem.

Header. One or more lines of information printed along the top margin of every page in a document.

Helvetica. The most popular typeface of the *sans serif* class of type (a sans serif font is a typeface whose strokes don't end in cross strokes).

Italic. A typestyle that somewhat simulates handwritten letters. In an italic font, letters slant to the right and have rounded lines, rather than rectangular corners. If your printer cannot print an italic font, WordPerfect substitutes underlined characters.

Justify. To align text along the margin on both the right and left sides. In WordPerfect, this alignment is called Full Justification.

Kern. In typesetting, to move two letters closer together so that the overhanging part of one letter (like a *W*) slightly overlaps an adjacent letter (like an *o*), producing a more attractive headline.

Keyline. An empty graphic box created within a word processing program as a positioning guide for the manual insertion of a photo half-tone or illustration.

Kilobyte. 1,024 bytes. *Kilobyte* is abbreviated as *K* (as in *640K*).

Laptop computer. A portable computer that usually weighs less than 12 pounds and has a self-contained power supply.

Laser printing. The term used to describe printing with one of the toner-based printers available for PCs. These printers use laser technology to project an intense light beam with a narrow bandwidth to create the electrical charge on the printer drum that picks up the toner and transfers it to the paper.

Layout. The arrangement of text and graphic elements on a page.

Leading. The amount of vertical white space (measured from baseline to baseline) between lines in a paragraph or block of text.

Light pen. An input device that uses a light-sensitive pointer connected by a wire to a video terminal.

LIM. Abbreviation of Lotus-Intel-Microsoft Expanded Memory Specification, a system by which extended memory is converted to expanded memory. Known also as EMS.

Line art. Illustrations containing only black and white areas, with no intermediate tones (shades of gray) in the illustration. Line art is the easiest to reproduce because it does not require the screening or patterning step that most printing processes need to produce a range of tones.

Line spacing. The distance between the bottom of one line and the bottom of the line above or below. Decreasing line spacing allows the user to put more lines on a given page.

Load. To open up or start a program by sending the program to the computer's *RAM*.

Logo. A shortened form of logotype, which is a combination of letters or a drawing treated as a single character. Today the term refers to the company, institutional, or publication symbol or stylized rendering of the organization's name.

M. See **Megabyte**.

Macro. A series of recorded keystrokes and/or menu selections that can be replayed repeatedly.

Mail merge. The process of merging a form letter, label form, or envelope form in one document with data (names, addresses, and so on) from a second document to create multiple copies of the original document.

Margin. The amount of white space reserved on a page where text and graphics are not printed.

Mechanical. A completed page of type and illustration ready to be photographed by the printer and made into printing plates. (See **Overlay**.)

Megabyte. One million bytes. *Megabyte* is abbreviated as *M*, as in *40M hard disk* or *4M of RAM*.

MegaHertz (MHz). A metric unit of speed used to measure the "clock speed" of a central processing unit. The original clock speed of the IBM PC was 4.77 MHz. Machines today contain processors that run at 33 MHz and higher.

Menu. A list of user options displayed on-screen.

MHz. See **MegaHertz**.

Microcomputer. A complete computer system small enough to fit on a desktop. Most personal computers now in use are microcomputers.

Microprocessor. A miniature silicone chip consisting of up to a million or more transistors and related circuitry that composes the brains of a computer. The device is called a "computer on a chip" because it contains all the elements of a central processing unit.

Minicomputer. An intermediate computer system sized between the microcomputer and the large mainframe computer housed in its own computer room.

Modem. A contraction of *modulating-demodulating*, the term refers to a device that links your computer with a telephone for communication with other computers. Information is broken down by a modem into pulses that can be transmitted on an ordinary phone line and reassembled on the other end into recognizable computer data.

Monochrome display. A video monitor with a single color, such as green or amber.

Monopitch. Referring to a font whose characters take up the same horizontal space in a line—generally either 10 characters per inch or 12 characters per inch.

Mouse. A device used to point, draw, or select objects or text on a computer screen.

Multiscan monitor. A monitor that works with many kinds of video adapter cards, including CGA, EGA, and VGA.

Multitasking. Capable of running two or more programs on the computer at the same time and copying or moving data from one program to another.

Network. A system consisting of two or more computers connected by high-speed communication lines.

Nonjustified. Describing text that has a ragged right margin.

Numeric keypad. The set of keys at the right of many keyboards, used to enter numbers. In WordPerfect these keys (such as PgUp, PgDn, End, and Home) are used to move around quickly within a document.

Overlay. A sheet of tracing paper taped to the front of a *mechanical*. Used for writing special instructions to the printer, for indicating crop marks, and so on.

Password. A word or code used to identify an authorized user of a computer or bulletin board.

Path. The route DOS uses to find a directory, subdirectory, or file on a disk, usually a hard disk. For example, in the full file name C:\WP51\LETTERS\SMITH.01, the path is C:\WP51\LETTERS\.

Peripheral. Any hardware device connected to a computer, such as a printer, mouse, or joy stick.

Photostat. A clean, crisp photographic reproduction of an original illustration made to the percentage (larger or smaller) that you request. Generally, a photostat is used when you need to resize an illustration for manual insertion into a camera-ready page.

Pica. A unit of measurement used to measure typeset material. Six picas make up one inch.

Pixels. The small dots of light (picture elements) displayed on the computer monitor as text letters or graphic images. Generally, the more pixels, the more readable the text displayed on the monitor.

Point. A measurement used in the layout of text on a page. One point equals one-twelfth of a pica, or about one seventy-second of an inch. Fonts are typically measured in points, with a standard font size being 10 point for a magazine, 12 point for a book, 48 point for everyday newspaper headlines, and as little as 6 or 8 point for legal notices and "fine print."

Pop-up menu. The horizontal menu and vertical submenus that appear at the top of the screen. In WordPerfect 5.1 you can activate the horizontal menu by pressing Alt-= or by pressing the right mouse button.

Preview. In WordPerfect, the on-screen display representing a page or pair of pages with fonts, graphic boxes, headers, footers, footnotes, and page numbers as they will print.

Program. See **Software**.

Prompt. An on-screen message that provides information about a WordPerfect operation or that requests a response from the user.

RAM. An abbreviation for random-access memory, a type of computer memory that can be changed or modified.

Record. A group of related *field*s that is used to store data about a subject. A collection of records is a file, and a collection of files is a *database*.

ROM. An abbreviation for read-only memory, a type of microchip that cannot be modified by the user.

Rules. Lines added to the page—for example, between columns—to enhance the design or readability of a publication. In WordPerfect 5.1, rules can be horizontal or vertical and can be of varying lengths, widths, and shades.

Sans serif. Describing a typeface without the small cross-lines, or *serifs*, that appear on the ends of characters. For example: This sentence is printed in a sans serif typeface. Sans serif typefaces are most commonly used in headlines.

Scroll. To move through a file to information not on the current screen display.

Serial port. A part of the computer, usually on the back, that sends or receives serial bits of data to and from a peripheral device such as a *modem*.

Serif. The small cross-lines that appear at the ends of characters. The typeface used throughout this book has serifs. Serif typefaces are most commonly used for body text because they are easier to read than *sans serif* faces.

Soft font. A font packaged on disk that is sent to the printer when the printer is turned on or when a file is being printed.

Software. Programs that enable a computer to carry out instructions. Software comes stored on floppy disks and can be transferred onto a hard disk within a computer.

Spreadsheet. A software program that simulates a paper spreadsheet, or financial worksheet, in which columns of numbers are manipulated and totaled.

Stat. See **Photostat**.

Status line. An on-screen line of information about the document on-screen and your cursor position.

Stripping. Placing an illustration or photo manually onto a camera-ready page of text.

Super VGA monitor. Also called the extended VGA or VGA Plus, Super VGA monitors provide 16 colors in an 800-by-600-pixel resolution. This monitor first appeared in 1988.

Telecomputing. Working at home and communicating by computer with the office.

TSR. An abbreviation for terminate-and-stay-resident programs, which operate in the background until activated with a special "hot key" combination. Then the software pops into the foreground and performs whatever special activity the user needs.

User-friendly. Describing hardware or software designed to help people use their computers with minimal reference to a manual or set of instructions.

Video Graphics Array (VGA). An adapter introduced in 1987 with the IBM PS/2 line of computers. The VGA provides 16 colors at 640-by-480-pixel resolution.

Virus. A "rogue" program that attaches itself to other programs, by disk or through links between computers, and carries out unwanted and sometimes damaging operations.

Weight. The boldness or thickness of a letter or font. Many typestyles have been designed with special bold, medium, or light forms, or weights.

White space. Empty space on a page, used for neither text nor graphics.

Window. A portion of a video display screen devoted to a certain program.

Word processor. A text-editing program or system that allows the electronic writing and correcting of articles and other text.

Word wrap. The automatic adjustment of the number of words on a line of text in order to match the margin settings and font selected. As text is typed on the screen, words "wrap" down to the next line automatically when there are too many words or characters for the line.

X-height. The height of the lowercase letter x in a particular font. This height is the normal height of the lowercase letters in that font.

Index

Computer Books From Que Mean PC Performance!

Spreadsheets

1-2-3 Database Techniques	$24.95
1-2-3 Graphics Techniques	$24.95
1-2-3 Macro Library, 3rd Edition	$39.95
1-2-3 Release 2.2 Business Applications	$39.95
1-2-3 Release 2.2 Quick Reference	$ 7.95
1-2-3 Release 2.2 QuickStart	$19.95
1-2-3 Release 2.2 Workbook and Disk	$29.95
1-2-3 Release 3 Business Applications	$39.95
1-2-3 Release 3 Quick Reference	$ 7.95
1-2-3 Release 3 QuickStart	$19.95
1-2-3 Release 3 Workbook and Disk	$29.95
1-2-3 Tips, Tricks, and Traps, 3rd Edition	$22.95
Excel Business Applications: IBM Version	$39.95
Excel Quick Reference	$ 7.95
Excel QuickStart	$19.95
Excel Tips, Tricks, and Traps	$22.95
Using 1-2-3, Special Edition	$26.95
Using 1-2-3 Release 2.2, Special Edition	$26.95
Using 1-2-3 Release 3	$27.95
Using Excel: IBM Version	$24.95
Using Lotus Spreadsheet for DeskMate	$19.95
Using Quattro Pro	$24.95
Using SuperCalc5, 2nd Edition	$24.95

Databases

dBASE III Plus Handbook, 2nd Edition	$24.95
dBASE III Plus Tips, Tricks, and Traps	$22.95
dBASE III Plus Workbook and Disk	$29.95
dBASE IV Applications Library, 2nd Edition	$39.95
dBASE IV Handbook, 3rd Edition	$23.95
dBASE IV Programming Techniques	$24.95
dBASE IV QueCards	$21.95
dBASE IV Quick Reference	$ 7.95
dBASE IV QuickStart	$19.95
dBASE IV Tips, Tricks, and Traps, 2nd Edition	$21.95
dBASE IV Workbook and Disk	$29.95
R:BASE User's Guide, 3rd Edition	$22.95
Using Clipper	$24.95
Using DataEase	$22.95
Using dBASE IV	$24.95
Using FoxPro	$26.95
Using Paradox 3	$24.95
Using Reflex, 2nd Edition	$22.95
Using SQL	$24.95

Business Applications

Introduction to Business Software	$14.95
Introduction to Personal Computers	$19.95
Lotus Add-in Toolkit Guide	$24.95
Norton Utilities Quick Reference	$ 7.95
PC Tools Quick Reference, 2nd Edition	$ 7.95
Q&A Quick Reference	$ 7.95
Que's Computer User's Dictionary	$ 9.95
Que's Wizard Book	$ 9.95
Smart Tips, Tricks, and Traps	$24.95
Using Computers in Business	$22.95
Using DacEasy, 2nd Edition	$22.95
Using Dollars and Sense: IBM Version, 2nd Edition	$19.95
Using Enable/OA	$24.95
Using Harvard Project Manager	$24.95
Using Lotus Magellan	$21.95
Using Managing Your Money, 2nd Edition	$19.95

Using Microsoft Works: IBM Version	$22.95
Using Norton Utilities	$24.95
Using PC Tools Deluxe	$24.95
Using Peachtree	$22.95
Using PFS: First Choice	$22.95
Using PROCOMM PLUS	$19.95
Using Q&A, 2nd Edition	$23.95
Using Quicken	$19.95
Using Smart	$22.95
Using SmartWare II	$24.95
Using Symphony, Special Edition	$29.95

CAD

AutoCAD Advanced Techniques	$34.95
AutoCAD Quick Reference	$ 7.95
AutoCAD Sourcebook	$24.95
Using AutoCAD, 2nd Edition	$24.95
Using Generic CADD	$24.95

Word Processing

DisplayWrite QuickStart	$19.95
Microsoft Word 5 Quick Reference	$ 7.95
Microsoft Word 5 Tips, Tricks, and Traps: IBM Version	$22.95
Using DisplayWrite 4, 2nd Edition	$22.95
Using Microsoft Word 5: IBM Version	$22.95
Using MultiMate	$22.95
Using Professional Write	$19.95
Using Word for Windows	$22.95
Using WordPerfect, 3rd Edition	$21.95
Using WordPerfect 5	$24.95
Using WordPerfect 5.1, Special Edition	$24.95
Using WordStar, 2nd Edition	$21.95
WordPerfect QueCards	$21.95
WordPerfect Quick Reference	$ 7.95
WordPerfect QuickStart	$21.95
WordPerfect Tips, Tricks, and Traps, 2nd Edition	$22.95
WordPerfect 5 Workbook and Disk	$29.95
WordPerfect 5.1 Quick Reference	$ 7.95
WordPerfect 5.1 QuickStart	$19.95
WordPerfect 5.1 Tips, Tricks, and Traps	$22.95
WordPerfect 5.1 Workbook and Disk	$29.95

Hardware/Systems

DOS Power Techniques	$29.95
DOS Tips, Tricks, and Traps	$22.95
DOS Workbook and Disk, 2nd Edition	$29.95
Hard Disk Quick Reference	$ 7.95
MS-DOS Quick Reference	$ 7.95
MS-DOS QuickStart	$21.95
MS-DOS User's Guide, Special Edition	$29.95
Networking Personal Computers, 3rd Edition	$22.95
The Printer Bible	$24.95
Que's Guide to Data Recovery	$24.95
Understanding UNIX, 2nd Edition	$21.95
Upgrading and Repairing PCs	$27.95
Using DOS	$22.95
Using Microsoft Windows 3, 2nd Edition	$22.95
Using Novell NetWare	$24.95
Using OS/2	$24.95
Using PC DOS, 3rd Edition	$24.95
Using UNIX	$24.95
Using Your Hard Disk	$29.95
Windows 3 Quick Reference	$ 7.95

Desktop Publishing/Graphics

Harvard Graphics Quick Reference	$ 7.95
Using Animator	$24.95
Using Harvard Graphics	$24.95
Using Freelance Plus	$24.95
Using PageMaker: IBM Version, 2nd Edition	$24.95
Using PFS: First Publisher	$22.95
Using Ventura Publisher, 2nd Edition	$24.95
Ventura Publisher Tips, Tricks, and Traps,	$24.95

Macintosh/Apple II

AppleWorks QuickStart	$19.95
The Big Mac Book	$27.95
Excel QuickStart	$19.95
Excel Tips, Tricks, and Traps	$22.95
Que's Macintosh Multimedia Handbook	$22.95
Using AppleWorks, 3rd Edition	$21.95
Using AppleWorks GS	$21.95
Using Dollars and Sense: Macintosh Version	$19.95
Using Excel: Macintosh Version	$24.95
Using FileMaker	$24.95
Using MacroMind Director	$29.95
Using MacWrite	$22.95
Using Microsoft Word 4: Macintosh Version	$22.95
Using Microsoft Works: Macintosh Version, 2nd Edition	$22.95
Using PageMaker: Macintosh Version	$24.95

Programming/Technical

Assembly Language Quick Reference	$ 7.95
C Programmer's Toolkit	$39.95
C Programming Guide, 3rd Edition	$24.95
C Quick Reference	$ 7.95
DOS and BIOS Functions Quick Reference	$ 7.95
DOS Programmer's Reference, 2nd Edition	$27.95
Oracle Programmer's Guide	$24.95
Power Graphics Programming	$24.95
QuickBASIC Advanced Techniques	$22.95
QuickBASIC Programmer's Toolkit	$39.95
QuickBASIC Quick Reference	$ 7.95
QuickPascal Programming	$22.95
SQL Programmer's Guide	$29.95
Turbo C Programming	$22.95
Turbo Pascal Advanced Techniques	$22.95
Turbo Pascal Programmer's Toolkit	$39.95
Turbo Pascal Quick Reference	$ 7.95
UNIX Programmer's Quick Reference	$ 7.95
Using Assembly Language, 2nd Edition	$26.95
Using BASIC	$19.95
Using C	$27.95
Using QuickBASIC 4	$22.95
Using Turbo Pascal	$22.95

For More Information, Call Toll Free!

1-800-428-5331

All prices and titles subject to change without notice. Non-U.S. prices may be higher. Printed in the U.S.A.

Free Catalog!

Mail us this registration form today, and we'll send you a free catalog featuring Que's complete line of best-selling books.

Name of Book _____

Name _____

Title _____

Phone ( ) _____

Company _____

Address _____

City _____

State _____ ZIP _____

Please check the appropriate answers:

1. Where did you buy your Que book?
   ☐ Bookstore (name: _____)
   ☐ Computer store (name: _____)
   ☐ Catalog (name: _____)
   ☐ Direct from Que
   ☐ Other: _____

2. How many computer books do you buy a year?
   ☐ 1 or less
   ☐ 2-5
   ☐ 6-10
   ☐ More than 10

3. How many Que books do you own?
   ☐ 1
   ☐ 2-5
   ☐ 6-10
   ☐ More than 10

4. How long have you been using this software?
   ☐ Less than 6 months
   ☐ 6 months to 1 year
   ☐ 1-3 years
   ☐ More than 3 years

5. What influenced your purchase of this Que book?
   ☐ Personal recommendation
   ☐ Advertisement
   ☐ In-store display
   ☐ Price
   ☐ Que catalog
   ☐ Que mailing
   ☐ Que's reputation
   ☐ Other: _____

6. How would you rate the overall content of the book?
   ☐ Very good
   ☐ Good
   ☐ Satisfactory
   ☐ Poor

7. What do you like *best* about this Que book?
   _____
   _____

8. What do you like *least* about this Que book?
   _____
   _____

9. Did you buy this book with your personal funds?
   ☐ Yes   ☐ No

10. Please feel free to list any other comments you may have about this Que book.
    _____
    _____
    _____

que

Order Your Que Books Today!

Name _____

Title _____

Company _____

City _____

State _____ ZIP _____

Phone No. ( ) _____

Method of Payment:

Check ☐   (Please enclose in envelope.)

Charge My: VISA ☐   MasterCard ☐

American Express ☐

Charge # _____

Expiration Date _____

Order No.	Title	Qty.	Price	Total

You can **FAX** your order to **1-317-573-2583**. Or call **1-800-428-5331, ext. ORDR** to order direct.
Please add $2.50 per title for shipping and handling.

Subtotal	
Shipping & Handling	
Total	

que